Charles Seale-Hayne Library
University of Plymouth
(01752) 588 588
LibraryandITenquiries@plymouth.ac.uk

ATTENTION
and
PERFORMANCE VI

Proceedings of the Sixth International Symposium
on Attention and Performance
Stockholm, Sweden, July 28—August 1, 1975

ATTENTION
and
PERFORMANCE VI

Proceedings of the Sixth International
Symposium on Attention and Performance
Stockholm, Sweden, July 28—August 1, 1975

Edited by
STANISLAV DORNIČ
University of Stockholm, Sweden

 LAWRENCE ERLBAUM ASSOCIATES, PUBLISHERS
1977   Hillsdale, New Jersey

DISTRIBUTED BY THE HALSTED PRESS DIVISION OF

JOHN WILEY & SONS

New York   Toronto   London   Sydney

Lawrence Erlbaum Associates, Inc., Publishers
62 Maria Drive
Hillsdale, New Jersey 07642

Distributed solely by Halsted Press Division
John Wiley & Sons, Inc., New York

Library of Congress Cataloging in Publication Data

International Symposium on Attention and Performance,
6th, Stockholm, 1975.
Attention and performance VI.

Includes bibliographies.
1. Attention—Congresses. 2. Performance—
Congresses. I. Dornic, Stanislav. II. Title.
BF321.I57   1975   153.7'33   77-9284
ISBN 0-470-99120-8

Printed in the United States of America

Contents

PART V: MEMORY ORGANIZATION AND RETRIEVAL

Preface

The Attention and Performance symposia started in 1966 as an informal and spontaneous venture. Six meetings have been held since that time, and five volumes of proceedings published. This volume is the sixth in the series. In order to oversee future symposia a *Stichting—International Association for the Study of Attention and Performance*[1] was recently founded. Its main objectives are "to increase and disseminate knowledge in the area of human attention, performance, and information processing, and to foster international communication in this area" (see the Appendix to this volume).

The research encompassed by the Attention and Performance symposia covers a very broad area, and a single meeting can only focus on a few topics. The content of each meeting is the combined outcome of what recent research problems that Organizer (or the Organizing Committee) has selected as being of special interest, and of the availability of the invitees to contribute to the symposium on the general topic suggested to them.

Within the general topic, contributors were free to choose their own theme as well as their own form of presentation, without the usual constraints imposed by journals, textbooks, or other edited volumes.

As far as the form of this book is concerned, three types of papers are included. Some authors emphasized a particular set of their latest experiments, some preferred to give an overview of their special fields, and some focused on theoretical issues. In general, the papers here presented stress the *review* aspect of the problems more than those in the previous volumes. This is an emphasis which, I hope, will render this latest publication more accessible to a wider audience.

---

[1] "Stichting" is a technical term in Dutch Law that denotes a legal entity that is something between a corporation and a foundation without being either. To the best of my knowledge the term is unique and has no translation.

Attention and Performance VI contains 34 chapters. The topical organization is rather arbitrary and is intended to provide the reader with a rough orientation through the material. Some of the topics necessarily overlap and blend into one another and some are dealt with in several parts of the volume, so that a preliminary glance through the subject index may be worthwhile.

Part 1 of the book contains chapters on an "evergreen" topic in experimental psychology: reaction times. Sensory and perceptual processes, coding, selective attention, visual search, masking, storage, and recognition are overlapping topics around which Parts 2 and 3 are organized. The last chapter in Part 3 focuses on the concept of activation. Part 4 deals with verbal inputs: the processing and recognition of visually presented words as well as the process of reading. The last part of the volume deals with memory topics, and, as usual, the bulk of this section is concerned with verbal memory. The final contribution is devoted to a topic whose importance for Performance Theory is now generally acknowledged: the mechanisms of motor memory.

I am indebted to many people for their aid in organizing this symposium and in editing this volume. In the first place, thanks are due to the participants who came to Stockholm from all over the world, presented their findings, ideas and models, and contributed to the volume of proceedings.

The routine manner of organizing these meetings has been to consult the Programming Committee. Before the Sixth International Symposium on Attention and Performance, the Committee consisted of Sylvan Kornblum (United States), Wim Koster (The Netherlands), Patrick Rabbitt (England), Andries Sanders (The Netherlands), Saul Sternberg (United States), and Alan Welford (Australia), as well as the present Editor. The first list of invitees was prepared together with P.M.A. Rabbitt, and I am truly grateful for his valuable advice concerning this matter as well as the topics. The final list of invitations was based on suggestions and comments from all the above members of the Committee. Their friendly help and counsel were indispensable to me.

A number of referees—experts in their fields—deserve our gratitude for their careful reviewing of papers. Their aid, and the full cooperation of all contributors, are gratefully acknowledged.

Needless to say, credit must be given to the Swedish Council for Social Science Research, whose generous support made it possible, *for the second time*, to organize this meeting in Stockholm.

The effort of the LEA staff, who worked diligently on this volume, is appreciated. Thanks are due to Larry Erlbaum for his sincere and helpful interest in this research field.

Finally, I would like to thank my wife and secretary Viera, who helped me with the work of organizing the meeting and editing the book.

S.D.

Contributors and Participants

Invited Contributors[1]

ALLPORT, D. A., Department of Psychology, University of Reading, England

BADDELEY, A. D., M.R.C., Applied Psychology United, Cambridge, England

BARON, J., Department of Psychology, University of Pennsylvania, Philadelphia, Pennsylvania, United States

BERNSTEIN, I. H., Department of Psychology, University of Texas, Arlington, Texas, United States

BREBNER, J., Department of Psychology, University of Adelaide, Aldelaide, South Australia

BROADBENT, D. E., Department of Experimental Psychology, Oxford University, Oxford, England

CHASE, W. G., Department of Psychology, Carnegie–Mellon University, Pittsburgh, Pennsylvania, United States

COLTHEART, M., Department of Psychology, Birkbeck College, London, England

CORCORAN, D. W. J., Department of Psychology, University of Glasgow, Scotland

CRAIK, F. I. M., Erindale College, University of Toronto, Mississauga, Ontario, Canada

DORNIČ, S., Institute of Applied Psychology, University of Stockholm, Solna, Sweden

DUNCAN, J., Department of Experimental Psychology, Oxford University, Oxford, England

[1] Drs. Sternberg and von Wright gave a talk but did not contribute to the volume. Drs. Nickerson's and Dornic's contributions, included in this volume, were on the symposium's program but could not be presented at the meeting. Dr Rydberg presented a demonstration of a new method for recording perceptual movements in the study of the development and training of attention–memory interplay.

EISLER, H., Department of Psychology, University of Stockholm, Sweden

HAGGARD, M. P., Department of Psychology, The Queen's University, Belfast, Northern Ireland

HAMILTON, P., Department of Psychology, University of Stirling, Stirling, Scotland

HAWKINS, H. L., Department of Psychology, University of South Florida, Tampa, Florida, United States

HOCKEY, B., Department of Psychology, University of Durham, Durham, England

KAHNEMAN, D., Department of Psychology, The Hebrew University of Jerusalem, Jerusalem, Israel

LABERGE, D., Department of Psychology, University of Minnesota, Minneapolis, Minnesota, United States

MASSARO, D. W., Department of Psychology, University of Wisconsin, Madison, Wisconsin, United States

NÄÄTÄNEN, R., Institute of Psychology, University of Helsinki, Helsinki, Finland

NICKERSON, R. S., Bolt, Beranek and Newman Inc., Cambridge, Massachusetts, United States

NILSSON, L.-G., Department of Psychology, University of Uppsala, Uppsala, Sweden

OLLMAN, R. T., Bell Laboratories, Holmdel, New Jersey, United States

PRINZ, W., Psychologisches Institut, Ruhr-Universität Bochum, Germany

RABBITT, P. M. A., Department of Experimental Psychology, Oxford University, Oxford, England

REQUIN, J., Département de Psychophysiologie Générale, Institut de Neurophysiologie et Psychophysiologie du CNRS, Marseille, France

RUMELHART, D. E., Department of Psychology, University of California, San Diego, La Jolla, California, United States

RYDBERG, S., Department of Psychology, University of Stockholm, Sweden

SANDERS, A. F., Institute for Perception TNO, Soesterberg, The Netherlands

SHIFFRIN, R. M., Department of Psychology, Indiana University, Bloomington, Indiana, United States

SMITH, G. A., Department of Psychology, University of Adelaide, Adelaide, South Australia

STELMACH, G. E., Motor Behavior Laboratory, University of Wisconsin, Madison, Wisconsin, United States

STERNBERG, S., Bell Laboratories, Murray Hill, New Jersey, United States

TREISMAN, A. M., Department of Experimental Psychology, Oxford University, Oxford England

VROON, P. A., Psychological Laboratory, University of Utrecht, The Netherlands

WELFORD, A. T., Department of Psychology, The University of Adelaide, Adelaide, South Australia

WRIGHT, J. von, Department of Psychology, University of Turku, Finland

Invited Observers[2]

FRANZÉN, O., Department of Psychology, University of Uppsala, Uppsala, Sweden

HOLLNAGEL, E., Institute of Psychology, University of Aarhus, Denmark

KOMORI, T., Kyoto Womens University, Kyoto, Japan

KORNBLUM, S., Mental Health Research Institute, The University of Michigan, Ann Arbor, Michigan, United States

KOSTER, W. G., Institute for Perception Research, Eindhoven, The Netherlands

LISPER, H.-O., Department of Psychology, University of Uppsala, Uppsala, Sweden

MICKO, H. C., Institute für Psychologie, Technische Universität, Braunschweig, Germany

MULDER, G., Institute of Experimental Psychology, University of Groningen, Haren, The Netherlands

OHTANI, A., Department of Medical Psychology, Hyogo, College of Medicine, Hyogo, Japan

SCHEERER, E., Psychologisches Institut, Ruhr-Universität, Bochum, Germany

STRANGERT, B., Department of Psychology, Umeå University, Umeå, Sweden

Co-authors[3]

ADEY, M., Department of Psychology, University of Texas, Arlington, Texas, United States

*BESNER, D., Department of Psychology, University of Reading, Reading, England

BONNET, M., Département de Psychophysiologie Générale, Institut de Neurophysiologie et Psychophysiologie due CNRS, Marseille, France.

BROADBENT, M. H. P., Department of Experimental Psychology, Oxford University, Oxford, England

CUMMING, G., Department of Psychology, La Troke University, Melbourne, Australia

DAVELAAR, E., Department of Psychology, University of Reading, Reading, England

GELADE, G., Department of Experimental Psychology, Oxford University, Oxford, England

HENIK, A., Department of Psychology, The Hebrew University of Jerusalem, Jerusalem, Israel

---

[2] A number of other observers, research fellows, and students participated in some of the conference sessions. We wish to thank them for their interest.

[3] An asterisk before a name indicates a coauthor who participated in the meeting.

HITCH, G., M.R.C. Applied Psychology United, Cambridge, England
JACKSON, A., Department of Psychology, University of Glasgow, Glasgow, Scotland
*JONASSON, J. T., Department of Psychology, University of Reading, Reading, England
KELSO, J. A. S., Motor Behavior Laboratory, University of Wisconsin, Madison, Wisconsin, United States
MERISALO, A., Institute of Psychology, University of Helsinki, Finland
NORDEN, M. J., Department of Psychology, University of Minnesota, Minneapolis, Minnesota, United States
*OHLSSON, K., Department of Psychology, University of Uppsala, Uppsala, Sweden
PETERSEN, R. J., Department of Psychology, University of Minnesota, Minneapolis, Minnesota, United States
*PRESSON, J. C., Department of Psychology, University of South Florida, Tampa, Florida, United States
REJMAN, M., Department of Psychology, University of Stirling, Stirling, Scotland
*RÖNNBERG, J., Department of Psychology, University of Uppsala, Uppsala, Sweden
SCHNEIDER, W., Department of Psychology, Indiana University, Bloomington, Indiana, United States
SEMJEN, A., Institute of Psychology, Szondy-u, 83-85, Budapest VI, Hungary
SMITH, D. B., Department of Psychology, University of Texas, Arlington, Texas, United States
SUMMERFIELD, Q., Department of Psychology, The Queen's University, Belfast, Northern Ireland
SYKES, M., Department of Experimental Psychology, Oxford University, Oxford, England
TEMPELAARS, S., Institute of Sonology, University of Utrecht, The Netherlands
TIMMERS, H., Psychological Laboratory, University of Nijmegen, The Netherlands
VYAS, S., Department of Experimental Psychology, Oxford University, Oxford, England

ATTENTION
and
PERFORMANCE VI

Proceedings of the Sixth International Symposium
on Attention and Performance
Stockholm, Sweden, July 28—August 1, 1975

Part I
REACTION TIME

1
Structural and Functional Aspects of the Reaction Process

A. F. Sanders

Institute for Perception TNO
Soesterberg, The Netherlands

ABSTRACT

This paper deals with the interplay between structural and functional factors in the reaction process. First some research on Sternberg's idea of processing stages is reviewed. The conclusion is that the results of most studies can be satisfactorily described as a simple sequence of three processing stages. However, it is difficult to incorporate the observed interactions between auditory signal intensity and time uncertainty, and between S–R compatibility (in tactual choice reactions) and time uncertainty. A variable criterion model can handle these exceptions but, in its turn, cannot easily account for several results – like additivity between visual signal intensity and time uncertainty – that fit the processing stages model. It is proposed that intense signals, that is, tactual signals and loud auditory signals, produce an orienting response, which may be labeled as immediate arousal. The effect of immediate arousal is to enhance readiness to respond. When the response made requires a choice the effects of immediate arousal are inhibited. Several implications of this view are discussed.

I. INTRODUCTION

It has long been recognised that behavior has structural as well as functional aspects. The terms "structural" and "functional" are used here, respectively, as loose references to hypothetical computational mechanisms for processing information, like encoding and choice, and to mechanisms affecting the efficiency of the computational mechanisms, like alertness. Thus Wundt's apperception had a functional counterpart in his attention concept as a state which accompanies the clear apprehension of a mental content (Wundt, 1896). In behavioristic theories, habits have been assigned excitatory potentials related to drive states. More recently the arousal concept has gained currency as an "energiser, not a guide" (Hebb, 1955). The continuing interest in functional factors is clear in Kahneman's recent book *Attention and Effort* (1973) and in the symposium volume *Man under Stress* edited by Welford (1974).

It is clear that structural and functional processes and their interplay in processing information are central themes of human performance theory. There has been and still is a tendency to treat them as separate classes of problems. Thus, there are typical functional topics such as vigilance, and effects of stressors and drugs on performance, in which questions about the structural requirements of the tasks play, at best, a minor role. On the other hand, functional aspects are usually not discussed in a predominantly structural topic such as the reaction process. Fortunately there are instances in which this is changing. I may mention Posner's components of attention, being investigated in the discrete reaction process (Posner & Boies, 1971; Posner & Klein, 1973). Lisper and Törnros (1974) work on sustained attention and, of course, Broadbent's *Decision and stress* (1971). I consider the joint treatment of structural and functional factors as important because both classes of factors may affect each other selectively. For instance, I do not think that stimulant and depressant drugs, in moderate doses at least, will have general unspecified effects on performance. They probably have specific effects on certain structural and functional factors and no effect on others. If this working hypothesis is correct, in the long run it would not be very useful to carry out drug research on batteries of tasks the structural processes of which are virtually unknown.

In this chapter I focus on the discrete reaction process. Some research on structural processing stages in the reaction process is summarized. A very simple picture of three stages appears to account for most of the data, but there are some serious inconsistencies that will be considered with reference to Grice's (1968) variable criterion model. I also argue that Grice's model cannot easily cover the whole set of available data. Finally, in an attempt to present a more comprehensive account, I describe the data in terms of interplay between structural and functional processes.

II. STRUCTURAL PROCESSING STAGES

It is almost trite to say that research on structural factors in the reaction process has received an important impetus from Sternberg's (1969) contribution to *Attention and Performance II* on the discovery of processing stages by considering whether task variables have additive or interacting effects on mean reaction time (RT), its variance, and its distribution. There are some well-known problems associated with Sternberg's idea. For example, additive contributions to RT do not necessarily imply the operation of different processing stages. Thus two variables may happen to contribute to RT additively, while still affecting the same processing stage. Another problem is that of accepting versus rejecting the null hypothesis in the presence of, say, insignificant trends toward an interaction between two variables. Still another problem is that interactions can often be easily removed or created by some transformation of the data and that there are no strict rules for deciding whether or not some transformation is appropriate. However, a practical test of Sternberg's idea would be to consider whether the experiments on the relations between the different possible variables lead to a consistent and intuitively reasonable picture of the reaction process.

There are a number of consistent results on mean RT which are summarized in Table 1. They suggest at least three additive components in the choice reaction process, which may be tentatively labeled as encoding, response choice, and motor adjustment (Fig. 1). However, several comments are necessary. It should be noted that most results of Table 1 were obtained from well-practiced subjects. Relatively unpracticed subjects may well show different relations between task variables. For example, Sternberg (1969) has observed an interaction between S−R compatibility and stimulus degradation which disappeared after practice. Rabbitt (1967) has also found an interaction between S−R compatibility and stimulus discriminability, again with unpracticed subjects.

TABLE 1

Additive effects	Source
Signal degradation × S−R compatibility	Sternberg (1969)
Number of alternatives × time uncertainty	Alegria & Bertelson (1970)
	Broadbent & Gregory (1965)
S−R compatibility × motor preparation	Sanders (1970)
Stimulus intensity × time uncertainty (visual)	Raab et al. (1961)
Stimulus intensity × stimulus modality	Howell & Donaldson (1962)
Signal degradation × relative signal frequency ($p \geqslant 0.07$)	Miller & Pachella (1973)
Signal degradation × time uncertainty	Frowein (1977)

Interactive effects	
Signal degradation × number of alternatives	Sternberg (1969)
S−R compatibility × number of alternatives	Brainard et al. (1962)
S−R compatibility × time uncertainty	Broadbent & Gregory (1965);
	Sternberg (1969)
S−R compatibility × relative signal frequency	Sanders (1970)
	Fitts et al. (1963)
Relative signal frequency × time uncertainty	Bertelson & Barzeele (1965)
Relative signal frequency × motor preparation	Sanders (1970)
Relative signal frequency × signal degradation ($p < 0.05$)	Miller & Pachella (1973)

Change in the composition of processing stages as a function of practice is in itself an interesting subject which should be investigated in more detail.

The picture given by Fig. 1 is probably not exhaustive. There may be more processing stages for which there is still a lack of evidence. One interesting possibility is stimulus preprocessing, which would require additive contributions of variables such as stimulus intensity and discriminability to RT. With regard to encoding, the question can be raised whether the effects of stimulus degradation interact with those obtained with more classical methods of investigating the effects of signal discriminability, such as differences in size or length (Crossman, 1955; Shallice & Vickers, 1964). In the case of a single encoding mechanism a strong interaction would certainly be predicted.

The next question concerns the relation between relative signal frequency and signal degradation. Miller and Pachella (1973), while finding reasonably additive contributions of signal degradation and relative signal frequency when signal frequencies were not too low, reported an interaction between these variables for infrequent signals with a probability of 0.025. The authors interpret these data as showing an effect of relative signal frequency on encoding. I would prefer to say that, in general, these variables affect different stages (Fig. 1), except at very low probabilities. Why would this occur? One possibility is that the interaction occurs only when subjects are relatively unpracticed, as was the case in Miller and Pachella's study. The low-probability items could suffer more from lack of practice when they are degraded than when they are not degraded. The authors' counterargument that there was no practice X degradation interaction is not convincing in view of the few trials given to the low-probability items.

Another possibility is that the degraded signals in particular require an activated internal code of the set of items to ensure efficient coding. Wagenaar (1972), in a series of studies on the production of random sequences as a function of set size, suggested that the subset of the alphabet, internally activated at a time, has a size of approximately six symbols. If this were true it could be that of the eight symbols which Miller and Pachella used, the two

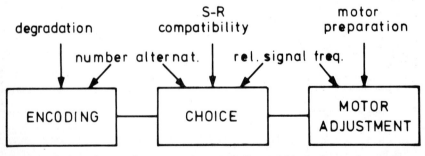

FIG. 1   Structural processing stages and corresponding variables in the reaction process.

low-probability items were not internally activated and, accordingly, required a longer encoding time.

A final issue — the relations between time uncertainty and the other variables — has not been included in Fig. 1. This is because of the rather complex relations between time uncertainty, motor preparation, S–R compatibility, and the number of alternatives. The interaction between the last two variables is a well-known and documented phenomenon (see, for example, Brainard, Irby, Fitts, & Alluisi, 1962) while both Alegria and Bertelson (1970) and Broadbent and Gregory (1965) found additive contributions of number of alternatives (varying between two and eight) and time uncertainty. Furthermore, Broadbent and Gregory (1965) reported a pronounced interaction between time uncertainty and S–R compatibility. Finally S–R compatibility and motor preparation seem to have additive effects on RT (Sanders, 1970). Motor preparation was varied in the last study by having responses in a letter naming experiment start with either a specific or a common phoneme, allowing, respectively, specific or unspecific preparation. Applying Sternberg's method, these findings, taken together, would require an additional stage, presumably between response choice and motor adjustment (Fig. 2).

On the other hand, Posner et al. (1973) have found additive effects of foreperiod duration and compatibility although it should be admitted that their experiment differed from Broadbent and Gregory's study in many respects. Yet, additivity between time uncertainty and S–R compatibility would obviously simplify the picture presented in Fig. 2. In that case, the effects of time uncertainty could be tentatively ascribed to motor adjustment, and there would be no need to assume an extra stage. That time uncertainty has also an effect on signal detection in a psychophysical setting (e.g., Klein & Kerr, 1974) does not necessarily contradict this view. Quite possibly, preparation for detecting a signal consists largely of motor adjustments. In the following, two experiments are re-

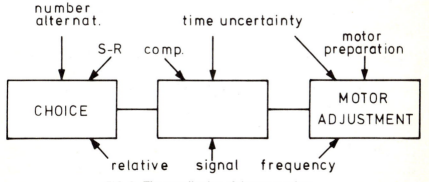

FIG. 2 The complication of time uncertainty.

ported with the aim to shed more light on the relation of time uncertainty and S–R compatibility.

III. TIME UNCERTAINTY AND S–R COMPATIBILITY

The major evidence bearing on the relation between time uncertainty and S–R compatibility derives from the study by Broadbent and Gregory (1965), who found a very strong interaction. They used tactual-choice responses, which are very highly compatible indeed when the subject responds with the stimulated finger. In their incompatible condition subjects were instructed to respond with the corresponding finger of the other hand. Time uncertainty was either low or very high (a constant 2 sec versus randomly varying intervals of 10, 20, 30, and 40 sec). In contrast, Posner *et al.* (1973) employed a two-choice visual reaction task with blocks of constant foreperiods of 50–800 ms separating an auditory warning tone from the imperative stimulus. Compatibility was varied by changing the spatial relations between stimuli and responses.

In the following experiments visual and auditory stimuli are used with differences in time uncertainty ranging between 1 and 10 sec.

A. Experiment I: The Relation of Time Uncertainty and S–R
    Compatibility in a Visual Choice-Reaction Task

1. Method and Procedure

Three lights and response keys were mounted on a sloping desk. The lights were equidistantly spaced (3 cm) in a horizontal row and were clearly visible. The keys were located below the lights in a convenient configuration and were operated by the index, middle, and ringfinger of either the right or left hand according to subject's preference.

Subjects were instructed to keep their fingers on the keys throughout a block of trials. A trial started with an auditory warning (70 dB, 1000 Hz, 500 msec); the signal (one of the lights with equal probability) appeared after a foreperiod of 2, 4, or 10 sec (constant within blocks). Subjects responded by pressing the appropriate key as quickly as possible and were allowed an error margin of 5%. In the compatible blocks, the key below the presented light was to be pressed. In the incompatible blocks the middle key corresponded to the left light, the right key to the middle light, and the left key to the right light. Testing took place in a sound-attenuating cubicle. The six experimental conditions (time uncertainty: 2, 4, and 10 sec; and S–R compatibility: high/low) were tested in six separate blocks per session in a counterbalanced within subjects design with the restriction that all compatible conditions were tested before the incompatible ones or vice versa. After performing the compatible (or incompatible) conditions, subjects had a 15-min break before starting the incompatible (or compatible) blocks of trials. Moreover, at a shift in compatibility, subjects received 15 practice trials prior to the experimental ones.

Twelve paid students from the University of Utrecht served as subjects. In each block of trials 22 correct reactions were obtained, the first two reactions of each block being always excluded from analysis. The mean RT per condition and subject was used as an individual cell in the Analysis of Variance (ANOVA). In order to trace possible interactions with practice, there were six experimental sessions for each subject, two sessions per day on three consecutive days.

2. Results

Mean RTs over subjects are presented in Fig. 3. The ANOVA showed highly significant effects of all main variables (S–R compatibility: $F = 518.6$; $df = 1$, 30; $p < 0.01$; time uncertainty: $F = 80.31$; $df = 2$, 30; $p < 0.01$; practice: $F = 5.56$; $df = 4$, 24; $p < 0.01$). There were two significant interactions: practice X

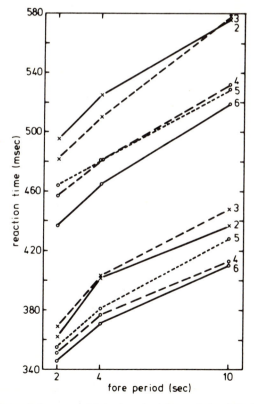

FIG. 3 The effects of time uncertainty (constant foreperiods of 2, 4, and 10 sec), S–R compatibility and practice (sessions 2–6) on visual choice reaction time.

S–R compatibility ($F = 4.63$; $df = 4$, 120; $p < 0.01$), and order of testing X practice ($F = 1.83$; $df = 20$, 120; $p < 0.05$) which are usually observed. The F values of S–R compatibility X time uncertainty was smaller than 1. Inspection of Fig. 3 confirms that at all stages of practice, the effects of S–R compatibility, and time uncertainty were virtually additive. Errors were within the limits set by the instructions and did not vary significantly between conditions.

B. Experiment II: The Relations between Time Uncertainty, S–R Compatibility, and Stimulus Intensity in an Auditory Choice-Reaction Task

1. Method and Procedure

Three auditory signals were used, all consisting of 1-sec bursts of noise (800–1000 Hz frequencies) but at different spatial localizations. The signals were presented through sound attenuating earphones, Signal 1 being presented only to the left ear, Signal 2 only to the right ear, and Signal 3 to both ears. Thus, Signal 3 appeared subjectively in the middle of the head. Intensity differences between Signals 1 and 2, and Signal 3 were corrected by increasing the intensity of Signals 1 and 2 to a level that was subjectively equal to that of Signal 3. The response keys were positioned and operated in the same way as in Experiment I. In the compatible blocks of trials reactions corresponded to spatial localization, the left key corresponding to Signal 1, the right key to Signal 2, and middle key to Signal 3. In the incompatible blocks the middle key corresponded to Signal 1, the right key to Signal 3, and the left key to Signal 2, which was analogous to the configuration in Experiment I. S–R compatibility, time uncertainty, and stimulus intensity were the three main experimental variables. There were two levels of time uncertainty: a constant 1-sec interval between warning and signal, and a variable interval of 1, 3, 5, 7, or 9 sec. The warning signal was the same as that used in Experiment I. There were also two levels of intensity: 85 and 35 dB (measured at Signal 3). Thus, the experiment included eight conditions which were all tested in separate blocks of 15 trials for the constant interval conditions and 40 trials for the variable interval conditions. In the latter conditions, the interval durations were randomly varied.

Eight paid students from the University of Utrecht served as subjects. In an experimental session, they were tested on all eight conditions in a counterbalanced within subject design, with the same restrictions as in Experiment I. Each subject was tested on two consecutive days. The first day was completely devoted to instruction and practice. On the second day each subject underwent six experimental sessions, separated by ample rest periods. The data of all sessions were pooled, mainly in order to get sufficient data on the variable intervals. The instructions on speed and accuracy were the same as in Experiment I. Individual mean RTs were used as cells in the ANOVA.

2. Results

A separate ANOVA on the variable intervals alone showed neither a difference between intervals nor any interactions with the other major variables (compatibility, intensity). In this analysis, the data were treated as if a randomized block design had been used. In view of the extended practice prior to the experimental blocks, this is probably justified. Thus, there were no significant practice effects between sessions.

Another ANOVA was carried out on all conditions with the results on the variable intervals pooled to one mean RT per condition and subject. The mean RTs over subjects are presented in Fig. 4.

The ANOVA showed significant effects of S–R compatibility ($F = 111.8$; $df = 1, 7$; $p < 0.01$), intensity ($F = 37, 9$; $df = 1, 7$; $p < 0.01$), and time uncertainty ($F = 39; 1$; $df = 1, 7$; $p < 0.01$). No interaction between these variables was significant or showed a trend toward significance. Again, errors did not vary systematically between conditions.

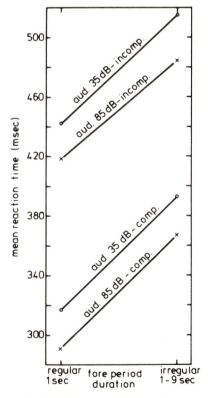

FIG. 4   The effects of intensity, time uncertainty (constant foreperiods of 1 sec versus irregular intervals of 1, 3, 5, 7, and 9 sec) and S–R compatibility on auditory choice reaction time.

C. Discussion

Experiments I and II suggest a different relation between time uncertainty and S–R compatibility than did Broadbent and Gregory's (1965) study. In fact, the present data are more in line with those from Posner *et al.* (1973). Thus it appears that with both visual and auditory choice reaction, S–R compatibility and time uncertainty show additive contributions. Moreover, in the auditory study, stimulus intensity proved to be a third additive component (Fig. 5).

There may be at least three possible reasons for the discrepancy with Broadbent and Gregory's results. First, an interaction might only appear at the very large degrees of time uncertainty used by Broadbent and Gregory and not at the "medium" degree of time uncertainty used in this study. However, inspection of the absolute effects of time uncertainty renders this explanation unlikely. Broadbent and Gregory found a 150-msec effect of time uncertainty in their incompatible, and only 30 msec in their compatible conditions. In comparison, the present data show about 70 msec, regardless of compatibility. Taking into account the difference in time uncertainty between Broadbent and Gregory's experiment and this one, the results of both studies could be quite comparable for the imcompatible conditions. The 70-msec effect at medium time uncertainty might easily extend to 150 msec under conditions of high time uncertainty. However, the effect of time uncertainty on the compatible signals is more pronounced in the present study. Thus, the discrepancy seems largely to be due to compatible tactual-choice reactions being less sensitive to the effect of time uncertainty, and compatible visual and auditory signals being more sensitive to such effect.

A second possible reason may lie in compatibility differences. Responses corresponding spatially to visual signals are less compatible than tactual-choice responses. Thus the RT-information function still has a slope of about .1 in the first case, while tactual choice responses have virtually a zero slope (Hick, 1952; Leonard, 1959). If this were the decisive factor it would mean a rather different structure of processing stages for very compatible signal–response connections

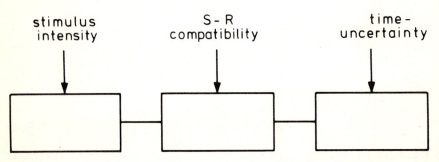

FIG. 5   Three additive processing stages derived from Experiment II.

as compared to all other degrees of compatibility. In turn this means a complication of Fig. 1.

A third reason may be the difference between tactual signals in the one case, and visual signals in the other. Obviously, this would imply a second-order modality X S–R compatibility X time uncertainty interaction, which is even more complicating for the additive stages of Fig. 1. A test for deciding between the last two suggestions might be to repeat Experiments I and II using naming of letters, a type of reaction test which shares the property of zero slope of the RT-information function with tactual-choice reactions.

IV. MODALITY, STIMULUS INTENSITY,
AND TIME UNCERTAINTY

The problem posed in the foregoing discussion can be summarized by the question of why compatible tactual-choice reactions are relatively insensitive to effects of time uncertainty. It may be interesting to relate this question to another set of results that also suggest differential sensitivities to effects of time uncertainty in the case of simple or selective reactions. I am referring here to the repeated observation of interactions between sensory modality, stimulus intensity, and time uncertainty. There are no problems with regard to simple or selective reactions to visual signals. In that case, stimulus intensity and time uncertainty have additive contributions to mean RT as would be expected from an input and a motor variable (Raab, Fehrer, & Hershenson, 1961; Sanders, 1975). However, the situation is different for simple or selective reactions to auditory signals. At Soesterberg we observed some years ago that mean RTs to 70 dB tones at constant foreperiods of 1 and 5 sec were often not significantly different. These results were obtained by accident, but in a more systematic study, again no reliable effect of constant foreperiod duration (1 versus 5 sec) on RT to 70 dB auditory signals was found; the experiment confirmed the usual effect of time uncertainty on visual signals (Sanders & Wertheim, 1973). This result is not due to sensory modality per se, however, since when using auditory signals below 50 dB, the effect of foreperiod duration was equally strong for auditory signals and for visual signals of high and low intensity, but the effect of time uncertainty almost vanished with auditory signals of 75 dB. These findings were obtained in a traditional *a*-reaction task with 20% catch-trials and in a *c*-reaction task in which 80% of the signals required an overt response (Sanders, 1975). Similar effects are reported in the data of Bernstein *et al.* (1973), Keuss (1969), and Trumbo and Gaillard (1975). Although the last study reported an effect on RT to a 70 dB click when comparing constant and variable foreperiods, the effect was significantly smaller than that obtained with visual signals.

In summary, the assumption that stimulus intensity, as an input variable, and time uncertainty as a supposed motor variable (see page 7) always have additive contributions to mean RT is not confirmed. More specifically, it is not true for auditory signals when an *a*-reaction or an overt-response biased *c*-reaction is involved. It seems to hold when equally probable auditory choice reactions are involved, as was shown in Experiment II. The inclusion of signal intensity in the latter study was intended to investigate this point.

V. THE VARIABLE CRITERION MODEL

There is a reaction-time model in the literature which predicts an interaction between stimulus intensity and readiness to respond. This model — a variant of McGill's (1963) decision model — has been mainly developed and tested by Grice and co-workers (Grice, 1968, 1972; Grice, Hunt, Kushner, & Morrow, 1974; Grice & Hunter, 1964). It assumes that a signal elicits a series of pulses, accumulating at a constant rate, until some criterion value is reached. The pulse rate depends on signal intensity and the setting of the criterion is variable, depending on subjects' preparedness and expectancy. When, for some reason, the criterion becomes more strict, low intensity signals should be affected more than high intensity signals, due to the difference in pulse rate.

The basic difference between the processing stages notion of Fig. 1 and the variable-criterion model is that the former assumes a series of computational stages, so that, say, signal intensity and readiness to respond should contribute additively to RT, while the latter assumes one stage affected by both pulse rate and criterion.

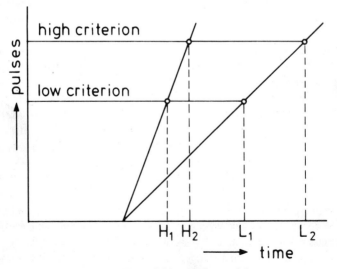

FIG. 6 The variable criterion model.

Hence the variable-criterion model predicts an interaction between signal intensity and readiness to respond. Several experimental results have been reported in favor of this idea. One consistent finding is that the effect of intensity is amplified when two intensity levels are randomly varied within a block of trials as compared to blocks of constant intensity (Grice & Hunter, 1964; Thrane, 1961). The criterion is assumed to rise in the mixed intensity blocks due to increased uncertainty. Speiss (1973) has recently found that in the mixed intensity conditions the criterion is very adaptive. If subjects receive knowledge about stimulus intensity prior to each trial, the RTs equal those obtained in blocks of constant intensity. Other types of variables which have been found to fit the model are the differential effects of various types of catch signals (Grice *et al.*, 1974) and of type of instruction. Thus Loveless and Sanford (1974) found that RT to a low intensity signal suffered more from a "perceptual set" instruction than did RT to a high intensity signal.

It seems clear that at least at a qualitative level the variable-criterion model faces no problem in explaining the auditory stimulus intensity X time uncertainty interaction as another instance of manipulating the criterion level. Time uncertainty should clearly have the effect of raising the criterion. The model has difficulties handling the additive contributions when auditory choice reactions are used (Experiment II). In defense, one should note that the model has only been meant to describe simple reactions. Yet it faces serious problems in explaining the additive contributions of intensity and time uncertainty with simple visual signals. Interestingly, all the research of Grice and co-workers was carried out with auditory stimuli. The problem is that there is no reason why the model should be valid only for auditory stimuli.

It would be difficult to explain the absence of an interaction in the visual case by assuming ceiling effects, either in pulse rate or in criterion variation, since both intensity and time uncertainty had clear effects on RT (Sanders, 1975). There is the theoretical possibility, however, that under certain circumstances subjects apply different criteria when reacting to intense visual signals as compared to weak signals. Thus, an intensity X time uncertainty interaction could be obscured when subjects have about the same criterion, irrespective of signal intensity, when time uncertainty is low but use a relatively low criterion for reacting to weak signals as compared to intense signals when time uncertainty is high.

An appropriate test of this possibility may be to study the effects of mixed versus constant level of intensity during a block of trials on RT to visual and auditory signals at different levels of time uncertainty. The idea is that, while subjects might use different criteria in blocks of constant intensity, the criterion would not depend on intensity when subjects are unaware of the intensity level at a particular trial (e.g., Speiss, 1973). Hence an interaction between time uncertainty and visual intensity could not be obscured when the intensity level varies during a block of trials.

A. Experiment III: The effects of stimulus intensity, time uncertainty, and blocked versus mixed intensity on auditory reaction time.

1. Method and Procedure

The auditory signal was a 1000 Hz tone, presented for 500 msec, with an intensity of either 85 or 35 dB. Upon onset of the signal, the subject responded by pressing a key that was mounted on a sloping desk. A signal was presented in 80% of the trials. In the remaining trials a catch signal was presented, which was a 400 Hz tone with an intensity of either 85 or 35 dB. Subjects were instructed to respond as fast as possible to the signal, to withhold response to the catch signal, and to avoid errors of commission.

There were six experimental conditions. In three conditions the signals were presented at constant 1-sec intervals, each interval starting immediately after the previous signal. In the other three conditions the interval varied randomly with durations of 1, 3, 5, 7, or 9 sec. The three constant and variable interval conditions differed with regard to signal intensity. In one condition signals and catch signals were always loud (85 dB); in another condition they were always weak (35 dB); while loud and weak signals, as well as loud and weak catch signals, occurred in the third condition. Thus in the mixed condition both the loud and the weak signal were each presented in 40% of the trials. Similarly, the loud and weak catch signal were each presented in 10% of the trials. The regular interval blocks contained 15 trials with constant intensity and 26 trials with mixed intensity. In the variable interval blocks there were 32 constant-intensity trials and 40 mixed-intensity trials. Six paid students from the University of Utrecht served as subjects. They performed all conditions in a counterbalanced order. In an experimental session subjects worked on all conditions with short breaks in between. Each subject was tested on two consecutive days. On the first day there were five experimental sessions, which were all considered practice. On the second day, there were another five experimental sessions, the data of which were pooled for analysis.

B. Experiment IV: The effects of stimulus intensity, time uncertainty, and blocked versus mixed intensity on visual reaction time.

1. Method and Procedure

The setup of this experiment was the same as that of Experiment III except for the signal, which was a light presented for 300 msec with an intensity of either 280 or 0.8 cd/m^2 on a virtually black background. The catch signal was another light, also with an intensity of either 280 or 0.8 cd/m^2, positioned 3 cm to the right of the signal. As in the auditory study, the intensities of signal and catch signal were either 0.8 or 280 cd/m^2 in the blocked conditions, while all four possibilities occurred in the mixed conditions. Signal, catch signal, and response key were all mounted on the earlier described sloping desk, the response key situated below the signal. Six new students served as subjects.

2. Results of Experiments III and IV

In the ANOVAs the data were analyzed as a randomized-block design, which seemed reasonable in view of the extensive practice preceding the experimental sessions. With regard to the auditory experiment, the ANOVA showed significant main effects of intensity level ($F = 71.3$; $df = 1, 5$; $p < 0.01$), interval ($F = 21.9$; $df = 5, 25$; $p < 0.01$) and blocked versus mixed intensity level ($F = 34, 5$; $df = 1, 5$; $p < 0.01$). Moreover, there were significant interactions of intensity level X interval ($F = 8.29$; $df = 5, 25$; $p < 0.01$), blocked versus mixed intensity level X interval ($F = 4.56$; $df = 5, 25$; $p < 0.01$), and blocked versus mixed intensity level X intensity ($F = 17.8$; $df = 1, 5$; $p < 0.01$). Finally there were the usual significant differences between subjects and some significant interactions between subjects and the main experimental variables.

Post hoc Newman—Keuls analysis of individual mean RTs showed significant differences between the constant 1-sec interval and all irregular intervals. The irregular intervals did not differ significantly among themselves except for the 1-sec irregular interval which had longer mean RTs than the other intervals.

A similar finding was obtained in the visual experiment. Therefore the data on intervals of 3—9 sec were pooled (Fig. 7) while the irregular 1-sec conditions were separately analyzed. This analysis showed that the effects of intensity level and of blocked versus mixed intensity level were more pronounced but not qualitatively different at the irregular 1-sec interval as compared to the pooled 3—9-sec intervals. Because this adds no new element to the argument the discussion is restricted to the data on the pooled 3—9-sec intervals. Errors of commission occurred significantly more with loud signals than with weak signals, irrespective of condition and time uncertainty, confirming the findings of earlier studies (Sanders & Wertheim, 1973; Sanders, 1975).

The auditory experiment shows two further replications of earlier findings. The intensity X interval interaction confirms the effect that weak auditory signals suffer more from time uncertainty than do loud auditory signals (Sanders, 1975). The blocked versus mixed intensity level X intensity interaction replicates the results of Grice and co-workers, in that loud signals are less affected by mixed intensity levels than are weak signals. Finally, the blocked versus mixed intensity levels X interval interaction indicated a larger effect of mixed intensities on RT in the case of some irregular intervals, this effect occurring exclusively at the irregular 1-sec interval.

The visual experiment, the ANOVA showed significant main effects of intensity ($F = 83.9$; $df = 1.5$; $p < 0.01$), intervals ($F = 33.7$; $df = 5, 25$; $p < 0.01$), and subjects. Furthermore, there was a significant second order interaction of intensities X intervals X blocked versus mixed intensity levels ($F = 2.75$; $df = 5, 25$; p

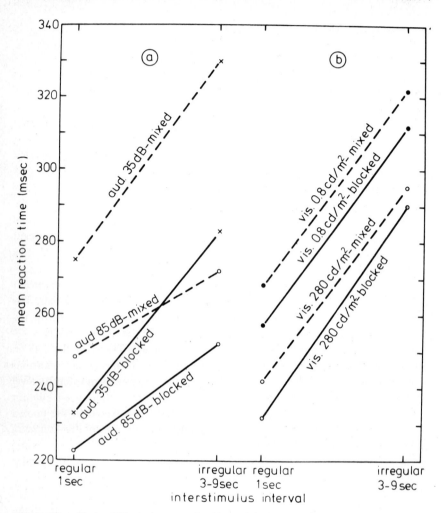

FIG. 7 The effects of blocked versus mixed intensity, signal intensity and time uncertainty (constant 1-sec intervals versus irregular intervals of 3, 5, 7, and 9 sec) on (a) auditory and (b) visual selective reaction time.

< 0.01). Post hoc Newman–Keuls analysis showed a lengthening effect of mixed intensities on RT in all conditions except those in which bright signals were presented at irregular intervals. The size of the effect of blocked versus mixed intervals was larger in the auditory study than in the visual experiment, considering only the 1-sec regular intervals for strong signals ($t = 2.72$; $df = 8$; $p < 0.01$). This effect might be due to differences in discriminability between signal and catch signal in the visual and auditory cases.

C. Discussion

The results of the auditory study are, at least qualitatively, in line with the assumptions of the variable criterion model, in that interactions were found between blocked versus mixed intensity levels and signal intensity and between signal intensity and time uncertainty.

Both effects were absent in the visual study and, consequently, there remains the question of why the variable-criterion model fails in the visual studies. There were appreciable effects on RT of both signal intensity and time uncertainty which should allow for sufficient variation in pulse rate and criterion for an interaction to show up. That the effect of blocked versus mixed intensity levels was stronger on auditory than on visual RT does not affect this last conclusion. At best, this might account for the absence of the intensity X blocked versus mixed-intensity interaction. One should keep in mind, however, that the main aim of using the mixed-intensity level conditions was to get the same criterion in reacting to weak and strong signals, thus avoiding the possibility of divergent criteria, which might have been used in the blocked conditions and which, indeed, could have obscured an interaction between signal intensity and time uncertainty. However, neither in the blocked nor in the mixed visual intensity conditions was there evidence for a signal intensity X time uncertainty inter-action (Fig. 7b). Thus it seems that a one-stage notion, like the variable criterion model does not suffice. Intensity and time uncertainty appear to have additive contributions to mean RT, at least with visual signals and with auditory signals of about 50 dB or less.

The similar effects of time uncertainty on RT in all these conditions also seem to contradict a description in terms of additivity when signals are highly discriminable and interactions when signals are poorly discriminable, – as was suggested by a referee. In this view, the visual signals are supposed to be highly discriminable, irrespective of the intensity range used in the cited studies. The auditory signals, particularly those of weak intensity, are supposed to be poorly discriminable.

Even if this were true and if the effect of time uncertainty depended on discriminability (see, however, Frowein, 1977, Table 1) one should still reason-ably expect a *stronger* effect of time uncertainty on RT when reacting to weak auditory signals as compared to visual signals.

VI. IMMEDIATE AROUSAL

As argued earlier, the processing-stages model of Fig. 1 copes well with additive contributions of signal intensity and time uncertainty. Signal intensity would affect the computations during the input stages – signal preprocessing, and perhaps encoding (see page 6) and time uncertainty would affect the degree of presetting motor adjustment. That is, time uncertainty would negatively affect preparatory state which, in turn, affects readiness to respond.

Obviously, there remains the problem that the effect of time uncertainty on RT is reduced when reacting to loud auditory signals. However, from the point of view of interplay between structural and functional factors in processing information, this may not be surprising. The stages of Fig. 1 are depicted as computational processes without any reference to arousing properties a signal may have. That such variables as stimulus intensity and time uncertainty are troublesome for a mere structural processing model is very reasonable, since they are the very RT variables that are most commonly linked to arousal. Stimulus intensity is always mentioned as important in eliciting an orientation reaction (e.g., Lynn, 1966) and time uncertainty is often considered a mere functional factor, with reference to the measurement of alertness (Posner & Boies, 1971).

It could be that loud tones exert an immediate arousing effect along with their cuing function, while weak tones and visual signals would not possess this property – at least not in a way observable in the above experiments – implying that their effects on RT are as expected from the structural processing stages. Possibly immediate arousal enhances in particular readiness to respond. Readiness to respond would then be a joint function of immediate arousal and level of preparation.

Immediate arousal is not altogether an ad hoc postulate. The term was used before by Bertelson and Tisseyre (1969) who found that a click, presented simultaneously with, or just before a visual signal requiring a response, canceled out the effect of time uncertainty on RT. This is in contrast to the condition in which the preceding signal was visual, in which case a time course of preparation was observed (about 200 msec). Bertelson and Tisseyre (1969) suggested that an auditory signal "might exert some immediate arousing effect besides its warning effect" (p. 151). Since this suggestion, Keuss (1972) has found the extent of the facilitating effect to depend on the intensity of the preceding auditory signal. I failed to find any facilitating effect of loud auditory signal on RT to a visual signal under conditions of low-time uncertainty, so we are not dealing with a mere modality effect (Sanders, 1972). Hence the literature on the time course of preparation is in strong agreement with an immediate arousal interpretation. Without immediate arousal, the effects of time uncertainty should only depend on preparatory state and, consequently, the effects should be about equal under a variety of experimental conditions. Indeed, the slopes in Fig. 7 are all very similar and, moreover, they do not deviate much from those found with choice reactions in Experiments I and II.

An immediate arousal notion can also account for the data on blocked versus mixed-intensity levels. If mixed intensities have a negative effect on preparatory state – an assumption also made by the variable-criterion model – the lower preparatory state is then at least partly compensated for by immediate arousal when a loud auditory signal is presented. Hence an interaction is found between loudness and blocked versus mixed-intensity levels in the auditory case and an additive effect in the visual case, as is observed in Fig. 7. Furthermore, it encompasses the finding that at moderate degrees of time uncertainty, RT to loud signals does not increase significantly, as reported by Sanders and Wertheim (1973) and by Sanders (1975), and as found incidentally in other studies (Keuss, 1969; Bernstein *et al.*, 1973). An effect on RT will appear only when the level of preparation drops below the value of full compensation by immediate arousal.

The last point raises an interesting question about the effect of immediate arousal in the case of low-time uncertainty when preparatory state is optimal. Will there be a floor at which immediate arousal does not add to readiness to respond? Alternatively, could there occur too much readiness to respond so that performance is actually degraded in the case of the combination of optimal preparatory state and immediate arousal? Some support for the last suggestion might be derived from the finding (Sanders & Wertheim, 1973; Sanders, 1975) that, in the case of loud auditory signals and low or medium time uncertainty, subjects tend to show rather large proportions of errors of commission, which is suggestive of their being too ready to respond.

Another possibility is that, when subjects know that immediate arousing signals will be presented, they are capable of voluntarily lowering their preparatory state in order to avoid a too high readiness to respond. This hypothesis, farfetched as it may seem, could account for the finding of John (1966) that visual RT in a selective reaction task slows down when the catch signal is a loud auditory signal as compared to a weak auditory signal. To avoid errors of commission, the level of preparation might be lowered when the catch signal is loud, while there is no need to do so with a weak auditory catch signal. The detailed relations between immediate arousal and preparatory state in determining readiness to respond are far from clear and require more research.

One obvious objection to the operation of arousal in this type of experiment could be that RT to loud auditory signals suffered from time uncertainty as much as from weak signals in the choice-reaction situation of Experiment II. *This result might suggest, however, that immediate arousal is not effective when the information flow involves the response–choice mechanism of Fig. 1.* This hypothesis might also serve as a possible interpretation of the divergent results on the interaction between the effects of time uncertainty and S–R compatibility (see page 12). It has been repeatedly suggested that with extreme compatibility, the response–choice mechanism is virtually bypassed (e.g., Broadbent, 1971).

Consequently, if a tactual signal shares the immediate arousing property with loud auditory signals – which is a reasonable supposition – then the effect of time uncertainty on compatible choice reactions should be considerably reduced, as was found by Broadbent and Gregory (1965). In contrast, if immediate arousal is not effective when the response–choice stage is involved, then the usual effect of time uncertainty should appear with incompatible tactual choice reactions. A strong prediction of this hypothesis is that reactions to loud auditory signals of extreme compatibility – for example, naming responses –

suffer at best slightly from time uncertainty, while reactions to weak auditory signals of the same extreme compatibility should suffer more strongly; to about the same degree as reactions to incompatible, loud auditory S–R relations. Pending this experiment, which has already been proposed (see page 15), the immediate arousal hypothesis seems able to account for the divergence between Broadbent and Gregory's study and Experiments I and II. Interestingly, so far the encoding stage has not been found to render immediate arousal ineffective. The requirement of discriminating among alternatives as in c-reactions delivered the same type of results as in the simple a-reactions.

There are some other incidental findings relating to immediate arousal that deserve consideration. Under conditions of moderate time uncertainty, Trumbo and Gaillard (1975) found a negative effect of a barbiturate on auditory RT but not on visual RT. In fact, after administration of the barbiturate, the interaction between time uncertainty and modality disappeared. This is one instance in which a drug appeared to have a selective effect on performance. As Trumbo and Gaillard suggest, one of the effects of barbiturate may be to suppress the arousing property of auditory signals. Another interesting result was obtained after a more refined analysis of Trunbo and Gaillard's data: the interaction between sensory modality and time uncertainty proved to depend on the time of the day a subject was tested, being most pronounced during the early afternoon and strongly reduced during the morning. During the morning, the effect of time uncertainty on auditory RT was more pronounced. This type of result supports the functional interpretation, as outlined in this section. This leads to a final consideration: the possible relations between immediate arousal and other arousal concepts. Immediate arousal has several properties in common with an orientation reaction (OR): It is brief in duration, it depends on stimulus intensity, and it is involuntary. One problem might be that OR is usually found to rapidly habituate, while the effects of immediate arousal on RT remained the same throughout a block of trials. However, habituation of OR is usually defined in terms of physiological variables – for example, G.S.R. – which may not always extend to behavioral data. Furthermore, there is recent evidence that the orientation wave of the CNV (Loveless & Sanford, 1975) does not habituate with repeated trials (Gaillard, 1976), so that the conditions under which habituation of OR occurs are still under discussion. It may be interesting to relate immediate arousal to the orientation wave of the CNV, the amplitude of which depends also on intensity and on modality of stimulation.

VII.   CONCLUDING REMARKS

The argument of this chapter, tentative and preliminary as it is, may be considered an example of the interplay between structural and functional aspects in the reaction process. There are the limitations set by processing stages.

There is also the efficiency of responding affected by the level of preparation as an intentional factor and by the intensity of the stimulus as an involuntary factor (e.g., Kahneman, 1973). It seems that man has an internal arousal dimension, sensitive to signal intensity, but having different values for different sensory modalities: least sensitive to visual-, more to auditory-, and still more to tactual-signal intensity (see also Posner, Nissen, & Klein (1976)). It would be interesting to know the relation of immediate arousal to efficiency in long-term performance. There are indications that auditory vigilance suffers less decrement over time than visual vigilance (e.g., Sanders, 1971, p. 206).

Much remains to be worked out, especially in view of the interaction between the operation of immediate arousal and the involvement of the structural-choice stage. Can one inhibit immediate arousal by changing the parameters of the internal arousal dimension? When and where would that occur if possible? These questions are intimately related to Broadbent's views on an upper and a lower state arousal mechanism (Broadbent, 1971). We should now initiate a systematic approach toward these types of problems.

ACKNOWLEDGMENT

I am indebted to A. W. K. Gaillard for useful suggestions and criticisms on earlier drafts of this paper.

REFERENCES

Alegria, J., & Bertelson, P. Time uncertainty, number of alternatives and particular signal—response pair as determinants of choice reaction time. In A. F. Sanders (Ed.), *Attention and performance III*. Amsterdam: North-Holland Publ., 1970. Pp. 36–44.

Bernstein, I. H., Chu, P. K, Briggs, P. B., & Schurman, D. L. Stimulus intensity and foreperiod effects in intersensory facilitation. *Quarterly Journal of Experimental Psychology*, 1973, 25, 171–181.

Bertelson, P., & Barzeele, J. Interaction of time-uncertainty and relative signal frequency in determining choice reaction time. *Journal of Experimental Psychology*, 1965, 70, 448–451.

Bertelson, P., & Tisseyre, F. The time course of preparation: Confirmatory results with visual and auditory warning signals. In W. G. Koster (Ed.), *Attention and performance II*. Amsterdam: North-Holland Publ., 1969. Pp. 145–154.

Brainard, R. W., Irby, T. S., Fitts, P. M., & Alluisi, E. A. Some variables influencing the rate of gain of information. *Journal of Experimental Psychology*, 1962, 63, 105–110.

Broadbent, D. E. *Decision and stress*. London: Academic Press, 1971.

Broadbent, D. E., & Gregory, M. On the interaction of S–R compatibility with other variables affecting choice reaction time. *British Journal of Psychology*, 1965, 56, 61–67.

Crossman, E. R. F. W. The measurement of discrimination. *Quarterly Journal of Experimental Psychology*, 1955, 7, 176–195.

Fitts, P. M., Peterson, J. R., & Wolpe, G. Cognitive aspects of information processing II:

Adjustments to stimulus redundancy. *Journal of Experimental Psychology*, 1963, **65**, 423–432.

Frowein, H. W. Signal degradation, foreperiod and S–R compatibility. *Acta Psychologica*, 1977, submitted for publication.

Gaillard, A. W. K. Effects of warning signal modality on the contingent negative variation (CNV). *Biological Psychology*, 1976, **4**, 139–154.

Grice, G. R. Stimulus intensity and response equivocation. *Psychological Review*, 1968, **75**, 359–373.

Grice, G. R. Conditioning and a decision theory of response evocation. In G. Bower (Ed.), *The psychology of learning and motivation*. Vol. 5. New York: Academic Press, 1972. Pp. 1–65.

Grice, G. R., & Hunter, J. J. Stimulus intensity effects depend upon the type of experimental design. *Psychological Review*, 1964, **71**, 247–256.

Grice, G. R., Hunt, R. L., Kushner, B. A., & Morrow, C. H. Stimulus intensity, catch trial effects and the speed–accuracy tradeoff in reaction time: A variable criterion theory interpretation. *Memory & Cognition*, 1974, **2**, 758–770.

Hebb, D. O. Drives and the C.N.S. (Conceptual nervous system). *Psychological Review*, 1955, **62**, 243–254.

Hick, W. E. On the rate of gain of information. *Quarterly Journal of Experimental Psychology*, 1952, **4**, 11–26.

Howell, W. C., & Donaldson, J. E. Human choice reaction time within and among sense modalities. *Science*, 1962, **135**, 429–430.

John, I. D. Intensity of non-key stimuli in the Donders' *c*-type reaction. *Australian Journal of Psychology*, 1966, **19**, 27–34.

Kahneman, D. *Attention and Effort*. Englewood Cliffs, N.J.: Prentice-Hall, 1973.

Keuss, P. G. M. The effect of time intervals between two shortly spaced acoustic signals on response times to the second. *Acta Psychologica*, 1969, **31**, 297–311.

Keuss, P. G. M. Reaction time to the second of two shortly spaced auditory signals both varying in intensity. *Acta Psychologica*, 1972, **36**, 226–238.

Klein, R. M., & Kerr, B. Visual signal detection and the locus of foreperiod effects. *Memory & Cognition*, 1974, **2**, 431–435.

Leonard, A. Tactual choice reactions. *Quarterly Journal of Experimental Psychology*, 1959, **11**, 76–83.

Lisper, H. O., & Törnros, J. Effects of intersignal interval regularity on increase in reaction time in a one hour auditory monitoring task. *Acta Psychologica*, 1974, **38**, 455–460.

Loveless, N. E., & Sanford, A. J. Slow potential correlates of preparatory set. *Biological Psychology*, 1974, **1**, 303–314.

Loveless, N. E., & Sanford, A. J. The impact of warning signal intensity on reaction time and components of the congingent negative variation. *Biological Psychology*, 1975, **2**, 217–226.

Lynn, R. Attention, arousal and the orientation reaction. London: Pergamon Press, 1966.

McGill, W. J. Stochastic latency mechanisms. In R. D. Luce, R. R. Bush, & E. Galanter (Eds.), *Handbook of mathematical psychology*. Vol. 1. New York: Wiley, 1963. Pp. 309–360.

Miller, J. D., & Pachella, R. G. Focus of the stimulus probability effect. *Journal of Experimental Psychology*, 1973, **101**, 227–231.

Posner, M. I., & Boies, S. J. Components of attention. *Psychological Review*, 1971, **78**, 391–408.

Posner, M. I., & Klein, R. M. On the functions of consciousness. In S. Kornblum (Ed.), *Attention and performance IV*. New York: Academic Press, 1973. Pp. 21–37.

Posner, M. I., Klein, R., Summers, J., & Buggie, S. On the selection of signals. *Memory & Cognition*, 1973, **1**, 2–12.
Posner, M. I., Nissen, M. J., & Klein, R. M. Visual dominance: An information-processing account of its origin and significance. *Psychological Review*, 1976, **83**, 157–171.
Raab, D., Fehrer, E., & Hershenson, M. Visual reaction time and the Broca–Sulzer phenomenon. *Journal of Experimental Psychology*, 1961, **61**, 193–199.
Rabbitt, P. M. A. Signal discriminability, S–R compatibility and choice reaction time. *Psychonomic Science*, 1967, **7**, 419–420.
Sanders, A. F. Some variables affecting the relation between relative signal frequency and CRT. In A. F. Sanders (Ed.), *Attention and performance III*. Amsterdam: North-Holland Publ., 1970. Pp. 45–55.
Sanders, A. F. *Psychologie der Informationsverarbeitung*. Berlin: Huber, 1971.
Sanders, A. F. Foreperiod duration and the time course of preparation. *Acta Psychologica*, 1972, **36**, 60–71.
Sanders, A. F. The foreperiod effect revisited. *Quarterly Journal of Experimental Psychology*, 1975, **27**, 591–598.
Sanders, A. F., & Wertheim, A. H. The relation between physical stimulus properties and the effect of foreperiod duration on reaction time. *Quarterly Journal of Experimental Psychology*, 1973, **25**, 201–206.
Shallice, T., & Vickers, D. Theories and experiments on discrimination times. *Ergonomics*, 1964, **7**, 37–49.
Speiss, J. M. Effects of preknowledge and stimulus intensity upon simple reaction time. *Journal of Experimental Psychology*, 1973, **101**, 109–115.
Sternberg, S. The discovery of processing stages: Extensions of Donders' method. In W. G. Koster (Ed.), *Attention and performance II*. Amsterdam: North-Holland Publ., 1969. Pp. 276–315.
Thrane, V. C. Sensory and preparatory factors in response latency: III. Preknowledge and regularity of stimuli as antecedent variables. *Scandinavian Journal of Psychology*, 1961, **2**, 30–44.
Trumbo, D. A., & Gaillard, A. W. K. Drugs, time uncertainty, signal modality and reaction time. In P. M. A. Rabbitt & S. Dornic (Eds.), *Attention and performance V*. London: Academic Press, 1975. Pp. 441–454.
Wagenaar, W. A. Sequential response bias. Rotterdam: Bronder-Offset, 1972.
Welford, A. T. Man under stress. *Ergonomics*, 1974, **16**, (Whole No. 5).
Wundt, W. *Grundriss der Psychologie*. Leipzig: Engelmann, 1896.

2

Studies of Compatibility and a New Model of Choice Reaction Time

Glen A. Smith

Department of Psychology
University of Adelaide
Adelaide, South Australia

ABSTRACT

The effect of different relationships between stimuli and responses, and of number of stimuli, on choice–reaction-times was investigated using an apparatus in which the stimuli consisted of vibrations delivered to the tips of the fingers through the keys used for making responses. The tasks involved either pressing the key which vibrated ("compatible") or one of the keys of the unstimulated hand ("mapped"). In some sessions all relationships between stimulus and responses were compatible. In other sessions, all were mapped, and in yet others half were compatible and half mapped. The fully compatible task was a replication of Leonard's (1959) experiment, which gave no increase of latency with degree of choice. This finding was supported, and evidence is given which suggests that these compatible latencies are at some minimum level. However, in the mapped conditions substantial increases of latency with degree of choice were found. In the mixed conditions the latencies of responses to the compatible stimuli were dependent on degree of choice, and increased logarithmically relative to the pure compatible conditions. The latencies to mapped stimuli, however, were found to decrease relative to the pure mapped case. The results raise difficulties for previous models of choice–reaction time. A new model is suggested which fits the results obtained here, and those of previous choice–reaction experiments. It also reconciles the conflicting formulations of Hick (1952a) and Hyman (1953), showing both to be limiting conditions of a general case.

I. INTRODUCTION

Hick (1952a) noted that in his own and in Merkel's (1885) data, choice–reaction times increased linearly with the logarithm of $n + 1$, where in n is the number of possible stimuli, that is,

$$RT = k \log(n + 1). \tag{1}$$

Adopting the approach of Shannon and Weaver (1949) on information processing, Hick considered that the subject extracts information from the stiuation at a constant rate. This finding has subsequently been replicated; the +1 has been explained by noting that the subject has to distinguish whether or not a signal exists at any point in time, in addition to which of the n possibilities it is, that is, to distinguish between $n + 1$ possible states. Reducing the temporal uncertainty of the stimulus onset would reduce this constant ideally to a limit of zero.

In place of Hick's Eq. (1), Hyman (1953) has proposed:

$$RT = a + b \log(n) \tag{2}$$

with a as the simple reaction time. The relative merits of these two formulations are discussed in Welford's (1968) comprehensive review of the field, where evidence is cited supporting each.

An exception to this has been reported by Leonard (1959), who found a rise in mean reaction time from a simple to a 2-choice task, but no difference between 2-, 4-, and 8-choice tasks, after some practice. He used a compatible association between stimulus and response by having the subject rest his fingertips on a set of armatures which could vibrate. The stimulus was vibration to a finger and the response was pressing the armature on which the vibrated finger rested.

Mowbray and Rhoades (1959) noted that, after 36,000 reactions, the early difference between degrees of choice disappeared, in a situation in which the stimuli were a set of lights set out in the same pattern as the response keys under the subject's fingers. Mowbray (1960) again found that mean reaction times differed little with the number of stimuli using a highly familiar stimulus–response set (reading aloud a digit from the set 0–9) which was displayed visually in front of the subject.

Welford (1968) has suggested that these results may be an artifact because in all cases only the reaction times of the one response common to all degrees of choice was measured, and greater amounts of practice were given with higher degrees of choice. The experiment described below aims partly to repeat Leonard's experiment, but seeks to avoid these criticisms.

It is, however, apparent that the directness of the relationship between stimulus and response affects the rate of increase of reaction time with degree of choice, whether or not it can be reduced to zero. This was indicated notably by Brainard, Irby, Fitts, and Allusi (1962) whose subjects had 2-, 4-, and 8-choice tasks with all possible combinations of 2-signal and 2-response types. An increase in rate was noted from least to most compatible. Various stimulus–response associations have therefore been included in this experiment to investigate the above effect further.

The main area of interest for this experiment, however, is *conceptual modeling*. Previous models of choice–reaction times can be classified as either *continuous* or *serial*. Continuous models contend that on each trial the subject chooses his reaponse by processing the stimulus array continually as time passes, without definite intermediary stages. The simultaneous scanning models suggested by Hick (1952b), and Laming (1966) are of this class. In these, all possible stimulus states are checked or scanned simultaneously by the processing mechanism. The time taken by each stimulus has a random component, so the response, made after all stimuli are fully checked, will be slower the more stimuli are possible.

Serial models suggest that the subject chooses his response in a series of discrete steps, each taking some unit of time. That is, the subject jumps from one state of stimulus knowledge to the next. One such model was proposed by Hick (1952a). On each step the subject eliminates half the possible stimuli as not given on this trial, and each step is assumed to take the same time. This successive dichotomization model is inadequate to explain some results; for example, that more probable stimuli are reacted to faster than others, and if n is not a power of 2 the proportion of stimuli rejected at each stage cannot be a half.

Welford (1971) has shown that continuous models do not cover facts from some of his experiments, but that a version of the serial model will do so. However, results presented here raise problems for this model, too.

The differing values of the slope constant, k in Eq. (1) and b in Eq. (2), and the related "information transfer" rate found in choice–reaction experiments have yet to be explained fully, or in well defined terms. Commonsense ideas of compatibility and naturalness are applicable here, but cannot a priori give other than possible rank relationships between tasks. Comparing the slopes from a set of tasks, all using the same apparatus but different amounts of compatibility, may cast some light on factors underlying rates of decision processing and enable at least approximate estimation of the slope constant.

II. THE EXPERIMENT

A. Method

1. Apparatus

A set of eight keys were arranged in two arcs of four in such a way that subjects could comfortably rest one finger (excluding the thumbs) on each. The keys themselves were perspex cylinders, 13 mm in diameter, dished on the top to fit finger tips, and projecting up 5 mm through a base board. Each key was connected to a microswitch via an armature beneath the board. A force of about 150 g was needed to trip the switch and register a response. Through the center of each key was a rod, 3 mm in diameter, which could be vibrated up and down at 100 cycles/sec independently of the rest of the key. This vibration was the stimulus used. Subjectively, it was a mild tingling sensation.

The presentation of stimuli, recording of responses, and response latencies were controlled by a PDP-8 computer in an adjacent room. The stimulus onset was always with the up phase of a vibration cycle, and was left on until a response, correct or not, was made. Only the first response was recorded if multiple responses were made. Each new stimulus appeared a constant time (RSI) after the key pressed in response to the previous stimulus was released.

2. Subjects

Twelve subjects were used, six male and six female. Two were middle-aged, the others were undergraduates aged between 18 and 26.

3. Procedure

There were six different tasks in the experiment, labeled T1–T6. The basic difference between them was the stimulus–response associations for correct responses. Three types of mapping were used:

1. *Compatible*: Each stimulus had to be responded to by pressing the key under the finger stimulated.
2. *Reflected:* The same figure on the other hand was correct; for example, a stimulus to the left index finger was responded to with the right index finger. The stimulus–response mapping was a reflection about the body midline.
3. *Shifted*: The correct response was described by shifting the stimulated position to the other hand and responded with, for example, the left index finger if the right little finger was stimulated.

The fingers, the stimuli to them, and responses by them are labeled 1–8 from right to left and referred to in this way.

The tasks in terms of their mappings were:

T1: all compatible;
T2: all reflected;
T3: half reflected, half compatible; that is, a left-hand stimulus had to be reflected to give its correct response, and a right-hand stimulus had to be responded to with the stimulated finger;
T4: all shifted;
T5: half shifted, half compatible. Again, left-hand stimuli had to be shifted and right-hand stimuli were compatible with their correct responses; and
T6: described below.

These tasks provided a range of compatibilities via different S–R associations which, unlike those of Brainard, Irby, Fitts, and Alluisi (1962), all used the same stimuli and same responses.

Each task was given in a separate session which lasted approximately one hour. Each set of stimuli consisted of 192 events, preceded by 14 practice trials which were ignored for analysis. The stimulus order was random except that each occurred equally often in blocks of 16 trials. Each session began with a practice set of 8-choice trials, after which 8-, 4-, and 2-choice sets were given in random order to balance for intrasession effects. The RSI used was 2 sec.

Two different subsets of fingers were used for the 4- and 2-choice trials: Subset (a), the 4-choice stimuli were to be the right hand (Stimuli 1–4) and the 2-choice stimuli were the right index and middle fingers (Stimuli 3 and 4), and Subset (b), the 4-choice stimuli were the index and middle fingers of each hand (Stimuli 3–6), and the 2-choice stimuli were the two index fingers (Stimuli 4 and 5). Obviously the half–half tasks could only be of Type (b).

Task T6 was a control to test the possibility that the compatible task was at some kind of minimal threshold of reaction time and to explore differences due to stimulus factors (such as slight differences in the intensity of the vibrations), and response factors. A set of 192 trials was given in which the subject had to respond to the first stimulus with Finger 8, the second with Finger 7, . . . the eighth with Finger 1, the ninth with Finger 8 and so on across the hands, every 8 stimuli, regardless of which stimulus was given. Thus there was no uncertainty in what response to make. There was still stimulus uncertainty, but stimulus *detection,* not full stimulus *identification* was needed. The stimulus sequence was arranged so that every stimulus was linked with every response four times. To lessen the possibility of anticipatory responses, impossible in other tasks, a random RSI of between 1.5 and 2.5 sec was used. These trials were followed after a break by two similar sets of trials in which only one hand was stimulated and responses were made sequentially with the other. For half of the subjects doing T6 the first of these was with stimuli to the right hand and responses with the left, and the second vice versa. For the remaining subjects the order of the trials was reversed.

T6 was preceded by 192 8-choice compatible trials with an RSI of 2 sec, and then the same but with a random RSI of 1.5 to 2.5 sec. The first set acted as orientation to the situation, and allowed intersubject comparisons (noted below), while the second enabled the effect of varying the RSI to be tested.

Each subject did three sessions on a different day (and thus three tasks). Four subjects did each type of task, for example, four did T1a, and four did T1b, with the order of the tasks balanced to minimize the effects of intertask transfer on the results. Each subject did either T1a, T1b, or T6 on Day 1. The four who did T1a also did T2a and T4a. Two of those doing T1b, and two doing T6 also did T2b and T3b, while the remaining four did T4b and T5b. At the start of each session the task for that day was explained and the first 8-choice set was given.

There was then a short break, the subject was told how many and which stimuli to expect in the next set, and then the task was resumed. This procedure was repeated between each set of trials. As mentioned, all subjects did either T1 or T6 in their first session to allow a degree of matching between subjects doing various combinations of tasks. This matching involved putting subjects with similar means on the first set of 8-choice compatible into different groups.

No consistent significant effect was found on comparing the preliminary trial sets in T6, that is, varying the RSI had little effect. There was no significant difference (unrelated samples t tests) between groups of subjects in T1a and T1b (p = .31, two-tailed) nor between T1a and T6 (p = .43). Thus subject groups were matched at least to this extent.

To minimize auditory cues from the buzzing of the keys, the subjects wore earmuffs.

B. Results

Only the times for correct responses were considered. All but two subjects responded with error rates of less than 15% and over all subjects and nonpractice tasks the mean error rate was 7%. More importantly, within any task there was no significant difference between the error rate for 2-, 4-, and 8-choice sets. So speed–accuracy tradeoff effects can be ignored within sessions.

1. Degree of Choice and Information Rate

Table 1 gives mean latencies for each task T1–T5, standard error of the mean, and percentage errors averaged over the four subjects in each task. The related set of tasks, T1b, T4b, and T5b (compatible, shifted, and half compatible–half shifted) are given graphically in Fig. 1–3 as representative of the others. The first set of 8-choice times is longer than the second in each case. It may be questioned, therefore, which set should be compared with the 4- and 2-choice times. However, practice effects appeared to have been reasonably stabilized within the initial practice 8-choice trials. The means of the last 48 of the first 8-choice set and the whole of the second 8-choice set (the second, third, or fourth set in the session) were compared using a related samples t-test. No significant differences were found (p = .18). So we can assume that this method eliminated the unfamiliarity with the task, and mainly, if not fully, stabilized performance. It was assumed that this would also be valid practice for the 4- and 2-choice situations. In the rest of this chapter, "8-choice trials" will therefore refer to the second such set given on each session and not the practice set.

Table 2 presents the two-tailed probabilities of related sample t-tests between the 8-- and 4-, and 4- and 2-choice sets. No more powerful test was thought necessary in light of the low ps obtained. All differences were in the direction 8->4->2-choice. Considering the full task comparisons (not "right hand only") it can be seen from the table that only two comparisons are not significant at p =

TABLE 1

Mean Correct Reaction Times in Msec, Standard Error of
the Mean and Percentage Errors for Each Degree of
Choice in the Various Tasks[a]

Task	Practice	Degree of choice		
		8	4	2
T1a (mean)	287	244	238	219
(standard error)	22	239	31	25
(% errors)	1.6	2.6	4.7	4.7
T1b	298	248	240	227
	21	19	18	20
	4.2	5.2	3.1	2.1
T2a	712	696	620	337
	51	51	48	27
	10.9	10.0	7.8	5.2
T2b	596	559	444	310
	32	29	27	20
	10.4	10.9	7.8	7.8
T3b	388	353	266	204
	25	27	20	24
	12.0	15.7	8.3	2.0
T4a	1077	1052	828	449
	43	45	37	32
	9.4	13.2	8.9	8.6
T4b	710	663	567	320
	41	41	39	17
	10.4	6.8	6.8	8.9
T5b	552	552	468	274
	38	38	36	23
	8.3	6.8	6.3	7.3

[a]Each mean is taken over 192 trials (less errors) and 4
subjects.

0.05. These are the 8-choice compared with the 4-choice for T1a and T1b, the compatible task. The next two highest probabilities are the 4-, 2-choice comparisons for the same task ($p < 0.05$, 0.03). This lends credence to Leonard's (1959) conclusions that, in a vibro-tactile compatible task, degree of choice greater than one has no effect on reaction times after some practice.

The means in Table 1 increase proportionally more with degree of choice in tasks T2–T5 than in T1. The obvious and accepted interpretation of this fact is that it is the translation from stimulus to its associated response that leads to the increase (usually logarithmic, as here) in response time with degree of choice. This has been held to be true even if there is merely a translation from visual position to the corresponding finger position as in Welford's (1971) experiments. Leonard (1961) mentions that this light–key relationship is not obvious to the

TABLE 2
Two-tailed Probabilities from *t*-tests between Different Degrees of Choice[a]

	T1a	T1b	T2a	T2b	T3b	T4a	T4b	T5b	Right hand T3b	T5b
8 cf 4	.54	.20	0	0	.002	0	0	.01	0	.17
4 cf 2	.05	.03	0	0	.001	0	0	0	.01	.01

[a]An entry of 0 means $p < .001$.

young or mentally retarded, and suggests that normal adults have for some reason assimilated it while growing up.

Best fitting straight lines which minimized the squared error, were fitted to mean reaction time versus $\log(n)$ for all tasks except T6. The reciprocal of the slope of these lines can be taken as a measure of the rate of transfer of information that the subjects achieved, ignoring errors. These values are given in Table 3. A wide range of results occurred, from 3.3 bits/sec to 95 bits/sec. These rates are within those found by other experimenters: 5–8 bits/sec in light–key studies (Merkel, 1885; Hicks, 1952a; Welford, 1971); about 15 bits/sec for verbal naming responses and up to 180 in Morin, Troxell, and McPherson's (1965) experiment, and infinite for Leonard (1959). The information rates are given here only for comparison with other experiments, without commitment to the theoretical standpoint of transmitted information as the determinant of choice RT.

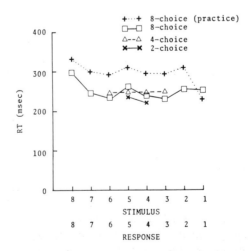

FIG. 1   Mean latencies of correct responses to each stimulus for Task 1b (compatible) taken over four subjects.

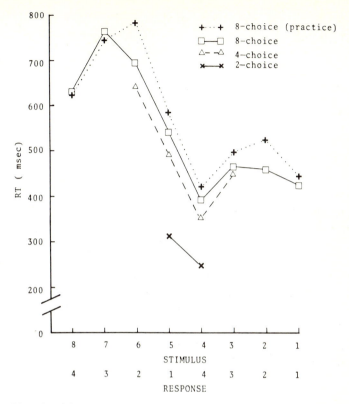

FIG. 2 Mean latencies of correct responses to each stimulus for Task 4b (shifted) taken over four subjects.

The rank order of these rates gives a comparison of the difficulties of the various tasks: with compatible the easiest; then half compatible–half reflected; half compatible–half shifted; reflected; and most difficult, shifted. Admittedly such a comparison involves comparisons between and across subjects, but the same order was found in three other subjects used during apparatus testing who did all six tasks. It confirms the results of Brainard *et al.* (1962) stressing the importance of the association between stimulus and response as seen here, even when the stimulus and response sets are constant.

Some further confirmation of Leonard's conclusions regarding highly compatible tasks comes from task T6. The main aim of this task was to separate out differences induced by the stimuli and by the responses. The set of 192 trials in which each stimulus was linked with each response three times was analyzed by a three-factor (subjects, stimuli, and responses) design analysis of variance. Table 4 lists the results of this. No interactions are significant, so using the within–cell variance as the error variance is justified (see Winer, 1962, p. 254). The response

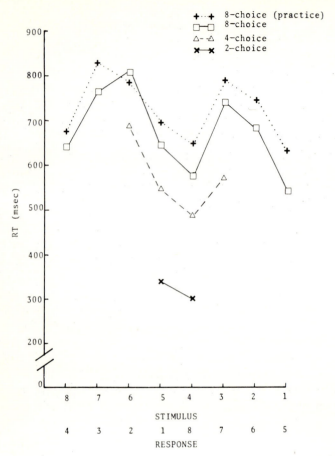

FIG. 3   Mean latencies of correct responses to each stimulus for Task 5b (half shifted—half compatible), taken over four subjects.

TABLE 3
Information Rates in Bits/Sec for Each Task, with Entries for Separate Hands for the Half—Half Tasks

									Left		Right	
Task	1a	1b	2a	2b	3b	4a	4b	5b	3b	5b	3b	5b
Info. rate	80	90	5.5	8.0	13.4	3.3	5.8	8.0	9.9	5.9	18.2	11.8

TABLE 4
Analysis of Variance on T6

Source	MS	df	F ratio	p
Subjects (S)	95531.10	3	7.0770	.003
Responses (R)	21597.25	7	1.5999	.1323
Stimuli (T)	33445.40	7	2.4776	.0165
S × R	13201.02	21	.9779	.5103
S × T	11670.23	21	.8645	.6389
R × T	10857.18	49	.8043	.8263
S × R × T	10821.7	147	.8017	.9465
Within	13498.90	512	–	–
Between	13007.78	255	–	–

factor was not significant, but the stimulus factor was, $p = 0.03$; that is, independent of what response was made there was a difference due to some stimulus property. Many subjects said that Stimulus 4 was most intense. The stimulus profile given in Table 5 shows that indeed this has a shorter latency, and Stimulus 8 is the slowest, each being about 25 msec above or below the level of the others. Post hoc comparisons showed that these two differences were significant at the .05 level. This is unfortunate, for Stimulus 4 is the right index finger and is used in all degrees of choice, while Stimulus 8 is used only in the 8-choice. This artificially increases the difference between degrees of choice. However, it is only likely to be of appreciable effect in T1 where otherwise the information rates shown in Table 3 would be even greater. In the others the effect of mapping stimuli to response is much greater than 25 msec.

TABLE 5
Stimulus and Response Profiles for the Predetermined Response Task, T6[a]

Stimulus	8	7	6	5	4	3	2	1
8 stimulus task	281	250	246	251	226	244	250	242
4 stimuli to left hand	216	214	220	207	–	–	–	–
4 stimulus to right hand	–	–	–	–	210	223	216	208
Response	8	7	6	5	4	3	2	1
8-stimulus task	271	235	233	244	236	237	249	227
4 stimuli to left hand	–	–	–	–	203	206	211	200
4 stimuli to right hand	212	205	204	206	–	–	–	–

[a]Each 8-stimulus value is the mean of 96 responses, being the 24 from each of four subjects (3 with each finger) made to that stimulus. Similarly for the 4-stimulus tasks, and response values.

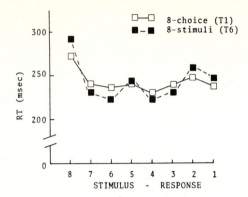

FIG. 4 Comparison of eight-choice means for Task 1a and Task 1b with average of the stimulus and response profiles for Task 6 with eight stimuli.

The two related four-stimulus tasks, in which one hand was stimulated and responses made with the other, were also to be analyzed in this way. However the variances were not homogeneous between cells and even after a square root transformation (following Winer, 1962, p. 220) this was still so. Hence, only indications from the data can be considered.

Regardless of which hand was stimulated, latencies were about 25 msec faster than for the 8-stimulus case, as is shown in Table 5. This may be a practice effect, but it is more likely that since the stimulus and response sets were separate, with a stimulated finger never used as the response, this compatible reaction may have been easier to suppress than in the 8-stimulus task, in which all fingers were used as stimuli and responses, and each compatible stimulus– response pair was correct on three trials.

Comparing the latencies of 8-choice T1 with this 8-stimulus T6 suggests that those of T1 are at some minimal level for responding (one of Leonard's, 1959, suggestions), since even making the required response completely determined before the stimulus arrives gives no lowering of latency. Another indicator of this is shown in Fig. 4 in which the stimulus and response profiles from T6 have been averaged and are compared with the mean times for the 8-choice from T1a and T1b. There is a high degree of similarity between the two curves.

2. Comparison of Compatible, Half–Half and Mapped Tasks

Figure 5 presents the mean latencies for T1b, T3b, and T2b. Similar plots hold for T1, T4, and T5 as can be seen by overlaying Figs. 1–3.

The order of the overall means as found here, T1b $<$ T3b $<$ T2b, is easily explained by any theory which can demonstrate different slope constants, b in Eq. (2), for different tasks, but other features are more difficult. For example, why is there a difference between the hands on the half–half tasks? There was even a 42-msec difference between response times to Stimuli 4 and 5 in the

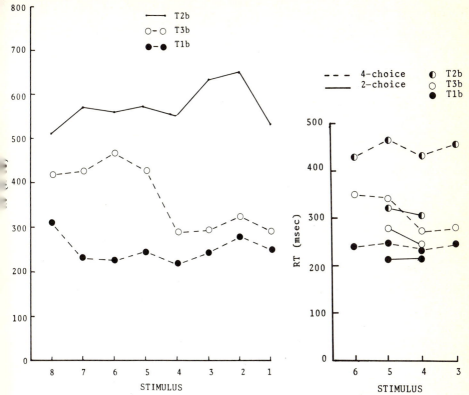

FIG. 5 (a) Comparison between mean RTs of the eight-choice condition of Task 1b and Task 2b, and the related half–half Task 3b, plotted stimulus. (b) Similarly for 4-1 and two-choice conditions.

2-choice task of T3b, although this effectively required the subject to make response 4 every two seconds.

These results replicate a finding of Morin and Forrin (1962) using pure and mixed tasks. The subject spoke a digit in response either to that digit (compatible) or to a geometric symbol (mapped). In three comparable 4-choice tasks (pure compatible, pure mapped, or half–half) they found that latencies for compatible responses in the pure compatible task were shorter than compatible in half–half, and that these in turn were shorter than mapped in half–half, which were again shorter (though not significantly) than in the pure mapped task — the same order as found here. Their experiment did not have the confounding effect of number of responses being less in the half–half case, so it seems probable that avoiding this here would not change the pattern of results. Clearly, in the mixed case the presence of incompatible mapping for some stimuli affects reactions to the stimuli for which mapping is compatible and vice versa, as was found by Kornblum (1965) in a 2-choice lights–keys task.

In addition, the linear regression of RT on Log N for the right-hand (compatible) stimulus subset accounted for 96 and 84% of the variance for T3b and T5b compatible, respectively, and the slopes were significantly greater than zero (p = 0.001, 0.003). Thus, not only did the mapped stimulus—response pairs increase RT, but this increase was probably logarithmic with N. Broadbent and Gregory (1965) also report an interaction of RT and N with different compatibilities using vibro-tactile apparatus. A model postulating a simple constant duration "which mapping" decision step during processing is therefore inadequate to describe these data.

3. Type a Compared with Type b

It was planned to compare T2a with T2b and T4a with T4b to assess the relative effects of all stimuli to one hand, and responses to the other (Type a), and stimuli (and responses) divided between both hands (Type b). It was hoped to find which of either additional distinctiveness within the stimulus and response sets or distinctiveness between the two sets would make the task more difficult.

For both Tasks 2 and 4 the (a) and (b) types were done by different groups of subjects, but since the 8-choice task was identical for (a) and (b), it was hoped that this common point would allow comparisons of slopes. Unfortunately, although the subjects' RTs on the compatible task were matched between groups, their RTs on the 8-choice mapped tasks were not. No comparison can easily be made under these circumstances, and none will be given here. However, the results do point out that caution is needed in generalizing matching on one task to a second, even closely related, task.

C. Models

A model applying to all the tasks in this experiment must fit the following results:

1. the linear increase of reaction time with the logarithm of the number of stimuli, with Task 1 a special case, (constant or almost so);
2. the relationship between compatible, half—half, and fully mapped tasks:

a. the decrease in latency for the mapped stimuli in the half—half case from the stimuli with the same S—R relationship in the fully mapped case;
b. similarly, the increase in latency for the compatible stimuli;
c. the difference between the compatible and mapped stimuli's times in the half—half case; these must hold for both spatial and reflected mappings, and for 8-, 4-, and 2-choice tasks, including the 2-choice half compatible—half reflected, in which both stimuli required the same response;

d. also, differences in the three above cases are proportional to log n, as are the means over all stimuli;

3. the longer reaction times for shifted as against reflected transformation must be allowed for, and this difference is proportional to log n, fitting Hyman's Eq. (2) to the data: the intercepts, a, are similar, and the slopes, b, differ between tasks, as observed in the data presented here;

4. of lesser importance is a significant difference between inner (middle and ring) fingers and outer (index and little) fingers; the outer stimuli are responded to faster in all tasks except the fully compatible and the 4-choice of T2b: that this difference is decreased by practice makes it less than essential to a model of the tasks.

5. results from other experiments, such as the effect of unequal frequencies, practice, and stimulus intensity should also be compatible with any model proposed.

There are two serious failings of serial subdecision models on these points. Consider linearity with log n: serial models satisfy this, but have difficulty in explaining the special case of high compatibility or long practice. For these cases with constant RT, the duration of each step in the process would have to be infinitesimally short. Such a limiting case is conceptually difficult in a search-type model, although a range of inspection times for a range of task difficulties would be expected.

To satisy Point 2 is even more difficult. It is not sufficient to postulate a single inspection time for all stimuli in the half—half tasks as this would not give the observed difference between hands. Nor does carrying over the inspection times for each mapping derived from the fully mapped tasks into the half—half tasks give the desired results, not at least without cumbersome assumptions on order of subgroup identification.

A New Model

This model, prompted by the inadequacies in existing models when applied to some aspects of the results generated by this experiment, can satisfy the above points (1)–(3) in its simple form and the rest in an extended version.

It assumes that the level of excitation for each possible stimulus is translated into a corresponding amount of excitation in the associated response, and accumulated. Each kind of mapping has a basic association time determining the time needed to perform the transformation required. This value, α, is low for compatible transformations and high for less natural ones. A response is made when it attains an excitation greater than a set value. Although the time needed for this translation is also proportional to the level of excitation with high level taking a longer time than a low level (a signal has more effect than noise), a response criterion is reached sooner the higher the level.

Considering the model in greater detail we define the following parameters, some of which are not critical to the model, but aid in its explanation:

1. n: the number of stimuli in use;
2. i: $i = 1, 2, \ldots, n$, a general stimulus set member;
3. j: the particular stimulus given on this trial;
4. k: $k = 1, 2, \ldots, n$, a general response set member;
5. m: the particular response made on this trial;
6. $r(i)$:   a function specifying the S–R pairs for the task;
7. $e(i)$:   the excitation on stimulus i;
8. $p(k,t)$: the response excitation of stimulus k at the time t;
9. $\alpha(i)$:   the association time for the mapping from i to $r(i)$;
10. $\delta(k)$: the response firing level for response k;
11. s: a variable representing iterations through the process of translating e into p

Consider an arbitrarily short time interval during the translation of e into p, which we shall call an iteration. In an iteration equal amounts of e are translated into p, and each of the possible stimuli takes some processing time. For mathematical convenience, we have the variable, s, as the continuous analog of the number of iterations performed (i.e., it can assume any real value greater than one, rather than just the integers).

The half–half tasks show that the nonstimulated fingers do affect the latency. To satisfy this we assume two sources of excitation, σ, that due to the signal, and ν, a measure of the neural noise unavoidable in the system. This noise is considered to be independent of n and evenly distributed between the stimuli. It can be conceived as being inherent in the translation mechanism and hence independent of n, so that before the signal is given all internal states have equal noise to which is added, for the given stimulus, the signal excitation at its onset. Mathematically we have:

$$e(j) = \sigma + \nu/n$$
$$e(i) = \nu/n; \quad i \neq j. \tag{i}$$

We now state that

$$\mathrm{RT}(j) = a + \int_1^x \sum_i \frac{\alpha(i)\, e(i)}{E \cdot s}\, ds. \tag{ii}$$

Where s is the time related variable of iteration, and x is defined as that value of s at which $p(m,s) = \delta(m)$, the iterations through the process required for the excitation of response m to accumulate to its firing level. Thus x satisfies $p(m, x) = \delta(m)$. E is the total excitation present; $E = \Sigma e(i) = \sigma + \nu$.

Thus Eq. (ii) states that the time for one iteration is proportional directly to the sum of the association times weighted with their initial levels (scaled by E to equal α in the simple case of a pure task) and inversely with the iteration variable, s. In addition the latency of the response is given by the sum of the durations of each iteration until the response criterion is met. It was mentioned in the brief outline of the model that time needed to convert energy was proportioned to association time and to excitation. The latter is seen in the results of the mixed tasks where, for example, the mapped stimuli latencies are a little faster than in a pure mapped task. This shows that the noise stimuli on a trial have an effect less than that of the signal. That the time should vary inversely with the iteration variable, s, has at least two possible explanations.

One is that time taken in an iteration by the translation of a stimulus into its corresponding response is proportional to the constant association time, and the level of stimulus excitation stored in short term memory. It is suggested that this falls off with iterations, and is given by $e(i)/s$. This fits at least qualitatively the fall off in neural reverbatory circuits with time. This, together with the assumption that each stimulus is serviced in an iteration, gives Eq. (ii).

A second approach is to link the α and $1/s$. Under this suggestion, the time to convert a unit of energy from stimulus into its response decreases with iterations within any trial. This would be like a within-trial practice effect; the task becoming faster as the neural pathways used become refreshed, more worn-in. Or, in attention terms, a gradual focusing of attention away from monitoring and other tasks and onto the translation process of that stimulus. Again, with each stimulus serviced in each iteration, this gives Eq. (ii). We can assume that the stimulus excitation level is constant, which is more in keeping with Eq. (v) below, where Δ must be independent of s.

It now remains to find the value of x in Eq. (ii). For latency to be proportioned to Log n, we need x proportioned to n:

$$x = C \cdot n \tag{iii}$$

as this, using the mathematical relation for natural logarithms,

$$\log y = \int_{1}^{y} \frac{ds}{s}$$

would give

$$RT(j) = A + B \log(n) \tag{iv}$$

where

$$A = a + \frac{\Sigma \, \alpha(i) \, e(i) \log(c)}{E}$$

$$B = \frac{\Sigma \, \alpha(i) \, e(i)}{E}$$

It is certainly plausible intuitively that x is proportional to n; a number of suggestions can lead to this. The simplest is that a constant amount of response excitation is allocatable to response on each iteration and that is shared equally between all n posibilities. This gives each $1/n$. However, this would have all responses reaching criterion together. A simple modification, weighting the $1/n$ with the stimulus excitation level, gives the increment in $\rho(r(i))$, denoted by Δ in Eq. (i).

$$\Delta(i) = \frac{e(i)}{n} \tag{v}$$

On any iteration this gives:

$$\rho(k,s) = \int_1^s \frac{e(i)}{n}\, ds$$
$$= \frac{e(i)}{n}(s-1)$$

at iteration s. So

(vi)

$$\rho(m,x) = \frac{e(j)\,(x-1)}{n}$$

But this is also $\delta(m)$, by the definition of x. Therefore,

$$x = \frac{\delta(m)\,n + 1}{e(j)} \tag{vii}$$

This is one way of satisfying Eq. (iii).

Combining Eqs. (ii) and (vii) gives:

$$RT(j) = a + \frac{[\Sigma\, \alpha(i)\, e(i)]}{E} \log \frac{(\delta(m)\,n + 1)]}{e(j)}$$

$$= a + \frac{\Sigma\alpha(i)\, e(i)}{E} \log \frac{\delta(m)}{e(j)} + \frac{\Sigma\alpha(i)e(i)}{E}\log \frac{(n+e(j))}{\delta(m)}$$

$$= A + B \log(n + \frac{e(j)}{\delta(m)})$$

We can assume that $\delta(m) > e(j)$, imposing the restraint that at least one iteration is needed to reach a response criterion, so that $e(j)/\delta$ ranges between 0 (low e, high δ) and 1 (equal e and δ): the model thus offers an explanation of why sometimes $\log(n)$ and sometimes $\log (n + 1)$ gives the better fit to experimental data. Low stimulus intensities (or more likely, discriminabilities) should give a better fit against $\log(n)$, while high intensities should be better fitted against $\log (n + 1)$. It does in fact appear that the stimulus intensities used by Hyman (1953) whose results are well fitted against $\log n$ were almost certainly less than those used by Hick (1952a) whose results are better fitted against $\log (n + 1)$. For the rest of this work we shall use $\log (n)$ for simplicity.

The model also offers a partial explanation for the intercept, A, in Eq. (iv). The given expression for A shows that part of this is inherent in the process, and is time dependent on C, that is, $\delta/e(j)$, is needed for a decision to be reached. It also gives the intercept as varying with α (weighted with log c). It is suggested below that α will decrease with practice, and therefore so will the intercept. Teichner and Krebs (1974), in a review of 59 visual choice reaction time studies, conclude that the intercept does in fact decrease with practice, and is a function of the stimulus coding required.

We let δ be constant across responses, that is no concentration or other biases, and so x is also indepencent of k. Now Eq. (iv) can be rewritten as:

$$RT(j) = A + \frac{\sum \alpha(i)\, e(i)}{E} \log n. \tag{ix}$$

So that for the mean reaction time over all stimuli we have

$$RT = A + \sum_j \frac{\sum_i \alpha(i)\, e(i)}{En} \log(n); \tag{x}$$

that is,

$$RT = A + \frac{\sum \alpha(i)}{n} \log(n). \tag{xi}$$

If α depends only on the transformation for that stimulus, we should expect that the same α would apply in a fully mapped task as for the same transformation in a half–half task. That is, from Eq. (xi) the slope constant for a half–half task would be the mean for the two αs for the component tasks. With α so determined, Point 1 is satisfied.

To test this, consider the slope values for T1b, T2b, and T3b; 10.5, 124.5, and 74.5, respectively. We find that the mean of the first two is 67.5, which is close to that of T3b. In addition, it would be expected that α for a mixed task in which two stimuli map onto each response would be lower than the simple mean of the αs incorporated in it, for $\rho(m)$ will have two increments (one signal and one noise) per iteration, and so will reach criterion faster (lower x). Thus this result is acceptable near the value predicted by this model.

The comparable α values for T1b, T4b, and T5b are 10.5, 171.5, and 124, respectively. The mean of the first two is 91. Although this differs appreciably from 124, one must bear in mind that two of the four subjects doing these mapped tests did T6, not T1b. Although these were roughly matched on the basis of performance on Task 1 or Task 6, some difference between them inevitably remained, especially noticable in the most difficult task, T5 (shifted). This could have lead to the kind of discrepancy involved.

Points 2a–d are also satisfied. Consider one subset of stimuli with the same transformation in two tasks, for example, the left hand in T2b and T3b. Let this set have an association time of α_1 and the other hand in the half–half task have one of α_2. Then the difference between the means for the same hand on different tasks will be (ignoring the slight effect of lowering of x noted above), from Eq. (ix):

$$RT_1 - RT_2 = \frac{\nu}{E}(\alpha_1 - \alpha_2)\log n. \qquad \text{(xii)}$$

This fits Points 2a, b, and d. For Point 2c we have similarly:

$$RT_1 - RT_2 = \frac{\sigma}{E}(\alpha_1 - \alpha_2)\log (n). \qquad \text{(xiii)}$$

So with appropriate choice of σ and ν we can get agreement between the means predicted by the model and the observed results. Indeed, these two equations could perhaps be used to determine relative levels of noise and of signals between subjects, which is of theoretical interest (see, e.g., Vickers, Nettelbeck, & Willson, 1972).

Point 3, that reaction times are longer for shifted than for reflected tasks, falls outside the model which is not designed to predict what value α will have in a given task, but the requirement of the model that the difference between the tasks is proportional to $\log(n)$ is obviously met.

Unequal stimulus frequencies effect latencies, with more probable stimuli responded to faster than others (La Berge & Tweedy, 1964; and others). This model handles this at least qualitatively if it is assumed that the $1/n$ in Eq. (v) is taken as a measure of some payoff function $p(j)$ for the stimuli. In the usual equal frequency, no special instructions choice task, all stimuli would have an equal payoff, $1/n$. If stimulus frequencies are unequal, the subject can obey the instruction to react as quickly as possible by changing this payoff to the probability of a signal. We can replace Eq. (v) with

$$x = \frac{\delta}{e(j)p(j)} + 1 \qquad \text{(xiv)}$$

where $p(j)$ is the payoff weighting given to stimulus j. This interpretation is reasonable in light of the explanation of Eq. (v) given above. Replacing Eq. (v) with Eq. (xiv) gives shorter response latencies for larger $p(j)$ as required.

The effect of concentration found by Welford (1973) – a decrease of response latency to the stimulus or stimuli concentrated on, and an increase in the others – can be obtained from this model in two ways. Perhaps concentration decreases δ for the emphasized stimuli and increases it for the others, respectively shortening or lengthening latencies; that is, some response presetting takes place. Alternatively concentration may bias the payoff, $p(j)$ of Eq. (xiv), in a like manner to unequal stimulus frequencies mentioned above, with the concentrated stimuli becoming favored [larger $p(j)$] as they are in some sense focused upon, and thus they have shorter latencies. However, the precise results in Welford's (1973) experiment and covered by his model are not explicable a priori by either of these ideas.

The decrease in RT with practice can be allowed for if α decreases with practice. Indeed, the explanation of α as association time would give this by analogy with paired-learning tasks and would be similar to the suggestion made by Welford (1968) that with practice the associations between stimulus and response become built in as a kind of transformation table. Whether α can reach zero for all tasks, as it appears to have in Mowbray and Rhoades' (1960) work with practice, and in Leonard's (1959) study is still not fully settled.

The model can also be extended to cover the point noted by Welford (1971), that reactions to stimuli in the middle of a row are slower than those at the ends. If $\sigma + v$ is not divided among the stimuli as suggested in Eq. (i), but according to some "neural distance" concept (see Welford, 1968, p. 80) with stimuli sharing the excitation in proportion to their differentiation in the brain from each other, then with an appropriate distribution we could get the designed effect. The size of this effect would depend on α, being low for T1 but more pronounced for the others, as found here.

Some features of sequential effects often noted in choice reaction times can be fitted with another assumption. If we assume that the stimulus and response excitation does not reset to zero immediately after a trial, but decays slowly, then repetitions of the same stimulus or response will be responded to more quickly, being as it were primed. Similar although lesser effects will be noted for successive trials in which the stimulus and response are not repeated but are in some way closely related. For example, a different response called for, but on the same hand, will be faster (Kirby, 1974). Also, long RSIs would give smaller sequential effects than would short RSIs, as has been found by Bertelson in 1961 and others subsequently.

Up to this point, we have considered the noise only as its mean value. By its nature, it varies from moment to moment, and this distribution of excitation with time introduces another testable prediction. It would introduce variance into the response times. Probably this would give a smooth increase with log(n) for n other than powers of 2, more in keeping with the results of Hick (1952a) than with a successive dichotomous model.

ACKNOWLEDGMENT

I wish to acknowledge the support and encouragement of my supervisor, Professor A.T. Welford, from the project's inception onward.

REFERENCES

Bertelson, P. Sequential redundancy and speed in a serial two–choice responding task. *Quarterly Journal of Experimental Psychology*, 1961, **13**, 90–102.

Brainard, R. W., Irby, T. S., Fitts, P. M., & Allusi, E. A. Some variables influencing the rate of gain of information. *Journal of Experimental Psychology*, 1962, **63**, 105–110.

Broadbent, D. E., & Gregory, M. On the interaction of S–R compatibility with other variables affecting reaction time. *British Journal of Psychology*, 1965, **56**, 61–67.

Hick, W. E. On the rate of gain of information. *Quarterly Journal of Experimental Psychology*, 1952, **4**, 11–26. (a)

Hick, W. E. Why the human operator? *Transactions of the Society of Instrumental Technology*, 1952, **4**, 67–77. (b)

Hyman, R. Stimulus information as a determinant of reaction time. *Journal of Experimental Psychology*, 1953, **45**, 188–196.

Kirby, N. H. Sequential effects in serial reaction time. *Journal of Experimental Psychology*, 1972, **96**, 32–36.

Kornblum, S. Response competition and/or inhibition in two-choice reaction time. *Psychonomic Science*, 1965, **2**, 55–56.

La Berge, D., & Tweedy, J. R. Presentation probability and choice time. *Journal of Experimental Psychology*, 1964, **68**, 477–481.

Laming, D. R. J. A new interpretation of the relation between choice-reaction time and the number of equiprobable alternatives. *British Journal of Mathematical and Statistical Psychology*, 1966, **19**, 139–149.

Leonard, J. A. Tactual Choice Reaction: I. *Quarterly Journal of Experimental Psychology*, 1959, **11**, 76–83.

Leonard, J. A. Choice reaction time experiments and information theory. In C. Cherry (Ed), Information Theory: Fourth London Symposium. London: Butterworth, 1961.

Merkel, J. Die Zeitlichen Verhältnisse der Willenshastigkeid *Philosophische Studien*, 1885, **2**, 73–127.

Morin, R. E., and Forrin, B. Mixing 2 types of S–R association in a CR task. *Journal of Experimental Psychology*, 1962, **64**, 137–141.

Morin, R. E., Troxell, N., & McPherson, S. Information and reaction time for "naming" responses. *Journal of Experimental Psychology*, 1965, **70**, 309–314.

Mowbray, G.H. Choice reaction times for skilled responses. *Quarterly Journal of Experimental Psychology*, 1960, **12**, 193–202.

Mowbray, G. H., & Rhoades, M. V. On the reduction of choice reaction times with practice. *Quarterly Journal of Experimental Psychology*, 1959, **11**, 16–23.

Shannon, C. E., & Weaver, W. *The mathematical theory of communication.* Urbana, Ill.: University of Illinois Press, 1949.

Teichner, J., & Krebs, P. Laws of visual choice reaction time. *Psychological Review*, 1974, **81**, (1), 75–98.

Vickers, D., Nettelbeck, T., & Willson, R. J. Perceptual indices of performance: The measurement of "inspection time" and "noise" in the visual system. *Perception*, 1972, **1**, 263–295.

Welford, A. T. Fundamentals of skill. London: Methuen, 1968.

Welford, A. T. What is the basis of choice reaction time? *Ergonomics*, 1971, **14**, 679–693.

Welford, A. T. Attention, strategy and reaction time: A tentative metric. In S. Kornblum (Ed.), *Attention and performance IV*. New York: Academic Press, 1973.

Winer, B. J. *Statistical principles in experimental design.* New York: McGraw-Hill, 1962.

3
Response Selection Rules in Spatial Choice Reaction Tasks

J. Duncan

Department of Experimental Psychology
Oxford University
Oxford, England

ABSTRACT

In spatial choice response tasks, reaction time (RT) depends on the mapping between a fixed set of stimuli and a fixed set of responses. This effect has been accounted for in terms of the "obviousness" of S–R relationships. Results show this account to be incomplete. Two different properties of the mapping influence spatial CRTs. One is the relationship between stimulus and response in individual S–R pairs. The other is the set of relationships represented in the whole mapping. Specifically, RT is short when the spatial relationship between stimulus and response is the same in all S–R pairs in the mapping. The results suggest that S–R mappings are not stored as sets of individual S–R associations. Rather they are stored as systems of rules that may each apply to several S–R pairs. The complexity of these systems does not depend only on the "obviousness" of individual S–R relationships.

I. INTRODUCTION

In spatial choice reaction time (CRT) experiments RT varies with the mapping between a fixed set of responses and a fixed set of stimuli. This variation has been named the effect of "S–R compatibility" (e.g., Fitts & Deininger, 1954). Of any two S–R mappings, that allowing the shorter RT is the more compatible.

It has been suggested (e.g., Broadbent, 1971) that compatibility is largely determined by how "obviously" responses correspond to their stimuli. "Obvious" correspondence may arise, for example, through long practice. It may be measured by asking subjects to pair on their own criteria sets of stimuli and responses.

There is in the original study of Fitts and Deininger (1954) a result which suggests that an additional factor should be considered. On each trial of their experiment, a light appeared in one of eight positions around the perimeter of a circle, and was answered by the movement of a joystick in one of eight possible directions. Three different S–R mappings were employed. In the first, response direction corresponded to stimulus position; for example, if the light appeared at the 9 o'clock position, the joystick was moved in the 9 o'clock direction. In the second, response direction was opposite to stimulus position; for example, if the light appeared at 9 o'clock, the joystick was moved to 3 o'clock. In the third, S–R pairing was random: no consistent relationship obtained between stimulus position and response direction.

RT was shortest under the first mapping, suggesting that compatibility is indeed high when stimuli and responses "obviously correspond." Though this was the result of most interest to the authors, it was not the most dramatic result of the experiment. RT under the third mapping was far longer than under either of the other two. This suggests that spatial CRT may be dominantly influenced, not only by whether individual stimuli and responses "obviously correspond," but by whether S–R relationships are the same in all the S–R pairs of the task.

In other words, the results suggest that spatial CRT is not influenced only by the spatial relationships of individual S–R pairs. A property of the set of S–R pairs making up the entire S–R mapping may also be important.

An alternative explanation of the results is possible. The "corresponding" responses of the first mapping and the "opposite" responses of the second may have been individually easy to make. RTs may have been short under these two mappings, not because all of the S–R pairs within them were similar, but because the relationship between stimulus and response in each individual pair was a relatively "obvious" one.

These alternatives may be distinguished by the following experiment. A single S–R pair should be embedded in two different S–R mappings, in one of which all S–R pairs are similar while in the other they are not. If the RT of this pair depends on the mapping in which it is embedded, then similarity between the various S–R pairs in a mapping is a factor influencing spatial CRT.

II. THE EXPERIMENT

A. Method

1. Task

The stimuli were four vertical lines, arranged in a horizontal row on an oscilloscope. Each was 0.8 cm high, and separated from the next by 1.8 cm (Fig. 1). Viewing distance was approximately 43 cm.

In Fig. 1 the stimuli have been numbered 1 to 4 from left to right. Stimuli 1 and 4 will be termed "Outer" and Stimuli 2 and 3 "Inner."

Responses were made with four keys arranged to lie under the fore- and middle fingers of each hand. In Fig. 1 the responses have been labeled A to D from left to right.

Figure 1 illustrates the four S–R mapping rules employed. Arrows connect stimuli to their appropriate responses.

In this chapter the following terminology will be employed. S–R pairs will be termed either "Corresponding" or "Opposite". An example of a Corresponding pair is "1–A," and of an Opposite pair "1–D." Mappings which contain only one type of pair will be termed "Pure," while those which contain both will be termed "Mixed."

Thus Condition P–C is Pure, and all S–R pairs are Corresponding. Condition P–O is Pure, and all S–R pairs are Opposite. Condition M–1 is Mixed, the S–R pairs of Inner stimuli being Corresponding and of Outer stimuli Opposite. Condition M–2 is Mixed, the S–R pairs of Inner stimuli being Opposite and of Outer stimuli Corresponding.

2. Procedure

Each subject served in a single 1-hr session, in one of the four experimental conditions. At the start the S–R mapping was described by numbering the stimuli from 1 to 4, and showing which key corresponded to each number. Instructions were given to go as fast as possible while making as few errors as possible. There followed six experimental runs, separated by short breaks during which the subject was shown his mean RT and error rate from the previous run. The subject was told to consider the first run as practice, and only data from the last five runs were analyzed.

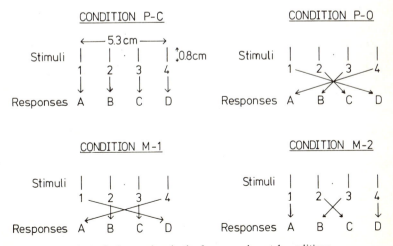

FIG. 1   S–R mappings in the four experimental conditions.

Each run consisted of 144 self-paced trials. The subject sat alone in a darkened room. The run began as follows: the word "READY" appeared for 2 sec; next the four stimuli appeared sequentially from left to right, each remaining for 3 sec, separated by intervals of 1 sec; finally the word "READY" reappeared for a further 2 sec, followed by the first trial. On each trial a single stimulus was presented, and remained until a response was made. There was a 1-sec R–S interval, during which a dot, intended to facilitate identification of the next stimulus, appeared in the center of the screen. Each successive block of 48 trials involved 12 presentations of each stimulus, in an otherwise random sequence.

The experiment was run on-line on a Linc-8 computer. Every stimulus, response, and RT was stored on magnetic tape. Summaries of the data were produced by various computer programs, all of which excluded trials immediately following error responses.

3. Subjects

There were 32 subjects aged 19–26 years. Eight, four of each sex, served in each condition.

B. Results

1. Mean RT

Figure 2 shows mean correct RT as a function of the type of mapping and the type of S–R pair. Responses to Inner and Outer stimuli have been separated. Each point of Fig. 2 is the mean of 8 subjects' means. The data have been pooled across Runs 2 to 6.

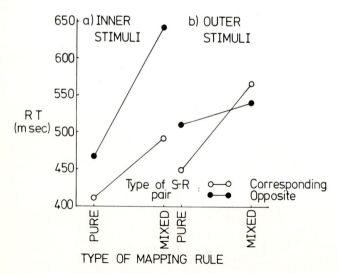

FIG. 2   Mean correct RTs as a function of type of mapping and type of S–R pair.

Figure 2 shows that both type of S–R pair and type of mapping influence RT. RT is generally shorter if the S–R pair is Corresponding than if it is Opposite. The RT of a given S–R pair, however, depends on the type of mapping in which it is embedded. RT is shorter if the mapping is Pure than if it is Mixed.

In Fig. 3 the data are replotted as a function of practice. Responses to Inner and Outer stimuli have been pooled.

The difference between RTs under Pure and Mixed mappings reduces sharply with practice. In Run 2 (Trials 145–288) the mean difference is 159 msec, and in run 6 (Trials 721–864), 75 msec. The data leave open the question of whether the difference would vanish with extended practice.

The difference between RTs of Corresponding and Opposite S–R pairs is, in contrast, insensitive to practice. This is at least so after the second experimental run. In Run 3 the mean difference is 59 msec, and in Run 6, 52 msec. There is no suggestion that the difference would vanish with extended practice, and the results do not suggest that the difference arises through a difference in practice.

The design of the experiment demanded that responses to Inner and Outer stimuli be examined by separate analyses of variance. Each of these analyses had the between-subjects factors "type of mapping" and "type of S–R pair." The levels of the first factor were Pure versus Mixed, and of the second, Corresponding versus Opposite. In addition each analysis had the 5-level within-subject factor "experimental run."

In the first analysis (Inner stimuli), all 3 main effects were significant: type of mapping, $F = 12.4$, $df = 1, 28$, $p < .01$; type of S–R pair, $F = 8.1$, $df = 1, 28$, $p < .01$; experimental run, $F = 24.6$, $df = 4, 112$, $p < .001$. The only significant interaction was type of mapping $\times$ experimental run, $F = 6.7$, $df = 4,112$, $p <$

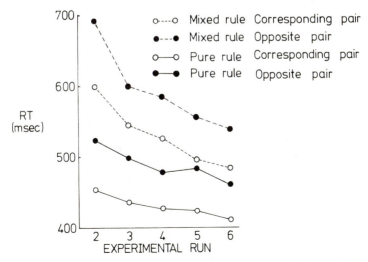

700

o---o   Mixed rule Corresponding pair
●---●   Mixed rule Opposite pair
o——o   Pure rule Corresponding pair
●——●   Pure rule Opposite pair

600

RT
(msec)

500

400

2   3   4   5   6
EXPERIMENTAL RUN

FIG. 3   Mean correct RTs as a function of type of mapping, type of S–R pair, and practice.

.001. In the second analysis (Outer stimuli), two main effects were significant: type of mapping, $F = 8.3$, $df = 1, 28$, $p < .01$; and experimental run, $F = 40.5$, $df = 4, 112$, $p < .001$. Type of S–R pair was not significant, $F = 0.4$. The only significant interaction was type of mapping × experimental run, $F = 8.5$, $df = 4, 112$, $p < .001$.

The first conclusion of this experiment is then that spatial CRT is influenced at least early in practice by the type of mapping in which a given S–R pair is embedded. RT is short when all S–R pairs are similar, that is, when the spatial relationship between stimulus and response is the same in each. Discussions of "compatibility" must take account of this.

To provide further insight into the phenomenon, more detailed analysis of the data will now be presented.

2. Sequential Effects

The present results are reminiscent of previous demonstrations that RT is raised when a task contains different categories of S–R pairs (Forrin, 1975; Forrin & Morin, 1966, 1967; Morin & Forrin, 1962). For example, Forrin (1975) has shown that symbol-naming RT is longer when the symbols may be either digits or letters than when only digits or letters can occur. In the present case, the relevant categories of S–R pair appear to be defined by the spatial relationships between stimuli and responses.

Another effect which appears when a task contains different categories of S–R pair is the "category repetition effect" (Forrin, 1975; Marcel & Forrin, 1974; Rabbitt & Vyas, 1973). The RT of a given S–R pair is shorter when this pair is immediately preceded in the sequence of trials by another pair from the same rather than from a different category; that is, category repetition RT < category alternation RT.

Even under Pure mappings, spatial CRTs show various "category repetition effects." For example, if successive responses are made with different hands, performance is facilitated when they are made with equivalent fingers (Rabbitt, Vyas & Fearnley, 1975). Under Mixed mappings an additional effect should appear. Performance should be facilitated by repetition of the spatial relationship between stimuli and responses, that is, when S–R pairs on two successive trials are either both Corresponding or both Opposite.

Figure 1 shows that, under the present Mixed mappings, repetition of S–R relationships occurs only when successive stimuli are opposites, for example, Stimuli 1 and 4. (For our purposes stimulus repetitions may be ignored.) Such opposite stimuli will here be termed "Equivalent," and other nonidentical stimuli "Nonequivalent."

Figure 4 shows RT as a function of the immediately preceding stimulus.

Consider first responses to Inner stimuli. Even under Pure mappings performance is facilitated by a preceding Equivalent stimulus. This is to be expected since Equivalent stimuli are responded to by the same finger on different hands. Under Mixed mappings the facilitation is exaggerated. This presumably reflects

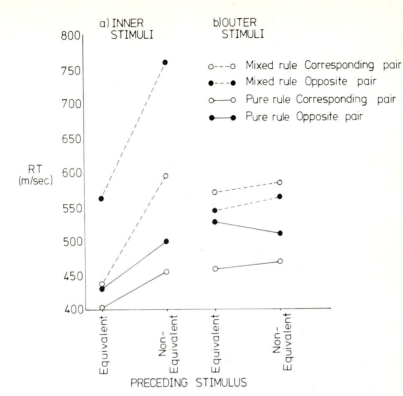

FIG. 4 Mean correct RTs as a function of type of mapping, type of S–R pair, and preceding stimulus. Note: Equivalent stimuli occur on opposite sides of the display, whereas nonequivalent stimuli may occur on the same side. In this analysis, cases in which successive nonequivalent stimuli occurred on the same side of the display were excluded.

the fact that, under these mappings, the S–R pairs of Nonequivalent stimuli fall into different categories, as defined by the spatial relationships between stimuli and responses. The data were examined by an analysis of variance, with the between-subjects factors "type of mapping" and "type of S–R pair" and the within-subject factor "preceding stimulus." The two levels of the third factor were Equivalent and Nonequivalent. In addition to all three main effects, the interaction type of mapping × preceding stimulus was significant, $F = 9.4, df = 1, 28, p < .01$.

Responses to Outer stimuli do not show category repetition effects. In the corresponding analysis of variance no interaction was significant.

3. Errors

Table 1 shows the total number of errors occurring in each experimental condition. Three major types of error are distinguished. Corresponding responses made when the correct response is Opposite are termed Corresponding errors.

TABLE 1
Total Numbers of Errors

			Error type			
Mapping	S–R pair	Stimulus	Corresponding	Opposite	Adjacent	Others
Pure	Corresponding	Inner	–	4	28	0
		Outer	–	0	82	0
	Opposite	Inner	87	–	27	3
		Outer	14	–	60	1
Mixed	Corresponding	Inner	–	98	18	–
		Outer	–	6	15	–
	Opposite	Inner	72	–	10	–
		Outer	43	–	20	–

Note: Values are total numbers of errors made by all subjects. Each is based on approximately 2,880 trials.

Opposite responses made when the correct response is Corresponding are termed Opposite errors. Two different types of response are termed Adjacent errors. These are "motor" Adjacent errors, that is, responses made with the incorrect finger on the correct hand, and "perceptual" Adjacent errors, that is, responses appropriate to the incorrect stimulus on the correct side. Under Pure mappings these two Adjacent errors cannot be distinguished; for example, given presentation of Stimulus 1 in Condition P–C, Response B is both the perceptual and the motor Adjacent error. Under Mixed mappings the two can be distinguished; for example, given presentation of Stimulus 1 in Condition M–1, Response B is the perceptual, and Response C the motor Adjacent error. Under Mixed mappings the properties of perceptual and motor Adjacent errors were indistinguishable.

Corresponding errors are most commonly made to Inner stimuli. The numbers of Corresponding errors made to Inner stimuli under Pure and Mixed mappings do not differ significantly. The number of Corresponding errors made to Outer stimuli is higher under Mixed than under Pure mappings ($p < .002$, Mann–Whitney U-test).

Opposite errors are also most commonly made to Inner stimuli. The number of Opposite errors made to Inner stimuli is higher under Mixed than under Pure mappings ($p < .001$, Mann–Whitney U-test). The numbers of Opposite errors made to Outer stimuli under Pure and Mixed mappings do not differ significantly.

Adjacent errors are most commonly made to Outer stimuli, and under Pure mappings. An analysis of variance with the between-subjects factor "type of mapping" and the within-subject factor "type of stimulus (Inner versus Outer)" gave significant main effects of type of mapping, $F = 24.9, df = 1, 30, p < .001$, and type of stimulus, $F = 26.5, df = 1, 30, p < .001$; and a significant interaction between the two, $F = 20.1, df = 1, 30, p < .001$.

TABLE 2
Differences between Correct and Error RTs (msec)[a]

| Mapping | | Error type | | |
		Corresponding	Opposite	Adjacent
Pure	Mean	− 8	−	+34[b]
	S.E.	13	−	9
	df	7	−	15
Mixed	Mean	− 3	−41	+16
	S.E.	20	30	32
	df	15	10	13

[a]Positive values indicate error RT < correct RT.
[b]$p < .01$; t-test.

To summarize: under Pure mappings the dominant type of error is Adjacent, though there is some tendency when the S–R pair is Opposite to make a Corresponding response. Under Mixed mappings Adjacent errors decrease in frequency, and Corresponding and Opposite errors become dominant. In other words, if the mapping contains both Corresponding and Opposite S–R pairs, the dominant type of error is a response bearing the wrong one of these two possible relationships to its stimulus.

Table 2 shows mean differences between correct and error RTs. These values were obtained as follows. Every response was classified by the finger used on both current and immediately preceding trials, and by experimental run. Mean differences between corresponding classes of error and correct responses were then obtained for each subject. The values shown are the means of these means.

TABLE 3
Differences between Total Correct and (Error − 1)
RTs (msec)[a]

| Mapping | | Error type | | |
		Corresponding	Opposite	Adjacent
Pure	Mean	+ 3	−	+14[c]
	S.E.	19	−	5
	df	7	−	15
Mixed	Mean	+25[b]	+ 5	+18
	S.E.	11	16	12
	df	15	10	13

[a]Positive values indicate (Error − 1) RT < total correct RT.
[b]$p < .05$; t-test.
[c]$p < .01$; t-test.

TABLE 4
Errors of 18 New Subjects. Condition M—1[a]

| | | Error type | | |
		Corresponding	Opposite	Adjacent
Total numbers of errors[b]		223	272	141
Differences between correct	mean	−45[c]	−21	+20
and error RTs (msec)	S.E.	13	14	20
	df	16	17	16
Differences between total	mean	+ 9	+11	+33[d]
correct and Error 1 RTs (msec)	S.E.	9	8	15
	df	16	17	16

[a]Positive values indicate error RT < correct RT; and (Error − 1) RT < total correct RT.
[b]Values are total numbers of errors made by all subjects. For Corresponding and Opposite errors, each value is based on approximately 9,360 trials. For Adjacent errors the value is based on approximately 18,720 trials.
[c]$p < .01$; t-test.
[d]$p < .05$; t-test.

Adjacent errors occurring under Pure mappings are significantly faster than correct responses (see Rabbitt, 1966). While no other effect is significant, there is a suggestion that Opposite errors occurring under Mixed mappings may be slower than correct responses.

Table 3 shows mean differences between total correct RTs, and RTs of those correct responses immediately preceding errors (here termed (Error − 1) responses). These values were obtained by a procedure equivalent to that previously described. All differences are positive; that is, correct responses immediately preceding errors are unusually fast.

For comparison, Table 4 shows the error data of 18 new subjects. These subjects served with the stimuli and mapping of the present Condition M−1, differing among themselves in the sets of fingers used for response, the degree of practice, and the experience of other similar experimental conditions. The results are similar to those from the main experiment. The dominant error types are Corresponding and Opposite. Both Corresponding and Opposite errors are slower than correct responses, in the former case significantly so. Adjacent errors are again insignificantly faster than correct responses. Correct responses immediately preceding all three types of error are unusually fast.

To summarize: Adjacent errors are faster than correct responses, possibly under both Pure and Mixed mappings. Corresponding and Opposite errors may both be slower than correct responses. Those responses which immediately precede errors are unusually fast, apparently independent of the type of error they precede.

C. Discussion

One component of CRT tasks is the choice of one of the possible responses as appropriate to the current stimulus. This will here be termed "response selection."

Some previous accounts of the process (e.g., Theios, 1975) have suggested it to be based on a set of individual S–R associations. The internal representation of each stimulus is associated to that of its correct response. "Natural" or highly practiced associations may be relatively strong, accounting for effects of compatibility.

The present results suggest an alternative account. Responses may be selected, not on the basis of individual S–R associations, but by use of a rule or system of rules.

Let us introduce the concept of a "spatial transformation." This is defined as an operation which, when applied to the internal representation of a stimulus in a spatial CRT task, produces a response bearing some fixed spatial relationship to that stimulus. Hence its use may be described by the equation:

$$R = T(S)$$

where R and S can be any response and stimulus in a spatial CRT task, and T represents some fixed spatial relationship between them. Examples of transformations are those producing respectively Corresponding and Opposite responses. Transformations as defined here have obvious similarities to those presumably used in tasks such as mental rotation (Shepard & Metzler, 1971).

It is suggested that a set of transformations, along with information as to which is correct for each stimulus, underlies response selection in spatial CRT tasks. Responses are selected by choice and use of the appropriate transformation.

This model accounts first for the difference between RTs under Pure and Mixed mappings. Under Pure mappings a single transformation is appropriate for all stimuli. Under Mixed mappings this is not so, and on each trial therefore a decision must be made between alternative possible transformations. This is presumably reflected in the longer RTs occurring under these mappings.

Second, the model accounts for the category repetition effect occurring under Mixed mappings, when on two successive trials S–R relationships are identical. It might be expected that, under these mappings, choice and use of the same transformation on two successive trials would facilitate performance.

Third, the model accounts for the occurrence of Corresponding and Opposite errors. These may arise through selection and use of the wrong transformation. They occur especially under Mixed mappings, though Corresponding errors also occur when all S–R pairs are Opposite (Condition P–O). Thus an incorrect transformation is most likely to be selected if it is appropriate to some other stimulus in the task; but it may also be selected if it is in some way "simpler" than the correct one.

The critical property of a transformation, as introduced here, is that it is a rule. It is an operation which will produce a response bearing some fixed relationship to any spatial stimulus. Use of a rule rather than individual S–R associations is beneficial when a task is ordered, that is, when S–R relationships are similar in several or all S–R pairs. Under these circumstances the number of rules needed is less than the number of S–R pairs.

The results of this experiment show that performance under some spatial S–R mapping is not a function only of the "obviousness" of the relationships between individual stimuli and responses. Spatial CRT is influenced by two different properties of the mapping. One is the spatial relationship of individual S–R pairs, that is, in terms of the proposed model, which transformation must be made. The other is the number of different relationships in the whole mapping; that is, the number of transformations from which selection must be made.

This conclusion is not surprising if response selection involves use of rule systems rather than individual S–R associations. Performance in a given CRT task will then be a function, not of how easy each response is to associate to its stimulus, but of the complexity of the rule system employed. This will not in general depend only on the "obviousness" of relationships between individual stimuli and responses.

Differences in performance under different S–R mappings, and even in different types of CRT task (e.g., light–key, digit–key), have been considered effects of "compatibility" (e.g., Brainard, Irby, Fitts, & Alluisi, 1962). Use of this single term may be misleading. An account of these differences in performance cannot be given only in terms of some factor such as "strength of S–R association." Such an account will probably demand description in detail of the "processing" mechanisms underlying performance in different CRT tasks. A first step toward such a description for spatial CRT has been reported here.

ACKNOWLEDGMENTS

The author is indebted to Mr. S. Fearnley, whose programs for the Linc-8 were used throughout, both for running the experiment and analyzing the results; and to Dr. P. M. A. Rabbitt, who supervised the work. The author was supported by MRC Research Studentship Number G.77/4610.

REFERENCES

Brainard, R. W., Irby, T. S., Fitts, P. M., & Alluisi, E. A. Some variables influencing the rate of gain of information. *Journal of Experimental Psychology,* 1962, **63,** 105–110.
Broadbent, D. E. *Decision and stress.* New York: Academic Press, 1971.

Fitts, P. M., & Deininger, R. L. S—R compatibility: Correspondence among paired elements within stimulus and response codes. *Journal of Experimental Psychology,* 1954, **48**, 483—492.

Forrin, B. Naming latencies to mixed sequences of letters and digits. In P. M. A. Rabbitt & S. Dornic (Eds.), *Attention and performance V.* London: Academic Press, 1975.

Forrin, B., & Morin, R. E. Effect of contextual associations upon selective reaction time in a numeral-naming task. *Journal of Experimental Psychology,* 1966, **71**, 40—46.

Forrin, B., & Morin, R. E. Effects of context on reaction time to optimally coded signals. In A. F. Sanders, (Ed.), *Attention and performance I.* Amsterdam: North-Holland Publ., 1967.

Marcel, T., & Forrin, B. Naming latency and the repetition of stimulus categories. *Journal of Experimental Psychology,* 1974, **103**, 450—460.

Morrin, R. E., & Forrin, B. Mixing two types of S—R associations in a choice reaction time task. *Journal of Experimental Psychology,* 1962, **64**, 137—141.

Rabbitt, P. M. A. Errors and error correction in choice—response tasks. *Journal of Experimental Psychology,* 1966, **71**, 264—272.

Rabbitt, P. M. A., & Vyas, S. What is repeated in the "repetition effect"? In S. Kornblum (Ed.), *Attention and performance IV.* New York: Academic Press, 1973.

Rabbitt, P. M. A., Vyas, S., & Fearnley, S. Programming sequences of complex responses. In P. M. A. Rabbitt & S. Dornic (Eds.), *Attention and performance V.* London: Academic Press, 1975.

Shepard, R. N., & Metzler, J. Mental rotation of three-dimensional objects. *Science,* 1971, **171**, 701—3.

Theios, J. The components of response latency in simple human information processing tasks. In P. M. A. Rabbitt & S. Dornic (Eds.), *Attention and performance V.* London: Academic Press, 1975.

4

The Search for Exceptions to the Psychological Refractory Period

John Brebner

Department of Psychology
University of Adelaide
Adelaide, South Australia

ABSTRACT

Recent studies attack the single-channel principle, which may be briefly stated as "a response is organised, and begun, before a second stimulus impinges upon the organizing centre" (Vince, 1948a, p. 86) in two ways. Herman and Kantowitz (1970) argue that the single-channel model fails to account for changes in RT1 when S2 is presented, and that this is evidence for their "response–conflict" theory. Allport, Antonis, and Reynolds (1972) and Greenwald and Shulman (1973) report failures to observe the psychological refractory period (PRP) which is predicted to occur by single-channel theory. This study argues against "response–conflict" theory on the grounds that the effects on RT1 are due to processes which take place before the onset of S2, and that the limited range of the effect supports the single-channel model. A replication of Greenwald and Shulman's (1973) study is undertaken which, by showing the typical PRP effect among subjects who did not "group" their responses, casts doubt on the interpretation of the above failures to find the PRP. Finally, a second experiment leads to the tentative suggestion that it is not feedback from a response which clears the channel (Welford, 1959), but execution of the program controlling the response.

I. INTRODUCTION

Ever since it was first proposed by Craik (1947, 1948) and subsequently reformulated into more precise terms by Welford (1952), there has been criticism of the theory that the central decision mechanisms function as a single channel of limited capacity, which acts so that, a "response is organized, and

63

begun, before the organizing centre is impinged upon by a second stimulus" (Vince, 1948a, p. 86). Support for the theory has derived from studies of the psychological refractory period (PRP) showing that RT to the second of two rapidly successive stimuli (S_2) decreases as the interstimulus interval (ISI) increases. Criticisms of the theory fall into two broad classes: either (1) arguing that single-channel theory fails to account for some important feature of the data, or some crucial aspect of the experimental situation (Annett, 1966; Elithorn & Lawrence, 1955; Herman & Kantowitz, 1970); or (2) presenting evidence that the PRP is not found under conditions for which single-channel theory predicts its occurrence.

Without adding another review of the PRP to the literature, recent examples of both sorts of criticisms can be cited. In the first category, Herman and Kantowitz (1970) have championed the cause of "response—conflict" theory in opposition to the single-channel model. These authors suggest that when stimuli for different responses are applied in rapid succession, the response tendencies aroused by the successive stimuli interact, and the RTs to both stimuli are affected. This view is an improvement over the single-channel explanation, they claim, since single-channel theory fails to predict an increase in RT to the first stimulus (S1). Herman and Kantowitz note the suggestions of Borger (1963) that S1 may be stored until the second stimulus (S2) arrives, and both be processed together, or the first response (R1) may be stored until R2 is prepared and both then executed together. In either case the result is the same, RT1 increases as ISI lengthens, but even if Borger's suggestion were accepted as modifications to the single-channel theory, it would still be wrong according to Herman and Kantowitz since what they find, in reviewing many studies, is that where RT to the first of two stimuli (RT1) is longer than RT to a single stimulus, RT1 first decreases as ISI lengthens up to approximately 100 msec and then remains constant.

"Competing response tendencies," which are the basis of response conflict theory, have been used extensively as an explanatory construct in the field of learning. In conditioning theory, for example, competing response tendencies exist as an alternative to the buildup of some form of response-mediated inhibition to explain extinction and spontaneous recovery. Applied to the PRP, however, the notion of competing response tendencies adds little beyond the general statement that the processes concerned with S1 and S2 interact. The theory offers no way of predicting the extent of the effects of such interaction on either RT1 and RT2. The finding that the *force* of the response may be affected by the arrival of a subsequent signal, up to 130 msec later, has recently been offered in support of response conflict theory (Kantowitz, 1973). Nevertheless, as an alternative to the single-channel view, response conflict theory depends entirely upon the argument that if RT1 is longer than that to a single stimulus, this implies that RT1 has been modified by events *following* the occurrence of S2. The main difficulty with such reasoning is the obvious one, it cannot be safely assumed that the central processes underlying RT to stimuli presented *singly,* are the same as those underlying RT to the first stimulus when a *pair* of stimuli are expected. It would be relatively easy to construct a model which added some time spent in sampling for the occurrence of a second stimulus if two stimuli were expected. This more complex process would be longer than that for single stimuli by the amount of time spent sampling for S2.[1] Evidence for this line of argument exists in Salthouse's (1970) finding that *RT*1 was increased when the likelihood of S2 occurring was high in comparison with other situations where the probability of S2 was low.

This simple model would also assume that, once S2 is detected, storing information about that signal takes up capacity, thereby reducing the capacity available for decoding S1. From this it follows that the shorter ISI is, the longer the period of reduced capacity and, hence, the slower the RT. It might be argued that this model is now a version of response conflict theory since the storage of S2 competes with the analysis of S1. However, the evidence for the modification of RT1 by the occurrence of S2 (Gottsdanker, 1973; Herman & Kantowitz, 1970; Smith, 1969) seems *only* to be found within a short ISI range up to about 100 msec. The absence of such an effect at longer ISIs is consistent with the view that once the information has reached the translation mechanism, that is, once the organization of a response to *S1* has begun, there is no competition for capacity between the stimuli, and RT1 is not delayed. But this is what single-channel theory predicted more than 20 years ago. Craik (1948), Vince (1948b), and Welford (1952) all clearly state that it is the ongoing organization of a response that is protected from interruption from later stimuli which have to be stored until the single channel has cleared to accept them. So the model is perhaps better described as a stimulus-competition rather than a response-conflict model.

Finally, in connection with this, the pattern of decreasing latencies of RT1 as ISI rises, which Herman and Kantowitz (1970) discussed, is not always found by any means, and those authors are careful to note that it is observed when RT1 is greater than RT to a single stimulus. Early studies of the PRP went to some trouble to ensure that RT1 was approximately the same as the reaction time to a stimulus delivered singly, for example, as cited by Davis (1959) or Poulton (1950). But although Welford (1952) seems to have assumed that as a result of instructions to subjects, practice, and the experimental arrangements, RT1 would be the same as RT to a single stimulus, that does not mean that the single-channel model cannot handle the effect described by Herman and Kantowitz.

This chapter is mainly concerned, however, with some recent examples of this latter category in which the PRP is not observed.

---

[1] A simple mathematical treatment of this proposal is presented by Smith in the Appendix which follows this paper.

At the outset, it seems relevant to distinguish those exceptions to the PRP which are also exceptions to the single-channel theory and those which are not. As early as 1950 Vince showed (1) that stimuli could be grouped together and processed simultaneously, though this increased RT if dissimilar responses were required, and (2) she also confirmed Bryan and Harter's (1899) finding that "sensory overlap" could occur, that is, the organization of a second response could take place during the execution of a previous response.

What Vince demonstrated were some of the ways of circumventing the PRP rather than eliminating it, and from her work and later studies (e.g., Gottsdanker, 1973; Welford, 1959) it is clear (as Vince stated) that serial responding can be speeded up by grouping, by sensory overlap, or input–output overlap.

It seems necessary to make this point since many studies ignore these possibilities. To take one example, Raeburn and Corballis (1972) suggest that their failure to find the usual PRP in a task in which subjects responded "same" or "different" to the second of two closely spaced stimuli, if ISI was held constant, is evidence against single-channel theory. Although in their experiment only one response was made, previous research using two separate responses (Burns & Moskowitz, 1971) had already established that RT1 increased systematically as ISI lengthened, when ISI was held constant in blocks of trials. When ISI varied within blocks, on the other hand, RT1 did not change significantly over the ISI range. This result suggests that grouping of stimuli tends to be adopted if ISI remains constant, and is a possible explanation for Raeburn and Corballis' (1972) result.

Other apparent exceptions to the PRP pose more problems for the single-channel theory. Two, in particular – the report by Greenwald and Shulman (1973) that they have eliminated the PRP using "ideomotor" (IM) compatible relationships, and the demonstration by Allport, Antonis, and Reynolds (1972) that tasks which are very dissimilar from one another can be performed simultaneously – both seem to limit the generality of the single-channel principle.

Allport et al. (1972) report two experiments which challenge single-channel theory. The first showed that recognition of items presented while the subject performed an auditory shadowing task was no better than chance if the items were spoken words, was improved to around 30% errors using written words presented visually, and errors were further reduced to about 10% when the stimuli were complex pictures. That is, performance improved as the two tasks became increasingly dissimilar. The second experiment showed that subjects could combine playing the piano from a musical score with the auditory shadowing task. Here, there was no marked rise in errors on the shadowing task, no tendency for intermittent bursts of speech followed by periods of silence, and, finally, the piano playing performance was not judged worse, in terms of wrong notes and timing, when shadowing. It should be noted, however, that even when not shadowing, the auditory stimuli were still presented to the subjects who, in the "undivided attention" condition, were instructed to ignore the spoken prose passage.

While these are interesting results, it is probably an overstatement to claim that they constitute a disproof of the single-channel model. Taking the first experiment, it is noteworthy that performance at all three of the secondary tasks was significantly impaired under the shadowing condition. Allport *et al.* (1972) made the point that:

> It cannot be argued in defence of the single channel hypothesis that the shadowing task, even though at a very fast rate, might not have been such as to fully occupy the capacity of the hypothetical single channel, since in that case the hypothesis is unable to account for the almost complete failure to remember the auditory word list (and to a lesser extent the visual word list) under the same conditions of concurrent shadowing during presentation. (p. 229)

But the particular pattern of results could be due to several factors, the shadowing task may have masked the spoken words more effectively than it did the visual stimuli, which were, in any case available for inspection for a period of 1.7 sec. If the visual words tended to be recoded into auditory terms for storage, one might expect more interference from shadowing to these items than on the picture items.

In the piano playing experiment, there seem to be three possibilities:

1. Tasks which are very dissimilar are exceptions to the PRP since they use different, independent processors as the authors suggest. The effect cannot be due to different modalities, since auditory and visual stimuli like those used by Allport *et al.* (1972) have often been used and the usual PRP obtained (e.g., Davis, 1956). Even where a manual response is made to the visual stimulus and a dissimilar vocal response to the auditory stimulus, the PRP has still been found (Greenwald & Shulman, 1973; Smith, 1969).

2. The effect could be due to grouping and sensory overlap. If this is the case, then though shadowing 150 words in one minute can be coordinated with playing from a musical score with unlimited preview, increasing the information processing demands should result in disruption of one task by the other. Only further research can determine if this is the case or not.

3. The results obtained may be due not to the dissimilarity of the tasks but rather to the fact that the auditory shadowing task used is an "ideomotor" compatible one.

As defined by Greenwald (1972; Greenwald & Shulman, 1973) ideomotor (IM) compatible relationships exist when "the stimulus resembles sensory feedback from the response" (p. 70). The tasks selected as IM compatible by Greenwald and Shulman were: (1) responding to a visual arrow symbol by moving a switch in the indicated direction left or right; and (2) repeating a letter "A" or "B" which was heard through headphones.

This task parallels the auditory shadowing task used by Allport and co-workers. The arrow symbol preceded the spoken letter so that subjects performed two rapidly successive two-choice responses.

Thus, two similar experiments, both using different visual—motor and auditory—vocal tasks, report the absence of the PRP — but offer quite different explanations of this result.

In the first of two experiments Greenwald and Shulman failed to eliminate the PRP since RT1 increased and RT2 decreased over the ISI range. However, when they instructed subjects that stimuli would most often occur simultaneously, and did not indicate that different ISIs would be employed, they obtained the result (Fig. 1) that RT2 did not decrease as ISI increased.

Since any genuine elimination of the PRP is likely to extend our understanding of how information is processed, it seemed worth testing the IM compatibility hypothesis further. But it also seemed useful in doing this to use two stimulus—response tasks which were similar, on two grounds. First, if we could eliminate the PRP using IM compatible tasks which were similar, the operative factor would be pinpointed, as IM compatibility rather than dissimilarity. Second, if we could show that the absence of the PRP in Greenwald and Shulman's second experiment was not a genuine exception to single-channel theory, then the result

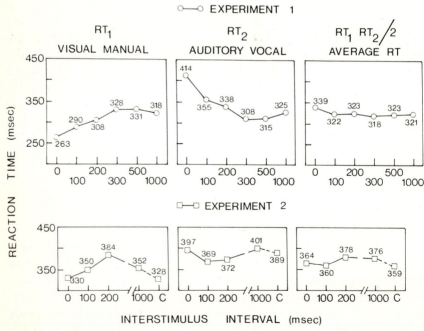

FIG. 1   Data show "elimination" of PRP with IM compatible tasks. (From Greenwald and Shulman, 1973). (Copyright 1973 by the American Psychological Association. Reprinted by permission.)

of their first experiment, in which they found the usual PRP using dissimilar visual—motor and auditory—vocal tasks, would cast doubt upon the "dissimilarity" hypothesis of Allport and co-workers. One good reason for believing it may be possible to explain the absence of the PRP in Greenwald and Shulman's second experiment is that it appears that grouping may have contaminated their data in Experiment 2 since RT1 tended to lengthen with ISI. Their instruction to subjects that stimuli would most often be simultaneous might well have led subjects to try to make two simultaneous responses, leading to a grouping strategy.

II. EXPERIMENT I

A. Method and Apparatus

To test the IM compatible hypothesis an experiment was performed using as stimuli the upward movement, against the subject's fingertips, of solenoid operated response buttons. In this way it was hoped to achieve an IM compatible situation in which the stimulus resembles sensory feedback from the response, in this case pressing the button down to operate a microswitch.

Four such stimulus—response keys were used in a successive two-choice PRP task like Greenwald and Shulman's. The first response was always made with the index or middle finger of the left hand, and the second response with the index or middle finger of the right hand. Stimuli were presented at 5 ISIs: 100, 160, 200, 260, and 300 msec. Presentation of stimuli and recording of RTs was controlled by a PDP8 computer housed in a separate room. The intertrial interval was set at 1.5 sec after the response to S2, and ISI order was random. All subjects performed in a practice session in which S1 and S2 were presented 80 times at each of the 5 ISIs. They then undertook the experimental session, in which 80 RTs to *S1* and *S2* were obtained at each ISI. All 13 subjects tested were students in the Psychology Department at the University of Adelaide.

B. Results and Discussion

Subjects were divided into two groups according to whether RT1 increased systematically with ISI (5 subjects), or did not (8 subjects). The upper curves in Fig. 2 show mean RTs for subjects whose RT1 increased with ISI. Using Friedman's nonparametric ANOVA (Siegel, 1956) confirms what is apparent from Fig. 2: differences in RT1 across the ISI range are significant ($X_r^2 = 19.4$, $p < 0.01$), but differences in RT2 are not ($X^2 = 8.8, p > .04$), although there is some increase in RT2 at the shortest ISI of 100 msec. The results from this group are consistent with the view that they "grouped" their responses by processing S1 and S2 together so that RT1 was delayed but RT2 was not.

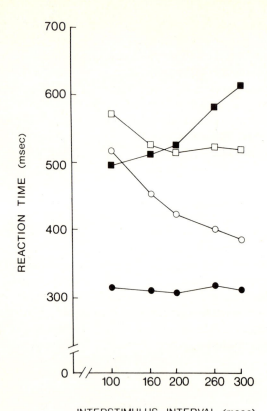

INTERSTIMULUS INTERVAL (msec)

FIG. 2   Mean RT1, RT2, and *SD* for subjects in Experiment I: ■, RT1 and □, RT2: Subjects who tended to delay processing of S1 until S2 arrived. ●, RT1 and ○, RT2: Subjects who tended to begin processing S1 immediately it arrived without waiting for S2.

Standard deviations:

ISI	100	160	200	260	300
■	96	95	100	120	125
□	108	118	122	140	140
●	60	60	55	65	65
○	95	90	95	95	95

The eight subjects whose RT1 was more or less constant across ISI exhibited the usual PRP effect as shown by the lower curves in Fig. 2. For this group the delay pattern is reversed and RT1 does not change across the ISI range ($X_r^2 = 7.9, p > .05$), but the decrease in *RT2* as ISI increases is statistically significant ($X_r^2 = 30.8, p < .001$). This latter result fails to substantiate the claim by Greenwald and Shulman (1973) that the PRP is eliminated under conditions of IM compatibility. Whether their result is due to pooling two opposite effects like those found here is not known, but it now seems a distinct possibility. If this interpretation of the outcome of their second experiment is accepted, then the failure to eliminate the PRP in their first experiment, which was not grossly unlike the experiment of Allport and co-workers, cast further doubt on the view that, in order to eliminate refractory delays in responding, it is sufficient to use tasks which are very dissimilar.

The experiment reported above supports the single-channel theory which predicts the usual PRP where the relationships between S1 and R1, and S2 and R2 are IM compatible. But it has been speculated (Welford, 1959) that the fact that the PRP lasts for the full duration of RT1 would be explained if "some minimum feedback from the responding action, indicating it had begun, was necessary for the decision mechanism to be 'cleared'" (p. 207). If we take Welford's suggestion seriously, single-channel theory could incorporate the IM compatibility hypothesis with the slight modification that the PRP may be eliminated if a stimulus resembles sensory feedback from a response *which is already organized*. The suggestion here is that the single channel may be selectively receptive to stimuli which resemble sensory feedback from a response which has been prepared but not executed. This differs from the original IM hypothesis by suggesting that the PRP may be eliminated if the relationship *between R1 and S2* is IM compatible.

A second experiment was performed to test this possibility.

III. EXPERIMENT II

A. Apparatus and Method

While some of the apparatus was the same as in Experiment I, the approach was different. Here, only two stimulus–response keys were used, one stimulating the index finger of the left hand by exerting pressure against the tip of the finger. This served as a warning signal (WS) that a visual stimulus (S1), the illumination of a light-emitting diode, would occur 400 msec after the onset of WS. The subject's task was to *synchronize* pressing the button under the index finger of his right hand with the onset of the visual S1.

In two conditions of this experiment the sequence just described occurred on 300 out of 500 trials, but on the remaining 200 trials, the subject's right index finger was stimulated (S2) at various intervals before the visual stimulus (S1) was due. In this way an attempt was made to have S2 approximate the sensory feedback from a prepared response. S2 was presented 150, 210, 250, 310, or 350 msec after WS.

Stimulus presentation and data recording was controlled by a PDP8 computer housed in a separate room. Each subject performed two runs under each of the three conditions described below, one for practice and one in which responses were recorded. All 15 subjects were students at the University of Adelaide.

B. Experimental Conditions

There were three conditions within the complete experiment:

1. *Synchronizing:* In the first, S1 followed WS after 400 msec and the subject tried to synchronize pressing the button under his right index finger with S1. There were 100 such trials in this condition.

2. *Canceling:* In the second condition the WS–S1 sequence occurred normally on 300 trials. On a further 200 trials, randomly distributed, S2 was presented at one of the ISIs after WS. The subject was instructed that when this happened he should cancel or inhibit any effort to respond when the visual S1 appeared.

3. *Substituting:* Condition 3 was similar to Condition 2 except that when S2 was presented it indicated to the subject that he should respond with the index finger of his left hand (in place of his right index finger) in synchrony with the visual S1.

C. Results and Discussion

Table 1 shows mean synchronizing RTs obtained in the three conditions. Using Friedman's nonparametric ANOVA, RT did not differ significantly across the three conditions ($X_r^2 = 3.0$, $p > .05$). Subjects were apparently trying to perform the synchronization task as instructed.

Turning to the attempt to cancel the synchronizing response (Condition 2), Table 2 shows the percentage of trials on which the response was correctly canceled for each WS–S2 interval. Evidently, the proportion decreases as the interval between WS and S2 increases, that is, as S2 approaches S1 ($X_r^2 = 53.7$, $p < .001$). It seems necessary to conclude that even where an IM compatible stimulus is used, a prepared response cannot be immediately canceled. As Hick

TABLE 1

Group Mean and *SD* (msec) for Synchronization RT in the Three Conditions of Experiment II[a]

	Time (msec)	
	Mean	SD
Condition 1 (synchronize)	378	66
Condition 2 (cancel)	416	81
Condition 3 (substitute)	394	77

[a]WS–S1 interval = 400 msec.

and Bates (1950) found, given 150 msec, there is a reasonable chance that the response can be stopped. As progressively less time than that is allowed, the probability of the response occurring increases. Table 2 also shows the mean RT and SD of the trials on which subjects failed to cancel the synchronizing response. RT (measured from WS) increases significantly across the range of WS–S2 intervals (X_r^2 = 45.7, p < .001). This is interpreted as showing that synchronizing responses having long latencies tend to be canceled, and are more likely to be successfully canceled the shorter the WS–S2 interval.

One might expect from this result that the attempt to substitute another response would share the same fate. But emitting a similar response with the other hand may involve only altering the response rather than revoking the decision to respond, and one cannot be sure the same pattern of results will emerge. Table 3 shows the number of successful attempts to substitute a left for a right response for each WS–S2 interval. Just as in trying to cancel a response, the attempt to substitute a different response for one in preparation meets with decreasing success as the WS–S2 interval increases, falling from nearly 70% to less than 7% when the interval increases from 150 to 350 msec (X_r^2 = 56.8, p < .001). The RTs of these substitute responses are measured from the onset of S2 – the instruction to "substitute" – and, while there is no significant change in RT across the range of WS–S2 intervals, substituted responses always occur much later than synchronized responses.

The RT on trials on which only the prepared right-hand response was made, despite a signal to substitute a left-hand response, are shown in Table 4. RT for these responses increases as ISI rises (X_r^2 = 20.6, p < .01), again showing that responses with long latencies are more likely to be substituted at shorter intervals.

Finally, it is possible that although a previous decision to respond cannot be substituted, nevertheless the signal for a substitute response might be accepted and processed without delay, if it was presented in IM compatible form.

TABLE 2
Canceling of Response in Condition 2 of Experiment
II[a]

	\multicolumn{5}{c}{Time (msec)}				
Interval between warning signal and signal to cancel	150	210	250	310	350
Percent trials on which response was cancelled	75	54	43	23	15
Group mean RT of failures to cancel	275	315	345	375	380
SD of the above	35	35	40	50	50

[a]WS–S1 interval = 400 msec.

TABLE 3
Mean RT and *SD* for Successful Substitutions.
Experiment II: Condition 3[a]

	Time (msec)				
WS–S2 interval	150	210	250	310	350
Number of successful substitutions	409	276	180	86	40
Mean RT	376	348	354	370	377
SD	89	59	59	60	90

[a]WS–S1 interval = 400 msec.

Moreover, as in all these possibilities, acceptance might only become possible at a relatively late stage of response organization when it has been "decided" what sensory feedback should be expected. In this case the frequency of both substitute and original responses occurring on the same trial should increase at longer WS–S2 intervals.

Table 5 shows the number of trials on which both the substitute (L) and the original (R) responses were produced and the RT of these responses. The overall pattern repeats itself in these data. The frequency of the substitute response occurring, even if the originally prepared response is also emitted, decreases from 22.3 to 8.7% as the WS–S2 interval increases from 150 to 350 msec. Within this pattern, however, the frequency of both responses occurring rises as the interval increases from 150 to 250 msec. Where a "substitute" instruction arrives within 150 msec of time when the prepared response should occur, the substituted response occurs only infrequently even if the prepared response is also emitted. The change in frequency of both responses across intervals is significant $(X_r^2 = 10.1, p < .05)$. The RT of substitute responses, measured from S2, shows no significant change across the range of WS–S2 intervals $(X_r^2 = 2.4, p > .05)$.

The RT of the prepared right-hand responses, measured from the onset of WS, increases with the WS–S2 interval in the same way as failures to cancel the right-hand response shown in Table 2 and failures to substitute (Table 4).

TABLE 4
Mean RT and *SD* for Failures to Substitute.
Experiment II: Condition 3[a]

	Time (msec)				
WS–S1 interval	150	210	250	310	350
Number of failures to substitutes	44	146	229	403	494
Mean RT	292	308	343	363	371
SD	39	31	49	49	60

[a]WS–S1 interval = 400 msec.

TABLE 5
Mean RT and *SD* for L and R Responses when Both L and
R Responses Were Made in the "Substitute" Condition.
Experiment II: Condition 3[a]

	Time (msec)				
WS–S2 interval	150	210	250	310	350
L response	–	–	–	–	–
Number	133	168	175	98	47
Mean RT	407	401	429	419	443
SD	98	82	107	88	89
R response	–	–	–	–	–
Number	134	171	177	100	52
Mean RT	298	337	368	441	472
SD	55	48	40	61	77

[a]WS–S1 ISI = 400 msec.

This experiment indicates that even when it is the R1–S2 relationship which is IM compatible, and S2 resembles the sensory feedback from a response which is being prepared, the IM compatible S2 cannot immediately overwrite a previous instruction for a different response. This supports the view that the organization of a response is protected from interruption by subsequent signals. The notion that the single channel might be selectively receptive to a stimulus resembling sensory feedback from a prepared response, which was derived from Welford (1959), was not supported. Among other possibilities it could be suggested that the single channel is cleared only by execution of the program which controls the responding activity rather than by feedback from that activity. This ad hoc hypothesis could explain both the present results, and why the PRP is often found to last for a full RT.

D. Conclusion

The present experiments fail to confirm Greenwald and Shulman's (1973) claim to eliminate the PRP using IM compatible S–R relationships. The possibility suggested by Allport *et al.* (1972), that, in order to eliminate the PRP, it is necessary to use tasks which are highly dissimilar from one another was not tested. However, since the two studies which come closest to meeting both conditions of task dissimilarity and IM compatibility (Greenwald & Shulman, 1973; Smith, 1969) both show the usual PRP, one cannot regard the dissimilarity hypothesis with confidence. Rather, it seems necessary to conclude that the single-channel principle still holds. However, since we stand to learn so much about how information from different sources, and for different responses, is handled by learning how to control the PRP, it is certain that the search for exceptions to the PRP will continue. And when, hopefully, genuine exceptions are found, then the single-channel model will have done its job, and will have made it possible to take one more step on the road to understanding the central decision processes.

IV. APPENDIX (BY G. A. SMITH)

Reaction Time in the Psychological Refractory Period: An Alternative to Response Conflict[2]

A mathematical exposition of possible processes involved in the Psychological Refractory Period (PRP) paradigm is given briefly, without appealing to the concept of response conflict.

It has been suggested by Brebner in this chapter that it is not necessary to postulate response conflict to explain the pattern of results found in PRP experiments, contrary to Herman and Kantowitz's (1970) claim. A simple model which avoids the assumptions of response conflict theory is presented here.

We can consider reaction time to consist of two components, the first of which, preprocessing, can be affected by the expectation and arrival of a subsequent stimulus, and the second which is the rest of the process. Let the amount of preprocessing needed for S_1 (the first of two stimuli given), be P_1 and the time taken by the rest of the process be Q_1. By preprocessing we mean that initial processing time of about 100 msec for which Herman and Kantowitz (1970) found a linear decrease in RT_1 (the reaction time to the first of two asynchronous stimuli) with the time between S_1 and the second stimulus, S_2. A possible description of Q_1 is the time taken for the organization of the response. (This is elaborated under Case 2 below.)

We now present the model:

Case 1 in which S_1 only is to be given on a series of trials (simple reaction). Let p_1 be the time needed to process one unit of S_1. When the processor is thus dedicated to S_1 we have:

$$RT_1 = P_1 \cdot p_1 + Q_1 \tag{i}$$

Case 2 in which two stimuli, S_1 and S_2, are presented on each trial, and the subject uses a program to deal with them as they arrive. That is, after the onset of S_1, some capacity is taken up in anticipating S_2 (e.g., checking for its arrival). This results in more time being needed per unit processed. Let this be p' where $p' > p$. After the arrival of S2 the preprocessing of S1 is slowed even further because S_2 takes capacity in just being stored (the single channel theory).[3] From Herman and Kantowitz (1970) this additional slowing of RT_1 does not seem to happen if S_2 arrives after the 100 msec of preprocessing is complete. This could

[2] This Appendix was written by Glen A. Smith of the Department of Psychology, University of Adelaide, Adelaide, South Australia.

be interpreted as showing that once the organization of a response to S_1 has begun the response organization is protected from interruption by the arrival and storing of S_2. Let this further increment in time per unit be d_1.

Thus:

$$RT_1' = P_1 \cdot x_1 \cdot p_1' + P_1(1 - x_1)(p_1' + d_1) + Q_1 \qquad \text{(ii)}$$

where x_1 is the proportion of P_1 completed before the arrival of S_2. This simplifies to:

$$RT_1' = P_1(p_1' + d_1(1 - x_1)) + Q_1 \qquad \text{(iii)}$$

Similarly for S_2, its processing is affected by ongoing S_1 processing (single channel would be the limiting case; the organization of a response to S_2 is prevented until the channel is cleared; Welford, 1959). We therefore have

$$RT_2' = P_2(p_2' + d_2(1 - x_2)) + Q_2 \qquad \text{(iv)}$$

where the definition of the symbols are as for Eq. (iii), but referring to Stimulus 2.

Case 3 in which the subject expects two stimuli, but uses a strategy for treating the two stimuli as one complex asynchronous complex stimulus. That is, S_1 is stored until S_2 arrives, and then both responses are organized together. Since this is a more complex task than processing either S_1 or S_2, time per unit of processing, p_3, will be larger than p_1 and p_2. Hence we have

$$RT_1'' = ISI + P_1 \cdot p_3 + Q_1 \qquad \text{(v)}$$

and

$$RT_2'' = P_2 \cdot p_3 + Q_2 \qquad \text{(vi)}$$

where ISI is the time between the arrival of S_1 and of S_2.

These equations quantify the observed results without reference to response conflict assumptions.

ACKNOWLEDGMENTS

The author wishes to thank Miss W. Gaetjens, Mr. G. Garcia-Barrio and Mr. R. Willson of Adelaide University for their technical and professional assistance throughout this project. Helpful discussions with Professor A. T. Welford on the topic of this paper are also acknowledged.

REFERENCES

Allport, D. A., Antonis, B., & Reynolds, P. On the division of attention: A disproof of the single channel hypothesis. *Quarterly Journal of Experimental Psychology*, 1972, **24**, 225–235.

[3] This increment could also be a slowing due to processing of S_2 although this assumption leads to a more complex interpretation of eq. (iv).

Annett, J. A note on Davis's refutation of the expectancy hypothesis. *Quarterly Journal of Experimental Psychology*, 1966, **18**, 179–180.

Borger, R. The refractory period and serial choice reactions. *Quarterly Journal of Experimental Psychology*, 1963, **15**, 1–12.

Bryan, W. L., & Harter, N. Studies on the telegraphic language: The acquisition of hierarchy of habits. *Psychological Review*, 1899, **6**, 345–375.

Burns, M. M., & Moskowitz, H. Reaction time to a 1st signal as a function of time relationship to a 2nd signal and mode of presentation. *Perceptual and Motor Skills*, 1971, **32**, 811–816.

Craik, K. J. W. Theory of the human operator in control systems: I. The operator as an engineering system. *British Journal of Psychology*, 1947, **38**, 58–61.

Craik, K. J. W. Theory of the human operator in control systems: II. Man as an element in a control system. *British Journal of Psychology*, 1948, **38**, 142–148.

Davis, R. The limits of the "psychological refractory period." *Quarterly Journal of Experimental Psychology*, 1956, **8**, 24–38.

Davis, R. The role of "attention" in the psychological refractory period. *Quarterly Journal of Experimental Psychology*, 1959, **11**, 211–220.

Elithorn, A., & Lawrence, C. Central inhibition – Some refractory observations. *Quarterly Journal of Experimental Psychology*, 1955, **7**, 116–127.

Gottsdanker, R. Psychological refractoriness and the organization of step-tracking responses. *Perception & Psychophysics*, 1973, **14**, 60–70.

Greenwald, A. G. On doing two things at once: I. Time sharing as a function of ideomotor compatibility. *Journal of Experimental Psychology*, 1972, **94**, 52–57.

Greenwald, A. G., & Shulman, H. G. On doing two things at once: II. Elimination of the PRP effect. *Journal of Experimental Psychology*, 1973, **101**, 70–76.

Herman, L. M., & Kantowitz, B. H. The psychological refractory period effect: Only half the double stimulation story? *Psychological Bulletin*, 1970, **73**, 74–88.

Hick, W. E., & Bates, J. A. V. The human operator of control mechanisms. Ministry of Supply Research and Development Monograph, 1950, No. 17, 204.

Kantowitz, B. H. Response force as an indicant of conflict in double stimulation. *Journal of Experimental Psychology*, 1973, **100**, 302–309.

Poulton, E. C. Perceptual anticipation and reaction time. *Quarterly Journal of Experimental Psychology*, 1950, **2**, 99–112.

Raeburn, B. J., & Corballis, M. C. Refractoriness in same-different judgements. *Quarterly Journal of Experimental Psychology*, 1972, **24**, 406–413.

Salthouse, T. Human performance as a function of future demands. *Perceptual and Motor Skills*, 1970, **30**, 327–336.

Siegel, S. *Non-parametric statistics*, New York: McGraw-Hill, 1956.

Smith, M. C. The effect of varying information on the psychological refractory period. *Acta Psychologica*, 1969, **30**, 220–231.

Vince, M. A. Corrective movements in a pursuit task. *Quarterly Journal of Experimental Psychology*, 1948, **1**, 85–103. (a)

Vince, M. A. The intermittency of control movements and the psychological refractory period. *British Journal of Psychology*, 1948, **38**, 149–157. (b)

Vince, M. A. Some exceptions to the psychological refractory period in unskilled manual responses. *Medical Research Council Applied Psychology Unit Report* 124/50, 1950.

Welford, A. T. The "psychological refractory period" and the timing of high-speed performance – A review and a theory. *British Journal of Psychology*, 1952, **43**, 2–19.

Welford, A. T. Evidence of a single-channel decision mechanism limiting performance in a serial reaction task. *Quarterly Journal of Experimental Psychology*, 1959, **11**, 193–210.

5

Serial Reaction Times, Continuity of Task, Single-Channel Effects, and Age

A. T. Welford

Department of Psychology
University of Adelaide
Adelaide, South Australia

ABSTRACT

Experiments are described that were designed to test a theory that the disproportionate slowing of performance by older subjects in continuous (as opposed to discontinuous) tasks is due to aftereffects of neural activity which increase in duration with age. At long interstimulus or interresponse intervals these effects would have time to dissipate, and thus would not affect the speed with which responses were initiated. At very short intervals, however, they would impair the making of different responses but have less effect on, or even facilitate, the making of repeated responses. It was argued that if the theory was correct, reaction times for repeated responses should tend to be faster than those for different ones, and that this tendency should increase with age. The results showed clearly that this did not happen but that, instead, there was an increased tendency with age for times for repeated responses to be slower than for different ones. The increase could be accounted for in terms of older subjects taking longer to discriminate repeated signals, and tending to monitor their responses more than young subjects. The results appear to endorse certain aspects of the single-channel hypothesis that were proposed many years ago but have not hitherto gained much attention, and to suggest that previously neglected factors of discriminability and monitoring of responses can influence serial effects in reaction times.

I. INTRODUCTION

The slowing of performance commonly observed from young adulthood onward appears to take several different forms. When, for example, reaction times for different finenesses of visual discrimination or varying degrees of choice are compared, age effects are usually the addition of a time to all tasks which is either constant or proportionate according to conditions of presentation. The slowing in these cases can be reasonably accounted for by assuming that age brings a lowering of signal-to-noise ratio in the central nervous system for which the subject tends to compensate, when he can, by accumulating data over a longer time (for a review see Welford, 1977). One finding, seemingly difficult to account for in this way, is that the slowing with age tends to be greater for continuous than for discontinuous tasks — for example, in serial reaction tasks in which each response brings on the next signal immediately or after a short interval, as opposed to tasks in which each signal and response are well separated in time from others (see Miles, 1931; Welford, 1958/1973, 1959b, 1977).

It has, however, been suggested that the longer reaction times found in continuous tasks may be due to effects of signals and responses affecting the processes of dealing with subsequent signals. The aftereffects are assumed to act as noise in relation to a signal and action occurring after a short interval, and thus make a longer accumulation of data necessary if an accurate decision and appropriate action are to be achieved. Such interference should apply mainly to actions which are different from those immediately preceding. When an action has to be repeated, the aftereffects would be likely to have less interfering, and perhaps even a facilitating, effect. In a discontinuous task these aftereffects would have time to die away between one signal or action and the next, and so would not affect performance. It is suggested that these aftereffects die away more slowly in older people, so that they not only operate over longer invervals of time, but have a greater effect at any given time before decay is complete. Evidence from EEG studies and from the tendencies of older people to perseverate in their responses makes this view at least plausible (for a summary see Welford, 1965).

The theory should be testable by means of the repetition or alternation effects observed in serial reaction times. If it is correct, there should be a tendency at short intersignal or interresponse intervals for repeated responses to be made more quickly than ones which are different from those preceding (repetition effect) and this tendency should increase with age. By the same tokens, if conditions favor, instead, the making of different responses more rapidly than repeated ones (alternation effect) the difference should diminish with age at short intersignal or interresponse intervals. It is true that Waugh, Fozard, Talland, and Erwin (1973) found no tendency for repetition effects to increase with age, but the intervals between signals they used were so long (10–15 sec) that their results do not constitute a test of the theory. At longer intervals the aftereffects would have died away so that one would expect no increase of repetition effect or reduction of alternation effect with age.

A series of experiments was accordingly undertaken to examine repetition and alternation effects in relation to age under several experimental conditions which have been found in previous researches to produce repetition effects in varying degrees. The results obtained are complex and difficult to interpret. They are offered here not so much because they prove anything as because they provide interesting suggestions, not only regarding age changes, but about serial reaction times in general, which it is hoped others may take up in the future.

II. EXPERIMENT I

A. Method

1. Apparatus

Eight lens-topped neon bulbs of 16 mm diameter were mounted with centers 22 mm apart in a horizontal row. The tops appeared through a 20 cm square panel painted matt black set at 2.8 m directly in front of the subject and about 20 cm below eye level. The panel was divided in halves by a pale grey vertical line 3 mm wide which ran between the fourth and fifth lights in the row. The subject sat at a table on which eight Morse keys were arranged in two arcs of four so as to be located conveniently under the fingers of the two hands. The tension on the keys was adjusted so that a pressure of about 140 g was required for operation. The tops of the keys were flattened so that the fingers could rest comfortably on them. Signals were presented and responses recorded by a PDP8 computer.

2. Subjects

One of the greatest difficulties in cross-sectional studies of aging is to secure reasonable comparability between subjects of different ages. Even if subjects are matched for such variables as occupational or educational level, the older tend to represent a "survival of the fittest," and thus to be more highly selected on biological grounds than the younger. Since there appears to be a substantial hereditary factor in longevity, an attempt was made to improve comparability by recruiting members of three generations from the same families: daughter, mother, and mother's mother; or son, father, and father's father, thus securing young and middle-aged subjects who had better than average chances of surviving to a fit old age, as their grandparents or parents, respectively, had done. The control of heredity was not, of course, perfect since everyone has two parents, but was thought to be the best practicable and an improvement on that of most previous studies. Ten such trios were recruited, 8 female and 2 male. Particulars of ages are given in Table 1.

3. Procedure

Only the central two lights, one on each side of the grey line, and their corresponding keys were used. The left-hand light was responded to with the left index finger and the right-hand light with the right index finger.

Each subject performed two tasks:

1. A discontinuous task in which each light came on without warning, 2 seconds after the key pressed in response to the previous light was released. The order of lights was random except that each appeared an equal number of times in every block of 16. They stayed on until a response key, whether correct or incorrect, was struck. Forty-eight trials were scored. This condition is referred to as RS2 (Release-to-Signal, 2 sec).

2. A continuous task which was the same as RS2 except that each light came on immediately the key pressed in response to the previous light was released, and that 96 trials were scored. This condition will be referred to as RS0 (Release-to-Signal, 0 sec).

Each task was carefully explained before a subject attempted it, and 16 practice trials were given before scoring began. There was a short pause after the practice trials, and any subject who so desired was given further blocks of 16 practice trials before embarking on those that were to be scored. Subjects were told to press the appropriate key as quickly as possible when each light came on and, while trying to be accurate, not to worry about occasional errors.

The two tasks were always given in the same order, first RS2 then RS0. This was thought to be justified in view of the practice given before each, and the indication from previous studies (see Teichner & Krebs, 1974) that practice effects were unlikely to be substantial with the number of trials involved.

The three members of most of the trios came to the laboratory together and stayed together in the same room during testing. The youngest member was tested first, followed by the middle member, and the oldest, last. This was done in order to ensure that the oldest member had had the tasks thoroughly demonstrated before attempting them. The young and most of the middle members understood quickly what had to be done. So did the older members when their turn came, but it seemed likely from previous experience of testing older people that many of them would have been at a disadvantage if they had been tested first.

B. Results

Severe difficulties arose, as they usually do in studies of aging, over statistical treatment of the results. There is not only a tendency for variances to rise sharply with age, but occasional wildly deviant performers cast doubt upon the applicability of normal procedures for analysis of variance and other parametric tests. It was decided, therefore, to rely on nonparametric tests of particular differences of theoretical importance. Such methods, although a little less powerful, have appeared in previous studies to be convenient and satisfactory in handling data comparing age groups.

Table 1 shows that in the RS2 condition there was a slight fall in overall reaction time from the young to the middle group, and a substantial rise from these groups to the older ($p < .02$ by U test). In the RS0 condition there were rises both from the young to the middle and from the middle to the older groups although only the latter was significant ($p < .02$ by U test). The rises with age were obviously not associated with increased accuracy in a speed–accuracy tradeoff. Every subject except one had a longer mean reaction time in the RS0 condition than in the RS2. The exception was the oldest subject, a man aged 87 whose performance in the RS0 condition was faster than that of any other subject except one in the young group. He seems to have been an example of the maverick older performer who often appears in aging studies. There was no

TABLE 1

Experiment I. Mean Correct Reaction Times and Times on Key (in msec) and Percentage Errors in 2-Choice Tasks with Intervals of 2 Sec (RS2) and 0 Sec (RS0) between the End of One Response and the Onset of the Next Signal

	Age group			Differences[a]	
	Young (Y)	Middle (M)	Older (O)	M–Y	O–Y
Range (years)	17–25	39–57	69–87		
Mean (years)	19.0	47.7	79.0		
Reaction time					
RS2	304	295	383	−9(−3)	+79(+26)
RS0	357	399	495	+42(+12)	+139(+39)
Serial effects					
RS2					
Repeated (R)	332	312	416	−20(−6)	+84(+25)
Different (D)	276	279	349	+3(+1)	+73(+26)
R–D[b]	+56(+18)	+33(+11)	+67(+17)		
RS0					
Repeated (R)	353	424	524	+71(+20)	+171(+48)
Different (D)	361	374	466	+13(+4)	+105(+29)
R–D[b]	−8(−2)	+50(+13)	+58(+12)		
Time on key					
RS2	149	140	200		
RS0	177	156	202		
Percentage errors					
RS2	1.1	2.0	4.5		
RS0	4.8	7.3	6.3		

[a]Percentage differences shown in parentheses.
[b]Differences as percentage of overall reaction time shown in parentheses.

apparent reason for his exceptional performance other than that he seemed unusually alert for his age.

In order to test whether the rise of reaction time with age in the RS0 condition was greater than in the RS2, the differences of times RS0–RS2 for individual subjects were ranked against age group. The overall rank correlation τ was positive, and significant at the 1% level. Since, however, the reaction times themselves rose with age, this result might merely indicate some overall factor that produced a proportionate rise of all reaction times with age rather than a factor which had a special effect in the RS0 condition. A more stringent test was therefore made by ranking the *ratios* of times RS0/RS2 for individual subjects against age group. In this case τ was still significant at the 5% level, indicating that the increase with age was more than proportionate. Comparing the age groups by U tests, the young group's ratios were significantly less than those of the middle ($p < .02$) but not of the older, owing to the exceptional subject already mentioned. If his results are omitted, the young did differ significantly from the older ($p < .05$). The middle and older groups did not differ significantly from each other.

When the reaction times to signals which were repeated and different from those immediately preceding were separated, as shown in Table 1, a substantial alternation effect was evident for all age groups in the RS2 condition. For the young subjects in the RS0 condition the effect disappeared, and was replaced by a small repetition effect. This is in line with previous work showing increased tendency to repetition effects as the interval between responses becomes shorter (Bertelson & Renkin, 1966; Hale, 1967). For the middle and older subjects, no such tendency was present – the alternation effects were approximately the same in both conditions. The ratio of times for Different/Repeated, was significantly greater in each of the middle and older groups than in the young ($p < .02$ in each case by U test).

The percentage changes with age for both Repeated and Different responses in the RS2 condition and for Different responses in the RS0 were closely similar. Those for Repeated responses in the latter condition were much greater. Evidently the whole of the disproportionate increase of reaction time with age in this condition was due to the longer time taken by middle and older subjects to react to Repeated signals. These results are, of course, quite contrary to our hypothesis that the greater slowing with age in continuous performance is due to aftereffects of the kind envisaged in this chapter's Introduction. If these operate at all, their influence is heavily masked by that of some other factor or factors. The results imply that older people have difficulty in reacting quickly to Repeated signals. Subjectively, in the RS0 condition, Repeated signals appeared less "insistent" than Different ones. The latter involved not only a light flashing on, but also a change of position which often produced an apparent movement effect. Perhaps the absence of this extra cue made Repeated signals less discriminable by older subjects.

III. EXPERIMENT II

The conclusion from Experiment I is problematical in that the results for the middle and older groups showed overall alternation effects in the RSO condition rather than the repetition effects which had been expected on the basis of previous work. This objection cannot, however, apply to the results of a second experiment in which subjects performed an 8-choice task which, in line with previous work (Kornblum, 1969; Kirby, 1975), yielded repetition effects for all three age groups.

A. Method

1. Apparatus

The apparatus and procedure were the same as in the RSO condition of Experiment I except that all 8 lights and keys were used. The leftmost light was responded to by pressing the leftmost key with the left little finger, the next light by pressing the next key with the left ring finger, and so on until the rightmost light was responded to by pressing the rightmost key with the right little finger.

2. Subjects

The subjects were the same as those in Experiment I, and the present experiment, involving 96 scored trials after practice, was carried out at the same session after a short break.

B. Results

As expected from previous work on reaction time in relation to degree of choice, and as shown in Table 2, all the mean reaction times were longer than for the 2-choice tasks of Experiment I. The times taken to respond to Repeated signals were shorter than to Different, but there was no significant increase of repetition effect with age, so that the results again do not support the theory outlined in the Introduction to this chapter.

The percentage changes with age in times to respond to Different signals were similar to those in Experiment I. As regards Repeated signals, the absolute rise of reaction time from the young group to the older was closely similar to that of the RSO condition in Experiment I, while the percentage rise was somewhat less. The rise from the young group to the middle was nil. Why this should be so is not clear. A possible reason might be, however, that slowing due to difficulty in discriminating Repeated signals was offset, in this multichoice condition, by the fact that Repeated signals would require less "work" for identification and choice of corresponding response.

TABLE 2

Experiment II. Mean Correct Reaction Times and Times on Key (in msec), and Percentage Errors in an 8-Choice task with 0 sec between the End of One Response and the Onset of the next Signal

| | Age group | | | Differences[a] |
	Young (Y)	Middle(M)	Older (O)	
Reaction time	651	659	820	+8(+1) +169(+26)
Serial effects				
Repeated (R)	573	574	749	+1(0) +176(+31)
Different (D)	662	671	830	+9(+1) +168(+25)
R–D[a]	−89(−14)	−97(−15)	−81(−10)	
Time on key	183	167	256	
Percentage errors	16.1	10.1	20.7	

[a]Percentage differences shown in parentheses as in Table 1.

IV. EXPERIMENT III

If the disproportionate age change in the RS0 condition of Experiment I was due to difficulty in discriminating Repeated signals, the change should be reduced if two signals were mapped onto each response and used in such a way that no signal was ever repeated. Experiment III was designed to examine the effects of this arrangement.

A. Method

1. Apparatus

This was the same as for Experiment I except that the display of eight light bulbs was replaced by one of four bulbs in two pairs. The bulbs in each pair were located one above the other with centers 22 mm apart. The pairs were separated horizontally with centers 66 mm apart. Both of the left-hand pair were responded to by the left index finger on the same key, and both of the right-hand pair by the right index finger on a second key.

2. Subjects

Ten trios were recruited, all female. Three of the trios had previously taken part in Experiments I and II, the remaining seven were new. Particulars of ages are given in Table 3.

3. Procedure

Each subject performed three tasks in the following order:

1. As in the RS2 condition of Experiment I. The lights of each pair were used alternately so that no signal was ever repeated immediately. In the place of

Repeated signals we can, therefore, speak of "Equivalent" signals which, although not repeated, call for repetition of the same response.

2. As Task 1 but under RS0 conditions.

3. The use of two lights alternately on each side made it possible to arrange for the next light to appear immediately on *pressing* instead of releasing the key used in response to the previous light. Ninety-six trials were scored under these conditions, which will be referred to as PS0 (Press-to-Signal, 0 sec).

Instructions, arrangements for practice and order of testing subjects of different ages were the same as in Experiment I.

B. Results

Table 3 shows a pattern of results for the RS2 and RS0 tasks, roughly similar to those in Experiment I except that, in the RS0 condition, the rise from the young to the middle group was absent and the rise to the older group was slightly reduced.

TABLE 3

Experiment III. Mean Correct Reaction Times and Times on Key (in msec), and Percentage Errors in 2-Choice Tasks with Intervals of 2 Sec (RS2) and 0 Sec (RS0) between the End of One Response and the Onset of the next Signal

	Age group			Differences[a]	
	Young (Y)	Middle (M)	Older (O)	M−Y	O−Y
Range (years)	17−26	40−56	67−86		
Mean (years)	19.4	46.0	72.9		
Reaction time					
RS2	278	273	340	−5(−2)	+62(+22)
RS0	393	398	520	+5(+1)	+127(+32)
Serial effects					
RS2					
Equivalent (E)	296	292	362	−4(−1)	+66(+22)
Different (D)	261	254	319	−7(−3)	+58(+22)
E−D[a]	+35(+13)	+38(+14)	+43(+13)		
RS0					
Equivalent (E)	402	407	558	+5(+1)	+156(+39)
Different (D)	384	389	482	+5(+1)	+98(+28)
E−D[a]	+18(+5)	+16(+4)	+66(+13)		
Time on key					
RS2	143	157	140		
RS0	166	176	157		
Percentage errors					
RS2	1.7	1.5	0.8		
RS0	7.5	7.5	7.8		

[a]Percentage differences shown in parentheses as in Table 1.

As regards serial effects, the young subjects showed some reduction of alternation effect in the RSO condition compared with the RS2, but not, as in Experiment I, an overall repetition effect. This is perhaps in line with the finding by Bertelson (1965) and Rabbitt (1968) that repetition effects were less with Equivalent than with Repeated signals, although the conditions of their experiments differed in some ways from ours. The middle subjects showed a reduction of alternation effect in the RSO condition similar to that shown by the young. The older showed a slight absolute rise but no proportionate change.

The percentage rises from the young to the older groups, for both Equivalent and Different responses in the RS2 and for Different responses in the RSO condition, were all similar to each other and to the corresponding rises in Experiment I. The percentage rise between the same groups' responses to Equivalent signals in RSO condition was, like that of responses to Repeated signals in Experiment I, higher, and the percentage differences of time between responses to Equivalent and Different signals rose significantly from each of the young and middle groups to the older ($p < .02$ in each case by U test).

Taking the results as a whole it seems reasonable to suggest that middle but not older subjects found Equivalent signals relatively easier to deal with than Repeated. As in Experiment I, however, there is no support for the hypothesis suggesting a tendency away from alternation effects towards repetition effects with age.

The results for the PSO task are set out in Table 4. The overall reaction times rose a little from the young to the middle group, and substantially from the middle to the older. The difference of reaction time PSO–RS2 correlated positively with age group ($p < .05$ by τ test), due largely to the very marked rise with age in the times taken to respond to Equivalent signals. Overall, the ratio of

TABLE 4

Experiment III. Mean Correct Reaction Times and Times on Key (in msec.), and Percentage Errors in a 2-Choice Task with an Interval of 0 Sec between the Beginning of One Response and the Onset of the next Signal (PSO)

	Age group			Differences[a]	
	Young (Y)	Middle (M)	Older (O)	Ms,nY	O–Y
Reaction time	321	342	472	+21 (+7)	+151 (+47)
Serial effects					
Equivalent (E)	328	377	536	+49 (+15)	+208 (+63)
Different (D)	315	308	409	−7 (−2)	+94 (+30)
E–D[a]	+13 (+4)	+69 (+20)	+127 (+27)		
Time on key	158	168	176		
Percentage errors	7.6	6.5	10.7		

[ab]Percentage differences shown in parentheses as in Table 1.

times PSO/RS2 did not rise significantly with age group, but it did so for Equivalent signals alone ($p < .02$ by τ test). There was again an overall alternation effect, and its rise with age, measured by correlating percentage effect with age group, was again significant ($p < .01$ by τ test).

The mean reaction times for the PSO task were, in all age groups, intermediate between those for the RS2 and RSO. Of the 30 subjects, 23 showed PSO times longer than their RS2 times, and 25 showed RSO times longer than their PSO times ($p \ll .001$ by W test of agreement that RS2 < PSO < RSO). This was a surprising result. Whatever factors made reaction times longer in the RSO task than in the RS2 might have been expected to operate even more strongly in the PSO, making reaction times even longer. However, the results are consistent with the single-channel hypothesis. It was suggested over 20 years ago following experimental results available at the time (Welford, 1952; for later confirmation see Leonard, 1953; Welford, 1959a, 1967, 1968), that if a signal came during the movement made in response to a previous signal, reaction to the new signal might be delayed because the subject's attention was taken up with monitoring the previous response. If, however, the new signal arrived at or before the point at which the responding movement to the previous signal began, this monitoring could be omitted and delay avoided on at least a proportion of occasions.

In such circumstances the lack of monitoring of action would tend to make the subject lose awareness of what he was doing. This occurred in Leonard's case, and was observed by several subjects of the third experiment in such terms as "In the first and second tasks (i.e., RS2 and RSO) you seem to be chasing the lights; in this one (i.e., PSO) they seem to be chasing you." The idea that new signals may take precedence in this way over monitoring, receives some support from the finding by Klein and Posner (1974) that visual data tend to take precedence over kinaesthetic in gaining attention.

The results for the PSO condition raise two further possible reasons why the older subjects were slower. One possibility, that they took longer to make responses and were therefore not ready in time to execute responses to new signals, can be dismissed at once: the mean times spent pressing the keys were all far shorter than their reaction times. A more likely reason is that older subjects were less able to suppress monitoring of their responses. The suggestion is the more plausible in that older people have been shown in many previous studies to be more likely than younger to check and monitor their actions (e.g., Szafran, cited in Welford, 1958/1973; Craik, 1969). A direct test in the present experiment is not possible, but it can be argued that if a subject suppressed monitoring every time, his average reaction time should be the same as in the RS2 condition. If, on the other hand, he always monitored, his reaction time should be the sum of his reaction time in the RS2 condition and his time on key in the PSO condition. The difference between time on key and reaction time in the PSO condition was calculated for each subject and divided by that subject's reaction time in the RS2 condition. The ratios ranged from just over 1, indicating no suppression of

TABLE 5
Experiment III. Numbers of Subjects Whose Difference
between Reaction Time and Time on Key in the PSO
Condition Was above or below .75 of their Reaction
Time in the RS2 Condition

	Age group		
	Young	Middle	Older
Below .75	7	7	1
Equal to or above .75	3	3	9

monitoring, to 0.15 indicating almost complete suppression. Numbers of subjects with ratios falling above and below the median shown in Table 5 indicate a significant tendency for the older subjects to have higher ratios ($p < .01$ when older compared with combined middle and young groups by τ test).

If this is the true explanation of the longer times taken by older subjects in the PSO condition, the further question arises of why their increased monitoring was associated with Equivalent signals. Is there a tendency, especially among older people, to monitor repeated responses more than different ones? We shall return to this question subsequently.

V. EXPERIMENT IV

The results of Experiment III confirm those of Experiment I in going against the theory stated in the Introduction. However, the serial effect is once again an alternation rather than a repetition effect. One further attempt was accordingly made to obtain repetition effects increasing with age under conditions comparable to ones which previous work had shown to be especially favorable for the emergence of repetition effects (e.g., Bertelson, 1963).

A. Method

1. Apparatus

Each subject performed two tasks, the arrangements for which were the same as in the RS2 and RS0 conditions of Experiment III except that the lights on the left side were responded to with the right hand and vice versa. It has been assumed that, under these conditions, the complex translation from perception to action does not have to be made de novo for a repeated response, which is therefore made more quickly.

2. Subjects

The subjects were the same as in Experiment III, and the readings were taken after those of Experiment III at the same session, following a few minutes' break.

B. Results

These are shown in Table 6. Taking first the times for the RS2 condition, the percentage differences between the overall reaction times and those for the corresponding condition in Experiment III rose significantly when ranked against age group ($p < .05$ by τ test), indicating that the older subjects were more affected than the younger by the indirect relationship between signal and response. At the same time, although an overall alternation effect remained, the percentage effect was, in contrast to Experiment III, less for both middle and older subjects than for young ($p < .02$ and $p < .002$, respectively by U test).

TABLE 6

Experiment IV. Mean Correct Reaction Times and Times on Key (in msec), and Percentage Errors in 2-Choice Tasks with Signals on the Right Responded to by the Left Hand and Vice Versa in RS2 and RS0 Conditions

	Age group			Differences[a]	
	Young (Y)	Middle (M)	Older (O)	M–Y	O–Y
Reaction time					
RS2	425	448	608	+23(+5)	+183(+43)
RS0	527	545	732	+18(+3)	+205(+39)
Serial effects					
RS2					
Equivalent (E)	458	453	627	−5(−1)	+169(+37)
Different (D)	392	443	590	+51(+13)	+198(+51)
E–D[a]	+66(+14)	+10(+2)	+37(+4)		
RS0					
Equivalent (E)	520	557	754	+37(+7)	+234(+45)
Different (D)	534	535	712	+1(0)	+178(+33)
E–D[a]	−14(−3)	+12(+2)	+42(+6)		
Time on key					
RS2	139	153	155		
RS0	162	170	162		
Percentage errors					
RS2	4.2	3.3	8.1		
RS0	10.9	8.8	12.3		

[a]Percentage differences shown in parentheses as in Table 1.

In the RS0 condition, the young subjects showed a repetition effect in place of the alternation effect they showed in the RS2 condition – a result already mentioned as being in line with that to be expected from previous work. The middle and older subjects, however, showed no such trend. Proportionately the rises of time with age in the RS0 condition, both overall and for Equivalent and Different responses separately, were not significantly greater than in the RS0 condition of Experiment III. Nor was there any significant percentage change with age in sequential effects.

Taking the results for the RS2 and RS0 conditions together, the simplest interpretation seems to be that sequential effects in the RS0 conditions of Experiments I and III were partly offset by a tendency, increasing with age, for a repeated signal-response mapping to have been achieved more quickly than a new one. This tendency is unlikely to be due to any short-lasting aftereffect facilitating repetition, since it seemed to operate under RS2 conditions as well as RS0. Presumably, it should rather be attributed to a strategy, such as, perhaps, remembering the last signal and response and, if the previous signal is repeated, giving the same response as before without working out afresh which response corresponds to which signal (or pair of signals).

VI. DISCUSSION

The results of these experiments indicate that with the transition from discontinuous to continuous tasks, young subjects tended – in line with previous work – to change from alternation effects toward repetition effects. No such tendency was evident, however, among middle-aged and older subjects. Therefore, either the theory is wrong that aftereffects of previous signals and responses tend to lessen alternation effects or increase repetition effects among older subjects, or the aftereffects are masked by other factors. Also some doubt is cast upon the generality of serial effects found by previous experimenters, all of whom appear to have used subjects entirely or mainly in young adulthood.

The experimental results reported here do, however, offer two positive leads. First is the tendency in the RS0 conditions of Experiments I and III for reaction times to Repeated and Equivalent signals to lengthen more with age than those to Different signals – a tendency which, as already noted, suggests that older subjects have special difficulty with these signals. Second is the implication in the PS0 results of Experiment III that older subjects tend to monitor their performance more than do young.

Are the two tendencies distinct, or is one the result of the other? When seeking an answer to this question it is perhaps relevant to remember that a reason is also required for the longer reaction times in the RS0 conditions than in the RS2 to both Repeated (or Equivalent) and Different signals and regardless of age. These obviously cannot have been due merely to longer times taken to discriminate Repeated and Equivalent signals. Nor can they have been due to difficulty in discriminating *all* signals coming in quick succession, because if they had been, the reaction times in the PSO condition should have been at least as long as those in the RSO. As they were not, a different explanation seems to be required. Any explanation must be speculative, but the facts appear to be consistent with findings obtained in previous experiments concerned with the single-channel hypothesis. We may present the argument in the following six steps:

1. There is a spontaneous tendency to monitor responses. Such monitoring prevents immediate attention to signals which arrive during the making of a response and thus lengthens reaction times to them (Welford, 1952, 1959a).

2. However, when a new signal arrives during the reaction time to a previous signal, attention appears to be switched to the new signal as soon as the response to the previous signal has begun, and monitoring of the response to the previous signal is omitted as shown in Fig. 1A. When the new signal arrives simultaneously with the beginning of the response to the previous signal, experimental results have indicated that dealing with the new signal is sometimes delayed by monitoring the previous response and sometimes not. In the latter case the feedback from the response is either ignored or in some way combined ("grouped") with the new signal so that both are reacted to together. Whether the feedback is ignored or combined, monitoring as a separate operation which delays dealing with a new signal is suppressed (Welford, 1959a). The reason for the variability of result appears to lie in the fact that the "gate" which leads to single-channel operation in the central mechanisms lies between the detection of the signal and the choice of response to it (Welford, 1967, 1968). If, therefore, a signal arrives at the moment the response to a previous signal begins, as in the PSO condition, a short time will elapse while the signal is being detected. If this is shorter than the time required to detect feedback from the previous response, the new signal will occupy the single channel at once and monitoring will be suppressed. If, however, detection of the new signal takes longer than detection of feedback, monitoring of the response can capture the central mechanisms and thus delay choice of response to the new signal. The events envisaged are shown in Fig. 1, B and C.

3. Such delays may occur regardless of type of signal, but insofar as Repeated and Equivalent signals are less discriminable than Different ones, the detection process for them will take longer and the chance of delay by monitoring will be correspondingly greater, leading to longer average reaction times to Repeated and Equivalent signals. Any increase with age of difficulty in discriminating these signals will accentuate the chance of such delays in older subjects. Some indications on this point can be obtained by comparing Tables 3 and 4. If the assumption is correct and if Equivalent signals are less discriminable than

TIME →

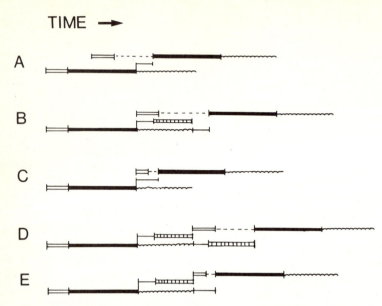

FIG. 1   Delays and monitoring postulated according to the single-channel hypothesis:

=== Detection of signal
▬ Choice and initiation of response
— Detection of beginning or end of response
ɪɪɪɪɪɪ Monitoring of response
〜〜〜 Execution of response
---- Signal held in store

A. Events envisaged when a signal arrives near the middle of the reaction time to a previous signal. (After Welford, 1967, 1968.) Monitoring of the response to the previous signal is suppressed.   B.   PS0 condition when the beginning of a response takes less time to detect than the next signal. Monitoring of the response delays reaction to the next signal. C. PS0 conditon when the beginning of a response takes longer to detect than the next signal. Reaction to the next signal suppresses monitoring of the previous response. D. RS0 condition when the end of a response takes less time to detect than the next signal. Monitoring of the response delays reaction to the next signal.   E.   RS0 condition when the end of a response takes longer to detect than the next signal. Reaction to the next signal suppresses monitoring of the end of the previous response.

Different, the difference between the times in PS0 and RS2 conditions should be greater for Equivalent than for Different signals. This is so for the middle and older subjects, but not for the young. The differences for Equivalent and Different signals respectively were 174 and 90 msec for the older subjects, 85 and 54 for the middle, but 32 and 54 for the young, implying that for the young subjects Equivalent signals were no more difficult – if anything a little easier – to discriminate.

4. In RS0 conditions the response will normally always be monitored, for a time which previous work suggests will be roughly equal to the time for which the key is pressed. Monitoring appears, however, in at least some cases to be initiated not only at the beginning of a response but at the end, presumably signifying that attention may be given not only to its commencement but also to its completion (Welford, 1952, 1959a). Such monitoring appears to be suppressed virtually always in PS0 conditions, presumably because there is always a signal waiting to be dealt with when the end of the response occurs. However, in RS0 conditions it can cause delays in responding to signals which come at the end of a response, similar to the delays in PS0 conditions in responding to signals which come at the beginning of a response. The events envisaged are shown in Fig. 1, D and E. Delays would have occurred especially with older subjects if they had had difficulty in discriminating Repeated or Equivalent signals, and could have led to their showing larger alternation effects than young subjects in the RS0 conditions of Experiments I and III. In these conditions young subjects showed, in one case, a relatively small alternation effect and in the other a small repetition effect implying again that they did not find the discrimination of Repeated and Equivalent signals especially difficult. This last result is consistent with that obtained by Rabbitt (1969) who found no differences of absolute repetition effects among subjects aged 18–20 with response–stimulus intervals of 20, 120, and 220 msec. His results cannot, however, be fully compared with the present ones because his signals were digits all displayed in the same position.

5. The detection stage is likely to be faster in the case of the end of a response than the beginning because, at the beginning, there will be uncertainty about which response has been initiated, but at the end there will be none. Detection of the end of a response is, therefore, the more likely to be complete before detection of the new signal, and thus to capture attention and cause monitoring delays in the RS0 condition more than in the PS0.

6. No delays of these kinds should occur in RS2 conditions since, by the time a new signal arrives, monitoring will have been completed.

If this model is correct, the fact that response to new signals in the RS0 and PS0 conditions would sometimes be delayed by monitoring and sometimes not, should result in the variance being higher in these conditions than in the RS2. This was clearly so: all the group mean variances and almost all those of individual subjects were higher under RS0 and PS0 conditions than under RS2.

Discriminability of signals and monitoring of responses are factors that have not hitherto been considered in relation to serial effects in reaction times, probably because previous studies have used highly discriminable signals and simple, ungraded responses with young subjects. The results obtained with our older subjects suggest, however, that these factors can be important and would be worth thorough investigation.

ACKNOWLEDGMENTS

I wish to express sincere gratitude to Dr. P. M. A. Rabbitt for his thorough, penetrating, and constructive criticism of a preliminary draft of this paper, but must add that any shortcomings still remaining are my responsibility, not his.

My thanks are due also to Dr. N. H. Kirby for helpful discussions, to Mr. R. Willson and Mr. P. Barnes for technical assistance, and to the Australian Research Grants Committee for financial support.

REFERENCES

Bertelson, P. S–R relationships and reaction times to new versus repeated signals in a serial task. *Journal of Experimental Psychology*, 1963, **65**, 478–484.

Bertelson, P. Serial choice reaction-time as a function of response versus signal-and-response repetition. *Nature*, 1965, **206**, 217–218.

Bertelson, P., & Renkin, A. Reaction times to new versus repeated signals in a serial task as a function of response–signal time interval. *Acta Psychologica*, 1966, **25**, 132–136.

Craik, F. I. M. Applications of signal detection theory to studies of ageing. In A. T. Welford & J. E. Birren (Eds.), *Decision making and age*. Basel: Karger, 1969. Pp. 147–157.

Hale, D. J. Sequential effects in a two-choice serial reaction task. *Quarterly Journal of Experimental Psychology*, 1967, **19**, 133–141.

Kirby, N. H. Sequential effects in an eight choice serial reaction time task. *Acta Psychologica*, 1975, **39**, 205–216.

Klein, R. M., & Posner, M. I. Attention to visual and kinaesthetic components of skills. *Brain Research*, 1974, **71**, 401–411.

Kornblum, S. Sequential determinants of information processing in serial and discrete choice reaction time. *Psychological Review*, 1969, **76**, 113–131.

Leonard, J. A. Advance information in sensori-motor skills. *Quarterly Journal of Experimental Psychology*, 1953, **5**, 141–149.

Miles, W. R. Measures of certain human abilities throughout the life span. *Proceedings of the National Academy of Science*, 1931, **17**, 627–633.

Rabbitt, P. M. A. Repetition effects and signal classification strategies in serial choice-response tasks. *Quarterly Journal of Experimental Psychology*, 1968, **20**, 232–240.

Rabbitt, P. M. A. Psychological refractory delay and response–stimulus interval duration in serial, choice-response tasks. *Acta Psychologica*, 1969, **30**, 195–219.

Teichner, W. H., & Krebs, M. J. Laws of visual choice reaction time. *Psychological Review*, 1974, **81**, 75–98.

Waugh, N. C., Fozard, J. L., Talland, G. A., & Erwin, D. E. Effects of age and stimulus repetition on two-choice reaction time. *Journal of Gerontology*, 1973, **28**, 466–470.

Welford, A. T. The "psychological refractory period" and the timing of high-speed performance – A review and a theory. *British Journal of Psychology*, 1952, **43**, 2–19.

Welford, A. T. Evidence of a single-channel decision mechanism limiting performance in a serial reaction task. *Quarterly Journal of Experimental Psychology*, 1959, **11**, 193–210. (a)

Welford, A. T. Psychomotor performance. In J. E. Birren (Ed.), *Handbook of aging and the individual*. Chicago: University of Chicago Press, 1959. Pp. 562–613. (b)

Welford, A. T. Performance, biological mechanisms and age: A theoretical sketch. In A. T.

Welford & J. E. Birren (Eds.), *Behavior, aging and the nervous system.* Springfield, Ill.: Charles C Thomas, 1965. Pp. 3–20.

Welford, A. T. Single-channel operation in the brain. *Acta Psychologica,* 1967, **27,** 5–22.

Welford, A. T. *Fundamentals of skill.* London: Methuen, 1968.

Welford, A. T. *Ageing and human skill.* Westport, Conn.: Greenwood Press, 1973. (Originally published, 1958.)

Welford, A. T. Motor performance. In J. E. Birren (Ed.), *Handbook of the psychology of aging.* New York: Van Nostrand Reinhold, 1977.

6

Choice Reaction Time and the Problem of Distinguishing Task Effects from Strategy Effects

Robert Ollman

Bell Laboratories
Holmdel, New Jersey, United States

ABSTRACT

This paper examines how we use choice RT measurement to make inferences about mechanisms for processing stimulus information. Distinguishing strategy effects from task effects is a major problem. One approach, which is widely used, supposes that if the probability of a correct response remains constant across experimental conditions, strategy also remains constant and so differences among RTs are purely task effects. It strongly appears that this approach is based on tacit acceptance of a special case of the fast guess model. Specifically, it can be shown that this approach is consistent with the fast guess model but inconsistent with the deadline model, for example. The adjustable timing model, which is suggested by the Schouten and Bekker (1967) study, commends the opposite approach: if the distribution of RTs remains constant across experimental conditions, then strategy remains constant and so differences in the probability of a correct response arise purely from task effects. Particular methods for distinguishing effects are based on particular models and there is no universally accepted model at this time. To decide which method is best suited to a particular problem, it is necessary to conduct factorial experiments in which both "task" and "strategy" variables are manipulated. A particular method for distinguishing types of effects should not be chosen until after alternative models have been fitted and tested. An approach to the statistical problem of testing the adjustable timing model is briefly sketched.

I. INTRODUCTION

In this chapter I will discuss the method of choice reaction time and how it is used as an investigative tool. Usually, we regard the reaction time (RT) as a dependent variable and we manipulate what I refer to as "task" variables to observe their effects on the RT. From an analysis of these effects, we have drawn various conclusions — some of them surprising — about human capabilities for processing information.

Without intending to challenge any specific findings, I would like to question whether this approach is correct in general. Some interesting results from studies of the speed—accuracy tradeoff suggest that the usual approach is sometimes wrong. There are even some results — admittedly fragmentary — that suggest we have been doing things backward much of the time. Perhaps there are occasions when we should treat the RT as an independent variable, to be actively controlled and manipulated rather than passively observed. If we are interested in "task" effects (as distinguished from "strategy" effects), we should take the probability of a correct response as the dependent variable and we should attempt to control the RT. This would be a reversal of the usual approach, which is based on controlling the probability of a correct response and using the RT as a dependent variable.

I will first review the usual approach to RT and propose that it is implicitly based on the rather doubtful assumption that a special case of the fast-guess model (Ollman, 1966; Yellott, 1971) is correct in general. Advancing this proposal requires a brief review of the already familiar fast-guess and deadline models. It also requires a somewhat oversimplified description of current experimental practices. In truth, there may be no single experimenter who wholly practices or believes what will be called "the RT method." Hopefully it will be accepted that the foregoing description of "the RT method" is something of a caricature that is meant to focus on a one basic problem: to control the speed—accuracy tradeoff strategy. For a description that is more general, yet attentive to this particular problem, see Pachella's (1974) review.

After the "RT method" has been discussed, the adjustable timing model will be introduced. Then, using the adjustable timing model as the motivation, I propose alternative methods of experimentation and data analysis. They are almost directly opposite to what we are accustomed, but closely related to the methods advocated by Lappin and Disch (1972a, 1972b), and Reed (1973). For situations in which the adjustable timing model applies, they are the proper methods for measuring the effects of task variables.

It is not the purpose of this contribution merely to propose that accustomed methods should be discarded in favor of new ones. My basic point is that particular methods for performing experiments and for analyzing data all take their justification from particular models. We now have a considerable range of possible models to consider but we have no way of anticipating which of them will be appropriate for a particular application. Any model is potentially wrong and therefore we should not committ ourselves to any particular "method" without first testing the applicability of the particular model that informs it.

To test the applicability of specific models, it appears we shall have to conduct experiments that are substantially more complex and difficult than those to which we are accustomed. Our plight is an instance of the general one that Fisher (1966, Chapter 6) describes: there is a phenomenon (RT performance in this case) that admits effects from several factors and there is a question about how these factors interact. In such circumstances, Fisher argues, single factor experimentation is futile because there is always a question whether the remaining factors have been controlled correctly. Multiple factor experiments at least permit us to test our assumptions about the interaction of experimental variables. By conducting multiple factor experiments, we expose our assumptions to test and thereby avoid the risk of proceeding with assumptions that are false.

In the context of RT, there is great uncertainty about the interaction of "task" (the term is still vague here) variables with "strategy" variables. Thus we should conduct two-factor experiments in which "task" and "strategy" variables are independently manipulated. Before we draw conclusions, we should test our hypotheses about their interaction. In principle, this reduces the risk of error and in practice it gives rise to the difficult statistical problem of deciding how RT models should be evaluated against the data from multifactor experiments. For the adjustable timing model, this contribution will sketch one possible approach. It connects in an interesting way with Sternberg's (1969) method of additive factors, which suggests that other models might be evaluated in a similar way.

II. THE "RT METHOD" AND THE PROBLEM
OF STRATEGY SHIFTS

To illustrate "the RT method," we may consider the familiar topic of memory scanning, as developed by Sternberg. (See Sternberg, 1975, for a recent review.) There are two responses, the "yes" response and the "no" response. In the "varied set" procedure, each stimulus presentation is a memory set, plus a test item, which follows immediately. The instructions are to respond yes or no, according to whether the test item was a member of the memory set. The subject is instructed to perform this task accurately but quickly and the RT is measured. Stimulus—response records are also made so that accuracy of performance can be evaluated.

The task variable in this case is the size of the memory set. In one condition, the memory set may contain only three items. In another, it may contain four, or five, etc. In the analysis of data, RT is selected as the dependent variable and a graph is made of how the RT varies with size of the memory set. Inferences about human information-processing capabilities are then drawn from such graphs.

Before conclusions are actually drawn, an important preliminary data analysis is performed. This preliminary analysis is required because it is well known that there is a potential problem with comparing RTs measured under separate experimental conditions. From studies of the speed–accuracy tradeoff, we know there is a second kind of effect. If we manipulate the instructions for speed versus accuracy, we can make the subject perform a given task more quickly but less accurately. There is an effect on the RT, but it is a strategy effect, not a task effect. By varying the instructions or the payoffs, we can produce strategy effects in a wide variety of task situations. In particular, we can produce them in the memory scanning situation.

Without doubt, the speed and accuracy of performance exhibit two types of effect. The question is whether we know how to produce them separately, which raises the question of whether we really know how to control strategy. If we had a universal theory of choice RT and if it were established as correct, then we could use it to discover exactly which experimental variables produce pure effects. But we do not have such an established theory and we select experimental variables largely on the basis of judgment and convenience. There is no assurance that our task variables do not have a strategy component, and vice versa. We do not really know, for example, that set size is a pure task variable. Indeed, it seems quite likely that many of our present task variables also have effects on strategy and that if we manipulate a task variable, we may also alter the optimal speed–accuracy tradeoff strategy, even if the speed–accuracy instructions remain constant. Therefore, when we alter a task variable, we may inadvertently produce a combination of effects. First, there is the intended task effect. Second, there is the possibility of a strategy shift: in the new experimental situation, a subject may prefer a different speed–accuracy tradeoff than before. Increasing the memory set from three to four items, for example, might encourage a strategy shift, as well as producing a task effect.

We know that strategy shifts are a problem and we try to exclude them, by controlling the speed–accuracy instructions. There is some uncertainty whether this method of control is completely effective and so, having conducted the experiment, we examine the data to verify that strategy actually remained constant. The question is, what aspect of the data do we examine? We look at the probability of error responses. We say that if the error probabilities are about the same in each condition, the same speed–accuracy tradeoff strategy was used throughout. With memory scanning, for example, we might find a 2% error rate with a three-item set, a 3 % error rate with a four-item set, and a 2 % error rate with a five-item set. In this case, we would say that the error rates are about equal and that the speed–accuracy tradeoff strategy remained constant across experimental conditions.

We almost never ask whether the RTs remained constant. We expect the RTs to differ because we expect a task variable to affect the RT. There is an element of prejudgment in this. We have somehow decided that the task variable should affect the RT and we want only to know whether the RT differences are purely task effects or whether there is a contribution from strategy shifts. Our customary procedure is to say that if the various error rates are all about the same, then differences in RT are truly and purely task effects.

Following this procedure presumes several things. It presumes that the task variable, for example, set size, has no significant effect on the probability of a correct response. It presumes that task variables do affect the RT. It presumes that changes in strategy affect both speed and accuracy. Most important of all, it presumes that if strategy remains constant, accuracy also remains constant, even if a task variable affects the RT.

These are very strong and specific assumptions and it appears that they can be identified with a very particular model. Specifically, they can be identified with a special case of the fast guess model (Ollman, 1966; Yellott, 1971), which supposes that only two types of response are possible. Fast guess responses are made immediately upon detection of the stimulus and are correct only by chance. The speed of a guess response is not affected by task variables or by strategy shifts. Deliberative, or stimulus controlled, responses take longer to make and are more accurate. The speed, and possibly the accuracy, of deliberative responses is affected by task variables but not by strategy. Deliberative responses, because they are supposedly affected by task variables, are interesting to study. Fast guess responses, by contrast, are merely a nuisance. (In memory scanning for example, the time to search through memory is the deliberation time. Supposedly, memory search cannot be accelerated voluntarily: the time to search memory is supposedly determined exclusively by the set size, which is supposedly a task variable.) In the fast guess model, the only role of strategy is to determine what fraction of responses will be deliberative responses, as opposed to guess responses. As the fraction of deliberative responses increases, performance becomes more accurate but slower.

Consider two experimental conditions that differ in the value of some X variable. For example, the size of the memory sets might be different. In each condition, according to the fast guess model, the mean RT is a weighted average of two components. One component, the guessing time, is the same for both conditions. The other component includes the hypothetical deliberation time, which may be different for the two experimental conditions. In addition, the relative weights may differ, meaning that there may be different fractions of guesses in the two situations.

We would like to know whether the same strategy was used in both X conditions. If the strategies are the same, then the difference between RTs must result entirely from the effect of the X variable upon the speed of the hypothetical deliberation process. This would mean that X is purely a task variable.

According to the fast guess model, strategies can be compared by examining the response probabilities because, according to the fast guess model, the probability of a correct response is also a weighted average of two components. One component is the probability .5, the accuracy of guess responses. This is the same for both task conditions. The other component corresponds to the accuracy of deliberative, or stimulus controlled responses. In general, this second component may differ between the two conditions. As a special case, however, we may suppose that the experimental variable does not affect the accuracy of deliberative responses and so the second component is also the same for both conditions. To be concrete, we may suppose deliberative responses are always 100% accurate in both X conditions.

According to this special case of the fast-guess model, if the probability of a correct response is the same in two conditions, we know that guessing and deliberative responses have been mixed in the same proportion, that is, there has been no strategy shift. Therefore if the mean RTs are different, that difference arises exclusively from the effect of the X variable upon the deliberation time, which means that X is a pure task variable. Thus a special case of the fast guess model provides a rationale for our customary practice of selecting RT as the dependent variable and of using equal response probabilities to infer equivalent strategies.

Perhaps there is another model, distinct from the fast guess model, that also provides a rationale for our current practices. However, I tend to doubt it because it appears that the important feature of the fast guess model is this: if strategy (represented as a guessing probability) remains constant, it is possible for the probability of a correct response to remain constant, even if there is an experimental effect on the RT. This is one of the key assumptions behind our current practices and I do not know of any other model that proposes this to be possible.

Consider the deadline model (Ollman & Billington, 1972; Thomas, 1974; Yellott, 1971). In many respects it closely resembles the fast guess model. It also supposes the existence of a deliberation process. As with the fast guess model, there is supposedly no voluntary control over either the speed or the accuracy of the deliberation process, that is, the deliberation process is immune to strategy effects.

The only difference between the two models lies in the mechanism for deciding whether or not a particular response shall be deliberative. The fast guess model postulates a hypothetical coin toss and so the decision to respond deliberatively is made independently of variations in the deliberation time. The deadline model supposes there is a random time limit, or deadline. A response is made when processing is done or when the deadline expires, whichever comes first. If processing finishes before the deadline, the response is deliberative. If the deadline elapses before processing is complete, the response is a guess, and less likely to be accurate. The deadline is adjustable, which permits a speed—accuracy tradeoff. In a particular experimental situation, the choice of a deadline distribution is purely a matter of strategy.

Suppose the deadline model is correct and consider an experimental variable that affects the deliberation time but not the deliberation accuracy. Specifically, suppose that increasing the task variable simply makes the deliberation time slower and allows deliberative responses to be 100% accurate in all conditions.

Increasing the memory set might do this. Also suppose that the deadline does not shift, that is, strategy remains constant. Because deliberation is slowed, fewer responses will be deliberative and more will be guesses. This is because fewer races against the deadline will be won. The probability of a correct response must therefore decline. To maintain constant accuracy, the subject must relax the deadline. This is a strategy shift and it will contribute to lengthening the RT. Thus we come to the conclusion that according to the deadline model, if the probability of a correct response is the same in two experimental conditions, and if the RTs are different, then part of that difference must come from a strategy shift. Thus the deadline model explicitly denies the validity of our standard method for deciding whether strategy has remained constant. According to the deadline model, if the response probabilities are equal, differences in RT cannot be attributed purely to changes in the deliberation time. There must also have been a strategy shift, which also contributes to the difference between RTs.

When we use the RT method, we make a number of implicit assumptions. I doubt whether any of us has appreciated how strong they are and that these assumptions seem to add up to the fast guess model. In effect, we are presuming the fast guess model is correct and then applying it to classify experimental variables as producing either task or strategy effects. Studies of the speed—accuracy tradeoff have taught us to be skeptical about the fast guess model (Audley, 1973). Sometimes it seems to work well, but not always. Moreover there is one observation, discussed below, that it simply cannot explain. Although the fast guess model may be sometimes useful, it is highly doubtful that it is correct in general. This should make us cautious about inferring constant strategy from constant accuracy and then using RT differences to measure task effects.

Before leaving the RT method, I would like to use these two models to analyze a related argument, based on the speed—accuracy tradeoff. According to the fast guess model, changing the proportion of fast guess responses leads to a linear tradeoff relationship between the probability of a correct response and the mean RT. According to the deadline model, the tradeoff is accomplished by adjusting the distribution of deadline times and the probability of a correct response does not necessarily vary linearly with mean RT. But in the special case where both the deliberation time and the deadline are exponentially distributed, adjustment of the mean deadline produces a linear tradeoff relationship that is identical to that of the fast guess model (Thomas, 1974).

According to some commentators (e.g., Pachella, 1974; Wickelgren, 1974), the shape of the tradeoff function is central to whether the RT method is valid: they observe that if the probability of a correct response approaches an asymptote as the mean RT increases (which is observed in some tradeoff studies) then it is possible for substantial strategy differences to have large effects on the RT while having small effects on the probability of a correct response. Accordingly, nearly equivalent response probabilities need not correspond to nearly equivalent strategies. The premise of this argument seems to be that the validity of the RT method hinges exclusively on the shape of the tradeoff function. If the shape of this function were all that mattered, then the exponential case of the deadline model would also justify the RT method: its tradeoff function is identical to that of the fast guess model, which does justify the RT method.

But it appears the premise is incorrect because although the deadline model contains a special case where the tradeoff function is linear (like that of the fast guess model), the deadline model is inconsistent in general (and in particular for the exponential case) with the RT method. The shape of the tradeoff function is relevant to whether the RT method is valid, but it is not the only consideration.

III. THE ADJUSTABLE TIMING MODEL AND THE METHOD OF VIRTUAL PROBABILITIES

There are some indications that we should reconsider our assumptions about how strategy and task effects manifest themselves. Studies of the speed—accuracy tradeoff provide a hint that the RT is purely a matter of strategy and that task variables have an effect only on the relation between accuracy and particular values of RT. In particular, there is the study by Schouten and Bekker (1967).

They conducted a choice experiment in which task variables were held constant. The instructional request for speed versus accuracy was manipulated, that is, they conducted a speed—accuracy tradeoff experiment. Instead of using mean values to summarize their various RT distributions, Schouten and Bekker partitioned their data into intervals of RT. For each interval of RT, they calculated the probability that a response was correct when its RT fell in that interval. They performed this analysis separately for each level of speed—accuracy instruction. In each case the result is a graph that increases, which simply means that responses with RTs near the slower end of each distribution are likelier to be correct.

Significantly, all of their graphs seem to follow a common curve. It starts at the level of chance accuracy, increases for a time, and then levels off. Although the RT distributions have different mean values, and the overall response probabilities are different, the conditional probability that a response is correct, given that the RT has a particular value, always follows the same curve.

Their discovery almost directly suggests a new model. From probability theory, the joint probability that a response is of a specific type (correct versus error), and also has a particular RT, can be expressed as the product of two terms: the marginal probability that the RT has a particular value, and the conditional probability that the response is the specified type, given the particular value of RT. More precisely, if $f(r,t)$ is the joint density of response types ($r = c$ or $r = e$) and RTs, then:

$$f(r,t) = A(r|t)f(t), \quad r = c,e \text{ and } t > 0 \tag{1}$$

where

$$f(t) = \sum_r f(r,t)$$

$$A(r|t) = f(r,t)/f(t), \qquad f(t) \neq 0$$

The function $A(c|t)$ is what Schouten and Bekker computed for each of their experimental conditions.[1] I refer to it as the conditional accuracy function (CAF), although various other writers have used other names. For example, Lappin and Disch (1972a, 1972b) refer to it as the "latency operating character-istic." Since $A(c|t) + A(e|t) = 1$, a statement about the CAF is effectively a statement about the more general function $A(r|t)$, where r can assume the values c and e.

To be complete, a model for RT performance should describe the joint density $f(r,t)$, not just $f(t)$, the marginal density of RT values. Any model for $f(r,t)$ can then be factored in accordance with Eq. (1). Also, a model for $f(r,t)$ must contain separate task and strategy parameters if it is to account for the effects of both task and strategy variables. It is revealing to take a particular model, factor it in accordance with Eq. (1), and then examine the roles of task and strategy parameters. According to the fast guess and deadline models, the formulae for both $A(r|t)$ and $f(t)$ each contain a combination of strategy and task parameters (Thomas, 1974). Similarly with Stone's (1960) random walk model, and so on.

Because Schouten and Bekker manipulated a "strategy" variable and observed that $A(r|t)$ did not change appreciably, it appears that the appropriate model for their data is an unusual one that describes $A(r|t)$ purely in terms of task param-eters. Although a strategy parameter is not required for the description of $A(r|t)$, a strategy parameter is required for the description of $f(t)$ because their instruc-tional manipulation did have a substantial effect on the RT distribution. From their data it appears that the description of $A(r|t)$ requires a task parameter but not a strategy parameter and that the description of $f(t)$ requires at least a strategy parameter.

The design of their experiment leaves unanswered the question whether $f(t)$ requires a task parameter. As a conjecture, it is interesting to suppose that it does not and that the distribution of RTs, $f(t)$, is purely a matter of strategy.

These ideas may be formalized as the adjustable timing model, which is named for an interpretation that will given shortly. Let the subscript u indicate a quantity that requires task parameters and let the subscript v indicate a quantity that requires strategy parameters. The joint density $f(r,t)$ exhibits both task and strategy effects and so in general,

$$f_{u,v}(r,t) = A_{u,v}(r|t)f_{u,v}(t).$$

The Schouten and Bekker (1967) study suggests a restriction on this general

---

[1] Actually, they computed $A(e|t)$ but I have transposed the description of their results in order to simplify the task of relating them to other papers.

possibility, which is the adjustable timing model:

$$f_{u,v}(r,t) = A_u(r|t)f_v(t), \quad r = c,e \text{ and } t > 0 \tag{2}$$

Thus we are proposing a particularly simple multiplicative model for the joint distribution of response types and RTs. One multiplicative factor, $A(r|t)$, requires only task parameters for its description and the other multiplicative factor, $f(t)$, requires only strategy parameters.

Intuitively, the adjustable timing model supposes there is a memory where information about the stimulus is accumulated. The conditional accuracy function, $A(c|t)$, describes this accumulation of stimulus information in memory. It gives the probability that a correct response will result if memory is consulted at time t. It should be an increasing function of t and its complement, $A(e|t)$, should be decreasing. The absence of a strategy parameter for $A(r|t)$ means that the model supposes there is no capacity for voluntary adjustment of the memory process.

In addition, the model supposes that there is an adjustable timing device that the subject can preset to guarantee the production of RTs that are clustered about some target value; $f(t)$ is the probability density for the resulting RTs. That $f(t)$ has no task parameter means that the adjustability of the timer is unrestricted by the specifics of an experimental situation. According to the model, at the instant when the timing device calls for the rendition of some response, the content of memory is consulted and a response is chosen on the basis of whatever information has been accumulated up to that instant. The joint probability density for a correct response at time t is thus $f_v(t)A_u(c|t)$, and so on.

This interpretation suggests we should view the model as an approximation. Presumably, the RT actually contains a residual component associated with processing the memory content, executing a response, etc., and so there is a lag between consulting memory and making a response. If the residual delay is a constant, then $A(c|t)$ will differ from the curve of memory growth only by a displacement parameter. In this case all variability in the RT is assumed to result from variability in the adjustable timer. However, if the residual delay also has statistical variability, the observed $A(c|t)$ will be a "smeared" version of hypothetical memory curve. Thus Eq. (2) is an idealization that treats the residual delay as a constant and neglects the possibility of "smearing." The data of Wood and Jennings (1976) may indicate that the smearing can be substantial in some applications.

According to the adjustable timing model, the probability of a correct response is a weighted average CAF value where $f_v(t)$, the distribution of RTs, is the weighting factor:

$$P_{uv}(c) = \int_0^\infty f_{u,v}(c,t)dt = \int_0^\infty A_u(c|t)f_v(t)dt \tag{3}$$

If the experimenter manipulated a variable that affects the CAF, then the probability of a correct response will also be affected. If the RT distribution does not change, that is, if a strategy shift does not occur, then differences in $P(c)$ are purely task effects, arising purely from changes in $A(c|t)$. Thus, according to the adjustable timing model, our present methods for distinguishing task versus strategy effects are exactly backward. As an indicator of constant strategy, we should take constancy of the RT distribution. Then, if the RTs are identically distributed in all conditions, we may use the probability of a correct response as the dependent variable for summarizing task effects. This is opposite to the precepts of the RT method, which appears to be founded on the fast guess model.

According to the adjustable timing model, our present methods for instructing/paying subjects are similarly defective because they actually encourage the subject to make strategy shifts. Consider Eq. (3) and suppose the experimenter manipulates an experimental variable (for example, size of the memory set) that has an effect on $A(c|t)$. If the subject does not compensate by adjusting his RT distribution, the probability of a correct response will change. If the subject is instructed to produce the same response probability in every set-size condition, he must adjust $f(t)$ to compensate for the effect of set size on $A(c|t)$. In one condition, for example, $A(c|t)$ may increase quickly so that the subject can attain 95% accuracy by setting the timer to produce RTs with a mean of 500 msec. In another condition, it may increase more slowly so that the timer must be set to 600 msec if the same probability is to be attained. Adjustments of $f(t)$ are strategy shifts, according to this theory, and they are actually encouraged by the very procedure that was meant to discourage them. A better way to control strategy, according to the adjustable timing model, is offered by the method of band payoffs (Snodgrass, Luce, & Galanter, 1967), in which the subject is paid a premium for producing RTs that are concentrated in a prespecified RT region.

In this theory, if the RTs are not identically distributed in all experimental conditions, then variations in the probability of a correct response result from a combination of task and strategy effects. In this case, the experimenter may wish to know what the response probabilities would have been if the same strategy had been used in the various conditions. To answer this question, the experimenter may first estimate the conditional accuracy function by calculating

$$\hat{A}(c|t) = \hat{f}(c,t)/\hat{f}(t), \qquad \hat{f}(t) \neq 0$$

from the data of each experimental condition. According to the adjustable timing model this aspect of the data can exhibit only task effects. Then the experimenter can postulate some fictitious or "virtual" RT distribution, $\$(t)$, and use this virtual distribution for calculating the average height of each CAF. The result is a "virtual" response probability,

$$\hat{VP}(c) = \int_0^\infty \$(t)\hat{A}(c|t)dt = \int_0^\infty [\$(t)\hat{f}(c,t)/\hat{f}(t)]\,dt,$$

which can be interpreted as the probability that would have resulted if the RTs had followed the virtual RT distribution rather than the observed one. For example, the experimenter can estimate what the probability of a correct response would have been, if the RTs had followed a negative exponential distribution with a mean of .5 sec.

From the viewpoint of the adjustable timing model, this is a correction for strategy differences, since strategies correspond simply to RT distributions. It is exactly analogous to the "correction for guessing" that Yellott (1971) derives from the fast guess model. In this case, however, the correction is justified by the adjustable timing model and it is applied to response probabilities rather than to RTs.

Lappin and Disch (1972a, b) make a similar proposal but advance a different reason. Empirically, they point out, the CAF has striking similarities to the speed–accuracy tradeoff function, which describes how the marginal probability of a correct response varies with the mean RT when task parameters remain constant and strategy varies. This similarity is predicted by the adjustable timing model. For simplicity, suppose the RT has no statistical variability so that $f_v(t)$ is concentrated at the mean, $\overline{RT}_v$. In this case, according to the adjustable timing model,

$$P_{u,v}(c) = A_u(c \mid \overline{RT}_v),$$

and so the speed–accuracy tradeoff function is identical to the CAF. More realistically, the RT distribution has statistical variability and so this relation is an approximation. For other models, there is not even an approximate similarity. Thus it appears that the Lappin and Disch proposal takes its ultimate justification from the adjustable timing model.

IV. CONCLUSION

The problem is to distinguish correctly between task effects and strategy effects. We are concerned that the manipulation of a task variable might induce a strategy shift, even if the payoffs or instructions remain constant.

Customarily, we say that strategy has remained constant if the probability of a correct response remains constant. Differences in RT are then treated as pure task effects. We are dismayed to learn that this procedure is justified — thus far at least — only by the fast guess model. The fast guess model is not celebrated for its universal success and so there is doubt whether our customary procedures are valid. According to the adjustable timing model, we should proceed the opposite way and infer constant strategy from constant RT. According to the deadline model, neither approach is correct and something else — not yet known to us — is required.

There are many alternative models for choice RT and we do not know which is right. Perhaps none of them is. Perhaps each of them is applicable to particular types of situations. One thing is clear, however: if we simply pick a method (model) and apply it blindly, we are likely to draw false conclusions from our experiments.

This situation raises some basic questions about experimental method, experimental design, and statistical analysis. Briefly, each of these alternative models — the fast guess model, the deadline model, the adjustable timing model, etc. — may be seen as the basis for an analysis of variance procedure. There are two types of factor, strategy factors and task factors, and the various models are alternative proposals for the interaction of these factors.

To decide which model is appropriate to a particular problem we must conduct factorial experiments in which task variables and strategy variables are both manipulated. In effect, we must conduct a speed—accuracy tradeoff study for each level of the task variable. If a particular model interests us, we must fit it to the entire body of data and decide whether it is correct. This is hypothesis testing. If the model fits the data satisfactorily, we may then use it to interpret results. But if it fits badly, we should seek an alternative model for drawing conclusions.

The need to test multifactor RT models draws attention to the unfortunate fact that we do not now have satisfactory statistical techniques for evaluating any of the various models that are presently known. This is a serious lack and so to close this discussion, I briefly sketch how the experimenter might evaluate the adjustable timing model by an analysis of variance procedure. It appears that similar methods can and should be developed for the other models. It relates closely to Sternberg's (1969) method of additive factors.

For specificity, consider a memory scanning study where set size is the task variable and where payoff band is the strategy variable. It has a factorial design. The investigator believes the adjustable timing model could be correct and he has chosen the method of band payoffs for controlling the RT.

The results from this experiment may be arranged as a matrix, in which each row corresponds to a size of the memory set and each column corresponds to a payoff band. In a particular cell, there is a joint probability distribution that can be resolved, or decomposed, into a CAF and a marginal RT distribution (Eq. 1). Within a single row, all the CAFs should be identical, and within a column, the marginal RT distributions should be identical, according to the model.

Consider a particular cell within this matrix. It contains a marginal RT distribution and a CAF. Each of these may be reduced to a single number. The RT distribution can be summarized by its mean value, which should be the same for all cells in the same column, if the RT is purely a matter of strategy. The CAF can be similarly reduced to a single number by computing its average height with respect to a virtual distribution, $\$(t)$, introduced by the experimenter. The result is a "virtual" probability. If the experimenter always uses the same virtual distribution, $\$(t)$, and if the adjustable timing model is correct, the virtual probabilities should be the same for all cells in the same row.

Now the joint distribution in each cell has been reduced to a pair of numbers: a mean RT and a virtual probability. One number should be a function only of the row and the second should be a function of the column. The pairs of numbers may be added together. Now there is a matrix where each cell contains only a single number. That number should be an additive function of the row and column variables, if the adjustable timing model applies. Of course there are statistical fluctuations and so we must conduct an analysis of variance to determine whether the row and column effects are satisfactorily additive or whether there are statistically significant interactions.

Although the interpretation of mathematical terms is different, the logic is identical to that of Sternberg's (1969) additive factor method, which, as he points out, traces to the work of R. A. Fisher. If there are interactions, something is wrong. Perhaps the variability of residual delays cannot be neglected. Perhaps the model is fundamentally wrong. Perhaps the model is correct, but the use of band payoffs did not succeed in preventing strategy shifts. We cannot tell where the problem lies. We can only tell that the model has not worked and therefore we should refrain from using the model to interpret the data. We should refrain, in particular, from interpreting the CAF as a purely task-dependent quantity. Only if additivity is supported should we use the model to explicate the data. Only then have we successfully tested our principal assumption, namely, that the adjustable timing model applies.

ACKNOWLEDGMENTS

Several colleagues have made helpful observations on the material summarized by this paper. I am especially grateful to S. Sternberg and R. G. Swensson for their sustained and thoughtful attention.

REFERENCES

Audley, R. J. Some observations on theories of choice reaction time. In S. Kornblum (Ed.), *Attention and performance IV.* New York: Academic Press, 1973.

Fisher, R. A. *The design of experiments.* (8th ed.) New York: Hafner, 1966.

Lappin, J. S., & Disch, K. The latency operating characteristic: I. Effects of stimulus probability on choice reaction time. *Journal of Experimental Psychology,* 1972, **92,** 419–427. (a)

Lappin, J. S., & Disch, K. The latency operating characteristic: II. Effects of stimulus intensity on choice reaction time. *Journal of Experimental Psychology,* 1972, **93,** 367–372. (b)

Ollman, R. T. Fast guesses in choice reaction time. *Psychonomic Science,* 1966, **6,** 155–156.

Ollman, R. T., & Billington, M. J. The deadline model for simple reaction times. *Cognitive Psychology,* 1972, **3,** 311–336.

Pachella, R. G. The interpretation of reaction time in information processing research. In B. H. Kantowitz (Ed.), *Human information processing: Tutorials in performance and cognition.* Hillsdale, N.J.: Lawrence Erlbaum Associates, 1974.

Reed, A. V. Speed accuracy trade-off in recognition memory. *Science,* 1973, 181, 574–576.

Schouten, J. F., & Bekker, J. A. M. Reaction time and accuracy. In A. F. Sanders (Ed.), *Attention and Performance: Acta Psychologica,* 1967, 27, 143–153.

Snodgrass, J. G., Luce, R. D., & Galanter, E. Some experiments on simple and choice reaction time. *Journal of Experimental Psychology,* 1967, 75, 1–17.

Sternberg, S. The discovery of processing stages: Extension of Donders' method. In W. G. Koster (Ed.), *Attention and performance. II.* Amsterdam: North Holland Publ., 1969. Pp. 276–315.

Sternberg, S. Memory scanning: New findings and current controversies. *Quarterly Journal of Experimental Psychology,* 1975, 27, 1–32.

Stone, M. Models for choice–reaction time. *Psychometrika,* 1960, 25, 251–260.

Thomas, E. A. C. The selectivity of preparation. *Psychological Review,* 1974, 81, 442–464.

Wickelgren, W. A. Speed–accuracy tradeoff in information processing dynamics. Paper presented at the meeting of the Psychonomic Society, Boston, November, 1974.

Wood, C. C., & Jennings, J. R. Speed–accuracy trade-off functions in choice reaction time: Experimental designs and computational procedures. *Perception & Psychophysics,* 1976, 9, 92–102.

Yellott, J. I. Jr. Correction for guessing and the speed–accuracy tradeoff in choice reaction time. *Journal of Mathematical Psychology,* 1971, 8, 159–199.

7

Expectancy and Preparation in Simple Reaction Time[1]

R. Näätänen
A. Merisalo

Institute of Psychology
University of Helsinki
Helsinki, Finland

ABSTRACT

In this chapter, the work on the simple reaction time relevant to the concepts of expectancy and preparation carried out at the University of Helsinki during the last ten years is reviewed. The two main lines of this research involve: (1) studies on the effect of the temporal uncertainty of the imperative stimulus on reaction time (the foreperiods were randomly varied, using either rectangular or Bernoulli distributions of foreperiods); and (2) studies on the effect of imperative-stimulus probability on the reaction time (using within-block constant foreperiods). In the light of the results obtained, expectancy or the momentary subjective probability of the immediate delivery of the stimulus appears to be the most important determinant of preparation and, hence, of the reaction time, but the results also point to the existence of other kinds of determinants. As to expectancy, it follows rather well the momentary objective probability but there also exist interesting dissociation phenomena between the objective and subjective probabilities.

I. INTRODUCTION

There are, of course, many possible ways to characterize the daily life of human beings and other creatures in very broad terms, one of which is to stress the responding role of the organism with regard to various kinds of environmental

[1] This is a review on reaction-time research conducted at the Institute of Psychology, the University of Helsinki.

stimuli. Perhaps the most popular laboratory situation for studying the characteristics of human beings as responding agents is that involving reaction time (RT). Compared to the response situations of real life, the laboratory situations generally are, of course, simplified (and repetitive!) but nevertheless seem to simulate rather well many essential variables of real response situations such as different numbers of stimulus and response alternatives, different degrees of preresponse uncertainty as to the kind of the stimulus and the time of its occurrence, etc. It is essential to understand that although the RT is the principal dependent variable in such studies, the RT or speed as such is generally of no primary interest. Much of the popularity of the RT is explained by its being the most easily and most accurately measured aspect of many kinds of responses. On the basis of RT data, more or less indirect inferences are made with regard, for example, to such central aspects of responding and human-environmental interaction as learning, risk of erroneous performance, preresponse preparation, attention, vigilance, strategies adopted, etc. Consequently, rather than speaking about reaction time research it might be more appropriate to use the expression *reaction research.*

In our laboratory, we have so far used only the simple RT situation. Hence, there has been only one imperative stimulus and only one type of response. The major aspects which have been manipulated are the temporal predictability of the imperative stimulus (S2) and the certainty of its occurrence.

Studies on physiological processes related to RT have also been conducted (mainly in collaboration with the Institute for Perception TNO, Soesterberg, The Netherlands) but this work (Gaillard & Näätänen, 1973, 1976, in press; Näätänen, 1973a, b, 1975, in press; Näätänen & Gaillard, 1974a, b; Näätänen, Gaillard, & Mäntysalo, in press) is not reviewed here.

II. STUDIES ON TEMPORAL PREDICTABILITY
OF STIMULUS

Much of our work, as well as that of others, has involved foreperiods (FPs) of different durations given in an irregular order. Such work is mainly aimed at clarifying the effect of time uncertainty of the imperative signals on the RT.[2] In our first study, which was carried out in 1966 (Näätänen, 1970), the effect of the type of frequency distribution of three different FP alternatives on the RT was investigated. More specifically, we were interested in the well-known phenomenon involving shortening of the RT as a function of the FP when the rectangular FP distribution is used. (Such a relationship, of course, stands out in considerable contrast to the FP–RT relationship obtained when the FP is held constant within-block.) We thought, as did Elithorn and Lawrence earlier

---

[2] For discussions on the interpretation of these kinds of data, see Ollman and Billington (1972), and Kornblum (1973).

(1955), that this phenomenon is due to the increasing expectancy of the immediate delivery of the stimulus as time from the warning signal elapses, expectancy increasing because of the increased probability of the immediate termination of the FP as a function of its age. Consequently, the other FP frequency distribution employed was that of Bernoulli; these frequencies are designed so that the probability of the immediate termination of the FP is independent of its age. In each condition, the median FP was 3 sec but the range of the FP duration was either 1, 2, or 4 sec. The main results are seen in Fig. 1: with "nonaging" FPs, the shortest FP no longer yields the longest RTs. The slower RTs with the shortest FPs in the "nonaging" condition compared to the

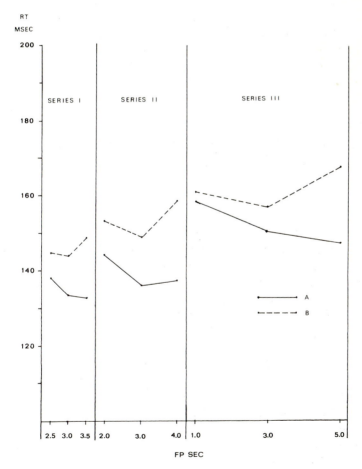

FIG. 1   RTs obtained by using randomized FPs of different durations in three FP series differing in range under Conditions A (rectangular distribution) and B (Bernoulli's distribution). (From Näätänen, 1970; reproduced by permission of the North-Holland Publishing Company).

respective RTs of the rectangular distribution are also of some interest, since the probability of S2 at the first possible stimulus moment is the same for both conditions. It appears that especially when the FP range is short the reduction in the probabilities of longer FPs prolongs the RT with the shortest FP. This reflects the subject's imperfect time estimation ability.

In Fig. 2, the results are given separately for inexperienced and highly experienced subjects. It appears as if practice were reducing the sensitivity of the RT to the three kinds of manipulations of experimental conditions in the present study: (1) the FP range; (2) the S2 probability; and (3) the relative length of the FP within the block in which it was embedded. The error variance was also considerably reduced.

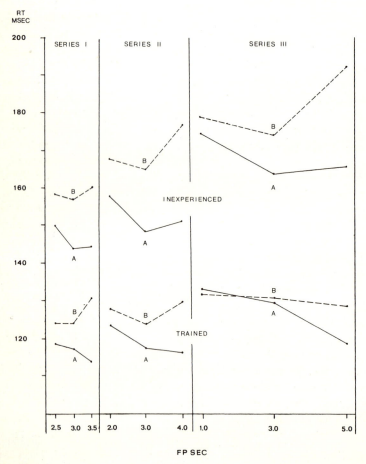

FIG. 2   The same data as in Fig. 1 given separately for trained and inexperienced subjects. (From Näätänen, unpublished data.)

The result involving the reduction in the systematic variance appears to suggest that in very well-trained subjects, strong expectancy is no longer a necessary condition for fast RTs. It might be that practice reduces the effort needed to maintain a high level of preparation, perhaps by cutting off the activation of irrelevant mechanisms. For example, it was shown by Tiffin and Westhafer (1940) that muscle tension in the uninvolved hand diminishes from session to session. The attenuation of the efforts to maintain a high level of preparation might lead to its continuous maintenance, regardless of the momentary fluctuations in expectancy, as long as the latter exceeds a certain limit. As to the inexperienced subjects, they can probably maintain a high degree of preparation only for a short period of time and, naturally, "invest" it in those periods of time when the expectancy is high.

Unfortunately, the "nonaging" FP condition of this study also involved occurrence or event uncertainty, that is, uncertainty as to whether the imperative stimulus will at all be presented at a trial. That form of uncertainty was eliminated in the next related study (Näätänen, 1971) in which real nonaging FPs were used. Each stimulus series lasted 30 minutes and the average ISI between stimuli (each of which was to be responded to) was varied. In Series A it was 5 sec, in Series B 10 sec, in C 20 sec, and in D 40 sec. The ISIs were made nonaging so that the probability of the delivery of the stimulus at each full second was in Series A 1/5, in Series B 1/10, in Series C 1/20, and in Series D 1/40. The main results are shown in Fig. 3. The data are, unfortunately, rather noisy, a problem which seems to be to a large extent inherent in this kind of experiment. The RT was highly significantly prolonged as a function of the ISI in Series A in which the mean ISI was 5 sec. (This result is in agreement with that of Gottsdanker, 1975, in an experiment with nonaging FPs of shorter mean durations.) Such an effect was not observed with longer mean ISIs. Instead, a trend ($p < .05$) in the opposite direction was found when the mean ISI was very long (40 sec). The RT became continuously longer with the increased mean ISI – a result in agreement with many previous studies (Klemmer, 1956; Nickerson, 1967; Nickerson & Burnham, 1969).

These two studies are consistent with the generally accepted conclusion that the RT follows rather closely the objective probability of the delivery of the stimulus when the subject has had an opportunity to learn the temporal structure of the task. The mediating organismic variable is generally understood to be the subjective probability or expectancy of the immediate delivery of the stimulus. The latter results, however, point to the possibility that other factors besides expectancy may also be important determinants of the RT: in Series A the RT was considerably increased and in Series D decreased as a function of the ISI irrespective of the constant objective stimulus probability. On the other hand, it is, of course, possible that expectancy does not always strictly follow the objective probability. Unfortunately, we lack the means to measure expectancy directly (see, however, Vroon, 1973, and Vroon & Vroon, 1973). The

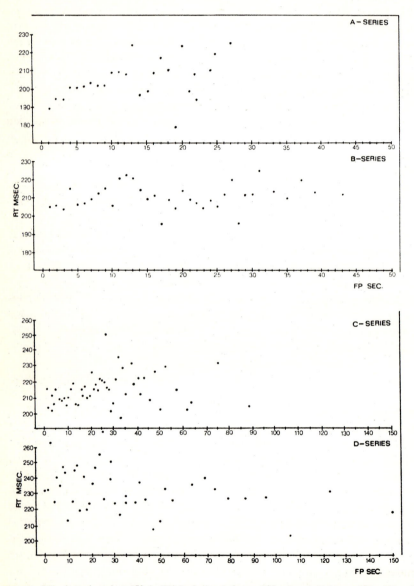

FIG. 3 RT plotted against ISI (= FP) in Series A (mean ISI = 5 sec), B (mean ISI = 10 sec), C (mean ISI = 20 sec), and D (mean ISI = 40 sec). (From Näätänen, 1971; reproduced by permission of The North-Holland Publishing Company).

works reviewed in the following were aimed at a more direct measurement of some aspects of it.

When a constant FP has been employed, a common observation has been that the longer the FP the longer will be the RT, except for very short FPs. The optimal FP seems to be approximately 0.5 sec or even less. The increase of the RT when the FP is prolonged beyond the optimal is generally explained as resulting from increased difficulty in correctly predicting the stimulus moment. Hence, when long FPs are used, the subjects have a considerable amount of time uncertainty (Klemmer, 1956) with respect to the stimulus moment and the time course of expectancy, consequently, has a long, flattened-out form. We (Näätänen, Muranen, & Merisalo, 1974) investigated the subject's accuracy in predicting the moment of the stimulus separately for each of five different FPs ranging from 0.25 to 4 sec by asking the subject to indicate the expected moment of the stimulus by a key press, that is to try to synchronize the key press with the onset of the stimulus. Hence, this was an attempt to determine the moment of peak expectancy of the stimulus for these different, within-block constant FPs. In Fig. 4, the temporal frequency distributions of presses in this task (distributions on the left side) are given separately for each ISI and subject. The frequency distributions on the right side indicate the results from a parallel RT task conducted with these FPs. It can be seen that the distribution in the anticipation task considerably flattens out when the FP exceeds 1 sec. Hence, we find that the precise prediction of the stimulus moment becomes more and more difficult as the FP is prolonged above a certain limit, which seems to be around 1 sec. On the other hand, the RT was only slightly affected by the increase of the FP.

In another related study (Näätänen, Vesalainen, Mäkinen and Merisalo, unpublished data), we tried another technique to map the subjective flow of the FP. Additionally, the RT was examined as a function of the subjective FP. Three FPs, which could not be easily discriminated among because of their small differences in duration, were randomly presented with the rectangular distribution. The subject's task, after responding to the imperative (auditory) stimulus, was to report which of the three FPs, short, medium, or long, he believed was used during that trial. The results are shown in Fig. 5. The RT was a much more steeply inverted function of the subjective than of the objective FP. This result stresses expectancy as a determinant of the RT. Another finding was that the rectangular FP distribution was experienced as biased in such a way that the subjective frequency of the median FP was remarkably increased. This might increase expectancy around the respective moment after the warning signal and thus cause, or contribute to, the rather common V form of the FP–RT relationship under such experimental conditions. The somewhat self-evident explanation of the subjective distribution is shown in Fig. 6 and verified by additional data from a similar experimental setting. (See the rightmost graph of Fig. 7.) This further experiment had five response categories for subjective FPs

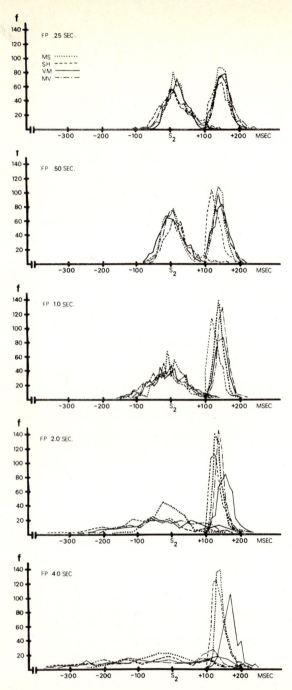

FIG. 4 Distributions of presses in the RT (right-side distributions) and in the anticipation (left-side distributions) tasks given separately for each ISI and subject. (From Näätänen, Muranen, & Merisalo, 1974; reproduced by permission of The North-Holland Publishing Company).

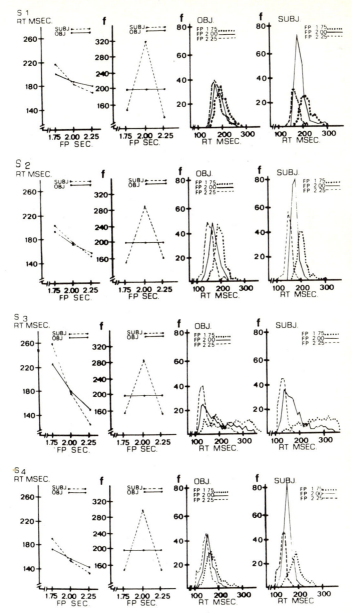

FIG. 5 From left to right: (1) RT as a function of objective and subjective FP; (2) frequencies of objective and subjective FP; (3) RT distributions for separate objective FPs; (4) RT distributions for separate subjective FPs. The four horizontal rows from top to bottom present the data for Subjects 1 to 4, respectively. (From Näätänen, Vesalainen, Mäkinen, & Merisalo, unpublished data.)

123

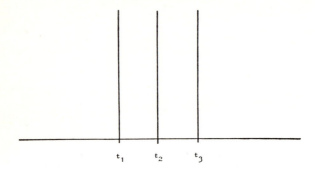

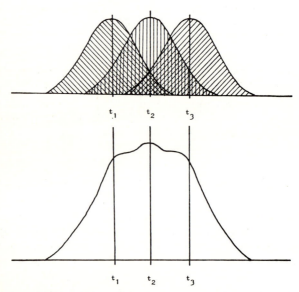

FIG. 6 The three small normal distribution curves in the middle row represent the imagined distributions of experienced durations of each ISI in an RT task with randomized ISIs. The curve on the left side represents the distribution of experienced durations of the shortest ISI, the middle that of the median ISI, and the curve on the right side that of the longest ISI. The objective (rectangular) distribution of the ISIs of the task is shown in the top row, and this distribution as assumed to be experienced by the subject in the bottom row. (The form of the sum curve of the bottom row is not, of course, intended to be generally valid, but depends on the parameters of the "small" distribution curves.) (From Näätänen, 1970; reproduced by permission of The North-Holland Publishing Company).

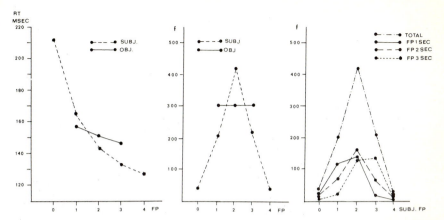

FIG. 7 The graph on the left represents RT as a function of objective FP (solid line) and subjective FP (dotted line). The middle graph represents distributions of objective (solid line) and subjective (dotted line) FP. The graph on the right represents distributions of subjective FPs given separately for each objective FP. (From Näätänen, Vesalainen, Mäkinen, & Merisalo, unpublished data.)

instead of three so that the subject could also indicate that the FP was exceptionally short (Response Alternative 0) or exceptionally long (Response Alternative 4). Consistently, the RT in the former case was longer and in the latter case shorter than with any of the other subjective FPs, including those with the same objective FPs.[3]

III. STUDIES ON OCCURRENCE UNCERTAINTY OF STIMULUS

In these studies, S2 was either delivered or not delivered at a trial; when it was delivered it was always at a fixed time interval from the warning signal.[4] The kind of uncertainty which now was varied has been called *event uncertainty* or *occurrence uncertainty*. Figure 9 shows results from a study (Näätänen, 1972) in

[3] During this symposium, the possibility was raised by Eisler that the subject's estimation of the FP duration at least partially reflected the degree of his subjective success in responding quickly. Hence, for example, if he experienced his response as slow, he might have inferred from this that the FP should have been short, that is, that S2 was delivered unexpectedly early. This possibility is not yet exhaustively explored but our tentative analyses show that this cannot be the whole truth. In Fig. 8 the RT distributions are given separately for each subjective FP. As is easily seen, the variance of RTs associated with the subjective surprise, Response Category 0, is very large; there were both fast and slow RTs associated with this response category.

[4] In one of the previously discussed studies (Näätänen, 1970), there was, however, a condition under which FPs of different durations and blank trials were randomly given (see above).

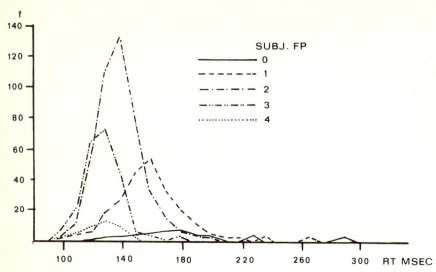

FIG. 8   Distributions of RTs given separately for each subjective FP. (The same data as in Fig. 7.)

which the probability was varied from 0.25 to 1.00. The RT appeared to be an almost linear function of the stimulus probability and this seemed to hold for all the different constant FPs used. This result was clearly in conflict with that obtained by Gordon (1967), according to whom the RT is a negatively accelerated function of the probability. This difference was explained by pointing to the fact that Gordon, as a result of his equalization of the response rate between the conditions, had very short intertrial intervals (ITIs) under his low-probability conditions, which presumably exhausted his subjects more than the other conditions.

In Gordon's study, the smallest probability used was 0.1 whereas it was 0.25 in our study – both still rather high values. In the next related study of ours (Näätänen & Koskinen, 1975), the RTs to stimuli with very small probabilities were deemed an essential and specific object of interest because many critical stimuli in our lives, such as many of those in traffic, are of precisely this kind. In this study, an FP of 1 sec and 5 different (within-block constant) probability values ranging from 1/256 to unity (39/40) were used. As to the results, the quadratic function had the strongest explanatory power so that the RT was relatively fast and practically independent of the S2 probability with very small probabilities (Fig. 10). When the probability is attenuated, there may be a certain limit beyond which the RT is no longer dependent on the probability. Estimating from the present data, this probability limit might be of the order of 0.01 or 0.001 under such experimental conditions. It may be that this probability limit signifies the value at which the zero level of expectancy is reached. As to whether any degree of preparation existed with these very small proba-

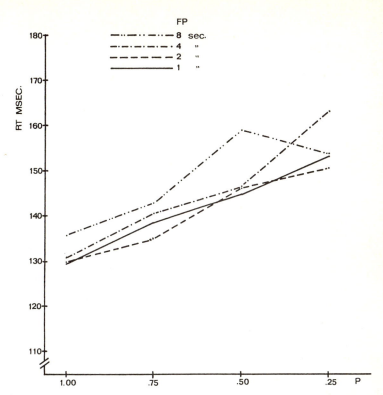

FIG. 9 RT as a function of the stimulus probability, given separately for each FP. (From Näätänen, 1972; reproduced by permission of The North-Holland Publishing Company).

bilities, the relatively short RT (288.6 msec) obtained even with the smallest probability suggests that there was some. It might be that preparation under such conditions is composed of merely those organismic processes which are not remarkably energy consuming and exhausting and do not have sharp temporal gradients.[5] Such preparation perhaps is only of sensory (and postural) rather than motor type (Tiffin & Westhafer, 1940; Henderson, 1952).

Under different probability conditions the subject worked at different levels of risk of making a premature response. Under the condition with the highest probability (39/40), some 10% of the catch trials were responded to. The mean of the RTs at trials (immediately) preceding the catch trials to which a response was given was significantly lower than that of the RTs at trials preceding the

---

[5] The latter suggestion is supported by the relatively small standard deviations of the condition with the smallest probability. Furthermore, the conditions involving the two smallest probabilities were the only ones with no failures to respond. With the highest probability, such failures amounted to 3.6% of all the trials. Three subjects had one or more failures to respond under the ¼ probability condition and under the ¹⁄₁₆ condition there were three trials altogether involving failure to respond.

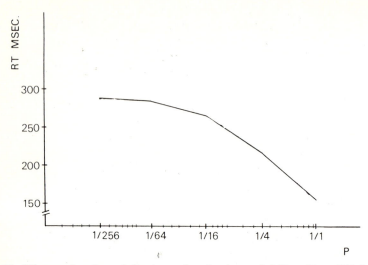

FIG. 10 RT as a function of the imperative-stimulus probability. (From Näätänen & Koskinen, 1975; reproduced by permission of The North-Holland Publishing Company).

nonresponded catch trials (the respective means were 133.0 and 160.7 msec). A similar comparison of the RTs following the responded catch trials and the unresponded catch trials yielded no statistically significant difference, although a tendency toward increased cautiousness can be observed after the responded catch trials (mean RTs 178.6 versus 168.9 msec, respectively). It was interesting that, when they did occur, the responses to the catch trials were delayed (mean 272.9 msec) with reference to the moment at which S2 would have been delivered compared to the RTs to S2 of this same probability condition.

It appears that the strong influence of the S2 probability on the RT is mainly mediated by expectancy. To have a closer look at the mediating mechanism, the next study (Näätänen & Sjölund, unpublished data) also involved a pretrial prediction of whether the stimulus would be delivered during that trial or not. To the best of our knowledge, no such study with the simple RT has been carried out. Figure 11 shows the frequencies of "yes" and "no" predictions separately for each probability value used. The data show that expectancy can vary between trials even when the objective probability is held constant (the subject knowing it via instruction). For small probabilities, there seem to be more and for high probabilities fewer positive predictions than would be expected from the probability values, but generally the correspondence was rather good. The effect of expectancy as such (the objective probability held constant) was very clear; the RTs generally were much shorter for the trials with positive predictions than for those with negative. This held true with respect to each probability value used (Fig. 12).

However, one reservation shall be made with respect to these results and to those of many similar studies: Can we use the prediction method without

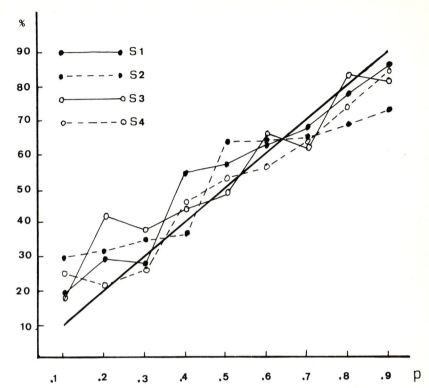

FIG. 11 The frequency of "yes" predictions plotted against the objective probability separately for each subject. The continuous solid line represents the relative frequency of "yes" predictions equal to the probability of a "yes" prediction being correct. (From Näätänen & Sjölund, unpublished data.)

interfering with the subject's performance? Would the RTs and the processes involved have been the same had we not asked him to give the predictions? It is possible, for example, that giving a "yes" prediction as such hastens the response and giving a "no" prediction might, similarly, slow down the response. Giving such a verbal prediction might, for example: (1) sharpen the differences in the subjective probability or expectancy between trials; or (2) amplify the effects of these differences on preparation. Figure 13 shows data from one subject in a control experiment now in progress (Näätänen, Virtanen & Merisalo, unpublished data). The RT distribution drawn with the solid line refers to a condition under which no predictions were given, the dotted line to a comparable condition with pretrial predictions. It is clearly seen that the addition of the prediction as such slowed down the RT (the mean for the latter condition was 149.9 msec and for the former 128.0 msec). The standard deviation was also greatly increased; the respective values were 39.4 and 17.3 msec. The three other subjects tested so far showed the same tendency but not to a statistically

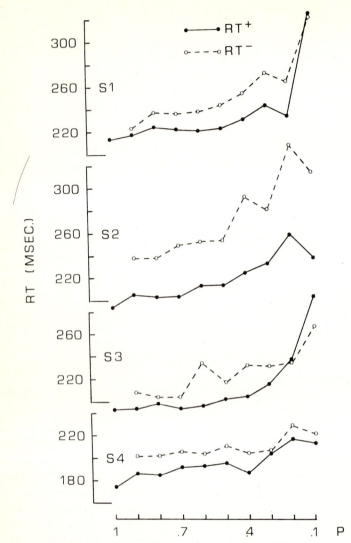

FIG. 12   RTs separately for "yes" (RT⁺) and "no" predictions (RT⁻) for each probability, separately for each subject. (From Näätänen & Sjölund, unpublished data.)

significant degree. (For two of these subjects, the standard deviation was about doubled, whereas for the third it remained the same.)[6]

[6] The implication of such results is evident: they increasingly give us reason to doubt whether the processes and relationships that take place or prevail during "normal" RT performance still exist undistorted when pretrial prediction is added. The general prolongation of RTs and increased standard deviations suggested by this control experiment are indications of distortion.

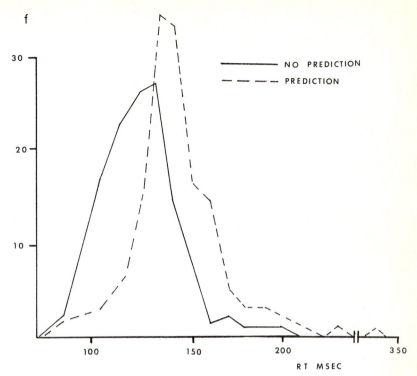

FIG. 13 Distributions of RTs under conditions with pretrial predictions (dotted line) and without pretrial predictions (solid line). (From Näätänen, Virtanen, & Merisalo, unpublished data.)

The possible contaminating effect on performance of such pretrial predictive activities should be taken very seriously. The problem with the prediction procedure seems to be largely the same as that with the classical introspection method: the observer and his object cannot be one and the same. The ensuing contamination is not necessarily limited to temporally coincident (observer and object) activities but might be extended to temporally adjacent activities. It is obvious that in any experiment in which such predictions are given the possibility of a contaminating effect should be seriously considered.

Another source of dissatisfaction with respect to the present prediction method lies in the binomiality of its response categories, as there apparently is no reason to doubt the continuous character of the expectancy variable.

Even the same significance of the same ("yes" or "no") prediction across different p conditions is to be seriously doubted: for example, to predict "yes" under the p condition of 0.1 would probably not signify the same degree of subjective certainty that the stimulus will be delivered as "yes" signifies when given under the 0.9 p condition. Paradoxically, a "yes" prediction under the 0.1

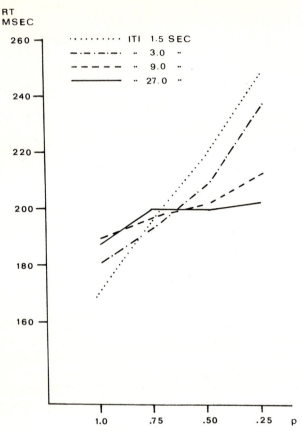

FIG. 14   The effect of the S2 probability on RT as a function of the ITI. (From Näätänen, Väistö, & Merisalo, unpublished data.)

p condition might, in fact, signify a lower degree of subjective probability of the delivery of the stimulus than a "no" prediction under the 0.9 p condition. The possible reasons for giving predictions which evidently do not correspond to the subject's real experience are various: for example, desire to gamble, tendency to avoid boredom, fear of irritating the experimenter by repeating the same prediction, etc.

All research work relevant to the relationship between expectancy and preparation we have so far conducted points to the importance of the former as a determinant of the latter (although some data were reviewed in the foregoing which suggested that the attenuation of this effect could be a function of practice). In fact, we have obtained some data which suggest that a subject cannot prepare himself by an effort of will for a not wholly certain event to the same degree as for an analogous certain event: although the subject under uncertain conditions is instructed to try to respond to the stimulus as fast as under conditions with full certainty of S2 delivery, he seems consistently to fail. There appears to be strong involuntary, stimulus, or situation control over the degree of preparation and its fluctuations. Recently we (Näätänen, Väistö, & Merisalo, unpublished data) obtained data which clearly suggested that the prolongation of the RT with the decrease of the S2 probability is a function of the ITI. In this study the ITI, which was either 1.5, 3, 9, or 27 sec, was kept constant within each block. It is seen in Fig. 14 that by prolonging the ITI the S2 probability effect can be destroyed. This is of special interest because the subject knew the S2 probability value used under each of the conditions. It is as if being exposed to a trial with an uncertainty as to the S2 delivery would exert a kind of temporary – lasting perhaps 10 or 20 sec – inhibitory effect on the subject's preparation for the next trial. (Such an effect was not selectively associated with blank trials as the S2 probability effect was approximately of the same order of magnitude after blank and nonblank trials.)

IV. CONCLUSION

The question of the nature of preparation or preparatory state is still far from settled. Even so, such a concept is undeniably justified, evidence for this coming from two main sources: (1) overt and covert changes taking place in the organism while waiting for an action signal under certain circumstances, for example, under pressure for a fast response to the signal; (2) preparatory kinds of effects on performance (difference between prepared and unprepared performance).

What, then, is the essential nature of preparation? It is suggested that it is *performing in advance what can be performed in advance of a response.* One can, for example, assume the appropriate posture and make the necessary peripheral sensory adjustments, such as the fixation of the gaze on the display on which the stimulus will appear. But preparation is more than that; it appears to include the facilitation of relevant sensory, motor, and central, integrative functions. There is plenty of experimental evidence, mainly psychophysiological, for the existence of facilitation of each of these three kinds of covert functions during the preparatory period of many kinds of activities, although much uncertainty still prevails with respect to these facilitatory processes (see, for example, Requin, in this volume, and Näätänen, 1973a). It is evident on the basis of an extensive body of data, some of which we have reviewed above, that expectancy, that is, the subjective probability of the immediate delivery of the (imperative) stimulus, is the most important determinant of preparation. Generally, the stronger the expectancy, the more preparation exists in the organism. As is clear from the preceding reviewed experiments, expectancy reflects rather well the objective probability. There are, however, some clear exceptions to this general rule, some of which are:

1. *Sequential effects:* There seems to exist in humans a general tendency to experience more dependency between adjacent events than exists in reality. Such a tendency is probably reflected by what are usually called sequential effects in RT. For example, when a trial with a certain FP was preceded by a trial with a longer FP, the RT usually was longer than when the preceding FP was the same or shorter (e.g., Karlin, 1959). Such sequential effects probably are mainly based on fluctuations in expectancy which do not follow changes in objective probability: in these experiments successive FPs generally are independent of each other which is often actually told to the subject in the instructions. Such sequential effects as that mentioned above have been explained by referring to a tendency to expect the delivery of S2 at about that moment at which the time elapsed since the warning signal approximately corresponds to the preceding FP.

Sequential effects have also been observed in many other kinds of human performance, for example, when one response at a time from among a set of a limited number of responses has been consecutively chosen by the subject in prediction experiments (for example, Wagenaar, 1972). One of the best known – and most expensive – of such biases is the so-called "gambler's fallacy," an increasing expectancy of alteration as a function of the number of consecutive repetitions.

2. *Modified subjective frequencies:* In the foregoing, studies have been reviewed which indicate that among a set of FPs of different durations given in randomized order, those FPs with the median duration are experienced more frequently than they are objectively. Probably this results in increased expectancy in the middle of the range of variation of the FPs used and hence causes, or contributes to, the common finding that the mean RT with the intermediate FP is the shortest or, at least, shorter than the average of the mean RTs with the extreme FPs.

3. *Long intertrial intervals:* Data have been reviewed (Näätänen, Väistö & Merisalo, unpublished data) which demonstrated that the S2 probability effect on the RT was attenuated or abolished by prolonging the ITI. This might indicate either a drastic dissociation phenomenon between the objective probability and expectancy or that, with long ITIs, expectancy has little or no control over preparation.

The foregoing list indicated some exceptions to the rule that the objective probability is veridically reflected by expectancy[7] which was regarded as the most important determinant of preparation. There are doubtlessly other de-

---

[7] The different forms of expectancy phenomena and their behavioral effects have been extensively discussed elsewhere (Näätänen & Summala, 1976).

terminants of preparation; if the organism is exhausted it might not be capable of developing a very high degree of preparation. This is but one example of the fluctuations in the basic state of the organism which might affect preparation independently of expectancy. Another suggested source of variation in preparation is related to the control of the activation state of the responding system. There is a decision-making aspect involved here. This suggestion is illustrated in Fig. 15, which represents an imagined time course of motor preparedness (motor excitation minus motor inhibition) with a premature response under conditions of *constant* expectancy. (No stimulus happens to be delivered, however, during the described sequence of events.)

The first wave ("increase preparedness") represents a motor excitatory process with a resulting increased preparedness to respond. This is followed by a more "cautious" period involving decreased preparedness. It is emphasized that the organism, evidently, has no direct way to "perceive" the moment-to-moment distance between the degree of motor readiness of the responding system involved and the limit of motor action; hence, the organism is obliged to use feedback information from the muscular effects of its excitatory and inhibitory commands in this control task. (It appears that there is no clear limit between the increasing motor readiness and the corresponding motor response, but somewhere during this increase, the cumulating motor readiness "flows over," as it were, into the corresponding motor action; see Meyer, 1953). Thus, in trying to maintain a high degree of motor readiness in order to be able to respond quickly to the awaited stimulus, the organism has to operate to a crucial extent on the basis of its "estimates" of the effects of the excitatory and inhibitory motor commands; these estimates are presumably based on delayed and rather vague feedback information. Hence, continuous corrections via excitatory and

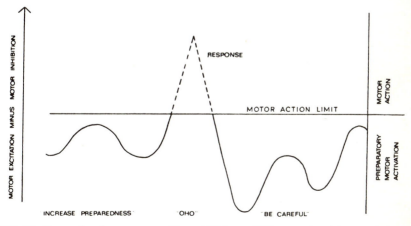

FIG. 15 For explanation, see text. (From Näätänen, 1971; reproduced by permission of The North-Holland Publishing Company).

inhibitory motor mechanisms are made in order to keep the motor readiness in the vicinity of the motor-action limit; these corrections induce the fluctuations in motor readiness described in the figure. It is as if motor readiness were sometimes pushed nearer to the motor-action limit and sometimes drawn backward to a safer distance. A step too far, leading to an unintended response ("Oho"), is illustrated in the middle of the figure. This is, of course, a negatively reinforcing experience, followed by a "Be Careful" phase during which the motor readiness is kept at a really safe distance from the motor-action limit.[8]

Generally, it appears that the mean distance from the motor-action limit of motor readiness which the subject maintains under such conditions is determined by the relative frequency of premature responses which the subject regards as "still tolerable," or as still tolerated by the experimenter. (The mean distance referred to represents the point of balance between the excitatory and inhibitory motivational components determining the safety margin and, hence, the probability of a premature response). Consequently, if the subject is strictly admonished to avoid premature responses, or is severely punished for them, their frequency naturally becomes very low and the RTs are long. On the other hand, if speed is stressed in the instructions with no emphasis on the avoidance of premature responses, the latter are frequent and RTs short. Hence, an important determinant of preparation is the subjective speed—accuracy tradeoff and its momentary fluctuations.

Expectancy can probably affect the RT also without affecting preparation, by affecting the subject's decision-making criterion with respect to S2. In order to respond quickly, he should in a very early phase after the S2 onset detect (decide) that S2 is present. Let us imagine an RT situation in which the imperative stimulus is the only stimulus and is delivered at regular ISIs of 3 sec. In such a situation the subject apparently already responds at the very early phase of the stimulus processing involving the experience of "something is happening"; his decision criterion is very low. It is a common observation in such reaction situations that any stimulus, for example, a sound from outside the laboratory, occurring at about the expected time of the signal, triggers the response; such a stimulus does not have even to be of the same modality as the signal. It might indeed be that by the expected moment of the signal the subject has abandoned all the other, more specific criteria for decision making: "someting," somewhat discrete from the background stimulation and neural noise is enough for the decision of "signal." (For details of, and evidence for, this explanation, see Näätänen, 1975, pp. 250, 292—293.)

---

[8] As mentioned earlier, the mean RT in the trials (immediately) preceding the responded catch trials was found by Näätänen and Koskinen (1975) to be considerably shorter than the mean RT in the trials preceding the nonresponded catch trials. And the RTs at trials immediately following the responded catch trials tended to be longer than the RTs at trials immediately following the unresponded catch trials.

ACKNOWLEDGMENTS

The research work reviewed in this chapter was supported by the Academy of Finland.

REFERENCES

Elithorn, A., & Lawrence, C. Central inhibition – Some refractory observations. *Quarterly Journal of Experimental Psychology*, 1955, **11**, 211–220.

Gaillard, A. W., & Näätänen, R., Slow potential changes and choice reaction time as a function of interstimulus interval. *Acta Psychologica*, 1973, **37**, 173–186.

Gaillard, A. W., & Näätänen, R. Modality effects on the contingent negative variation in a simple reaction-time task. In W. C. McCallum & J. R. Knott (Eds.), The Responsive Brain. *The proceedings of the third international congress on event-related slow potentials of the brain.* Bristol: Wright, 1976, Pp. 46–50.

Gaillard, A. W., & Näätänen, R. CNV and the law of initial value. In J. E. Desmedt (Ed.), *International Symposium on Cerebral Evoked Potentials in Man. Brussels, April 15–18, 1974.* (In press)

Gordon, I. E. Stimulus probability and simple reaction time. *Nature*, 1967, **215**, 895–896.

Gottsdanker, R. The attaining and maintaining of preparation. In P. M. A. Rabbitt & S. Dornic (Eds.), *Attention and performance V*. London: Academic Press, 1975; Pp. 33–49.

Henderson, R. L. Remote action potentials at the moment of response in simple reaction-time situation. *Journal of Experimental Psychology*, 1952, **44**, 238–241.

Karlin, L. Reaction time as a function of foreperiod duration and variability. *Journal of Experimental Psychology*, 1959, **58**, 185–191.

Klemmer, E. T. Time uncertainty in simple reaction time. *Journal of Experimental Psychology*, 1956, **51**, 179–184.

Kornblum, S. Simple reaction time as a race between signal detection and time estimation: A paradigm and model. *Perception & Psychophysics*, 1973, **13**, 108–112.

Meyer, D. R. On the interaction of simultaneous responses. *Psychological Bulletin*, 1953, **50**, 204–220.

Näätänen, R. The diminishing time-uncertainty with the lapse of time after the warning signal in reaction-time experiments with varying foreperiods. *Acta Psychologica*, 1970, **34**, 399–419.

Näätänen, R. Nonaging foreperiod and simple reaction time. *Acta Psychologica*, 1971, **35**, 316–327.

Näätänen, R. Time uncertainty and occurrence uncertainty of the stimulus in simple reaction time task. *Acta Psychologica*, 1972, **36**, 492–503.

Näätänen, R. Inverted U-shaped relationship between activation and performance. A critical review. In S. Kornblum (Ed.), *Attention and performance IV*. New York: Academic Press, 1973. Pp. 155–174. (a)

Näätänen, R. On what is the contingent negative variation (CNV) contingent in reaction-time experiments. In A. Fessard & G. Lelord (Eds.), I.N.S.E.R.M. 1er Colloque de Neurophysiologie humaine appliquée à la Psychologie et à la Psychiatrie: Activités Evoquées et leur Conditionnement chez l'homme normal et en pathologie mentale. Paris: INSERM, 1973. Pp. 121–152. (b)

Näätänen, R. Selective attention and evoked potentials in humans – A critical review, *Biological Psychology*, 1975, **2**, 237–307.

Näätänen, R. Components of physiological activation in psychophysiological performance and personality research. In J. Strelau (Ed.), *Proceedings of International Conference on Temperament and Personality, Warszawa, October 21–24, 1974.* (In press)

Näätänen, R., & Gaillard, A. W. The relationship between the contingent negative variation and the reaction time under prolonged experimental conditions. *Biological Psychology,* 1974, **2**, 277–291. (a)

Näätänen, R., & Gaillard, A. W. The relationships between certain CNV and evoked-potential measures within and between vertex, frontal and temporal derivations. *Biological Psychology,* 1974, **2**, 95–112. (b)

Näätänen, R., Gaillard, A. W., & Mäntysalo, S. S_2 probability and CNV. In *Proceedings of 2nd International Congress of C.I.A.N.S.* (Collegium Internationale Activitatis Nervosae Superioris), Praha, June 30-July 3, 1975. (In press)

Näätänen, R., & Koskinen, P. Simple reaction time with very small imperative-stimulus probabilities. *Acta Psychologica,* 1975, **39**, 43–50.

Näätänen, R., Muranen, V., & Merisalo, A. The timing of expectancy peak in simple reaction time situation. *Acta Psychologica,* 1974, **38**, 461–470.

Näätänen, R., & Sjölund, M. Prediction outcome and simple reaction time for different constant imperative stimulus probabilities. Unpublished manuscript; Institute of Psychology, University of Helsinki, 1973.

Näätänen, R., & Summala, H. Road-user behavior and traffic accidents. Amsterdam: North-Holland Publ., and New York: American Elsevier, 1976, 270 pp.

Näätänen, R., Vesalainen, M., Mäkinen, M., & Merisalo, A. Simple reaction time as a function of the objective and subjective foreperiod. Unpublished data; Institute of Psychology, University of Helsinki, 1974.

Näätänen, R., Virtanen, M., & Merisalo, A. The effect of prediction on simple reaction time. Unpublished data; Institute of Psychology, University of Helsinki, 1975.

Näätänen, R., Väistö, L., & Merisalo, A. The effect of imperative stimulus probability on simple reaction time – A short-term inhibition phenomenon? Unpublished data; Institute of Psychology, University of Helsinki, 1974.

Nickerson, R. S. Psychological refractory phase and the functional significance of signals. *Perceptual and Motor Skills,* 1967, **21**, 3–10.

Nickerson, R. S., & Burnham, D. W. Response times with nonaging foreperiods. *Journal of Experimental Psychology,* 1969, **79**, 452–457.

Ollman, R. T., & Billington, M. J. The deadline model for simple reaction times. *Cognitive Psychology,* 1972, **3**, 311–316.

Requin, J. Is there a specificity in the supraspinal control of motor structures during preparation? In S. Dornic, *Attention and performance VI.* Hillsdale, N.J.: Lawrence Erlbaum Associates. 1977.

Tiffin, J., & Westhafer, F. L. The relation between reaction time and temporal location of the stimulus on the tremor cycle. *Journal of Experimental Psychology,* 1940, **27**, 318–324.

Vroon, P. A. Tapping rate as a measure of expectancy in terms of response and attention limitation. *Journal of Experimental Psychology,* 1973, **101**, 183–185.

Vroon, P. A., & Vroon, A. G., Tapping rate and expectancy in simple reaction time tasks. *Journal of Experimental Psychology,* 1973, **98**, 85–90.

Wagenaar, W. A. Sequential Response Bias. A Study on Choice and Chance. Rotterdam: Bronder-Offset N.V., 1972.

8

Is There a Specificity in the Supraspinal Control of Motor Structures During Preparation?

Jean Requin
Michel Bonnet
András Semjen[1]

Département de Psychophysiologic Générale
Institut de Neurophysiologie et Psychophysiologie du CNRS
Marseille, France

ABSTRACT

From the general hypothesis that preparatory adjustments set up before a motor task depend upon the response probability, and are patterned according to the biomechanical requirements of the movement to be performed, four experiments were designed in order to analyze, using reflexogenic methods, the changes in the excitability of spinal motor structures during the preparatory period of different RT paradigms. Principally, it was found that the general depressive control exerted from central nervous structures upon the spinal reflex pathway during preparation was strengthened when the muscle was involved in the execution of the response and when the muscle was located on the preferred body side. However, the depth of such a control did not depend, in a choice–RT condition, upon the probability for the muscle to be involved. Moreover it was only slightly modified when the role played by the muscle in the response–movement was changed from agonistic to antagonistic as well as when the expected force of the movement was increased. In relation to the likely neurophysiological mechanisms underlying inhibitory central influences acting at the spinal level, the functional significance of this relatively widespread depression of the reactivity of spinal reflex pathways is discussed. It is mainly concluded that such a phenomenon has to be considered as the negative component of the preparatory process, that means an active suspension of the execution of the response, and/or a temporary protection of spinal motor structures

---

[1] Present address: Institute of Psychology, Szondy-u. 83-85, Budapest VI, Hungary

against exogenic influences able to prematurely trigger or disturb the execution of the motor program. Finally, the weak specificity of the changes observed at the spinal level during preparation is regarded as sustaining the idea that preparatory adjustments mainly intervene at earlier stages of the response information processing.

I. INTRODUCTION

When looking at a living organism, it is obvious that a large part of its behavior, especially in the form of explicit attitudes, cannot be understood without reference to the notion of anticipation. If one defined anticipation as a permanent, short-term process of adaptation to the requirements of more or less expected changes in the conditions of life, it can be considered, with an intentional teleologic point of view, that the function of anticipatory behavior is to set up preparatory adjustments to a given event at a given time at the different stages of information processing, in order to increase the efficiency of an explicit or implicit response. In this extended meaning, preparation thus includes more restricted concepts such as prevision, attention, or expectancy, which, nevertheless, cover more or less separate psychological components underlying the involvement of the organism in an oriented behavior.

Whereas the time course of preparatory processes has been extensively studied (for a review, see Alegria, 1975), some of the important remaining questions are, first, whether or not these processes and their underlying mechanisms depend upon the characteristics of the task performed, and, secondly, what are the amount and extent of such a specificity. Considering the experimental facts obtained in this direction during the last thirty years, a noticeable difference appears between experimental psychology and psychophysiology. Many experiments designed by psychologists have provided results relevant to the general hypothesis that preparation, as an intervening variable, has not only a quantitative dimension but also some qualitative aspects depending upon the nature of the task that the subject is performing. When faced with the prolificacy of psychological studies and the relative coherence of the results obtained in this area, one can be impressed by the remaining difficulty to find and analyze some indices of the specificity of preparatory processes at the level of nervous structure activity, as it was, for instance, underlined in a pessimistic conclusion by Moray (1969): "Reading over the physiological work of the last few years which has either deliberately or accidentally been relevant to attention, one cannot help but be disappointed. The truth of the matter seems to be that we know almost nothing" (p. 178).

Moreover, in the field of psychophysiological investigation, a large number of studies focused especially upon nervous processes underlying a differential control of sensory inputs at the various stages of sensory pathways, according to the perceptual requirements of the subject's task. On the contrary, there were only a few attempts to demonstrate that the excitability or reactivity states of the efferent pathways or structures would be patterned according to the biomechanical requirements of the motor activity to be performed. Such a difference between the interest respectively given to the sensory and motor sides of the covert concomitants of behavioral changes probably cannot be explained by theoretical or methodological considerations only.

After the very promising discovery of the spontaneous electrical activity of the brain structures, it progressively appeared that the classical electroencephalographic method was of limited fecundity in the understanding of the neurophysiological substrate of psychological processes. Then, the possibility of recording the potentials evoked in the brain by sensory inputs allowed an anatomically focused, precisely timed, and relatively sensitive testing of the sensory and associative nervous structures. In spite of often inconsistent results, the method was extensively used in order to study the physiological substrate of selective attention (Karlin, 1970; Näätänen, 1975) with, however, severe limitations: "... it seems clear that at present, we cannot expect physiology to help our understanding of selective attention at complex levels of analysis ..." (Moray, 1969, p. 178).

A somewhat identical, but not so well known, story developed in the study of changes in the activity of nervous motor structures related to psychological processes. Passive electromyographic methods first appeared very promising for the investigation of the covert responses of efferent systems to various experimental conditions. Beyond the classical finding that the level of tonic muscular activity was related to the general level of alertness (see Duffy, 1962), it was found that any kind of sensory input was able, when it reached a sufficient physical intensity, to trigger a transient increase of this basic activity, the so-called "startle pattern" (Landis & Hunt, 1939), the time course, morphology, and adaptation of which were precisely studied by Davis (1948, 1950, 1953), Davis, Buchwald, and Frankmann (1955), and Dawson and Davis (1957). When the cognitive aspects of the situation were manipulated, especially by giving a warning significance to the stimulus, this change in electromyographic activity was amplified and lengthened until the expected event occurred. Moreover, it was progressively clear that this phenomenon could not be described, according to the framework of activation theory, as being only nonspecific, but rather as depending upon the biomechanical requirements of the response. The increase of electromyographic activity was centered upon the muscles which had to be involved in performing the movement (Davis, 1940, 1952; Requin, 1965). At last, while the level of muscular activity during the preparatory period (PP) in RT experiments was generally considered as having a predictive meaning for the RT performance, there were some discrepancies about the sign and strength of this covariation. It was mainly concluded that RT decreased as electromyographic activity increased, either in the involved muscles (Davis, 1956a; Fink,

1956; Freeman, 1933; Patton, 1957; Requin, 1965) or even in the noninvolved muscles (Daniel, 1949; Henderson, 1952; Travis & Kennedy, 1947), whereas in other experiments, either an inverted correlation (Davis, 1956b, c) or a lack of correlation (Meyer, 1953) was observed. Here too, methodological limitations, the extent of interindividual differences and the intraindividual versatility of patterns of muscular activities explained that these more or less successful studies have justified somewhat pessimistic conclusions and finally were discontinued (Davis, 1957; Requin, 1965).

But reflexogenic methods are in a similar position with regard to electromyography as cortical evoked potentials methods are with respect to electroencephalography (see Paillard 1955, who emphasized the advantages of investigating Hoffmann (H) and tendinous (T) spinal reflexes to study the effects of psychological factors at the level of motor structures). In addition to the methodological benefits of an active testing compared to a passive recording, especially the precise control of the different parameters of the experiment, spinal reflex methods lead to a selective exploration of a functionally well-defined motoneuron pool. The possibility was so offered to differentiate between generalized, focused, or more complex patterns of supraspinal effects, by comparing the data observed from different motoneuron pools. Lastly, it is important to underline the general interpretive value of the indices obtained during the course of an exploration of spinal reflexes. This appears to be, in fact, the essential justification of an extensive use of this method in the analysis of behavior. Its interest results primarily from the large amount of information known about the spinal processes and the supraspinal control of reflex activity. It is not only a question of results concerning the neurophysiological mechanisms underlying the modifications of the spinal motor structure activity but also the functional role of such modifications. The control of muscular contraction by alpha motoneurons, the role of gamma motoneurons in the regulation of postural tone or that of interneurons in the transmission, and selection of peripheral and central influences (see Fig. 1) are all essential elements for discussion of the experimental facts. The very large body of knowledge in this field appears to lend itself to proposing a psychophysiological interpretation of the observed findings.

Reflexogenic methods thus appear as particularly suitable to the examination of the general hypothesis that the specificity of the preparatory process for a defined motor activity would result in variations of efferent structure activity or excitability, the patterning of which would depend upon the information given the subject about the requirements of the movement. Nevertheless, the number of experiments designed along this line is still surprisingly small, suggesting that the implicit idea remains that the electrode is farther from psychology when spinal rather than cortical activity is recorded.

This work was an attempt to investigate, by means of these methods, the indices of preparatory adjustments to the execution of a motor program. It was mainly guided by the major issues of experimental psychology, emphasizing the

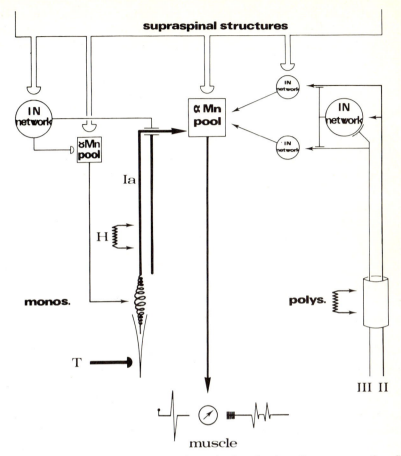

FIG. 1 Simplified diagram of the spinal organization showing: the monosynaptic reflex pathway brought into play by either an electrical stimulation of *Ia* fibers (H reflex) or a stretch of the muscle (T reflex); the control exerted by the gamma motoneurons (γ Mn) upon spindle sensitivity; the polysynaptic reflex pathways brought into play by an electrical stimulation of cutaneous afferents (fibers from groups II and III); the roles played by the different interneuron (IN) networks in the transmission of reflexogenic afferences to alpha motoneurons (α Mn); the distribution of supraspinal influences upon spinal motor structures; and the morphology of electromyographic responses evoked when the different reflex pathways are sollicited. Activatory effects are indicated by arrows, inhibitory effects by lines perpendicular either to structures (postsynaptic inhibition) or to fibers (presynaptic inhibition), and mixed influences by semicircles.

role of response factors in RT experiments. The first experiment was a reply to previous works showing that the distribution over spinal structures of changes in excitability is related to the question of whether or not the muscle is involved in the response to be performed. The second experiment was especially designed in order to see whether or not such an index of the motor structure involvement could be modulated by manipulating the relative S–R probability. The third and fourth experiments were concerned with the patterning of preparatory adjustments according to the biomechanical aspects of the intended response movement, especially its direction and force.

II. GENERAL METHODOLOGY

This set of experiments was designed in order to investigate, using reflexogenic methods, the modifications of the excitability of spinal motor structures during the PP of simple or choice RT paradigms.

A. Apparatus

The subject sat in a reclined position in an armchair especially designed to test spinal reflexes, located in a slightly illuminated, but only sound-attenuated box. In order to mask completely auditory information from the experimental room, a white noise at 59 dB intensity was continuously used during the experiment.

The warning signal (WS) was given by a loudspeaker and response signals (RS) by two diode light sources situated on a panel 1.5 m in front of the subject. The loudspeaker provided a 1000 Hz, 68 dB tone of 50 msec duration. The illumination of the diode light sources lasted 50 msec.

The response was either an extension or a dorsal flexion of the right or left foot which was fixed upon a moving pedal in order to restrict the movements to a rotation of 3° angular amplitude around the axis of the ankle. The extension movement was especially controlled by the soleus muscle, which was antagonistic to the flexion movement.

B. Physiological Recordings

H reflexes were evoked and recorded in the right and left soleus muscles, according to the method developed by Paillard (1955) and more recently by Hugon (1973).

The stimulation of the tibialis posterior nerve by percutaneous means was obtained by a 1-msec rectangular electrical pulse delivered through an isolated unit, between a cathodal electrode situated in the fossa poplitea and an anodal electrode located just above the knee joint. The intensity of this stimulation was adjusted in order to obtain an amplitude of the electromyographic response of about 50% of the maximum amplitude reached when this intensity was increased. These conditions were not changed within a single series of trials.

The reflex responses were recorded through a pair of electrodes formed by two pieces of synthetic sponge, 1 cm in diameter, fixed upon the surface of the muscle, 3–4 cm apart.

C. Experimental Design

The subjects performed under different conditions during two or four sessions at a few days' interval. In each session there were successive series of 48 trials, the sequential organization of which was electronically controlled as follows:

1. The intertrial interval (ITI) was between 8 and 14 sec graduated in steps of 2 sec, with the same probability. The presentation order of ITIs was arranged to counterbalance the sequential effects related to ITI duration.
2. The preparatory period (PP) was always of 1 sec duration.
3. The reflexogenic stimulation was delivered with 6 equiprobable and randomly distributed latencies with respect to the WS. In order to obtain samples of reflex amplitude by steps of 100 msec during the PP, the latencies were −100, 100, 300, 500, 700, and 900 msec, in a first type of series, and 0, 200, 400, 600, 800, and 1000 msec in a second type of series, alternately presented to the subject.

D. Analysis of the Data

Reaction time was given by an electronic timer triggered by the RS and stopped by a photocell darkened by a displacement of the moving pedal.

H reflexes were amplified (Tektronix FM 122), then transmitted to a two-channel oscilloscope (Tektronix 565) in order to be continuously checked and then transmitted to a special digital voltmeter in order to measure their amplitude with about a 1% precision. Digital data were stored on punch cards that were later analyzed by a UNIVAC 1110 computer.

In order to obtain comparable data within a group of subjects, notwithstanding the irreductible differences in the conditions of physiological recordings from one subject to another, the mean amplitude of the reflexes recorded at each latency in the PP was transformed into z score. For each subject, the mean and standard deviation of the distribution of the reflex amplitudes triggered either before (−100 msec) the WS in the first type of series, or simultaneously to the WS (0 msec) in the second type of series, served as references.

III. EXPERIMENT I: EFFECTS OF THE MUSCLE INVOLVEMENT IN MOTOR PERFORMANCE

A. Introduction

In a previous series of experiments (Requin, 1967, 1969; Requin et al., 1968a, b), the variations of spinal excitability in human subjects during the PP of a simple RT task were determined by measuring the amplitude of T and H reflexes. They were evoked in the soleus muscle of both legs, while an extension of the right foot was used as the response in the RT task. During the first part of 1-sec PP, a bilateral increase of H reflex was observed, reaching its maximum value between 100 and 300 msec after the WS. Whereas in the left noninvolved muscle this increase was maintained or slightly declined until the end of the PP, a steep decrease was found in the right involved muscle during the same period.

Such variations in the excitability of spinal structures before movement were found again by Gerilovski and Tsekov (1971), Pierrot-Deseilligny et al. (1971), and Papakostopoulos and Copper (1973). Their functional significance and physiological basis were discussed elsewhere (Bonnet & Requin, 1972; Requin & Paillard, 1971). The main conclusion was that the time course of the fluctuations of spinal excitability between the WS and RS depended upon the role played by the muscle in the motor performance. Thus, there was some evidence for a specific component of preparation to act, expressed by a differential supraspinal control of the motoneuron pools, respectively involved and noninvolved in the execution stage of the movement. Moreover, only the amplitude of spinal reflexes in the evoked muscle had a predictive meaning for the RT performance (Requin, 1969; Requin & Paillard, 1971; Semjen, Bonnet, & Requin, 1973).

However, it must be noted that in all the experiments quoted above, the subjects performed the RT task with the right foot. Because there was no reason to expect a difference between the right and left sides, such a procedure, which always makes the right soleus the involved muscle, was systematically used. But many experiments now suggest that supraspinal nervous structures exert a differential control upon the motoneuron pools, according to motor dominance. We occasionally used the left foot of right-handed subjects to perform the response in an experiment designed to study the time course of H-reflex amplitude as a function of the PP duration (Semjen et al., 1973). No difference was observed between the left involved and the right noninvolved muscles. Nevertheless, a clear conclusion as to the part played by the subject's lateralization was difficult to make because of the "go—no go" procedure used. While the "go" signal was presented on the left side of the panel, triggering the response of the left foot, a "no go" signal was presented on the right, prohibiting not only the response of the left foot but probably also, because of the high spatial S—R compatibility, a tendency for the subject to respond with the right foot, which could hence not really be considered as simply "noninvolved".

More recent experiments have given supplementary evidence as to a possible right—left difference in the accessibility of the motoneuron pools to supraspinal influences, at least those exerted through the reticulospinal and vestibulospinal pathways. The classical activatory effect of a brief nonsignificant tone of high intensity upon the activity (Davis, 1948, 1950, 1953; Davis et al., 1955; Landis & Hunt, 1939), or excitability (Bowdich & Warren, 1890; Coquery, 1969; Paillard, 1955; Semjen et al., 1973) of spinal motor structures appears stronger in the nonpreferred leg of left-handed and right-handed subjects (Bonnet & Lacour, 1973). Similarly the increase of H reflexes following a monaural galvanic vestibular stimulation was found to be asymmetrical, that is, always greater in the soleus muscle of the nonpreferred leg, regardless of what side was stimulated (Lacour, Bonnet, & Roll, 1974).

These data strongly suggest that in our previous results on the spinal organization of the preparatory set to a motor response the effects of two factors were possibly confounded. On the one hand, it is the permanent asymmetry in the supraspinal control exerted on the left and right sides according to handedness, and on the other hand, the transient functional difference between spinal structures according to the part they play in the execution of the response.

B. Method

Ten right-handed male subjects, 25 to 37 years old, performed a simple RT task during two sessions. From one session to another, the responding foot, which had to perform an extension movement, was changed from right to left for 5 subjects and in the reversed order for the 5 other subjects. In each session, there were 8 series of trials alternating between a classical simple RT condition and a control condition in which the subject was instructed to do nothing but relax. In the latter case the tone, which served as WS in the RT condition, was presented alone.

C. Results

The evolution of H reflex amplitude during the PP is shown in Fig. 2 for each muscle (right or left soleus) when the response movement was performed by either the right or left foot. The results of a three-way (delay of H reflex in the PP X muscle: right or left X involvement: yes or no) analysis of variance are presented in Table 1. The respective effects of the two main factors (side and involvement of the muscle) are shown in Fig. 3, which includes data obtained in the control condition, without taking into account the strong difference between the mean levels of H-reflex amplitude observed in the control and experimental conditions. At the time of the WS there is, in fact, a mean decrease of 1.00 (expressed by z score) from the control to the experimental condition.

When the response was performed by the right foot, the time course of H-reflex amplitude during the PP clearly differs, depending on the muscle recorded. The slight increase which follows the WS continues for the left noninvolved muscle, while the amplitude progressively decreases in the right-involved muscle until the RS occurs. When the response side was changed from right to left, it is clear that this pattern is neither reversed nor canceled, but only attenuated. H-reflex amplitude is less depressed in the right noninvolved muscle and more depressed in the left involved muscle, but nevertheless remains greater

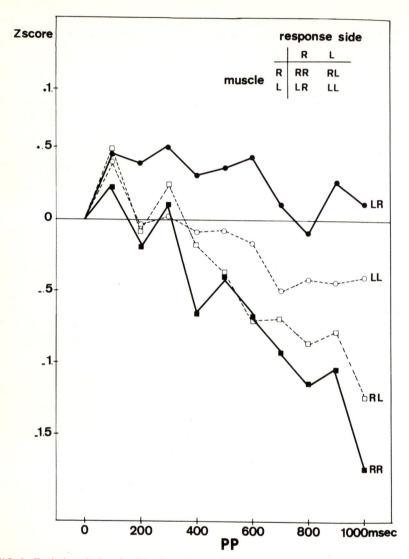

FIG. 2 Evolution during the PP of H-reflex amplitude in the right and left soleus when they are involved or not in the response performance. On the right of the curves, the first letter indicates the side of the muscle, the second letter the side of the response.

in the left than in the right soleus. The general significant decrease of excitability during the PP course ($F = 10.69$, $p < .01$) thus appears modulated by two factors, the side of the muscle on one hand ($F = 3.38$, $p < .01$), which is already slightly present in the control condition, and the involvement of the muscle in performing the response on the other hand ($F = 6.08$, $p < .001$). Moreover, the effects of these two factors do not interact ($F > 1.00$).

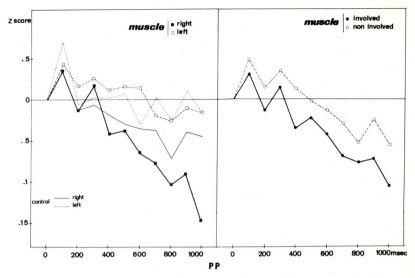

FIG. 3   Same data as in Fig. 2, but separating the effects of, respectively, the side of the muscle, regardless of the role played in the response (on the left), and the muscle involvement in the response performance, regardless of the side of the muscle (on the right). Data obtained in the control condition are shown in the left part of the figure.

TABLE 1

Experiment I: Analysis of Variance of H Reflex
Amplitude in the Experimental Condition

Origin	MS	df	F
Delay (D)	6.142	9	10.69*
S × D	.574	81	
Muscle (M)	21.580	1	20.61**
S × M	1.047	9	
D × M	.988	9	3.38**
S × D × M	.292	81	
Involvement (I)	17.476	1	21.20**
S × I	.824	9	
D × I	1.092	9	6.08*
S × D × I	.179	81	
M × I	2.419	1	2.03
S × M × I	1.189	9	
D × M × I	.294	9	.79
S × D × M × I	.372	81	

*$p < .001$.
**$p < .01$.

However, it must be noted that the different patterns of spinal excitability observed according to the response side are not clearly related to the RT performance, which does not significantly differ depending upon whether the response was performed by the right (206 msec) or the left (202 msec) foot.

D. Discussion

These results provide some clarification of the discrepancies observed in our previous experiments, without, however, contradicting the main finding that the excitability state of motoneuron pools is modified during the PP, depending on the part these structures play in the motor performance. Taking into account some supplementary precisions obtained concerning the setting up of central influences exerting themselves upon reflex pathways, it is now possible to propose a likely description of the changes which occur in spinal motor structures during a task involving an anticipatory behavior.

As soon as the subject becomes engaged in the task, a nonspecific depressive control of these structures appears, as the difference between control and experimental conditions shows. This finding confirms the results we have previously obtained in a choice-RT experiment by comparing the mean level of H and T reflex amplitude during rest periods before and after the task, intertrial interval (ITI), and PP. Spinal excitability was found to decrease from rest to ITI, and from ITI to PP (Brunia & Requin, unpublished results). On the contrary, Bathien and Hugelin (1969), Bathien (1971), and Brunia (1971, 1972) have generally found an increase of H or T reflexes when subjects were engaged in sensory–motor tasks involving attentional processes. However, their results differed according to the type of task, especially depending on the amount of motor activity required, suggesting that samples of reflex amplitude taken during task periods probably confused the depressive effects of the involvement of the subject in an anticipatory activity and the activatory effects resulting from sustained motor performance itself.

Then, after the transient increase of excitability triggered by the WS, the time course and morphology of which were discussed elsewhere (Semjen et al., 1973), the strength of the depressive supraspinal control progressively increases as the PP elapses until the RS occurs. This phenomenon differentially affects motoneuron pools, according to the body side involved on the one hand, the decrease of excitability being sharper on the preferred side, at least in our right-handed subjects, and to the part played in the motor performance by the corresponding muscle on the other hand, the decrease of excitability being sharper when the muscle has to perform the response movement. Hence, it is obvious that one must consider with caution conclusions based upon results obtained in experiments in which these two factors were not balanced.

While we have not yet obtained confirmatory data in left-handed subjects, especially because in these subjects the notion of motor dominance is not clear at the level of inferior limbs, the likely difference in the central influences exerting themselves upon motor structures of both sides is undoubtedly related to the functional asymmetry underlying handedness. This adds to some recent physiological findings emphasizing a preferential lateralization of the influences transmitted to the spinal level by descending reticular and vestibular pathways. Moreover, it can be noted that the difference between the amplitude of the motor potential recorded on the contralateral and ipsilateral cortex just before a movement is not exactly the same depending on the body side of the performing limb in left-handed subjects (Donchin & Kutas, 1974). One can therefore suggest that there is possibly a similar asymmetry for corticospinal pathways, taking into account the likely hypothesis that the motor potential is closely related to the amount of discharge of tonic and phasic motor cortex neurons (Evarts, 1973; Gantchev, 1977).

The fact that at the spinal level such an asymmetry appears as a more marked excitability decrease for the preferred side, in the same way as a short-term involvement in the response, suggests a common functional explanation, if one considers handedness as mainly resulting from a long-term asymmetrical involvement in skilled performance. However, in both cases, the reactivity of spinal motor structures seems to be surprisingly reduced at the time when the response starts and, moreover, to be not closely related to the RT performance. The functional meaning of such a phenomenon cannot be understood without an extended analysis of its possible neurophysiological basis, as are made in the concluding remarks.

IV. EXPERIMENT II: EFFECT OF
THE S–R RELATIVE FREQUENCY

It is well known that RT increases with either an increase of the number of S–R alternatives (Crossman, 1953; Hyman, 1953) or a decrease of the relative probability of a particular S–R alternative (Fitts, Peterson, & Wolpe, 1963; Hyman, 1953; Leontiev & Krinchik, 1963).

With explicit or implicit models referring to expectancy or preparatory states, psychologists have tried to separate the respective parts played in these effects by perceptual factors, as preparatory adjustments to stimulus input and/or signal identification, and response factors, as preparatory adjustments to response selection and/or execution, by independently manipulating stimulus and response relative frequency. Some of them have come to the conclusion of either a perceptual bias only (Bertelson & Tisseyre, 1966; Hawkins & Friedin, 1972; Hawkins & Hosking, 1969; Hawkins, Thomas, & Drury, 1970), or a perceptual bias principally (Hinrichs, 1970; Hinrichs & Krainz, 1970; La Berge, Tweedy, & Ricker, 1967); whereas, in another set of experiments, the response bias was found effective in determining RT (Dillon, 1966; Keele, 1969; Morin & Forrin, 1963; Rabbitt, 1959).

As suggested by Bernstein, Shurman, & Forester (1967), La Berge and Tweedy (1964), and La Berge, Legrand, & Hobbie, (1969), a more recent series of experiments has shown that preparatory adjustments probably intervene at both perceptual and motor stages, when the relative frequency effect is observed by manipulating either the number of S–R alternatives (Hawkins & Underhill, 1971) or the frequency imbalance (Hawkins et al., 1973, 1974). The interactions of the frequency effect with the S–R compatibility, the difficulty of response requirements, and, lastly, the effect of practice, seem to be crucial factors explaining the discrepancies between the results mentioned above and, thus, supporting the hypothesis of a response bias, as was emphasized by Posner (1966), Sanders (1970), and, more recently, by Theios (1975). Similarly, the fact that sequential effects, especially the repetition effect, could be found selectively related to the nature of the response (Bertelson, 1965; Kornblum, 1973; Smith, Chase, & Smith, 1973) strongly suggests that preparatory adjustments can modify the time required for the different stages of the response information processing.

As noted in the introductory remarks, physiological correlates of the event-probability effect were investigated in studies devoted to selective attention processes and, therefore, mainly concerned with the changes observed in the activity of sensory and perceptual systems. For instance, Hillyard (1974), Sutton, Braren, and Zubin (1965), Tueting and Sutton (1973), and Tueting, Sutton, and Zubin, (1971) have shown that the amplitude of the late components of the evoked potentials partly depended on S–R probability. As far as we know, no attempts were made to find such a relationship by recording the activity or the reactivity of nervous motor structures. An indication in this direction can be nevertheless found in a study by Davis (1952), showing that the increase of electromyographic activity during the foreperiod of an auditory RT task was less centered upon the muscles involved in performing the response when a choice paradigm was used than when a simple one was used.

This experiment was designed to determine whether or not the strength of the depressive control exerted by the supraspinal structures upon the involved motoneuron pool during the PP could be modulated according to the response probability in a classical choice-RT with unequally likely SR alternatives.

A.   Method

Twelve right-handed subjects, six males and six females, 25 to 37 years old, performed a two-choice RT task during two sessions. In each session there were 8 series of 48 trials. Within each series, the response was an extension either of the right or left foot, respectively, when the visual RS was presented, in random order, either 5 cm to the right or 5 cm to the left of the median plane of the display panel. The subject had to keep his eyes fixed on an intermediate point during the whole experiment. For six subjects relative probabilities of the right and left RSs were .75 and .25 in the first, and .25 and .75 in the second session. Probability assignments were reversed for the other six subjects.

B. Results

The evolution of H-reflex amplitude during the PP is shown in Fig. 4 for the right and left soleus, when the probability for each of them to perform the movement was either .75 or .25. The results of a three-way (H-reflex delay during the PP X muscle:right or left, X probability assignment:.75 or .25) analysis of variance are presented in Table 2. The effects of the two main factors upon H-reflex amplitude (side of the muscle and probability of performing the response) are shown in Fig. 5.

It appears that the decreasing course of excitability during the PP ($F = 6.56, p < .001$) is mainly, if not only, modulated by the side of the muscle ($F = 5.28, p < .001$), while the interaction between the delay and probability effects is significant ($F = 2.24, p < .05$). It must be noted that RT performance strongly differs according to the S–R relative probability ($F = 24.21, p < .001$), the low probability resulting in slower RT (285 msec) than the high probability (245 msec).

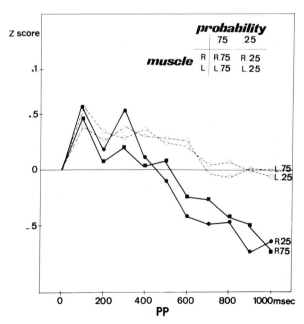

FIG. 4 Evolution during the PP of H-reflex amplitude in the right and left soleus according to the probability for each of them to be involved in the response performance.

TABLE 2

Experiment II: Analysis of Variance of H Reflex
Amplitude

Origin	MS	df	F
Delay (D)	3.312	9	6.56*
S × D	.505	81	
Muscle (M)	11.072	1	6.64**
S × M	1.667	9	
D × M	.665	9	5.28*
S × D × M	.126	81	
Probability (p)	.001	1	.00
S × p	.207	9	
D × p	.093	9	2.24**
S × D × p	.042	81	
M × p	.048	1	.16
S × M × p	.292	9	
D × M × p	.120	9	1.37
S × D × M × p	.087	81	

*$p < .05$.
**$p < .001$.

C. Discussion

These results confirm the laterality effect pointed out in the first experiment, but do not lead to any positive conclusion as to a differential modulation of the supraspinal depressive control according to the probability to respond, in other words, to the degree of involvement in the execution of the task.

While the interaction between H delay and probability effects is statistically significant, it is rather difficult to claim that the changes in the probability for the muscle to respond result in a differential time course of H-reflex amplitude. The slope of the two curves is slightly different because they cross at the middle of the PP course, but it is obvious too that the excitability level reached at the time of the RS does not differ according to the probability for the muscle to perform the response.

Considering the simple RT paradigm used in the first experiment as a limiting case with a probability bias of 1:0, it could be possible to predict that a probability bias of .75:.25 would result in similar but reduced effects, that is, a depressive control more marked in the more often involved muscle than in the less often involved one. In fact, when the right soleus was less involved, a slight strengthening of the depressive effect was observed (Fig. 4), while no clear tendency appears for the left soleus. Thus, with a probability bias of .75:.25, the depressive control of spinal excitability does not seem to reflect the changes in the involvement of the muscle, at least in an experimental condition in which

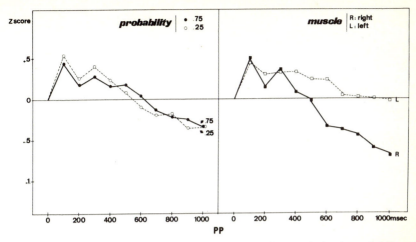

FIG. 5 Same data as in Fig. 4, but separating the effects of, respectively, the probability of response involvement, regardless of the side of the muscle (on the left), and the side of the muscle, regardless of its involvement probability (on the right).

the two limbs differentially involved in the motor performance were bilaterally symmetrical.

By changing the absolute rather than the relative probability to respond, Gerilovski and Tsekov (1971) have compared the evolution of H-reflex amplitude during the 1-sec PP of a simple RT task ($p = 1.0$) and a "go–no go"-RT task ($p = .50$ or $.25$ according to conditions). They found that the depression of the H-reflex amplitude during the second half of the PP was more accentuated with the high-response probability than with low-response probabilities. Nevertheless, their data do not give any evidence for a monotonous relationship between the degree of involvement and the depth of the depressive control. By replicating such an experiment (Requin *et al.,* unpublished results) we observed only a slight difference in the time course of spinal excitability, the decreasing course of H-reflex amplitude being a little sharper in the simple RT condition. However, it is not clear that such comparisons between experimental conditions in which the absolute probability of the response is manipulated with a "go–no go"-RT paradigm are relevant to the study of the covariations between the strength of the depressive supraspinal control and the probability for the muscle to be involved in the motor performance. The lack of the RS in a large number of trials, with different ratios, probably introduces corresponding decreases in the amount of information making the subjective estimation of the PP duration possible. The changes observed in the time course of H-reflex amplitude could be therefore related to time-uncertainty effects only.

Moreover, it must be underlined that, in any case, the large effect of S–R probability upon RT performance, regularly found in those experiments, does not result in corresponding changes at the level of the excitability of spinal motor structures. These negative data are in accord with the more recent conclusions of psychologists, previously quoted, that the response bias which partly explains the relative probability effect probably intervenes very early in the response information processing, for instance, at the levels of the S–R coding or even of the presetting of the motor program. In both cases, this does not necessarily imply any consequence at the terminal stage of the response organization.

V. EXPERIMENT III: EFFECT OF THE INVOLVEMENT OF THE MUSCLE AS AGONIST OR ANTAGONIST

There is increasing evidence in the field of experimental psychology for the part played in choice-RT experiments by event uncertainty, defined as the probability of events to which the subject is instructed to give precise responses. In contrast, there are few data concerning the changes in choice-RT depending upon the biomechanical aspects of the motor responses to be performed in conditions in which event uncertainty per se remains fixed. This lack of information can be explained, in part, by the methodology generally used in RT experiments, in which the complexity of the response is intentionally reduced as much as possible by using a key-pressing task. But here, too, the low interest in investigating the motor side of information processing is probably a more likely explanation.

However, from the results obtained by Fitts et al. (1963), Gibbs (1965), Megaw (1972), and Semjen (1970), it appears that, all things being equal, a greater impairment of RT results from an increase in the uncertainty related to the direction of the movement to be performed than from an increase in the uncertainty related to the amplitude of the movement. Such a relationship, first shown in step-tracking tasks, has been found again and specified by Fiori, Semjen, and Requin (1974) in a visuo–manual pointing task. The effect of direction uncertainty was found to be related to the angle formed by the courses of the movements that the subject had to perform in a two-choice RT paradigm. RT increased from $0°$ to $135°$, and then very slightly decreased for $180°$. These results were interpreted in terms of preparatory pattern incompatibility, from the hypothesis that the specificity of the preparation set up before the movement was lower, and thus RT was slower, when the alternative responses given to the subject were reciprocally more exclusive in terms of the underlying neuro-muscular synergies.

One could therefore suggest that the specificity of these neuromuscular synergies would appear in the supraspinal control of spinal excitability during the preparatory process. The third experiment was designed in order to see whether or not the course of H-reflex amplitude in the same motoneuron pool differs

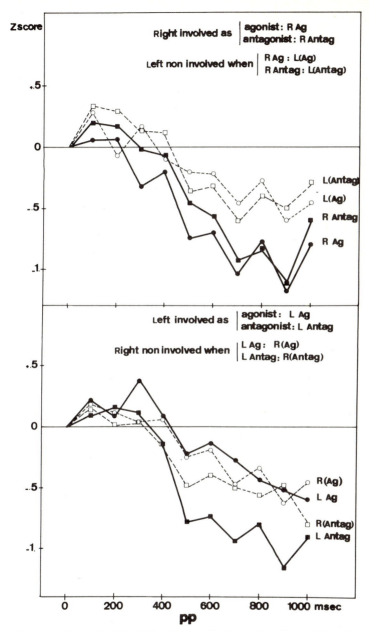

FIG. 6 Evolution during the PP of H-reflex amplitude in the right and left soleus, when either the right one (above) or left one (below) was involved, either as agonist or as antagonist in the movement. Corresponding data for the muscle of the opposite side were shown.

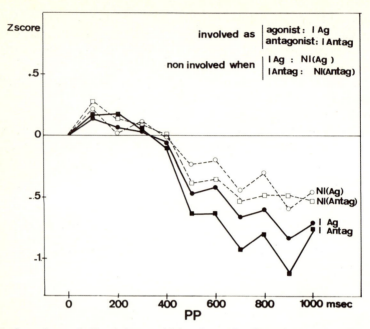

FIG. 7   Same data as in Fig. 6, but combining the results observed when the right and the left soleus were involved in the movement.

when the corresponding muscle is involved as agonistic or antagonistic to the movement.

A. Method

Ten right-handed subjects, 25 to 37 years old, performed a simple RT task during two sessions. From one session to another the responding foot was changed from right to left for five subjects and in the reversed order for the five other subjects. In each session there were 8 series of 48 trials. When the subject was at rest, the position of the pedal was adjusted by two antagonistic spiral springs, allowing the subject to make extension or flexion movements of the foot of the same angular amplitude. The response movement was an extension during four series and a dorsal flexion during the four other series, alternately presented to the subject.

B. Results

The evolution of H-reflex amplitude during the PP is shown in Fig. 6 for the right (above) and left (below) soleus, when they were involved either as agonists or as antagonists in the response movement. In both cases, the corresponding evolution of H-reflex amplitude in the noninvolved muscle of the opposite body side is shown. A sum of these results, combining the data obtained when the right or left soleus was involved in the response performance, is presented in Fig. 7. The results of a four-way analysis (H-reflex delay during the PP, X muscle: right or left, X involvement:yes or not, X function of the involved muscle: agonist or antagoinst) are shown in Table 3 for H-reflex data.

The decreasing course of H-reflex amplitude during the PP $(F = 9.08, p <$ .001) appears slightly modulated by the motor function played by the involved muscle, but only when the response movement was performed by the left foot:

TABLE 3
Experiment III: Analysis of Variance H Reflex
Amplitude

Origin	MS	df	F
Delay (D)	6.139	9	9.08
S × D	.675	45	
Muscle (M)	.011	1	.00
S × M	2.820	9	
D × M	.146	5	.29
S × D × M	.503	9	
Involvement (I)	5.106	45	1.90
S × I	2.682	5	
D × I	.227	9	1.23
S × D × I	.184	45	
M × I	2.618	1	.70
S × M × I	3.732	5	
D × M × I	.063	9	.24
S × D × M × I	.261	45	
Involved: Function (F)	.693	1	1.57
S × F	.439	5	
D × F	.105	9	1.01
S × D × F	.104	45	
M × F	3.942	1	10.54*
S × M × F	.373	5	
D × M × F	.112	9	.88
S × D × M × F	.127	45	
Noninvolved: Function (F)	.307	1	.72
S × F	.425	5	
D × F	.080	9	1.08
S × D × F	.074	45	
M × F	.017	1	.05
S × M × F	.368	5	
D × M × F	.103	9	1.90
S × D × M × F	.054	45	

*$p < .001$.
**$p < .05$.

the depression of H-reflex amplitude during the second half of the PP is greater when the left soleus is involved as an antagonist in the response movement than when it is involved as an agonist. In the latter case, the course of excitability does not differ from that observed in the right noninvolved muscle. Once again, this difference between right and left sides explains the summarized results shown in Fig. 7 and the significant interaction between the side of the muscle and its functional role in the movement (F = 10.54, $p < .05$).

C. Discussion

As previously mentioned, knowledge of the direction of the response movement to be performed results in an improvement of RT. Concerning a pair of movements in opposite directions, this knowledge thus implies that the functional role of the muscle involved as either agonist or antagonist in the control of the movement can be anticipated. Suppose, first, that such a preselection of the functional role of the muscle is included in the preparatory adjustments to the execution stage of the response, and, second, that the decreasing course of spinal excitability is a peripheral aspect of such adjustments, then a differential modulation of the depressive control could be expected when the subject knows that the muscle will be involved as either an agonist or an antagonist in the response.

Such advance information concerning the functional role of the soleus muscle does not result in a distinct difference in the decreasing course of H-reflex amplitude during the PP. Although this decrease is a little sharper when the left soleus is involved as an antagonist than when it is involved as an agonist, a slightly reversed tendency is observed in the right soleus, but both these effects probably do not attain statistical significance. In a similarly designed experiment, Gerilovski and Tsekov (1972) did not find any difference in the time course of H-reflex amplitude in the gastrocnemius muscle involved either as an agonist or as an antagonist in extension or flexion movements of the foot. Analyzing the course of spinal excitability before and during the same movements performed spontaneously without any WS or RS, Coquery and Coulmance (1971) observed that H-reflex amplitude just before the electromyogram of the response was relatively higher when the soleus was involved as an antagonist than when it was involved as an agonist, but this difference was not significant.

Therefore one must conclude that the effect of the muscle involvement on the course of spinal excitability before the response is not only focused upon the motoneuron pool controlling the muscle whose contraction moves the body segment, but probably also affects spinal structures corresponding to the synergistic or antagonistic muscles acting upon the same joint or even located in the same limb. However, because of the characteristics of the motor system analyzed, which obviously was chosen merely for imperative technical reasons, this conclusion has to be taken with some reservation.

First of all, the soleus muscle and its functional antagonist, the tibialis anterior muscle, cannot be merely considered as antagonistic muscles in the same way as, for instance, extensors or flexors of the fingers or of the arm. They are, in fact, mainly concerned with the postural stabilization of the body, in which their coactivation is the rule, but rarely with rapid movements involving their phasic and isolated contraction. Moreover, the antagonistic motor system can be considered, as regards the problem of preparatory adjustments to the execution of the motor program, as a limiting and special case. Because antagonistic muscles are controlled through the fixed nervous circuits of the reciprocal innervation, it can be suggested that a differential preparation is useless, at least prior to the execution of one of the two opposite motor programs. An indication in this direction can be found in the results of our previous experiment concerning the effect of direction uncertainty of arm movements upon a two-choice RT (Fiori et al., 1974). While a monotonous increase of RT was observed when the angle between the course of both movements increased from $0°$ to $135°$, a relative decrease appeared for $180°$, for antagonistic movements, which suggested, according to our hypothetical background, a decrease in the incompatibility of the corresponding preparatory patterns.

VI. EXPERIMENT IV: EFFECT OF THE EXPECTED FORCE TO PERFORM THE MOVEMENT

As previously stressed, direction uncertainty was found to be an important factor determining choice RT, but there were some discrepancies between the results concerning the effect of uncertainty related to the amplitude of the response movement. While such a factor seemed to have no effect upon choice RT in step-tracking tasks (Gibbs, 1965; Megaw, 1972; Semjen, 1970), the response latency in a visuo–manual pointing task was found to grow when the sum of the distances of the targets from the common starting point of both movements was increased (Fiori et al., 1974).

Although, in the latter study, the effects of varying uncertainty related to the amplitude of movement were found on choice RT but not on simple RT, the interpretation of the data remained difficult. Because the diameter of the targets was fixed in this experiment, the changes experimentally introduced in the distance of these targets resulted in covariations of the relative accuracy required by the pointing movements. On the other hand, the speed of these movements was found to be greater when the distance of the targets was increased, suggesting that corresponding changes were induced by the dynamic conditions of triggering the movement. It was thus possible to suggest two different explanations for RT impairment with amplitude uncertainty, emphasizing either the initial stage of the movement, in which dynamic conditions of triggering would be crucial, or the terminal stage of the movement, in which accuracy of pointing would be crucial.

The fourth experiment especially focused upon the examination of the first hypothesis. It was designed in order to see whether or not the dynamic conditions in triggering the movement are specifically prepared and, thus, appear in a differential organization of the changes in spinal excitability during the PP. In order to control more precisely this experimental factor, the dynamic conditions in the initiation of the movement were manipulated by varying the elastic force opposed to the rotation of the ankle, rather than by varying the angular amplitude of such a movement.

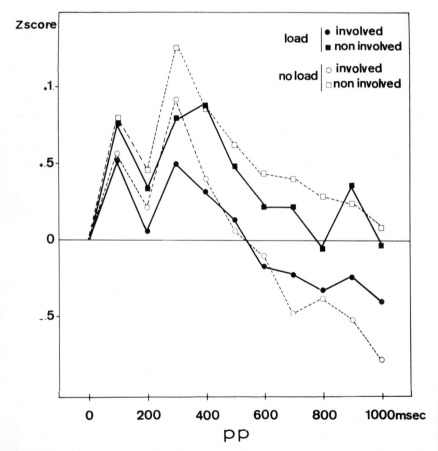

FIG. 8 Evolution during the PP of H-reflex amplitude in the right-involved and left-noninvolved soleus in the two conditions of loading.

A. Method

Sixteen right-handed subjects, 25 to 37 years old, performed a simple RT task during one session. There were 8 series of trials, alternatively performed by the subject in two different conditions. In the first condition, requirements of the response—movement were the same as in the previous experiments ("no load" condition), whereas in the second condition, the force that the subject had to develop to move the pedal was strongly increased by adding a weight of 7 kg in opposition to the rotation of the ankle ("load" condition). The response—movement was always an extension of the right foot.

B. Results

The evolution of H-reflex amplitude during the PP is shown in Fig. 8 for the right-involved and left-noninvolved muscles in both conditions. The results of a three-way (delay of H reflex in the PP, X condition:"load" or "no load", X involvement:yes or no) analysis of variance are shown in Table 4 for H-reflex data.

Although the activatory effects of the WS, peaking 300 msec later, seem to be reduced when the load was added, the decreasing course of H-reflex amplitude ($F = 10.18$, $p < .001$) does not differ according to the conditions of motor performance ($F = 1.21$). Only the muscle involvement had a significant effect

TABLE 4
Experiment IV: Analysis of Variance of H Reflex
Amplitude

Origin	MS	df	F
Delay (D)	6.921	9	10.18*
S × D	.680	135	
Condition (C)	3.119	1	2.82
S × C	1.105	15	
D × C	.262	9	1.21
S × D × C	.215	135	
Involvement (I)	25.993	1	10.22**
S × I	2.544	15	
D × I	.327	9	1.17
S × D × I	.279	135	
C × I	1.440	1	2.08
S × C × I	.692	15	
D × C × I	.083	9	.57
S × D × C × I	.145	135	

*$p < .001$
**$p < .01$

upon excitability ($F = 10.22$, $p < .01$), but one must recall that it could only be due to a right—left difference effect which was not balanced in this experiment.

On the other hand, it can be noted that RT is significantly slower ($F = 21.87$, $p < .001$) in the "load" condition (257 msec) than in the "no load" condition (239 msec).

C. Discussion

We must note that changes of dynamic conditions in the triggering of the response, as well as the response probability and the variations of the direction of the movement, do not result in a clear differential modulation of the motor spinal structure reactivity during preparation.

If the dynamic conditions in the triggering of the response had been manipulated by changing the amplitude of the movement to be performed, this negative result would be in accord with the suggestions of Megaw (1972) and Semjen (1970). According to these authors, the programming of movement amplitude is relatively late in the timing of the reaction process. Therefore, it would not be surprising if such programming were not preceded by early preparatory adjustments, especially during the PP.

In this experiment, the increase of the elastic resistance that the subject had to overcome in order to perform the response presupposes, prior to foot displacement, a development of isometric contraction in the muscle. During this time period, the progressive recruiting of active motoneurons permits the muscle to attain the force necessary to overcome the resistance. If the developed force closely depends upon the corticospinal control, especially through the pyramidal tract (Evarts, 1968), it is also true that the proprioceptive regulating system, especially from muscular spindles, assumes an important part in the recruiting of motoneurons during the isometric contraction before the movement. Several aspects of this servoassistance have been recently emphasized by neurophysiologists.

Taking these underlying mechanisms into account, the preparatory adjustments to motor performance would imply the setting up of peripheral conditions allowing the proprioceptive regulating system to provide a maximal assistance to the movement execution. In this experiment, this would suppose a weakening of the depressive supraspinal control in the "load" condition. The possible neurophysiological basis for such an hypothesis is discussed in the Conclusion. But, from this point of view, the slight dissociation between the excitability curves obtained in both conditions for the involved muscle cannot be neglected. Moreover, such a dissociation, that is, a depression of H-reflex amplitude less marked in the "load" condition than in the "no load" condition, was already found in a preliminary experiment (Semjen, unpublished results). Hence, it appears that supplementary investigations, using a more extended range of loads or of movement amplitudes, are necessary.

VII. CONCLUSION

In all these experiments the major finding is a widespread depression of the monosynaptic reflex pathways during the PP, while the elements of these pathways are involved in the motor performance. However, such a surprising conclusion that motor preparation would be expressed by an excitability decrease on motoneurons whose activity underlies the response execution, can, in fact, be contested, according to the possible neurophysiological mechanisms involved. The functional significance which can be attributed to an inhibitory supraspinal control, whose strength does not appear closely related to RT performance, also depends, in part, upon the solution given to this physiological problem. Finally, this weak specificity of the changes observed at the spinal level during preparation raises, in psychophysiological terms, the question of the locus in the response process of the WS effects, which, according to psychological data, undoubtedly result in precise preparatory adjustments to response requirements.

A. The Neurophysiological Mechanisms of the Decrease of
    H-Reflex Amplitude

As demonstrated in Fig. 1, a depression of a monosynaptic reflex response can result either from a postsynaptic inhibitory mechanism involving a genuine decrease of motoneuron excitability or from a presynaptic inhibitory mechanism acting upon the afferents to motorneurons, Ia fibers included. Incidentally, one must note that methodological implication of the later hypothesis, questioning the basis of reflexologic methods which postulate that reflex amplitude is directly related to the excitability state of motoneurons. A more correct formulation would be the reactivity state of spinal reflex pathways, without any possible direct inference concerning the motoneuron excitability itself. In a previous experiment we found that polysynaptic reflexes triggered by a stimulation of cutaneous afferents were also depressed during the PP of a simple RT task, thus excluding a presynaptic inhibitory mechanism selectively blocking the primary afferents from muscle spindles. Nevertheless, from these results the hypothesis of an extended presynaptic inhibition intervening upon all the afferents to motoneurons cannot be rejected (Bonnet & Requin, 1972).

Unfortunately, it seems clear that this neurophysiological problem could only be solved by microphysiological investigations which, obviously, cannot be performed in human subjects. However, it remains that many indirect arguments converge to sustain the presynaptic hypothesis. We have previously observed (Requin, 1965, 1967) an increase of the integrated electromyogram recorded in the involved muscle during the PP, that is, when monosynaptic reflexes are depressed. Such a dissociation between the activity and reactivity of spinal motor structures could only be understood by a presynaptic inhibitory mechanism decreasing the reflexogenic effect of the electrical stimulation, but maintaining the accessibility of motoneurons to central influences, if one excludes the unverified hypothesis that spontaneous activity and reflex activity would not be controlled by the same motoneurons within spinal motor structures. But it was also noted that the slight depression of H reflexes either just before the movement performance (Pierrot-Deseilligny *et al.,* 1971), or at the end of the PP (Requin, 1967), as well as the reflexes triggered in the preferred side soleus (Bonnet & Lacour, 1973), are associated with an increase in the variability of the response amplitude. This phenomenon could be explained by a general disconnection of the motoneuron pool from its afferents, which, by reducing exogenic sources of variance, would increase the correlation between motoneuron unitary activities and, thus, would increase the variability of the global response of the motor structure. Finally, the present set of experiments shows no clear covariation between the depth of the H-reflex depression observed in different conditions and RT performance. However, looking at the relationship between H-reflex amplitude and RT within a series of trials, we generally found, for the involved muscle, a slight correlation of negative sign, the greater the reflex amplitude the faster the RT (Requin, 1969; Semjen *et al.,* 1973). Such a discrepancy would be easily explainable if an extended presynaptic inhibitory control during the PP would not suppress the motoneuron pool accessibility to activatory influences which increase the motoneuron reactivity to the central command triggering the motor program execution. Such an hypothesis is closely related to the problem of the functional meaning of the depressive control.

B. The Functional Significance of a Depressive Supraspinal Control During Preparation

These results clarify to some extent the possible functional meaning of a depressive control upon either the spinal motor structure excitability or the spinal reflex pathway reactivity during preparation.

One of the three hypotheses which we previously suggested (Requin & Paillard, 1971) can certainly be rejected. Suppose that the decrease of H-reflex amplitude in the involved muscle could result either from a very slight activity of the antagonistic muscle involving a preparatory flexion of the foot in order to assist the extension by a previous "winding up" movement, or, even, from an excitability increase of the corresponding motoneuron pool which would make the antagonistic muscle ready to repress an early triggering of the response. In both cases, the depression of H reflexes in the involved muscle would be explainable by the postsynaptic motoneuron inhibition through activation, either from central structures or from muscular afferents, of the reciprocal innervation system. But we never found any increase of the electromyographic activity of the tibialis anterior muscle during the PP; moreover, it is clear now, from the results of the third experiment, that when the soleus muscle acts as an antagonist in the movement, H reflexes are also depressed.

It was hypothesized that such depression could reflect a selective isolation of motoneurons from their muscular afferents, in relation to the necessity for the motor structures involved in performing the response to free themselves from stabilizing myotatic influences contributing to the locking of the position of joints which have to remain fixed during the movement. Unfortunately, it appears that the reflex pathway reactivity depression is not limited to mono-synaptic reflexes involving muscular afferents, but also affects polysynaptic reflexes (Bonnet & Requin, 1972). Moreover, in the fourth experiment, the changes in the resistance opposed to motor performance undoubtedly resulted in variations of the role played by the postural stabilizing system. In the "load" condition, for instance, because the performance of a strong lateralized move-ment disturbing the body equilibrium certainly involved a strengthening of this system, either a relative increase of H-reflex amplitude reflecting a muscular afferent input increase, or, on the contrary, a strengthening of the depressive control in opposition to such activatory influences could be expected. The lack of change in spinal excitability observed when loading conditions were varied would thus be reconcilable with such an hypothetical interpretation only if one supposes that the strength of the inhibitory control is adjusted to the amount of muscular afferences, in order to maintain the motoneuron excitability, or reflex pathway reactivity, fixed just before the movement.

Finally, whereas the latter interpretation cannot be excluded, it very likely has to be included in a more general hypothesis. The widespread supraspinal control of the spinal motor system during preparation — depressing monosynaptic as well as polysynaptic reflexes, overlapping the structures which are not directly or primarily involved in the movement execution, and intervening even when the response has a low probability to be performed — could reflect a large isolation of the active spinal motor structures from all irrelevant inputs of peripheral origin, this could possibly trigger an anticipated response or disturb the prepara-tory patterning of these structures. The interpretative value of a possible presyn-aptic inhibitory mechanism in this direction must be underlined. In such a case, the transient protective isolation of the motoneuron pool, reflecting an active suspension of the response process until the RS occurs, could be insured without a real decrease of motoneuron accessibility to facilitatory influences of central origin and, obviously, to the future motor command.

C. The Locus of WS Effects Making Preparatory Adjustments Specific

This set of experiments was designed according to the hypothesis that the preparatory adjustments triggered by the WS would result in spinal motor structure excitability changes, modulating the execution of the motor program. From the weak specificity of these changes in function of response require-ments, it cannot be concluded that the WS does not trigger preparatory adjust-ments in the motor system, but only that these adjustments could intervene at different stages in the response organization, not necessarily resulting in a corresponding patterning of spinal structure excitability (Fig. 9).

In this direction, cortical structures and reticular formations of the brain stem could be especially involved, not only because the role they play in the control of spinal activity through corticospinal and reticulospinal pathways is well known, but also because they are potentially multispecific, that is, characterized more by their extended possibilities of short-term functional reorganization than by their anatomically fixed nervous circuits. One can, for instance, suggest that the information given by the WS is primarily used in a presetting of the motor program, intervening at the highest level in nervous organization. Such a preset-

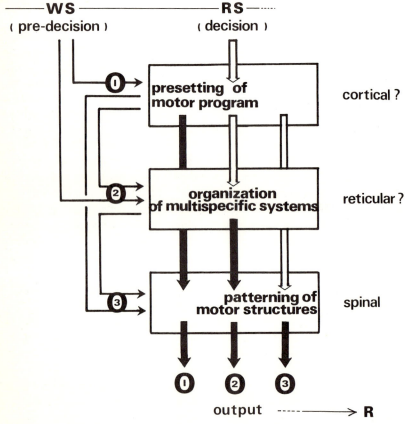

FIG. 9 Schematization of the three possible levels in the motor organization in which the preparatory adjustments triggered by the WS could intervene. This diagram takes into account the likely nervous pathways (on the left) and structures (on the right) involved. In each hypothetical mechanism, the vertical arrow corresponding to the execution stage of the response is changed from white to black as soon as preparatory adjustments are effective in modulating the motor program.

ting could imply either an assembling of elementary subroutines in the motor memory register or, on the contrary, a specification of a more suitable program taken from a more standard one, that, in both cases, would make this preselected motor program more easily available. In this way, the motor command triggered by the WS would already have the benefit of preparation before being executed by spinal motor structures, without any change in the excitability state of these latter structures beforehand. A similar suggestion can be made at the intermediary level of reticular formations which, regardless of their role in the regulation of activation level, could be, in part, functionally reorganized, directly or through cortico–reticular pathways, depending on WS significance. In such a case, the motor program execution triggered by the RS would not, or not only, be preceded by relatively specific reticulospinal influences, but rather accompanied by such influences, acting simultaneously with the cortical command at the spinal level.

Moreover, these three hypotheses concerning the locus of WS effects in the response process are compatible and even suggest a hierarchical organization, implying that the different preparatory adjustments to response factors are not taken into account at the same level in the motor system. For instance, according to psychological data showing that the response bias in the relative frequency effect intervenes at the S–R coding stage or even at the motor program selection stage, it could be proposed that the cortical level is mainly involved in these preparatory adjustments. Similarly, the preparatory modifications of the postural system which had to be remodified, or adjusted, in order to be compatible with the biomechanical requirements of the movement, would be insured by a preorganization of the brain stem reticular system, according to the relative specificity now admitted for reticulospinal effects. Finally, the preparatory patterning at the spinal level would be restricted to the weakly specific protective control of spinal structures which we have principally found. Whereas its central origin seems to be unquestionable, its precise neurophysiological mechanism remains to be found. One can, nevertheless, suggest that it could be cortically controlled, resulting in an overregulation of the WS alertness effects.

Unfortunately, from a methodological point of view, the possibilities of investigation suggested by such hypotheses are still limited. While, as we underlined in the Introduction, reflexologic methods were very suitable and easily utilizable to analyze the changes in spinal structure excitability, the experimental access to reticular or cortical preparatory processes remains problematic. An analysis of the functional organization of brain stem reticular formations requires difficult chronic experiments in animals, especially due to unavoidable limits in the manipulation of psychological factors. Investigations of the concomitants of motor preparatory adjustments at the level of cortical activity would probably be easier, especially when the relative specificity of the motor potentials which precede the movement execution is taken into account (Vaughan & Ritter, 1973).

ACKNOWLEDGMENTS

We are indebted to N. Fiori, G. Reynard and N. Viton for technical assistance in various aspects of this work.

REFERENCES

Alegria, J. *Contribution expérimentale à l'étude des ajustements préparatoires à court terme.* Doctoral dissertation, Brusells, 1975.

Bathien, N. Réflexes spinaux chez l'Homme et niveaux d'attention. *Electroencephalography and Clinical Neurophysiology,* 1971, **30,** 32–37.

Bathien, N., & Hugelin, A. Réflexes monosynaptiques et polysynaptiques de l'Homme au cours de l'attention. *Electroencephalography and Clinical Neurophysiology,* 1969, **26,** 604–612.

Bernstein, I. H., Shurman, D. L., & Forester, G. Choice reaction time as a function of stimulus uncertainty, response uncertainty and behavioral hypotheses. *Journal of Experimental Psychology,* 1967, **74,** 517–524.

Bertelson, P. Serial choice reaction time as a function of response versus signal and response repetition. *Nature,* 1965, **208,** 217–218.

Bertelson, P., & Tisseyre, F. Choice reaction time as a function of stimulus versus response relative frequency of occurrence. *Nature,* 1966, **212,** 1069–1070.

Bonnet, M., & Lacour, M. H-reflex variations and motor dominance. *Electroencephalography and Clinical Neurophysiology,* 1973, **34,** 810.

Bonnet, M., & Requin, J. Variations des réflexes polysynaptiques cutanés au cours de la période préparatoire au temps de réaction chez l'Homme. *Psychologie française,* 1972, **17,** 101–112.

Bowdich, H., & Warren, J. W. The knee-jerk and its physiological modifications. *Journal of Psychology,* 1890, **11,** 25–64.

Brunia, C. H. M. The influence of a task on the Achilles tendon and Hoffmann reflex. *Physiology and Behavior,* 1971, **6,** 367–373.

Brunia, C. H. M. The influence of Metamphetamine and Diazepam on the amplitude changes of the Achilles tendon and Hoffmann reflex during a mental task. *Physiology and Behavior,* 1972, **8,** 1025–1028.

Coquery, J.-M. Attitude préparatoire et variations de l'excitabilité spinale induites par un son. *Physiology and Behavior,* 1969, **4,** 297–302.

Coquery, J.-M., & Coulmance, M. Variations d'amplitude des réflexes avant un mouvement volantaire. *Physiology and Behavior,* 1971, **6,** 65–69.

Crossman, E. R. Entropy and choice time: The effect of frequency unbalance on choice response. *Quarterly Journal of Experimental Psychology,* 1953, **5,** 41–51.

Daniel, R. S. Some observations on Meyer's study of reaction time and muscle tension. *Journal of Experimental Psychology,* 1949, **39,** 896–898.

Davis, R. C. Set and muscular tension. *Indiana University Publications Sciences V series,* 1940, n° 10.

Davis, R. C. Motor effects of strong auditory stimuli. *Journal of Experimental Psychology,* 1948, **38,** 257–275.

Davis, R. C. Motor responses to auditory stimuli above and below threshold. *Journal of Experimental Psychology,* 1950, **40,** 107–120.

Davis, R. C. The stimulus trace in effectors and its relation to judgment responses. *Journal of Experimental Psychology,* 1952, **44,** 377–390.

Davis, R. C. Response and adaptation to brief noises of high intensity. *USAF School Aviation Medicine Report,* 1953, *55* (Whole No. 127).

Davis, R. C. Electromyographic factors in aircraft control. Experimental investigation of the effect of a muscle tension reflex upon simple instructed movements. *USAF School Aviation Medicine Report,* 1956, *55* (Whole No. 122). (a)

Davis, R. C. Electromyographic factors in aircraft control. Muscular activity during steady noise and its relation to instructed responses evoked by auditory signal. *USAF School Aviation Medicine Report,* 1956, *55* (Whole No. 124). (b)

Davis, R. C. Electromyographic factors in aircraft control. Muscular activity during steady noise and its relation to instructed responses evoked by visual signals. *USAF School Aviation Medicine Report,* 1956, *55* (Whole No. 126). (c)

Davis, R. C. Response pattern. *Trans New York Academy of Sciences,* 1957, **19,** 731–739.

Davis, R. C., Buchwald, A. M., & Frankmann, R. W. Autonomic and muscular responses and their relation to simple simuli. *Psychological Monographs,* 1955, *69* (Whole No. 20).

Dawson, H. E., & Davis, R. C. The effects of an instructed motor response upon somatic responses to a brief tone. *Journal of Comparative and Physiological Psychology,* 1957, **50,** 368–374.

Dillon, P. J. Stimulus versus response decisions as determinants of the relative frequency effect in disjunctive reaction time performance. *Journal of Experimental Psychology,* 1966, **71,** 321–330.

Donchin, E., & Kutas, M. Motor potentials, force of response and handedness. In *Proceedings of the International Symposium of Cerebral Evoked Potentials,* Brussels, 1974, 72–73.

Duffy, E. *Activation and behavior,* New York: Wiley, 1962.

Evarts, E. V. Relation of pyramidal tract activity to force exerted during voluntary movement. *Journal of Neurophysiology,* 1968, **31,** 14–27.

Evarts, E. V. General discussion. In J. Paillard & J. Massion (Eds.), *Motor aspects of behavior and programmed nervous activities. Brain Research,* 1973, **71,** 558.

Fink, J. B. Electromyographic factors in aircraft control. The development and loss of a muscle tension set to an incidental stimulus. *USAF School Aviation Medicine Report,* 1956, *55* (Whole No. 130).

Fiori, N., Semjen, A., & Requin, J. Analyse chronométrique du pattern préparatoire à un mouvement spatialement orienté. Résultats préliminaries. *Le Travail Humain,* 1974, **37,** 229–248.

Fitts, P. M., Peterson, J. R., & Wolpe, G. Cognitive aspects of information processing. II. Adjustments to stimulus redundancy. *Journal of Experimental Psychology,* 1963, **65,** 423–432.

Freeman, G. L. The facilitative and inhibitory effects of muscular tension upon performance. *American Journal of Psychology,* 1933, **45,** 17–52.

Gantchev, G. N. Neuronal activity and average evoked potential in the sensori-motor cortex of monkey related to the preparation for performing movement. *Brain Research,* 1977, in press.

Gerilovski, L., & Tsekov, T. Amplitude changes of H-reflex during a fixed waiting period as a function of absolute probability of the response signal. In *Visual Information Processing and Control of Motor Activity,* Sofia: Bulgarian Academy of Sciences, 1971. Pp. 397–401.

Gerilovski, L., & Tsekov, T. Amplitude changes of the H-reflex during a fixed waiting period when the tested muscle is agonist, antagonist or does not take part in the movement. *Agressologie,* 1972, **13,** 31–35.

Gibbs, C. B. Probability learning in step-input tracking. *British Journal of Psychology,* 1965, **56,** 233–242.

Hawkins, H. L., & Friedin, B. D. The relative frequency effect and S–R compatibility. *Psychonomic Science,* 1972, **28,** 329–330.

Hawkins, H. L., & Hosking, K. Stimulus probability as a determinant of discrete choice reaction time. *Journal of Experimental Psychology,* 1969, **82**, 435–440.

Hawkins, H. L., MacKay, S. L., Holley, S. L., Friedin, B. D., & Cohen, S. L. On the locus of the relative frequency effect in choice reaction time. *Journal of Experimental Psychology,* 1973, **101**, 90–99.

Hawkins, H. L., Snippel, K., Presson, J., MacKay, S. L., & Todd, D. Retrieval bias and the response relative frequency effect in choice reaction time. *Journal of Experimental Psychology,* 1974, **102**, 910–912.

Hawkins, H. L., Thomas, G. B., & Drury, K. B. Perceptual versus response bias in discrete choice reaction time. *Journal of Experimental Psychology,* 1970, **84**, 514–517.

Hawkins, H. L., & Underhill, J. R. S–R compatibility and the relative frequency effect in choice reaction time. *Journal of Experimental Psychology,* 1971, **91**, 280–286.

Henderson, R. L. Remote action potentials at the moment of response in a simple reaction-time stiuation. *Journal of Experimental Psychology,* 1952, **44**, 238–241.

Hillyard, S. A. Long-latency evoked potentials and selective attention. In *Proceedings of the International Symposium on cerebral evoked potentials in man,* Brussels, 1974, 105–108.

Hinrichs, J. V. Probability and expectancy in two-choice reaction time. *Psychonomic Science,* 1970, **21**, 227–228.

Hinrichs, J. V., & Krainz, P. L. Expectancy in choice reaction time: Stimulus vs response anticipation? *Journal of Experimental Psychology,* 1970, **85**, 330–334.

Hugon, M. Methodology of the Hoffmann Reflex in man. In J. E. Desmedt (Ed.), *New developments in electromyography and clinical neurophysiology.* Vol. 3. Basel: S. Karger, 1973, 277–293.

Hyman, R. Stimulus information as a determinant of reaction time. *Journal of Experimental Psychology,* 1953, **45**, 188–196.

Karlin, L. Cognition, preparation and sensory evoked potentials. *Psychological Bulletin,* 1970, **73**, 122–136.

Keele, S. W. Movement control in skilled motor performance. *Psychological Bulletin,* 1969, **70**, 387–403.

Kornblum, S. Sequential effects in choice reaction time: A tutorial review. In S. Kornblum (Ed.), *Attention and performance IV,* New York: Academic Press, 1973. Pp. 259–288.

LaBerge, D., Tweedy, J. R., & Ricker, J. Selective attention: Incentive variables and choice time. *Psychonomic Science,* 1967, **8**, 341–342.

LaBerge, D., Legrand, R., & Hobbie, R. K. Functional identification of perceptual and response biases in choice reaction time. *Journal of Experimental Psychology,* 1969, **79**, 295–299.

LaBerge, D., & Tweedy, J. R. Presentation probability and choice time. *Journal of Experimental Psychology,* 1964, **68**, 477–481.

Lacour, M., Bonnet, M., & Roll, J. P. Effets spinaux d'une stimulation vestibulaire électrique chez l'Homme. Mise en évidence d'une prévalence vestibulaire et du rôle de la latéralisation motrice. *Acta Otolaryngologia,* 1974, **78**, 399–409.

Landis, C., & Hunt, W. A. *The startle pattern.* New York: Farrar and Rinehart, 1939.

Leontiev, A. N., & Krinchik, C. P. On certain aspects of human information processing. *Sovietskaia Psychologia and Psychiatria,* 1963, **1**, 24–31.

Megaw, E. D. Direction and extent uncertainty in step-input tracking. *Journal of Motor Behavior,* 1972, **3**, 171–186.

Meyer, D. R. On the interaction of simultaneous responses. *Psychological Bulletin,* 1953, **50**, 204–220.

Moray, N. *Attention: Selective processes in vision and learning.* London: Hutchinson, 1969.

Morin, R. E., & Forrin, B. Response equivocation and reaction time. *Journal of Experimental Psychology,* 1963, **66**, 30–36.

Näätänen, R. Selective attention and evoked potentials in humans. A critical review. *Biological Psychology,* 1975, **2**, 237–307.

Paillard, J. *Réflexes et régulations d'origine proprioceptive chez l'Homme. Etude neurophysiologique et psychophysiologique.* Paris: Arnette, 1955.

Papakostopoulos, D., & Cooper, R. The contingent negative variation and the excitability of the spinal monosynaptic reflex. *Journal of Neurology, Neurosurgery and Psychiatry,* 1973, **36**, 1003–1010.

Patton, R. M. Electromyographic factors in aircraft control. The effect of induced tension upon muscular activity during simple voluntary movement. *USAF School Aviation Medicine Report,* 1957, **55** (Whole No. 33).

Pierrot-Deseilligny, F., Lacert, P., & Cathala, H. P. C. Amplitude et variabilité des réflexes monosynaptiques avant un mouvement volontaire. *Physiology and Behavior,* 1971, **7**, 495–508.

Posner, M. I. Components of skilled performance. *Science,* 1966, **152**, 1712–1718.

Rabbitt, P. M. A. Effects of independent variations in stimulus and response probability. *Nature,* 1959, **183**, 1212.

Requin, J. Quelques problèmes théoriques et méthodologiques posés par l'étude psychophysiologique de l'attitude préparatoire à l'action. *Cahiers de Psychologie,* 1965, **8**, 101–113.

Requin, J. Organisation de l'activité motrice préparatoire. In M. Richelle (Ed.), *Hommage à André Rey.* Bruxelles: Charles Dessart, 1967. Pp. 337–366.

Requin, J. Some data on neurophysiological processes involved in the preparatory motor activity to reaction time performance. *Acta Psychologica,* 1969, **30**, 358–367.

Requin, J., Bonnet, M., & Granjon, M. Evolution du niveau d' excitabilité médullaire chez l'Homme au cours de la période préparatoire au temps de réaction. *Journal de Physiologie,* 1968, **60**, 293–294. (a)

Requin, J., Granjon, M., & Bonnet, M. Confrontation des données obtenues par l'exploration simultanée des réflexes tendineux et de Hoffmann au cours de la préparation à l'activité motrice chez l'Homme. *Journal de Physiologie,* 1968, **60**, 529–530. (b)

Requin, J., & Paillard, J. Depression of monosynaptic reflexes as a specific aspect of preparatory motor set in visual reaction time. In *Visual information processing and control of motor activity.* Sofia: Bulgarian Academy of Sciences, 1971. Pp. 391–396.

Sanders, A. F. Some variables affecting the relation between relative stimulus frequency and choice reaction time. In A. F. Sanders (Ed.), *Attention and performance III,* Amsterdam: North Holland Publ., 1970. Pp. 45–55.

Semjen, A. Phase organization of amplitude regulated movements. The "action threshold" of movement, the programming of its direction and amplitude. *Magyar Pszichologiai Szemle,* 1970, **28**, 355–363.

Semjen, A., Bonnet, M., & Requin, J. Relation between the time course of Hoffmann Reflexes and the preparatory period duration in a reaction time task. *Physiology and Behavior,* 1973, **10**, 1041–1050.

Smith, E. E., Chase, W. G., & Smith, P. G. Stimulus and response repetition effects in retrieval from short-term memory: Trace decay and memory search. *Journal of Experimental Psychology,* 1973, **98**, 413–422.

Sutton, S., Braren, M., & Zubin, J. Evoked potential correlates of stimulus uncertainty. *Science,* 1965, **150**, 1187–1188.

Theios, J. The components of response latency in simple human information processing tasks. In S. Dornic (Ed.), *Attention and performance V.* New York: Academic Press, 1975. Pp. 418–440.

Travis, R. C., & Kennedy, J. L. Prediction and automatic control of alertness. I. Control of lookout alertness. *Journal of Comparative and Physiological Psychology,* 1947, **40**, 457–461.

Tueting, P., Sutton, S., & Zubin, J. Quantitative evoked potential correlates of the probability of events. *Psychophysiology,* 1971, 7, 385–394.

Tueting, P., & Sutton, S. The relationship between prestimulus negative shifts and poststimulus components of the averaged evoked potential. In S. Kornblum (Ed.), *Attention and performance IV.* New York: Academic PRess, 1973. Pp. 185–207.

Vaughan, H. G., & Ritter, W. Physiological approaches to the analysis of attention and performance, In S. Kornblum (Ed.), *Attention and performance IV.* New York: Academic Press, 1973. Pp. 129–154.

Part II

MASKING AND EARLY PROCESSING

9
Perceptual and Response Interdependencies in Visual Masking

Ira H. Bernstein
Dan B. Smith
Michael Adey

Department of Psychology
The University of Texas
Arlington, Texas, United States

ABSTRACT

Most theories of visual masking view the mask in relatively literal terms as a stimulus which destroys information to impair perception. Consequently, definitions of visual masking are phrased solely in terms of this perceptual impairment. In this chapter we consider the possibility that impairment results because the mask both creates misleading cues and destroys valid ones. A consequence of this view is that one need study more than just impairment, for example, one need explore the subject's criterion content (Kahneman, 1968). Hake, Rodwan, and Weintraub's (1966) noise reduction model, which emphasizes the misleading effects of irrelevant but compelling cues, formed the basis for a theory of metacontrast suppression. It was hypothesized that the reason the test appears dim is that information about its brightness is extracted by comparing its rapidly fading trace to a subsequently presented mask. Garner and Morton's (1970) related views on perceptual independence were applied to a task involving recognition of a sequentially presented pair of letters, each of which could be a B or D, independently of the other. The obtained masking function was symmetric for forward and backward masking conditions.

I. INTRODUCTION

Visual masking is typically defined as a "class of situations in which the effectiveness of a visual stimulus . . . is reduced by the presentation of another . . . in close temporal contiguity [Kahneman, 1968, p. 404]." Though most investigators recognize that the two stimuli exert mutual though not necessarily equal influences upon one another, response measures are typically obtained for only one of the stimuli (the test) and not for the other (the mask). In this chapter, we will follow the terminology used by Kahneman (1968) to describe the concepts used in the masking literature and consider, in two specific cases, why impairment arises. The first case involves a U-shaped masking function in which maximum impairment occurs when the mask is delayed rather than presented concurrently. In so doing we also hope to show why limiting discussion to impairment obscures several processes basic to visual information processing.

II. TWO GENERAL APPROACHES TO MASKING

Many theories of visual masking tend to view the role of the mask in essentially literal terms. That is, the mask is conceptualized as something that hides (obscures, covers, etc.) the test in one way or another. In so doing, the mask is assumed to destroy cues furnished by the test that would normally be available. The specifics of this process differ among the various theories. Sperling (1963) argued that the mask interrupts the readout of a visual image of the test and prevents its verbal encoding. This interruption causes the mask to replace the test in the visual system. Bridgeman (1971) and Weisstein (1968, 1972) argued that the destruction arises from lateral inhibition which prevents contour formation from occurring. Eriksen (1966), in discussing masking by a homogenous light flash, argued that the test and mask became integrated into a composite or montage having a lower contrast ratio than that possessed by the test alone.

A smaller but more important class of alternative theories hypothesize that the mask may create cues which are misleading or which conflict with other cues. Kahneman (1967, 1968) noted that test–mask interactions in metacontrast configurations provide contradictory movement cues. Suppression of the test prevents violation of perceptual stability by preventing an object from seeming to move to two places at once.

Eriksen (1966; Eriksen, Becker, & Hoffman, 1970; Eriksen & Eriksen, 1971) has also noted how a mask may create cues in some cases, although he tends to view the effects of these created cues as extrinsic to masking effects proper. For example, Eriksen et al. (1970) used the letters O and D as test alternatives in one study and the letters H and K as test alternatives in another study. Masking was more pronounced in the latter case. The authors indicated that this was due to the cue furnished by the relation of the left side of the test to the mask in the first study that was not present in the second study. Thus, with O versus D, the mask would serve as a frame of reference to see whether the left side of the test was straight or curved.

We view masking effects present in the literature as a collection of various processes. Hence, we do not see cue destruction and cue creation as necessarily mutually exclusive. In some cases, most specifically masking by a light flash, cue destruction effects seem a sufficient explanation. However, we see cue creation in pattern masking and, especially, in metacontrast as an overlooked process intrinsic to performance.

There are two important consequences of investigating masking in terms of cues created by the mask that we now consider. One of these is that judgments about the test may be made on the basis of some cues that are relevant to the requisite judgment and others that are irrelevant. The subject's task may be viewed as one of attempting to separate these two sets of cues, and masking may be viewed as an incorrect resolution of this separation problem. The other consequence arises if we ask the subject to make some form of judgment about what is nominally called the mask as well as the test. Here, covariances may well arise between the judgmental processes for the two stimuli. The first of these topics has been considered by Hake and his associates (Hake *et al.,* 1966; Hake & Rodwan, 1967; Hake, Faust, McIntyre, & Murray, 1967; Rodwan & Hake, 1964; Friden, 1973; Weintraub, 1971) and the second by Garner and Morton (1970). Both approaches suggest powerful analytic tools to investigate how well a subject can disentangle a complex of information and respond to what is relevant and emerged from the approach to perception stated in the work of Garner, Hake, and Eriksen (1956). Alternatively, Hake's approach emphasizes the problem of focusing attention, and Garner and Morton's approach emphasizes the problem of divided attention (Treisman, 1969). We feel that the reason these approaches have not been properly applied to masking is because of the traditional emphasis upon impairment. It is the purpose of this chapter to explore the application of these approaches.

III. NOISE REDUCTION
AND PSYCHOPHYSICAL JUDGMENTS

Following Weintraub (1971), assume that a subject is tachistoscopically presented with one of several rectangles varying only in width and that the task is to judge this variation. By proper choice of stimulus differences, it is possible to have a subject achieve a high but not perfect level of discrimination accuracy.

The judgmental process may be conveniently described in the manner of a response-conditional receiver operating character (ROC) curve in signal detection theory.[1] Consider a physical axis of width. One may conceptualize a probability distribution on this axis corresponding to each of several response categories. For simplicity, assume that these distributions have different means but are equal variance and Gaussian. Thus, there will be a mean energy for a response of "wide," a second mean energy for a response of "medium," and so on. However,

---

[1] Use of an accuracy measure in this example does not necessarily limit consideration to this type of indicator. The present discussion applies to phenomenological measures as well.

the distributions for any one of these response categories will be a simple translation along the energy axis for any other. Any one of several accuracy measures can be used to describe the subject's judgmental ability. All, in general, describe a stimulus–response covariance in terms of the overlap of the distributions and, by assumption, overlap is slight in this case.

Suppose that something is now added to induce variation along a second dimension, height, independently of width variation. Each observation now may be regarded as a vector in two-space instead of a scalar in one-space. This attribute vector will be of the form (relevant magnitude, irrelevant magnitude). However, as the subject's response is constrained to be a scalar, a second weighting vector of the form (relevant weight, irrelevant weight) needs to be applied to the attribute vector. If this weighting vector is not of the form $(1, 0)$ and the subjects thereby attend to "noise," accuracy will be poorer than it could be given the information contained in the attribute vector and the assumed width–height independence.

This suggests a second way to describe the difference stated above between destructive and creative theories of masking. Destructive theories of masking treat impairment as if it results from an increase in random variance, which produces an increase in overlap among the response distributions. In essence, the subject responds less systematically but with an appropriate weighting vector. In contrast, creative theories treat impairment as if it results from an inappropriate weighting vector. The subject may respond in a highly systematic manner but to the wrong cues. If this is so, one needs to consider what a subject is attending to, that is, the *criterion content* (Kahneman, 1968) of the weighting vector as well as the resulting accuracy.

Figure 1 illustrates this latter possibility. Here we assume that the subject gives equal weight to the relevant and the irrelevant cues. Three response categories having bivariate normal distributions are also assumed (we further assume that the subject's response is unidimensional with respect to this oblique axis or *discriminant,* though it is not necessary for our argument). Accuracy is a function of the overlap of the projections of these bivariate distributions onto the relevant axis, which will be greater than the overlap along the discriminant. Hence, accuracy will be poorer than it could be with optimal weighting.

An important consequence of this point of view is that it illustrates presence of systematic as well as random error in judgments. That is, the subject's responses may covary with values along the irrelevant dimension. In this example, the correlation is negative, but in some situations it can be positive or negative depending upon the subject's strategy (Friden, 1973).

It is natural to ask why the subject chooses these nonoptimal weightings and responds to an irrelevant attribute. There are several reasons why this might happen. Perhaps the main reason is that subjects do not necessarily know what is relevant and what is irrelevant. This is particularly true for dimensions that are not defined in physical terms. A second factor is that the resulting set of

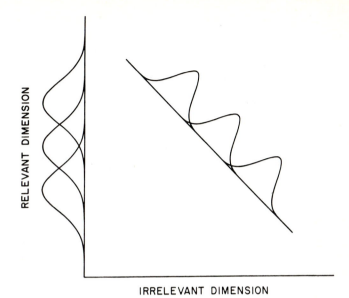

IRRELEVANT DIMENSION

FIG. 1 Hypothetical distribution of three response categories as a function of the magnitude of the relevant and irrelevant dimension along with the projections of these distributions onto the relevant axis.

response distributions overlap less than they do along the single, relevant dimension. In the univariate case, random error causes a subject to assign different responses to the same stimulus (equivocate, in an information theoretic sense) and vice versa. This attenuates the mean differences in responses. Figure 1 illustrates that the differences along the discriminant are greater than their projections along the relevant axis. This allows the subject to gain *coherence* or internal consistency of judgments, though it sacrifices accuracy (Hake & Rodwan, 1967). It implies that the various responses will be made to stimuli that may be subjectively more different than in the univariate case and, at the least, more different than they would be with an appropriate weighting vector.

Two more considerations giving rise to the use of irrelevant information are: (a) variation along some dimensions is more readily resolved into sensory differences than equal physical variation in other dimensions, that is, there is *grain* to the judgment space (Friden, 1973) and (b) variation in irrelevant dimensions may be made to exceed variation along a relevant dimension by the experimenter or by nature (Hake *et al.*, 1967).

The studies by Hake and his associates cited above give ample evidence that subjects are quite easily influenced to respond on the basis of an irrelevant attribute. Specifically, Hake *et al.* (1967) showed how estimates of the size of a square are influenced by the size of the background on which it appears and how increasing variation in the size of the background caused this irrelevant variable to be given a higher weighting, that is, to be attended to more by most but not all subjects (see Hake *et al.*, 1967, for a discussion of the source of these individual differences). Friden (1973) showed how judgments of illumination and judgments of reflectance essentially were made to the same physical dimension, reflectance.

Hake *et al.* (1967) point out that this apparently aberrant behavior is merely the reverse side of a highly adaptive coin. Basing their work on the tradition of Brunswik (1956), they point out that under more optimal conditions where several dimensions of stimulation covary (as they do in the nontachistoscopic world), responses based upon these partially or totally redundant dimensions are both more stable and more accurate than responses based only upon one, a process they term "noise reduction." Put in quite traditional terms, the core to which judgments should be directed cannot, and usually should not, be isolated from the context because the context normally provides evidence about the core. It is primarily the use of unnatural orthogonal designs that makes reliance upon context lead to impairment. For generality, then, two physical dimensions need not be labeled "relevant" and "irrelevant" and need not be orthogonal.

IV.   NOISE REDUCTION AND METACONTRAST

Consider one familiar display used to produce metacontrast, the three-object display (Kahneman, 1968), in which the test is a square and the mask is a pair of flanking squares. If test and mask are of equal energy, presentation of the mask concurrently with the test has little or no effect on judgments of brightness. As the stimulus onset asynchrony (SOA) separating test from mask increases, the test appears to dim up to an SOA of 50–200 msec. Further increases in the SOA lead to increases in the brightness of the test to an asymptote equal to the "no mask" control. The well-known term for this is U-shaped masking, which may also be obtained in nonmetacontrast masking (Stewart & Purcell, 1974).

We feel that this situation lends itself quite well to the preceding analysis and will now attempt to show how (a more detailed treatise on this theory, including a formal, mathematical model is in preparation; hence, we only describe the outlines of this theory in this chapter; Bernstein & Proctor, 1974, represent an earlier and slightly different view). On "no mask" trials, the subject must obtain information about brightness from the perceived energy change at the test or from the relation of test to background. We call cues of this type *absolute information.*[2] We further assume that this information is also available on test—mask (experimental) trials and is unaffected by the mask.

We hypothesize that the introduction of the mask creates a second cue in the form of the brightness of the test relative to the mask. We call this cue the

---

[2] From our standpoint, it does not matter whether this information is extracted from the test alone or the luminance difference between test and mask background.

comparative information. With concurrent stimulation, this provides a highly veridical cue to brightness for the usual reasons that comparative judgments are more sensitive than absolute judgments. For example, suppose the subject is to discriminate between one test energy equal to the mask energy and another that is slightly lower, as is true of the type of judgment we employ (Bernstein, Proctor, Proctor, & Schurman, 1973; Bernstein, Proctor, Belcher, & Schurman, 1974). The subject can use the mask as a frame of reference or adaptation level to make same–different judgments to which our sensory system is highly tuned. Hence the mask can provide noise reduction with respect to variation in overall retinal sensitivity, as the difference in brightness between test and mask is not affected by this variation.

The problem with comparative information, though, is that a time error results when the subject employs it with a delayed presentation of the mask. The subject must compare a fading trace of the test with an intact representation of the mask. This makes the test look dimmer than it would if it were judged on an absolute basis. Since different test energies all fade to a common zero level, the overlap among various alternatives increases. Increasing the delay is analogous to rotating a comparative judgment axis in the relevant–irrelevant space of Fig. 1 from a vertical to a horizontal position to describe its progressive independence from the test's energy.

We further assume that the subject has some information to tell him/her to decrease the weighting of comparative information as SOA increases. Given the relational nature of perception, though, we need not assume that comparative information is disregarded to the extent that it should be, although eventually it is when SOA is sufficiently long. Thus, the theory attributes the initial decline in brightness to overdependency upon comparative information, that is, an inappropriate weighting vector, and the eventual return to the baseline to eventual independence. The advantage of this approach is that a formal model may be constructed from traditional and rather general assumptions about the nature of trace decay rather than any of the controversial neurophysiological assumptions present in other formal models. We specifically do not need to make the assumption that Weisstein (1968, 1972) has that lateral inhibition has a shorter latency than excitation.

The comparison stimulus hypothesis was stated initially by Bernstein *et al.* (1973). In that study, subjects judged whether a bright (68 Cd/m^2 × 50 msec) or dim (40 Cd/m^2 × 50 msec) test had been presented. These alternative energies were selected because pilot research had indicated that they could be discriminated with nearly perfect accuracy in the absence of a mask. The mask was also 68 Cd/m^2 × 50 msec. Hence the task could also be viewed as determining whether the test and mask were of the same or different energy. The results were that accuracy in discriminating between the two alternatives was a U-shaped function of SOA in two experiments, one in which SOA was held constant within trial blocks and the other in which it varied randomly over trials. In the former case, in which subjects could adjust their criteria to each trial block (SOA), response bias was constant across SOA. In the latter, in which the response criterion would presumably be the same for each SOA, the bias measure declined from 0 to 25 msec, indicating that subjects increased their frequency of "dim" responses. This is consistent with the use of cues derived from a comparison of the fading trace of the test with the mask, though it is also predictable from other theories.

A somewhat more explicit test of this hypothesis was made by Bernstein *et al.* (1974). This differed from the preceding study in that the mask was also bright or dim independently of the test. Consequently, brightness mismatches provided a veridical cue to judgment, since they could only arise from the bright test/dim mask or dim mask/bright test pairings. Brightness matches, on the other hand, could come either from a bright test/bright mask or dim test/dim mask pairing. Hence, if subjects were using brightness match/mismatch information at short SOA, accuracy should be higher on trials involving different energy levels for test and mask than on trials involving the same energy levels. The difference in accuracy was in fact observed when test and mask were concurrent. The advantage on brightness mismatch trials decreased as the mask delay increased, as one would expect from trace decay effects.

A more elegant application of the noise reduction paradigm involves the linear discriminant function methodology described in Hake *et al.* (1967). A study employing this methodology is currently in progress.

V. THE EXPERIMENT:
PERCEPTUAL INDEPENDENCE AND MASKING

It was earlier noted that most workers recognize that the test may influence the mask as well as vice versa. Yet there are relatively few studies in which a series of two or more stimuli are presented to the same or adjacent retinal loci and judgments are obtained about each. Eriksen and Eriksen (1971) did such a study using a three-stimulus sequence. They found accuracies of all three stimuli to be above chance at all delays. This is contrary to an erasure hypothesis (Sperling, 1963), which predicts that the first and second stimuli should not be reached until a critical delay is reached to allow readout from visual storage. Eriksen and Eriksen (1971) analyzed only the accuracies of the individual stimuli though, and thus did not examine possible covariances in the judgmental process. These covariances are to be expected if a noise reduction process is operative.

In the most general definition of the term, visual masking studies are concerned with interdependencies among overlapping or adjacent stimuli presented in rapid sequence. Garner and Morton (1970) discussed the various types of dependencies that generally might exist between two separate judgments and described their measurement. They began by drawing a distinction between a *state* correlation and a *process* correlation. A state correlation involves the accuracies of two or more judgments. Higher (or lower) accuracy in judging one stimulus when the other is correctly as opposed to incorrectly judged defines a state correlation. A process correlation involves the underlying act or judgmental process and may exist at a sensory level, a response level, or both. The authors point out that typical assessments of perceptual independence are centered around determination of state correlations. Yet they described a hypothetical set of data in which strong joint response biases operated. These involved the tendency to use certain combinations of responses over others. Despite the fact that this falsely implied lack of perceptual independence, the consequent accuracies were uncorrelated.

Garner and Morton (1970) indicate that the most effective way to explore perceptual independence is to employ a design in which the alternatives for the two stimuli are presented independently of each other and a response is made to each stimulus. In terms of present application to masking, each alternative is thus a test in its own right and potentially a mask for the other stimulus. The two stimuli are labeled S1 and S2, and their associated responses will be labeled R1 and R2.

In the study to be described, both the S1 and S2 alternatives were the letters B and D. The B and D were so positioned that the outer contours of the two were superimposed when one was used as S1 and the other as S2. Adey (1972) developed this task and found that the masking function inferred from accuracy in recognizing S1 was U-shaped. We decided to examine this task to see if the same general factors were operative as those we feel are responsible for metacontrast suppression of brightness. One goal of the study was therefore traditional in that we studied perceptual impairment, that is, changes in accuracy, as a function of the delay between S1 and S2. This was extended to infer both forward and backward masking functions from R1 and R2 accuracies.

In addition to accuracy measures describing the covariances between the two stimuli and their associated responses, two other classes of covariances could plausibly exist. These are mask–response covariances between S1 and R2 and between S2 and R1 and a response–response covariance between R1 and R2. In general, cue destruction theories ignore these possible covariances. In order to explore them, two interdependent analyses were performed: a signal detection analysis following from our own previous work, and a four-dimensional uncertainty analysis described by Garner and Morton (1970).

A. Method

Subjects.   They consisted of two paid undergraduates and two paid graduate students in psychology at the University of Texas at Arlington. Each had normal or corrected-to-normal visual acuity. Prior to the gathering of experimental data, each participated in approximately 2000 practice trials spread over 9 sessions.

Apparatus and Stimuli.   The stimuli were presented monocularly by trans-illumination in an Iconix four-channel tachistoscope. Sylvania F6T5/CW bulbs were used. A telegraph key was used by the subject to self-initiate trials. A continuous dim fixation point was externally illuminated so that all four exposure fields could be utilized for presentation of the test alternatives. The fixation point appeared approximately in the middle of the visual field.

Exposure Fields I and II respectively contained the B and D used as the S1 alternatives and Exposure Fields III and IV respectively contained the B and D used as the S2 alternatives. The circuit allowed the experimenter to present a stimulus in either Field I or II, impose a variable delay, and then present a stimulus in either Field III or IV.

The letters were designed so that only the center bar of the B differentiated it from the D. They appeared with their base at fixation and subtended .64° of arc in height by .51° of arc in width. The base of the figures appeared .13° of arc above fixation. Neutral density material (Kodak) was used to reduce their luminance to 4 Cd/m². They were presented at a duration of 3 msec.

Procedure. Each subject served in 13 one-hour sessions. In each session, the first 15 minutes was allocated to practice and dark adaptation and the remaining time to 192 experimental trials. In all cases, the experimenter made the adjustments necessary to select S1 and, in the Double Stimulus/Double Response and Double Stimulus/Single Response conditions, S2. The purpose of the Double Stimulus/Single Response condition was to see if making two responses, a task traditionally not imposed upon the subject, had any influence upon performance. Only S1 was presented in the Single Stimulus condition, the traditional "no mask" control. When these adjustments were made and afterimages from the previous trial had disappeared, the subject focused, fixated, and initiated the trial.

All responses were made using a 6-point confidence-rating scale (1 = very sure that a B had been presented, 2 = sure that a B had been presented, 3 = guess that a B had been presented, 4 = guess that a D had been presented, 5 = sure that a D had been presented, and 6 = very sure that a D had been presented). In the Double Stimulus/Double Response condition, a pair of these ratings were made which, in all cases, were in the order R1, R2. In the remaining conditions, only a single response was made.

Data for the Double Stimulus/Double Response and Single Stimulus Conditions were gathered in nine of the sessions during which eight blocks of the former and one block of the latter trials were run. A block in all cases consisted of 24 trials divided equally among the possible stimulus alternatives. These were B–B (read as "B followed by B"), B–D, D–B, and D–D in the Double Stimulus/Double Response condition and simply B or D in the Single Stimulus Condition. One block was run at each of 8 stimulus onset asynchronies (SOA) in the Double Stimulus/Double Response condition (3, 5, 10, 20, 40, 80, 160, or 320 msec). These SOA values may be converted to the interstimulus interval measure of delay by subtracting 3 msec (the S1 exposure duration) and the shortest SOA thus involves consecutive presentation.

The four stimulus combinations (B–B, B–D, D–B, and D–D) were presented in the Double Stimulus/Single Response condition which was run in the remaining four sessions. During each session, the subject responded to S1 on one block and to S2 on another block at each of 4 SOA (3, 10, 40, and 160 msecs).

In all cases, blocks were randomized over sessions and subjects. The Double Stimulus/Single Response sessions were also randomly intermixed among the other sessions.

B. Results

Single-Stimulus Condition. A total of 216 Single Stimulus or "no mask" control trials were run per subject divided equally between the alternatives B and D. Presentation of a B was considered "signal plus noise" and presentation of a D was considered "noise" for purposes of a signal detection analysis. The 6-category response scale was used to generate confidence-rating ROC curves. The sensitivity and the bias separating the "3" and "4" categories were respectively inferred from the area measure and the negative natural logarithm of Luce's (1963) beta measure. These two indices are directly related to accuracy and to a tendency to use the B as opposed to D response category, respectively. A two-way uncertainty analysis was also performed by disregarding confidence ratings and classifying response categories "1" to "3" as "B" responses and response categories "4" to "6" as "D" responses. The resulting S1 X R1 frequencies over trials defined the confusion matrix.

The mean area measure over the four subjects was greater than .99 and no subject fell below this value. This indicates that there was negligible error when only a single stimulus was presented. The mean bias index was −.07, and three of the subjects had biases of 0, indicating nearly equal use of the B and D categories. Finally the mean information transmitted was .95. The reasons that this measure (as well as percent correct responses) is slightly less than the area is that the confidence ratings within the two broad response categories contained information not considered in the uncertainty analysis.

Double Stimulus/Double Response Condition. The data of major interest are from the condition in which R1 and R2 were respectively obtained to S1 and S2. Over the course of the experiment, 216 trials were run per subject per SOA divided equally among the four combinations of S1 and S2 alternatives. These 216 trials were used to obtain four ROC curves. The R1 data were separately analyzed as a function of whether S2 (the mask for S1) was a B or a D and vice versa for the R2 data. The bias and sensitivity indices were the same as those used in the Single Stimulus condition. By again disregarding confidence within "B" and "D" categories, a four-way uncertainty analysis was performed by taking the resulting S1 X S2 X R1 X R2 frequencies to form a confusion matrix in the manner suggested by Garner and Morton (1970).

Figure 2 contains the composite area measures as a function of SOA, forward masking of S2 versus backward masking of S1 and type of mask (B versus D). In this as well as other analyses presented below, the composite data are most representative of individual subjects. A four-way repeated measures analysis of variance (ANOVA) supported the following relations in evidence in the figure. First, there was no difference between forward and backward masking, indicating that masking in this particular task is symmetric. Second, very little masking occurred at short SOA when the mask was a D, but masking did occur when the mask was a B. Accuracy conformed to the control condition at long SOA regardless of mask. This is confirmed by the significant main effects of SOA, type of mask and their interaction ($p < .01$, .05, and .01, respectively). Whether the masking function for trials on which a B was the mask is U-shaped or flat to 40 msecs ISI is not clear. The linear component of the SOA by type of mask interaction accounted for 74% of the variance and the quadratic component accounted for 14% ($p < .01$). Partitioning of the main effect of SOA led to substantially the same results.

These accuracy data indicate a symmetry of forward and backward masking. This symmetry argues against an interruption theory of the type formulated by

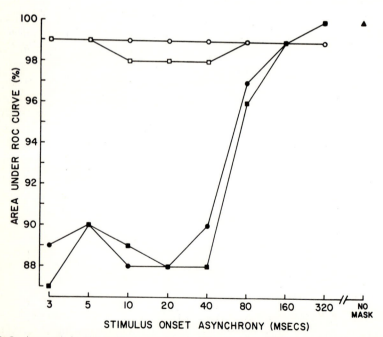

FIG. 2   Accuracy in terms of area under confidence-rating ROC curves as a function of interstimulus interval. (Filled points are based upon trials in which the mask was the letter B; open points are based upon trials in which the mask was the letter D; circles are R1 data; squares are R2 data; and the filled triangle is the "no mask" control.) The abscissa is spaced logarithmically solely for clarity.

Sperling (1963) which predicts backward but not forward masking and neglects luminance summation effects (Eriksen & Eriksen, 1971). Similar relations held for the accuracy indices obtained from the uncertainty analysis and for percentage of correct responses, but these data are subsequently considered in a different context.

Figure 3 contains the composite bias data as a function of ISI, forward versus backward masking, and type of mask. As was the case for accuracy, there were no differences between backward and forward masking. At short SOA, the type of mask has a strong effect on bias such that subjects are more likely to respond to S1 with a "B" if S2 is also a "B" and vice versa. Likewise, they also were more likely to respond to S1 with a "D" if S2 is also a "D" and vice versa. This implies that the subjects tend to "see" the S1 and S2 as correlated even though they are orthogonal. This effect disappears with SOA. The main effect of type of mask and SOA by type of mask interaction were both highly significant ($p <$ .01). The bias functions are essentially flat up to 40 msec SOA but the slight rise in the "B" function and drop in the "D" function is relatively consistent over subjects. The linear component accounted for 78% of the interaction and the quadratic component accounted for 8% ($p < .01$).

Figure 4 contains what Garner and Morton (1970) term the direct contingencies and the partial cross contingencies. The direct contingencies, symbolized as U(S1:R1) and U(S2:R2), describe the covariance between the stimulus and its associated dichotomized response. The partial cross contingencies, symbolized as

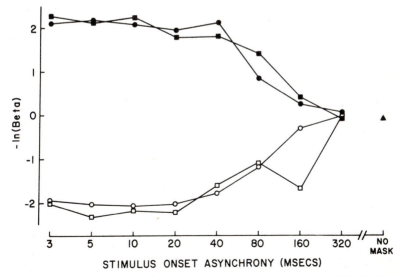

FIG. 3 Bias in terms of −ln (Beta) as a function of interstimulus interval. (Filled points are based upon trials in which the mask was the letter B; open points are based upon trials in which the mask was the letter D; circles are R1 data; squares are R2 data; and the filled triangle is the "no mask" control.) The abscissa is spaced logarithmically solely for clarity.

U(S1:R2/S2) and U(S2:R1/S1), describe the covariance between a stimulus and the dichotomized response to the other stimulus in the sequence, partialing out the direct contingency between the latter response and its appropriate stimulus. Thus, U(S1:R2/S2) is the relation between S1 and R2 independent of their possible dependencies upon S2. Each is portrayed as a composite as a function of SOA. Two separate ANOVAs were performed, one on the direct and the other on the partial cross contingencies. The factors were SOA, forward versus backward masking and subjects in all cases.

The ISI effect was the only significant effect in each analysis ($p < .01$), once again consistent with the symmetry previously noted. As in the other analyses, the direct and partial cross-contingency functions are essentially flat up to 40 msec SOA, but there is a slight drop in the former and rise in the latter. The linear components accounted for 84% and 74% of the direct and partial cross contingencies, respectively, and the quadratic components accounted for 13% and 5% (all $p < .01$).

The points of especial interest in this analysis are that accuracy, in terms of the direct contingencies, were quite low at short SOA (this was also true in an analysis of percentage correct responses which will not be presented) and that the subjects tended to report the mask rather than the test at short SOA. The

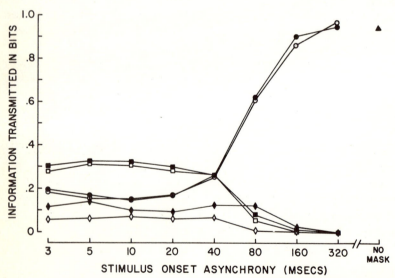

FIG. 4 Direct contingencies (circles), partial cross contingencies (squares) and response–response contingencies (diamonds) as a function of interstimulus interval. (The filled circles and squares are for the backward masking of S1 by S2; the filled diamonds are corrected for stimulus–response contingencies; the unfilled diamonds are incorrect; and the filled triangle is the information transmitted between stimulus and response in the "no mask" control.) The abscissa is spaced logarithmically solely for clarity.

former, taken in conjunction with the higher accuracies obtained using the area measure, also indicate that the confidence ratings contained a substantial amount of information.

In order to see whether the relatively large partial cross contingency contribution was due to a tendency to lose order information, the confusion matrix was examined in detail. This was in part true although, as the bias data indicated, the dominant effect was to respond with the same response to S1 and S2 rather than reverse two correct responses. Thus, subjects who erred were more likely to respond "B–B" to a B–D sequence rather than to respond "D–B." The "B–B" response combination was also much more likely than the "D–D" response when S1 and S2 differed. The reason that the overall "B" and "D" rates were nearly equal was that more errors arose on B–B trials than on D–D trials.

Figure 4 also contains the cross-response contingency data. Two such measures may be obtained from the data. One is based upon the zero-order contingency between R1 and R2 and is symbolized U(R1:R2). The other removes the stimulus-related variance and is symbolized U(R1:R2/S1,S2). The two were combined into a single ANOVA with SOA and subjects as the other factors. There is a tendency for U(R1:R2) to be lower than U(R1:R2/S1,S2). This is what one would expect because the stimuli are presented orthogonally, and stimulus-related variance would attenuate the correlation. However, the difference was not significant. Again, the function is essentially flat up to 40 msecs though there is a slight rise ($p < .01$). The linear component of the trend accounted for 86% of the variance ($p < .01$) and the quadratic component accounted for 4% ($p < .05$).

Other measures were extracted from the uncertainty analysis, but these fail to add to what has been presented. In short, we find that not only accuracy changes over SOA but bias, mask–response, and response–response covariance changes as well. We also found that the use of symmetric tests and masks gave rise to symmetric masking functions.

Double Stimulus/Single Response Condition. The measures obtained from this condition were analyzed, both separately and in terms of the difference between the Double Stimulus/Double Response condition for those SOA in common. All trends observed previously were observed in these control conditions and differences between corresponding indices in the two conditions were negligible and nonsignificant. In short, we may conclude that our use of two responses did not in itself affect performance.

C. Discussion

The main finding was that subjects acted as if S1 and S2 alternatives presented at short ISIs were correlated despite the fact that they were orthogonal. This is an aspect of a noise reduction process illustrated in Fig. 1. Consequently, the data supplement the metacontrast findings of Bernstein *et al.* (1974) in support of a cue creation approach to masking.

Cues furnished by luminance summation seem to underlie the perceived covariance. For simplicity, assume that the brightness of the single stimulus was one unit. Because brightness is not a linear function of energy, the outer contour of a consecutive combination would have a brightness less than 2 units, say 1.5 units. The brightness of the crossbar, which is a basic cue in the task, would be 0 units if the stimuli were D–D, 1.0 units if the stimuli were mixed (B–D or D–B), and 1.5 units if the stimuli were B–B, assuming no lateral inhibition. This nonlinearity of brightness seems sufficient to cause more confusions between a mixed sequence and B–B than between a mixed sequence and D–D. Cue destruction effects would lead to the converse expectation. As ISI lengthens this would not occur because the stimuli would be processed independently. The data suggest that little independent processing occurred for shorter ISIs than 40 msec.

Evidence for U-shaped masking was equivocal, but we would hesitate to say that the data conflict with Adey's (1972). Furthermore, temporal integration effects can account for a slight nonmonotonicity. As Schurman and Colegate (1970) indicated, the dark interval between stimuli would disrupt temporal integration. This would cause the brightness of the outer contour common to the B and D to decrease from 1.5 units and enhance confusions between mixed sequences and B–B more than under consecutive presentation.

VI. CONCLUSIONS

One basic need in the area of visual masking is to consider the various ways that errors may arise. Turvey (1973) has discussed the role of peripheral (retinal) and central factors in masking. Yet the term "central" applied in this and related contexts has frequently implied a sensory locus. The sensory process may be veridical to the extent that both appropriate and inappropriate cues are encoded. The term "response" effect has been generally limited to such factors as response biases in the signal detection sense. These biases are either disregarded or (preferably) minimized through techniques such as forced choice indicators. Attempts to control for factors like bias are certainly necessary, but they are not sufficient to rule out the judgmental factors we stress. Indeed, only after it can be shown that the kinds of errors made in accuracy tasks are unsystematic can judgmental theories like ours be ruled out in favor of a pure cue destruction approach. We feel that this is unlikely. In essence, the recognition that "noise" may be systematic as well as unsystematic needs be more fully utilized in masking theories.

The particular type of theory that we feel has been most negligent of the possible presence of multiple, conflicting cues is neurophysiological in origin

(Weisstein, 1968, 1972; Bridgeman, 1971). We strongly concur with the need to conceptualize masking in a broad framework that integrates it with other literatures. However, to achieve integration with biology at the expense of a vast portion of the psychological literature on judgment making, such as the covariances with irrelevant aspects of stimulation, is, we feel, a serious error.

This argument is quite separate from other criticisms that one might make about their use of the lateral inhibition concept (Uttal, 1970) and the failure to find U-shaped masking at the very neurophysiological level that gave rise to the theories. The core of our objection may be exemplified using a typical metacontrast experiment. All too often a subject is asked "How bright is the test?" or even more complicated questions like "What proportion of the test do you see remaining?" (Weisstein, 1971). Implicit in this assumption is that the single number verbalized exhausts the subject's perception. Yet as we have attempted to note that as long as a mask is present, the question may be legitimately defined in at least two ways, absolutely and on a comparative basis. By the time that a judgment is made, this ambiguity may or may not be sensed. Not to sense an ambiguity does not, of course, mean it is lacking. Pertinent to the judgmental literature is the point that successful conflict resolution can eliminate the sensation of conflict even though the conflict may be ascertained in other ways.

ACKNOWLEDGMENTS

The authors are indebted to Professors Bruce Ambler, Subastiano Fisicaro, and Robert Proctor for their useful comments and encouragement. They are also indebted to Dean Howard Arnott and Ms. Barbara Coots for their assistance.

This study was supported by the Organized Research Funds of the Graduate School of the University of Texas at Arlington.

REFERENCES

Adey, M., Metacontrast, Unpublished B.A. dissertation, University of California at San Diego, 1972.

Bernstein, I. H., and Proctor, R. W. The role of criterion content in U-shaped masking. Paper presented at the convention of the Psychonomic Society, Boston, October, 1974.

Bernstein, I. H., Proctor, J. D., Proctor, R. W., & Schurman, D. L. Metacontrast and brightness discrimination. *Perception & Psychophysics,* 1973, **14**, 293–297.

Bernstein, I. H., Proctor, R. W., Belcher, J., & Schurman, D. L. An analysis of U-shaped metacontrast. *Perception & Psychophysics,* 1974, **16**, 329–336.

Bridgeman, B. Metacontrast and lateral inhibition. *Psychological Review,* 1971, **78**, 528–539.

Brunswik, E. *Perception and the representative design of psychological experiments.* Berkeley: University of California Press, 1956.

Eriksen, C. W. Temporal luminance summation effects in backward and forward masking. *Perception & Psychophysics,* 1966, **1**, 87–92.

Eriksen, C. W., Becker, B.B., & Hoffman, J. E., Safari to masking land: A hunt for the elusive U. *Perception & Psychophysics,* 1970, 8, 245–250.

Eriksen, C. W., & Eriksen, B. A. Visual perceptual processing rates and backward and forward masking. *Journal of Experimental Psychology,* 1971, 89, 306–313.

Friden, T. P. Whiteness constancy: Inference or insensitivity? *Perception & Psychophysics,* 1973, 14, 81–89.

Garner, W. R., Hake, H. W., & Eriksen, C. W. Operationalism and the concept of perception. *Psychological Review,* 1956, 63, 149–159.

Garner, W. R., & Morton, J. Perceptual independence: Definitions, models, and experimental paradigms. *Psychological Bulletin,* 1970, 72, 233–259.

Hake, H. W., Faust, G. W., McIntyre, J. S., & Murray, H. G. Relational perception and modes of perceiver operation. *Perception & Psychophysics,* 1967, 2, 469–478.

Hake, H. W., & Rodwan, A. S. Perception and recognition. In J. B. Sidowski (Ed.), *Experimental methods and instrumentation in psychology.* New York: McGraw-Hill, 1967.

Hake, H. W., Rodwan, A., & Weintraub, D. Noise reduction in perception. In K. R. Hammond (Ed.), *The psychology of Egon Brunswik.* New York: Holt, Rinehart & Winston, 1966. Pp. 277–316.

Kahneman, D. An onset-onset law for one case of apparent motion and metacontrast. *Perception & Psychophysics,* 1967, 2, 577–584.

Kahneman, D. Method, findings and theory in studies of visual masking. *Psychological Bulletin,* 1968, 70, 404–425.

Luce, R. D. Detection and recognition. In R. D. Luce & E. Galanter (Eds.), *Handbook of mathematical psychology.* Vol. 1. New York: Wiley, 1963.

Rodwan, A. S., & Hake, H. W. The discriminant function as a model for perception. *American Journal of Psychology,* 1964, 77, 380–392.

Schurman, D. L., & Colegate, R. L. Dark intervals as stimulus events and their effect on visual masking and time-intensity reciprocity. *Journal of Experimental Psychology,* 1970, 85, 278–287.

Sperling, G. A model for visual memory tasks. *Human Factors,* 1963, 5, 19–31.

Stewart, A. L., & Purcell, D. G. Visual backward masking by a flash of light: A study of U-shaped detection functions. *Journal of Experimental Psychology,* 1974, 103, 553–566.

Treisman, A. M. Strategies and models of selective attention. *Psychological Review,* 1969, 76, 282–299.

Turvey, M. T. On peripheral and cerebral processes in vision: Inferences from an information-processing analysis of masking with patterned stimuli. *Psychological Review,* 1973, 80, 1–52.

Uttal, W. R. On the physiological basis of masking with dotted visual noise. *Perception & Psychophysics,* 1970, 7, 321–327.

Weintraub, D. J. Rectangle discriminability: Perceptual relativity and the Law of Pragnanz. *Journal of Experimental Psychology,* 1971, 88, 1–11.

Weisstein, N. A Rashevsky–Landahl neural net: Stimulation of metacontrast. *Psychological Review,* 1968, 75, 494–521.

Weisstein, N. W-shaped and U-shaped functions obtained for monoptic and dichoptic disk-disk masking. *Perception & Psychophysics,* 1971, 9, 275–278.

Weisstein, N. Metacontrast. *Handbook of Sensory Physiology,* 1972, 7, 233–272.

10
Masking and Preperceptual Selectivity in Auditory Recognition

Harold L. Hawkins
Joelle C. Presson

Department of Psychology
University of South Florida
Tampa, Florida, United States

ABSTRACT

The results of several experiments on auditory recognition masking are discussed in terms of their implications for a general theory of auditory masking. The task entails the presentation of two brief pure tones in rapid succession. The subject is instructed to categorize the first of these with respect to pitch and to disregard the second. The basic finding is that categorization performance is poor, approaching chance, at short stimulus onset asynchronies (SOA), but systematically increases as SOA is incremented. Manipulations of the laterality relationship between the tones, and other considerations, specifically reveal (1) that distinctly different and identifiable forms of masking occur at the peripheral and the central levels of the auditory information-processing sequence; and (2) that a clearly delineated process of selective attention operates prior to the point of contact between input and categorization processes in memory.

I. INTRODUCTION

A view at one time prominent among theories of stimulus masking is that the effect of the masking stimulus can be adequately described primarily in terms of a simple interruption process. Following this notion, an optimal masker attacks the target representation at some point, or point series, along the information-processing sequence and, in essence, erases or overwrites it. Masking extent is known to be responsive to a number of factors, among these the relative amplitudes of target and masker, the temporal relation of the two, and their formal similarity. The effects of such variables, according to the interruption hypothesis, is a simple matter of erasure extent. Indeed, considerable appeal attaches to the idea that the perceptual consequence of any set of masking conditions can be represented as a single point along an interruption continuum anchored at one end by complete erasure, at the other by no measurable erasure, and in between, by varying degrees of partial erasure. However, research recently emerging from a number of laboratories (Eriksen, 1966; Kahneman, 1968; Turvey, 1973; Bernstein, Proctor, Belcher, & Schurman, 1974) has amply established the inadequacy of the simple erasure notion as a sufficient account of recognition masking effects in vision. The primary objective of this chapter is to demonstrate the inadequacy of the erasure notion as a sufficient account of recognition masking effects in audition. Closely related to this demonstration are two specific theoretical points we wish to make regarding the determinants of masking the auditory recognition. One of these points stems from the well-known Broadbent—Treisman notion of a preperceptual mechanism of selective attention (Broadbent, 1958; Treisman, 1964). Recent conceptualizations of the data on selective attention no longer assume that selectivity is the exclusive property of precategorical processes, for clearly it is not. Rather, the current question concerns whether it is necessary to assume *any* selectivity prior to the point of memory contact (Keele, 1973). The evidence presented in this chapter provides strong support for the idea of precategorical selectivity within the auditory modality. However, the selectivity process identified here does not appear to be strictly equivalent to that postulated earlier by Broadbent or Treisman.

The second specific theoretical point closely parallels an argument elaborated by Turvey in his (1973) paper on the loci of masking effects in vision. We will propose that in audition, as in vision, two important and clearly discernable forms of recognition masking phenomena can be identified. The first of these phenomena apparently occurs peripheral to the point at which binaural input is partitioned into separate laterality, or spatial, channels, whereas the second occurs subsequent to lateralization but in advance of the point at which input is categorized. We will argue that test tone—masker interactions occurring peripherally follow a *subtractive rule* (Egan & Meyer, 1950), whereas those occurring subsequent to lateralization but in advance of categorization follow an *additive-rule*.

II. THE BASIC AUDITORY-RECOGNITION
MASKING EFFECT

The procedure used in the experiments is the highly analytic, and controversial, auditory recognition masking paradigm developed by Massaro (1970). The subject's task in this procedure is to categorize a brief acoustic stimulus along

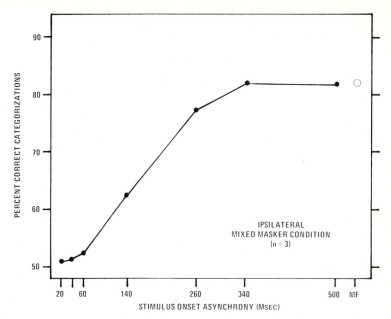

FIG. 1 Percentage correct categorization responses in backward auditory recognition masking as a function of stimulus onset asynchrony (SOA). Masker frequency varied randomly
across trials. MF denotes performance on masker-free trials.

the sensory dimension associated with a particular physical continuum, such as
frequency or wave form. Most of the data we will describe come from backward
masking situations in which the stimulus presented on each trial is one of two
brief sinusoidal tones which are to be categorized along a two-valued pitch
dimension, either as "high" or "low." In these situations, the test tone whose
pitch is to be judged is followed after a variable silent interval by an equally
intense masker tone that differs from the first both in duration and frequency.
The interval between onsets of the test tone and the masker typically ranges
between 20 and several hundred msec. Both tones are delivered to subject
through headphones. A brief warning light initiates each trial, and informative
feedback is provided immediately following the subject's response. Prior to the
beginning of the experimental sessions, subjects are given extensive training.
During training trials the test tones are presented with feedback and in the
absence of a masker.

    Figure 1 summarizes results obtained in a prototypic backward auditory
recognition masking situation.[1] These data were gathered under conditions in

---

[1] Further details on the design of this and all subsequently described experiments will be
provided in an article by Hawkins, H. L., Lutfi, R., and VanDercar, D. on central and
peripheral auditory masking, currently in preparation.

which the frequencies of the 20 msec, 81 dB, test tone alternatives were 787 Hz ("low") and 863 Hz ("high"). The frequencies of the 500 msec, 81 dB, masker tones were 749, 825, and 901 Hz. Each trial contained one of the two test tones randomly paired with one of the three maskers. The two tones paired on each trial were monaurally channeled to the same ear.

As can be noted from Fig. 1, performance is quite poor, approaching the chance level, at the shortest stimulus onset asynchronies (SOA), systematically improves as SOA is increased, and reaches an asymptotic level at SOAs of between 240 and 320 msec. Beyond this point, no masking effects are present, as is evidenced by the equivalence of performance on trials with SOAs equal to or greater than 320 msec and on trials in which no masker is presented. These masker-free (MF) trials, we should note, constitute 25% of the experimental trials and are randomly intermixed with trials containing a masker.

One clear implication of these results, like others (e.g., Massaro, 1972a) reported in the masking literature, is the optimal categorization performance under conditions of this kind requires considerably more processing time than is available during stimulus presentation. Since the categorization process does appear to gain information for several hundred msec beyond test tone termination, we assume the existence of a precategorical sensory holding mechanism in the auditory modality. After Morton, Crowder, and Prussin (1971) we call this mechanism the *precategorical acoustic store* (PAS). (We do not intend, by the way, that our use of Morton and coworkers' term "PAS" be construed as an endorsement of their contention that experiments on the stimulus suffix effect have adequately demonstrated the existence of a sensory storage mechanism in addition.) The PAS presumably holds a relatively unanalyzed echoic representation of acoustic input for some period of time following stimulus offset and continues to transmit information regarding this representation to the subsequent categorization process. In these terms, *one* effect of the masker may be conceptualized as the disruption of test tone processing prior to categorization – perhaps at the level of the PAS. The earlier the disruption occurs within the several hundred milliseconds interval of test tone processing, the less information will be available for test tone analysis, and therefore the less accurate categorization performance will be.

III. SELECTIVE ATTENTION
IN AUDITORY RECOGNITION MASKING

Given the masker has its disruptive effects prior to categorization, it follows from the Broadbent–Treisman notion of preperceptual selective attention that the effect of a masker presented through a prespecified input channel differing from that receiving the test tone should be less than that observed when the two tones share a common input channel. The extent of the masking shown in Fig. 1 illustrates the fact that our subjects have considerable difficulty evading the ipsilateral masker of uncertain frequency. Indeed as shown in Fig. 2, close to an equivalent degree of ipsilateral masking is observed even when the subject is fully preadvised of masker frequency by presenting masker frequency in a blocked, as opposed to mixed, fashion. Now, what happens to the masking effect when test tone and masker are separately channeled to the subject? The results of an initial experiment in which the masker was channeled either to the ipsilateral ear relative to the monaural test tone, to the contralateral ear, or binaurally, provided no apparent support for the Broadbent–Treisman model. Figure 3 summarizes these data. Masker frequency varied randomly from trial to trial in mixed fashion, and the test tone-masker laterality relation was presented in block fashion. As can be seen, no measurable attenuation of masking effects occurs under either contralateral or binaural, relative to ipsilateral, masker conditions.

These findings would appear to be at odds with the idea of a precategorical selectivity process possessing the capacity to inhibit unwanted and potentially disruptive stimuli received through a unique and anticipated input channel. A slight variation in the procedure, however, yields markedly different results.

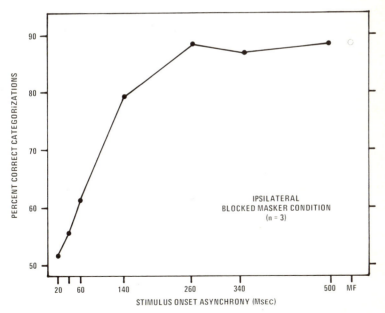

FIG. 2 Percentage correct categorization response in backward auditory recognition masking as a function of SOA. Masker frequency remained invariant within trial blocks and was varied in counterbalanced order across subjects, trial blocks, and days.

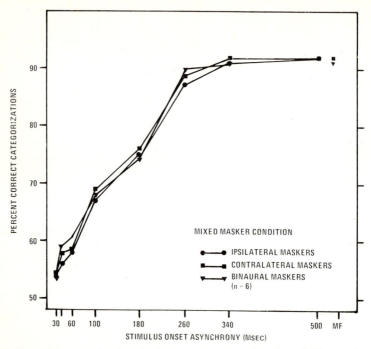

FIG. 3 Percentage correct categorization responses as a function of SOA, under three different laterality conditions. In this figure the ipsilateral masker function summarizes data from trial blocks in which both the test tone and the masker were presented to the right (R–R) ear together with those on which both tones were presented to the left (L–L). The contralateral function summarizes data from R–L and L–R blocks, and the binaural function summarizes R–LR and L–LR blocks data. Masker frequency varied randomly across trials within blocks.

Figure 4 summarizes data taken under conditions identical to those just described with the exception that masker frequencies were presented in blocked, rather than mixed, fashion. Thus, we may assume the subject was in some sense aware of the masker's pitch prior to the beginning of each trial. Here, as before (Fig. 2), extensive masking is observed during ipsilateral masker trial blocks. Under both contralateral *and* binaural masker blocks, however, masking is minimal in magnitude and short lived.

The implications of these results — which replicate and extend earlier findings from our laboratory (Hawkins, Thomas, Presson, Cozic, & Brookmire, 1974) — are readily apparent. A selectivity process functions in the auditory system to diminish the effects of unwanted input prior to that point in the system at which categorization occurs. Furthermore, this process appears effective in attenuating the effects of an acoustic mask only under conditions in which the mask is channeled separately from the test tone and which permit the mecha-

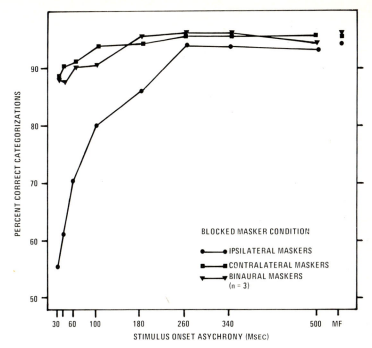

FIG. 4 Percentage correct categorization responses as a function of SOA under three different laterality conditions. Masker frequency remained invariant within trial blocks, and was counterbalanced across subjects, trial blocks, and days.

nism to be pretuned to the frequency of the unwanted stimulus. For these reasons, we might view the selectivity mechanism as analogous to an imperfect narrow band-reject filter.[2] Note that such a mechanism is considerably more restricted in function and effectiveness than the more omnibus, channel-wide, selectivity processes postulated by Broadbent (1958) or Treisman (e.g., 1964).

Massaro (1972a), Norman (1968), and others have argued that much, if not all, the data that have been offered as evidence for precategorical selectivity in fact

[2] An interesting alternative to the notion of an active, cognitively mediated, filter is the idea that a portion of the auditory nervous system habituates to the masking stimulus under blocked masker conditions. The repetitive presentation of an invariant stimulus such as the blocked masker constitutes optimal conditions for the occurrence of habituation (Thompson & Spencer, 1966). Pursuant to this analysis, the absence of habituation effects in the blocked ipsilateral masker case can be interpreted through two assumptions: (1) habituation occurs subsequent to the point in the auditory system at which input is partitioned into separate laterality, or spatial, channels; and (2) The variable and task-relevant test tone functions as a dishabituating stimulus. Test tone preparation thus serves to maintain the sensitivity of the laterality channel shared by test tone and masker in the ipsilateral case, effectively precluding masker habituation.

may reflect processes operating at or beyond the point of memory contact. A particularly pertinent objection raised by these investigators is that precategorical selectivity has been inferred using procedures containing no satisfactory basis for estimating the location of the interference effects that the selectivity process presumably reduces or eliminates. The problem is obvious: in the absence of evidence that the interference occurs precategorically, it becomes difficult to argue that its attenuation is necessarily a precategorical process. On both logical and empirical grounds, it seems highly improbable that the masker used in the auditory recognition masking task exerts its effects *after* the test tone has been categorized as "high" or "low." As we subsequently demonstrate, the masker clearly and systematically influences events leading up to categorization, rather than those which follow it. Moreover, interpretations of selectivity that are based on short-term memory disruption (Massaro, 1972a), pertinence considerations (Norman, 1968), or the demands of subsequent mental operations (Keele, 1973), seem totally irrelevant to the auditory recognition-masking situation. None of these factors differentiates among the laterality conditions shown in Fig. 4.

One further point regarding the Fig. 4 data requires comment. Asymptotic levels of performance are somewhat higher under the binaural (97.1%) and contralateral (96.3%), relative to the ipsilateral (94.6%), masker conditions. In this chapter we argue that enhancement of the stability of the test tone representations in memory (as indexed by asymptotic categorization accuracy) will yield reductions in the extent of masking. However, it seems highly improbable that differences in asymptotic performance as small as those shown in Fig. 4 could produce the large differences obtained in masking extent across laterality conditions. If the differences in asymptote are real, they are most reasonably interpreted as a result, rather than as a cause, of the obtained differences in masking. During practice, prior to the institution of masking trials, our subjects show accuracy in excess of 99%. The errors they do make tend to occur at the very beginning of practice. However, as can be noted in all figures shown in this chapter, performance on masker-free trials within experimental sessions is usually well below the 99% level. The reduced level of asymptotic performance during experimental sessions is undoubtedly due to the effects of masking on subjects' memory for the two test tone alternatives. That is, the test tone representations maintain their stability to the extent that they are enhanced across trials by repeated test tone exposure. However, when masking is effective (as under the ipsilateral masker condition in Fig. 4), the memory mechanism is much less frequently provided with valid (unmasked) test tone information. Accordingly, we should expect that asymptotic performance will be somewhat lower under the ipsilateral masker condition, in which masking is extensive, than under the binaural and contralateral masker conditions, in which it is not.

IV. LOCUS OF AUDITORY RECOGNITION MASKING

The second point we consider relates more directly to where the auditory recognition masking effect is taking place. The principal focus of the masking research reported in the psychoacoustics literature has been on situations in which signal and masker are presented simultaneously. Consequently, the two acoustic sources present on each trial may be assumed to exert a simultaneous influence on the auditory system, beginning at the extreme periphery. Indeed, the weight of evidence (see Kryter, 1970) is that the detection masking effects observed under conditions of relatively continguous stimulus presentation are primarily the result of signal—mask interactions occurring along the basilar membrane, and perhaps as far beyond that as the cochlear nuclei. Consistent with this analysis, little or no masking is obtained when the masker is presented contralateral to the signal (see Kryter, 1970), or when temporal delays in excess of 20—30 msec are inserted between the signal and an ipsilaterally presented masker (Penner, Robinson, & Green, 1972). Relevant to this view is the simultaneous recognition masking study reported by Egan and Meyer (1950). Listeners were presented each trial with a 1.6 sec pure tone, either 300 or 620 Hz in frequency. The tone was presented simultaneously with a comparably intense narrow band noise, 410 Hz at center, and 90 Hz wide. Following offset of the tone—masker pair, an unmasked comparison tone was presented. The task was to adjust the frequency of the unmasked tone so that its perceived pitch matched that of the masked tone. Egan and Meyer found that identity judgments consistently placed the unmasked comparison tone *below* the frequency of the lower masked tone and *above* the frequency of the higher masked tone. In other words, the effect of the masker under simultaneous recognition masking conditions is to displace the perceived pitch of the masked tone *away* from the masker's center frequency.

Just the opposite occurs under temporal auditory-recognition masking conditions. Figure 5 provides a more detailed rendering of the data earlier summarized in Fig. 1. Recall that test tone frequencies were 787 and 863 Hz and masker frequencies were 749, 825, and 901 Hz. The function labeled "adjacent masker" in Fig. 5 depicts performance averaged across trials on which the 787 Hz test tone was followed by the 749 Hz masker and those on which the 863 Hz test tone was followed by a 901 Hz masker. The "remote masker" function designates the average of 787 Hz test tone—901 Hz masker trials and 863 Hz test tone—749 Hz masker trials. (The 825 Hz "interior" masker data are excluded from this analysis). The observed error patterns which we have obtained consistently across subjects indicate that the perceived pitch of the test tone is governed not only by *its* frequency but also by the frequency of the masker. More specifically, it appears that the categorization process is cumulative, basing its output decision on the seemingly indiscriminant averaging of all acoustic

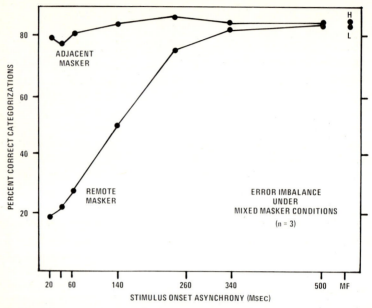

FIG. 5 Percentage correct categorization responses as a function of SOA and test tone–masker frequency relation under mixed, ipsilateral, masker conditions.

input received over a period extending several hundred milliseconds beyond test tone onset. We assume that test tone processing is interrupted at, or closely following, masker onset. Accordingly, the foregoing considerations may be taken to imply that the categorization process continues to gain information from the test tone residual in PAS up to the point of masker onset, at which time it begins to gain information from the masker. The gain of irrelevant masker information, we believe, continues until the completion of a present sampling interval. Thus, the resultant categorization decision is largely determined by the relative proportions of the total (preset) sampling interval devoted to processing the test tone and masker, respectively. The shorter the SOA, the greater will be the proportionate contribution of the masker, and therefore, the greater will be the likelihood that categorization will reflect masker, as opposed to test tone, frequency.

The above reasoning implies that error rate will be relatively low on the higher frequency test tone when followed by the highest frequency masker, for instance, because the confluence of the two high frequency inputs compels a correct "high" decision. Conversely, when the higher frequency test tone is closely followed by the lowest frequency masker, the masker-dominated combination of the two inputs leads toward an incorrect "low" decision. This analysis argues that the masking effect under auditory recognition masking conditions is diametrically opposed to that obtained under the simultaneous recognition masking procedures studied by Egan and Meyer. Interference in auditory recognition masking may be characterized in terms of an additive rule: the product of the test tone—masker interaction at the categorization level consists of an additive combination of the features of both. Interference in simultaneous recognition masking, on the contrary, has been characterized by Egan and Meyer in terms of a subtractive rule in which the interaction residual is given by the difference between neural activation patterns generated by the two simultaneous inputs. That is, that portion of the distribution of neural elements captured by an unmasked signal which overlaps that captured by the mask becomes unavailable for the subsequent analysis of the signal. As a consequence, the categorization process gains a sample of signal frequency data that is biased away from the center frequency of the masker.

Previously we have indicated why the effects obtained in simultaneous masking are interpreted as peripheral in origin. In contrast to this, three relatively independent sources of evidence argue for the centrality of auditory recognition masking effects. First, under the mixed masker condition, in which the subject cannot precategorically inhibit the masker, the effects of a contralateral binaural masker are as extensive as those produced under ipsilateral masker conditions. This finding effectively precludes a peripheral interpretation. Second, consider the ipsilateral and binaural masker functions shown in Fig. 4. Up to the point in the auditory system at which the binaural input is separated into a unique laterality, or spatial, channel, the state of the auditory pathway receiving the test tone is unchanged across these two conditions. Yet the ipsilateral case shows extensive masking, whereas the binaural case shows relatively little. On this basis, one must conclude that the masking effects obtained with the ipsilateral masker have their origins beyond the lateralization mechanism. Third, auditory recognition masking effects extend out several hundred msec beyond the 20–30 msec bound characteristic of peripheral masking. Thus, the effects apparently persist well beyond the point following test tone termination at which the neural correlates of the test tone have cleared the peripheral portion of the auditory nervous system (Davis, Deatherage, Eldredge, & Smith, 1958).

Aside from demonstrating an important characteristic of the central masking phenomenon, the data shown in Fig. 5 lend additional evidence for the presence of a precategorical selectivity process in auditory recognition masking. These data demonstrate that masker frequency information feeds into, and markedly influences, the categorization process. Thus, the finding shown in Fig. 4, that neither contralateral nor binaural blocked maskers produce appreciable masking, strongly implies masker attenuation *prior* to the point at which masker information could feed into and bias the categorization process.

If backward maskers are capable of a peripheral attack on the test tone residual to intertone intervals of 20 to 30 msec, as suggested by the psychoacoustics literature, we might expect to see evidence of this attack at the shortest intervals in auditory recognition masking. Such evidence appears in the data. Both Massaro (1970) and we have obtained a curious U-shaped function under certain auditory recognition masking conditions which seems inexplicable in terms of central masking. Figure 6 illustrates this effect. The data depicted in the figure were drawn from mixed ipsilateral masker trials containing an 825 Hz interior masker. As can be noted in Fig. 6, more extensive masking is obtained at SOAs of 40 and 60 msec than at 20 msec. This effect occurs only on trials containing an interior masker, which is precisely what would be expected were the U-shaped function a manifestation of peripheral masking phenomena. Recall Egan and Meyer's (1950) finding that a peripherally operating masker displaces the perceived pitch of the test tone away from the masker's center frequency. Placed in the auditory recognition masking context, the Egan and Meyer result implies that one consequence of peripheral interactions between the test tone and a very closely following, and equally intense, interior masker is an *increase* in test tone discriminability: the higher frequency test tone will emerge from the peripheral interaction even higher, and the lower frequency test tone will emerge even lower. This effect should, of course, hold only across the 20–30 msec interval following test tone offset during which peripheral effects are evidenced. The data shown in Fig. 6 are clearly consistent with this expectation.

We have performed one test of the peripheral masking interpretation of the short interval U-shaped function, and the results of this test provide further

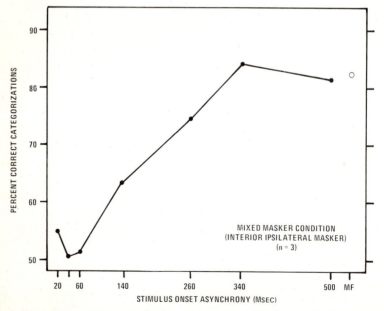

FIG. 6 Percentage correct categorization responses as a function of SOA on those trials within mixed, ipsilateral, masker blocks in which the masker's frequency lay midway between those of the two test tone alternatives (interior masker).

support for our analysis. Figure 7 shows the interior masker data obtained under the mixed masker condition discussed previously in connection with Fig. 3. As would be expected from the peripheral masking interpretation, the U-shaped function appears under both ipsilateral and binaural masker conditions, where peripheral interactions are possible, but not under contralateral masker conditions, where they are not. Based on these results, we tentatively conclude that the auditory recognition masking paradigm can serve as a useful tool for the investigation of peripheral as well as central masking phenomena.

To summarize, we have noted that closely adjacent or temporally overlapping acoustic events can give rise to neural patterns which interact at the peripheral portion of the auditory system and mutually interfere in a subtractive manner. We have labeled this type of interference *peripheral recognition masking*. Consequent to lateralization, input makes contact with a selectivity mechanism that inhibits the impact on subsequent processes of unwanted acoustic information exhibiting a unique and predictable channel of input and a prespecified pitch. Inputs successfully passing the selectivity process gain access to a sensory store (PAS) which functions to preserve an echoic representation of the input for at least several hundred milliseconds beyond termination of the external source,

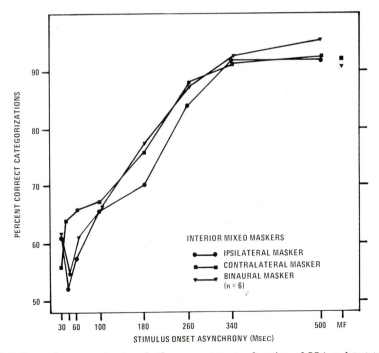

FIG. 7   Percentage correct categorization responses as a function of SOA and test tone—masker laterality on interior masker trials drawn from mixed—masker blocks.

and to transmit data concerning this representation for subsequent processing in memory. To perform optimally under any given set of listening conditions, the categorization mechanism requires some minimum interval for sampling from the acoustic stimulus or its residual. If the wanted stimulus is followed by an unwanted input with a delay less than this minimum sampling interval, the unwanted input interrupts and *replaces* the first as the dominant source of information feeding categorization. As a consequence, the categorization decision will reflect the character not only of the wanted stimulus, but also that of the masker. The degree to which the decision is influenced by the masker directly corresponds to the proportion of the sampling interval given to masker processing. These two effects – the termination of test tone processing by the masker at the precategorical level, and the sequenced, additive contribution of the two tones in categorization – constitute *central recognition masking* as we presently conceptualize it.

V. CONCLUSIONS

We noted the controversy surrounding the auditory recognition masking procedure. In concluding, we wish to comment on the objections that have fed this controversy. At the 1973 Attention and Performance Conference Crowder (1975) expressed concern regarding the actual cause of errors in the auditory recognition masking situation. As an alternative to Massaro's (1970, 1972a) view that the masker disrupts processing of the test tone residual in the sensory store, Crowder noted the possibility that a subject may simply confuse the two tones, mistakenly judging the pitch of the masker rather than of the test tone. According to this analysis, as the interval between the test tone and masker increases, the probability that the subject will judge the wrong tone decreases, and therefore errors will systematically decline. Certainly our error imbalance data, taken at face value, do little to discourage this view. However, it is well known that the temporal resolution of the auditory system is extremely fine (Green, 1971), and consequently, temporal order errors of the kind Crowder has suggested seem highly unlikely across the intervals used in auditory recognition masking. We have data from a comparative judgment task that bear on this issue. The subjects were exposed to stimulus conditions identical in all respects to those used in the mixed masker procedure described in this chapter. The task, however, was to indicate which of the two tones presented on each trial was higher in pitch. If the possibility raised by Crowder were correct, the probability of comparative judgment errors in this task should increase with decreasing SOA. To the contrary, accuracy remained essentially invariant, fluctuating around 90%, across the range of SOA values studied. We conclude, therefore, that the auditory recognition masking data do not reflect a breakdown in the temporal resolution of the auditory system. Yet our subjects clearly *do* incorporate properties of both tones in their categorization decisions. This effect, however, constitutes an important aspect of central masking, and the temporal course of the effect makes sense only through the assumption that a sensory storage system exists prior to auditory categorization.

Objections appearing in the psychoacoustics literature (e.g., Leshowitz & Cudahy, 1973; Watson, Wroton, Kelly, & Benbassat, 1975) have focused on the fact that several seemingly minor variations in the auditory recognition masking procedure have been found to markedly reduce the degree of the masking obtained. More specifically, both the magnitude and duration of masking have been significantly reduced by (1) substantially increasing the number of preexperimental training trials beyond the several hundred to several thousand used by Massaro and by us (Leshowitz & Cudahy, 1973); (2) holding invariant the SOA or masker frequency parameters which we often allow to vary across trials (Watson et al., 1975); or (3) employing paradigms such as the two alternative forced-choice procedure rather than the single interval procedure we have used (Yost[3]; Leshowitz & Cudahy, 1973). The results of these manipulations have led Leshowitz and Cudahy (1973) to contend that the auditory recognition masking data are adequately interpreted in terms of the peripheral sensory masking phenomena long discussed in the psychoacoustics literature rather than in terms of cognitive-perceptual models of the type advocated by Massaro (1972b) or by us. However, their analysis is clearly undermined by the data we have presented which argue for the centrality of the auditory recognition masking effect. We take the results reported by these investigators as important for quite another reason. They make it abundantly clear that the extent of central recognition masking is closely governed by the quality of the representation in memory against which the acoustic input on each trial is compared during categorization. If memory for the sensory properties of the test tone alternatives is in a highly stable state at test tone onset, as is likely the case following extensive overlearning, or when judgments can be based on the comparison of stimuli presented a few hundred milliseconds apart, then a relatively modest sample of the input will be sufficient to insure accurate performance. One implication of our analysis is that one should be able to reinstate masking effects under the conditions described by Leshowitz and Cudahy (1973) and by Watson et al. (1975) by simply reducing the discriminability of the test-tone alternatives the subject must distinguish. This experimental tactic should increase the necessity for extensive input sampling on each trial and should thereby enhance masker effectiveness. Massaro[4] has recently obtained results consistent with this expectation.

---

[3] Unlike Leshowitz and Cudahy (1973) and Watson et al. (1975), Professor Yost (personal communication) shares our view (see following text) that categorization accuracy in auditory recognition masking is importantly determined by the stability, or structural goodness, of the internal representation against which the acoustic input on each trial is referenced.

[4] D. Massaro, personal communication, 1975.

The auditory recognition masking data Massaro (1970, 1972b) and we have obtained are highly systematic and consistent across both subjects and experiments. This finding suggests that we are dealing here with some relatively basic phenomena which offer little opportunity for the use of complex, individualized cognitive strategies. For our purposes, which are behavioral and mechanistically inclined, this is a highly desirable state of affairs. This feature is also desirable from the electrophysiological perspective, which is one direction we believe should be pursed in the future. Indeed, the auditory recognition masking task would seem to be well adapted to the study of alert, behaving, subhuman primates. Moreover, the pure tone stimuli and the tightly controllable temporal parameters of the situation are directly comparable to those used in many investigations of auditory neural physiology. Thus, this line of research should provide a useful and needed point of contact between the literature on neural processing and that on attention and performance.

ACKNOWLEDGMENTS

This work was supported in part by a research grant from the National Science Foundation (BMS 75-09574) to Harold L. Hawkins. Some of the experiments described were conducted at the University of Oregon where the first author held a visiting appointment during the 1973–1974 academic year.

REFERENCES

Bernstein, I. H., Proctor, R. W., Belcher, J., & Schurman, D. L. An analysis of U-shaped metacontrast. *Perception and Psychophysics,* 1974, **16**, 329–336.

Broadbent, D. E. *Perception and Communication.* Oxford, England: Pergamon Press, 1958.

Crowder, R. G. Inferential problems in echoic memory. In P. M. A. Rabbitt & S. Dornic (Eds.), *Attention and performance V.* London: Academic Press, 1975.

Davis, H., Deatherage, B. H., Eldredge, D. H., & Smith, C. A. Summating potentials of the cochlea. *American Journal of Psychology,* 1958, **195**, 251–261.

Egan, J. P., & Meyer, D. R. Changes in pitch of tone of low frequency as a function of the pattern of excitation produced by a band of noise. *Journal of the Acoustical Society of America,* 1950, **22**, 827–833.

Eriksen, C. W. Temporal luminance summation effects in backward and forward masking. *Perception and Psychophysics,* 1966, **1**, 87–92.

Green, D. M. Temporal auditory acuity. *Psychological Review,* 1971, **78**, 540–551.

Hawkins, H. L., Thomas, G., Presson, J., Cozic, A., & Brookmire, D. Tonal specificity and masking in auditory recognition. *Journal of Experimental Psychology,* 1974, **103**, 530–538.

Kahneman, D. Method, findings and theory in studies of visual masking. *Psychological Bulletin,* 1968, **70**, 404–425.

Keele, S. W. *Attention and human performance.* Pacific Palisades: Goodyear, 1973.

Kryter, K. D. *The effects of noise on man.* New York: Academic Press, 1970.

Leshowitz, B., & Cudahy, E. Frequency discrimination in the presence of another tone. *The Journal of the Acoustical Society of America*, 1973, 54, 882–887.

Massaro, D. W. Preperceptual auditory images. *Journal of Experimental Psychology*, 1970, 85, 411–417.

Massaro, D. W. Perceptual images, processing time, and perceptual units in auditory perception. *Psychological Review*, 1972, 79, 124–145.   (a)

Massaro, D. W. Stimulus information vs. processing time in auditory pattern recognition. *Perception and Psychophysics*, 1972, 12, 50–56.   (b)

Morton, J., Crowder, R. G., & Prussin, H. A. Experiments with the stimulus suffix effect. *Journal of Experimental Psychology*, 1971, 91, 169–190.

Norman, D. A. Toward a theory of memory and attention. *Psychological Review*, 1968, 75, 522–536.

Penner, M. J., Robinson, C. E., & Green, D. M. The critical masking interval. *The Journal of the Acoustical Society of America*, 1972, 52, 1661–1668.

Thompson, R. F., & Spencer, W. A. Habituation: A modal phenomena for the study of neuronal substrates of behavior. *Psychological Review*, 1966, 173, 16–43.

Treisman, A. M. Monitoring and storage of irrelevant messages in selective attention. *Journal of Verbal Learning and Verbal Behavior*, 1964, 3, 449–459.

Turvey, M. On peripheral and central processes in vision: Inferences from an information-processing analysis of masking with patterned stimuli. *Psychological Review*, 1973, 80, 1–52.

Watson, C. S., Wroton, H. W., Kelly, W. J., & Benbassat, C. A. Factors in the discrimination of tonal patterns. I. Component frequency, temporal position, and silent intervals. *The Journal of the Acoustical Society of America*, 1975, 57, 1175–1185.

11

Capacity Limitations in Auditory Information Processing

Dominic W. Massaro

Department of Psychology
University of Wisconsin
Madison, Wisconsin, United States

ABSTRACT

An information processing model serves as a heuristic to understand capacity limitations and attentional effects in auditory-processing tasks. Experiments in backward recognition masking show no selective perception along the dimensions of spatial location, loudness, or sound quality. Some capacity limitation is shown, however, when an auditory perception task must be performed concurrently with visual recognition. Selective attention also occurs when observers are required to integrate and count a sequence of sounds although these same sound sequences can be monitored on a perceptual level without an attentional effect. Attentional effects in processing dichotic speech inputs are also described in terms of the model.

I. INTRODUCTION

The goal of this chapter is to utilize an information processing model in order to understand capacity limitations and attentional effects in auditory processing tasks. This approach rests on the idea that a model of attention can only follow rather than precede models of information processing. Accordingly, we begin by describing the development of an auditory processing model and the empirical support for the model. We then consider the implications of the model for attentional effects at successive stages of auditory processing.

Figure 1 presents a flow diagram of the auditory processing model utilized in our research. Auditory input is funneled through the ears so that although the

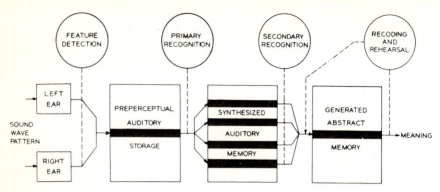

FIG. 1   Successive stages of auditory information processing.

atmosphere is filled with sound, our contact with it is limited to these two organs. The transduction of the sound-pressure fluctuations passes on featural information which is detected and stored centrally in preperceptual auditory storage. Preperceptual auditory storage holds the featural information given by the detection process for a short time after a stimulus is presented. The primary recognition process involves a resolution of this information, producing a synthesized percept held in synthesized auditory memory. Primary recognition accomplishes the phenomenological outcome of perceiving sound of a definite loudness and quality at some location in space. Preperceptual auditory storage appears to be centrally located with a capacity of just one sound; a second sound appears to replace the featural information stored there about the earlier sound. The information about the first sound passed on by primary recognition is limited to that processed between the onset of the first sound and the onset of the second. The quality of the information in synthesized auditory memory is, therefore, a direct function of the processing time between the onsets of the two sounds.

II.   RECOGNITION MASKING

Evidence for this conceptualization of preperceptual auditory storage and primary recognition comes from a number of results in recognition masking. Massaro, Cohen, and Idson (1976) provided a direct comparison of forward and backward recognition masking. On each trial the subject was required to identify a sine-wave test tone as high or low. The high and low test tones were 860 and 790 Hz, respectively. In forward masking, the test tone was preceded by a masking tone, whereas the masking tone followed the test tone in backward masking. The masking tone was either high (900 Hz), middle (825 Hz), or low (750 Hz). The test and masking tones were 20 msec in duration and were presented at a normal listening intensity.

Each trial began with the visual presentation of a Cue 1 or 2, signifying whether the test tone would be presented first or second. The cue was presented 1 sec before the onset of the test tone presentation. On masking trials, the test tone was preceded or followed by a masking tone with a 0-, 20-, 40-, 80-, 160-, 250-, or 350-msec silent interval between the test and masking tones. On 1/8 of the trials no masking tone was presented. These trials were cued with the digit "1." The subject had 1.5 sec to make a response after the offset of the test tone. Subjects pushed 1 of 2 buttons labeled "H" and "L," respectively, indicating whether the test tone was high or low. Feedback was given after this interval by illuminating for 250 msec a visual display with the symbol H or L depending on whether the high or low tone was presented. The intertrial interval was 1.5 sec.

Figure 2 presents the forward and backward masking functions for eight subjects. The results show an insignificant amount of forward masking at silent intervals longer than 20 msec whereas significant backward masking occurs out to intervals 250–350 msec. Asymptotic performance under forward and backward masking averaged about 5% less than performance under the no-mask condition. This result contrasts with a number of previous results showing that backward masking at 250 msec is equivalent to the no masking case (Hawkins & Presson, this volume; Massaro & Cohen, 1975; Massaro & Kahn, 1973). One explanation might be that the subjects missed or forgot the visual cue on a small proportion of trials in this study. When this occurred on masking trials, the subject might have categorized the masking tone rather than the test tone. This mixup could not occur on no-masking trials, leading to the slight asymptotic advantage of the no-mask condition.

The results given in Fig. 2 can be interpreted in terms of the properties of preperceptual auditory storage and the primary recognition process. Recognition of a short sound may not be complete at the end of the stimulus and can continue to occur during the silent period after the sound presentation. Backward masking occurs because a second sound interferes with the recognition process by replacing the first sound in preperceptual auditory storage. Very little forward masking is found since the test sound replaces the masking sound in preperceptual storage and recognition can continue during the silent interval after the test sound presentation.

The recognition masking results appear to require some assumption of a preperceptual storage before recognition has taken place. Crowder (1975) suggested that backward masking may occur because subjects confuse the order of the test and masking tones and judge the pitch of the masking rather than the test tone. Increasing the silent interval between the tones decreases the likelihood of the temporal confusion and, therefore, performance will improve. Crowder's temporal confusion hypothesis predicts that backward and forward masking should be equally effective since temporal confusions must be bidirectional. The large asymmetry in backward and forward masking in Fig. 2 argues against a simple temporal confusion hypothesis.

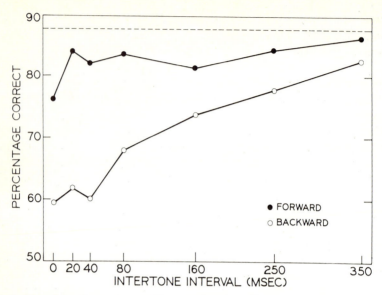

FIG. 2   Percentage of correct recognitions as a function of intertone interval under forward and backward masking. The dotted line gives performance when no masking tone was presented. (After Massaro, Cohen, & Idson, 1976.)

III.   SELECTIVE PERCEPTION

The following experiments asked to what extent capacity limitations and attentional effects occur at the initial stage of primary recognition. The experiments are carried out in a backward recognition masking task for a number of reasons. Since the masking stimulus terminates processing of the test stimulus, attentional effects can be measured at different processing times of the test stimulus. This procedure tests for attentional effects across the whole range of performance levels, allowing the experimenter to avoid floor and ceiling effects. The significant improvement in performance with processing time will provide a measure of the dynamic aspect of attentional effects if they are found, and will help silence potential criticisms of an inadequate test if no attentional effects are observed. If attentional effects are shown to interact with processing time, the results can be safely located at the primary recognition, rather than some later stage of information processing.

A.   Spatial Location

The results of recognition masking support the idea that a second sound can replace an earlier sound held in preperceptual auditory storage. There is also good evidence that the storage is located centrally after the inputs from the two ears are combined in the auditory system. (see Hawkins & Presson, this volume;

Massaro, 1975b; Massaro & Cohen, 1975). A masking tone presented to the opposite ear of a test tone presentation produces as much interference as one presented to the same ear as the test tone.

If the structure of preperceptual auditory storage is a single channel that receives inputs from both ears, primary recognition should not be capable of selective attending to one spatial location or blocking out another. To test this hypothesis, subjects were asked to recognize a test tone as high or low (Massaro, 1975a). The test tone was a 20-msec sine wave of either 720 or 780 Hz. The test tone could be presented to either of the two ears followed after a variable silent interval by a masking tone presented to the opposite ear. The masking tone was a 100-msec square wave tone of 750 Hz. Before each trial, subjects were cued that the test tone would be presented to the right, to the left, or to either ear. These practiced subjects also knew that the masking tone would be presented to the opposite ear. Therefore, given the cues right or left, subjects attempted to attend to the designated ear and to block out the unattended ear. Given the either cue, however, subjects had to divide their attention between the two ears as the test tone could occur on either ear.

If subjects can selectively attend to spatial location at the level of primary recognition, we should find significantly less masking in the selective than the divided attention conditions. On the other hand, the spatial location of a sound may not be available until primary recognition of spatial location has occurred. In this case, sounds coming in different ears cannot be differentiated and

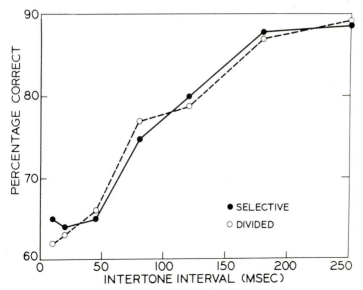

FIG. 3 Percentage of correct recognitions as a function of intertone interval under selective and divided attention. (After Massaro, 1975a.)

selective attention to spatial location should not be possible. Therefore, primary recognition of the pitch of the test tone should not be facilitated by a precue indicating the spatial locations of the test and masking tones. Figure 3 plots performance under the selective- and divided-attention conditions as a function of the intertone interval. Supporting earlier dichotic masking studies, pitch recognition improved with increases in processing time before the masking tone. And in agreement with the experimental hypothesis, no differences were found between the selective- and divided-attention conditions.

B. Loudness and Sound Quality

Spatial location information is not immediately available at the level of preperceptual storage but must be resolved by primary recognition. Similarly, loudness and sound quality are not differentiated at the level of preperceptual storage. Moore and Massaro (1973) asked whether observers could selectively process one dimension of an auditory stimulus. On each trial, subjects identified either the loudness, sound quality, or both dimensions of a short test tone in a backward recognition masking task. Performance improved with increases in the silent intertone interval, but was not dependent on whether subjects identified one or two dimensions of the test tone. This result shows that the primary recognition process cannot selectively attend to certain features of sound quality or loudness to improve its performance relative to the situation in which both dimensions must be identified.

The results of Massaro (1975a) and Moore and Massaro (1973) show that subjects may not be able to selectively attend to an auditory dimension of spatial location, loudness, or sound quality at the level of primary recognition. The reason for this, in our model, is that these dimensions are not differentiated at the level of preperceptual auditory storage. An alternative explanation would be that the dimensions are differentiated but that the primary recognition process is automatic and unlimited in capacity. This hypothesis also predicts that multiple dimensions can be processed in parallel without a performance deficit. One way to distinguish between these two explanations is to measure auditory recognition when subjects are required to perform some other nonauditory task. If auditory recognition were unlimited in capacity, a second task should not limit its efficiency. Given a limited capacity, however, a second task might interfere with auditory recognition even though subjects cannot selectively attend to certain dimensions of a sound at the level of primary recognition.

C. Auditory and Visual Recognition

Massaro and Kahn (1973) asked whether auditory recognition could be disrupted by an additional visual processing task. Simultaneously identifying the duration of a light decreased tone identification relative to the selective attention case in which just the tone had to be processed. This result is consistent with the idea that the process of primary recognition itself is limited in capacity and identifying the duration of the light can subtract from the process capacity available for primary auditory recognition. Within the process of auditory recognition, however, no further division of processing capacity may be possible because of the structure of preperceptual auditory storage. In this case, it may not be possible to selectively process one auditory dimension at the expense of another.

Shiffrin and Grantham (1974) have argued that duration judgments require short-term memory and decision capacity which cannot be divided without loss. Given the difficulty of the duration task, processing the duration of the visual stimulus may delay the decision about the pitch of the test tone until the appropriate information is lost. It is difficult to see, however, why the subject would forget the pitch of the test tone since it can be categorized as high or low. If making two decisions instead of just one produces a short-term memory loss, we might also have expected an attentional effect in the Moore and Massaro (1973) study.

If one argues that recognition is automatic and does not have capacity limitations, any deficit observed in some divided-attention situation might be claimed to occur at some later stage of processing. The evidence indicates, however, that recognition masking measures the temporal development of auditory recognition and does not depend on decision or short-term memory limitations (Hawkins & Presson, this volume; Massaro, 1976a). Accordingly, the recognition masking paradigm is ideal for studying attentional effects and capacity limitations at the primary recognition stage of processing. If some attentional manipulation is observed to interact across the temporal course of recognition, we are somewhat confident in assuming that its effect is occurring at the recognition stage of processing. Shiffrin (1976) agrees that backward masking occurs before short-term memory; if capacity limitations or attentional effects interact with backward masking, their effect should be located at the recognition, not the short-term memory, stage of processing.

Massaro and Warner (unpublished manuscript, 1976) asked whether primary recognition was limited in capacity. Subjects were asked to selectively attend to a visual recognition task, an auditory recognition task, or to divide their attention between the two tasks. The visual task required the subject to recognize a letter as "U" or "V." The subjects identified the test tone as high or low in the auditory task. Both the visual and auditory test stimuli were followed by masking stimuli after a variable interval. Each trial was initiated with a visual cue indicating whether the subject should identify the tone, the letter, or both the tone and the letter. All other experimental conditions were exactly analogous to the Moore and Massaro (1973) study.

Figure 4 presents the results of four subjects under the selective- and divided-attention conditions. Performance improved with increases in the processing

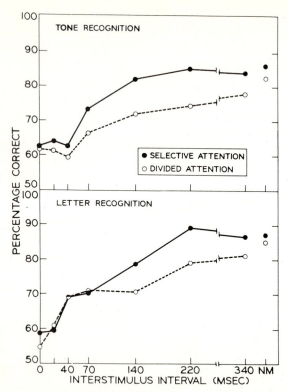

FIG. 4   Percentage of correct recognitions as a function of interstimulus interval under selective and divided attention. (After Massaro & Warner, unpublished manuscript, 1976.)

interval between the test and masking stimuli in both letter and tone recognition and under selective and divided attention. Overall performance was better in the selective- than the divided-attention condition in both visual and auditory recognition. These results provide some support for the hypothesis that auditory recognition may be limited in capacity. Even though auditory recognition has a capacity limitation, however, it may not be possible to selectively enhance processing of one auditory dimension at the expense of processing another dimension.

IV.   MONITORING AND COUNTING SOUNDS

We have argued that, although primary recognition may be limited in capacity, it is not possible to selectively attend to certain auditory dimensions at this stage of processing. The outcome of primary recognition is the perception of some sound at some location in space. Synthesized auditory memory holds the outcome of primary recognition. The storage capacity of synthesized auditory memory is larger than preperceptual auditory storage. Synthesized auditory memory can hold a number of items over the time span of seconds. Given that a sound is stored in synthesized auditory memory with perceptual information about spatial location, loudness, and pitch quality, it should be possible to selectively attend to some dimension at this stage of processing. Secondary recognition involves an analysis for meaning and this analysis should be dependent on the structural properties of the information in synthesized memory. The following experiments were aimed at showing that, although selective attention to spatial location and tone frequency are not possible at primary recognition, these dimensions can be selectively attended to at the level of secondary recognition.

A. Spatial Location

Previous studies of primary recognition have required subjects to process just a single test tone. In order to compare primary and secondary recognition, we asked observers to process sequences of test tones. First, the experiment on selective attention to spatial location (Fig. 3) was extended to monitoring a sequence of test tones (Massaro, 1976b). Subjects heard a sequence of 5, 6, 7, or 8 20-msec tones. The tones in a sequence were either presented to the same ear or alternated between the ears. The tones could be presented at any of 8 rates of presentation ranging between 20 and 3.5 per second. All of the tones but one were 800 Hz. The frequency of the different tone, called the probe tone, was either slightly higher or lower than 800 Hz. The task was to indicate whether the probe tone was higher or lower than the other tones in the sequence regardless of the rate of presentation or whether the tones alternated between ears. The subjects were practiced and were given feedback after each trial.

Subjects should be able to perform this task at the level of primary recognition. The sequence of tones can be monitored by listening for the higher or lower probe tone. If subjects cannot selectively attend to spatial location at this stage of processing, no decrement in performance should be observed when the tones are alternated between ears relative to being presented to the same ear.

The bottom panel of Fig. 5 plots the percentage of correct recognitions of the frequency of the probe tone as a function of the rate of presentation and whether the tones are presented to the same ear or alternated between ears. The rate of presentation is described in terms of processing time defined as the time between the onsets of the successive 20-msec tones. Performance improved about 20% with increases in the silent interval between successive test tones. This result demonstrates that backward recognition masking also occurs with a sequence of successive tones. Each tone in the sequence functions as a masking tone terminating any further resolution of the pitch of the previous tone. More importantly, probe recognition is not disrupted when the tones are alternated

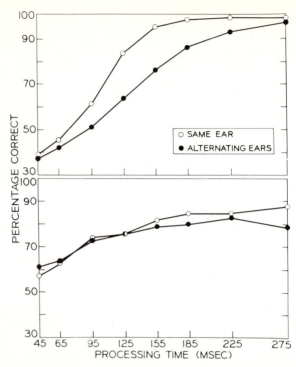

FIG. 5 Percentage of correct probe recognitions (bottom panel) and correct counts (top panel) as a function of processing time for each tone. The parameter indicates whether the tones were presented to the same ear or alternated between the ears. (After Massaro, 1976b.)

between the ears relative to being presented to the same ear. (The advantage of the same ear condition at the 275-msec processing interval will be discussed subsequently.)

The goal now was to take these same sequences of tones and require them to be processed at the level of synthesized auditory memory and secondary recognition. The task we chose was a counting task. The sequences were the same as in the probe monitoring task except that all tones were 800 Hz. Accordingly, subjects now heard a sequence of 5, 6, 7, or 8 20-msec tones, reported which of the four sequences occurred, and were informed of the number of tones actually presented. The top panel of Fig. 5 presents the percentage of correct counts as a function of processing time under the two types of presentation. Counting performance improved with increases in processing time but at a much faster rate when the tones were presented to the same ear than when the tones were alternated between the ears. The deficit in counting performance when the tones are alternated between the ears is consistent with the idea that perceptual dimensions at the level of synthesized auditory memory can be utilized for selective processing during secondary recognition. Given that no decrement was found in the monitoring task, alternating the tones between the ears did not interfere with the perceptual resolution of each of the test tones. The decrement in the counting task with alternating tones must, therefore, mean that subjects have trouble counting or integrating sequences of tones that are perceived at different locations in space. Harvey and Treisman (1973) reached similar conclusions from an analogous set of studies.

B. Frequency

Two additional experiments explored the possitility that the frequency dimension would operate similar to spatial location. These experiments replicated the previous two experiments, but the 20-msec tones were presented binaurally, and were either presented at the same frequency or alternated between two different frequencies. The different frequencies were slightly over one octave apart; the notes A_4 (440) and B_5 (988 Hz) were used.

The monitoring task required subjects to listen for a probe tone that was either slightly longer or shorter than the other 20-msec tones in a sequence. (A change in duration produces a timbre difference.) On each trial, subjects indicated whether the probe tone was longer or shorter and were given feedback on their decision. The bottom panel of Fig. 6 shows that recognition improved with increases in processing time and was somewhat poorer at the longer processing intervals when the tones alternated in frequency. This deficit, which contradicts the experimental hypothesis is discussed subsequently.

The counting task required the subjects to count the tones in the sequence regardless of whether they were presented at the same frequency or alternated between frequencies. The top panel of Fig. 6 plots counting performance as a function of the rate of presentation under the same and alternating frequency conditions. Counting performance was significantly poorer when the tones alternated in frequency relative to being presented at the same frequency but this effect did not emerge until the tones were presented at 8 per second or slower. Analogous to the experiment in which tones can alternate between the ears, subjects show a deficit in counting sounds that have been presented at alternating frequencies.

The monitoring results in Figs. 5 and 6 show a slight decrement at the slowest rate of presentation in the alternating relative to the same ear or frequency condition. This result shows that subjects may have switched to a comparison judgment between successive test tones at the slowest rate of presentation. In this case, the subjects would be at a disadvantage in the alternating relative to the single frequency or ear condition. Consider the monitoring experiment in which the tones could alternate in frequency. The change in duration of the probe tone produces a change in timbre and the timbre also depends on the frequency of the probe tone. To perform the monitoring task correctly, subjects

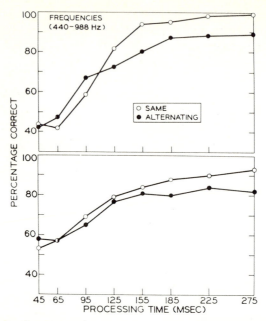

FIG. 6 Percentage of correct probe recognitions (bottom panel) and correct counts (top panel) as a function of processing time for each tone. The parameter indicates whether the tones were presented at the same frequency or alternated between frequencies. (After Massaro, 1976b.)

would have to remember the timbre of the longer and shorter probe tones at both frequency values. If subjects made successive comparison judgments, however, it would be easier to compare the timbre of successive notes when the notes are at the same frequency than when the notes alternate in frequency. An analogous argument can be made when the tones alternate between the ears since a tone of a given frequency may give a different pitch impression to one ear than to another. This argument is not critical for our purposes since *no* monitoring deficit was observed at those rates of presentation that gave the largest counting deficit.

Primary recognition involves the readout of a single preperceptual store that receives information from both ears and different frequencies. In the monitoring task, subjects can evaluate the output of primary recognition to observe whether a probe frequency or duration was presented. The critical variable is the processing time available for primary recognition. Given the central preperceptual store, primary recognition shows very little decrement when sounds are alternated between the two ears or between different frequencies. Secondary recognition, on the other hand, is necessary to abstract meaning from synthesized auditory memory. Given that sounds are perceived at different spatial locations or different pitches in the alternating conditions, secondary recognition has more difficulty integrating and counting these sounds than sounds perceived at the same pitch and spatial location (cf. Fig. 1). This analysis illuminates the differences found in the monitoring and counting experiments and provides a processing model of the stages of processing at which selective attention will and will not occur.

Information is most easily processed along a temporal dimension in synthesized auditory memory. The perceptual dimensions such as spatial location or pitch cannot be used to organize auditory inputs. If the inputs from the different ears could be processed by location rather than by temporal order, then we wouldn't have expected such a substantial counting deficit in the alternating ear condition. Subjects would have been able to count the number of tones along one location and then those along the other location. Evidently, synthesized auditory memory did not maintain all of the items along their spatial locations for the 1 or 2 seconds necessary to perform the task in this way.

V. SPEECH PROCESSING

The tone experiments and this analysis have implications for the processing of speech stimuli presented simultaneously to the two ears. Previous investigators have assumed that the analysis for meaning of a list of items presented to one ear can be delayed for 1 or 2 seconds until the list on the other ear is processed (Broadbent, 1958, 1971; Darwin, Turvey, & Crowder, 1972). One test of the capacity and structure of synthesized auditory memory has been to present simultaneous lists of items to different spatial locations preceded or followed by a probe cue asking the subjects to recall some subset of the items. If the items are indeed maintained along separate locations in synthesized auditory memory and semantic analysis is delayed for 1 or 2 seconds, cuing recall of the items according to spatial location should produce better performance than cueing recall along some semantic dimension such as category name. Semantic analysis is not delayed for 1 or 2 seconds in our model but occurs on the order of every syllable (see Massaro, 1975c). Therefore, we predict that spatial location will not be a more effective partial report cue than category name even if the cue is given immediately after the test lists.

In one experiment (Massaro, 1976c), two lists of four items each were recorded by different speakers at a rate of 4 items per second. These lists were presented simultaneously to the two ears. Each list on each ear contained two one-syllable words and two letters chosen randomly without replacement from respective master sets of 25 one-syllable words and 25 letters. When subjects were asked to recall by location the cue indicated whether they should report the items presented to the left or right ears. When subjects were asked to recall by category, the cue indicated whether they should report the words or letters. The exact same lists and cues (pure tones) were used in both report conditions.

The cue was presented immediately after the last items in the lists. In both report conditions there were two possible report cues and the subjects were required to report four items. Therefore, if the items are maintained along separate auditory dimensions according to spatial location and semantic analysis is delayed for 1 or 2 seconds, recall cued by location should be superior to recall cued by category name.

The results showed no advantage of a report by spatial location over that by category name when the cue was given immediately after the test list (Massaro, 1975b, 1976c). This result shows that the separate lists are not maintained for 1 or 2 sec in a precategorical form according to spatial location of presentation. The spatial location of an item does not appear to be preserved in a precategorical form but must be remembered by way of association (the letter "E" comes from the left).

On the other hand, we might expect that recall by spatial location would be much better if the report cue is given before the test lists. In this case, subjects can utilize the report cue during the processing of the lists. Figure 7 presents the mean number of items recalled when the location and category cues were given before or after the test list. Recall by spatial location was much better than

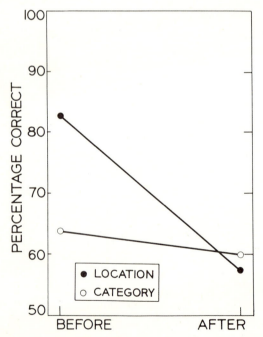

FIG. 7 Percentage of items correctly recalled as a function of whether the report cue was given seconds before or immediately after the test list. The parameter specifies whether recall was cued according to spatial location or category name. (After Massaro, 1976c.)

recall by category name when the cue was given before the list presentation. Delaying the report cue until immediately after the test list decreased recall by spatial location by 25% but had an insignificant effect on recall by category name. Replicating the earlier study, no difference in recall occurred when the cues were given after the test list.

The results of the partial report experiments clarify the temporal course of successive stages of auditory information processing. Simultaneous items are first stored centrally in preperceptual storage. Primary recognition resolves the items at a perceptual level and locates them at different locations in space. Secondary recognition then processes the items for meaning. If the report cue for spatial location is given before the test list, secondary recognition can devote most of its processing capacity (but not all of it) to items perceived at a given location in space. In recall by category name, the cue before the list does not reduce the processing required by secondary recognition. Each item must still be processed for meaning to determine if it belongs to the appropriate category for recall. Accordingly, more items can be reported correctly in recall by spatial location than in recall by category name when the cue is given before the test list. If subjects are not cued until after the test list, the items have been processed by both primary and secondary recognition. In this case, retrieval by spatial location no longer shows an advantage over recall by category name.

VI. SUMMARY AND CONCLUSION

A simplified version of the model proposed earlier is shown in Fig. 8. The model distinguishes between three stages (levels) of auditory processing: detection, primary recognition, and secondary recognition. The detection of sound refers to the listener's experience that some sound was present. In this case, detection means the observer is able to state when sound is present or absent. After a sound is detected, the listener does not necessarily have any information about

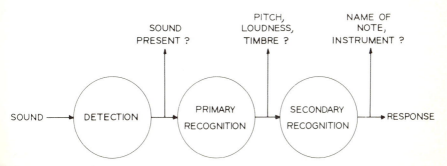

FIG. 8 Detection, primary recognition, and secondary recognition stages of auditory processing.

the nature of that sound. Having heard a sound, primary recognition refers to the listener's ability to resolve some attribute of the sound, such as its pitch, timbre, loudness, or spatial location. Finally, the listener's ability to identify a particular pitch as middle C is called secondary recognition. It is assumed that the onsets of these three stages of processing are successive although the stages themselves may overlap in time. Given the successive nature of detection and primary and secondary recognition, a listener might detect a tone but not resolve its pitch, or resolve its pitch but fail to identify its name. Furthermore, a later stage of processing usually does not occur unless each earlier stage is successful. For example, the pitch of a sound could not be resolved without detection of the sound.

The stage analysis appears to provide a worthwhile heuristic for studying capacity limitations and selective attention effects in auditory processing. Although primary recognition may be limited in capacity, it may not be possible to selectively attend to certain dimensions of sound at this stage of processing. On the other hand, integrating successive sounds at the level of secondary recognition is dependent on selective attention to dimensions of the sound sequence. Therefore, selective attention to some auditory dimension can facilitate processing for meaning. Given that the analysis for meaning is not delayed for 1 or 2 seconds, however, retrieval along an auditory dimension shows no advantage over retrieval along a semantic category when the retrieval cue is given immediately after the auditory input.

ACKNOWLEDGMENTS

The preparation of this paper was supported by National Institute of Mental Health Grant MH-19399 and a grant from the Wisconsin Alumni Research Foundation.

REFERENCES

Broadbent, D. E. *Perception and communication.* New York: Pergamon Press, 1958.
Broadbent, D. E. *Decision and stress.* London: Academic Press, 1971.
Crowder, R. G. Inferential problems in echoic memory. In P. M. A. Rabbitt & S. Dornic (Eds.), *Attention and performance V.* London: Academic Press, 1975.
Darwin, C. J., Turvey, M. T., & Crowder, R. G. An auditory analogue of the Sperling partial report procedure: Evidence for brief auditory storage. *Cognitive Psychology,* 1972, **3**, 255–267.
Harvey, N., & Treisman, A. M. Switching attention between the ears to monitor tones. *Perception & Psychophysics,* 1973, **14**, 51–59.
Hawkins, H. L., & Presson, J. C. Masking and perceptual selectivity in auditory recognition. This volume.
Massaro, D. W. Backward recognition masking. *Journal of the Acoustical Society of America,* 1975, **58**, 1059–1065. (a)

Massaro, D. W. *Experimental psychology and information processing.* Chicago: Rand Mc—Nally, 1975. (b)

Massaro, D. W. *Understanding language: An information processing analysis of speech perception, reading, and psycholinguistics.* New York: Academic Press, 1975. (c)

Massaro, D. W. Auditory information processing. In W. K. Estes (Ed.), *Handbook of learning and cognitive processes Vol. 4: Attention and memory.* Hillsdale, N. J.: Lawrence Erlbaum Associates, 1976. (a)

Massaro, D. W. Perceiving and counting sounds. *Journal of Experimental Psychology: Human Perception and Performance,* 1976, **2**, 337–346. (b)

Massaro, D. W. Perceptual processing in dichotic listening. *Journal of Experimental Psychology: Human Learning and Memory,* 1976, **2**, 331–339. (c)

Massaro, D. W., & Cohen, M. M. Preperceptual auditory storage in speech recognition. In A. Cohen & S. G. Nooteboom (Eds.), *Structure and process in speech perception.* New York: Springer-Verlag, 1975.

Massaro, D. W., Cohen, M. M., & Idson, W. L. Recognition masking of auditory lateralization and pitch judgments. *Journal of the Acoustical Society of America,* 1976, **59**, 434–441.

Massaro, D. W., & Kahn, B. J. Effects of central processing on auditory recognition. *Journal of Experimental Psychology,* 1973, **9**, 51–58.

Massaro, D. W., & Warner, D. Dividing attention between auditory and visual recognition. Unpublished manuscript, 1976.

Moore, J. J., & Massaro, D. W. Attention and processing capacity in auditory recognition. *Journal of Experimental Psychology,* 1973, **99**, 49–54.

Shiffrin, R. M. Capacity limitations in information processing, attention, and memory. In W. K. Estes (Ed.), *Handbook of learning and cognitive processes Vol. 4: Attention and memory.* Hillsdale, N. J.: Lawrence Erlbaum Associates, 1976.

Shiffrin, R. M., & Grantham, D. W. Can attention be allocated to sensory modalities? *Perception & Psychophysics,* 1974, **15**, 460–474.

12

On the Hemispheric Representation of Time

Pieter A. Vroon

Psychological Institute
University of Leiden
Leiden, The Netherlands

Han Timmers[1]

Psychological Laboratory
University of Nijmegen
Nijmegen, The Netherlands

Stan Tempelaars

Institute of Sonology
University of Utrecht
Utrecht, The Netherlands

ABSTRACT

It is well known that subjective duration is related to cognitive processes. Also, differences between the information processing and analyzing systems of both cerebral hemispheres have been reported. This study attempts to determine whether or not the left brain is superior in the encoding of time. In Experiment I the subjects reconstructed the durations of simple reaction time tasks carried out predominantly by either the left or the right brain half in the visual and auditory modality. It appeared that the variances of the time estimates of the right brain considerably exceeded those of the left. Consequently, there is a relatively great time uncertainty

[1] The second author participated in Experiment I as partial fulfillment of the M.A. requirements of the University of Nijmegen; the third author participated in Experiment III by programming the computer system.

in the right brain. This difference was clear for the auditory modality but it was not observed for visual stimuli. In Experiment II the subjects reacted to visual stimuli with irregular intervals as well as to regularly presented auditory stimuli. The visual task primarily loaded either the left or the right hemisphere, the other being mainly involved in the auditory reactions. With respect to the auditory RTs, the left brain showed a faster training effect over trials, indicating a better discovery of the internal structure of a time series and a relatively superior prediction of events in time. In Experiment III it was observed that the left hemisphere is also better in the detection of short interruptions in noise bursts. The findings suggest that one of the structural differences between the cerebral hemispheres stems from the degree to which processed information is analyzed and encoded in time.

I. INTRODUCTION

This study attempts to relate two fields of research, time psychology and the lateralization of cortex functions. Of the many phenomena comprising time psychology (Fraisse, 1963), the experience of duration has attracted most interest. Two theories attempt to explain the phenomenon that subjective time varies with respect to the clock. The first theory proposes a pulse counter based on the hypothesis that time is experienced via an internal time keeper, driven by physiological or hypothetical periodic processes. The speed of the time keeper is assumed to be some function of (physiological) arousal. The theory was first proposed by Hoagland (1933) and is able to account for the effects of, for example, body temperature, activation and some drugs. The second theory is a cognitive approach based on an information processing view of behavior. Time means information to man (Michon, 1972) and subjective time is a function of processes such as the coding, storing, and retrieving of information (Ornstein, 1969). For example, Michon (1965, 1967) and Vroon (1970) showed that apparent time is a decreasing function of the information transmission rate and that curves relating apparent duration to physical time show an inflection point at the transition between sensory and short-term memory. Thus, duration experience appears to be closely dependent on the characteristics of information processing and memory mechanisms. The cognitive theory does not exclude the first model, but is the more plausible of the two approaches in that it not only explains physiological effects but also the influences of, for example, specific coding and memory processes. Apart from this positive evidence, some basic assumptions of the first theory have been questioned (Vroon, 1974).

With respect to information processing in general, research during the last two decades suggests that both hemispheres possess qualitatively different analyzing systems (Dimond, 1972; Dimond & Beaumont, 1972b) and that both structures may even work independently of each other to some degree (Dimond & Beaumont, 1972a). However, in spite of numerous reports on hemispheric differences in the processing of verbal and nonverbal, auditory, visual, and tactual stimuli, there are few theories in which the precise nature of the double mechanism is outlined. There are anatomical reasons for a relative superiority of the left brain with verbal material, but the background of the right brain's superiority in the perception of complex visual forms and visual directionality (Fontenot & Benton, 1972), human nonspeech sounds, dot location, stereoscopic depth perception, and nonvisual location (Kimura, 1966, 1973) remains unclear. One could argue that a general difference between the hemispheres is defined by a distinction between serial and parallel types of processing (Neisser, 1967) inasmuch as the left brain plays a major part in understanding and producing speech. With respect to verbal material, this viewpoint, implying a fine temporal resolution power in the left brain, is defended by Bosshardt and Hörmann (1975). Corcoran (1971) argues, however, that the parallel processes which Neisser (1967) assumes to be responsible for some visual pattern recognition tasks might be explained instead as very rapid sequential processes. Consequently, as Dimond (1972) concludes, there seems to be no equivocal evidence to suppose extreme differences (1) between the processing and analyzing systems for every type of sensory material; and (2) with respect to hemispheric specialization in general. It seems expedient to concentrate first on differences between sensory modalities rather than on gross distinctions between the brain halves. With respect to the latter, we hypothesize that the left hemisphere is somewhat superior in the internal analysis of auditory stimuli.

As far as auditory material is concerned, a left brain superiority is clear for verbal material. Since producing and understanding speech calls for internal stimulus analysis and a fine temporal discriminatory ability, one could argue that time is better encoded in the left brain. In the visual modality no difference is expected in this respect. It is not certain that the better recognition of nonverbal material by the right brain is caused by a parallel or "holistic" processing system in which time-order variables would be less important. Moreover, part of the reported visual differences can be ascribed to effects of reproduction order (Bryden, 1960). Dimond and Beaumont (1972a) found that figural material is processed somewhat faster by the right hemisphere. They suggest that there is some qualitative difference in the method of analysis of both visual systems. However, the data do not warrant the expectation of definite differences in terms of the temporal encoding process in both visual cortex halves. A faster analysis of certain stimuli is not the same as a different method of analysis.

There is a very little research relating the internal representation of time to possible hemispheric differences. Efron (1963), and Carmon and Nachson (1971) found that patients with left hemisphere lesions were less able to discriminate between the temporal order of events, and that there were no differences between subjects with right hemisphere lesions and control subjects in this respect. These data are consistent with our hypothesis that there is less temporal encoding of information in the right brain. Recently a first study on the hemispheric representation of time was reported by Hicks and Brundage (1974). These authors compared time estimates of subjects involved in three situations: one involving recognition of words, another involving recognition of faces, and a control condition. They found that the time judgments were shorter with both recognition tasks than in the control condition, thus replicating results found by Michon (1965) and Vroon (1970). However, there was no difference in the time judgments between the word recognition and the face recognition tasks. Inasmuch as verbal memory is assumed to be primarily mediated by the left hemisphere (Milner, 1971) and memory for nonverbal patterns such as faces is mediated by the right brain (Yin, 1970), the authors conclude that there is no indication for a lateralization of function with respect to time. However, this study does not refute the possibility that some lateralization of time might exist. First, the subjects were free to move their eyes over the stimulus material so that the information had direct access to both hemispheres. Second, the formation content of words versus faces is not known whereas this factor is of considerable importance with respect to the amount of apparent time (Michon, 1965; Ornstein, 1969; Vroon, 1970). Third, in both experimental conditions the subjects were asked to give their time estimates in verbal units (mentioning seconds), a task which "translates" the processes going on in the right hemisphere into the language system of the left brain. Consequently, it is not likely that in both conditions the responses were mainly controlled by the hemisphere under study. A fourth point is that the authors studied differences between the means of the time estimation curves whereas Michon (1967, 1972) showed that the variances of estimates particularly present significant information about underlying processes. Finally, the method of verbal reconstruction of time is reported to be an indirect and rather unreliable measure of experienced duration (Michon, 1972; Ornstein, 1969). In fact, verbal estimation implies more cross-modality matching than, for example, the method of reproduction.

Thus, the Hicks and Brundage (1974) study is important, though not a dismissal of the case. In Experiment I of this chapter it is attempted to account for possibly contaminating factors by: (1) presenting the information primarily to separate hemispheres; (2) choosing a simple decision task which could be carried out equally well by each brain half; (3) attempting to measure time estimates of each hemisphere separately; (4) choosing a direct method for measuring time experience, that is, reproduction of the interval; and (5) comparing the variances of the estimates of both brain systems.

Bosshardt and Hörmann (1975) found that verbal items were recalled better in the order they were presented when the material had been presented to the right ear and that recall starts slowly and is rather irregular in the right hemisphere. On the basis of current memory research they assume that the temporal encoding pattern for verbal material might be better in the left brain. Within the framework of the cognitive theory of time, Ornstein (1969) showed that the amount of reconstructed time increases with memory content. It seems likely that experienced duration is also related to retrieval effort. Thus, we expect that the left brain's estimates of task durations will show less variance than those of the right hemisphere.

II. EXPERIMENT I

A. Method

Thirty-six subjects, enrolled in an introductory psychology course, were divided into two equal groups, one group receiving an auditory condition, the other a visual condition. Three subjects in the auditory group and two in the visual group were left-handed. All subjects were placed in front of a panel and fixated a dot in its center. At a distance corresponding to 6° to the left and to the right of the fixation point, a light bulb was mounted with a visual angle of 0.5°. A punch tape reader fed signals to the lights at randomized intervals of 2, 3, and 4 sec. Every signal was converted into a 100-msec flash of the left or right light. During the visual condition, the subjects wore soundproof ear coverings in order to avoid uncontrolled auditory stimulation (the experimental room also dampened 40 dB external noise). In the auditory condition the same procedure was used to present 100-msec 30 dB clicks to either the right or the left channel of a pair of headphones. Every subject served as his own control for comparing the time judgments. In the "left" conditions the stimuli were presented to the left of the fixation point or to the left ear, and the subject pressed a reaction time key with the left hand as soon as a stimulus had been presented (and vice versa). The presentation order of the left and right conditions was balanced over the subjects. Each of the four conditions (auditory, visual, left, right) was split up into three task periods of 20, 40, and 60 sec. Per subject and per series (left and right) each task period was performed five times in a random order. Immediately after a task period, the subject reproduced the task duration by pressing a key twice with the same hand used for the reactions to the stimuli.

B. Results

The reaction times were not recorded since there is evidence that these types of "split brain" reactions do not show differences when the hemisphere not under study is not loaded with another task (Poffenberger, 1912; Davis & Schmit, 1971). With respect to simple reaction time it is known that in the case of randomized foreperiods no training effect occurs over trials (Vroon & Vroon, 1973) and in the present experiment no subject reported having discovered the temporal structure of the stimulus series. Figure 1 shows the mean time estimation curves of the four conditions.

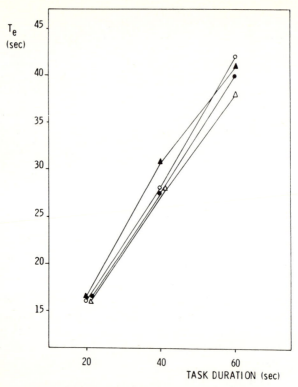

FIG. 1   Mean time estimation curves (T_e) and linear regression coefficients (m) as functions of task duration for the visual, auditory, left and right conditions. Open circle: visual-left, m = 0.66; open triangle: visual–right, m = 0.55; solid circle: auditory–left, m = 0.56; solid triangle: auditory–right, m = 0.65.

It appears that the functions are linear and that differences in slope and height are negligible. Table 1 presents the results of a hierarchical four-factor analysis of variance of the data (Winer, 1970). The factors are visual–auditory, subjects, left–right, and task duration. All factors are fixed, except for subjects which are nested under the visual–auditory factor. With respect to the main effects only the subjects and the task durations show significant results. No left–right or visual–auditory differences is observed, but several interactions with the left–right factor are significant.

The hypothesis of the greater time uncertainty of the right brain was tested by calculating the variances per task duration and condition (left–right) for every subject. Subsequently, a Wilcoxon matched pairs signed rank test was carried out over the subjects. For the visual condition no difference between left and right is found (T = 751, z = 0.08, $p \leqslant 0.93$, two-tailed). In the auditory condition a considerably greater variance for the left presentations (right brain) is observed

TABLE 1
Analysis of Variance of the Time Estimates

Source	df	MS	F
Visual–auditory	1	201	0,13
Subjects	34	1595	39,68[a]
Left–right	1	7	0,03
Task duration	2	53547	255,00[a]
Left–right × subjects	34	219	5,45[a]
Left–right × visual–auditory	1	572	2,61
Task duration × visual–auditory	2	19	0,09
Task duration × subjects	68	210	5,23[a]
Task duration × left–right	2	153	3,81[a]
Task duration × left–right × visual–auditory	2	260	6,50[a]
Task duration × left–right × subjects	68	40	1,00

[a] $p \leqslant 0.01$.

over all task durations ($T = 222$, $z = 4.25$, $p \leqslant 0.00006$, two-tailed). A comparison between the auditory and the visual conditions shows that the mean variance of the auditory right condition over subjects is also consistently smaller than those of the visual left and visual right conditions for all task periods (F test, $0.10 \leqslant p \leqslant 0.05$).[2]

C. Discussion

The data are in agreement with earlier findings in time psychology as well as with our hypothesis about the time uncertainty in the right hemisphere. Michon (1965) and Vroon (1970) demonstrated that apparent time decreases with the amount of transmitted information. The data of Hicks and Brundage (1974) are also in accordance with this tendency. The mean estimated durations show no modality effect. The functions are linear because per task duration a proportionally greater number of stimuli are converted into (reaction) decisions. Consequently, the T_e curves in Fig. 1 increase linearly but they remain below the physical equivalents as a result of the information processing task.

As mentioned previously, Michon (1967) found an inflection point in time estimation curves at the transition between sensory and short-term memory (STM). This finding is in consistent with the hypothesis that the reconstruction

---

[2] These variance differences hardly have consequences for the results shown in Table 1. Box (cited in Winer, 1970) demonstrated that inhomogeneous variance bias the F-test only slightly in an analysis of variance.

of time follows both memory content and type of storage/retrieval. Our own data show that there is no inflection in the curves, although a deviation at 60 sec might be expected since the transition between STM and LTM is usually localized aroung 30 sec (Wickelgren and Berian, 1971). Interestingly, such a transition occurs in patients with mediotemporal cortex lesions (Richards, 1973). These subjects possess a short-term store but the long-term memory does not function. Combining this evidence with the present data and those of Hicks and Brundage (1974) suggests that in normal subjects the reconstruction of durations longer than about 400 msec is determined by one storage system only.

It appears that the right brain is more uncertain about the amount of elapsed time in that its estimates are unreliable. This phenomenon is reflected by the greater variance of the auditory left versus the auditory right condition. Apart from this, the variance of the auditory right condition is smaller than those of both visual conditions. Seeing that differences between the visual conditions are lacking, the temporal uncertainty primarily holds for the auditory modality. This effect is most likely associated with the fact that the right brain is generally mute and (also) less involved in analyzing speech. But how are the unreliable time estimates to be related to the memory processes in the right brain which can be assumed to be a basis of the reconstruction durations? A first possibility is that the memory contents are less available in the right hemisphere. However, in this case it is to be expected that the means of the auditory left condition would have been smaller than those of the auditory right condition, which is not the case. This expectation is based on data showing that reconstructed time closely follows memory content (Ornstein, 1969). A second possibility is related to the finding of Bosshardt and Hörmann (1975) that the recall of auditory (verbal) information by the right hemisphere is not inferior, but that it occurs rather irregularly in time. This might mean that the right brain experiences difficulties in the retrieving process and that the amount of effort invested in retrieving varies over time. When relatively short task periods are used, the latter may be responsible for the variance of the time estimates. If this possibility is correct, it follows that the variances of the left and right auditory conditions will be equal when very long task durations are used. A third possibility is, that the right hemisphere's unreliable time estimates originate from an inferior temporal coding of stimuli. The earlier mentioned reversal effects in the recall of auditory material (Bosshardt & Hörmann, 1975) point in this direction. If an hypothesis about a basic time uncertainty in the right hemisphere is correct, the left brain will show a better time keeping ability in, for example, predicting events by being superior in discovering the internal structure of a time series. When constant foreperiods are used in a simple reaction time task, RT tends to decrease with trials as the subject learns to predict the moments of stimulus presentation (Michon, 1967; Vroon & Vroon, 1973). Since a better "timing" of and expectancy for subsequent events rest upon a better encoding of the temporal dimension, the left hemisphere will show a more pronounced training effect in such a task.

III. EXPERIMENT II

A. Method

Forty students, enrolled in an introductory psychology course, were split up into two equal groups: A and B. All subjects were right-handed. A double task method was used. The subjects fixated a dot in the center of a panel. At a distance corresponding to $6°$ to the left and to the right, a small light bulb was mounted. A punch tape reader fed 100-msec signals to a light bulb at randomized intervals of 2, 3, and 4 sec. A tape recorder presented 100-msec 30 dB clicks at equal intervals of 7 seconds to the left and to the right channel of a pair of headphones. There were no separate foreperiods. In both cases the stimuli also functioned as warning signals for the succeeding stimuli. Group A fixated the dot on the panel. The visual signals were presented to the left light and the subjects were to respond to each flash by pressing a microswitch with the left hand. The auditory stimuli were concurrently fed to the right channel of the headphones and the subjects reacted as fast as possible to them by pressing a second key with the right hand. For Group B the reverse procedure was used (right light–right hand; left ear–left hand). The subjects were informed that the auditory reaction time task was of greater significance than the visual reaction task. The auditory RTs were recorded in milliseconds and the experiment was terminated after an uninterrupted series of 50 clicks/reactions.

B. Results

Figure 2 presents the mean RTs for the auditory series. Both curves show the usual decrease of RT with trials. The stimuli presented to the left ear have higher RTs than those presented to the right ear ($t = 2.08$, $df = 38$, $p \leqslant 0.05$, two-tailed). The difference mainly originates from a faster training effect over the first 20 trials in the right ear.

C. Discussion

The visual reaction task was used as a distractor to ensure that the hemisphere not under study was restricted in influencing the expectancy for and reacting to the auditory stimuli. The ear–hand combination for the clicks was chosen in such a way that the brain half receiving most of the auditory information also primarily carried out the reactions.

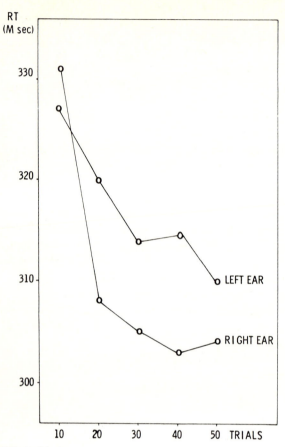

FIG. 2 Mean RTs in blocks of 10 as functions of trials for the groups receiving left and right ear stimulation.

At first sight, the data are inconsistent with those discussed by, for example, Davis and Schmit (1971), who observed that simple RTs of both hemispheres do not differ. However, in these studies the second hemisphere is not loaded with another task. Consequently, it may contribute to the reaction decisions and responses of the other brain half. Moreover, in the latter situation both hemispheres have (some) access to the motor control system of one hand (Filbey & Gazzaniga, 1970). It is clear that these two types of interference were improbable in this experiment since both hemispheres were loaded with different tasks.

In the discussion of Experiment I two hypotheses were put forward: (1) the unreliable time estimates originate from irregular retrieving, and (2) there is an inferior temporal coding system in the right brain. The data suggest that second hypothesis is more plausible. It is not clear how a better timing of events over short periods (7 sec) originates from a general factor such as "retrieval effort." On the contrary, both the ease of timing and the ease of retrieving information can be explained on the basis of a better temporal encoding system since time is also a cue for retrieval. One could argue that the less decreasing RT function for the left ear is simply caused by using the nondominant hand. This possible conjecture is invalidated by Davis and Schmit (1971) as well as by one of our pilot studies with binaural stimulation in which no differences between the RTs of both hands were observed.

Both the considerable variance of time estimates by the right brain and its poorer ability to predict events in time reflect somewhat molar phenomena. It is to be expected that differences are also present on a molecular level. For example, in understanding and generating speech one is able to distinguish between words like "fist" and "fits," which calls for a distinct temporal analysis of auditory information. Blakemore, Iversen, and Zangwill (1972) found that the left hemisphere is better in the recognition of fricatives and explosives. Thus, we hypothesize that the left brain processes auditory signals by a moment-to-moment analysis of the signal whereas the right hemisphere tends to deal with larger temporal "chunks." If this is true, it follows that the left brain is also superior in the detection of short gaps in an auditory stimulus.

IV. EXPERIMENT III

A. Method

A PDP 15-20 computer generated 3-sec 80-dB noise bursts, delivered by earphones. The system was programmed to interrupt the bursts at 1, 1.5, or 2 sec after the onset of the signal. The durations of the interruptions ranged between 1 and 4 msec in steps of .5 msec. Twenty-eight students served as subjects. The noise was presented monaurally by earphones. Every subject received a total of 180 stimuli, equally divided over both ears. In 54 cases the stimulus consisted of a blank (noise without interruption). Ear stimulated, moment of interruption and gap duration were randomized. The task was self-paced, that is, the subject received a stimulus 500 msec after pressing a button and indicated his decision by pressing either a "yes" or a "no" button with the hand on the side of the stimulated ear.

B. Results

Subjects with a false alarm rate for either ear higher than 15% were excluded from the group, leaving 20 subjects for further analysis. Their mean false alarm rate for the right and left ear was 11 and 10%, respectively. Figure 3 shows the

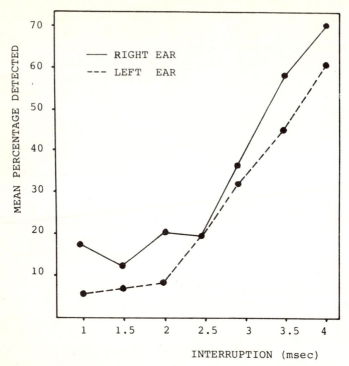

FIG. 3   Mean percentage of gap detection as functions of interruption time for both ears.

mean percentage detected interruptions as a function of interruption time. It appears that the gaps are more easily detected when presented to the right ear (sign test over subjects, $p \leqslant 0.01$, two-tailed).

C. Discussion

In contrast to Experiment II, it was possible that the hemisphere ipsilateral to the stimulated ear was also involved in the detection of the interruptions. Nevertheless, a left brain superiority is observed and the data confirm the hypothesis of a better temporal discriminatory process in the left brain on a "molecular" level.

As far as temporal variables are concerned, we conclude that the left brain is more reliable in the reconstruction of the duration of events, the discovery of the internal structure of a time series, as well as in the temporal analysis of auditory stimuli. The better encoding of time in general holds primarily for auditory stimuli and possibly originates from the lateralization of language functions. These effects are not limited to explicit verbal material (as suggested by findings of Bosshardt & Hörmann, 1975; Blakemore et al., 1972) but characterize the auditory processing system in general.

V. CONCLUSION

The perception of music is often mentioned as an exception to usually defined left—right differentiations of the human brain since melodic patterns are better recognized by the right hemisphere (Kimura, 1973; Kinsbourne, 1975). This exception is remarkable in that music as well as speech consists of an ordered series of pitches. Hence, music should also be analyzed better by the left brain. Bever and Chiarello (1974) found that excerpts from a tone sequence were recognized better by musically experienced listeners. These subjects also performed better when the sequences were presented to the right ear. Bever and Chiarello conclude that the left brain is superior in the recognition of music when the internal relations of a melodic sequence have to be analyzed, which is the case when short fragments are used. The left ear superiority of naive subjects is explained by the hypothesis that they treat simple melodies as unanalyzed wholes. This also explains why these subjects are not good in recognizing the short fragments. Consequently, the controversy about the difference between speech perception and the recognition of melodic patterns seems merely an apparent one: the internal and temporal analysis of both types of acoustic patterns occurs mainly in the left hemisphere.

There are two theories about hemispheric differences. Kimura (1966, 1973) holds a structural viewpoint, in that the left and right brain correspond with a verbal and a spatial processor, respectively. The better recognition of verbal material in the right visual field and by the right ear is explained by a direct access hypothesis to the relevant brain half. On the other hand, Kinsbourne (1970, 1975) offers a functional explanation in terms of attentional variables. There is evidence that these theories complement each other. For example, Mainka and Hörmann (1971) found that focusing attention cannot completely compensate for ear asymmetry. Hence, these authors conclude that there is some basic asymmetry. The reported experiments suggest that one of the structural differences depends on the degree to which processed information is encoded in time, and this asymmetry appears to hold for the auditory modality.

ACKNOWLEDGMENTS

The authors are indebted to Marjan Elzer who conducted Experiment III.

REFERENCES

Bever, T. G., & Chiarello, R. J. Cerebral dominance in musicians and nonmusicians. *Science,* 1974, **185,** 537–539.
Blakemore, C., Iversen, S. D., & Zangwill, O. L. Brain functions. *Annual Review of Psychology,* 1972, **23,** 413–456.

Bosshardt, H. G., & Hörmann, H. Temporal precision of coding as a basic factor of laterality effects in the retention of verbal auditory stimuli. *Acta Psychologica,* 1975, **39**, 1, 1–12.

Bryden, M. P. Tachistoscopic recognition of non-alphabetical material. *Canadian Journal of Psychology,* 1960, **14**, 2, 78–86.

Carmon, A., & Nachson, I. Effect of unilateral brain damage on perception of temporal order. *Cortex,* 1971, **7**, 410–418.

Corcoran, D. W. J. *Pattern recognition.* Hammondsworth, London: Penguin Books, 1971.

Davis, R., & Schmit, V. Timing the transfer of information between the hemispheres in man. *Acta Psychologica,* 1971, **35**, 335–346.

Dimond, S. J. *The double brain.* Edinburgh: Churchill Livingstone, 1972.

Dimond, S. J., & Beaumont, J. G. On the nature of the interhemispheric effects of fatigue. *Acta Psychologica,* 1972, **36**, 6, 443–449. (a)

Dimond, S. J., & Beaumont, J. G. Processing in perceptual integration between and within the cerebral hemispheres. *British Journal of Psychology,* 1972, **63**, 4, 509–514. (b)

Efron, R. Temporal perception, aphasia and déjà vu. *Brain,* 1963, **86**, 403–424.

Filbey, R. A., & Gazzaniga, M. S. Splitting the brain with reaction time. *Psychonomic Science,* 1970, **17**, 336–336.

Fontenot, D. J., & Benton, A. L. Perception of direction in the right and left visual fields. *Neuropsychologia,* 1972, **10**, 447–454.

Fraisse, P. *The psychology of time.* New York: Harper & Row, 1963.

Hicks, R. E., & Brundage, R. M. Judgments of temporal duration while processing verbal and physiognomic stimuli. *Acta Psychologica,* 1974, **38**(6), 447–454.

Hoagland, H. The physiological control of judgments of duration. Evidence for a chemical clock. *Journal of General Psychology,* 1933, **9**, 267–287.

Kimura, D. Dual functional asymmetry of the brain in visual perception. *Neuropsychologia,* 1966, **4**, 275–285.

Kimura, D. The asymmetry of the human brain. *Scientific American,* 1973, March, 70–79.

Kinsbourne, M. The cerebral basis of lateral asymmetries in attention. *Acta Psychologica,* 1970, **33**, 193–201.

Kinsbourne, M. The mechanism of hemispheric control of the lateral gradient of attention. In P. M. A. Rabbitt & S. Dornic (Eds.), *Attention and performance V,* London: Academic Press, 1975.

Mainka, G., & Hörmann, H. Genügt der Begriff 'Aufmerksamkeit' zur Erklärung des sogenannten Lateralitätseffekts? *Psychologische Forschung,* 1971, **34**, 295–311.

Michon, J. A. Studies on subjective duration II: Subjective time measurement during tasks with different information content. *Acta Psychologica,* 1965, **24**, 205–219.

Michon, J. A. *Timing in temporal tracking.* Assen, The Netherlands: Van Gorcum & Comp.N.V., 1967.

Michon, J. A. Processing of temporal information and the cognitive theory of time experience. In J. T. Fraser, F. C. Haber, & G. H. Müller (Eds.), *The study of time.* Berlin: Springer-Verlag, 1972.

Milner, B. Interhemispheric differences in the localization of psychological processes in man. *British Medical Bulletin,* 1971, **27**, 272–277.

Neisser, U. *Cognitive psychology.* New York: Appleton-Century-Crofts, 1967.

Ornstein, R. E. *On the experience of time.* Hammondsworth: Penguin Books, 1969.

Poffenberger, A. T. Reaction time to retinal stimulation with special reference to the time lost during conduction through nerve centres. *Archives of Psychology,* 1912, no. 23.

Richards, W. Time reproductions by H. M. *Acta Psychologica,* 1973, **37**, 279–282.

Vroon, P. A. Effects of presented and processed information on duration experience. *Acta Psychologica,* 1970, **34**, 115–121.

Vroon, P. A. Is there a time quantum in duration experience? *American Journal of Psychology,* 1974, **87**, 237–245.

Vroon, P. A., & Vroon, A. G. Tapping rate and expectancy in simple reaction time tasks. *Journal of Experimental Psychology,* 1973, **1**, 85–90.

Wickelgren, W. A., & Berian, K. M. Dual trace theory and the consolidation of long-term memory. *Journal of Mathematical Psychology,* 1971, **8**, 404–417.

Winer, B. J. *Statistical principles in experimental design.* London: MacGraw-Hill, 1970.

Yin, R. K. Face recognition by brain-injured patients: A dissociable ability. *Neuropsychologia,* 1970, **8**, 395–402.

13
Attention to Visually and Auditorily Presented Durations

Hannes Eisler

Department of Psychology
University of Stockholm
Stockholm, Sweden

ABSTRACT

The results of three experiments (Brown & Hitchcock, 1965; Goldstone, 1968; Stevens & Greenbaum, 1966) in which a time interval presented as sound was reproduced as a time interval of light, and vice versa, were investigated in terms of a new model for time perception (Eisler, 1975). It is proposed (a) that the subject in both tasks attends exclusively to the subjectively more intense modality and thus treats *both* durations as if they were either sound or light; and (b) that the two subjective durations are weighted according to the subject's relative uncertainty between them by his "applying" different scale units in the psychophysical power function.

I. INTRODUCTION

In his paper delivered at the First Conference of the International Society for the Study of Time at Oberwolfach, West Germany, Michon (1970) recommended to theorists of time psychology to "stay close to the trend toward the formulation of functional, quantitative models" (p. 264). An attempt at such a model can be found in a recent article by Eisler (1975), though the quantification is carried out within a psychophysical frame of reference, which probably is not quite what Michon had in mind.

This model accounts for a number of phenomena in time perception, like certain peculiarities in discrimination of time intervals and the time-order error for time, but the typical experiment considered is the reproduction of time intervals. As shown subsequently in the presentation of the model, from data of this kind one can determine the exponent of the psychophysical power function (Stevens' Law), that is, β in:

$$\psi = \alpha\,(\Phi - \Phi_0)^\beta \tag{1}$$

where ψ denotes subjective and Φ physical duration, and α and Φ_0 are constants, the scale unit and the subjective zero, respectively. A survey of about one hundred studies, comprising several hundred experiments (Eisler, 1976) that allowed the determination of exponents for duration demonstrated that the exponent is about the same for all sensory modalities used for presenting the durations, including empty time intervals, with one exception: light. In almost all comparable experiments, the exponent for light is slightly higher than for the other modality, which usually is noise or a tone. In these experiments the modality by which the stimulus durations (the standard) and the response durations (the variable) were presented, was always the same. However, it has been observed by a number of investigators (e.g., Cohen, 1967, p. 87) that when a visually presented duration is reproduced by one presented auditorily, the reproduced durations are shorter than when the order between the modalities is reversed. The aim of this study is to investigate this phenomenon theoretically on the basis of the model mentioned above, and in the light of the only three pertinent experiments I could find in the literature. In these experiments the exponents for light and sound are either given or can be determined separately, and data from sound–light and light–sound reproduction experiments are reported.

II. THE MODEL

Traditionally, it has been supposed that in a duration reproduction task, the subject stores the first (standard) duration in memory, and compares the second (variable) duration with these memory contents. As soon as this second duration agrees with the memory of the first one, he indicates that the two durations are equal. Since necessarily the whole process takes place with subjective magnitudes, one could say that the percept of the second duration is compared with the memory of the percept of the first duration. (The term "percept" need not to be taken literally — here it does not make any difference whether we regard a duration percept as a simple sensation or as the result of an active reproduction of stored information, the latter in accordance with a cognitive theory; see, for example, Michon, 1970).

The model proposed disposes of any memory. Instead, it makes use of two sensory registers. The *total* subjective time, that is, the subjective time for the sum of the standard and the variable, is accumulated in one, and the *variable* subjective time, in the other. When the difference between the contents of the two registers equals the contents of the register containing the variable time, the two durations are experienced as equally long. The model is perhaps understood most easily if we assume time perception to be veridical. In this case the difference between the total and the variable duration would equal the standard, which in its turn would equal the variable duration. [See Eq. (4) with $\beta = 1, \alpha = 1$, and $\Phi_0 = 0$.] Figure 1 describes the model for an exponent below unity. Mathematically we have (subscript T refers to total duration, V to variable duration):

$$\psi_V = \psi_T - \psi_V, \tag{2}$$

yielding

$$\psi_V = \frac{1}{2}\psi_T. \tag{3}$$

We can thus regard a duration reproduction experiment as a duration halving experiment: the reproduced subjective duration is half the total subjective duration. Making use of Stevens' Law, we can rewrite Eq. (2) in physical terms:

$$(\Phi_V - \Phi_0)^\beta = \alpha(\Phi_T - \Phi_0)^\beta - (\Phi_V - \Phi_0)^\beta, \tag{4}$$

that is,

$$(\Phi_V - \Phi_0)^\beta = \frac{\alpha}{2}(\Phi_T - \Phi_0)^\beta. \tag{5}$$

Note that the total duration is physically equal to the sum of the standard and variable durations: $\Phi_T = \Phi_S + \Phi_V$, but that this relation does not hold for the

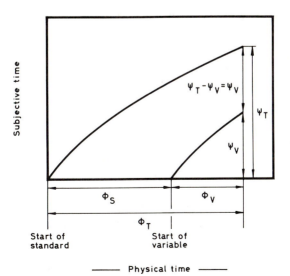

FIG. 1 The duration reproduction task described in psychophysical terms. Subscripts S, V, and T refer to standard, variable, and total duration, respectively.

corresponding subjective durations ψ except for veridical time perception, that is, when $\beta = 1$, $\Phi_0 = 0$. An $\alpha \neq 1$ value means that the scale units for the total and the variable duration are different. Since scale units are arbitrary, the scale unit of the variable is always set to unity. Thus α really denotes the ratio of the scale unit for the total duration to the response duration. Also the values of Φ_0 could be different for total and variable duration; this possible difference can, however, be neglected in the present context.

The reasoning leading to the present model, as well as experimental evidence supporting it, can be found in Eisler (1975) and will not be repeated here. Solving for Φ_V in Eq. (5) yields:

$$\Phi_V = \left(\frac{\alpha}{2}\right)^{\frac{1}{\beta}} \Phi_T + \left[1 - \left(\frac{\alpha}{2}\right)^{\frac{1}{\beta}}\right] \Phi_0,$$

that is, the reproduced physical time is a linear function of the total physical time:

$$\Phi_V = a\, \Phi_T + b.$$

If the scale unit for standard and variable, that is, for total and reproduced time, is the same, $\alpha = 1$, the exponent β can be computed from the slope a of the straight line; since $(1/2)^{1/\beta} = a$:

$$\beta = \frac{\log(1/2)}{\log a}. \tag{6}$$

On the other hand, if β is known, α can be computed from $(\alpha/2)^{1/\beta} = a$:

$$\alpha = 2\, a^\beta. \tag{7}$$

There is one complication in the present model with rather important implications for the problem we are going to deal with. It is more the rule than an exception that a subject changes his frame of reference at some point within the range of durations under study; such a change of reference entails a break in the psychophysical function and may be due to a change in the subjective zero Φ_0, a change in the scale unit α, or both, so that one value describes the psychophysical function for short durations, say for durations $< \Phi_1$ sec, and another value for long durations, $> \Phi_1$ sec. In time reproduction, in which our experimental variables are physical time intervals measured in seconds, say, *subjective* duration must be regarded as an intervening variable. How would such a shift in the frame of reference of this intervening variable, showing up as break in the plot of subjective time against physical time, manifest itself in the data obtained? If, in accordance with the model, we plot Φ_V against Φ_T, two breaks are obtained, dividing the points into three groups: those in which both standards and variables lie on the upper segment of the psychophysical function, that is, both above its break; those in which the standards lie on the upper and the variables on the lower segment, that is, on both sides of its break; and finally those in which standards and variables lie on the same segment of the psychophysical function, but the lower one below its break. (Here the standard corresponds to total and the variable to reproduced duration.) The line s–l in Fig. 2a shows such an instance. Here the discontinuity of the psychophysical function is at 6.5 sec, corresponding to one break at the y- and another one at the x-axis at this value. (A more detailed description of breaks in psychophysical functions is found in Eisler, 1958, 1975). For this plot the lowermost group of points consists of one point only; the other figures show examples without breaks, and with just a single break. The latter case arises when the duration range of the experiment is so restricted that one of the three groups of points is lacking. If one experimental duration value is exactly at the break, the subject may oscillate between the two segments, yielding a bimodal distribution of response durations (cf. Richards, 1964); a mean value would then lie somewhere between the straight lines on both sides of the break: see, for example, the sixth point of the function l–s in Fig. 2a.

If both standard and variable durations are presented by the same modality, the exponent for duration can be computed from the slope of the outer lines, for which total and response time lie on the same segment, using Eq. (6); the ratio of the scale units, α, can then be determined from the slope of the middle line by Eq. (7). When the experiment yields only two straight lines, one has to decide which of these corresponds to the "outer" and which to the "middle" one before applying Eqs. (6) and (7). If the data do not show any break, Eq. (6) is used, because this implies that the same scale unit is used by the subject throughout the experimental range.

III. THE CASE IN WHICH STANDARD AND VARIABLE ARE PRESENTED BY DIFFERENT MODALITIES

There are several alternative ways of conceiving of the process in a subject who is given the task of reproducing a time interval in another modality than the one by which it is presented. We will first explore the four alternatives demonstrable from a formal point of view. After that the alternatives are evaluated by data and an attempt is made at psychological interpretations.

A. Alternative 1

Consider Eq. (2). The problem consists of how the total subjective duration ψ_T is built up when we have different exponents for the two modalities. Let us assume that the total subjective duration is composed of two parts, the subjective duration for the standard, and the subjective duration for the variable, the latter starting from zero. Leaving open all possibilities of different subjective zeros and different scale units, we obtain:

$$(\Phi_V - \Phi_{01})^{\beta_2} = \alpha_1 (\Phi_S - \Phi_{02})^{\beta_1} + \alpha_2 (\Phi_V - \Phi_{03})^{\beta_2} - (\Phi_V - \Phi_{01})^{\beta_2}$$

or

$$2(\Phi_V - \Phi_{01})^{\beta_2} = \alpha_1 (\Phi_S - \Phi_{02})^{\beta_1} + \alpha_2 (\Phi_V - \Phi_{03})^{\beta_2}, \tag{8}$$

where β_1 and β_2 correspond to the exponents of the first and second, that is, of the standard and variable durations, respectively.

We see that what has been called the traditional model is a special case of Eq. (8), the case in which $\Phi_{03} = \Phi_{01}$ and $\alpha_2 = 1$. We also see that, even with the exponents known, Eq. (8) features five parameters; and when we have two experiments with the two modalities as standard and variable and vice versa, there are as many as ten. However, since the numerical values of the subjective zeros Φ_0 do not make much difference in terms of fit, we may set $\Phi_{03} = \Phi_{01}$, yielding:

$$\Phi_V = \left(\frac{\alpha_1}{2\,\alpha_2}\right)^{1/\beta_2} (\Phi_S - \Phi_{02})^{\beta_1/\beta_2} + \Phi_{01}, \tag{9}$$

or

$$\Phi_V = c\,(\Phi_S - \Phi_{02})^{\beta_1/\beta_2} + d. \tag{10}$$

This expression has only three parameters and is also much more tractable than Eq. (8). Note that Φ_V here is *not* a linear function of Φ_S (and thus neither of Φ_T). Eisler (1974) has shown that there is linearity between variable and standard if the exponents are equal, and, vice versa, that equal exponents imply linearity.

B. Alternative 2

Alternative 2 differs from the previous one in the buildup of ψ_T. Rather than assuming that the part of ψ_T corresponding to the second duration starts from zero, it is put on top of the first duration. This is done most easily by integrating the derivative of ψ,

$$\psi' = \alpha\,\beta\,(\Phi - \Phi_0)^{\beta-1}.$$

Accordingly

$$\Psi_T = \int_{\Phi_{01}}^{\Phi_S} \alpha_1\beta_1 (\Phi - \Phi_{01})^{\beta_1-1}\,d\Phi \;+\; \int_{\Phi_S}^{\Phi_T} \alpha_2\beta_2 (\Phi - \Phi_{02})^{\beta_2-1}\,d\Phi$$

yielding:

$$\psi_T = \alpha_1 \, (\Phi_S - \Phi_{01})^{\beta_1} + \alpha_2 \, (\Phi_T - \Phi_{02})^{\beta_2} - \alpha_2 \, (\Phi_S - \Phi_{02})^{\beta_2} \, . \tag{11}$$

Inserting into Eq. (2) yields:

$$2 \, (\Phi_V - \Phi_{03})^{\beta_2} = \alpha_1 \, (\Phi_S - \Phi_{01})^{\beta_1} + \alpha_2 \, (\Phi_T - \Phi_{02})^{\beta_2} - \alpha_2 \, (\Phi_S - \Phi_{02})^{\beta_2} \, . \tag{12}$$

Equation (12) cannot be simplified like Eq. (8) and contains five parameters. Again, Φ_V is not a linear function of Φ_T (or Φ_S).

C. Alternative 3

The remaining two alternatives differ from the previous ones in that linearity is supposed to hold between Φ_V and Φ_T, entailing the same exponent for standard and variable. In this alternative it is thus supposed that the same exponent governs the whole experiment, and accordingly both parts of the total duration as well as the variable duration. For instance, this exponent could be a compromise between the one for sound and the one for light.

D. Alternative 4

Finally, we might assume that, in spite of different modalities for standard and variable, either modality determines the exponent, but the scale units for the total and the variable durations are different throughout the whole experimental range. This interpretation of the data seems the most appealing and is discussed at some length in the next section.

IV. DATA AND THE FOUR ALTERNATIVES

Table 1 gives pertinent parameters for the three studies mentioned in the introduction. Figures 2–4 show the data. The exponents for sound and light were determined from sound–sound and light–light reproductions by Eq. (6) for the Brown and Hitchcock (1965) and the Goldstone (1968) investigations. For the Stevens and Greenbaum (1966) investigation the magnitude estimation exponents were used. Though these authors also report exponents from magnitude production, Eisler (1975, 1976) has shown that magnitude estimation exponents agree well with exponents computed from reproduction data, and that magnitude production data yield somewhat higher exponents.

Goodness of fit should serve to evaluate Alternatives 1 and 2 relative to each other, as well as to the remaining alternatives. Alternatives 3 and 4 assume the same straight line and can only be evaluated relative to each other by interpretation of the results.

TABLE 1
Parameter Values for Three Experiments

Reference	Experiment	Experimental data						Inferred from Alternative 4: Ratio α of scale units			
		Exponent		Slope		Exponents		Based on sound		Based on light	
		s^a	l^a	$s-l$	$l-s$	$s-l$	$l-s$	$s-l$	$l-s$	$s-l$	$l-s$
Brown & Hitchcock, 1965	Constant signal	.87	.91	.4009	.4790	.76	.94	.90	1.05	.87	1.02
	Patterned signal	.94	.91	.4812	.4748	.95	.93	1.01	.99	1.03	1.02
Goldstone, 1968	Group 1[b]	.89	.92	.4682	.4532	.91	.88	1.02	.99	1.00	.97
	Group 2[b]	.86	.89	.4758	.4454	.93	.86	1.06	1.00	1.03	.97
Stevens & Greenbaum, 1966		.87	.93	.4332	.3491	.83	.66	.97	.80	.92	.75

[a] s stands for sound, l for light. The denotation s–l refers to the experiment where a duration presented as sound was to be reproduced by light.
[b] The two groups differed only in the order in which the four tasks were given.

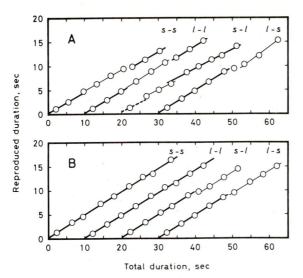

FIG. 2 Reproduced durations as a function of total durations in sec. (A: signal constant, B: signal patterned.) Sound and light are denoted by s and l, respectively. (The origin of each new curve is moved 10 sec to the right.) (Data from Brown & Hitchcock, 1965.)

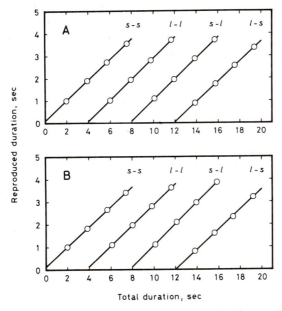

FIG. 3 Reproduced durations as a function of total durations in sec. (A: Group 1, B: Group 2.) Sound and light are denoted by s and l, respectively. (The origin of each new curve is moved 4 sec to the right.) (Data from Goldstone, 1968).

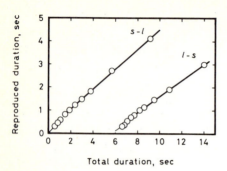

FIG. 4 Reproduced durations as a function of total durations in sec. Sound and light are denoted by *s* and *l,* respectively. (The origin of the second curve is moved 6 sec to the right.) (Data from Stevens & Greenbaum, 1966.)

All three figures show that the data for the mixed reproductions can be well described by straight lines, a fact that immediately speaks against Alternatives 1 and 2. However, the values of the two exponents are rather close in all studies, so that the curvatures expected from the first two alternatives may not become apparent. The following procedures were applied. (Throughout, only the thick straight lines in the figures were considered. The slopes of the other, "middle" lines – see Section II – are composed of both the exponent and the scale unit.) Both straight lines of Fig. 4 were fitted simultaneously with three parameters – two slopes, but the same Φ_0 value. Since this leads to nonlinear equations, Chandler's (1969) program STEPIT was used. Thereby the fit for Alternatives 3 and 4 can be evaluated. Alternative 1 was investigated by regarding $(\Phi_S - \Phi_{02})^{\beta_1/\beta_2}$ in Eq. (10) as the independent variable, in which β_1/β_2 was .87/.93 for the sound–light, and .93/.87 for the light–sound conditions (see Stevens & Greenbaum's 1966 data in Table 1). Equation (10) was fitted for different values of Φ_{02} by least squares for both data sets. Though this procedure makes use of six parameters (Φ_{02}, c, and d for each condition) compared with three in the previous procedure, the fit was somewhat worse.

Alternative 2 was tested by fitting Eq. (12), for which again STEPIT had to be used because of nonlinearity. Though the number of parameters was still larger (I attempted also to let the program determine the two exponents) the fit was again worse, compared to the first procedure. Therefore, Alternatives 1 and 2 were rejected for Stevens and Greenbaum's (1966) data, and since the straight lines in the other figures did not show any hint of curvilinearity, Alternatives 1 and 2 were not even tried for these data.

Let us see whether the parameter values given in Table 1 can help in choosing between the two remaining alternatives. First, note how little scatter the exponents show. For sound they are .87, .89, .86, .87; only the exponent for patterned sound, .94, deviates. For light the exponents are: .91, .92, .89, .93; and .91 for patterned light. The finding mentioned in the Introduction again holds: for every single experiment the exponent for light is slightly higher than that for sound. The only violation occurs when both signals are patterned. A look at the four exponents for the experiments with patterned signals shows that they are very close. It does not seem to make any difference for the exponent whether the signal consists of sound or light, and whether the modalities for standard and variable are the same or not. A tentative conclusion would be that when a duration is composed of a sequence of delimited events (a pattern extended in time), these events determine subjective time, however they are produced.

Goldstone's (1968) data show only small differences in the exponents throughout and thus do not give much of a clue. They will be discussed subsequently.

That leaves us with Brown and Hitchcock's (1965) study of constant signals and Stevens and Greenbaum's (1966) investigation. Of all four exponents for the different modality experiments, none constitutes a compromise, because none falls between the exponents for the single modality experiments. Accordingly, this interpretation of Alternative 3 fails. Since the exponents in the mixed tasks are lower (with one exception), one could argue that a mixed task is more difficult and the exponent becomes smaller with increasing difficulty. This might parallel the finding (Eisler, 1976) that the exponents for children are smaller than for adults. When the task is difficult, we may get more childish, so to speak. Though this idea cannot be rejected on the basis of the data, it seems rather unsatisfactory and has little explanatory value.

To interpret Alternative 4, I would consider an argument proposed by Hellström (1977) regarding the time-order error. According to his theory, when, for example, two tones of equal intensity are heard in succession, their percepts are weighted differently, entailing an experienced difference in loudness. The weights are conceived of as connected with the information the subject feels he has about them at the moment of comparison, that is, with his relative uncertainty regarding them. Technically, these weights correspond to the scale units mentioned before. If we assume that the total subjective time is experienced as more uncertain when composed of different modalities, the subject might assign a lower weight — a smaller scale unit — to it than to the variable subjective time: α would be less than unity.

The last columns of Table 1 give these α values, computed by Eq. (7), assuming that both sensory registers are geared either to sound or to light. But to which? One could argue that the registers become geared to the first, the standard signal. This hypothesis would yield the values .90 and 1.02 for Brown and Hitchcock (1965), which are quite reasonable, and .97 and .75 for Stevens and Greenbaum (1966). Here it is more difficult to understand why the subject feels so uncertain for the light—sound sequence. One could argue the other way round, that it is the modality which the subject controls himself that determines the exponent. In that case we would have α values of 1.05 and .87 for one set of data, and .80 and .92 for the other. Here the value of 1.05 does not seem to fit. Why should the subject feel more confident in the composed duration than in the one he controls?

I am inclined to believe that a subject has the same modality as his basis, irrespective of the order between sound and light. In the experiments of Brown and Hitchcock (1965) it is light, yielding α values of .87 and 1.02; in the experiments of Stevens and Greenbaum (1966) it is sound, with α = .97 and .80. In both cases the subject feels practically certain when the *first* duration is given in the modality of his choice: α = 1.02 and .97, both close to unity. If the standard is not this modality, he feels less confident: α = .87 and .80.

There is still one problem left: why do Brown and Hitchcock's subjects direct their attention to light, and Stevens and Greenbaum's to sound? The answer probably lies in the experimental setup. Brown and Hitchcock used quite intense light of 22 apparent ft-c and a rather soft 1000-Hz tone of 60 dB sound pressure level (SPL). Stevens and Greenbaum do not give a precise description of their stimuli. Their light, however, seems to have been weak — a 15-W red bulb. The sound consisted of noise. Presumably it was louder than the tone in the other experiment, and besides, noise in itself seems to be a stronger stimulus than a tone.

What about Goldstone's (1968) data? The differences in exponents are too small to allow any conclusion except that these subjects felt fairly confident: all α values are high. This might be the result of a better balance between sound and light; the light was 6 apparent ft-c, and thus weaker than Brown and Hitchcock's (1965), and the sound louder: a 1000-Hz tone of 84 dB SPL.

V. CONCLUSION

Though other interpretations of the data dealt with cannot be excluded, it appears that when a subject is faced with the task of reproducing a time interval, presented by one modality, by a time interval of another modality, he gears both his sensory registers — "attends" — to the modality experienced as stronger or more intense. Since the total duration — with which he compares the response duration — is experienced as more uncertain, he attaches a lower weight to it. This lower weight manifests itself as a ratio of the scale units for total and variable subjective durations below unity.

This conclusion must be regarded as tentative and should be tested with experiments designed for this purpose, for instance by varying the relative intensity of sound and light, or randomizing the four reproduction tasks within a single experimental series.

ACKNOWLEDGMENT

This work was supported by the Swedish Council for Social Science Research.

REFERENCES

Brown, D. R., & Hitchcock, L., Jr. Time estimation: Dependence and independence of modality-specific effects. *Perceptual and Motor Skills,* 1965, **21,** 727–734.

Chandler, J. STEPIT – Finds local minima of a smooth function of several parameters. *Behavioral Science,* 1969, **14**, 81–82. (CPA 312)

Cohen, J. *Psychological time in health and disease.* Springfield: Charles C. Thomas, 1967.

Eisler, H. A note on treatment of ratio setting data for constructing psychological scales. *Reports from the Psychological Laboratory,* University of Stockholm, 1958, No. 54.

Eisler, H. The derivation of Stevens' psychophysical power law. In H. Moskowitz, B. Scharf, & J. Stevens (Eds.), *Sensation and measurement.* Dordrecht: D. Reidel, 1974.

Eisler, H., Subjective duration and psychophysics. *Psychological Review,* 1975, **82**, 429–450.

Eisler, H. Experiments on subjective duration 1868–1975: A collection of power function exponents. *Psychological Bulletin,* 1976, **83**, 1154–1171.

Goldstone, S. Production and reproduction of duration: Intersensory comparison. *Perceptual and Motor Skills,* 1968, **26**, 755–760.

Hellström, Å. Differential sensation weighting as the basic cause of time–errors. Reports from the Department of Psychology, University of Stockholm, 1977, No. 498.

Michon, J. Processing of temporal information and the cognitive theory of time experience. *Studium Generale,* 1970, **23**, 249–265.

Richards, W. Time estimates measured by reproduction. *Perceptual and Motor Skills,* 1964, **18**, 929–943.

Stevens, S. S., & Greenbaum, H. B. Regression effect in psychophysical judgment. *Perception & Psychophysics,* 1966, **1**, 439–446.

14

Perceptual Calibration for Parameters of Speaker Differences—Measures from Sequential Reaction Time Increment Studies

Mark Haggard
Quentin Summerfield

Department of Psychology
Queen's University
Belfast, Northern Ireland

ABSTRACT

Two manual choice reaction-time experiments are reported in which subjects identified vowels in consonant–vowel–consonant (CVC) syllables. Specific acoustical relationships were considered between the voices in which the syllables were spoken. For pairs of voices having different average formant frequencies, and hence involving a perceptual adjustment to a different vocal tract size, there was a substantial increase in RT on trials when the voice changed but the response did not. Such increments did not occur for voice differences such as pitch, even though these were perceptually salient; dichotic masking experiments also confirm a distinction between the perceptual effects of these two aspects of voice differences. It is concluded that sequential RT increment measures are capable of providing estimates of the processing demand of decoding operations in perception of speech sounds, but interpretative power derives chiefly from directional predictions for these measures enabled by an understanding and control of stimulus structure.

I. INTRODUCTION

In the last decade information-processing psychologists have presented subjects with an impressive diversity of tasks and obtained a depressing diversity of results. These results tell us quite a lot about "what people can do" and should allow us to draw valuable generalizations about how their strategies typically adapt to variations in the task parameters. There has been less concern for what aspects of tasks are typically represented in natural performances and it may be that basic limits and operations in information processing, if such exist, will be more accessible when laboratory tasks are simple analogues of real-life performances. In attempting to approximate "what people really do" we can use the methodologically valuable findings from diverse laboratory tasks to provide leverage on processing operations from the response end, while at the same time getting leverage from the stimulus end by the variation of structural parameters informationally relevant to the task. In this chapter we attempt to achieve such a classical balance. In this attempt we have had to abandon the contemporary ideal that experiments, or at least the subsequent debriefings, should be spiritually enlightening for the subjects and use a rather boring task. The subject identifies a single stimulus word by pressing an associated button, and the differences between experimental conditions are so opaque as to not even elicit and hence not risk to defy subjects' speculations about the purpose of the experiment. This is because stimulus composition and response sequence decomposition realize the analytical power more normally assigned to the task and the experimental design.

Our experiments were begun in 1972, stimulated by the lack of any very direct tests of the concept of "encoding." Briefly, this concept refers to the fact that speech perception is a complicated business because there is no invariant relationship between the obvious first order acoustic parameters of speech stimuli and the linguistic categories (phonemes) implicit in identification responses. Like most good ideas it had first to be overstated (Liberman *et al.*, 1967), and then generated an overreaction. In an extraordinary amalgam of elementary phonetics, misused terms, and tape-splicing techniques, Cole and Scott (1974) have purported to displace encoding from the range of theoretical concepts deemed useful in understanding what goes on in speech perception. Darwin and Baddeley (1974) have elegantly freed the encoding issue from dependence upon the issue of behavioral differences between the phonemic classes vowels and consonants, which has limited its apparent explanatory power, while not challenging it directly. We do not attempt here to review the encoding issue fully but it is demonstrated that its usefulness is partly reinstated by our results. We set out to see if the hypothetically greater complexity of perceptual decoding required for sets of stimuli displaying encoding (acoustical noninvariance) could actually be measured as an increase in choice reaction time. Previous demonstrations had only shown the existence of certain decoding operations, that is, perceptual adjustments to the variable context through the distribution of particular identification responses or through error rates. We felt that the interest and accessibility to further analysis of these operations depended upon some measure of the apparent extra processing load which they create. This is the sort of measure that reaction-time increment methodology is ideally placed to provide. Wood (1974) was the first to apply this methodology to speech studies. An irrelevant stimulus variable in an enlarged experimental set is made to vary between trials in addition to the variations in the primary discriminandum for the task. The degree of interdependence in processing is inferred from the increase in RT obtained for blocks of trials with this irrelevant variation over and above blocks with the primary variation alone. Presence or absence of these increments may enable us to infer serial or parallel stages; but in the present work a better concept is of an extra feedback loop that may be implemented to modify the transfer function of a stage when its output is insufficiently distinct or a feedforward loop activated when an input displays certain key properties.

II. EXPERIMENT I

We chose differences in voices as our contextual variable rather than variations in an adjacent phoneme because we had prior experience of its ability both to generate identification errors and to influence the degree of right ear advantage, hypothetically a measure of specifically phonetic—linguistic processing (Haggard, 1971, 1974). It seemed essential to separate two quite distinct ways in which voices can differ on the grounds of their distinct psychoacoustical consequences and the distinct types of phonetic and linguistic information that they carry. Figure 1 shows the extreme example of both types of difference occurring, between a male and female voice. The first salient difference is in the fundamental frequency, $F0$; this is the voice pitch and is manifest in the broadband type of spectrogram by the horizontal separation between the vertical striations corresponding to the individual glottal pulses. Despite evidence that such low pitches are conveyed psychophysiologically by periodicity they are for convenience specified by frequency. This variable carries semantic, syntactic, and paralinguistic information and results chiefly from varying tension on the vocal cords but its long-term mean in a single speaker is related to the size of his larynx. The considerable male—female difference in larynx size has biological antecedents and musical consequences.

The other chief difference is in the average values of the formant frequencies manifest in the vertical location of the broad horizontal bands of energy. These are resonant frequencies, depending on the size and shape of the vocal tract. The pattern of their change specifies the lexical items of language and arises from movements of the articulators through target regions for the phonemes of the language. However, the long-term mean formant values depend upon the size of the individual's head. Hence linguistic and individual information are encoded onto the same small set of acoustical parameters and, where more than one speaker is present, extra perceptual operations may be required to separate the intimately related types of information. Differences in fundamental frequency

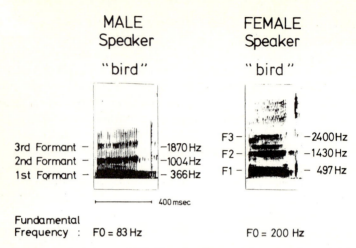

FIG. 1 Spectrograms of the word "bird" spoken by an adult male and an adult female of the same dialectal group (English RP).

are highly discriminable and serve (Broadbent & Ladefoged, 1957) to define which formants belong to which speaker; they are hence a clear stamp of individuality. However, the within-sex statistical association between head size and larynx size is overridden by the male–female difference, hence, informationally, the average $F0$ is not bound up with the fomant variations necessary for identifying vowels and consonants in quite the same way that the average value of the formants is. These distinctions in our ecological psychophysics can be justified phonetically and linguistically so it would be surprising if we could not show that they have performance correlates. However, such demonstrations are a necessary inroad to understanding the underlying information flow.

Details of the first experiment have been published elsewhere (Summerfield & Haggard, 1973) but a summary will be given here to show how the concepts and methodology developed and to demonstrate the compatibility of results between two rather different situations.

As stimuli we chose the set of English words "bed, bird, bored"; in British English the "r" is not pronounced and hence this set differ in only their vowel phonemes. These can, furthermore, be arranged with virtually no loss of fidelity along a single acoustical continuum: the average $F2$ in the vowel steady state between the trajectories that largely define the abutting /b/ and /d/ consonants. Such a situation is atypically simple and the point is to see whether such impoverishment with which a simple acoustical filter could easily cope elicits a similarly limited acoustically unidimensional analysis from the human listener. This was tested by having not only a basic voice defined by $F1, F3$, and a set of $F2$ frequencies but three other voices with the same patterns specifying the words but different acoustical details. These voice details had various degrees of relationship to the critical $F2$ information. Figure 2 shows the acoustical differences between the various voices that were embodied by synthesizing the entire set on a parallel formant synthesizer. (Henceforth, when speaking of one voice differing from another in terms of a particular acoustic component, we are implying that phonemically identical stimuli representing the two voices differ in that component). Voice 1 differed from Voices 2, 3, and 4 in mean fundamental frequency. This was the only difference between Voice 1 and the basic Voice 2. The average formant frequencies in Voice 3 were higher than those in Voice 2 by a factor of 1.2 in $F1$ and $F3$. For the $/\varepsilon/$, $/\mathrm{3}/$, and $/\mathrm{o}/$ vowels, respectively, $F2$ was higher in Voice 2 by the ratios: 1.1; 1.2; and 1.3. Voice 4 had the same $F1$ and $F3$ as Voice 2 and the same $F2$ as Voice 3. This design allowed us to dissociate the effects of voice differences in $F0$, $F2$, and $F1$ and $F3$; that is, in unrelated information, in supposedly "critical," information and in vocal tract scaling information respectively. After each of the eighteen subjects performed the word identification conditions in balanced order, they were recalled for a second session involving the speeded classification of *voices*. Here, after preliminary practice in which words from the voices in each pair were labeled by the experimenter as belonging to the voice "high" or "low," subjects responded in the same manner. This provided control data upon the discriminability of differences between pairs of voices irrespective of the effect of such differences upon normal processing in an identification task. In the speeded word identification task, subjects had to press three buttons to identify the three words. One-voice and two-voice blocks were presented within the same counterbalancing of order and finger-button assignment was also permuted. Reaction times were logged and tabulated for correct responses only.

There were five important aspects of the results:

1. Mean response times (RTs) to the stimuli representing a particular speaker were longer when those stimuli appeared in a mixed-voice rather than a single-voice block of trials.

2. The overall mean RTs in the three mixed-voice blocks which included the set of stimuli representing Voice 3, and in which, therefore, $F1$ and $F3$ differed

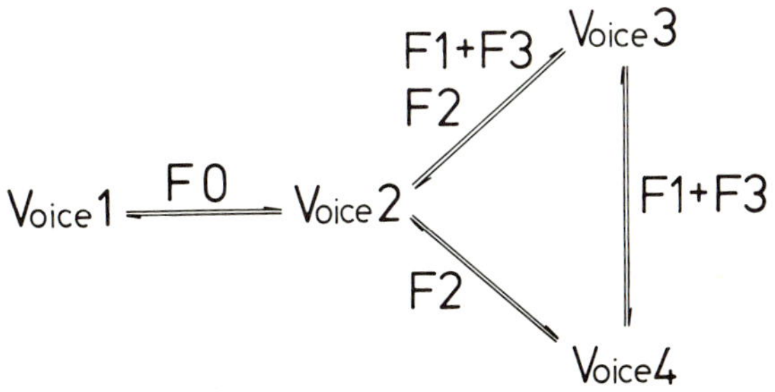

FIG. 2   Acoustic components differing between voices in Experiment 1.

between the pair of voices, were approximately equal to one another and averaged 477 msec. Collectively, they were significantly longer than the overall mean RTs in the other three mixed-voice blocks which were also approximately equal to one another and averaged 459 msec.

3. The data from the mixed-voice blocks were broken down according to the sequential contingencies between the stimulus presented on Trial $n+1$ and the stimulus presented on Trial n. The overall pattern noted in the previous result appeared in each individual sequential condition. It was especially large for repeated words in changed voices where the difference in RT between the three blocks which had included stimuli representing Voice 3 and the other three blocks was 50 msec; this provides a relative measure of extra processing complexity (Table 1).

4. The increases in RT observed in Result 1, and the differences observed in Results 2 and 3 were obtained for responses to the stimuli representing both of the voices in mixed-voice blocks and not simply for responses to the stimuli representing Voice 3, which happened to have shortest absolute RTs and hence largest increments (Fig. 3).

5. The control condition, in which subjects classified the stimuli in the mixed-voice blocks by voice rather than by word, showed that Results 1, 2, 3, and 4 were not directly a function of the discriminability of the pairs of voices.

Result 1 showed that RT was a measure sensitive to changes in processing demand. This was not simply a reflection of the increase in difficulty of mapping six stimuli rather than three stimuli onto three responses, nor a measure of a specific difficulty due to voice changes, because of Result 2. In those blocks in which stimuli representing Voice 3 were not present, the increases in RT observed in Result 1 were small (less than 10 msec) while, in those blocks in which stimuli representing Voice 3 were present, the increases were larger (more than 15 msec). We concluded that the increases in RT that occurred when Voice 3 was present reflected the fact that this voice represented a genuinely shorter vocal tract than did any of the other three voices. The shift in the frequency of $F1$ and $F3$ between stimuli representing this voice and the stimuli with which it

TABLE 1

Experiment I. Mean Absolute Three-Choice RTs for Voice Pairs Differing in Vocal-Tract Scaling Information and in Other Ways, in Two Types of Trial Sequence

Sequential contingency type	Voice pairs involving different vocal-tract information ($F_1 + F_3$)	Voice pairs involving other differences
Same voice/same word	435	416
Different voice/same word	500	450

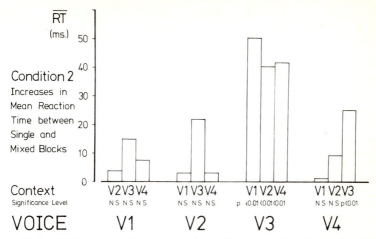

FIG. 3 Choice RT increments for various voice pairings, over the basic reaction time for identification with a single voice. For further details, see text.

was paired required, and triggered a recalibration of those parameters that represented the vocal tract length of the current speech source.

That a representation of vocal tract length should not only be extracted but also maintained in the perceptual process was shown by the different sequential effects in Result 3. Results 2 and 3 also showed that the recalibration was, in part, task specific. It was not triggered by the acoustic difference that resulted whenever $F0$ differed between voices, even though this was previously found to be the most effective means of discriminating the stimuli by voice.

In general, in identifying vowels the perceptual processor appeared to be responding to the overall spectral shape of the vowel portions of the stimuli rather than to an array of individual formants, and the results expressly ruled out an acoustic mode of processing in which the task was performed simply on the basis of the frequency of $F2$. A device consisting of an array of three acoustic bandpass filters tuned to the $F2$ frequency regions used to represent the three vowels could have performed the task of vowel identification with the same efficiency regardless of variations in $F0$ or in $F1$ and $F3$, though it might have proved slightly less efficient with $F2$ voice differences. Objectively, the task favored an acoustic processing strategy. However, the relative unimportance of voice differences in $F2$ showed that the listeners were not performing in such a way within the experiment.

In addition to extending the range of generalization over stimulus and response conditions, subsequent experiments had to remove minor inelegancies such as the imbalance of single-voice reaction times in favor of the short vocal tract; Voice 3 (high $F1$ and $F3$) and the basic Voice 2 had mean RTs of 435 and 452 msec, respectively. Although the error rate was low and did not vary significantly from condition to condition or in a way that vitiated the above interpretations, more precise control would also have been desirable. These two points are related in that error rates in the single voice blocks were 4.63 and 6.48%, respectively, for Voices 3 and 2. The voice with different (lower) $F0$, Voice 1, produced a mean RT of 457 msec and 7.52% errors, further confirming a very slight association of time and error measures. Finally, we did not determine whether listeners with extended exposure to a single pair of voices can come to respond in the fashion of a simple acoustical filter. But before recounting our progress to experimental impregnability in these respects we comment upon the apparent advantage for short vocal tracts as an interesting phenomenon in its own right.

III. A DICHOTIC PARALLEL

Two rather different considerations could underlie the advantage for the voice with higher formant frequencies. First, it could be better formed, with its three vowels' $F2$ frequencies further away from the ambiguous phoneme boundary regions for a vocal tract with those average formant frequencies, though pilot experimentation rendered this unlikely and the difference in errors was small. Second, it could have a greater attention demand for biological reasons that are intuitively acceptable, corresponding, for example, to the help calls of children. If the attention demand view is reasonable, then other paradigms such as dichotic listening should show similar dominance for voices with higher formant frequencies. Haggard (1971) showed no significantly greater rate of intrusions from an unattended voice with higher $F1$, $F2$, and $F3$ plus $F0$ despite a slight tendency to greater identification accuracy. Darwin's (1971) higher voice with higher formant frequencies was the more accurately responded to; although a direct breakdown into intrusion and simple errors is not available, because two responses were taken, differences between conditions indicated lower proneness to intrusions for the voice with higher $F1$, $F2$, and $F3$. Perl (1975) and others have found faster reaction times to high tones than to low in nonspeech tasks. There is thus an issue which needs clearing up.

Some relevant data are available from a dichotic study by Haggard and Paul (1975). As it also supports a distinction between effects of $F0$, and $F1$, $F2$, and $F3$ voice differences upon perceptual performances, we will summarize it here.

A dichotic simultaneous masking paradigm was employed. The particular stimuli to be identified as to both consonant and vowel on a predesignated ear were synthetic /b ɜ/, /d ɜ/, /b ɛ/, /d ɛ/. However, the predesignated target and "mask" ears had four possible relationships: same voice; $F0$ different; $F1$, $F2$, and $F3$ different; and both $F0$ and $F1$, $F2$, and $F3$ different. The frequency scaling factors of $F0$ and $F1$, $F2$, and $F3$ replicated the voice differences of

Experiment I exactly, except that there was no anomalous voice like Voice 4 giving voice differences in $F2$ alone, and the basic voice now had the lower rather than the higher fundamental. Eight subjects were run with voice varying between trials on the ear designated target for that block, while the mask-ear voice remained fixed; eight were run with the reverse pattern. The fixed voice was always the basic voice. For both groups of subjects an $F0$ voice difference facilitated the selective report of the vowel aspect of the syllable (i.e., it depressed intrusion errors) while depressing the percentage of correct report of the consonants (i.e., increasing the chance of an intrusion). However, the two groups displayed interesting differences. Presumably because intrusions were a high proportion of errors, the subjects with the varying-target/fixed-mask voices performed better than the subjects with the fixed-target/varying-mask voices. This observation should be of some interest to attention theorists. What is of interest here, however, is that trials with $F1$, $F2$, and $F3$ higher in *target* voices brought about a substantial reduction in the intrusion rate of both consonants and vowels, while trials with $F1$, $F2$, and $F3$ higher in *mask* voices did not have either a similar reduction in intrusions nor the complementary increase that might have been expected from the idea that voices with high $F1, F2$, and $F3$ are simply more intrusive.

As in Experiment I, therefore, we have a tendency, in the dichotic situation for $F0$, and $F1, F2$, and $F3$ voice differences to produce rather different distinct patterns of results over task conditions. These different patterns cannot be ascribed to the attention-demanding properties of the voice with higher average formant frequencies. For the group with varying-target voice, simple errors were fewest on trials with high $F1$, $F2$, and $F3$ voice, with a suggestion of further improvement when the $F0$ was also raised. This pattern, together with the results on single-voice blocks in Experiment I, suggests that voices with higher formants are more accurately perceived. As the particular stimuli differed between the experiments, well-formedness of the set is not a likely explanation.

There remains an alternative not considered at the outset which is both plausible phonetically and consistent with the data of both experiments: that accuracy and speed are related to the compatibility of the relationship between $F0$ and $F1$, $F2$, and $F3$. If confirmed, this would ascribe some perceptual importance to the statistical association between the variables over individual speakers. Specifically interesting would be whether the analytical distinction of the kind we created between related $F1$, $F2$, and $F3$ information and independent $F0$ information can, after all, be reduced to one of degree. In resuming the topic of reaction time increment for voices differing in average formant frequencies, we should point out that the possible small effects of compatibility between $F0$ and $F1$, $F2$, and $F3$ do not restrict the conclusions to be drawn from Experiment I, in which the trends in sequential effects on the mean RTs of the two voices were not affected by adding an $F0$ difference to an $F1$, $F2$, $F3$ difference.

IV. EXPERIMENT II

In Experiment I, both voices and responding requirements varied from block to block. The ability to develop an acoustical processing strategy might depend on the perceptual system acquiring a more detailed knowledge of the voices as represented by the stimuli and of the acoustic relationships between them, though it is unlikely that any amount of experience would result in behavior totally consistent with the "acoustic filter" hypothesis. In Experiment I, $F2$ could be designated the "task-critical" formant and $F1$ and $F3$ the "contextual variations" in vocal tract length. To simplify interpretation there, "critical" and "contextual" information were carried on separate formants. This might have allowed a greater degree of parallel processing of formant information than would be possible when critical and contextual information were carried on the same formant. We might, therefore, expect more RT increment in an experiment in which a change in vocal tract length was implied by a formant also critical to the vowel identification task, than in the experiment already described where the two sorts of information were generally carried on different formants. In the previous experiment, pairing Voices 2 and 4, which differed only in $F2$, produced negligible RT increment. It could be said that "critical" and "contextual" information were carried on the same formant but this is a limited design on which to base a general conclusion about critical–contextual relationships.

A. Method

1. Stimuli

Stimuli were synthetic versions of the monosyllables /bId/, /b ɛ d/, and /b ɜ d/. They were generated by the OVE 111b serial formant synthesiser under the control of our SPEX programming system (Draper, 1973). Four versions of each monosyllable were synthesised so as to represent the outputs of four dimensionally different vocal tracts. The stimuli bore a specific and constrained acoustic relationship to one another. *Within* each of the four sets of stimuli defining a particular voice, /bId/ was distinguished from /b ɛ d/ only by a difference in the frequency contour of $F1$. /b ɛ d/ was distinguished from /b ɜ d/ only by a difference in the frequency contour of $F2$. The four sets of stimuli formed two pairs, one differing in the contours of $F2$ and $F3$, and one in the contours of $F1$ and $F3$.

The stimuli were all 240 msec in duration, of which 110 msec comprised the vowel steady state. The first 25 msec of each stimulus comprised parabolic formant frequency transitions whose frequency loci were appropriate to the vocal tract length implied by the vowel formants. The formant frequencies of the vowel steady states in each of the twelve stimuli are tabulated in Table 2. In all respects other than their mean formant frequencies the stimuli were identical.

TABLE 2

Stimuli for Experiment II. Formant Frequencies (Hz) of the Vowel Steady-States of the Stimuli Comprising the Two Voice Pairs[a]

Voice differs in:	Stimulus	F_1	F_2	F_3	F_1	F_2	F_3
		Voice A			Voice B		
F_2 & F_3	/bɪd/	351	2300	2770	351	1916	2263
	/bɛd/	550	2300	2770	550	1916	2263
	/bɜd/	550	1610	2770	550	1345	2263
		Voice C			Voice D		
F_1 & F_3	/bɪd/	351	1990	2770	330	1990	2263
	/bɛd/	570	1990	2770	476	1990	2263
	/bɜd/	570	1500	2770	476	1500	2263

[a]Within each voice pair, /bɪd/ is distinguished from /bɛd/ only by a difference in F_1, and /bɛd/ is distinguished from /bɜd/ only by a difference in F_2.

2. Subjects

Subjects were eight postgraduate students whose first language was English learned in the U.K., who declared themselves to be right handed and to have normal hearing. They ranged in age from 22 to 26 years of age.

3. Procedure

The experiment was composed of two major conditions, involving $F2, F3$, and $F1, F3$ voice differences; four subjects performed $F2, F3$ then $F1, F3$, while four performed in the reverse order.

The subjects' task was to identify each stimulus by pressing one of three horizontally arranged buttons labeled "BID," "BED," and "BIRD" from left to right. The allocation of both stimuli and fingers to buttons was constant across subjects so that all subjects identified /bɪd/, /bɛd/, and /bɜd/ with the index, middle, and fourth fingers of their right hands.

At the start of each subexperiment subjects identified the six stimuli from the appropriate voice pair on a 24-item random sequence with feedback. No subject made more than one error in these pretests. For the experiment proper, instructions encouraged the subject to respond as fast as was compatible with a zero error rate. Mean RTs and number of errors were displayed at the end of each block.

The order of administration of the blocks was as follows:

Blocks 1–4: All six stimuli from one voice pair occurred requiring a 6:3 S–R mapping.

Blocks 5—12:   Only stimuli from the same voice pair presented in Blocks 1—4 occurred. In each block examplars of either /bId/ and /bɛd/ *or* examplars of /bɛd/ and /bɜd/ occurred. Four of the eight blocks involved stimuli from only one voice requiring a 2:2 S—R mapping. Four blocks involved stimuli representing both voices requiring a 4:2 S—R mapping.

Blocks 13—14:   Same as blocks 1—4 but with the other voice pair.
Blocks 15—22.   Same as blocks 5—12 but also with this other voice pair.

In Blocks 1—4 all six stimuli in a particular voice pair were presented in pseudorandom sequences of 72 trials introduced by header blocks of 18 trials, responses to which were discarded. The sequences contained 12 examples of each stimulus and were constrained so that each first-order sequential stimulus contingency occurred twice. There were 12 occurrences of each of the sequential conditions involving repeating a response, and 24 occurrences of contingencies involving alternation. As well as giving general and specific practice, these blocks provided data on numbers of errors, sequential effects, and learning effects for particular voices in a three-choice task similar to Experiment I.

In each of Blocks 5—12 and 15—22, the subjects' task was either to identify /bId/ and /bɛd/ or to identify /bɛd/ and /bɜd/. Eight blocks were required to permute these two tasks with each voice on the pair singly plus two occurrences of mixed voices. Each block consisted of 64 trials introduced by a header block of 16 trials. Trial-to-trial sequential stimulus contingencies were constrained up to the second order in two-voice blocks and up to the fourth order in one-voice blocks.

Blocks 13 and 14 were preceded by a second pretest with the stimuli representing the voice pair not presented in Blocks 1—12. Finally, subjects received another eight two-choice blocks consisting of the eight Conditions 1—8 and constituting the second major condition of the voice pair.

Throughout the experiment, the intertrial interval was fixed at two seconds. The algorithm described by Summerfield (1975) controlled stimulus presentations; it only recorded a response as correct when it involved the correct S—R mapping, its RT was less than 1000 msec, and it had been preceded by four correct, similarly fast, responses. Feedback was provided to the subjects by a light after any response which involved an incorrect S—R mapping. The entire experiment was run on line under the control of a suite of programs running under SPEX.

B. Results and Discussion

1. Errors

Averaged over both subexperiments and all subjects, the average number of errors in the 72-trial (6:3 S—R) blocks was 2.0, that is, 2.8%. This compares favorably with the 6.5% error rate in the mixed-voice blocks of the previous experiment which did not employ the algorithm. The average number of errors was 1.7 in the (4:2 S–R) 64-trial blocks and was 1.5 in the (2:2 S–R) 64-trial blocks. The error data will not be considered further since they did not reflect any trends that are not displayed more sensitively by the RT data. The raw RT scores were averaged for each condition to be compared and parametric statistical analyses were performed on these average scores. The results of Blocks 1–4 and Blocks 13 and 14 are considered first.

2. Two-Voice, Three-Choice Blocks

Of all the blocks in Experiment II, the one most comparable with Experiment I in terms of task, overall degree of practice, and stimulus unfamiliarity is Block 13. The mean absolute RTs in the four sequence types for Block 13 displayed a pattern similar to that observed in the previous experiment's $F1–F3$ mixed-voice blocks differing in $F1$ and $F3$. The figures for the same- and different-voice sequences with repeated response were 480 msec and 545 msec, as compared with 435 and 500 msec in Experiment I. Thus the mean difference was 65 msec for both experiments.

There are two connected ways in which practice with the set of stimuli defining a voice might be manifest in the absolute RT data, in the absence of a single-voice condition. RTs might show an abrupt increase for the block at which subjects experienced a new voice pair and might then decline with experience of a particular voice pair. The former tendency was evident, but not significant, in the contrast between Blocks 4 and 13. In Blocks 13 and 14, the main effect of *voice* was significant, $(F1,6 = 6.91, p = 0.038)$ and interacted significantly with *blocks* $(F1,6 = 6.94, p = 0.038)$. This shows that the perceptual difficulty experienced when only the voice changes reduces with familiarity to the stimuli defining the voices.

These results replicate the finding of the previous experiment for both of the voice pairs used here. However, the effect appears to be dependent, at least in part, on unfamiliarity with the stimuli used to define the voices. Whether we should interpret the process previously termed vocal tract normalization as being more rapid when these familiarities are established, or, as becoming less necessary, is not yet clear.

3. One- and Two-Voice, Two-Choice Blocks

The graphs in Fig. 4 show the overall mean RTs in the two subexperiments with different voices according to the task and the number of voices represented. In each graph, four points are plotted. Each point indicates the mean RT over two stimulus words and two voices. Each point plots the mean of 1024 RTs.

An analysis of variance examined the factors: *groups* (2) $\times$ *subjects* (4) $\times$ *conditions* (2) $\times$ *number of voices* (2) $\times$ *tasks* (2:1–ε or ε–3). Again, the *groups* factor, and its interactions, were not significant. The overall mean RTs for the two subexperiments with the two different voices were very nearly equal: 376.8 and 377.4 msec. Given the general ease with which the subjects identified the

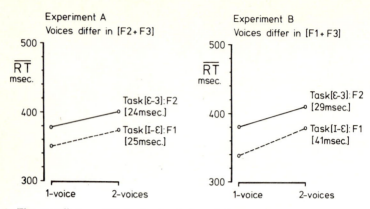

FIG. 4   The overall mean RTs in the two halves of the experiment having different voice pairs.

two sets of stimuli in the pretests and the low error rates across all conditions, we can be reasonably sure that the acoustic constraints which the experimental design imposed upon the stimuli did not render either subset unnatural to the extent that stimulus unnaturalness, per se, was an important factor in determining the results.

The *voices* factor ($F1,6 = 12.07, p = 0.013$) shows that responses were made more slowly in the two-voice conditions; the *tasks* factor ($F1,6 = 107.5, p = 0.0002$) shows that responses were made more slowly when the task was identify /bɛd/—/bɜd/ rather than /bɪd/—/bɛd/. The two-voice increments are again compatible with Experiment I.

There was no significant interaction corresponding to the slight divergence from parallel of the lines in Fig. 4. The two-voice RT increment was not greater either for the $F1-F3$ voice differences or for tasks in which critical and contextual information was carried on the same formant. However, we saw in Experiment I that effects in the macrostructure of results may be unevenly and explicably distributed in the microstructure (as in different sequence types) and the possibility that opposing effects in the microstructure may underlie some negative results suggests closer scrutiny. Felfoldy (1974), for instance, in a visual categorization task, found that RT increases between a one-dimensional condition and a two-dimensional orthogonal condition, in which the unattended dimension could also vary, were manifest mainly on trials in which the response changed. It is most revealing, therefore, to tabulate the two-voice increment as a function of sequence type. This is done in Table 3.

Consider first the fifth column in which the increases in RT resulting for each of the sequence types are averaged across the four voice-pair/task conditions. Two-tail *t*-tests showed that these averages differ significantly from 0 at the 5% level in only the two types with the highest average: different voice/same word (ii) and same voice/different word (iii). This suggests that the basis of the

TABLE 3

Experiment II. Two-Choice RT Increments (msec) for Eight Subjects in Mixed-Voice Blocks over Single-Voice Blocks for Tasks Related and Unrelated to Voice Difference, by Trial Sequence Type

Sequential contingency type	Voice difference $F_2 + F_3$ Task effectively identification of:		Voice difference $F_1 + F_3$ Task effectively identification of:		Average
	F_1 (I–E) (unrelated)	F_2 (E–3) (related)	F_1 (I–E) (related)	F_2 (E–3) (unrelated)	
Same voice/same word[a] (i)	7	11	32	17	17
Different voice/same word[b] (ii)	54	57	50	66	57
Same voice/different word[c] (iii)	38	25	40	20	31
Different voice/different word[a] (iv)	0	9	37	11	14
Average	25	26	40	29	30

[a]"Acoustical" microtask soluble on the basis of physical identity or difference.
[b]Microtask involving perceptual recalibration for a new vocal tract.
[c]Microtask soluble on the basis of normal phonetic-linguistic decoding.

response decision in the two-voice blocks may differ between these contingencies and the others. We may explain these observations by postulating that the speed of a subject's response is controlled by the first terminating of a number of parallel processes, one of which is effectively a same/different judgement on the basis of a physical match. In the two-voice blocks, acoustical identity of two successive stimuli would be sufficient to determine that the response to the first should be repeated, rapidly, to the second. (Processing would continue after response initiation to check the accuracy of the decision and bring about a change in response strategy should an error have occurred). If a preset criterion of *acoustic difference* between successive stimuli were exceeded (implying that both the vowel and the voice had changed) then the alternative response could be made. A problem would arise for the processor when the acoustic difference between successive stimuli was intermediate. In this case, either the voice or the vowel might have changed and a response could not be made purely on acoustic criteria. Phonetic analysis would be required to distinguish the two possibilities. First, therefore, the increases in RT in Contingencies (i) and (iv) should be small and approximately equivalent since responses in these contingencies can be based on the outcome of acoustic analyses. Second, the increase in RT in Contingency (iii) might be larger since responses in this contingency must be based on the outcome of phonetic analysis. Third, the increase in Contingency (ii) should be larger still since additional processing to achieve vocal tract recalibration should be required before phonetic analysis can be completed. This is the pattern shown by the average increases in Table 3.

In a 4-treatments by 8-subjects analysis of variance, the difference between the four sequential stimulus contingencies was significant ($F3,21 = 13.38, p < 0.0001$). The difference between the increases of 17 and 14 msec in Contingencies (i) and (iv), in which the primary basis for the response is presumed to have been acoustic, is not significant ($F1,21 = .12$, n.s.). The comparison between these two increases jointly and the 31 msec increase in Contingency (iii), where phonetic processing was presumably required for response initiation, is significant if assessed against an *a priori* criterion ($F1,21 = 5.18, p < 0.05$), but not if assessed against the *least* stringent *a posteriori* criterion recommended by Scheffe (1953) which requires an F ratio of 8.88 for significance at the 10% level. The difference between this 31 msec increase and the 57 msec increase found in Contingency (ii), where response initiation required additional processing for vocal tract recalibration, is significant when assessed against both *a priori* and *a posteriori* criteria ($F1,21 = 12.29$). We may perhaps explain the marginal effect for Contingency (iii) by positing that some of the acoustical differences are large enough to meet criterion and to trigger an alternation response before complete phonetic processing. Thus, these sequential data appear to show effects of three components of the perceptual process: the two-voice increment is least when responses are adequately determined by acoustic intertrial differences (assuming that the error rate is low, as it was here, and that some checking activity can occur after response initiation); the increment is greater when responses require phonetic analysis; the increment is even greater when parameter tuning to recalibrate vocal tract length must precede or accompany phonetic analysis.

We have established a rationale for the pattern of interference exhibited in the average data and now examine the extent to which this pattern varies with the relatedness of critical and contextual formant information. Of the various tendencies implied by the relative magnitudes of the increases in Table 3, only the within-task comparison for the $/I-\epsilon/$ task is significant. For Contingencies (i) and (iv), hypothetically favoring acoustical processing, significantly less two-voice increment occurred when critical and contextual information were carried on different formants; but this advantage was shown only in the $/I-\epsilon/$ task, that is, for identification of stimuli differentiated by a change in $F1$.

An explanation may lie in the overall discriminability of the stimuli. The generally shorter RTs for the $/I-\epsilon/$ task could reflect greater discriminability of the formant frequency differences in $F1$. This would favor application of an acoustical strategy and greater importance for the task-given relatedness of critical and contextually varying information. The pattern of performance may also reflect the greater long-term information load on $F2$ in speech, and the data do not allow these alternatives to be distinguished.

We regard the foregoing interpretations as well within the range of postdiction that psychological and phonetic knowledge render profitable. Their first test must be in their application to other data. Our analysis of Experiment I did not tabulate increments by sequential condition. This is done in Table 4. The column of means for the $F1-F3$ differences is analogous to the "unrelated" columns in Table 3 and shows a fairly similar pattern. The split into low and high $F1-F3$ trials confirms that the pattern over sequential conditions is resistant to differences in absolute RT between voices. For voices differing in $F1-F3$ the means differ significantly ($F3,51 = 16.4$, $p < 0.01$) but on a strict a posteriori criterion only the 75-msec increment in Contingency (ii) is significantly different from those in the other contingencies. This again pinpoints the occurrence of perceptual recalibration for particular types of voice difference in just that sequential contingency in which it is required for task execution.

For voices differing in $F2$ and $F0$ the pattern of increments is different. The means are also more homogenous ($F3,51 = 3.64$, $p < 0.05$). On a strict a posteriori criterion, sequential Contingency (ii) does not differ individually from any other. However, if we apply an a priori criterion, justifiable in view of the preceding discussion of situations favoring acoustical processing, Contingencies (ii) and (iii) differ jointly from Contingencies (i) and (iv) ($F1,51 = 8.14$, $p < 0.01$). The data obtained with exclusively $F2$ voice differences here are only to a limited extent comparable with Experiment II data in the "related" columns of Table 3. However, the different voice/same word increment is not as large as it is

TABLE 4

Experiment I. Three-Choice RT Increments (msec) for Eighteen Subjects in Mixed-Voice Blocks over Single-Voice Blocks for Particular Voice Pairs, by Trial Sequence Type[a]

Sequential contingency type	Voice pairs involving difference in vocal-tract scaling information ($F_1 + F_3$)			Voice pairs involving other differences: F_0 irrelevant; F_2 "critical" (Averages of trials in both voices)			
				Voice pairs differ in:			
	Low $F_1 + F_3$ trials	High $F_1 + F_3$ trials	Mean	F_0	F_2	Both F_0 & F_2	Mean
Same voice/same word[b] (i)	8	14	11	−11	−9	−16	−12
Different voice/same word[c] (ii)	66	85	75	8	31	17	19
Same voice/different word[d] (iii)	34	37	35	24	13	9	15
Different voice/different word[b] (iv)	13	38	25	−1	4	10	5

[a]Only the means are directly comparable between the left and right halves of this table.

[b]"Acoustical" microtask soluble on the basis of physical identity or difference.

[c]Microtask involving perceptual recalibration for a new vocal tract.

[d]Microtask soluble on the basis of normal phonetic-linguistic decoding.

for the $F1-F3$ voice differences and the column of $F2$-determined increments as a whole contains smaller values than Table 3 or the $F1-F3$ columns of Table 4. We may infer that these lower values are due to lack of $F3$ variations which are not "critical" but are important for recalibration.

Three further interesting trends deserve comment. Where voices differ in $F0$ a qualitatively different pattern emerges, with very small RT increment in the sequence type held to reflect vocal tract recalibration. Second, The RT increments for voice pairs differing in both $F0$ and $F2$ are smaller (except plausibly in the sequential contingency most like a physical-match "different" judgment) than the averages of increments on one-dimensional voice-pair differences. This suggests that RT increments do not simply accrue to conditions most favoring general distraction by perceptible sources of nontarget variation. Rather, there appears to be an alerting effect. Finally, facilitation rather than interference in the same word/same voice sequential contingency (a corollary of the approximately 20 msec smaller RT increments in this subset of the data) could likewise reflect an overall alerting function of voice differences as such, or simply a range effect of a type commonly observed in within-subjects designs (Poulton, 1975).

In conclusion, it is evident that the phonetically justified rationale for sequential effects in RT increments applies well to both experiments, despite some differences in stimuli and tasks. We should not make too much of the absolute magnitude of the increments shown on the same word/different voice trials because they vary in predictable fashion with the relative probability of repetition responses. However, as they appear to reflect perceptual operations which other aspects of the data suggest to be automatic, their magnitudes are sufficient to generate optimistic interest in measuring stages of perceptual processing of speech by RT methods. The results confirm a perceptual distinction, also justifiable linguistically, phonetically and psychoacoustically, between the larynx pitch and the vocal tract resonant frequency aspects of voice differences.

V. GENERAL DISCUSSION

Our results relate to experimental issues of contemporary interest in three ways.

Pisoni and Tash (1974) have shown that another form of acoustical variation in speech, phonemic context, generates extra processing demand. These authors used same—different judgements about initial consonants and found that RTs were longer by approximately 100 msec on "same" responses when the vowel also varied than when it did not. Together with our results, this study suggests that decoding of encoded phonemic information remains a useful concept in understanding speech perception.

On the more restricted problem of perceptual recalibration to different voices, Strange, Verbrugge, & Schankweiler (1974), and Verbrugge, Strange, & Shankweiler (1974) have found that the accuracy decrement with multiple speakers for vowel identification in natural speech is only appreciable for isolated vowels, not for vowels in consonant—vowel—consonant (CVC) context. They conclude in favor of the Gibsonian view that higher order stimulus variables are present that diminish the need to talk about inferential processes in perception or computational stages such as recalibration for vocal tract size. The conflict between their results and ours is only superficial, although it would be desirable to be able to ascribe it unambiguously to a difference in sensitivity of time and error measures or to a difference between natural and synthetic speech (unlikely, given our low error rates) by a further experiment. We do not wish to deny that the stimulus contains complex coherences that elicit rapid and accurate but unconscious operations in perception; rather we seek methods for determining the nature of those operations.

Finally, the difference between voices has been used as an index of the acoustical basis of inferred types of memory representation. Cole, Coltheart, and Allard (1974) found that same—different RTs to spoken letter names could be influenced by the speaker's voice: specifically a switch in sex of voice produced about 70 msec RT increment at 8 sec interitem interval. Part of this increment may be a recalibration delay in the identification of the second syllable. Indeed it is not surprising that parameters of perceptual analysis should remain set over such an interval provided no other speech or speechlike sounds are presented, because such parameters cannot be conceived exclusively of as being the information that is "stored in" or "passed through" any of the variously postulated forms of short-term memory stores of perceptual processing stages. Rather they must be an adjustable part of the linkages between stages. In a study of natural speaker verification as an ergonomic problem, we have concluded that speaker parameters are estimated and available for same—different judgements of speakers over several seconds (Summerfield, Paul, Margrain, & Haggard, 1974). In that experiment, increasing the number of syllables in the phrase spoken by the second of two speakers increased the accuracy of judgement of identity/difference with the first speaker even if the first phrase was not similarly augmented. However, it appears that the importance of acoustic and phonetically based parameters does not stop at identifying words and speakers. Surprisingly, Cole and associates' result was more marked with an interitem interval of 8 sec than of 2 sec, and Craik and Kirsner (1974) have shown accuracy and latency advantages in recognition memory for spoken words in the same as opposed to different-sex voices at presentation intervals up to two minutes. Whether there is any close connection between the particular speaker parameters important in perception and those important in this more enduring form of memory is yet to be established, and whether this form of memory is indeed echoically based must be determined first. Kirsner (cited in Craik, 1975) obtained similar results in a visual experiment in which words were accompanied by an extra word, "male" or "female," suggesting a categorical semantic tagging process. As memory for such semantic tags inevitably accompanies acoustical differences, interference from them could explain why the RT increment grows in the Cole *et al.* (1974) study for the longer interval. It might also account for the occurrence of an RT increment on "different" judgments that would not be expected from the present short RTs in sequential Contingency (iv) on any acoustical memory basis.

REFERENCES

Broadbent, D. E., & Ladefoged, P. On the fusion of sounds reaching different sense organs. *Journal of the Acoustical Society of America,* 1957, **29**, 708–710.

Cole, R. A., Coltheart, M., & Allard, F. Memory of a speaker's voice: Reaction time to same- or different-voiced letters. *Quarterly Journal of Experimental Psychology,* 1974, **26**, 1–7.

Cole, R. A., & Scott, B. Toward a theory of speech perception. *Psychological Review,* 1974, **81**, 348–374.

Craik, F. I. M. Personal communication, August 1975.

Craik, F. I. M., & Kirsner, K. The effect of speaker's voice on word recognition. *Quarterly Journal of Experimental Psychology,* 1974, **26**, 274–284.

Darwin, C. J. Ear differences in the recall of fricatives and vowels. *Quarterly Journal of Experimental Psychology,* 1971, **23**, 46–62.

Darwin, C. J., & Baddeley, A. D. Acoustic memory and the perception of speech. *Cognitive Psychology,* 1974, **6**, 41–60.

Draper, G. SPEX: A system to run speech perception experiments. *Proceedings of 9th Seminar of DECUS, Europe: 89–93. 1973.*

Felfoldy, G. F. Repetition effects in choice reaction time to multidimensional stimuli. *Perception & Psychophysics,* 1974, **15**, 453–459.

Haggard, M. P. Encoding and the REA for speech signals. *Quarterly Journal of Experimental Psychology,* 1971, **23**, 34–45.

Haggard, M. P. Selectivity for distortions and words in speech perception. *British Journal of Psychology,* 1974, **65**, 69–83.

Haggard, M. P., & Paul, D. J. Parameter-specific voice-difference effects in dichotic CV identification. Paper presented at the 90th meeting of the Acoustic Society of America, San Francisco, November 1975.

Liberman, A. M., Cooper, F. S., Shankweiler, D. P., & Studdert-Kennedy, M. Perception of the speech code. *Psychological Review,* 1967, **74**, 431–461.

Perl, N. T. Peripheral masking and bihemispheric processing of auditory information. Unpublished doctoral dissertation. Queen's University, Belfast, 1975.

Pisoni, D. B., & Tash, J. "Same–different" reaction times to consonants, vowels and syllables (Research on Speech Perception, Progress Report No. 1, 1974; Department of Psychology, Indiana University).

Poulton, E. C. Range effects in experiments on people. *American Journal of Psychology,* 1975, **88**, 3–32.

Scheffe, H. A method for judging all contrasts in the analysis of variance. *Biometrika,* 1953, **40**, 87–104.

Strange, W., Verbrugge, R., & Shankweiler, D. Consonant environment specifies vowel identity. Haskins Laboratories Status Report, 1974, **SR-37/38**, 209–216.

Summerfield, A. Q. A process-control algorithm for reaction time experiments allowing 'perfect responding' with errors. *Speech Perception,* 1975, **4**, 145–148.

Summerfield, A. Q., & Haggard, M. P. Vocal tract normalisation as demonstrated by reaction times. In G. Fant & M. Tatham (Eds.), *Proceedings of the Leningrad Symposium on auditory analysis and the perception of speech.* London: Academic Press, 1975. (Originally published 1973.)

Summerfield, A. Q., Paul, D. J., Margrain, S., & Haggard, M. P. Human factors in speaker verification. *Speech Perception,* 1974, **3,** 75–86. (Department of Psychology, Queen's University, Belfast).

Verbrugge, R., Strange, W., & Shankweiler, D. What information allows a listener to map a talker's vowel space? Haskins Laboratories Status Report, 1974, **SR-37/38,** 199–208.

Wood, C. C. Parallel processing of auditory and phonetic information in speech perception. *Perception & Psychophysics,* 1974, **15,** 501–508.

Part III

ATTENTIONAL PROCESSES

15
Exploring the Limits of Cueing

David LaBerge
Rohn J. Petersen
Michael J. Norden

Department of Psychology
University of Minnesota
Minneapolis, Minnesota, United States

ABSTRACT

This investigation is an attempt to determine what kinds of information-processing structures attention can operate upon in a selective way to facilitate processing. The three classes of structures considered were pattern identification codes, structures which interrelate patterns, and structures which select levels of processing of a given pattern. Attention was controlled by presenting a cue prior to the display on each trial. The function of a pattern cue was to facilitate processing of that pattern when it appeared in the display. The function of a relation or operation cue was to facilitate selectively either the matching of two digits or the ordering of them. The function of the "levels" cue was to determine whether a pair of letters was to be processed as a unit or as component letters. While evidence has been available in the literature to support the facilitation effect of cueing on pattern identification, only recently have data shown that tasks interrelating patterns can be selectively facilitated by a cue. Efforts to cue effectively the selection of a particular level of processing were unsuccessful in the experiments reported here.

I. INTRODUCTION

In the previous volume of this series, attention was represented as an activation process (LaBerge, 1975). This model assumed that attention could be directed to structures located not only at early stages of the information processing system, but also at processes operating later in the system. When attentional activation is allocated to a particular structure, for example, a pattern code, a color analyzer, or a sensory channel during or shortly after stimulus onset, we assumed that the level of activity in the structure is raised beyond that normally produced by incoming signals from the environment. In this way the processing by the structure itself is facilitated. However, another interpretation is that its output is amplified and therefore is more likely to activate subsequent structures in the system. For example, when we are shown a photograph of a group of people, a particular face may stand out as being somewhat familiar, but the name escapes us. However, when we allocate attention to it for a moment, we may increase the activation of the visual code of the face so that it elicits its name by way of an associative link output to the phonological system. Highly learned face-to-name associations, on the other hand, should occur automatically, that is, without additional activation by attention, just as highly learned letter names "pop into our heads" when we are shown a series of single visual letters (LaBerge & Samuels, 1974).

In a similar fashion, deployment of attention may assist connections between feature detectors and higher order pattern codes. When a pattern is unfamiliar, component feature detector outputs to the pattern code are weak or nonexistent, and attention to these outputs assists in the activation of the new code, and perhaps assists somehow in the organization of the code. When a pattern is familiar, we assume that the connections between feature analyzers and the pattern code are already strong enough to permit automatic activation of the pattern code when the stimulus is presented. The progressive strengthening of these connections is considered to be a form of perceptual learning (LaBerge, 1973), and because attentional involvement is reduced as a direct consequence of this strengthening, we regard perceptual learning of this kind and automatic processing to be closely related.

Thus far we have considered some effects of attentional activation when it occurs during or immediately following the presentation of a stimulus. Now we turn to the case when attention is directed to a structure just prior to stimulus onset. The experimental operation commonly used to direct attention to a structure in this case has been termed *cueing* (LaBerge, Van Gelder, & Yellott, 1970), sometimes *priming* (Beller, 1971), and sometimes simply *preknowledge* (Kohfeld & Morris, 1976).

In the typical task in which this operation is employed, a trial contains two stimuli. The first stimulus, which we will term the *cue*, may sometimes be used to predict one of the alternative displays (or part of a display) which could follow on that trial. The basis of this prediction is the probability distribution of the alternative displays given a particular cue. If, given a cue, a particular display (or a set of displays) is more likely to follow than others, the cue is termed an *informative* cue. If the cue carries no predictive information, then the cue is considered *uninformative*. When an informative cue correctly predicts the display, we will say that the display which occurred on that trial was *cued;* when an informative cue incorrectly predicts the display, we will say that the display which occurred on that trial was *miscued*. Uninformative cues are termed *neutral cues.* In summary, the first stimulus of the trial is termed the *cue,* and the task of the subject is simply to observe it but not to respond to it.. The second stimulus may be termed the *display,* and the subject's task is to make the appropriate response to it.

The informative cue is of main interest here, because it apparently induces the subject to *expect to perceive* the particular display which the cue indicates will most likely follow. In the case of cueing patterns, we represent this expectation as attentional activation of the particular pattern code to a level of excitation above the code's base rate of activity. Subsequently, when the pattern is presented to the subject, the pattern code processes the information more rapidly than would be the case without attentional activation. Therefore, re-action times should be faster to cued displays than to neutral cued or miscued displays. Some studies which show the facilitative effect of cueing are those of LaBerge, Van Gelder, and Yellott (1970), Darley, Klatsky, and Atkinson (1972), and Posner and Synder, (1975).

If it is reasonable to infer that faster reaction times to cued patterns indicates that attention can be directed to the perceptual structures corresponding to those patterns, then the cueing technique might be effectively employed to search for other structures in the processing system to which attention can be directed. It could be even more interesting to find a processing structure that resists cueing, because failures might reveal properties of attention which successes do not. The purpose of the experiments reported in this chapter was to explore the cueing of a variety of processing structures in order to determine which of these would accept attentional activation, and which, if any, would not. The three structures tested for cueing are those involved in identifying a pattern, operating on patterns, and determining the level at which patterns are processed.

The first process under consideration, that is, cueing of patterns, has been studied using a matching task, and the results with this paradigm led to the development of the notion of cueing. To determine that a cue affects processing of a pattern requires a comparison of response latencies under two conditions. The first condition is simply a trial in which the display follows an informative cue. The second condition is a trial in which the display either follows a neutral cue or is miscued. The difference between mean latencies of the cued and the miscued or neutral cued trials serves as the indicator of the effect of cueing. The magnitude of the latency difference seems to be about 121 msec for cued versus miscued and about 85 msec for cued versus neutral cued, when simultaneous matching of letter pairs is the stimulus, and a single letter is the cue (Posner & Synder, 1975). For matching tasks in which a single digit is the display and a single digit is the cue, the latency difference is about 167 msec for cued versus miscued conditions, and 45 msec for cued versus neutral conditions (Thorsen, 1975). The longer latency difference in the case of cued versus miscued compari-sons is attributable to the relatively long latencies obtained under miscued conditions. Apparently, when a subject is directing attention to a particular pattern code prior to the presentation of the stimulus and then some other, unexpected, pattern is presented, considerable time is required to withdraw attention from the expected pattern code and shift it to the particular pattern code activated by the stimulus on that trial. Posner and Snyder (1975) have analyzed this situation in terms of costs and benefits. When the display is cued, there is a benefit in the form of shorter latencies, compared to the neutral-cue condition; but whenever it is miscued, there is cost compared to the neutral-cue condition. Of course, the overall cost—benefit over a block of trials would depend upon the percentage of cued to miscued trials.

For these experiments which treated patterns and operations, the indicator of cueing effects was the latency difference between cue and neutral-cue trials. However, the indicator of cueing for the experiments dealing with cueing levels of processing was different because these experiments involved a somewhat more complex paradigm. A detailed description of that indicator is given in Section III.

II. CUEING PATTERNS AND OPERATIONS

When a pattern is perceived by a sensory system, processing usually does not terminate at that level, but continues at higher levels which operate on the results of perceptual processing. For example, a word pattern code may output a signal to its name or meaning code. This process is usually termed an *associative operation.* The pattern code might also be read into a memory store by rehearsal operations. In the case in which two digits are presented simultaneously, the subject may be instructed to perform a matching operation or an arithmetic operation on the two digits and then respond appropriately.

All of these examples illustrate operations which may be performed on information which has been processed by the perceptual system. Figure 1 is a schematic representation of the structures of pattern codes and operations, along with a representation of the attention activation center. The main question raised here is whether specific operations can be cued in the same way that patterns are cued. If attention can be directed to specific operations, we expect that, as in the case of pattern cueing, facilitation of processing will result. A recent experiment by LaBerge and Norden (1975) was designed to answer this question.

There were two types of operations or tasks that the subject was required to perform on display patterns. In the first task the subject was to respond when two digits matched, and in the second task he was to respond when the values of the digits increased from left to right. Sample displays and cues are shown in Fig. 2. The displays were called *targets* and *catches.* Target displays contained either vertical pairs of digits for the matching task, or horizontal pairs for the ordering task (e.g., 5–6, or 4–6). The subject was instructed to respond with a single button press when target displays appeared. He was instructed not to respond to

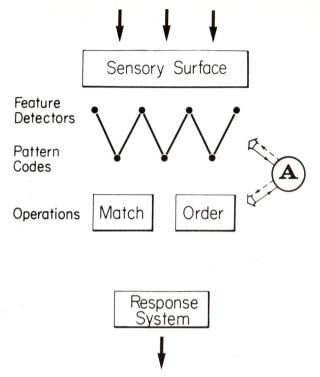

FIG. 1   Representation of perceptual memory structures and simple operations. Solid dots denote perceptual codes at the feature and pattern levels. Arrows from the attention center (A) to codes and operations indicate that attention can activate these structures, and in turn can be activated by them.

catch displays, which were either vertical pairs of digits which did not match, or horizontal pairs of digits which were not ordered from left to right. There were four categories of cues: three of these were informative and one neutral. The informative cues were: (1) task operations of matching or ordering, indicated by "+" symbols arranged vertically or horizontally; (2) patterns which were displayed as single digits selected within the range 2 to 6; and (3) both pattern and task, cued simultaneously with a digit and a "+" symbol in the orientation appropriate to the task. The neutral cue was simply a circle. Each of the four categories of cues occurred 12 times in the test block of 48 trials. For each of the four categories of cues, the display which followed the cue was a vertical pair of digits on 6 trials and a horizontal pair of digits on 6 trials. Four of these 6 trials were targets and 2 were catches. Therefore the target-to-catch ratio was 2:1.

Target displays were never miscued, but half of the catch displays following informative cues were miscued. This assured that under all cue conditions the subjects processed both the orientation of the display and the component digit

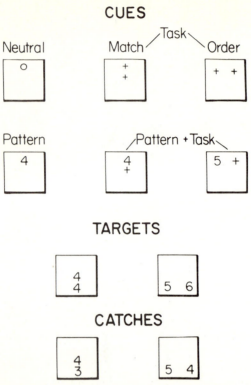

FIG. 2   Sample stimuli of the experiment in which operations and patterns were cued. The first stimulus of a trial was a cue; and the second stimulus was either a target or a catch display.

patterns before responding. If the information in the cues had been perfectly reliable the subjects might have ignored one of these two aspects of the display.

Prior to the test block each subject was given two practice blocks: a short one of 36 trials, and a longer one of 72 trials. These two blocks contained each type of cue and display, except that letters were used instead of digits. The durations of events within a trial were as follows: The cue was presented for 1300 msec, followed by a blank interval of 500 msec, and the stimulus was displayed for 1000 msec unless terminated by a response. The intertrial interval was 500 msec. The subjects were 32 volunteers from an introductory psychology course who were given $2 or 2 credit points for their services.

The results from the test block of 48 trials are shown in Fig. 3, in which mean latency of response to a target is given as a function of type of cue. Since the set of target displays was balanced across the four cueing conditions, it was appropriate to compare performance of each task across these conditions. An analysis of variance showed significant effects across cueing conditions and between types of task. Linear contrasts revealed highly significant differences

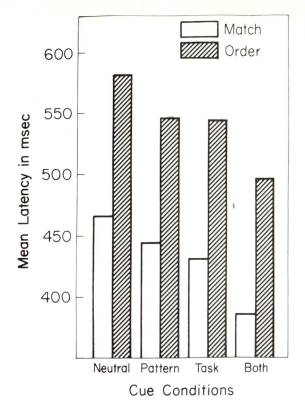

FIG. 3 Results of the experiment in which operations and patterns were cued. Mean latency to targets is plotted as a function of type of cue. The patterns were digits 1 to 9 and the tasks were matching and ordering.

between all pairwise comparisons except between task and pattern cueing conditions.

The indicator of the effect of cueing was a comparison of the latencies of the neutral-cue condition with each of the other cue conditions. The results showed that cueing was effective for tasks; in fact, it was about as effective as it was for patterns. In particular the latency difference found between neutral and pattern cueing for matching was 22 msec, compared with Posner and Snyder's (1975) difference of 85 msec. However, their data were obtained from capital letters, whereas our results are based on digits. Moreover, the experiments differ with respect to the types of other tasks included within a block.

A somewhat surprising result is that cueing *both* task and pattern produced substantially lower latencies than cueing either alone. In fact the effect appears to be additive in this particular design. Apparently it is possible to cue more than one structure at a time if one is a pattern and the other is an operation on that pattern. However, it seemed here that one cannot effectively cue more than one structure at a time if the structures are of the same type, that is, two patterns or two tasks. In Fig. 3 the neutral-cue condition could be regarded as cueing both matching and ordering, but the obtained latency was clearly greater than when only one of these tasks was cued. Similarly, the neutral cue condition could represent the cueing of the whole range of digit patterns, but the obtained latency for the neutral cue condition was greater than the single pattern cue condition. Similar comparisons have been shown by studies using the Sternberg paradigm (Sternberg, 1966), in which latency to a probe given a positive set of one is shorter than to probes of positive sets of two or more.

Before interpreting the present results as favoring the hypothesis that operations can indeed be cued, one must be sure that subjects were not simply cueing the orientation of the digits as a pattern itself. In all cue conditions the subject had to process the orientation of the display before he could determine which operation to perform. When he was cued for task by the orientation of the cue, he could have expected this orientation as a pattern and, when it occurred in the display, process it faster. But if this had been the case in the combined cue condition the subject would have been cued for two patterns, namely, the orientation pattern and a particular digit pattern. This possibility seems unlikely in view of the evidence previously discussed.

Nevertheless, to insure that the main results are not attributable to the cueing of an orientation pattern, we repeated the experimental design but presented all digit pairs horizontally. Matching operations were indicated by inserting either = or ↔ between the digits, and ordering operations were indicated by inserting either < or → between the digits. The reason that two symbols instead of one were used for each operation was to prevent the subject from expecting a particular symbol when a task was cued. The cue for the task was simply the word "match" or "order." When both pattern and task were cued, a typical cue was "4 match" or "5 order."

The results of this second experiment confirmed the cueing effects shown in Fig. 3. Neutral-cue trials were slower than task-cue trials and pattern-cue trials. The only deviation from the configuration of results shown in Fig. 3 was that for the ordering task, cueing both task and pattern did not produce a significantly faster latency than cueing task or pattern alone. Therefore, it would seem unlikely that when a subject was cued for a task in these experiments, he was in effect being cued to process a particular orientation in the display. Rather, it seems reasonable, in view of these results, that the subject could cue a task and therefore that attention can be directed to the operation structures shown in Fig. 1.

III. CUEING LEVELS OF PROCESSING

The information-processing system shown in Fig. 1 provides for the processing of feature codes into pattern codes and for the subsequent operations which must be performed on the outputs from these codes to produce an appropriate response. However, there is no provision in this model for determining which level of codes is read out for further processing and eventual determinations of a response. For example, when a pair of digits is presented in a matching task, the matching operation may be performed on the set of features corresponding to the two digits or on the two patterns taken as units. Of course, component features would require many matching operations, whereas unit codes would require only one match. Quite possibly, matching operations might be carried out at both levels simultaneously, with the first level to produce a match generating an output from the operation stage to the response stage. Without ruling out the possibility of parallel operations on codes at different levels, one can consider the possibility that outputs from codes at one level are somehow favored or facilitated over codes from other levels. Whatever the mechanism by which this is done, could the facilitation of output from one level of processing ever come about by direct attentional activation? Or, put in the context of the present paradigm, could the cueing procedure which apparently can facilitate processing of patterns and operations also directly facilitate or select a particular level of processing of a pattern?

One way to represent a mechanism which could mediate the selection of a level of perceptual processing is given in Fig. 4. A cluster code corresponds to pairs of letters such as "ph," "sc," or "fr." The column of three symbols, c_f, c_l, and c_{cl} represent nodes which, when activated, will in turn activate all detectors or codes in their respective rows. The two-way arrows provide for the possibility that a node may be activated by any code in its row. This scheme is very similar to one proposed by Estes (1975), in which it is assumed that an output from a perceptual code to subsequent stages of processing requires activation both from the sensory surface and from such "context" nodes. In particular, Estes assumed that the two sources of activation combine multiplicatively to produce an output from the code.

A finding that seems to be related to the selection of levels of processing is that of Aderman and Smith (1971). They investigated the word superiority effect with the Reicher–Wheeler tachistoscopic forced-choice procedure, and used two different kinds of lists. In one list, the display was made up of spelling patterns; in the other list of the displays were unrelated letters. Following each list, test trials were given with both types of displays. They found that a letter was identified better in spelling patterns than in unrelated letter strings only when the test items followed a list of spelling patterns. Apparently, when the subjects had a long series of unrelated letters, and then were given a spelling pattern test, they processed the spelling pattern as if it were another unrelated letter string. But when they had experienced a long list of spelling patterns, and were then given a spelling pattern test, subjects showed the superiority effect.

In another experiment which used a matching task instead of forced choice detection, Petersen and LaBerge (1975) found somewhat similar effects. Subjects were asked to press a button when two pairs of letters matched. The pairs they tested were familiar digraphs and blends, for example [ch ch] and [gl gl],

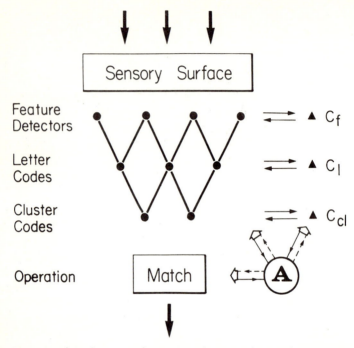

FIG. 4 Representation of perceptual memory codes, operations, and context nodes, c_f, c_l, and c_{cl}. Direct activation by attention is denoted by arrows from the attention center (A) to these structures. Arrows directed toward the attention centre indicate that these structures may attract attention.

termed *Clusters,* and unfamiliar pairs, for example [hc hc] and [lg lg], termed *Letters.* All stimulus items were presented in lower case. These two types of test items were inserted in lists in which the remaining items or "fillers" were either Clusters or Letters. In other words, test items were inserted randomly in lists made up predominantly of either Clusters or Letters. One third of the test items and filler items were catch trials, in which the pairs of stimuli did not match. Subjects were instructed to withhold their response to these displays.

The results of this experiment are shown in Fig. 5. In the Letters list, the mean latencies to Cluster and Letters test items were not significantly different. However, in the Clusters list, mean latency to Letters test items were significantly and substantially longer than mean latency to Cluster test items. Response latencies to Letters items were significantly different across lists, but latencies to Cluster items were not. One interpretation of these findings is that a Letters list induces the subject to process and match familiar Cluster test items in the same way that he processes and matches unfamiliar Letter pairs, that is, letter-by-letter. On the other hand, the Cluster list induces him to process and match Letters test items in the same way that he processes familiar Cluster

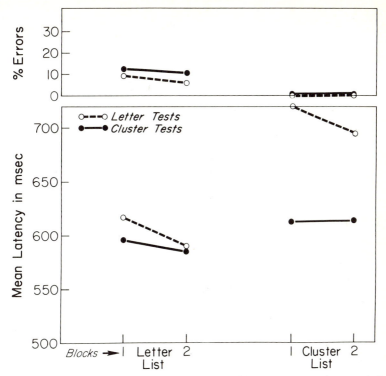

FIG. 5 Mean latencies and percentage errors of matching responses to letter and cluster pairs as a function of type of list items. Data are shown from the two test blocks. (From Petersen and LaBerge, 1975.)

items, that is, as a temporary unit at the cluster level. However, to process unfamiliar letter pairs takes additional time, either because a new unit is being integrated, or because attention must be shifted from the cluster level back to the letter level, where a match is performed on separate letters. It is noteworthy that the obtained latency to Cluster test items did not change appreciably between the lists. One explanation is that the time to match two letters to two letters is not much greater than time to match a cluster to a cluster. However, if the clusters had containing more than two letters, then the difference in latency should have diverged more sharply. Nevertheless, for letter strings of length two, Letter test items seem to be a stronger indicator of the level at which the items are being processed.

Returning to Fig. 4, we may recall that the code outputs of a particular level of processing are facilitated by means of activation of a node, and in the case of this experiment, the relevant nodes are c_l and c_{cl}. Presumably as the subject proceeds through successive displays of a list, the activity of one node is raised above that of the others by means of repeated presentations of a particular type

CUES

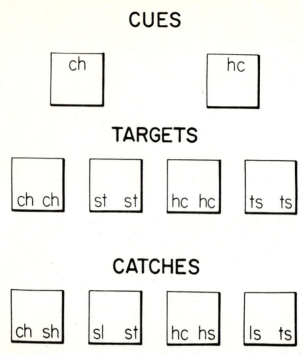

TARGETS

CATCHES

FIG. 6 Sample of stimuli in Experiment I. The first stimulus of a trial was a cue, and the second stimulus was either a target or a catch display.

of item at the sensory surface. Items which are familiar clusters activate node c_{cl}; items which are unfamiliar pairs of letters activate node c_l. But if letter codes are automatically processed first and then their outputs sent to cluster codes, why does not a cluster item activate both c_l and c_{cl} nodes? We would not attempt to propose an answer to this question here because it involves the very old and complex issue of the relationship of a unit to its components (cf, Wertheimer, 1974; LaBerge, 1976). The main point here is that the selective activation of the levels nodes is somehow induced from stimulation at the sensory surface by a series of displays of items of a particular type.

IV. EXPERIMENT I

Now we are ready to ask whether these level nodes can be activated by attention in the same way that the attention mechanism apparently activates patterns and operations (Fig. 4). Attempting to answer this query, we again employed the cueing procedure as one way of probing the properties of the attention process. However, the indicator of cueing a particular level of processing is more involved than a simple comparison of latencies to cued versus neutral-cued or miscued patterns. The indicator we adopted is based on the configuration of latencies shown in Fig. 5. In particular, the indicator of cueing is based on the difference between Letters test items and Cluster test items. If the latency difference is near zero, then we infer that it is the outputs of the item codes at the *letter* level that are being facilitated (i.e., presumably node c_l is dominant). If the latency to Letters test items is substantially longer than the latency to Cluster test items, facilitation is to item code outputs at the *cluster* level (i.e., node c_{cl} is dominant).

The procedure initially employed to cue a level of processing was the same as the one shown in Fig. 2 for cueing patterns and operations. In order to cue the cluster level, we presented a familiar cluster prior to presenting a pair of items for matching. Similarly, to cue the letter level, we presented an unfamiliar pair of letters as a cue. This procedure is illustrated in Fig. 6. To induce the subject

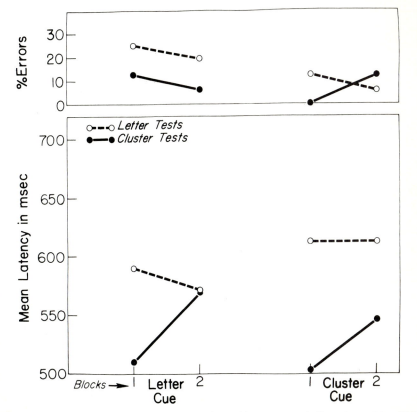

FIG. 7 Mean latency and percentage errors of matching responses in Experiment I in which Letter and Cluster test items were mixed within a block and cued with items from a Letter or Cluster list.

to observe and "use" the cue, the display pattern was the same as the cue 80% of the time. For example, a cue [ch] was followed most frequently by [ch ch], and the cue [hc] was followed most frequently by [hc hc]. Occasionally, either cue was followed by [st st] or [ts ts], which were test items. If the familiar cue [ch] successfully activates the cluster level, then the latency to [ts ts] should be appreciably longer than the latency to [st st]. Similarly, if the unfamiliar cue [hc] successfully activates the letter level, then the latency to [ts ts] should be same as [st st]. These two kinds of cues were randomized within a block.

Sixteen subjects were given a block of 80 practice trials followed by two test blocks of 100 trials each. Mean latencies and percentage of errors to the test items are given in Fig. 7. An analysis of variance of the latency data indicated a significant main effect only for type of test item, $F(1, 15) = 16.19, p < .01$. Significant interactions were found for: (1) type of test items by blocks, $F(1, 15) = 8.46, p < .05$; and (2) type of test item by type of cue, $F(1, 15) = 5.47, p < .05$. When latencies were averaged across the two blocks, the difference between Letters test items and Cluster test items was 41 msec on the Letters cue trials and 90 msec on the Cluster cue trials. Both of these differences were significantly different by Scheffé post hoc comparisons, $F(1, 30) = 9.36, p < .01$, for Letters cues and $F(1, 30) = 32.37, p < .01$, for Cluster cues. An analysis of variance of the error data yielded no significant results.

While the interaction between type of test item and type of cue indicates that cueing has an effect here, the effect fails to approximate the expected pattern of latency differences of list context shown in Fig. 5.

V. EXPERIMENT II

Considering the overall difference in mean latencies under both cueing conditions of Experiment I there was some suspicion that presenting a pair of letters alone in the cue display somehow favored unitization (perhaps by the Gestalt principle of proximity) even when the pair of letters was unfamiliar. This would account for the difference in latency obtained on trials in which letters were cued. To test this possibility, the experiment was repeated in all respects except that the two types of cues were separated by blocks and each presented to a separate set of 16 subjects. Therefore, the design was the same as the initial experiment (whose results are shown in Fig. 5) except that a pair of letters was given as an informative cue replacing the neutral cue. Since all cues and a large proportion of the displays were of the same type for a given subject, it would appear that there was adequate opportunity for the list to induce activation of the corresponding level.

In Fig. 8 are shown the results of this experiment. The analysis of variance of the latency data indicated a significant effect only for type of test item, $F(1, 30) = 26.49; p < .01$. No significant interactions were found. The difference between

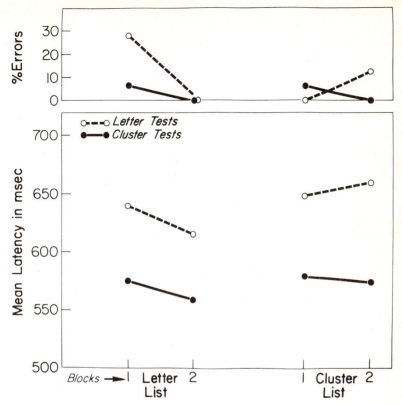

FIG. 8 Mean latency and percentage errors of matching responses in Experiment II, in which cued Letters and Cluster items were presented in separate blocks to separate subjects.

Letters test items and Cluster test items was, on the average, 61 msec for the Letters list group and 73 msec for the Cluster list group. The analysis of variance of error data indicated a significant main effect for: (1) type of test item, $F(1, 30) = 9.88$, $p < .01$; and (2) blocks, $F(1, 30) = 6.79$, $p < .05$. Significant interactions were found for: (1) type of list by blocks, $F(1, 30) = 14.16$, $p < .01$; and (2) type of list by type of test item by block, $F(1, 30) = 16.35$, $p < .01$. Apparently using a pair of letters as the cue induces cluster level processing over letter level processing, even when the list of items is predominantly Letters items.

VI. EXPERIMENT III

In view of the failure to reveal successful cueing for the letter level, we decided on an attempt to make the display more salient with respect to the differences between a Letters list and a Cluster list. To do this we displaced vertically the two letters of each pair in the Letters list. Sometimes the second letter was one line higher, sometimes one line lower than the first letter and occasionally it was on the same line as the first letter. The second pair of letters of a display was similarly "broken" with respect to alignment, and the patterns of misalignment were independent on a given display. In the Cluster list, the pairs of letters were also misaligned to determine whether alignment was critical for the Clusters effect to occur. It was hoped that misalignment would have the greatest effect on the processing of Letters, by encouraging the subjects to process them in a letter-by-letter manner. The test items occurred 20% of the time and were always in the normal horizontal alignment for both groups. One group of 10 subjects received a practice block plus two test blocks with the Letters list, and another 10 subjects were given the same treatment but with the Cluster list.

In Fig. 9 are shown the mean latencies and percentage errors from this experiment. The analysis of variance of the latency data indicated a significant main effect for type of test item, $F(1, 18) = 6.34, p < .05$; and a significant

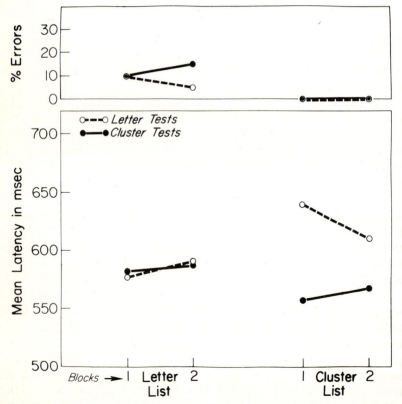

FIG. 9 Mean latency and percentage errors of matching responses in Experiment III, in which the filler letters were misaligned.

interaction for type of list by type of test item, $F(1, 18) = 7.27, p < .05$. Error differences were not significant. The differences between Letters test items and Cluster test items was 2 msec for the Letters list group and 64 msec for the Clusters list group. Only the second difference was significant. The obtained difference of 2 msec under the Letters list condition was the smallest difference we obtained in experiments of this sort, and we were encouraged to continue to use the letter-misalignment technique in subsequent studies to facilitate processing at the letter level. The fact that the latency difference between test items was significant for the Cluster list indicates that the clustering effect may not depend solely upon perceptual configurations of the letters in a pair. In fact, in another experiment, the test items as well as the filler items were misaligned in a list of familiar clusters, and the latency difference was significant and about the same value, 72 msec.

VII. EXPERIMENT IV

The last experiment described here was our strongest attempt to cue letters and cluster levels of processing. Not only did we employ the misalignment variable, but we also positioned the Letters and Cluster lists in different places on the display screen. Thus there were two perceptually distinctive characteristics related to the levels of processing.

Each block of trials in this experiment contained pairs of test and filler items constructed in a similar manner to those in the first experiment of this series. The cue was always the neutral symbol 0. However, when the cue appeared in the upper part of the screen, it indicated that the display pair which followed would always appear in the upper part of the screen, and similarly when the cue appeared in the lower part of the screen, the display pair would appear in the lower part of the screen. Stimuli which appeared in the upper part of the screen were predominantly Letters, those in the lower part of the screen were predominantly Clusters. Moreover, the Letters fillers in the upper location were always misaligned, while the Cluster fillers in the lower position were always aligned horizontally. Test items, which occurred on 20% of the trials, were always aligned horizontally in both upper and lower screen positions.

Each of the 32 subjects was given nine blocks of trials. The nine blocks represented three conditions. The first condition consisted of three blocks in which one type of list was presented in its particular location on the screen. In the next condition, there were three blocks in which the other type of list was presented in its location on the screen. The type of list given in the first and second conditions was balanced across subjects. In the last three blocks both types of lists in their specific locations were presented randomly within a block, and the cue (a circle) indicated which type of list would occur on each trial by its position in either the upper or lower part of the screen.

Each condition of three blocks included a practice block of 48 trials and two test blocks of 60 trials each. The trials were randomized across test and filler items with the following restraints: The test trials were always separated by at least two filler trials, and for the first two conditions, the first six trials were always filler trials.

The results from the first two conditions in which the type of item was separated by blocks are shown in Fig. 10. The data from the last condition, in which the type of item was mixed within a block, but cued on each trial, are shown in Fig. 11. The analysis of variance of the data of Fig. 10 indicated significant main effects for: (1) type of test item, $F(1, 30) = 48.78$, $p < .01$; and (2) type of filler list, $F(1, 30) = 8.76$, $p < .01$. Significant interactions were found for: (1) type of test item by type of filler list, $F(1, 30) = 32.11$, $p < .01$; (2) order of list type by replication, $F(1, 30) = 4.45$, $p < .05$; and (3) order of

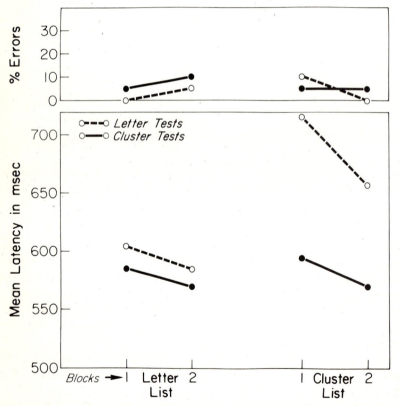

FIG. 10   Mean latency and percentage errors of matching responses in the first two conditions of Experiment IV, in which Letters and Cluster lists were presented in separate blocks.

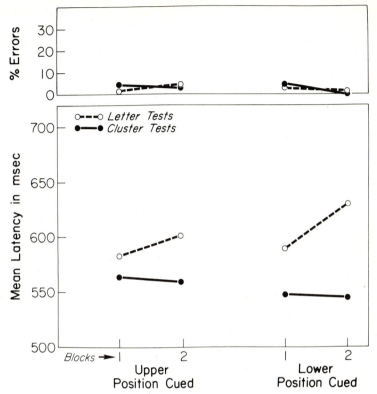

FIG. 11   Mean latency and percentage errors of matching responses in the last condition of Experiment IV, in which Letters and Clusters lists were mixed within blocks and cued.

filler list by replication by type of test item, $F(1, 30) = 11.93, p < .01$. The interaction between type of test item and type of filler list was elaborated by Scheffé post hoc comparisons. The difference obtained between Letters test and Cluster test latencies in the Letters list condition was 10 msec, and the difference was not significant, $F(1, 18) = 0.01, p > .05$. The difference obtained between Letters and Cluster test item latencies in the Cluster list condition was 91 msec, which was significant, $F(1, 18) = 14.15, p < .01$. The analysis of variance of the error data given in Fig. 10 indicated a significant main effect only for type of test item, $F(1, 30) = 6.55, p < .05$.

The analysis of variance of the mean latencies in Fig. 11 revealed a significant effect only for the latency of the type of test item, $F(1, 30) = 18.38, p < .01$. The analysis of variance of the error data indicated significant interaction for (1) order of list type by blocks, $F(1, 30) = 6.25, p < .05$; and (2) order of list type by type of test item, $F(1, 30) = 4.87, p < .05$. A comparison of the composite latency means across blocks of the Letters test Cluster tests revealed a difference of 31 msec in the Letters position and 63 msec in the Cluster position, but the difference between these differences was not significant. Apparently the cue used on each trial was not very effective in changing the level of processing.

While we cannot rule out the possibility that other procedures might produce a clear cueing effect, it would seem that the cueing of levels of processing is relatively difficult compared to the cueing of patterns or operations.

Our tentative interpretation of these generally negative findings is that the attention source, shown in Fig. 4, does not directly activate the context nodes, c_f, c_l, c_{cl}. How, then, are they typically activated so that readout from perceptual codes is facilitated at the appropriate level? Evidence shown in Figs. 5 and 10 have suggested one way already, that the presentation of a list of items of one particular type may determine the level of processing. Selection of level is represented in the theory by activation of the appropriate node. Letters lists facilitate letter level nodes and familiar Cluster lists facilitate cluster level nodes. The precise manner in which these stimuli activate one or the other node has not been specified here other than to suggest that an accumulation of several stimuli of the same type is required to produce a dominance of one particular node.

We should like to suggest also that there may well be internal sources of activation of the nodes other than indirect activation by stimuli. Consider the case in which one is checking a galley proof for spelling or for omission of a word or sentence. Most readers state that they can do only one of these tasks at a time. The two tasks seem to require processing outputs from two different levels, and it would seem that we can internally control (i.e., cue) which way we wish to process a given paragraph. What seems to happen in this case is that we direct our attention to some other part of the processing system, which in turn activates the visual level nodes. The phonological system may provide this capability when a task induces naming letters on the one hand and naming words on the other. This system, in turn, may have direct access to corresponding codes in the visual system. However if internal controls such as these do not exist, then we are left with the conclusion that the control is produced only by contextual factors in the environment.

Another interpretation of the failure to effectively cue levels of processing is that subjects simply find it easier to maintain a holistic cluster level of matching than to shift levels from trial to trial. Consider that matching operations may be carried out simultaneously at the letter and cluster levels in the manner described earlier in this paper. Since cluster matching requires one matching operation, while component letter matching requires two, the cluster level may be favored, even in view of the added time and attention required to chunk unfamiliar pairs of letters. Add to this the consideration that cueing requires a shift from one level to the other many times within a block. Taken together, these factors might very well induce the subject to stay with the easier strategy and maintain processing at the cluster level. Occasional shifts to the letter level may account for the fact that the differences in latencies in the Cluster list of Fig. 11 are less than the corresponding differences in Fig. 10.

Extrapolating this problem somewhat, we might ask how one can teach someone to perceive a pattern at a higher level for the first time. In terms of the model shown in Fig. 4, we are asking how a person constructs a new unit at level $n + 1$ from codes already formed at level n. If a readout from the code at $n + 1$ requires simultaneous activation by the subordinate codes at n and the levels node at $n + 1$, then the levels nodes at $n + 1$ must also be in existence if he is going to use the new code at $n + 1$ for any further operations. But how is a new levels node acquired by a person? Or are such structures innate? Whatever is the case, it would seem that a very interesting and perhaps quite powerful kind of learning is that of perceiving or considering things in new ways or contexts (Jenkins, 1974). Teaching someone to do this may be difficult partly because we may not be able to instruct or cue a person to deploy attention directly to levels. Teaching someone new patterns, for example, a new word, a new face, or even new operations, seems to be much easier, perhaps because the student's attention can be relatively easily directed by instructions to the structures involved.

ACKNOWLEDGMENTS

This research was supported by the United States Public Health Service Grant MH-16270-07, and in part by HD-06730-03 and the Center for Research in Human Learning through National Science Foundation Grant G13-35703X. The authors are indebted to Lee Brownston, Diana Randall, Ken Schultz, Dan Ansel and Dean Dreblow for their assistance in many phases of the study.

REFERENCES

Aderman, D., & Smith, E. E. Expectancy as a determinant of functional units in perceptual recognition. *Cognitive Psychology,* 1971, **2**, 117–129.

Beller, H. K. Priming: The effects of advanced information of letter matching. *Journal of Experimental Psychology,* 1971, **87**, 176–182.

Darley, C. F., Klatsky, R. L., & Atkinson, R. C. Effects of memory load on reaction time. *Journal of Experimental Psychology,* 1972, **96**, 232–234.

Estes, W. K. Memory, perception, and decision in letter identification. In R. L. Solso (Ed.), *Information processing and cognition: The Loyola symposium,* Hillsdale, N.J.: Lawrence Erlbaum Associates, 1975.

Jenkins, J. J. Remember that old theory of memory? Well, forget it! *American Psychologist,* 1974, **29**, 785–795.

Kohfeld, D. L., & Morris, F. E. Stimulus preknowledge and reaction time: Application of a variable criterion and attention switching model. *Memory and Cognition,* in press.

LaBerge, D. Attention and the measurement of perceptual learning. *Memory and Cognition,* 1973, **1**, 268–276.

LaBerge, D. Acquisition of automatic processing in perceptual and associative learning. In P. M. A. Rabbitt & S. Dornic (Eds.), *Attention and performance V,* London: Academic Press, 1975.

LaBerge, D. Perceptual learning and attention. In W. K. Estes (Ed.), *Handbook of learning and cognitive processes.* Vol. 5. Hillsdale, N.J.: Lawrence Erlbaum Associates, in press.

LaBerge, D., & Norden, M. J. Cueing patterns and operations. Technical Report. Information Processing Laboratory. Minneapolis, University of Minnesota, 1975.

LaBerge, D., & Samuels, S. J. Toward a theory of automatic information processing in reading. *Cognitive Psychology,* 1974, **6,** 293–323.

LaBerge, D., Van Gelder, P., & Yellott, J. I., Jr. A cueing technique in choice reaction time. *Perception & Psychophysics,* 1970, 7(1), 57–62.

Petersen, R., & LaBerge, D. *Contextual control of letter perception* (Technical Report No. 15). Minnesota Reading Research Project. University of Minnesota, 1975.

Posner, M. I., & Snyder, C. R. R. Facilitation and inhibition in the processing of signals. In P. M. A. Rabbitt & S. Dornic (Eds.), *Attention and performance V,* London: Academic Press, 1975.

Scheffé, H. A. A method for judging all possible contrasts in the analysis of variance. *Biometrika,* 1953, **40,** 87–104.

Sternberg, S. High-speed scanning in human memory. *Science,* 1966, **153,** 652–654.

Thorsen, E. doctoral dissertation University of Minnesota, 1975.

Wertheimer, M. The problem of perceptual structure. In F. C. Carterette & M. P. Friedman (Eds.), *Handbook of perception.* Vol. 1. New York: Academic Press, 1974.

16
Effects of Visual Grouping on Immediate Recall and Selective Attention

Daniel Kahneman
Avishai Henik

The Hebrew University of Jerusalem
Jerusalem, Israel

ABSTRACT

A phenomenon labeled "group processing" is observed when arrays of letters or digits organized in perceptual groups are presented for immediate recall. Recall probabilities are similar within each group and vary sharply between groups. Grouped items tend to be recalled in all-or-none fashion, but there is evidence of competition between groups in recall. Adding an item to the last group in the array depresses performance in that group. The interference is equally severe when the added item is a relevant digit or an irrelevant suffix. These effects are predicted by a model of allocation rules for attention or processing resources. Alternative interpretations, in terms of visual interference or hierarchical coding, are tested and rejected. Grouping structure has very strong effects in a task of selective attention by color: total performance depends on the complexity of grouping, and the groups that occur late in the processing queue are affected most severely by the presence of irrelevant material.

I. INTRODUCTION

In this chapter we are concerned with several aspects of a single question: How does perceptual grouping affect the recall of tachistoscopically exposed arrays of digits or letters? We report experiments in which subjects are shown arrays of unrelated items, variously organized in groups by manipulations of similarity or proximity. In some experimental conditions, all the material that is presented is

307

to be reported. In others, the subjects are instructed to select relevant items from an array which also includes irrelevant material that is to be ignored. Variations of grouping have large effects on performance in both the full-report and the selective-attention tasks.

We describe in some detail results of three experiments, and briefly mention findings from several other studies conducted in our laboratory. All these experiments share several features of method. They are conducted in a group setting, in a dimly illuminated room. The subjects face a screen on which a frame is constantly in view. The sequence of events on each trial is as follows: an oral warning by the experimenter; a 200-msec warning tone; a delay of 500 msec; a 200-msec exposure of the stimulus material in the area indicated by the frame on the screen. The subjects write their answer immediately after each exposure. No feedback is given. A typical session lasts about 30 minutes, during which the subjects receive brief instructions, are shown examples of the various types of arrays to which they are to be exposed, have a brief block of practice trials, and several experimental blocks in which various stimulus patterns are presented in random order.

II. THEORY

We have observed in a large number of experiments, within the general design described above, a phenomenon that we label *group processing*. The two main manifestations of group processing are:

1. The probability of recall of items varies relatively little within perceptual groups, but sharp discontinuities of performance occur between successive groups. For example, an array of digits grouped into three pairs, e.g., 12 34 56, yielded the following probabilities of correct responses for successive positions: .94, .91, .87, .90, .41, .48. In the same experiment, structuring the array into two triads, for example, 123 456, produced quite a different position effect: .98, .93, .90, .61, .56, and .52. In this example, the main difference in performance occurs on the fourth item, which is recalled as well as the third item in the pair structure, and almost as poorly as the fifth item in the triad structure.

2. The items that constitute a perceptual group tend to be recalled or omitted in all-or-none fashion. When any member of a group is included in the subject's report, other members of the same group are very likely to be reported as well. In contrast, correlations between items that belong to different groups are almost always negative.

The investigation of grouping effects in tachistoscopic perception was suggested by an approach to the study of attention (Kahneman, 1973), which combined a limited-capacity view of attention with the assumption that the allocation of attention is constrained by the operation of an early stage of perceptual analysis. The physical variables that determine perceived grouping are assumed to affect this stage of processing, which was labeled "preattentive" by Neisser (1967), and was called the "unit-formation" stage by Kahneman (1973). The theory proposes that attention can be selectively allocated only to groups that have been isolated at the unit-formation stage, but not to individual elements within such groups. It also assumes that the groups which have been defined at the unit-formation stage normally retain their integrity in subsequent phases of processing.

This general approach to attention can be given a more precise interpretation in the restricted context of the tachistoscopic perception of arrays of letters or digits. Our present version of such a model consists of the six assumptions listed below. The first two assumptions define the conditions in which group processing is expected to occur. The remaining assumptions describe a process which could explain this effect. The terms "attention" and "processing resources" are used interchangeably in our treatment.

1. *Resource limitation:* This model applies to relatively favorable conditions of exposure, in which the probability that a particular item will be reported depends primarily on the attention that is allocated to it (by instruction, or because of its position in the processing order), rather than on sensory factors, such as acuity or lateral interference among neighboring items. The manifestations of group processing may be obscured when performance is data limited rather than resource limited (Norman & Bobrow, 1975).

2. *Group size:* Unrelated items that constitute a perceptual group will be processed as a group, provided that (a) the number of items in the group does not exceed four; and (b) the items are arranged in conformity with prevailing reading habits.

3. *Group allocation:* When an array consists of several groups, a limited pool of attention, or processing resources, is distributed among the groups.

4. *The queueing rule:* The distribution of attention among groups follows a queueing rule: the amount allocated to the first group is determined mainly by the processing requirements of that group, and is essentially independent of the requirements of other groups. The allocation to subsequent groups, on the other hand, also depends on the amount which remains after the allocations to earlier groups in the queue.

5. *Fluctuations of allocation:* The queueing order and the distribution of attention among the groups that constitute a particular structure are subject to random variations, when the same structure appears on different trials.

6. *The homogeneity rule:* The distribution of the processing resources allocated to a group among the elements of that group is nonselective and homogeneous. The same amount of attention is allocated to all items in the group, regardless of whether or not they are relevant to the task.

The assumptions of the group-processing model entail a number of specific predictions concerning performance in tachistoscopic recall tasks, when the array is physically organized into groups of four or fewer items. The major predictions and the rationale for these predictions are given below. Possible alternative explanations of these effects are discussed in following sections, where the effects are described in detail.

(i) The tendency toward all-or-none recall of perceptual groups is explained, in this model, by the hierarchical process in which attention is allocated to individual items, and by the fluctuations of attentional allocation. The fluctuations cause the allocation of attention to vary from trial to trial. The hierarchical distribution, first to groups and only then to individual items, causes the amounts of processing resources assigned to different members of the same group to covary over trials. This interpretation differs from the notion of hierarchical coding, which is commonly applied to explain all-or-none recall of chunks in other memory tasks (Bower, 1972b; Estes, 1972a; Johnson, 1970, 1972; Miller, 1956; Simon, 1974). We return to this issue in Section IV.

(ii) The homogeneity of performance within groups is explained by the equal allocation of resources to all members of each group. Large differences between successive groups are entailed by the assumption that resources are assigned to groups according to a queueing rule. Some recent publications (Estes & Wolford, 1971; Wolford & Hollingsworth, 1974a) have attributed discontinuities of performance at group boundaries to the factors of retinal position and lateral interference. Reasons for rejecting this alternative explanation of our findings are discussed in Sections III and VI.

(iii) The model predicts that the addition of an extra item to the last group in an array will reduce the recall of other elements of that group, but will not affect performance for earlier groups. This follows from the queueing rule. The homogeneity rule implies, in addition, that an irrelevant suffix and an added item which is to be included in the report will have similar effects on the recall of other items. Finally, a suffix that is not perceptually grouped with relevant elements of the array will cause little or no interference. These predictions are tested in Section VI.

(iv) The decrement of performance that is observed when irrelevant items are included in the array is interpreted as a reduction of the processing resources allocated to relevant items. It is expected that overall performance in the focused-attention task will depend on the grouping structure of the array, and that the interference will be more severe for groups that occur late in the processing queue than for earlier groups. Relevant results are presented in section VI.

The interpretation of the group-processing effect cannot be isolated from the more general issue of what determines the tachistoscopic span in the full-report procedure. If the tachistoscopic span is limited by the number of items that can be "read" in a single glance, in the sense of activating corresponding structures in long-term memory or generating appropriate codes (Coltheart, 1972), then the phenomenon of group processing tells us something about the nature of reading. Perhaps it should be called *group reading*. If the span is limited by the characteristics of some type of short-term storage system (for example, the recognition buffer suggested by Sperling, 1967), the phenomenon would be most appropriately labeled *group storage*. The choice of the neutral term, group processing, reflects our indecision in this regard. Section VI includes some evidence that presents difficulties for both the reading and the storage views, as presently formulated. It leads us to the tentative conclusion that the limiting factor in tachistoscopic performance is found in the resources that are allocated to reading, rather than in the number of items that can actually be read, or in the competition of the outputs of reading for the limited capacity of a storage system. This view is generally compatible with the model of tachistoscopic perception developed by Rumelhart (1970).

A possible alternative to the group-processing model should be mentioned, although we do not believe this alternative to be tenable. In the alternative model, the concepts of *reading time* and *iconic decay* replace the concept of *attentional allocation*. The major assumptions of the model are that successive groups of items are read serially; that all items in each group are read in parallel; that the time at which a group is read depends on how many items that group contains (for the first group), and also on the time required to read preceding groups (for later groups); that the time at which groups are read fluctuates over trials; and that the likelihood that an item will be correctly reported depends on the duration of the interval allocated to the processing of its group, and on the quality of the icon during that interval.

This model appears to be an attractive alternative to our formulation of group processing, because the concepts of reading time and iconic decay are far less vague than the concepts of attention and processing resources. Our only reason for rejecting this alternative is that iconic decay cannot be the factor that limits performance in our experiments. The tachistoscopic span is achieved after 50–100 msec exposure even under conditions of masking (Merikle, Coltheart, & Lowe, 1971; Sperling, 1963). Since we employ an exposure duration of 200 msec, it is unlikely that iconic decay plays a major role in our results.

III. HOMOGENEITY OF RECALL WITHIN GROUPS

The observation that recall performance is generally homogeneous within perceptual groups and varies mainly among groups has recurred in a large number of experiments conducted in our laboratory. In this section, we illustrate this effect by an analysis of relevant results from a recent study, which was specifically designed to test the group-processing model against the lateral-interference interpretation of discontinuities of performance at group boundaries (Wolford, 1975).

The subjects ($N = 41$) were students in a Perception course, naive with respect to the purpose and hypotheses of the study. The experiment described was the second in a session. Before it began, subjects had 48 trials in the same basic task, whole report of tachistoscopic arrays of digits. The experiment consisted of seven blocks of trials. In the first, fourth, and seventh blocks, subjects were shown arrays of seven digits. Each block of nine trials included three examples of each of three grouping structures, for example, 12345 67, or 1234 567, or 123 4567, in random order. The other six blocks consisted of 12 trials, and each block included two examples of six different patterns. In three of these patterns, the array contained six digits, for example, 12345 6, or 1234 56, or 123 456. In the other three patterns, a lower case "k" was added to the right of the sixth digit, for example, 123 456k. As measured on the screen, the height of each character was 8 cm, and the center-to-center distance between adjacent characters was 7 cm. The subjects were instructed to ignore the "k" when it appeared, and to recall the digits in writing immediately after each trial, in any order which they found convenient. They were informed before each block of the number of digits that should appear in a fully correct report. Other details of the procedure were as described in the Introduction.

To test the importance of acuity factors in determining performance in this experiment, separate analyses were conducted for the 10 subjects who sat nearest the screen (average distance 3.4 m) and for 10 subjects who were furthest from it (average distance 7.7 m). The grand mean of digits correctly reported, over all conditions, was 3.90 for the near subjects and 4.31 for the far subjects. The inferior performance of the near subjects is due to their viewing the screen from a sharper angle than the far subjects. All qualitative aspects of performance were identical for the two groups of subjects. The relative unimportance of retinal size as a determinant of performance is an observation that recurs consistently in our experiments. It confirms the assumption that performance in our general experimental situation is resource limited rather than data limited (Norman & Bobrow, 1975).

Table 1 presents the percentage of items correctly reported, for each position in six of the nine patterns used in the experiment. The patterns included in the table are those in which the first group consisted of three or four items. Results for the three patterns in which the first group consisted of five items are discussed in Section V. To facilitate comparisons of performance for different items in the following discussion, we label each item by the pattern to which it belongs, and by its position within that pattern. Thus, item A2-5 is the fifth digit in an array of type A-2.

The most striking aspects of the results shown in Table 1 are the relative homogeneity of report probabilities within groups, and the sharp discontinuities at group boundaries. The magnitude of the effect can be appreciated by

TABLE 1
Recall of Digits in Various Patterns

Type	Example	\multicolumn{7}{c}{Percent recall}						
		1	2	3	4	5	6	7
A_1	1234 56	93	83	86	86	29	39	–
A_2	123 456	94	89	88	48	43	45	–
B_1	1234 56k	97	90	91	94	14	12	–
B_2	123 456k	96	95	92	36	27	17	–
C_1	1234 567	94	88	89	92	18	15	27
C_2	123 4567	96	94	92	32	23	17	29

comparing performance on adjacent digits when these belong to the same group or to different groups. The mean difference in probability of recall between the third and fourth item is 52% when they belong to different groups, and −2% when both belong to the first group. Similarly, the mean difference between the fourth and the fifth digits is 70% when these digits belong to different groups, and 8% when both are included in the second group.

Another way of looking at the same data is to compare performance on the fourth item when it is the last member of the first group and when it is the leading member of the second group. The mean advantage of belonging to the first group is 52%.

The discontinuities of performance at group boundaries that occur in every row of Table 1 were predicted from a theory which invokes the concepts of perceptual grouping and attention. However, an alternative interpretation of the same type of effect has been proposed, in which neither grouping nor attention are mentioned at all (Estes & Wolford, 1971; Wolford, 1975; Wolford & Hollingsworth, 1974a). In this view, the discontinuities at group boundaries are due to the combined effects of retinal position and lateral interference. The relevant aspects of the model proposed by Wolford (1975) may be summarized as follows: (a) the probability that an item will be reported is strongly dependent on its retinal position; (b) there are substantial effects of lateral interference among neighboring letters; (c) lateral interference is asymmetric; an item is subject to more interference from a neighbor that lies further in the periphery than from a neighbor that is presented closer to the point of fixation.

This model, of course, does not entail the prediction that performance will be homogeneous within groups of items. However, it must be considered carefully, because its predictions concerning performance on the fourth item in our experiment are qualitatively similar to the predictions from the group-processing model. Compare, for example, items A1-4 and A2-4. The latter is displaced toward the periphery, relative to the former, and it also has an immediate neighbor that is further in the periphery, while the only immediate neighbor of A1-4 is located more centrally. These sensory factors could combine to yield a lower level of performance on A2-4 than on A1-4, as is indeed observed.

An interpretation of our results in terms of sensory factors appears unlikely, in the light of the observation made earlier, that viewing distance (and therefore retinal size) had little effect on performance. Furthermore, the design of the experiment provides a direct test of the lateral-interference and group-processing models. Compare, for example, items A1-5 and A2-5. The two items occupy the same retinal position, and the latter has immediate neighbors on both sides, while the former has only one immediate neighbor. Consequently, the lateral-interference model entails that performance can only be worse for A2-5 than for A1-5. The group-processing model entails the opposite prediction. Because the first group in the processing queue is smaller in pattern A2 than in pattern A1, the model states that more resources will be allocated to the second group in the former case than in the latter. Since these resources are assumed to be shared equally among the elements of a group, more resources will be available for the processing of A2-5 than of A1-5, and the report probabilities are expected to reflect this difference. Similar differences are expected for the sixth and seventh items as well.

The results strongly confirm the prediction of the group-processing hypothesis. In all three sets of patterns, performance on the fifth digit is better in pattern 2 than in pattern 1. The pooled effect is highly significant ($t = 5.20, df = 40, p < .001$). The difference in performance on the sixth and seventh items is also significant, in the predicted direction ($t = 4.09, p < .001$). The conclusion of this experiment, of course, is not that sensory interactions play no role in tachistoscopic perception, but merely that the homogeneity of performance within groups, which we find in our studies, cannot be explained as an artifact of such interactions.

The similarity of performance levels within perceptual groups and the discontinuities at group boundaries are highly reproducible results, which we have observed in many different experiments, using a variety of grouping arrangements and different ways of inducing grouping. The discontinuities of performance between groups are most pronounced when the groups are segregated by blank spaces, but similar effects can be induced by color grouping. In one of the experiments in this series, we presented arrays of six letters, colored blue or red, which were variously structured as triads, for example, BBBRRR, or as pairs, for example, BBRRBB. The group-processing hypothesis entails that performance on the fourth item should be better in the pair structure, and that performance on the fifth item should be better in the triad structure. Both predictions were confirmed. The mean percentage of letters reported from the fourth position was 56% for pairs and 47% for triads ($t = 3.00, df = 28, p < .01$). The corresponding values for the fifth letter were 30 and 41% ($t = 4.49, p < .01$).

Retinal position was the same for the two items in both comparisons, and the pattern of results appears to defy explanation in terms of lateral masking.

These results indicate that grouping is an important determinant of performance on individual items, even when retinal position, lateral interference and position in the reporting order are controlled. To a good first approximation, performance levels tend to be the same for items that constitute a single group, if that group contains four items or less. However, it is important to note that homogeneous performance within groups is only an approximation, and that systematic violations of this prediction are often observed. For example, a downward trend of performance in the second group is evident in Table 1, although it is dwarfed by the discontinuity of performance between the groups. An end effect is also common, and the last item in the array is often reported more accurately than its immediate predecessor. Finally, under difficult conditions of exposure, marked differences in report probabilities can be found even between immediately adjacent members of small groups (Estes and Wolford, 1971; Wolford & Hollingsworth, 1974a). When performance is data-limited rather than resource-limited, group processing evidently fails to occur.

As already noted in the Section II, group processing also fails when perceptual organization violates reading habits. Consider, for example, patterns (i) and (ii), from a study in which arrays of six consonants were presented in various spatial arrangements:

$$\text{(i)} \quad \text{AB} \ C_D \ \text{EF} \qquad \text{(ii)} \ A_B \ C_D \ E_F$$

The mean percentages of letters correctly reported (in left to right order) were 83, 72, 77, 48, 10, and 15 for pattern (i); 74, 65, 50, 56, 14, and 13 for pattern (ii). The retinal location of items C and D was the same in both patterns. Note the highly significant difference in performance between items C and D in pattern (i), although these items clearly form a group in the Gestalt sense. Note also that the group-processing effect is restored in pattern (ii), although at a much depressed level of performance.

Systematic departures from homogeneous performance within groups can arise either from sensory factors that favor some members of a group over others or from systematic violations of our hypothesis that all members of a group share equally in the attention or processing resources allocated to the group. Indeed, we view this hypothesis itself as a first approximation, which is to be refined by further research. In some instances, both sensory and attentional factors could be operative. The end-item effect may well be a case in point. The end items of a tightly spaced line are more legible than their neighbors, even with prolonged exposures (Woodworth, 1938, p. 720), an observation which has been interpreted by several authors as evidence for lateral masking (Taylor & Brown, 1972; Townsend, Taylor, & Brown, 1971; Wolford & Hollingsworth, 1974b). The end item, of course, is subject to lateral masking from only one neighbor, and this could explain its greater visibility. However, the results of this section and the pattern of visual suffix effects that are discussed in Section VI both show that lateral masking does not in fact provide an adequate account of interactions among neighboring items. In the light of these results, the conjecture that the end item in an array may also have an advantage in the allocation of attention is not altogether implausible.

IV. CORRELATIONS AMONG ITEMS IN RECALL

The group-processing model entails the prediction that the successful report of items will be positively correlated, over trials, for items that belong to the same group, and negatively correlated for members of different groups. The positive correlations among members of a group are due, in this model, to the hierarchical nature of attentional allocation. Attention, or processing resources, is distributed among the groups, in a manner that fluctuates from trial to trial; the amount allocated to each group is then shared equally among its members. The fluctuations in the allocation of resources to groups on different trials affect equally all the items within each group, and thereby induce positive correlations among them. The negative correlations between members of different groups reflect the competition for the limited pool of processing resources.

Table 2 presents average values of contingency coefficients computed within the data of individual subjects, between the success achieved on selected pairs of items, for six of the structures presented in the experiment. The N for the computation of an individual coefficient is the number of trials on which each structure is repeated in the experiment. It should be noted that not all 41 subjects contribute to the entries shown in Table 2: the contingency coefficient between two items is undefined for a subject who invariably recalls or invariably fails one or both of these items. The number of subjects who contributed to the

TABLE 2
Average within-Subject Correlations in Recall[a]

Example	3–4	4–5	2–4	4–6
1234 56	(75)	−25	(52)	04
123 456	−27	(27)	−28	(25)
1234 56k	(50)	−27	(31)	−36
123 456k	−16	(18)	−20	(16)
1234 567	(59)	−32	(36)	−32
123 4567	−28	(25)	−31	(12)

[a]Correlations for pairs of items that belong to the same group are identified by parentheses.

values shown in Table 2 varies from 10 to 32, with a mean of 19. The table presents average correlations for all pairs of items which are included in the same group in some patterns, and in different groups in others.

The group-processing model predicts a positive correlation in 12 of the 24 entries in Table 2, and a negative correlation in the remaining cases. Entries for which a positive correlation is predicted are identified by parentheses. The mean values shown in the table have the predicted sign of 23 of the 24 cases, and differ significantly from zero in 19 cases. The results provide unequivocal support for the hypothesis that the members of each group tend to be recalled in all-or-none fashion, and that the two groups compete as teams for access to the subject's report.

The group-processing model identifies two sources of variation in the allocation of attention on different trials: (i) variations of the order of groups in the processing queue; (ii) fluctuations in the amount of attention allocated to the groups, for a given queueing order. It was of interest to establish the relative contributions of the two sources of variation to the pattern of correlations in performance.

Variation of queueing order may be expected to show up in the subject's written report, since the order of report was not constrained by instructions. Indeed, a consistent finding in all our studies is that when the subject's report does *not* begin with the leftmost item in the array, it is more likely to start with the leading member of some other group than with any other item. Inversions of the normal queueing order are relatively frequent when the left-to-right and top-to-bottom reading tendencies are in conflict, as in the following examples of six-letter arrays:

$$\text{(i)} \quad _{\text{ABC}} \text{DEF} \qquad \text{(ii)} \quad _{\text{AB}} \text{CD} \text{EF}$$

In such cases, the second group in left-to-right order may lead the report in up to 25% of trials. Within the linear arrangement of the present study, however, such inversions are rare. Over 93% of the reports start with the first item, and only 3.2% start with a member of the second group. The basic pattern of correlations is retained, although substantially attenuated, even when these trials are removed from the analysis. When the analysis of correlations is restricted to trials on which the report began with any item from the first group, 23 of the 24 values corresponding to the entries of Table 2 have the predicted sign, although only 9 are significant. We conclude that even when the basic queueing order is maintained, there are fluctuations in the relative amount of attention which is allocated to the two groups. These fluctuations induce positive correlations between members of the same group and negative correlations between groups. The observed pattern of correlations cannot be regarded as an artifact of variations of order in the overt report.

While the within-subject analysis of the correlations of performance provides the most direct test of our hypothesis, a different and independent correlational analysis is possible, which utilizes individual differences among subjects in the shape of the position curve. In this analysis, the score of each subject for items in a particular position is defined as the difference between his probability of recalling items from that position and his average probability of recall over all positions. The sum of these differences is zero for each subject, so that differences in total performance are removed from the analysis. A correlation is computed, over subjects, between the scores for different positions. The obtained coefficients provide an answer to the following question: if the serial position data of an individual is marked by especially high recall of items in a given position, which other positions are likely to show an advantage, and which are the positions where performance suffers? A slight bias toward negative correlations is induced by the constraint that the sum of the scores is set to zero for every subject.

The within-subject and between-subject analyses are mathematically independent, and it is entirely possible for the two types of correlations to exhibit different patterns. However, the group-processing model entails the same predictions for the two analyses. In this model, individual differences in the shape of the serial position curve reflect differences in the policies that the subjects adopt in allocating resources to the two groups in the array. Since this allocation has the same effect on all members of a group, the correlations should be uniformly positive within groups, and uniformly negative between groups.

The results of the between-subject analysis are very similar to those of the within-subject analysis, and equally clearcut. For entries corresponding to those of Table 2, 11 of 12 correlations involving members of the same group are positive, and 7 are significant. All correlations involving members of different groups are negative, and all are significant. Evidently, much of the systematic variance of individual differences in the shape of the positive curve can be explained by differences in the degree to which the subjects favor one group at the expense of the other.

The group-processing model explains the pattern of these results by two main ideas: that processing resources or attention can be viewed as a pool of limited capacity; and that the allocation of attention is hierachical, first to groups by the queueing rule, then to individual items by the homogeneity rule. The principal alternative to this account invokes the notions of the limited capacity of short-term memory and of a hierarchical process of recoding.

A tendency toward all-or-none recall of perceptually grouped items has been observed in a variety of memory tasks, and the common interpretation of this finding has been in terms of a process of chunking, or coding (e.g., Bower, 1972a,b; Estes, 1972a; Johnson, 1970, 1972). This conception assumes that the subject produces a unitary code for each chunk, stores these codes, and performs a decoding operation at the time of retrieval, which restores the original format of the input. The recall of the constituents of a chunk is dependent on the retrieval of the code of that chunk, and this dependence entails a tendency toward all-or-none recall of chunk members. The notion that the subject need store only the codes for the various chunks, rather than the codes of all their elements, explains the dramatic improvements of performance which are often associated with chunking, when the codes for the chunks are highly familiar (Miller, 1956; Simon, 1974). Perhaps the best demonstration of this effect in the domain of tachistoscopic perception is the classic observation that people retain many more letters from a brief exposure when these letters form words than when they do not (Cattell, 1885).

The notion of hierarchical coding has much appeal when the codes for higher-order units are available in advance. In that case it explains both all-or-none recall of chunks and the improvement of recall by chunking. However, a tendency toward all-or-none recall of perceptual groups has been observed even in the absence of familiar codes (Bower, 1972a). For example, Bower (1972b) showed subjects for five seconds a linear array of 12 letters, divided into 4 groups by variation of color. Recall was much better when the groups corresponded to familiar acronyms than when they did not, but in either case a shift from a correct response to an error, or vice versa, was more likely to occur at a group boundary than within a group. Bower (1972b) proposed a hierarchical coding interpretation for these results. A unitary code is formed for each perceptual group, which is associated with the corresponding position in the structure of the array. The elements of the group, in turn, are associated to the group code. All-or-none recall is explained by the necessity to retrieve the code of the group before its elements can be retrieved. The effects of familiarity are explained by the number of new associations that the subject is required to form during the limited time available.

Bower's theory appears to run into difficulties even in the domain of experiments for which it was advanced. Specifically, it implies that any subdivision of a group must be detrimental to performance, since it requires the formation of an additional association. This is an intuitively implausible prediction, for which no evidence is available. Estes (1972a) seems to have ignored the problem in his important attempt to achieve a synthesis of the coding and association approaches to short-term memory. Estes (1972a) writes "The new assumption to be made is that there is available in the memory system . . . a pool of elements which we may term control elements," and goes on to say "I wish to assume firstly that a new control element is set up at each discontinuity in the input sequence. The discontinuities may result form the input procedure, as those between letters in a string or between words in a sequence, or they may be generated by the subject when he groups or 'chunks' subsets together in rehearsal" (p. 175). These statements gloss over the essential distinction between situations in which the control elements for perceptual units are already available in memory and situations in which new control elements must be set up, when the subject encounters an unfamiliar sequence. It seems fair to say that the problem of the nature of grouping effects in short-term memory tasks still awaits a fully adequate solution.

A recoding approach appears particularly implausible in the context of tachistoscopic presentation, where there is simply no time for the subject to engage in activities that would normally be labeled recoding. For this situation, at least, a concept of hierarchical allocation of attention appears to provide a more adequate explanation of the positive correlations within perceptual groups than does the concept of hierarchical coding. A question for future investigation is whether this approach can be generalized to other short-term memory tasks. It does not appear impossible to apply to these tasks the basic ideas of the present treatment, namely that the positive correlations in recall arise because the members of each group are normally processed to the same depth or degree, and that the negative correlations arise from a limitation of processing resources.

V. THE PROCESSING OF OUTSIZE GROUPS

In terms of the perceptual appearance of grouping, a line of five or six regularly spaced items is at least as unitary as a line of three or four items. In terms of performance in the tachistoscopic situation, however, the manifestations of the phenomenon that we have labeled group processing invariably break down for groups that include more than four items. We have no theoretical treatment to offer for the allocation of attention or processing resources in such cases, and must content ourselves with a summary of empirical results concerning the serial position curves and the correlations among items for groups that consist of five or more items.

The typical serial-position curve for lines of six items consists of a flat portion for the first three items, and a gradual drop in probability of report for the fourth and fifth items. The decrement in performance between the third and fourth item is less sharp than when the six digits are grouped as two triads. We recently reviewed data from five different experiments, involving a total of 185 subjects, in which both a line and a triad structure had been presented. The stimuli were letters in four of these experiments, digits in the fifth. The same pattern appeared consistently in all these studies: the average drop in performance between the third and fourth item was 24% in the line structure, 35% in the triad structure. As we have already noted, a very different result is obtained when the array is divided into three pairs, or into a group of four items followed by an additional pair: in these cases, there usually is little or no decrement of performance between the third and fourth items.

Similar results are obtained for groups of five items. For example, the study described in the preceding sections included patterns in which the initial group consisted of five digits, followed after a blank space by a single digit, two digits, or a digit and a "k" suffix. The mean percentages of correct responses for items in the first group were 93, 86, 84, 71, and 66. Here again, note the drop of performance between the third and fourth items. A much sharper discontinuity of performance is observed between the fifth digit, which still belongs to the first perceptual group, and the sixth digit, which does not. Averaging over conditions, the difference in recall between these two items was 44%.

The similarity of performance levels over the first three items suggests the possibility that subjects tend to process the initial members of a line as a group, which includes at least three items for all subjects, and may include more items for some subjects. The results of the correlational analysis confirm this impression. In all the studies we have reviewed, the within-subject correlations among the first three items are invariably positive, although lower than in the triad structure (.25 for lines versus .48 for triads over the five studies). The other correlations in the line structure are almost always positive between immediately adjacent items, and generally negative for pairs of more distant items.

These results suggest that items in a tachistoscopic array are not processed independently, even when the physical structure of the array does not allow for group processing, as it has been described here. Specifically, the subjects appear to treat the first three items of a longer line as a group, and they may group other items as well, in a manner that is likely to fluctuate over trials and between subjects, and is therefore not readily amenable to analysis. The finding of group processing for the first three items in line structures is probably related to the well-known tendency of subjects to rehearse series of items in groups of three (Broadbent, 1975; Estes, 1972a). From the point of view of this chapter, the significant fact is that the spontaneous organization tendencies which come to light with the line structures are completely dominated by physical grouping factors, when the conditions for group processing apply.

VI. THE EFFECTS OF ADDING AN ITEM
TO AN ARRAY

We now study the effects of adding a seventh item to a six-item array, when that added item is a seventh digit which is to be reported, or an irrelevant "suffix" which is to be ignored. The effects of a visual suffix were originally investigated in an experiment designed in collaboration with Neisser (Kahneman, 1973, pp. 133–135). The study demonstrated that the interfering effects of the suffix on the report of neighboring relevant items can be predicted from observations of perceptual grouping: suffix interference occurs when the suffix is perceptually grouped with its relevant neighbors and it fails to occur when the suffix is perceptually segregated from its neighbors. The results of earlier studies of the interfering effects of auditory suffixes (Morton, Crowder, & Prussin, 1971) are consistent with this view: the magnitude of the suffix effect depends on perceptual grouping in the auditory as well as in the visual case (Kahneman, 1973, p. 133). In this section we discuss the visual suffix effect within the more detailed framework of the group-processing model. As will be shown, the most important implications of the suffix effect concern the nature of the factors that limit the span of recall in the tachistoscopic situation.

Let us first compare the results which are obtained when a seventh relevant digit or an irrelevant suffix (a lower-case "k") are added to an array of six digits. This comparison was obtained in the main experiment with which this part of the paper is concerned. It should be noted that the two conditions were presented in different blocks of trials. The suffix arrays were randomly mixed with other arrays or six digits, while the seven-digit arrays were presented separately, in order to prevent any uncertainty concerning the number of digits that were to be included in a fully correct report.

The group-processing model entails specific predictions concerning the effect of adding an item to the second group of a six-item array; (1) The effects on the recall of the six leading items should be the same, regardless of whether the added item is a seventh digit or an irrelevant suffix. (2) The addition of an item to the second group should cause an impairment of performance for all members of that group. (3) There should be no effect on performance for the first group. The first and second predictions follow from the assumption that resources are shared equally among members of a perceptual group. The third follows from the hypothesis that resources are allocated to groups according to a queueing rule. The relevant data are shown in Table 3, which presents the differences in the percentage of correct responses between various types of seven-item arrays and the corresponding six-digit arrays. The data in Table 3 are the same as were shown in Table 1, arranged to facilitate the relevant comparisons.

The data of Table 3 provide clear support for the first two of our three hypotheses. The results for corresponding positions in the seven-digit arrays and in the suffix arrays are virtually identical. The largest difference is 5%, and none of the differences is statistically significant. As expected, performance is impaired for all members of the second group when an extra item is added to that

Table 3

Differences between Seven-Item Patterns and Six-Item Patterns

	Differences in percentage correct					
Type	1	2	3	4	5	6
1234 56k	4	6	5	8	−15	−27
123 456k	2	5	4	−13	−16	−27
1234 567	1	5	3	6	−10	−24
123 4567	2	4	4	−16	−20	−27

group, regardless of whether or not that item is to be reported. However, our third hypothesis is disconfirmed, in quite unexpected fashion. The addition of an extra item to the second group of a six-digit array appears to produce a consistent *improvement* of performance on the first group (overall, $t = 5.96$, $df = 40$, $p < .001$). If substantiated by further research, this result will require a modification of our hypothesis concerning the queueing rule in the allocation of processing resources. It suggests that attention may be focused more exclusively on the leading group in the queue when it is followed by a group which appears forbiddingly difficult than when the second group is relatively easy.

The most important result in Table 3 is surely the identity of the effects of a relevant and an irrelevant seventh item on the report of the six leading digits. The significant aspect of this observation is not that the suffix acts like a seventh digit, but rather that a seventh digit, in its effects on other relevant items, acts like a suffix. Thus, by probing the nature of the suffix effect it becomes possible to learn about the nature of the interactions among relevant items that normally determine the span of tachistoscopic recall.

The view that the span reflects an interaction among the items in the array is imposed by the finding (Sperling, 1963) that for many different conditions of exposure, the total number of items recalled is virtually independent of the number of items shown. The same total performance, however, is distributed differently as the size of the array increases (Sperling, 1967). This pattern also hold in our results. For six-digit arrays, the mean number of digits recalled is 4.06, 4.17, and 4.42, respectively, for arrays where the first group consists of three, four, or five items. The corresponding values for seven-digit arrays are 3.83, 4.24, and 4.34. The values agree fairly closely. The seventh digit is reported on 28% of trials, but its inclusion in the array depresses performance on other items within the same group, as shown in Table 3, and the net result is that total performance remains approximately constant. Some kind of antagonistic interaction among items is clearly implied.

What is the nature of this antagonistic interaction, which is apparently the same for a seventh digit and for an irrelevant suffix? Three major hypotheses should be considered:

1. *Visual interference:* Neighboring items interact at the level of feature detectors, and by a loss of spatial information about the location of features, which makes identification impossible (Wolford, 1975). This interaction prevents some items from being "read," that is, from activating corresponding units in long-term memory.

2. *Competition for storage capacity:* If an item is to be included in the subject's report, a code corresponding to that item must gain access to some storage system that has a capacity of about four items. For example, Sperling's (1967) treatment of tachistoscopic performance implies that the bottleneck is to be found in a Recognition Buffer, which stores programs for rehearsal. If an item

is entered into this storage system, other items are less likely to gain access to it, because its overall capacity is limited.

3. *Competition for processing resources, or attention:* In contrast to the preceding hypothesis, where the competition occurs between *outputs* of an encoding stage, this hypothesis asserts that the competition occurs for a limited pool of *inputs,* which facilitate the processing of items in encoding, storage, or both. Rumelhart's (1970) model of tachistoscopic perception presents a detailed version of this hypothesis. The group processing model developed earlier also belongs in this class.

The visual interference hypothesis can be tested by studying the effects of physical variables on the extent of suffix interference. If this hypothesis does not adequately account for the effects of an irrelevant suffix on its relevant neighbors, it is unlikely to explain the mutual interactions among relevant items. The storage hypothesis can be tested by comparing the effects of codable and uncodable suffixes. An uncodable suffix is one for which a rehearsal program cannot be set up. If such a suffix interferes with its neighbors, the interference must occur before the level of competition among rehearsable codes.

Relevant evidence is shown in Fig. 1, which presents probabilities of correct report of the sixth digit, for several different suffixes. The study was conducted with 24 subjects, following the general procedure described in the introduction. Suffix trials were randomly mixed with control trials, on which no suffix was shown. There were 12 control trials, 12 trials on which the suffix was the digit "zero" printed in the same color as the other items, and 6 trials for each of the other types of suffix. The zero was never relevant, and it could appear only as a suffix.

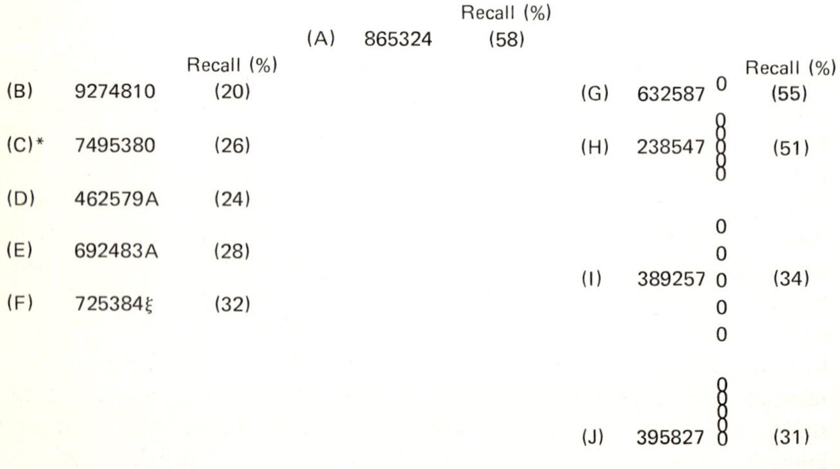

		Recall (%)					Recall (%)
(A)	865324	(58)					
(B)	9274810	(20)		(G)	632587	0	(55)
(C)*	7495380	(26)		(H)	238547	0 0 0 0	(51)
(D)	462579A	(24)					
(E)	692483A	(28)		(I)	389257	0 0 0 0 0	(34)
(F)	725384ξ	(32)		(J)	395827	0 0 0 0	(31)

*The zero is printed in red.

FIG. 1   Probability of recall of sixth digit for various suffixes.

The suffixes illustrated in Fig. 1 caused a highly significant decrement in the correct recall of the sixth digit, with patterns G and H as the only exceptions. These exceptions confirm results already reported (Kahneman, 1973, p. 134).

The results of this experiment appear impossible to reconcile with any interpretation in terms of visual interference. Perhaps the most compelling argument is the highly significant difference between the amount of interference observed in patterns B and I. Although any factor of visual interference which is present in the former pattern is surely present in even greater abundance in the latter, the interference is less severe with a line of zeroes than with a single zero ($t =$ 4.05, $df = 23$, $p < .001$). In conjunction with the standard observation that suffix effects in our experimental situation are essentially independent of viewing distance, the pattern of suffix effects illustrated in Fig. 1 allows us to rule out visual–sensory factors as major determinants of suffix interference. If the effects of a suffix and an added relevant item are identical, as suggested by the preceding experiment, the same conclusion can be extended to the interactions among relevant items in the array.

The hypothesis that the suffix and its neighbors interact at the level of verbal-acoustic codes can be rejected with equal confidence. An unfamiliar Greek letter which few subjects could name produces about as much interference as an easily codable letter. In another experiment in our laboratory, Bar-Niv found that letter-like nonsense shapes are highly effective suffixes. Thus, the suffix does not interfere with performance because its name competes with the names of relevant items for access to a storage system of limited capacity. Once again, it is reasonable to extend the same conclusion to the interactions among relevant items. Thus, we are led to agree with the suggestion by Wolford and Hollingsworth (1974b) that the tachistoscopic span is not limited by the characteristics of short-term memory, although we reject their alternative hypothesis, that the span is determined by visual imitations.

Coltheart (1972) has proposed that the tachistoscopic span represents the number of visual codes that can be simultaneously retained. This view is consistent with our findings about the unimportance of verbal coding in the suffix effect, since a visual code can be set up even for an item that cannot be named. However, an informal observation that we have made in the course of running studies of the suffix effect raises a difficulty for this view. The observation is simply that some of the suffixes that we employ are highly memorable, and that it is quite easy for a subject to recall what the suffix had been on a particular trial, even after completing his report of the relevant items. Furthermore, suffixes that cause virtually no interference (see patterns G and H) are at least as memorable as suffixes that cause severe interference with the report of relevant items. Thus, it appears that a visual code is set up even for an ineffective suffix, and this makes it unlikely that the interaction among items is due to a limitation on the number of visual codes that can be retained simultaneously.

In summary, the observations of the suffix study cast doubt on the interpretation of the tachistoscopic span in terms of sensory factors, and on two formulations of the span as a characteristic of some storage system for outputs of coding. The attention hypothesis concerning the nature of the span, and the group-processing model were not specifically tested in this study, but they are generally consistent with its results. However, the observation that an ineffective suffix may be stored implies that attention, or processing resources, are not *necessary* for the formation of a visual code.

While the results presented so far provide support for the group-processing model, and for the importance of perceptual grouping as a determinant of selective attention, they also indicate the need for caution in applying the concept of grouping. The converging operations that are required for an adequate definition of grouping are yet to be developed, and the interaction of reading habits and purely visual factors is not well understood. Two of the results shown in Fig. 1 bear on this point. In both patterns J and C (where the suffix is a red zero), the amount of suffix interference was substantially greater than we had anticipated. Routh and Walker (1975) have also reported that a red zero is a highly effective source of prefix interference although such an item clearly stands out on the background of the relevant black digits. Reading habits appear to be a powerful determinant of performance in this task and the conditions under which perceptual grouping overcomes this factor are yet to be worked out.

In spite of these qualifications, the concepts of perceptual grouping and attention provide a generally adequate treatment of the visual suffix effect. Can this treatment be generalized to the auditory suffix? In arguing against this possibility, Crowder (1975) mentioned the failure of these concepts to account for the so-called modality effect in short-term memory: the existence of a pronounced recency advantage in auditory presentation, which is absent when the items to be recalled are visually presented in sequence. However, the relevant visual analogue to sequential auditory presentation may be the case in which visual items are presented simultaneously rather than sequentially. In some fundamental respects, the role of temporal factors in audition is equivalent to the role of corresponding spatial factors in vision. This is the case, for example, in the comparison of binaural and binocular depth perception. Although the current literature interprets the end-item advantage in vision as evidence for lateral masking, and the recency advantage in audition as evidence for precategorical acoustic storage, it is quite possible that both effects may reflect the same attentional emphasis on terminal items.

VII. GROUPING AND SELECTIVE ATTENTION

The suffix effect with which the preceding section was concerned is a special case of a more general paradigm, in which the subject is required to focus attention on some stimuli and to ignore others. The hypothesis that factors of perceptual grouping determine the ease with which attention can be focused on relevant stimuli applies to the general class of focused attention tasks (Kahneman, 1973, Chapter 7). This section reports an investigation of this hypothesis, in the context of selective attention to items defined by their color, in a tachistoscopic display that includes an equal number of relevant and irrelevant items. This study was designed as an extension of experiments by von Wright (1968, 1970), who demonstrated that selective attention by color is possible, and pointed out that the variables which permit adequate selective report also induce strong perceptual grouping. Von Wright, however, did not systematically vary proximity as a grouping variable in interaction with color similarity. This was done by Fryklund (1975) in an experiment that was published after the present study was carried out. Fryklund's major finding was that proximity of the relevant items has a dominant effect on performance in a selective attention task. Wherever our data can be compared to Fryklund's, the agreement is quite close. However, some differences in design and in theoretical background led us to perform quite different analyses of the data.

The basic display employed in our study consisted of two rows of six upper-case letters. The projected height of the letters was 7 cm, and the center-to-center distance between adjacent letters was 12 cm, in both the vertical and horizontal directions. In the Blue/Red condition, the array consisted of six blue and six red letters. Six basic structures were used, each represented by two complementary variants in which the positions of red and blue letters were interchanged. The capital letters in the display of Table 4 indicate the location of blue letters in one of the variants, and of red letters in the other. The 12 patterns used in the Blue/Only condition were the same, with vacant spaces instead of red letters. The Blue/Red and Blue/Only conditions were alternated on successive blocks of trials, with every pattern represented once in each block, The subjects were instructed to report only blue letters. The data that will be shown are pooled over two replications of the experiment. Each pattern was represented by five slides in the first study ($N = 25$), and by a new set of six slides in the replication ($N = 26$). Some major results of the experiment are shown in Table 4. They may be summarized as follows:

1. The effects of pattern on performance in the Blue/Only condition are slight in absolute terms, although highly significant by analysis of variance ($F = 11.66$, $df = 5/250$, $p < .001$). Fryklund (1975) also observed that the effects of pattern on total performance are small, in the absence of interfering stimuli. The only striking effect in our results is the inferior performance with triads. A similar inferiority of a 3–3 arrangement to a 4–2 arrangement could be noted in the data of Table 1, where the stimuli were digits, presented on a single line.

2. In the presence of red letters, the effects of variations of pattern are huge, and highly significant ($F = 65.87$, $df = 5/250$, $p < .001$, in an analysis of variance on the difference between scores in the Blue/Red and Blue/Only conditions).

TABLE 4
Interference in the Recall of Letters

	Blue/Only	Blue/Red	Difference	Intrusions
A B C D E F a b c d e f	3.51	2.99	0.52	0.29
A B C d e f a b c D E F	3.20	2.63	0.57	0.28
A B c d E F a b C D e f	3.61	2.38	1.33	0.39
A a C c E e B b D d F f	3.52	2.16	1.36	0.39
A b c D E f a B C d e F	3.39	2.29	1.10	0.36
A b C d E f a B c D e F	3.58	2.01	1.57	0.40

These results are again similar to findings reported by Fryklund (1975). The differences are smallest where the items are clustered in large groups (lines and triads), and largest for the relatively isolated items in the checkerboard pattern.

3. The frequency of intrusions varies significantly for different patterns ($F = 4.27$, $p < .001$), but the intrusion rate is generally low. The conditions that lead to the smallest loss of correct items are also associated with the lowest frequency of intrusions, but the hardest condition differs from the easiest by only 35% in overt intrusions, while the corresponding difference in recall loss is 300%. The absence of proportionality between intrusions and omissions is, we believe, an important observation. It demonstrates that the selection of blue letters does not occur *in* the short-term memory system, but *prior* to that system. When exposed to an array of blue and red letters, subjects do not store a number of letters, irrespective of their color, and later decide which of these letters to report. If they were to do so, the rate of intrusions of red letters should be at least roughly proportional to the loss of blue letters from the report, and this is clearly not the case. The severely impaired recall of blue letters in some Blue/Red patterns is mainly due to a deficiency in the encoding and storage of blue letters, not to an excess in the encoding and the storage of red letters.

What is the anatomy of the interference effect in this situation? How does it relate to group processing? Analyses of performance in the Blue/Only and the Blue/Red conditions confirm that group processing occurs in both cases. For example, the average within subject correlation for items that belong to the same group in the triad pattern is .53 in the Blue/Only condition and .56 in the Blue/Red condition. The corresponding value for members of different groups are −.43 and −.54.

To obtain a more detailed analysis of the interference effect, we defined a measure of interference for individual items. This measure is the difference between recall probabilities for a given position in the Blue/Red and Blue/Only patterns, divided by the recall probability for the Blue/Only condition. This measure of proportional impairment was studied as a function of the position of the item in the modal order of report for each pattern, which is represented by the alphabetical order of positions in Table 4. It was immediately apparent that the results for lines and for triads differ qualitatively from the results for all other patterns. The nature of the difference is illustrated in Fig. 2. For lines and triads, the proportional impairment of recall does not appear to vary systematically with position; for all other patterns, there is a pronounced left-to-right gradient in the severity of interference. In the terms of the group-processing model, the groups that appear late in the queue for processing resources tend to suffer most from the presence of irrelevant material in the array. The failure of this generalization in the case of the triad pattern arises from frequent violations of the normal left-to-right queueing order in the Blue/Red condition, and from the

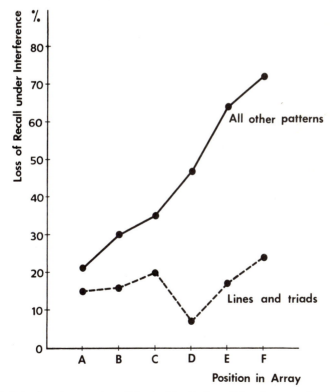

FIG. 2 Relative impairment of recall in the Blue/Red condition for successive positions in the normal processing order.

fact that subjects rarely reported more than one complete triad even in the Blue/Only condition.

In the terms that have been used in this chapter, the presence of irrelevant red items in the array appears to produce a sharp reduction in the amount of resources that are available for the processing of relevant blue letters. The reduction appears to be related to the number of different groups of relevant items that must be extracted from the background of irrelevant material. The intrusion results strongly suggest that the lost resources are not diverted to the production of name codes for the irrelevant letters. It is hardly plausible that the subjects maintain a low intrusion rate even in the conditions of most severe interference by deleting remembered irrelevant letters from the report. A possibility that deserves consideration is that the search for groups of relevant items draws on the same pool of limited resources that is also applied to the processing of these items when they are found. Interference is most severe in complex arrays, where a large number of separate groups of relevant items must be found, and where the small size of these groups may make them hard to find.

As was noted by Fryklund (1975), pattern effects present a challenge to current models of tachistoscopic perception, which commonly ignore factors of perceptual organization. The similarity of relevant to irrelevant items, for example, is usually discussed as a determinant of confusability, which affects a decision process, rather than as a determinant of perceptual grouping (e.g., Estes, 1972b; Gardner, 1973; Shiffrin, 1975). A difficulty for this view has been noted by Banks, Bodinger, and Illige (1974), who observed that increased cluttering of a display with irrelevant stimuli actually facilitates the detection of a target, if the greater density of irrelevant items improves their grouping in perception.

The dominant effect of grouping factors on the efficiency of selective attention shares a characteristic of many other so-called Gestalt effects: it surprises no one, and the subjects least of all. When a checkerboard pattern is shown for unlimited viewing during the introductory instructions, there are frequent giggles and exclamations: "This is going to be hard." Nevertheless, no current model of tachistoscopic perception easily incorporates this effect. The aversion for Gestalt concepts in modern cognitive psychology is often justified on the grounds that these concepts are circular or merely descriptive. Because the Gestalt psychologists were the great masters of the obvious, the neglect of their observations is sometimes associated with theorizing that has greater difficulty in explaining large and obvious effects than small and obscure ones.

ACKNOWLEDGMENTS

This research was supported by the Center for Human Development at the Hebrew University of Jerusalem. We thank J. Windzberg and V. Bar-Niv for allowing us to cite their data and Y. Schul, I. Bader, and S. Nemerow for their help in the experiments.

REFERENCES

Broadbent, D. E. The magic number seven after fifteen years. In: A. Kennedy and A. Wilkes (Eds.), *Studies in long term memory*. New York: Wiley, 1975.

Banks, W. P., Bodinger, D., & Illige, M. Visual detection accuracy and target–noise proximity. *Bulletin of the Psychonomic Society*, 1974, **2**, 411–414.

Bower, G. H. A selective review of organizational factors in memory. In: E. Tulving and W. Donaldson (Eds.), *Organization of memory*. New York: Academic Press, 1972. (a)

Bower, G. H. Perceptual groups as coding units in immediate memory. *Psychonomic Science*, 1972, **27**, 217–219. (b)

Cattell, J. Mck. Ueber die zeit der erkennung und benennung von schriftzeichen, bildern und farben. *Philos. st.*, 1885, **2**, 635–650.

Coltheart, M. Visual information-processing. In: P. C. Dodwell (Ed.), *New Horizons in Psychology 2*. Harmondsworth: Penguin, 1972.

Crowder, R. G. Inferential problems in echoic memory. In: P. M. A. Rabbitt and S. Dornic, (Eds.), *Attention and performance V*. London: Academic Press, 1975.

Estes, W. K. An associative basis for coding and organization in memory. In: A. W. Melton and E. Martin (Eds.), *Coding processes in human memory*. Washington, D.C.: V. H. Winston, 1972. (a)

Estes, W. K. Interactions of signal and background variables in visual processing. *Perception and Psychophysics*, 1972, **12**, 278–286. (b)

Estes, W. K., & Wolford, G. Effects of spaces on report from tachistoscopically presented letter strings. *Psychonomic Science*, 1971, **25**, 77–80.

Fryklund, I. Effects of cued-set spatial arrangement and target–background similarity in the partial-report paradigm. *Perception and Psychophysics*, 1975, **17**, 375–386.

Gardner, G. T. Evidence for independent parallel channels in tachistoscopic perception. *Cognitive Psychology*, 1973, **4**, 130–155.

Johnson, N. F. The role of chunking and organization in the process of recall. In: G. H. Bower (Ed.), *The psychology of learning and motivation*. Vol. 4. New York: Academic Press, 1970.

Johnson, N. F. Organization and the concept of a memory code. In: A. W. Melton and E. Martin (Eds.), *Coding processes in human memory*. Washington, D.C.: V. H. Winston, 1972.

Kahneman, D. *Attention and effort*. Englewood Cliffs, N.J.: Prentice–Hall, 1973.

Merikle, P. M., Coltheart, M., & Lowe, D. G. On the selective effects of a patterned masking stimulus. *Canadian Journal of Psychology*, 1971, **25**, 264–279.

Miller, G. A. The magical number seven, plus or minus two: Some limits on our capacity for processing information. *Psychological Review*, 1956, **63**, 81–97.

Morton, J., Crowder, R., and Prussin, H. A. Experiments with the stimulus suffix effect. *Journal of Experimental Psychology Monograph*, 1971, **91**, 169–190.

Neisser, U. *Cognitive psychology*. New York: Appleton-Century-Crofts, 1967.

Norman, D. A. and Bobrow, D. G. On data-limited and resource-limited processes, *Cognitive psychology*, 1975, **7**, 44–64.

Routh, D. A., and Walker, D. J. "Next-to-nothings" and nothingness: A study of attention, attenuation and the stimulus prefix effect. *Quarterly Journal of Experimental Psychology*, 1975, **27**, 393–403.

Rumelhart, D. E. A multicomponent theory of the perception of briefly exposed visual displays. *Journal of Mathematical Psychology*, 1970, **7**, 191–218.

Shiffrin, R. M. The locus and role of attention in memory systems. In: P. M. A. Rabbitt and S. Dornic (Eds.), *Attention and performance V*, London: Adacemic Press, 1975.

Simon, H. A. How big is a chunk? *Science*, 1974, **183**, 482–488.

Sperling, G. A model for visual memory tasks. *Human Factors,* 1963, **5,** 19–31.

Sperling, G. Successive approximations to a model for short-term memory. *Acta Psychologica,* 1967, **27,** 285–292.

Taylor, S. G., & Brown, D. R. Lateral visual masking: Supraretinal effects when viewing linear arrays with unlimited viewing time. *Perception and Psychophysics,* 1972, **12,** 97–99.

Townsend, J. T., Taylor, S. G., & Brown, D. R. Lateral masking for letters with unlimited viewing time. *Perception and Psychophysics,* 1971, **10,** 375–378.

von Wright, J. M. Selection in visual immediate memory. *Quarterly Journal of Experimental Psychology,* 1968, **20,** 62–68.

von Wright, J. M. On selection in visual immediate memory. *Acta Psychologica,* 1970, **33,** 280–292.

Wolford, G. Perturbation model for letter identification. *Psychological Review,* 1975, **82,** 184–199.

Wolford, G., & Hollingsworth, S. Lateral masking in visual information processing. *Perception and Psychophysics,* 1974, **16,** 315–320.   (a)

Wolford, G., & Hollingsworth, S. Evidence that short-term memory is not the limiting factor in the tachistoscopic full-report procedure. *Memory and Cognition,* 1974, **2,** 796–800.   (b)

Woodworth, R. S. *Experimental psychology.* New York: Holt, Rinehart and Winston, 1938.

17

Selective Attention and Stimulus Integration

Anne M. Treisman
Marilyn Sykes
Gary Gelade

Department of Experimental Psychology
Oxford University
Oxford, England

ABSTRACT

Perception of multidimensional stimuli composed of separable attributes requires some process of integration to combine the attributes into the correct compounds. We hypothesize that when more than one such stimulus is presented, subjects avoid perceiving illusory conjunctions composed of wrongly paired attribute values by focusing attention on one location at a time and thus processing the stimuli serially. Any of three conditions should then allow parallel processing with divided attention: (1) the stimuli vary along one attribute only (and acuity does not limit performance); (2) the stimuli are multidimensional but the correct conjunctions are irrelevant; (3) the stimuli are multidimensional but share no attributes which could be wrongly recombined. We report two experiments designed as first attempts to explore the implications of this hypothesis for perception in a visual search task and for memory in a successive matching task. Latencies to detect targets in arrays of varying size suggested that parallel processing could occur when the target differed from nontargets either in color alone or in a shape feature (curvature) alone, but that when a particular conjunction of color and shape defined the target, subjects were forced to scan the stimuli serially. In the successive matching task, two multidimensional targets (colored letters in one experiment and schematic faces in another) were compared with two multidimensional test stimuli. When a test stimulus wrongly combined two attribute values from the target stimuli, errors were frequent and response latencies increased by a constant duration. This suggests that: (1) attribute values are poorly integrated in memory when the physical stimulus is no longer present, and (2) a separate stage of processing is required to check whether two matching values which are spatially combined in the test stimulus were also combined in a memorized target.

I. SYNTHESIS OF ATTRIBUTES
AND SERIAL PROCESSING

What are the perceptual mechanisms that ensure that when presented, for example, with a green square and a red circle we usually see these stimuli correctly, and do not mistakenly perceive a green circle and a red square? In other words, how are the various attributes or features of complex stimuli perceptually combined into the correct compounds and held together as such in memory? This question presupposes that separate processing does occur, at least for some attributes, although, as Garner (1970) has pointed out, other physical attributes may in fact be processed integrally as unitary perceptual dimensions. Indeed Lockhead (1972) suggested that even with separable attributes there may be an initial holistic processing of objects as "blobs," which will be followed by separate analysis of attributes only if the task requires it. However, there is now considerable evidence that at least some attributes of multidimensional stimuli are processed in parallel by independent analyzers (Hawkins, 1969; Saraga & Shallice, 1973; Garner, 1974). It is perhaps surprising then how little attention has been paid to the consequent question of how the analyzed attributes are subsequently synthesized into the correct multidimensional compounds.

One obvious hypothesis is that the subset of attribute values which co-occur in the same spatial location are those selected for integration into unitary percepts. However, this presupposes some method of registering *which* location any particular value or feature occupies. It is unlikely that we have spatially distinct detectors for most of the complex stimuli that we recognize. Moreover, Gouras (1972) states that "the probability of a cell being color-sensitive decreases as its spatial complexity increases." This implies, he suggests "that there are separate and presumably hierarchical channels in foveal striate cortex selecting either for form or for color, but not both" (p. 430). If these conclusions are correct, some other means of recombining the information in different channels to allow perception of complex, multidimensional objects would be required.

One way of solving the problem without directly coding the conjunction of place and features would be to process *serially* stimuli in different spatial locations. The conjunction of attribute values which were identified in any one temporal interval would then be integrated as a single perceptual object without any need directly to code or store their spatial location. Minsky (1961) and Neisser (1967) argued that, since the number of possible conjunctions of features increases very rapidly with the number of features present in a display, some mechanism of focal attention is economically necessary, following an earlier preattentive stage at which "objects" are segregated. We suggest an additional benefit of testing serially for feature conjunctions in one spatial area at a time, namely, that this would reduce the chance of detecting illusory conjunctions which did not belong together in the real world. Our hypothesis therefore points to this additional important function for selective attention to stimuli in different spatial locations, which may even replace the usual assumption that it is needed to protect a limited capacity system from overloading. Milner (1974) recently advanced a similar notion in an attempt to solve the problem of how one achieves stimulus equivalence across different retinal locations while still retaining information about the location of each stimulus. He suggests that "some mechanism of selective attention must be postulated to keep the signals from the different objects separate" (p. 523).

Tasks in which attention is to be divided between spatially discrete stimuli can be of two kinds. Certain tasks can be performed without the identification of conjunctions of attribute values. For example, to detect a red letter in a field of blue letters one need only register its color. Other tasks force the subjects to register a conjunction of values; for example, to detect a red "H" in a field of blue "H"s and red "O"s, the particular combination of shape and color must be specified. From our hypothesis that the correct identification of conjunctions requires successive processing of different spatial locations, it follows that parallel processing will be found only in tasks of the first kind, whereas the processing of stimuli in tasks of the second kind will be serial. Is there any evidence to support this hypothesis?

Review of Previous Findings

We shall look briefly at three types of tasks.

1. *Tasks requiring divided attention with two simultaneous stimulus sequences.* Whenever the two sequences contain stimuli which vary along the same attributes, the possibility of mistaken spatial or temporal conjunctions arises. The task will therefore typically require conjunctions to be detected and labeled as such. If the stimuli are in the same modality, they require conjunctions of attribute values to be identified whenever the response is made contingent on the particular combination of input channel and item identity. For example subjects may be asked to shadow the items on the right ear (or in a man's voice) and monitor those on the left (or those in a woman's voice). Divided attention to both of two speech messages has been shown to be very difficult, unless the task can be performed on the basis of detecting a single property, such as change of voice (Treisman & Riley, 1969). Errors involving incorrect conjunctions in dichotic listening tasks have been reported. For example Treisman and Riley (1969) found that subjects made about 12% intrusion errors from the wrong ear in shadowing accurately synchronized digits. Day (1967) and Treisman (1970) reported fusion responses in which phonemes from each ear were combined into a single speech item (e.g., "back" and "lack" were heard as "black"). Similar illusions can occur with nonverbal stimuli: for example Efron and Yund (1974) described a striking dissociation between the pitch and loudness of two dichotic tone sequences, such that subjects sometimes heard the tonal sequence delivered

to the right ear at the loudness level of the left ear. In contrast, in a task requiring the detection only of a single attribute value (a tone of a different frequency embedded in a string of monaural or dichotically alternating tones), Harvey and Treisman (1973) found little impairment due to dividing attention between the ears; the decrement due to dichotic presentation was much less here than in subjects' report of the number and temporal location of the tones.

Another way of reducing the risk of perceiving wrong conjunctions is to reduce the number of attributes which are shared by the two inputs. When one message is auditory and one visual, there are fewer shared attributes which could allow illusory conjunctions to occur. This should facilitate parallel processing of two inputs in different modalities, even when processing *within* each input involves conjunctions and may be serial. Treisman and Davies (1973) showed, in fact, that divided attention to different complex verbal stimuli presented simultaneously to ear and eye is more efficient than when they are presented either to ear and ear or to eye and eye. At the time, we attributed this to the possibility that early processing by modality-specific analyzers could occur in parallel without interference because it drew on different limited-capacity analyzers rather than the same one, and therefore increased the total capacity available for the tasks. The present discussion suggests a further (not incompatible) reason for the better performance with two modalities instead of one.

2. *Classification tasks with multidimensional stimuli.* These tasks can also be considered in relation to whether they require the identification of conjunctions of attribute values or not. Checkosky (1971) asked his subjects to match a test item (a colored shape) to a previously presented set of two or three memory items. The number of attributes of the test stimulus which matched attributes of the memory items could be 0, 1, or 2. He found that the number of memory items and the number of attributes to be integrated had independent effects on response latency. There is however one feature of his results which he leaves unexplained: in the trials with two matching attributes (e.g., a trial on which a red circle and a blue square were in the memory set and a red square was the test stimulus), the results of the two comparisons of attributes would both be positive. Why then should subjects make a negative response? Clearly some extra operation is required to determine whether the attributes were combined or separate in memory. This might explain why the increase Checkosky obtained from 1 to 2 matching attributes was considerably greater than the increase from 0 to 1 (averaging 96 instead of 34 msec).

Marcel (1970) compared a classification task in which two memory targets were defined in one case by two values each on two *different* attributes (e.g., red and circle, solid and vertical) and in the other case by two mutually exclusive values on the *same* two attributes (e.g., red and circle, green and square). After practice the latter task remained much slower than the former. Marcel concluded that subjects can process values on different attributes in parallel but cannot assign values on a single attribute to two stimuli at once. Treisman (1969) had tentatively drawn a similar conclusion from a review of other experiments on divided attention and stimulus classification and related it to differences in the demands made on processing capacity within and between perceptual analyzers. However, again, a possible alternative reason for the difficulty of Marcel's shared-attribute task is that it allows the possibility of wrongly paired positive attributes; these could not occur when values on four different attributes defined the targets.

3. *Visual search tasks and feature analysis.* A demonstration that illusory conjunctions can occur in visual search was offered by Lawrence (1971). His subjects, attempting to report the identity of an upper-case target word embedded in a rapid, sequentially presented list of lower-case words, often reported instead the word which followed the target, feeling convinced that they had seen this presented in upper-case letters. Thus the problem of identifying conjunctions is a real one for the visual as well as the auditory system.

The problem of detecting correct conjunctions is not confined to different attributes of stimuli, such as color and shape, or case and meaning. Most visual shapes can themselves be described as specific conjunctions of simpler or elementary *local* features, for example, lines at particular orientations, curves, or perhaps angles. Our hypothesis then suggests that parallel processing should be more difficult with multifeatured shapes than with simple colors, sizes, line orientations and so on. Peeke and Stone (1973), indeed, reported that the effect of array size on the detection of a target was much greater if the target was defined by shape than if it was defined by color.

It is likely, however, that some shape discriminations can be performed on the basis of a single feature while others require response to conjunctions. Unfortunately it is not always easy to know in advance what the elementary features are. For example, is an angle a conjunction of two lines or a feature in its own right? It may even be the case that the features are not predetermined, but can vary, within limits, with the task requirements. For example, the presence of curvature is sufficient to discriminate "O" from "N" and "T," while to distinguish "O" from "C" and "U" it is necessary to check that the curve is a closed one, and this could involve checking for the absence of a gap in each of the two possible gap locations. To test the prediction of parallel processing for single features and serial processing for conjunctions it will be advisable initially to choose those examples that are intuitively most clearcut. However, if the hypothesis is confirmed, the method may be added to the tests for separability versus integrality which have been proposed by Garner (1970). It will be of considerable interest to see whether the same classifications of stimuli result.

An intriguing experiment by Beck and Ambler (1973) provides a test of our hypothesis. They found an interaction between focused and divided attention and the difficulty of two discrimination tasks: discrimination of "L" from "T" was more difficult than discrimination of tilted "T" from "T" under conditions of distributed attention, although with focused attention there was no differ-ence. They attributed the effect to a difference in confusability, a change in orientation being simpler, more distinctive and faster to "read out" from VIS than a change in the spatial arrangement of lines. Focal attention, they suggest, counteracts decreased discriminability by lowering thresholds and/or by "bring-ing to bear interpretive processes" which select one of several possible interpreta-tions of unclear sensory information. Our discussion suggests an alternative explanation, or perhaps rather an elaboration, of Beck and Ambler's account. Let us assume that the component lines in the shapes are elementary features. The letter "L" then differs from "T" only in the spatial arrangement of the component lines, while a tilted "T" differs from a "T" on the single feature of line orientation. We have argued that in order to avoid detection of incorrect conjunctions, serial processing of spatial locations may be necessary, while detection of a unidimensional difference is compatible with parallel processing. This may be the critical difference between the "L" and the tilted "T" in conditions in which more than one stimulus was presented.

The hypothesis may also help to explain results reported by Gardner (1970). He used the more general notion of confusability to predict whether or not interference would result from increase in display size. His confusable stimuli were "T" or "F" and "Ⴈ" and "D" or "ᗡ" and "O," in which the arrange-ments of the component lines are crucial, while his nonconfusable stimuli were "T" or "F" and "O," where a single feature will suffice to reject the irrelevant stimuli. Other experiments have also shown parallel processing of shapes, indi-cated by constant response latencies despite an increase in the number of items in the display, (Donderi & Case, 1970; Donderi & Zelnicker, 1969). The shapes used in these experiments were circle, square, triangle, and semicircle. Again, it appears likely that any pair of these shapes could be discriminated by the presence of a single feature rather than by a conjunction of shared features.

Experiments in which a letter is to be detected in digits or vice versa have also sometimes shown parallel processing (e.g., Egeth, Jonides, & Wall, 1972; Jonides & Gleitman, 1972). It has often been assumed that alphanumeric characters are analyzed perceptually into conjunctions of more elementary features. However this preconception may not be correct, or it may not represent a universal strategy; these highly familiar shapes may in fact be recognized as unitary wholes by higher-order feature detectors rather than necessarily decomposed into lines, curves, and angles. LaBerge (1973) reports evidence and a model suggesting that recognition of highly familiar stimuli can become automatized, in the sense of no longer requiring "focused attention." In this context LaBerge is using attention in the sense of expectancy or priming. However an interesting parallel can be drawn between LaBerge's finding that expectancy affects only unfamiliar stimuli, his hypothesis that this is because they have not yet become "unitized," and our suggestion that spatially focused attention may be necessary chiefly or only when conjunctions must be formed from separable features.

II. CONJUNCTIONS IN MEMORY

A further question of interest concerns the form in which information about conjunctions of attributes or features is held in memory. If coexistence in space and time provides the "glue" which holds together the different attributes of each perceptual object, the glue might tend to dissolve in memory when the object is no longer physically present. Some way of retaining conjunctions in memory is certainly necessary. One method would be to tie a spatial tag on each attribute value, the tags matching for values which had appeared in the same location when the stimulus was present. However we have suggested that the shared spatial location may simply be used to allow a temporal sequencing of focal attention to different stimuli and then need play no further part in holding together the features of each stimulus.

Another way in which we might retain conjunctions in the absence of spatial tags, would be to associate their component features to a single higher-level unit, perhaps a distinct verbal label. Santa (1975) offers evidence that a verbal label can facilitate the maintenance of an integral visual memory and suggests that it serves as the "address of a multicomponent array . . . which identifies the set of components as a unique perceptual experience" (p. 294). If some such form of associative bonding mediates retention of conjunctions, it would also of course be vulnerable to normal forgetting. The component features would retain their identity and might break loose and recombine, giving rise to errors in the form of illusory conjunctions in memory rather than perception. Thus a blue "O" and pink "H" might be retrieved as a blue "H" and pink "O," even when they were initially correctly perceived. False positives to wrong conjunctions in a successive matching task would be unlikely to occur if the attributes had coalesced into unitary gestalt or Lockheadian "blob." For example, the set of stimuli in Fig. 1 vary orthogonally in height and width rather than shape and color. These seem intuitively more likely to form integral units than do shape and color, since the variations in height and width give rise to changes in other perhaps unitary dimensions like orientation and area. It seems clear even without doing the experiment that the pair of targets A and B would not give rise to confusions with the negatives C and D in which their height and width are wrongly recombined. Any attributes or features which *can* give rise to illustory conjunctions in memory, then, must at some level still exist as independent components.

There is evidence suggesting that spatial coherence during presentation may facilitate retention of an arbitrary association. Thus, Asch, Ceraso, and Heimer (1960) showed that "unitary" percepts were better recalled and recognised than "nonunitary" ones; for example, a shape whose contours consisted of smaller replications of a different shape was easier to recall than the same large shape in solid outline with a row of the different smaller shapes beside it, or than an array of them forming a background to it. Thus there does appear to be something in the memory representation which makes two attributes of a single stimulus

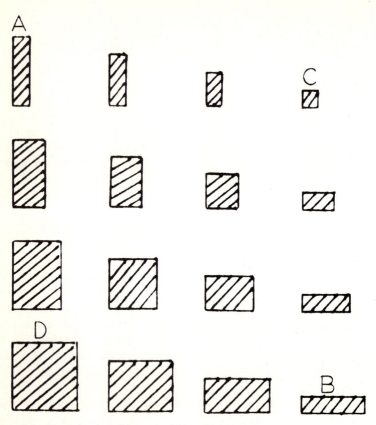

FIG. 1 Stimuli varying in height and width, which probably do not function as separate dimensions.

cohere better than an arbitrary association of two separate attributes, even for stimuli for which no unitary verbal code is available.

III. EXPERIMENT I: VISUAL SEARCH

The first experiment we report tested the predictions that perceptual processing can be spatially parallel in a visual search task if the target items are distinguishable from nontargets on the basis of a single feature, while if targets are defined by a particular conjunction of properties, however easily discriminable each is individually, processing will be forced into the serial mode.

The target we used was always a dark pink "O." Four ways of distinguishing the nontargets from the same target item were examined: (1) in the "color" condition the nontargets were purple and brown "O"s, and color was the single distinguishing feature; (2) in the "straight-line" condition the nontargets were pink "N"s and "T"s, which can be discriminated from a pink "O" by the absence of curvature; (3) in the "open-curve" condition the nontargets were pink "C"s and "U"s, which have gaps in the curve at the right or at the top; and (4) in the "conjunction" condition the nontargets were pink "N"s and green "O"s, which differed from the target either in shape or in color, but not in both features, so that the combination of features identifying the target had to be detected.

The crucial question was whether there would be differences in the functions relating RT to display size when subjects were asked to make a positive or negative decision about the presence of a target in the display. The conjunction condition (and possibly the open-curve condition) should require serial processing and therefore produce linear increases, while the color and the straight-line conditions, both of which could be distinguished from the target by a single features, should produce some function consistent with parallel processing. Parallel processing would not, however, preclude some increase in search times: this could occur for the negative displays if there were appreciable variance and stochastic independence of the processing times for different items; it could occur for both negatives and positives if there were interference between stimuli in different spatial positions, for example peripheral or central lateral inhibition. (Visual acuity was approximately equated by placing the items quasi-randomly within the same total area for all display sizes. This of course resulted in an increase in the density of items as the number increased.) One further factor which might produce a steeper increase with display size in the conjunction condition than in the single attribute ones is that each item in the conjunction condition would require an average 1.5 attributes to be checked rather than 1 (if processing of attributes were self-terminating; 2 if it were exhaustive). However none of these factors should change the shape of the function from nonlinear to linear. Moreover if shape and color can be processed in parallel, as recent experiments suggest (Hawkins, 1969; Saraga & Shallice, 1973), one would not expect even a nonlinear increase of RT with display size in the conjunction condition.

A. Method

1. Materials

Stimulus cards were made by hand using colored inks and stencils. The target and nontarget items were scattered over the card in positions, which to the eye, appeared random, although no systematic randomization procedure was used. The letters each subtended .83° and the whole area subtended 16.4° × 11°. Four different display sizes consisting of 1, 5, 15, and 30 items, were used in each condition. Sixteen cards were made for each display size in each condition, of which half contained a single target and the other half none.

2. Procedure

The experiment was run in two parts. The first part, run on 8 subjects, tested the color condition, the open-curve condition, and the conjunction condition. A second part of the experiment was run with 6 of the same subjects on the straight-line, open-curve, and conjunction conditions. The aims were: (1) to explore a shape condition in which the presence of a single feature (a straight line) could distinguish nontargets from targets, and (2) to investigate the effects of practice on the open-curve and the conjunction condition. Each part of the experiment consisted of three sessions, each containing three blocks, one for each condition. The order was counterbalanced across subjects. The first session was treated as practice. Any subjects who made more than 12% errors in any practice condition were encouraged to be more careful and to go more slowly in that condition; (this in fact only occurred in the conjunction condition, in which some subjects initially made a large number of false negative responses).

The different display sizes were randomly mixed within a block, and the three different nontarget conditions in each part of the experiment were presented in separate blocks of 64 trials each. Thus subjects knew what the nontargets would be on any trial, but not how many there would be. They were asked to press one key if the card contained a pink "O" and the other key if it did not, as quickly as possible without making errors. Half the subjects used their dominant hand for the positives and half for the negatives.

B. Results

The mean correct RTs and error rates are shown in Fig. 2. Nearly all the errors were false negatives. Mean RTs for the single-item displays in Part 1 were 438 msec for both the open-curve and the color conditions and 449 msec for the conjunction condition; in Part 2 they were 410 msec for the straight-line condition, 432 msec for the conjunction condition, and 439 msec for the open-curve condition. These differences were not significant on analysis of variance. Thus the difficulty of discrimination with a single stimulus was matched across conditions, and the differences appeared only when nontargets were added to the display.

Analysis of variance on the search times with all display sizes for each part separately showed significant effects ($p < 0.001$) of all the main factors except blocks (i.e., conditions, display size, positive versus negative response) and of all their two-way and three-way interactions. Newman–Keul's tests showed that all conditions within each part differed significantly from one another except that the difference between the open-curve and conjunction conditions failed to reach significance in Part 2 of the experiment. An analysis of practice effects in the open-curve and the conjunction conditions for the 6 subjects who did both parts of the experiment showed significant effects of blocks ($F(3, 15) = 5.29, p$

TABLE 1
Proportion and Significance of Variance with Display Size Due to Linearity and to Deviations from Linearity

		Part 1				Part 2		
		Linearity	Deviations	Slope (msec)	Intercept (msec)	Linearity	Deviations	Slope (msec)	Intercept (msec)
Color	Positives	0.431[a]	0.569[a]	2.76	451				
	Negatives	0.957[a]	0.043	10.63	476				
Straight-line	Positives					0.534[a]	0.466[b]	1.32	402
	Negatives					0.995[a]	0.005	4.41	429
Conjunction	Positives	0.964[a]	0.036	21.1	419	0.977[a]	0.023	14.8	402
	Negatives	0.995[a]	0.005	36.1	449	0.995[a]	0.005	25.4	454
Open-Curve	Positives	0.966[a]	0.034	9.26	419	0.900[a]	0.100[b]	7.31	428
	Negatives	0.999[a]	0.001	29.42	455	0.996[a]	0.004	22.9	462

[a] = p < 0.001.
[b] = p < 0.01.

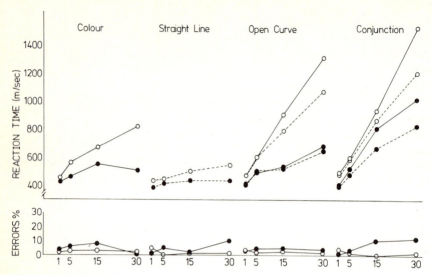

FIG. 2   Search times for Parts 1 and 2 and overall error percentages in Experiment I. Open circles: negatives; solid circles: positives. Solid lines: Part 1; dotted lines: Part 2.

< 0.025) and a significant interaction of blocks with display size ($F(9,45) = 3.50$, $p < 0.01$), reflecting the reduction in slopes in Part 2, but no other significant interaction with blocks. Thus the change in slopes did not differ significantly for the open-curve and the conjunction conditions. There was a significant overall difference between these two conditions and significant interactions of conditions both with positive versus negative response and with display size, and of positive versus negative with display size.

Linear regressions were calculated for each condition, and the proportion of the variance due to display size accounted for by linearity and by deviations from linearity are shown in Table 1, together with their significance levels and the estimated slopes and zero intercepts.

C.   Discussion

The hypothesis we proposed was that parallel processing should be possible for the two single attribute conditions (color and straight-line) and that serial processing would be necessary for the color—shape conjunctions, and perhaps also for the open-curve condition in which curvature was a shared feature of targets and nontargets. One strong indication that stimuli are processed serially is a strictly linear increase in RT with display size, although this can be mimicked by some versions of a capacity-limited parallel process (Atkinson, Holmgren, & Juola, 1969; Townsend, 1971). However, we have a theoretical framework predicting serial processing and no good reason to expect a *change* in the way capacity limits in a parallel process determine response times for conjunctions as

opposed to equally difficult discriminations on single attributes. We shall therefore, at present, treat a linear increase in RT with display size as evidence
for a serial search, although we recognize that an alternative account is not ruled
out. On the other hand, flat or markedly bowed RT functions are much more
difficult to reconcile with serial processing.

The slopes of the positive RT functions differ dramatically between conditions, and do so in the direction we had predicted. Deviations from linearity
were highly significant for both color and straight-line conditions and the linear
component accounted for only 43% and 53% of the variance due to display size
compared to 97% in the conjunction condition. Moreover the positive RTs
in both the single attribute conditions actually decreased as the display size
increased from 15 to 30 items. Thus the positive RTs in these two conditions
suggest that parallel processing is possible with a single attribute discrimination.
(Of course this could break down if peripheral factors like acuity were to limit
performance to foveal processing.)

These single attribute conditions differ strikingly from the shape—color conjunctions. However, it is important to note that the difference was limited to
displays with more than one item; with single-item displays, of course, the
question of serial versus parallel processing cannot arise. As soon as more items
were added to the display, their effect diverged dramatically in the single
attribute and in the conjunction conditions. The linear component of the
increase in RT with display size accounted for 97% of the variance in the
conjunction condition, and deviations from linearity were insignificant in both
parts of the experiment and in both positive and negative RTs. Thus the
hypothesis that serial processing would be necessary in this condition appears to
be largely confirmed by the results.

However, the negative RT functions pose a problem. They increase linearly
with display size in the single attribute as well as in the conjunction conditions.
How do we account for the difference between positive and negative RT
functions in the two single attribute conditions for which parallel processing was
predicted? This finding is reminiscent of the now familiar observation in
"same—different" classification tasks, that "same" RTs are fast and relatively
unaffected by the number of features or elements to be compared, while
"different" RTs suggest a serial comparison process. Bamber (1969) suggested
that different strategies determine the response latency on positive and on
negative trials; that positive responses can be triggered after a fast, holistic,
identity match, while negative responses must follow a serial check of features or
elements to determine *where* the mismatch occurs. Similarly it is possible that
positive and negative RTs in these single attribute conditions are determined by
two different processes which are carried out in parallel. The visual-search task
differs from a same—different comparison task in that all displays of more than
one stimulus contain mismatching stimuli, which preclude a holistic identity
match of the complete display. Instead, positive RTs in the single attribute

conditions may be mediated by a parallel check for the target feature, as we have proposed, while a serial comparison process determines the negative responses even in the single attribute conditions.

Two further alternative accounts of the difference between single attribute and conjunction conditions are worth considering: (1) that the number of attributes which are relevant to the task and shared by target and nontargets is greater in the conjunction condition; and (2) that the nontargets are more heterogeneous in the conjunction condition than in the single attribute conditions. Regarding the first alternative the experiment was designed to equate the number of nontarget attribute values that matched the target and the number that differed from it in each condition. However in the conjunction condition the nontargets all match the target on one relevant attribute, while in the straight-line and color conditions, the attributes on which nontargets match the target are not relevant to the task. This difference could have a number of consequences: It might induce greater conflict in reaching a negative decision about nontargets in the conjunction condition, causing the steeper increase in decision latency with an increase in the number of nontargets. It might result in greater overall similarity of the nontarget set to the target item, if similarity is determined by the number of task-relevant attribute values which are shared between targets and nontargets. Finally, it might force attention to switch between the relevant attributes within each nontarget stimulus. However these hypotheses all predict only that the increase in RT with display size will be steeper for the conjunction than for the single attribute conditions; none of them explains why the increase is linear for the conjunctions and nonlinear for the single attribute positive displays. It is this evidence for serial processing that is crucial to our hypothesis that identification of conjunctions requires focal attention. The time taken for each target-to-nontarget comparison may well vary with the degree of response conflict, or of similarity, or of attention switching involved, but the important point for this hypothesis is that these differences should be additive for each display stimulus when processing is assumed to be serial.

The nontargets differ from one another on only one attribute in the color and straight-line conditions while they differ in both color and shape in the conjunction conditions. One could control for this factor by doing an experiment in which the nontargets remained constant across conditions and only the targets varied. However, again it is not obvious how the heterogenity of nontargets would explain the qualitative difference between the positive RTs for the single attribute and the conjunction displays, the increase being linear only for the conjunctions.

What of the results in the open-curve condition? Here, too, the negative RTs increase linearly with display size. The positive RT functions however, deviate significantly from linearity in Part 2 and are much less steep than the function for conjunction positives, although steeper than the functions for the straight-line and color positives. The results suggest a possible mixture of strategies on positive trials: some are determined by a parallel check for a target (as in the color and straight-line conditions) and some by the same serial check as determines the negative response. We had initially assumed that these two nontargets, "C" and "U", would be rejected simply on the basis of the gap in the curve. One could conclude that the theory was incorrect or incomplete, and that some other factor such as similarity of shape could also induce serial processing, even when a single feature could mediate the discrimination. Alternatively, the error might be in our initial analysis of the shapes as varying by a single feature. This dilemma illustrates the point made in the Introduction, that we cannot know a priori what the functional features are for a given task. However, since the predictions were confirmed for positive RTs in the other three conditions (whose a priori description was less equivocal), it is worth considering the latter alternative. The main difference between the two nontargets, "C" and "U", is the spatial arrangement of curve and gap; moreover the absence of a gap in either position *alone* (top or right) is not sufficient to identify an item as a Target O. Thus, in the context of this discrimination, the functional description of an "O" might consist of a conjunction of arcs spanning each possible gap position. Further research is clearly needed to determine how far our predictions hold up in other less equivocal cases of feature conjunctions. If the hypothesis were supported, the method might then be used to throw light on cases (such as "O" versus "C" and "U") where there is doubt whether one or several features are used to encode the shapes.

IV. EXPERIMENTS II AND III:
CONJUNCTIONS IN MEMORY

The second pair of experiments reported here were attempts to compare the way conjunctions are handled in memory and in a physically present stimulus. We used a perceptual matching task in which two test stimuli were compared with two target stimuli, presented immediately before them. The stimuli varied along two attributes (shape and color) or by two features (eyes and mouth of schematic faces) with a range of four different values on each. The same attribute value never appeared more than once in any pair of stimuli. Subjects were required to press one key if one or both of the test stimuli exactly matched one or both of the target stimuli, and the other key for all other test displays. The negative test displays (i.e., pairs of negative stimuli shown together) could contain one, two, or no matching values on each of the two attributes, giving nine different types of negatives. In the case in which one value on each attribute matched the targets their spatial arrangements could take three different forms: they could be separate in both target and test displays, combined in the target and separate in the test display (t), or separate in the target and combined in the test display (d).

There were two main questions of interest: (1) Would there be a special difficulty with target—display combinations which allowed the possibility of illusory conjunctions because they contained at least one matching value on each attribute? Or would the overall similarity, that is, the number of matching values, be the only important variable? (2) Would this extra difficulty vary as a function of whether the matching values were spatially combined or separated in either the targets or the test displays? These conditions should give further evidence to supplement Experiment I on the method of testing for conjunctions when the stimuli are physically present (test display), and also throw light on the way subjects retrieve conjunction information from memory (targets). Experiment I suggested that with physically present stimuli which contain matching values on *both* dimensions, false conjunctions are avoided by serial processing of display positions. If subjects used this strategy in the following two experiments they would avoid any additional difficulty due to the possibility of illusory conjunctions in the display. However, it is not clear whether the same serial scanning strategy can be used for stimuli which are no longer physically present in different spatial locations. Thus the present paradigm allows us to explore the possibility of illusory conjunctions arising in memory, and to throw light on the strategy used by subjects to avoid errors of this type.

We chose colored letters and schematic faces in order to probe two very different classes of stimuli and to see how generally our predictions would apply. These stimuli differ in several respects: color and shape are integral in Lockhead's sense of coexisting spatially; on the other hand they are perhaps more likely to be processed by distinct neural channels than are the spatial patterns of eyes and mouth, both of which consist of lines, curves, angles, and so on. Thus even the features *within* the faces may themselves be defined by conjunctions of more elementary features, and may therefore require serial processing. On the other hand it has been plausibly suggested that faces are among the stimuli most likely to be directly perceived as gestalts. Evidence for this is found in Smith and Nielsen's (1970) data, which suggest that a unitary representation is set up initially and maintained over a short delay, although it is transformed to a feature list, perhaps verbally coded, by 10 seconds after presentation. They found that the number of relevant features had no effect on the time taken to code two successively presented faces as "same" at delays of 1 or 4 seconds but did at 10 seconds. Bradshaw and Wallace (1971) on the other hand found increased latencies with increased number of relevant features, and, like Tversky and Krantz (1969) (who used similarity scaling data) concluded that the features of schematic faces function as independent perceptual components. It seems of interest to use our method to provide further evidence on the question of separability versus integrality for facial features.

These experiments, together with others, will be reported more fully elsewhere. Here we will briefly outline the method and the main conclusions we draw from the results.

B. Method

1. Materials

The target items in Experiment II were a blue "O" and a pink "H". The nontargets included every other combination of the colors blue, pink, orange, and green with the letters "O", "H", "X", and "N". The letters were drawn with stencils in colored inks. Each letter subtended .8° and was centered .7° from the fixation point. The two target letters were placed above and below the fixation point and the two test letters on each trial were to the left and right of the fixation point. Each test display contained two different letters in two different colors. The target items in Experiment III were always the two faces shown at the top of Fig. 3. The nontargets included every other combination of the same eyes and mouths and the additional eyes and mouths shown in the lower half of Fig. 3. The faces were drawn in black ink using stencils for the outline and features. They subtended 2.3° and were centered 2.2° from the fixation point. Targets

FIG. 3   Examples of the faces used in Experiment III.

and test stimuli were otherwise shown in the same spatial arrangements as the colored shapes in Experiment II.

There were 15 different types of test trials, of which 11 were negatives and 4 positives. They are labeled by pairs of digits: the first digit gives the number of values (0, 1 or 2) that were shared by target and test display on the first attribute (color for Experiment II, eyes for Experiment III) and the second digit gives the number of matching values on the second attribute (shape for Experiment II and mouth for Experiment III). These are prefixed by the letters "N" for negative or "P" for positive. The N (1, 1) trials are further subdivided by using the two letters "t" and "d" to indicate whether the two matching values (one on each attribute) were spatially combined in the targets (t) or in the test displays (d). If they were spatially separate in both, no further symbol is used. Thus, for the targets blue "O" and pink "H" in Experiment II an example of the test trials labeled N(1, 1) would be blue "N" and green "H", an example of N(1, 1)t trials would be blue "N" and green "O" and an example of N(1, 1)d trials would be blue "H" and green "N." The negative trials N(1, 2) in which one color and two shapes matched and N(2, 1) in which two colors and one shape matched necessarily contained a shape and color which were combined in memory but separate in the test display and a shape and color which were combined in the test display but separate in memory (e.g., N(1, 2) might be blue "H" and green "O"). In trials N(2, 2) both shapes and colors matched but were wrongly paired (blue "H" and pink "O"). In the positive trials at least two matching values were always correctly combined, although in P(2, 1) trials there would be an additional matching color whose shape did not appear in the targets and in P(1, 2) trials the reverse. P(2, 2) trials had both target shapes and colors correctly combined.

Eight examples of each type of negative test card were made and 16 of each type of positive, giving 88 negatives and 64 positives altogether. The positions of the matching values in the test display were balanced.

2. Apparatus

The cards were presented in a three-field tachistoscopic. The background field contained a small black square in the center of the card, and was used to control fixation. The illumination of each field was the same. The onset of the test display also triggered a timer, which was stopped by the subject pressing one of two response keys.

3. Procedure.

The instructions required the subject to press the positive (right-hand) key if one or both of the test stimuli exactly matched one or both of the targets and the negative (left-hand key) otherwise. He was asked to respond as quickly and accurately as possible. Each subject was shown several examples of positives and of negatives to ensure that he understood the task. Different subjects were used in the two experiments, nine in Experiment II and six in Experiment III.

Each trial consisted of the following sequence of events: the subject fixated the background card; the experimenter said "Ready" and started the target display, which was presented for 1 sec. This was immediately followed by a test card, also presented for 1 sec. The RT was recorded and the subject was told whether it was correct or an error, the test card was changed, and the next trial was begun. The set of 152 test cards was presented in a different random order to each subject in each block.

Each subject was tested for three sessions consisting of about 20 practice trials on a random selection of the test cards, followed by the complete set of 152 test cards. A five-minute rest was allowed half-way through, plus any further breaks the subject requested. Each session took about 45 minutes.

C. Results

Figures 4 and 5 show the mean RTs for correct responses only and mean error rates on each type of test trial, averaged across subjects and blocks. The fitted lines are predicted by a model which is described below. In all the analyses of variance there was a highly significant effect of practice (blocks) but no interaction of practice with any other factor.

The results with the faces seem simpler and we will summarize these first. The parallel lines suggest that three factors have additive effects on RT (Sternberg, 1969). Let e be the number of matching pairs of eyes, m be the number of matching mouths, t be the number of pairs of matching values conjoined in the same target, and d be the number conjoined in the same test display. Then the data appear to fit the equation

$$\overline{RT} = \alpha + \beta_1 e + \beta_2 m + \gamma_1 t + \gamma_2 d.$$

An analysis of variance on the three types of N(1, 1) trials showed a significant effect of conditions; however Newman–Keuls tests showed that while N(1, 1)d differed significantly from the other two trial types the difference between N(1, 1)t and N(1, 1) was not significant. Thus it appears that $\gamma_1 = 0$, and that this term can be omitted from the equation. This indicates a clear asymmetry between the effects of conjunctions of matching values appearing in the targets and in the test displays.

On positive trials, P(2, 2) latencies were faster than all the others ($p < 0.001$), and P(2, 1) trials were significantly slower than P(1, 2) trials.

Similar results are shown with the colored shapes. The main difference between the two experiments appears to be in the effect of adding a second spatially separate match on a dimension which already has one matching value. With the faces, the increment in RT is almost as great as with the first match, while with

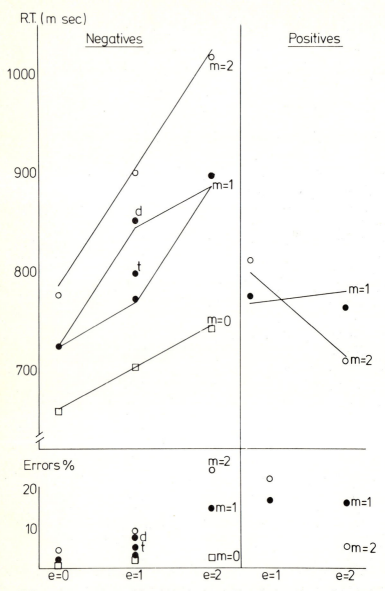

FIG. 4 RTs and error rates with schematic faces. The abscissa shows the number of matching pairs of eyes, and the parameter is the number of matching mouths.

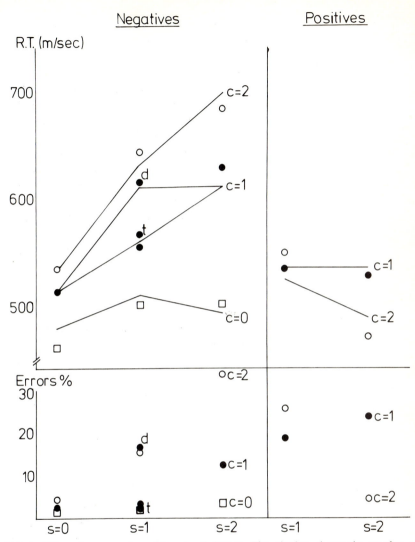

FIG. 5 RTs and error rates with colored letters. The abscissa shows the number of matching shapes and the parameter is the number of matching colors.

the colored shapes it is not. In fact a second matching shape leaves the latency almost unchanged unless it involves a potential conjunction error. Thus the equation here replaces the additive constants β_1 and β_2 by some other functions f_1 and f_2, and becomes $\overline{RT} = \alpha + f_1(c) + f_2(s) + \gamma_1 t + \gamma_2 d$, where c is the number of matching colors and s the number of matching shapes. Again, an analysis of all N(1, 1) trials showed a significant effect of γ_2 but no evidence that $\gamma_1 > 0$.

The error rates are also of interest. Subjects made a large number of errors on N(2, 2) trials, 33% in Experiment II and 25% in Experiment III. Thus on a quarter or a third of all trials they failed to detect that the four matching values in the test display were wrongly combined. Errors on P(2, 2) trials were very low suggesting a strong bias to respond "yes" when all 4 attribute values matched the targets. Errors on N(1, 1)d, N(2, 1), N(1, 2), and P(1, 1), P(1, 2), and P(2, 1) trials were also high, around 17% for colored shapes and 15% for the faces. These were more symmetrical across positive and negative trials. Errors on the other trial types were uniformly low.

D. Discussion

The error rates varied quite widely across trial types. Thus we need to consider whether comparisons of the associated latencies are valid. The discussion in the Appendix gives reasons why we feel that RTs can be meaningfully compared despite the differences in errors.

The main findings with respect to RTs are (1) a consistent increment in negative RT whenever a pair of matching values are conjoined in the test display; (2) no evidence that conjunction in the targets increases decision latencies when the matching values are spatially separate in the test display; (3) independent effects of adding matching values on each of the two different attributes, provided that their spatial separation or conjunction in the test display is controlled. The difference between the effects of conjunction in the targets and in the test displays suggests that subjects use the following ordered strategy. They first look for the presence of target features in the test display, checking each display position serially. In this way they avoid detecting illusory conjunctions among the stimuli which are physically present (as suggested by Experiment I). If they find a matching pair of features which are conjoined in the test display, they only then check whether these matching features were also conjoined in memory. The large number of errors on trials containing test display conjunctions of wrongly paired matching features suggests that the features do tend to break loose in memory. The errors on positive trials suggest that the features recombined to form incorrect conjunctions in memory. Thus neither the colored shapes nor the schematic faces formed stable, well-integrated memories, even with targets that remained constant over several hundred trials. This may explain why subjects apparently checked memory conjunctions last and only if it proved necessary.

A possible objection to this explanation of the difference in the way subjects treated targets and test stimuli is that the targets were constant from trial to trial while the test stimuli were varied. Any alternative account based on this factor was, however, excluded by a subsequent experiment (to be reported in more detail elsewhere), in which the same procedure was carried out except that the targets were varied within blocks as well as the test stimuli. There were no significant differences between the results from the two experiments.

1. A Possible Model

Figure 6 shows a model which would account quite well for the data with schematic faces. It assumes that subjects make a serial self-terminating check of the features in the test display, starting equally often (at least over the group as a whole) with eyes and with mouths. If the first feature tested proves negative in both display stimuli, the response is "no"; if one or both of the two is positive, they check the second feature only for the particular test stimuli on which the

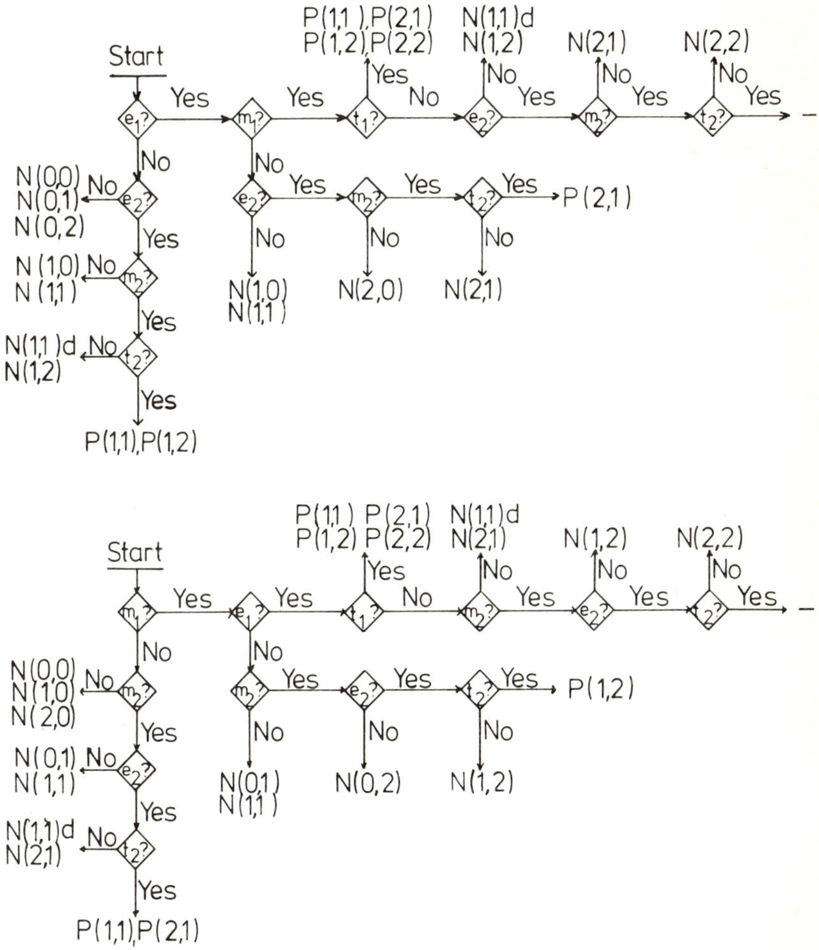

FIG. 6 Model for stages involved in successive matching of schematic faces. Subjects are assumed to follow equally often the stages shown in the top and in the bottom half of the figure. Key: $e_{1(or2)}$? Do the eyes in Display Position 1 (or 2) match those in either target face? $m_{1(or2)}$? Does the mouth in Display Position 1 (or 2) match that in either target face? $t_{1(or2)}$? Is the conjunction of matching features in Display Position 1 (or 2) also a conjunction in the target stimuli?

first feature was positive; if the second feature is also positive they check whether that particular conjunction occurred in memory. These operations are carried out in a serial, self-terminating sequence.

We can derive equations for these hypothesized additive components to predict the RTs in each condition. A successive-iteration program was used to estimate the best fitting times taken by each of 8 hypothetical components: β_1 (the time taken to check one pair of eyes), β_2 (the time taken to check one mouth), γ_2 (the time taken to check whether a positive conjoined pair of these display features were also spatially conjoined in the same target face), α (the other components of the RT which were not affected by differences between the experimental conditions). Each of these components could differ in duration depending on whether the outcome was negative or positive; this will be indicated by the subscript P or N. Thus, for example, the model predicts that $N(1, 1)d$ trials consisted equally often of the following four sequences of operations:

$$\beta_{1N} + \beta_{1P} + \beta_{2P} + \gamma_{2N} + \alpha_N;$$
$$\beta_{1P} + \beta_{2P} + \gamma_{2N} + \beta_{1N} + \alpha_N;$$
$$\beta_{2N} + \beta_{2P} + \beta_{1P} + \gamma_{2N} + \alpha_N;$$
$$\beta_{2P} + \beta_{1P} + \gamma_{2N} + \beta_{2N} + \alpha_N.$$

On average the number of each type of operation would be $.5\,\beta_{1N} + .5\,\beta_{2N} + \beta_{1P} + \beta_{2P} + \gamma_{2N} + \alpha_N$, which in the experiment gave a mean total RT of 852 msec. The data do not allow us to separate γ_{2P} and α_P, but the remaining seven components were estimated and gave the following values (all in msec): $\beta_{1N} = 116$, $\beta_{1P} = 100$, $\beta_{2N} = 101$, $\beta_{2P} = 109$, $\gamma_{2N} = 82$, $\alpha_N = 444$, $\gamma_{2P} + \alpha_P = 505$. The lines fitted to the data in Fig. 4 are those predicted by the model. Analysis of variance showed that the data did not depart significantly from the predictions. A regression of observed subject means on the predicted means for each trial type showed that the model accounted for 98.8% of the variance due to trial types.

We return now to the results with shape and color. What modification of the model would predict the slightly different pattern of results obtained here? The main difference appears to be that adding a second matching shape has little or no effect on RT unless it is spatially combined with a match on color. An obvious change to make in the model is to assume spatially parallel checking of the test display for the present of matching colors. Experiment I showed that parallel search for a target is possible for colors. If a matching color were found, all subsequent checks would still, if our arguments are valid, need to be spatially serial in order to ensure that only conjunctions of matches in the test display were checked for conjunction in memory.

The lines fitted in Fig. 5 show the predicted results with this one change in the model. We made the partly arbitrary assumption (as a first approximation) that the parallel decision that one color is negative and one positive takes the same time as the decision that both colors are negative. The reason for equating it with the time for two negative rather than two positive decisions was simply that we tried both and this gave a better fit to the data. However the assumption that the time taken when the decisions differ is equal to either of the times when the decisions are the same may not be justified. Nevertheless, we note that although the fit is slightly less good than for the faces, the model does account for 95.0% of the variance due to trial types, and the data do not depart significantly from the predictions on analysis of variance. (One of the biggest departures from the prediction is on P(2, 2) trials, which we suggest in the Appendix may reflect curtailed processing, with the check for conjunction in memory omitted on some proportion of occasions.) Thus this modified model may be along the right lines, although more detailed changes (to be discussed elsewhere) could perhaps improve the account given so far.

V. CONCLUSIONS

What general conclusions can we draw from these experiments? The visual search results suggest that identifying conjunctions of separable dimensions or features is one of the main factors precluding parallel processing and requiring focal attention to particular spatial locations at particular moments of time. It may be worth pushing the hypothesis to its extreme and stating the conditions under which attention limits would appear if this were their *only* determinant. If this were the case, one should fail to divide attention and be forced to process serially if and only if all three of the following conditions hold: (1) the discrimination required by the task involves conjunctions of properties; (2) these properties are separable rather than integral or unitized; and (3) the same properties are shared by the competing inputs and so would risk being inter-changed to form illusory conjunctions if they were registered in parallel. Further research is clearly needed to see how far this new formulation of the role of attention will go in accounting for past and future results.

The results of the successive matching experiments suggest that conjunctions of separable properties cannot always be held as unitary representations in memory, that they tend to dissolve into free-floating features which may wrongly recombine, and that retrieving and matching their conjunctions to a current input when the task requires it constitutes an independent and identifi-able stage of processing. These conclusions apply both to the different dimen-sions of shape and color and to different features *within* shapes, even when these are parts of schematic faces.

What then of normal, everyday perception? We handle complex multidimen-sional scenes at quite high rates with apparently little difficulty or error (e.g., Potter & Levy, 1969). We read prose at very high rates which seem to preclude serial identification of each letter. Are the present results restricted to the highly artificial and impoverished laboratory tasks we have tested, and if so why? We can offer two suggestions about these more complex stimuli. First, they are highly redundant: in order to perceive them correctly, a few diagnostic features are often sufficient. When this redundancy is removed or reduced it can be shown that many specific details fail to register (Rock, Halper, & Clayton, 1972), and that perception is considerably slower, possibly even serial rather than parallel (Biederman, 1972). The prolonged search through school photographs which is often needed to find one's own son or daughter offers further anecdotal evidence that parallel processing for highly familiar stimuli is not always possible (despite the one example to the contrary given by Neisser, 1964).

Second, it may be the case that the features we extract in identifying words or phrases, or in recognizing complex but familiar scenes are higher-order, relational ones. In other words we may solve the problem of integrating low level features or attributes by setting up higher-level units which respond directly to their conjunctions and which can therefore operate in parallel rather than serially. Fox (1975), for example, presents data suggesting that vertical symmetry may be responded to directly, in that its presence facilitates the matching of simultaneously presented letters and shapes. LaBerge's suggestion that familiarity produces "unitization" which allows "automatic processing" has already been mentioned. It is interesting to relate his finding to our suggestion that unitization may also remove attention limits in the sense of allowing parallel intake of simultaneous inputs. Further research is needed to discover how far our empirical criteria for unitization (parallel processing of a display, no conjunction errors in memory) correlate with the very different criteria proposed on the one hand by LaBerge (1973), and on the other by Garner (1970).

VI. APPENDIX

One possible explanation of the wide variation in error rates is that a speed—error tradeoff is operating, such that conditions with high error rates give mean correct latencies which are based on incomplete processing. If this is the case, the error latencies should on average be shorter than the correct latencies. In fact we found that in Experiment II errors on all negative trials and on P positive trials were faster than correct RTs. Grouping them according to approximately equal error percentages, the differences (correct minus error RTs) averaged 51 msec for N(0, 0), N(1, 0), N(2, 0), N(0, 1), N(0 2), N(1, 1), and N(1, 1)t trials, 59 msec for N(1, 1)d, N(2, 1), and N(1, 2) trials, and 181 msec for N(2, 2) trials. On P(1, 1) trials they were also 56 msec faster than correct RTs but on P(1, 2), P(2, 1), and P(2, 2) trials they were about the same as correct RTs. In Experiment III all the error RTs were about the same as the correct RTs (averaging 13 msec faster for N(0, 0), N(1, 0), N(2, 0), N(0, 1), N(0, 2), N(1, 1), and N(1, 1)t; 29

msec slower for N(1, 1)d, N(2, 1), and N(1, 2) trials, and 12 msec slower for P(1, 1) trials) with the exceptions again of N(2, 2) trials in which errors were 210 msec faster than correct RTs, and P(1, 2), P(2, 1), and P(2, 2) trials where errors were on average 70 msec slower than correct RTs.

Thus possible differences between conditions in speed–error tradeoff are suggested only by the results of condition N(2, 2), in which the processing appears to have been much curtailed on error trials. The slower errors in conditions P(2, 1), P(1, 2), and P(2, 2) may have resulted from wrong decisions at the final stage leading to further unnecessary processing. The question arises whether latencies on the *correct* N(2, 2) trials were also distorted by occasional incomplete processing. The answer depends on whether the curtailed processing, when it occurred, always led to an erroneous positive response, or whether it sometimes resulted in a negative response, which would of course be included in the correct RTs for that condition. If there were no bias to make a positive response after this curtailed processing, one should expect an equal number of fast negative errors on equivalent *positive* trials. This apparently did not occur on more than a small proportion of trials, if any, since the mean error latencies on positive trials were equal to or slower than the correct latencies. Thus it seems likely that curtailed processing on N(2, 2) trials always resulted in an erroneous positive response, and that the correct negative responses all reflect full processing. However the correct positive responses on any trial types which gave the same outcome as N(2, 2) trials up to the premature stopping point could include some trials with curtailed processing. P(2, 2) trials would be the ones most likely to match N(2, 2) trials up to the final stage, and the obtained mean P(2, 2) RT times may therefore underestimate the true processing time necessary. We conclude that RTs on all other trial types can probably be meaningfully compared, despite the differences in error percentages.

REFERENCES

Asch, S. E., Ceraso, J., & Heimer, W. Perceptual conditions of associations. *Psychological Monographs,* 1960, **74** (3, Whole No. 490).

Atkinson, R. C., Holmgren, J. C., & Juola, J. F. Processing time as influenced by the number of elements in a visual display. *Perception & Pyschophysics,* 1969, **6,** 321–326.

Bamber, D. Reaction times and error rates for "same"–"different" judgements of multi-dimensional stimuli. *Perception & Psychophysics,* 1969, **6,** 169–174.

Beck, J., & Ambler, B. The effects of concentrated and distributed attention on peripheral acuity. *Perception & Psychophysics,* 1973, **14,** 225–230.

Biederman, I. Perceiving real-world scenes. *Science,* 1972, **177,** 77–80.

Bradshaw, J. L., & Wallace, G. Models for the processing and identification of faces. *Perception & Psychophysics,* 1971, **9,** 443–448.

Checkosky, S. F. Speeded classification of multidimensional stimuli. *Journal of Experimental Psychology,* 1971, **87,** 383–388.

Day, R. S. Fusion in dichotic listening. *Psychonomic Bulletin,* 1967, **1,** 18.

Donderi, D., & Case, B. Parallel visual processing: Constant same–different decision latency with two to fourteen shapes. *Perception & Psychophysics,* 1970, **8,** 373–375.

Donderi, D. C., & Zelnicker, D. Parallel processing in visual same–different decisions. *Perception & Psychophysics,* 1969, **5,** 197–200.

Efron, R., & Yund, E. W. Dichotic competition of simultaneous tone bursts of different frequency: I Dissociation of pitch from lateralisation and loudness. *Neuropsychologia,* 1974, **12,** 249–256.

Egeth, H., Jonides, J., & Wall, S. Parallel processing of multielement displays. *Cognitive Psychology,* 1972, **3,** 674–698.

Fox, J. The use of structural diagnostics in recognition. *Journal of Experimental Psychology, Human Perception and Performance,* 1975, **104,** 57–67.

Gardner, G. T. Evidence for independent parallel channels in tachistoscopic perception. *Cognitive Psychology,* 1970, **4,** 130–155.

Garner, W. R. The stimulus in information processing. *American Psychologist,* 1970, **25,** 350–358.

Garner, W. R. *The processing of information and structure.* New York: Wiley, 1974.

Gouras, P. Color opponency from fovea to striate cortex. *Investigative Opthalmology,* 1972, **11,** 427–434.

Harvey, N., & Treisman, A. M. Switching attention between the ears to monitor tones. *Perception & Psychophysics,* 1973, **14,** 51–59.

Hawkins, H. L. Parallel processing in complex visual discrimination. *Perception & Psychophysics,* 1969, **5,** 56–64.

Jonides, J., & Gleitman, H. A conceptual category effect in visual search: O as letter or as digit. *Perception & Psychophysics,* 1972, **12,** 457–460.

LaBerge, D. Attention and the measurement of perceptual learning. *Memory & Cognition,* 1973, **1,** 268–276.

Lawrence, D. H. Two studies of visual search for word targets with controlled rates of presentation. *Perception & Psychophysics,* 1971, **10,** 85–89.

Lockhead, G. R. Processing dimensional stimuli: A note. *Psychological Review,* 1972, **79,** 410–419.

Marcel, A. J. Some constraints on sequential and parallel processing and the limits of attention. In A. F. Sanders (Ed.), *Attention and performance III.* Amsterdam: North Holland Publ., 1970.

Milner, P. M. A model for visual shape recognition. *Psychological Review,* 1974, **81,** 521–535.

Minsky, M. Steps towards artificial intelligence. Proceedings of the Institute of Radio Engineers, 1961, **49,** 8–30.

Neisser, U. Visual search. *Scientific American,* 1964, **210,** 94–102.

Neisser, U. Cognitive Psychology. New York: Appleton-Century-Crofts, 1967.

Peeke, S. C., & Stone, C. C. Focal and non-focal processing of color and form. *Perception & Psychophysics,* 1973, **14,** 71–80.

Potter, M. C., & Levy, E. I. Recognition memory for a rapid sequence of pictures. *Journal of Experimental Psychology,* 1969, **81,** 10–15.

Rock, I., Halper, F., & Clayton, T. The perception and recognition of complex figures. *Cognitive Psychology,* 1972, **3,** 655–673.

Santa, J. L. Verbal coding and redintegrative memory for shapes. *Journal of Experimental Psychology,* 1975, **104,** 286–294.

Saraga, E., & Shallice, T. Parallel processing of the attributes of single stimuli. *Perception & Psychophysics,* 1973, **13,** 261–270.

Smith, E. E., & Nielsen, G. D. Representations and retrieval processes in short-term memory: Recognition and recall of faces. *Journal of Experimental Psychology,* 1970, **85,** 397–405.

Sternberg, S. The discovery of processing stages: Extensions of Donder's method. In W. G. Koster (Ed.), *Attention and performance II.* Amsterdam: North Holland Publ., 1969.

Townsend, J. T. A note on the identifiability of parallel and serial processes. *Perception & Psychophysics,* 1971, **10,** 161–163.

Treisman, A. M. Strategies and models of selective attention. *Psychological Review,* 1969, **76,** 282–299.

Treisman, A. M. Perception and recall of simultaneous speech stimuli. In A. F. Sanders (Ed.), *Attention and performance III.* Amsterdam: North Holland Publ., 1970. Pp. 132–148.

Treisman, A. M., & Davies, A. Divided attention to ear and eye. In S. Kornblum (Ed.), *Attention and performance* IV. London: Academic Press, 1973. Pp. 101–117.

Treisman, A. M., & Riley, J. G. Is selective attention selective perception or selective response? A further test. *Journal of Experimental Psychology,* 1969, **79,** 27–34.

Tversky, A., & Krantz, D. H. Similarity of schematic faces: A test of interdimensional additivity. *Perception & Psychophysics,* 1969, **5,** 124–128.

18

An Analysis of Visual Search:
Entropy and Sequential Effects

Patrick M. A. Rabbitt
Geoffrey Cumming[1]
Subhash Vyas

Department of Psychology
Oxford University
England

ABSTRACT

A review of some experiments demonstrating sequential effects in serial choice-reaction tasks suggests that there are two distinct ways in which the presentation of one display may facilitate perceptual processing of another: (1) A current display may be compared for physical identity with its predecessor. Detection of identity will then allow a very fast response. (2) When successive signals are not physically identical, but nevertheless belong to a set to which the same response is made, recognition of the first may "prime" complex processes involved in recognition of the second. Transition analyses of visual search tasks show that in such situations, also, facilitation effects observed may be described under one or the other of these two headings. Further work on sequential effects shows that "a two-stage model" of perceptual processing, implying that successive signals are always compared for physical identity ("matching") as well as being subjected to more complex forms of perceptual processing ("analysis"), may be of general use in interpreting perceptual processing in sequential tasks.

I. INTRODUCTION

All theories of selective attention assume that the perception of one signal may affect the nature of judgements made about the next. None state this assumption clearly or attempt to explain how this can occur. Perhaps this is because

---

[1] Now at Department of Psychology, La Troke University, Melbourne, Australia.

theories are based on a very limited range of experiments on dichotic listening, in which the effects of context on recognition of particular items are difficult to determine, and the information-processing rate is never adequately controlled.

The most direct investigations of this phenomenon have been undertaken by Posner and Snyder (1975) using binary classification, "same–different" tasks. Posner and Snyder (1975) showed that "priming" by presentation of a word or symbol shortly before a binary comparison is made facilitates or slows the comparison depending on whether the "priming" display matches, or does not match the pair of signals subsequently presented for comparison. Posner and Snyder (1975) conclude that "all signals produce a temporary facilitation in the processing of items which share the same pathway" (Abstract, p. 699). The appropriately cautious phrasing of this statement underlines the fact that a problem has here been raised rather than solved.

It seems evident that if two successive displays D1 and D2, are identical, then the same set of functional operations (same *pathway*) will be undertaken in the analysis of both. These operations (it is assumed) will be carried out faster (and possibly more efficiently) for D2 than for D1 because they are repeated on the second occasion. What remains in question is what occurs when D1 and D2 are not identical, but similar. We may then say that *some* of the same functional operations (part of the same pathway perhaps) will be involved in processing D2. How we define "similarity," or assess "degrees of similarity," and whether we can empirically separate some functional operations (parts of the pathway) from others, or independently calibrate the effects of the repeated use of any one pathway independently of others, remain as open questions.

A study by Nickerson (1975) can be considered in these terms. Visual dot patterns representing English letters were presented for matching under various degrees of degradation by "noise" (extra dots). The patterns of "noise" dots were either correlated or uncorrelated between members of the pair to be compared. Times for both "same" and "different" judgments increased with noise level, increased more sharply when noise was uncorrelated than correlated, but increased at the same rate whether patterns were simultaneously or successively presented. Nickerson (1975) infers that even with successive presentation (1-sec interstimulus interval) the match between trace for D1 and input for D2 is made (at least partly) in terms of the degree of similarity of the *visual* representations of the two traces. For our present argument we may say that the greater the complexity of the patterns (the more noise dots there are in the field) the longer the comparison between displays will take. Given this, the greater the visual similarity between the patterns (noise "correlated" rather than "uncorrelated" between displays) the faster the comparison will be.

It will be seen that the implications of these results are rather different from those of Posner and Snyder (1975). The latter authors showed the effect of priming by presentation of a display D1 on a judgment *about* a complex display D2 (this did not involve a match or comparison *between* D1 and D2). Nickerson (1975) shows that if the decision about D2 concerns its comparison with D1, this comparison is faster when the two displays are identical, and becomes slower as the degree of difference between them increases. We may take a paper by Corcoran and Besner (1975) as illustrating a useful extension of this distinction.

Letter pairs were presented for matching. They differed in size, brightness, and contrast. These incidental variations in the physical representations of the letters affected times taken to make matches for physical identity (i.e., letter shapes) but did not affect the times taken to compare the *names* of letters which had different shapes (because they were in different cases). This emphasizes a distinction between *priming* experiments and *matching* experiments. In priming experiments we may say that the time taken to recognize D2 is reduced to the extent that analysis of D2 requires the same functional operations (the same pathways) as did analysis of a previous D1. In matching experiments, D1 and D2 will *not* generally require the same analyses. D1 may be "analyzed," de novo, as an entity in its own right. However D2 must be analyzed in terms of its similarity to or discrepancy from D1. Thus D1 determines the *way* in which D2 is analyzed. The same functional operations (the same pathways) *may* be used in the analysis of both D1 and D2. This may result in facilitation of analysis of D2, and we can *suggest* that this is one of the reasons why RTs are faster for "same" than for "different" judgements (in the former case identification of D2 will involve partial or complete repetition of processes employed in identification of D1). It must be emphasized that this is not a logically necessary assumption, nor one yet forced on us by empirical data.

Two cases of "identification" must be distinguished:

1. A display is identified as a particular one of a set of N possible different displays, and one of N possible responses is accordingly selected. This is the standard assumption in choice RT experiments with one-to-one stimulus-to-response mapping. This type of process is referred to here as "Type A," or *analytic processing.*

2. A display need not be identified as a particular one of N possible displays, but is only judged in terms of its physical similarity or difference to a single other display, presented simultaneously or shortly before it. This is the standard assumption in "binary comparison" experiments such as those we have described above. This type of process will be referred to as "Type B" or physical identity matching.

Posner and Snyder's (1975) results raise the possibility that in Case 1 the time taken to identify any particular display T in a series of N successively presented displays will vary, depending on whether identification of the immediately previous display $T-1$ required use of the same, or of different pathways. That is, whether recognition of display $T-1$ primes the subject to identify display T.

Facilitation of recognition of one display in a series by previous recognition of another identical display has long been considered as one possible source of facilitation (among others) giving rise to "repetition effects" in serial, self-paced choice RT tasks (see Bertelson, 1961; 1963; 1965; Rabbitt, 1968; Rabbitt & Vyas, 1973). It is interesting to note that explanations of repetition effects have been offered, without precise distinction, both in terms of analytic identification models of Type A and in terms of matching models of Type B. Thus Rabbitt and Vyas (1973) pointed out that facilitation might occur even when successive signals and successive responses were physically different, if rules of S–R mapping were repeated on successive trials. Duncan (in this volume) elegantly endorses this. The facilitation, like Posner and Snyder's (1975) "priming," could be categorized as referring to Type A analytic identification processes. A quite distinct suggestion by Bertelson (1963) may be taken as an example of a model of Type B. In fast serial tasks subjects may compare each new display received with their memory trace of the immediately preceding display. If input matches trace no further analysis is necessary, and the same response can be very rapidly repeated (the *repetition effect*). If input and trace do not match then subjects make some more exhaustive perceptual analysis of the current display to decide which of the N possible displays is, in fact, present. (Note that here, by definition, the size of N has no effect, or very little effect, on repetition RT, but alternation RT will vary directly with N.) We may call this the "two-test" model, in which both Type A and Type B processes are carried on. A previous paper discussing serial binary classification tasks has reviewed many of its implications, and empirically documented some of them (Rabbitt & Vyas, 1974).

The experiments described below are considered as tests as to whether the "priming hypothesis" or the "two-test" hypothesis better describes facilitation of identification of successively presented displays, and as to whether these hypotheses are necessarily mutually exclusive. Some of the experiments are briefly referred to because they are published elsewhere. Others are described in detail because they are not.

II.   IDENTITY OF CRITICAL AND OF INCIDENTAL CHARACTERISTICS OF SUCCESSIVE COMPLEX DISPLAYS

The first "test" assumed by the "two-test" hypothesis is essentially a binary same–different comparison, the memory trace of a previous event being compared for identity against current input. We have seen that when successive displays are compared for physical identity, variations in size, brightness, and nature of contrast (Corcoran & Besner, 1975) and in the amount and degree of correlation of visual noise (Nickerson, 1975) affect the time taken to make a match. We may consider whether an analogy in serial choice RT tasks can be found.

Rabbitt, Jordan, and Vyas (1977) required subjects to respond with one forefinger to appearances of the symbol "+" and with the other to the symbol "−." Symbols appeared on an in-line display, were $3/4$ in. across, and were illuminated in white light centered on a 1-in. background circle. Background circles were, with equal probability, and in random sequence, red, amber, or green. Subjects were told that variations in background color were introduced merely to relieve boredom during a long experiment (4 runs of 500 trials each). They were instructed to ignore the colors and to respond only to the symbols.

Each display, in turn, disappeared as soon as it was responded to, and the next came on within 50 msec. The analysis of interest concerned transitions between displays. Successive displays might have the same critical feature (symbol shape) and so would require the same response, but they might be either identical or different in terms of the incidental characteristic (background color). When successive symbols were different, the background color could, likewise, either be the same or different.

Analysis showed that RTs were faster when both symbol shape and background color were repeated than when shape was repeated but color changed. When symbol shape changed, however, RTs were unaffected by identity or change in background color.

A second experiment extended the first, using a many-to-one mapping task in which one response was made to either of the digits 1 or 2, and another to either of the digits 3 or 4. Digits occurred with equal probability in random order, and were presented against 1-in. diameter color patches as before. Subjects were again instructed to ignore color.

In this case three kinds of transitions were of interest. First, symbols (shapes) on successive displays might be identical. In this case background color might also be repeated, or might change. Second, successive symbols might be physically different (1 followed by 2, or 4 by 3) but might be "equivalent" in the sense that they required the same response. Background color might also be the same or change. Finally, successive symbols might both be physically different (1 followed by 3, or 4 by 2) and require different responses. The background color might, of course, change or not as before.

The point of interest was again the effect of identity or change in incidental display characteristics. When identical symbols followed each other, RTs were again some 51 msec faster if background colors were identical than if they were different. However, if successive symbols were not identical, whether they required the same response (i.e., were equivalent) or not (i.e., were new) variations in background color did not affect RT.

This is consistent with the "two-test" hypothesis. We may assume that each display is compared against the memory trace of its predecessor. If there is a match, the same response can immediately be repeated. In both the experiments described above RTs were faster when successive displays were identical in terms of both critical (symbol shape) and incidental (color) characteristics than when the incidental characteristic changed. In contrast, when successive displays were different because the *symbol* had changed (whether or not the new symbol required the same response) variations in the incidental characteristics (color) made no difference to RT. This is consistent with the assumption that if the match between display N and display $N-1$ fails, whether in terms of a critical *or* in terms of an incidental characteristic, some more extended perceptual analysis is necessary to identify the new display. Evidently this latter analysis is sufficient to identify the signal as a particular member of the signal set. The background color makes no difference to this analysis. We may note, in passing, that Corcoran and Besner (1975) also found that variations in symbol size, contrast, or brightness, which affected times taken for physical identity matching, had little or no effect when matching was for name between physically different (upper and lower case) letters.

A general distinction between "matching" (Type B) and "analytic" (Type A) processes can thus be derived. With matching processes subjects cannot ignore redundant information. Displays are compared "holistically." In contrast, analytic processes involve the separation of redundant from critical information, and it seems are capable of optimization by practice, the number of critical cues employed being reduced by practice (Rabbitt, 1967).

It also seems a defensible position that both Type B and Type A analysis is involved in serial identification of displays. Each display is matched against the memory trace of its predecessor (Type B match). If this match is successful no further analysis is necessary (though of course it may take place). If the match is unsuccessful, then Type A analysis is necessary to identify the new display. Note that if we adopt a "two-test" hypothesis this commits us to two distinct descriptions of the way in which the presentation of one display can facilitate response to the next. We may have facilitation by matching (Type B). We may also have facilitation by priming; and this must involve processes of Type A, that is, of analytic rather than matching processes.

III. DISPLAY IDENTITY, RESPONSE EQUIVALENCE, AND THE EFFECTS OF PRACTICE

Rabbitt, Jordan, and Vyas' (1976) results cannot be taken as evidence that in *all* many-to-one signal-to-response mapping experiments transitions between equivalent displays, to which the same response is repeated. This question was first asked by Bertelson (1965) following a technique introduced by LaBerge (1963). Practiced subjects showed no difference between RTs on "identical" and "equivalent" transitions. RTs for both these transitions were faster, however, than for "new" transitions between displays to which different responses had to be made. Rabbitt (1968) showed that practice was a critical variable. As can be seen from Table 1, early in practice RTs for equivalent transitions are as slow as RTs for "new" transitions, and RTs for identical transitions are much faster than either. Later in practice Bertelson's (1965) results were again obtained.

TABLE 1

RTs for Transitions between Signals and Responses in
Three Many-to-One Mapping Tasks, Early and Later in
Practice[a]

	Responses 301–600		Responses 1201–1500	
Two responses 4 signals	Mean	S.D.	Mean	S.D.
New signal/new response	584	219	424	182
Equivalent signal/same response	567	231	394	126
Identical signal/same response	491	184	383	142
Two responses 8 signals				
New signal/new response	608	251	484	197
Equivalent signal/same response	580	237	416	159
Identical signal/same response	510	219	377	162
Four responses 8 signals				
New signal/new response	725	270	592	201
Equivalent signal/same response	720	284	532	215
Identical signal/same response	652	247	416	224

[a]After Rabbitt (1968).

Early in practice it seems that matching procedures (Type B) are faster than analytic processes (Type A). Late in practice there is no advantage when identical displays follow each other, and consequently no reason to assume that each display is initially matched for physical identity against the memory trace of its predecessor. Identical and equivalent transitions may remain faster than new transitions simply because responses are repeated, and we need not assume any facilitation of perceptual identification. This seems a perverse assumption since as Table 1 shows, differences between identical and equivalent transitions which disappear with 1300-trials practice when the signal and response entropy is small are retained for conditions of greater entropy. Moreover, RTs to equivalent transitions after practice are faster than RTs to identical transitions *before* practice. Thus, after practice, identification RTs are faster than matching RTs were when practice began. A hypothesis to account for the effects of practice must account for the gradual change in the *efficiency*, and more importantly also in the *nature* of perceptual processing.

If we use the "two-test" hypothesis as a working basis for discussion there are alternative descriptions. We may assume that early in practice the first test (match) always precedes the second test (identification). The second test determines initiation of a response only conditionally upon failure of the first. If we believe that tests are successive in time, and conditional in their control of the response, we might assume that the first test (match) is no longer made when subjects are highly practiced. This would imply that practiced subjects identify signals only by the second test (analytic procedure, Type A) and that transitions between identical signals are dealt with no faster than transitions between equivalent signals (since there is, in effect, no longer any advantage for identical transitions).

The entailments of this hypothesis are more complex than first appears, since we see from Table 1 that RTs for equivalent transitions late in practice are faster than RTs for identical transitions early in practice. An Analysis of Variance and Scheffe's S^2 on the individual subjects' data from which mean RTs in Table 1 were derived confirmed this difference ($p < 0.01$). This would mean that late in practice identification by "Test 2" (Type A) procedures is *faster* than was identification by "Test 1" (Type B matching) procedures early in practice. A more parsimonious hypothesis, therefore, is that at all stages in practice Test 1 and Test 2 procedures are both carried out, not successively, but rather in parallel. Late in practice both procedures may take the same time, or Test 2 procedures may actually be faster. Thus responses are initiated by the outcomes of Test 2 rather than by the outcomes of Test 1 procedures, simply because "identification" is now faster than "matching," whether successive displays are physically identical or not.

This raises the obvious question as to why practice should reduce the time taken for Test 2 (Type A) procedures more than the time taken for Test 1 (Type B matching) procedures? Is it not rather more logical to suppose that *both* tests become faster with practice so that tests of Type B continue to be faster than tests of Type A?

Rabbitt (1967) investigated the effects of practice upon the efficiency with which subjects learned to distinguish between two sets of complex symbols (target and background letters) in visual search tasks. It appears that, with practice, subjects learn to use an optimally small number of cues, specific to distinctions between target and background sets. In other words they learn to ignore redundant or misleading aspects of complex displays. We have seen that the physical identity matching comparisons described as "Test B" procedures do *not* allow the subject to discard redundant information (Rabbitt, Jordan, & Vyas, 1976). If holistic comparison procedures of this type are employed, there is thus no scope for improvement in their efficiency by selective use of some display features and selective neglect of others. In contrast we know that the development of economical identification procedures (Type A) results in faster discriminations among complex symbols (Rabbitt, 1967). It is therefore a reasonable assumption that practice should reduce the time taken for Type A matches more than it should reduce the time taken for Type B matches, so that at some point, Type A matches would be as fast, or even faster than Type B matches. At this point in practice, physical identity of successive displays, concerning Type B matches only, would neither convey any advantage nor any handicap.

The evidence so far considered does not allow us to verify these speculations, but allows us to adopt them as plausible guidelines for the interpretation of the experiments described below. One caveat is clear. We cannot allow ourselves the naivete of supposing that practice simply reduces the time taken for processes of perceptual identification, but does not affect the nature, nor the relative efficiencies of these processes. On the contrary, it is clear that practice not only does affect the duration but also changes the nature of processes of perceptual analysis. A model of functional processes in perceptual identification which is valid at one stage of practice cannot necessarily be assumed to be so at another. All further discussions of experimental results must take this into consideration.

IV. MATCHING AND ANALYTIC PROCEDURES IN VISUAL SEARCH

Visual search experiments are paradigm cases of selective attention in perception. We may therefore consider how far our hypotheses of matching (Type B) and analytic (Type A) processes help us to interpret the effects of one display upon the next in visual search.

A. Experiment I

1. Equipment and Method

A Linc 8 computer was programmed to present arrays of five capital letters of the alphabet simultaneously in a horizontal line across the center of a 20 cm X 15 cm rectangular cathode ray tube display. The letters were from the standard Linc 8 character set, averaging 4 mm in width and 5 mm in height, spaced at 2 mm apart. Subjects observed the screen through a light-tight tunnel 50 cm long, placing their foreheads against a padded rest. The letters appeared upon the scope, illuminated in green, and were very clearly visible under these dim conditions. (The equipment was in a darkened room and subjects were dark adapted before testing.)

Each display of five letters with equal probability might, or might not, contain one member of a target set of four letters, A, B, C, or D. Target letters might occur with equal probability at any display position (i.e., 1 to 5 from left to right). The remaining (background) letters on displays were obtained by random equiprobable sampling of the 22 capital letters E through Z, with the constraint that no letter was repeated on the same display.

When subjects located any target letter on a display they pressed a key under one of their forefingers (T response). As soon as they were sure that no target letter was present they pressed a key under the other forefinger (N response). When either key was pressed the display disappeared (within 1 msec) and was followed by a new display 100 msec later (R–S Condition 1); or 2000 msec later (R–S Condition 2). This continued for a run of 200 successive displays and responses, subjects being given knowledge of results and urged to work as fast and accurately as possible. The computer recorded all symbols present on each display, the time elapsed between the onset of each display, and the response to it (to within 1 msec) and the response actually made (T or N, identified as correct or wrong). Each subject experienced eight runs of 200 responses, four in each R–S interval condition, during a single testing session. Displays were generated by a randomizing program so that no two runs were the same. R–S conditions were run in order balanced across subjects.

Subjects were 8 women and 4 men, students at the Oxford Polytechnic, aged between 17 and 22 years. They were paid 30 pence for the single experimental session.

2. Results

The results from the two conditions are here analyzed separately, those from Condition 1 (R–S intervals of 100 msec) being considered first.

A data-sort program identified errors. These averaged 4.7% of all responses made. All these errors, and the responses immediately following them, were disregarded. The remaining correct responses were sorted into four kinds of transitions between displays (i.e., TT, NT, NN, and TN). Mean RTs for each of these transitions are given in Table 2. Wilcoxon's tests across individual subjects' data showed that TT transition RTs were significantly faster than NN transition RTs ($p < 0.001$, two-tailed) and NT transitions faster than TN transitions ($p < 0.001$, two-tailed). In other words, taking comparable cases, subjects responded faster when a target was present than when it was not.

This may be expected, on the assumption that if no target is present all letters on a display must always be inspected, while if a target is present it will, on

TABLE 2
Mean RTs for Each of the Four Kinds of Transitions

	Mean RT	
Successive displays contain targets (TT transitions)	879 msec	194
Target display follows nontarget display (NT transitions)	908 msec	214
Nontarget display follows nontarget display (NN transitions)	1094 msec	218
Nontarget display follows target display (TN transitions)	1108 msec	201

average, be located after three letters have been inspected. We thus have an estimate for the average time taken to decide that any background letter is *not* a target letter, that is, (N RT − T RT)/2. This gives us an estimated scanning time of 100 4 − 908 msec/2, that is, 92 msec per letter. This is (perhaps surprisingly) very close to the similar estimate of 100 msec obtained by Neisser (1963). It also confirms that in this task, as in Neisser's, displays were scanned in a serial, self-terminating fashion.

Our interest in these data is the effect one display has upon the time taken to analyze the next. Individual subjects' mean RTs for TT, NT, NN, and TN transitions were subjected to a two-way Analysis of Variance (ANOVA). Main terms for subjects ($p < 0.01$) and transition classes ($p < 0.001$) were significant, but there was no interaction between them ($p > 0.2$). Scheffe's S^2 test was used to rank order mean RTs for the 4 transition classes. This was:

$$\text{RT(TT)} \overset{***}{<} \text{RT(NT)} \overset{**}{<} \text{RT(NN)} \overset{+}{<} \text{RT(TN)}$$

where *** = $p < 0.01$, ** = $p < 0.05$, and + = not significantly different ($p > 0.05$).

It seems, therefore, that there is a "repetition effect," in that a target is located faster if the preceding display also contains a target than if it does not. It seems that this effect must be due to perceptual rather than to response factors. The same key is also pressed twice in succession for NN transitions, but these are no faster than TN transitions.

This prompted a further analysis to compare runs of T transitions with runs of N transitions.

Individual subjects' mean RTs were obtained for runs of two to five successive T responses or successive N responses. Means of these means are set out in Table 3.

While RT(T) declines with (T) run length, RT(N) does not appear to decline with (N) run length. This was checked by a three-way ANOVA across individual subjects' means. Main terms for differences between subjects ($p < 0.001$), differences between (T) and (N) RTs ($p < 0.001$), and for differences in RT with run length ($p < 0.01$) were all significant. The only significant interaction term was that between response type (T versus N) and run length ($p < 0.05$). We may gather from this that T responses are, as we know, faster than N responses, and also that RT(T) declines with the length of a run of successive T displays, but RT(N) is not affected by run length (N).

It seems that identification of a target on one display facilitates identification of a target on the next. We may now enquire whether this facilitation is due to changes in the efficiency with which Type A (analytic) processes are carried on, whether it rather implies that Type B (matching) processes are possible, and occur, or whether both kinds of process are involved.

When two T displays follow each other they may both contain the identical target letter (TT_I) or may contain different target letters (TT_D). Further, the

TABLE 3

Experiment I. RTs (in msec) for Runs of Displays Containing Targets, and of Displays Not Containing Targets (R–S interval 100 msec)

Number of repeated responses		1	2	3	4	5
Successive displays do not contain targets (N runs)	$\bar{X}$	1081	1076	1062	1098	1139
		(σ 249)	(σ 250)	(σ 218)	(σ 200)	(σ 312)
Successive displays contain targets (T runs)	$\bar{X}$	908	909	853	802	–
		(σ 182)	(σ 194)	(σ 172)	(σ 112)	

target letters in both displays may occur in identical display positions (so that the letter in the second display is shifted 0 positions with respect to the first) or they may occur in different target positions (the letter in the second display being shifted 1, 2, 3, or 4 positions to the left or right with respect to the first). A data sort separated TT_I from TT_D transitions, and within each case separated transitions with 0, 1, 2, and $\geqslant 3$ relative positional shifts. Means of individual subjects' mean RTs for each of these cases are presented in Table 2.

A three-way ANOVA was run across individual subjects' mean RTs. Main terms for differences between subjects ($p < 0.01$), between TT_I and TT_D transitions ($p < 0.01$), and for differences in degrees of positional displacement ($p < 0.01$) were all significant. The only significant interaction term was that between transition type and degree of displacement ($p < 0.01$). We conclude that TT_I transitions are significantly faster than TT_D transitions, and that RT rises with degree of positional displacement. Further, the effect of positional displacement upon RT is more substantial for TT_I than for TT_D transitions.

Inspection of Table 4 suggests that this letter interaction occurs only because RT (TT_I) is exceptionally fast when successive displays occur in identical positions. Apart from this data point, the increase in RT with extent of positional displacement seems to be the same for both types of transition.

To check this, difference RTs ($TT_D - TT_I$) were obtained at each degree of positional separation from each individual subject's mean RTs. These were

TABLE 4

Experiment I. Times (msec) for Transitions between Displays with Identical or with Different Targets as a Function of Relative Positional Separation of Targets in Successive Displays (R–S Interval = 100 msec)

	Target in identical position	Target shifted ±1 position	Target shifted ±2 positions
Successive displays have identical targets	676 (σ54)	875 (σ112)	971 (σ179)
Successive displays have different targets	830 (σ114)	882 (σ152)	1049 (σ242)

compared by Wilcoxon's tests. It emerged that ($TT_D - TT_I$) at a positional separation of 0 is greater than at any other ($p < 0.01$, two-tailed). In contrast $TT_D - TT_I$ difference RTs were not significantly different between other positions.

Physical identity of successive targets thus markedly reduces RT when they follow each other in identical display positions. This might occur because subjects had no time to change their points of fixation between successive displays (the R–S interval was 100 msec). Recurrence of an identical target at this point of fixation allowed comparison by Type B (matching), and hence very fast RTs. However, if successive targets were physically different immediate matching was not possible so that RTs were slower. This was also the case if successive targets were identical but followed each other in different positions. In this case the first letter fixated on the new display would be a background letter. Matching would therefore not be possible at this point, nor as the display was subsequently scanned, since the "last stimulus" encountered would be whatever background letter had last been inspected.

On these assumptions the "two-test" hypothesis fits these data quite well.

The main question begged is the dependence of this pattern of results upon stability of fixation – that is, the assumption that when a subject locates a target on a display he begins his scan of the next display at the same location. This is plausible, because the interval between successive displays (100 msec) is some 50 msec shorter than minimum intersaccadic intervals generally reported in the literature. Analysis of Condition 2, in which the RS interval was 2000 msec, permitted a test of this assumption. The first analysis carried out was over individual subjects' RTs for runs of target and nontarget responses. Means of these means are presented in Table 5.

A three-way ANOVA revealed significant differences in RT between subjects ($p < 0.01$) between T RTs and N RTs ($p < 0.001$), and significant overall changes in RT with run length ($p < 0.01$). The only significant interaction was between RT type (T or N) and run length ($p < 0.01$). As in Condition 1 we find that RT reduces with runs of successive targets, but not with runs of successive nontargets. There are, again, clear signs of facilitation of perceptual analysis by recurrence of target letters in successive displays.

TABLE 5

Experiment I. Runs of Repeated Responses When Successive Displays (in msec) Did and Did Not Contain Targets (R–S interval = 2000 msec)

Number of repeated responses		1	2	3	4
Successive displays do not contain targets	$\bar{X}$	1021	1028	1041	1000
(N runs)		(σ 184)	(σ 172)	(σ 161)	(σ 152)
Successive displays contain targets (T runs)	$\bar{X}$	859	824	821	809
		(σ 178)	(σ 154)	(σ 158)	(σ 169)

A more detailed data-sort separated transitions between TT_I and TT_D transitions and degrees of positional displacement from 0 to $\geqslant \pm 3$. Means of individual subjects' means are plotted in Table 6.

A three-way ANOVA gave significant main terms for differences between subjects ($p < 0.01$) between transition types (TT_I transitions are faster than TT_D, $p < 0.001$) and for effects of positional displacement on RT ($p < 0.001$). There were no significant interaction terms.

When the interval between successive displays is so brief that it is not likely that a subject has time to refixate (Condition 1), RTs are especially fast if identical targets follow each other in identical positions. We have suggested that this is because the last symbol inspected on the earlier display (a target) can be immediately compared against the first symbol inspected on the later display (also a target). Where the interval between successive displays is as long as 2000 msec this is not the case. Nor would we expect it to be, since it is quite unlikely that the same point of fixation will be maintained on a blank CRT screen for two seconds between displays. The literature on binary comparisons further suggests that RTs for physical identity matches increase sharply with ISIs between 0 and 2000 msec. It has sometimes been suggested that this is because an "iconic" memory trace for the physical characteristics of a particular display cannot be maintained as long as this (Posner, 1969). This might imply that Type B physical identity matching cannot take place with R–S intervals of 2000 msec, whether fixation is maintained on a display or not. Consistent with this view are findings such as those by Bertelson and Renkin (1966) that "repetition effects" which are very marked at R–S intervals of 150 msec almost disappear when R–S intervals are increased to 1500 msec or longer.

Although Condition 2 (2000 msec R–S intervals) shows no apparent reduction of RT due to Type B matching, both Condition 1 and Condition 2 show reduction in RT for transitions between displays containing identical targets in cases in which matching cannot occur (gross spatial displacements of targets on successive displays). We have inferred that where matching does not occur, identification is by some more complex (Type A) analytic process. We must now

TABLE 6

Experiment I. Times (msec) for Transitions between Displays with Identical or with Different Targets as a Function of Relative Positional Separation of Targets on Successive Displays (R–S interval = 2000 msec)

	Target in identical position	Target shifted ±1 position	Target shifted ±2 positions
Successive displays have identical targets	715 (σ178)	792 (σ184)	873 (σ114)
Successive displays have different targets	843 (σ192)	851 (σ174)	945 (σ177)

also infer that this process of perceptual analysis can be facilitated by recency effects. That is, a target is recognized faster if the subject has recent experience of it, even though he may have scanned other symbols on a display (background symbols) in the interim. We shall refer to this recency effect as *priming* of Type A perceptual analysis, after Posner and Snyder (1975).

Two empirical distinctions between RT reduction due to matching and to priming are already apparent. First, as we have seen, matching is only possible when the last symbol fixated on one display is identical with the first symbol fixated on the next *without intervening fixations or scans of other symbols.* It may also be the case that even if these conditions are met, matching cannot occur if the time elapsed between successive displays is as long as 2 sec. In contrast priming can occur if targets on successive displays are identical, even though other symbols (such as background symbols) are scanned and identified between successive presentations. As can be seen from Table 2, the priming effects in this case are equally strong whether the interval between successive displays is 100 msec or 2 sec.

The main logical distinction between Type B matching processes and Type A signal identification processes is that the former cannot be affected by overall signal entropy, while the latter evidently are. If the trace of one signal is matched against another subsequently perceived the number of all other possible signals on the display is irrelevant to this *particular* comparison. Thus we would not assume that Type B matches are affected by variations in signal entropy. If a signal is to be identified as a unique entity among a range of other possibilities, the extent of this range (signal entropy) will certainly have an effect (Rabbitt, 1964). Thus we should expect Type A signal analysis to be affected by variations in signal entropy. A further test of the explanatory value of a distinction between "Matching" and "Analytic" procedures in visual search is, therefore, to compare effects of variations in signal entropy upon target detection times in cases in which identical targets followed each other in identical display positions at very brief R—S intervals, and in cases in which either the identity of the target, or its position, or both, changed on successive trials.

B. Experiment II

1. Equipment and Method

The Linc 8 system was used as before to present displays of five items with R—S intervals of 100 msec. There were two conditions of signal entropy. During four runs of 200 displays subjects again searched for the four target letters A, B, C, or D among background letters from the vocabulary of 22 letters, E through Z. During another four runs of 200 displays subjects again searched for these four target letters, but among a vocabulary of only five background letters, E, F, G, H, and I. Thus at least four, and sometimes five background letters were repeated (though in different positions) on successive displays. Half the displays contained target letters, the other half did not. The individual target letters were equally frequent, and occurred equally often in all display positions. The same was true of the background letters. Half the subjects began with the high-entropy condition and half with the low-entropy condition. Runs were alternated between conditions until practice was completed.

Subjects were 8 men and 12 women, aged 17 to 23, students at the Oxford Technical College, each paid 30 pence to serve for a single experimental session.

2. Results

The comparison of interest here concerned only transitions between successive displays which both contained targets. These transitions were extracted from the data to separate transitions between identical and dissimilar targets and within each of these classes to separate transitions in which targets on successive displays occurred in identical positions and transitions in which successive targets were displaced one, two, three, or four display positions relative to each other. Means of individual subjects' means are given in Table 7.

The hypothesis guiding analysis of these data was that when the vocabulary of background letters was small targets would be more quickly located (because target letters would be more quickly distinguished from background letters, and possibly also from each other; see Rabbitt, 1967). This difference would be evident when identical targets followed each other in different positions, and when different targets followed each other in different positions. It might also be evident when different targets followed each other in the same position (see Rabbitt, 1967). This is because in all these cases targets are identified by some (Type A) analysis, and the complexity (and so the duration) of this analysis might be expected to vary with the sizes of sets of stimuli between which discriminations must be made.

In contrast, when identical targets follow each other in identical display positions we would assume that direct physical-identity matching (Type B matching) occurred. Since this matching concerns only the two symbols (trace and input) compared at any time, and *not* the entire range of other possible

TABLE 7
Experiment II. Transitions (in msec) between Displays Containing Targets when the Vocabulary of Background Letters Varied from 5 to 22 Items: Effects of Target Identity and Difference, and of Spatial Separation (R–S interval = 100 msec)

	Identical targets Identical positions	Identical targets displaced	New targets identical positions	New targets displaced
Background vocabulary of 22 letters	684 (σ88)	952 (σ184)	843 (σ212)	981 (σ210)
Background vocabulary of 5 letters	662 (σ50)	886 (σ91)	801 (σ218)	904 (σ194)

symbols which *might* have to be compared, we would assume that matching time is independent of size of background vocabulary. In brief, when identical targets followed each other in identical display positions we would expect RT to be the same whether background letter vocabularies were 5 to 22. We would expect all other transitions to be faster with background vocabularies of 5 than of 22.

A four-way ANOVA gave significant main terms for differences between subjects ($p < 0.001$), for differences between background vocabulary sizes ($p < 0.001$), for differences between transitions between identical and different targets ($p < 0.001$), and for differences between the same and different display positions ($p < 0.01$). No interaction term involving subjects was significant. The second-order interaction for vocabulary size versus target identity or difference was significant ($p < 0.01$) as was the interaction between vocabulary size and same or different display position ($p < 0.01$). The second-order interaction term between target "identity"/"difference" versus "same" or "different" display positions was also significant ($p < 0.01$). Finally the third-order interaction term between these last three main terms was significant ($p < 0.05$).

The error term from this ANOVA was used to calculate Scheffe's S^2 rank order statistic to obtain estimates of the significance of differences between means for each of the different types of transitions investigated.

This allowed the main question to be answered. As can be seen from Table 3, mean RTs for cases in which identical targets follow each other in the same display positions are almost equal. The S^2 confirmed that they could not be considered to be significantly different ($p > 0.2$). However, both these RTs for identical transitions were significantly faster than for any other transitions ($p < 0.05$ to $p < 0.001$ in all cases).

In contrast, for every *other* type of transition examined, RT was faster for the small vocabulary displays than for the large vocabulary displays ($p < 0.05$ to $p < 0.001$).

Our working hypothesis is therefore supported. When identical targets follow each other in the same display positions, variations in the vocabulary of letters used upon displays does not affect RT. Moreover RT is shorter than for any other type of transition. This is what we should expect if these successive identical targets were matched against each other. Since only the trace of the last target and perceptual input from the currently located target are here involved, it is understandable that RT is not affected by the range of possible items (target or background) which *might* have occurred on the display.

In contrast, whenever targets on successive displays appeared in different locations, matching was not possible, and the entropy of displays affected RT. This is what we would expect if Type A analytic procedures were involved, since here any target must be identified as distinct from the entire, larger or smaller, set of background items.

It is interesting that variations in background set size should affect target identification RT when different targets follow each other in the same display location. In this case, one might at first think that variations in background target ensemble would be irrelevant. However further reflection shows that the contrary must be the case. The range of critical cues, features, or characteristics necessary to identify targets from background items will increase with the size of the set of background items, independently of the size of the target set (see Rabbitt, 1967). Thus more "evidence" will be required to identify any symbol as a member of the target set when the background set is larger than when it is small.

We have now shown that one experimental variable (R–S interval duration) affects the efficiency of (Type B) physical identity matching, but not of (Type A) analytic identification. Another variable (background-set size) affects the efficiency of Type B but not of Type A processes. These processes are therefore demonstrably distinct, and must be distinguished when assessing the effects of set in visual search.

There are two important gaps in this account. The first is that while Type B matching facilitation has been shown in conventional, serial, self-paced CRT tasks (see Rabbitt, Jordan, & Vyas, 1976) there is no evidence for facilitation of Type A analytic identification outside the context of the present experiments. Within these experiments evidence for this facilitation consists simply of the fact that targets are located faster when they have occurred in the previous display even though (presumably) some background items have been scanned between one identification of a target and fixation of the next. The relatively fast RTs for equivalent transitions in serial self-paced CRT tasks (e.g., Rabbitt, 1968) also cannot be taken as clear evidence for facilitation of perceptual processing of one signal by recognition of its predecessor. Since responses are repeated to successive equivalent signals motor facilitation alone may account for these effects.

V. SIGNAL RECENCY EFFECTS IN SERIAL CRT TASKS: PRIMING FOR PHYSICAL IDENTITY OR FOR CODE IDENTITY?

In these visual-search experiments we suspect a (Type A) "signal recency effect" as well as a (Type B) "matching" "signal repetition effect." That is, a particular target is identified faster if it has recently been encountered, even though some different background items may have been scanned between its first and the second appearance.

A parallel phenomenon in serial self-paced CRT would therefore be a demonstration that recurrence of a signal reduces RT even after an intervening signal had appeared and a response had been made to it. This was in fact found by Rabbitt, Rodgers, and Vyas (1977), using a task in which subjects made one response to either of the letters A or B and another response to either of the letters C or D. Subjects experienced runs of 200 such signals in random order with R–S intervals of 150 msec. Post hoc data sorts separated cases of double-response alternations. These were cases in which a subject responded with one hand, then with the other, and then again with the first. Within these identical response sequences two kinds of signal sequences could be compared. The signal A could be followed by the "identical" signal A. Alternatively the signal B might be followed by either of the signals C or D and then by the equivalent signal A. Rabbit, Rodgers, and Vyas (1977) found that repetition of a signal which thus had occurred "two places back" facilitated RT. That is, sequences of the Type A (C or D) A gave RTs which were about 50 msec faster than sequences of the Type B (C or D) A.

Two interesting features of this effect were apparent. First, its magnitude (i.e., RT nonrepeat–RT repeat) increased with the ensemble of signals employed: that is, this difference-RT was greater for two sets of four signals than for two sets of two, and greater still for two sets of eight. This is because RT rose with signal ensemble size, but less sharply when signals were repeated than when they were not.

A second, closely related, feature of the effect was its relationship to the degree of practice attained at a particular task. It was most marked early in practice, when subjects were comparatively unfamiliar with the signal–response allocations used. With easy tasks, for example, with two sets of two signals, the effect disappeared after subjects had experienced two runs of 200 signals and responses. The larger the size of the signal ensemble (e.g., 2 sets of 4 signals; 2 sets of 8 signals; and so on.) the larger was the initial effect, and the more practice was required before the effect disappeared. This is not surprising, since the larger the signal ensemble the longer subjects might be expected to take to learn it, and the greater the advantage of being "reminded" of a signal by its recurrence would be.

In terms of the models we have been discussing, a further obvious question was whether facilitation occurred because the physical characteristics of the signal were rendered easier to recognize by recent occurrence, or whether facilitation was due to activation of a particular signal–response allocation code (in less pompous jargon, because the subject had been reminded, recently, which response was appropriate to a particular signal).

This point was tested by using (among other tasks) a situation in which subjects had to respond with one forefinger to onset of any of the displays "3," "THREE," "5," or "FIVE" and with the other to "7," "SEVEN," "4," or "FOUR."

The question was whether RT was equally fast after sequences such as "3," "SEVEN," "THREE" and "3," "SEVEN," "3," and whether in both cases RT was faster than with sequences of the type "5," "SEVEN," "THREE" or "5," "SEVEN," "3." In other words, whether facilitation of RT by recent occurrence of a particular symbol occurred at all, and whether this facilitation depended upon recent presentation of a particular display with particular physical characteristics, or whether facilitation was mediated by the recurrence of the "name" of a display irrespective of its particular physical characteristics.

Allowing for other effects related to "1-back" rather than "2-back effects" (for an example of 1-back repetition of codes, see Rabbitt & Vyas, 1973) the answer was straightforward. There was a signal-recency effect, and it was equally strong whether a particular physical display, or whether a display "of the same name" (as "7" . . . "SEVEN") recurred. In other words this recency effect has little to do with the physical characteristics of particular displays. It appears to be mediated by activation of a particular S–R code; (less pretentiously, because subjects have recently been reminded what to do when a particular signal occurs).

It is this factor of "being recently reminded" which we fumble around in discussing "direction of attention," "set," or "priming." Here, priming, it seems, need not relate at all to the physical characteristics of successive displays, or to the speed with which these are "perceptually analyzed." Priming may rather concern the subject's knowledge of "what to do about" a particular display. A simple experiment was undertaken to test whether a similar effect might be demonstrated in visual search.

VI.   RECENCY EFFECTS IN VISUAL SEARCH UNRELATED TO REPETITION OF PHYSICAL FEATURES OF SYMBOLS

A.   Experiment III

1.   Equipment and Method

A computer was programed to type out lists in which all letters of the alphabet occurred with equal frequency and in random order. A further specification was that each letter, with equal probability, might be typed in upper or lower case. Resulting sheets of 1200 letters, typed with normal spacing (but without breaks as between "words") were Xeroxed. Subjects were required to search for the eight capital letters A, Q, N, R, B, D, E, and G, and for their respective lower-case forms a, q, n, r, b, d, e, and g. These letters were chosen their because upper- and lower-case versions are physically distinct. Subjects, under speed–stress instructions each scanned nine such different sheets of random letters, crossing out all occurrences of the eight target letters, whether in upper or in lower case. They were asked to scan methodically from left to right, starting at the top left-hand corner of each page and working down. All found this easy and natural.

Subjects were 12 women and 6 men, aged 17 to 20, students at the Oxford Technical College, paid 30 pence for a single experimental session.

2.   Results

We wished to determine the effects of recognition of a particular target letter upon the probability of recognition of the next target letter in the text.

Over all lists, subjects failed to cross, on average, 6.8% of all possible targets. That is, there were actually 3320 targets among a total of 10,800 letters. On the average subjects should have made 3320 responses. On the average they failed to detect 210 targets (6.325% omission error rate) and marked, on average, about eight nontarget symbols as targets (e.g., 3.81% of their incorrect responses were "false identifications" and 96.19% of their errors were omissions). This rather low error rate may be attributed to insistence on accuracy, knowledge of results given after each sheet was scanned, and to rest pauses given between successive lists during which previous work was checked (using a template). If the nature of a target which had recently been checked had no influence on the probability of missing the next target, we would expect that on 1/16 of occasions (that is, about 13 times) subjects should fail to check a target identical to one they had just checked. Similarly they would, on average, fail 13 times to check a target that was the opposite case version (lower or upper case) of a target they had just checked. The actual data were as follows:

1. Mean number of omissions made by each subject 210.9 (σ 46.2);
2. Mean number of cases in which omitted letter was identical to last target checked 1.9 (σ 0.8);
3. Mean number of cases in which omitted letter was opposite case version to last target checked 2.4 (σ 1.1).

Differences between observed and expected frequencies were tested by χ^2 across individual subject's scores. It appeared that when a particular target letter had been marked, and the next target in the scanning path was the identical letter, the probability that this repeated target would be missed was significantly less than would be expected by chance ($p < 0.001$). More interestingly if the next target letter scanned after a particular target letter had been marked was an opposite case version of that letter, the probability that it would be missed was also significantly less than would be expected by chance ($p < 0.001$).

The detection of a particular target therefore does affect the probability of detection of a subsequent target, even though a number of other intervening background letters are scanned in the meanwhile. This may be described as priming for one member of a target set. However our results show that priming in this context, does not seem to refer only to the physical characteristics of a particular item on a display. The detection of a target lowers the probability that a subject will miss another target which is physically dissimilar (different case) but has the same name. Perhaps the common language way of describing this finding is as good as any. When a subject locates a target he is reminded (during a confusing task) that this is one of the symbols for which he had to search. It is thus less likely that he will fail to respond to it as a target if he encounters it soon afterward. In keeping track of the letters for which he must search he is guided by their names, and not by their physical appearance. In this respect the present result agrees extremely well with that of Corcoran and Weening (1968), who found that when English text was scanned to locate particular target letters (e.g., "P") the probability that unpronounced letters (e.g., silent "p"s) would be missed was much greater than the probability that pronounced letters would be missed. We confirm this result, in a new context. Cuing, or priming, for one target by perception of another is shown to exist. This is clearly not *only* priming for physical characteristics of a symbol. It appears to be quite as effective when it concerns the name of the symbol. To this extent the recency effect in serial self-paced CRT experiments is shown to have a parallel in visual search tasks.

VII. GENERAL DISCUSSION AND CONCLUSION

It seems that, whether in visual search tasks or in serial CRT tasks, the perception of one signal can affect the speed, or the probability, of identification of a subsequent signal in two distinct ways.

First, if two signals succeed each other after a very short interval (50–150 msec in these experiments) they can be very rapidly compared for physical identity (Type B matching). Thus "identification" of the second, in the sense of production of an appropriate response to it, here may imply only recognition of its identity to the first.

Second, if successive signals do not match, a different process of perceptual analysis must be employed to identify a particular signal as one among an ensemble of all possible signals (Type A identification). The term "priming" properly applies to this type of analysis. While we have not, of course, shown that such priming *never* has anything to do with the analysis of physical characteristics of a particular signal; but we see that here priming in terms of particular physical characteristics is not necessary. Identification of one signal can be facilitated by recognition of a previous signal with the same name.

This characteristic distinguished priming of this kind from the type of facilitation of recognition implied in matching. Other distinctions are:

1. The effects of priming endure through R–S intervals for as long as 2000 msec. Matching was not observed to occur after so long a lapse of time between displays.

2. It is clear that priming but not matching effects are observed although one, and perhaps several, other symbols have been observed, or even responded to (Rabbitt, Rodgers, & Vyas, 1976) between the identification of one symbol and the inspection of another.

These results, collectively, suggest that the "two-test" hypothesis is a useful working hypothesis which allows us to describe performance in serial CRT tasks and in visual search tasks in terms of the same assumption, and which suggests profitable lines of further investigation. Adoption of this hypothesis, and examination of our data in terms of it, also forces our attention on the fact that both the *nature* as well as the *efficiency* of perceptual identification processes changes with practice. Clearly we do not need, merely, a model for perceptual identification or a model for priming and cuing. It is evident that no steady-state model for performance at any arbitrary level of practice (whether early or late) will answer the case. No model can be taken seriously unless it can also describe the way in which performance changes with practice. In this regard, also, the "two-test" hypothesis may be useful in guiding our consideration of the evidence available.

REFERENCES

Bertelson, P. Sequential redundancy and speed in a serial two choice responding task. *Quarterly Journal of Experimental Psychology,* 1961, **12**, 90–102.

Bertelson, P. S–R relationships and reaction times to new versus repeated signals in a serial task. *Journal of Experimental Psychology,* 1963, **65**, 478–484.

Bertelson, P. Serial choice reaction time as a function of response, versus signal-and-response repetition. *Nature,* 1965, **206**, 217–218.

Bertelson, P., & Renkin, A. Reaction times to new versus repeated signals in a serial task as a function of response-signal time interval. *Acta Psychologica,* 1966, **23**, 132–136.

Corcoran, D. W. J., & Besner, D. Application of the Posner technique to the study of size and brightness irrelevancies in letter pairs. In P. M. A. Rabbitt & S. Dornic (Eds.), *Attention and performance V.* London: Academic Press, 1975.

Corcoran, D. W. J., & Weening, D. L. Acoustic factors in visual search. *Quarterly Journal of Experimental Psychology,* 1968, **20**, 83–85.

LaBerge, D. Personal communication, 1972.

Neisser, U. Decision time without reaction time, experiments in visual scanning. *American Journal of Psychology,* 1963, **76**, 376–385.

Nickerson, R. S. Effects of correlated and uncorrelated noise on visual pattern matching. In P. M. A. Rabbitt & S. Dornic (Eds.), *Attention and performance V.* London: Academic Press, 1975.

Posner, M. I. Abstraction and the process of recognition. In G. H. Bower & J. T. Spence (Eds.), *The psychology of learning and motivation.* Vol. 3. New York: Academic Press, 1969.

Posner, M. I., & Boies, S. Components of attention. *Psychological Review,* 1971, **78**, 391–408.

Posner, M. I., & Snyder, C. R. R. Facilitation and inhibition in the processing of signals. In P. M. A. Rabbitt & S. Dornic (Eds.), *Attention and performance V.* London: Academic Press, 1975.

Rabbitt, P. M. A. Ignoring irrelevant information. *British Journal of Psychology,* 1964, **55**, 334–339.

Rabbitt, P. M. A. Learning to ignore irrelevant information. *American Journal of Psychology,* 1967, **80**, 1–13.

Rabbitt, P. M. A. Repetition effects and signal classification strategies in serial choice response tasks. *Quarterly Journal of Experimental Psychology,* 1968, **18**, 334–339.

Rabbitt, P. M. A., & Vyas, S. M. What is repeated in the repetition effect? In S. Kornblum (Ed.), *Attention and performance IV*. New York: Academic Press, 1973.

Rabbitt, P. M. A., & Vyas, S. M. Interference between binary classification judgements and some repetition effects in a serial choice reaction time task. *Journal of Experimental Psychology*, 1974, **103**, 1181–1190.

Rabbitt, P. M. A., Rodgers, M., & Vyas, S. M. Signal recency effects in serial CRT tasks. Manuscript submitted for publication, 1977.

Rabbitt, P. M. A., Jordan, T., & Vyas, S. M. Repetition effects in the coding of complex displays. Manuscript accepted by *Journal of Experimental Psychology*, Human Perception and Performance, 1977.

19
Basic Processes and Strategies in Visual Search

D. W. J. Corcoran
Alistair Jackson

Department of Psychology,
University of Glasgow,
Glasgow, Scotland

ABSTRACT

Search is considered to be conducted by the operation of a strategy, chosen from various potential solutions of the task problem by a high-level "planner." The planner takes into account task, situational, and instructional factors in its choice of strategy, and the major purpose of this chapter is to determine why the planner adopts a particular strategy in preference to others. The characteristics of the strategy are deduced from experimental data, being generally described as a model of the system. The characteristics of the planner can be deduced from the strategy; thus theoretical models of behavior are seen as intermediate stages in the understanding of behavior – the ultimate stage being a description of the parameters the planner considered in its decision between strategies. On the basis of findings by Egeth, Jonides, and Wall (1972), it was reasoned that the internal representation of the alphanumeric characters could be separated cognitively (partitioning) – a technique that allows in some instances for the rapid detection of targets of a different category to the background. The experiments were aimed at discovering the task variables determining whether the option to partition is taken up.

I. INTRODUCTION

It was interesting to read in Shaffer's recent article (1975) the following description of how a typist goes about her work:

There are two principles which seem to apply universally: a skill is organised 'from the top down' and action is continually monitored for its adequacy and correctness. The first principle supposes that any skilled performance begins in the brain as an overall plan, which is translated through a succession of more detailed abstract forms to the actual movement. The second principal supposes that ongoing movements are compared with the intention, making it possible for a movement to be modified or a mistake corrected. (p. 51)

Such opinions have, of course, been expressed before. But the passage serves well as an introduction to the underlying aims of our investigation by clearly distinguishing three behavioral concepts. First, the role of an intention; second, the plan which is designed to execute the intention; and, third, the monitoring of performance and the resulting modifications to the plan so that the gap between what is done and what should be done is narrowed.

On reading the previous paragraph one might be expected to observe that our discipline has not advanced very far if it has taken so long to arrive at such commonplace knowledge. This is an inappropriate comment because (1) we have *not* been ignorant of this general scheme, (2) it may be false (a mere rationalization of what we are doing when we engage in some task), and (3) it has been necessary to confine investigations within manageable proportions and it would be odd indeed to read the above sentiments prior to every investigation.

Philosophers warn us against reification, which is perhaps why cognitive psychologists refer so often to "levels" of cognitive activity. Nevertheless it is convenient for descriptive purposes to ascribe the functions of planning, overseeing, and modifying to a homunculus that we shall call the *planner*. To avoid the problem of infinite regression, we shall assume that the planner is determined, in the sense that given the sum total of environmental and organic factors there is no option other than to formulate the plan which is actually devised. Thus the planner is the ultimate mechanism.

Most cognitive psychologists are concerned with the form of the plan, and not with the reasons why the particular plan was adopted. To make this statement a little less obscure, let us suppose that the instruction for a particular task is somehow understood by the planner, who has the intention of conducting the task satisfactorily. An overall plan is formulated, that will only be an approximation until the task is actually met, since it has to be based wholly upon the experimenter's description of the task. The task may be accomplished by various methods and the primary task of the planner is to select that strategy which he believes will yield the optimal outcome. In the early trials quite substantial modifications to the plan are made, until a strategy is found which approaches optimum. But in many tasks the plan will undergo further change as more is learned about the task, about the strengths and limitations of the unique combination of tactics being used, and about the limitations of the hardware.

It is now possible to distinguish the plan from the reasons for adopting the plan. The plan itself corresponds to what are considered theories or models of behavior. By introducing a planner at a high level, we are simply calling to attention the fact that such theories represent only an intermediate step in the understanding of behavior, since we need also to know *why* the particular plan should have been adopted rather than (one assumes) other, perhaps logically equally viable solutions to the problem presented by the task. The cognitive model or theory is to the planner as the data are to the theory: the plan is deduced from data; the characteristics of the planner are deduced from the chosen plan. To date cognitive psychology has been tackling the former problem, which is logically prior and its contribution to overall understanding of behavior has therefore been very considerable, because without a description of the plan, one cannot proceed to a description of the planner. Of course, the planner can operate only if there is a choice about how the task can be handled. In such cases we speak of *strategies,* since the word implies choice. If there is no choice we shall refer to *basic processes.*

Iconic memory is an example of a basic process. As far as we can tell it is possessed by all people of normal vision; its characteristics seem to remain more or less constant irrespective of the procedures used to measure it (e.g., Averbach & Coriell, 1961; Eriksen & Collins, 1967; Haber & Standing, 1969; Sperling, 1960); finally, it would seem to be outside the subject's control in that he would appear to have little option other than to use it. Compare this with the longer term sensory memory demonstrated by Posner, Boies, Eichelman, and Taylor (1969), which requires "attention" for its operation (or utilization) that is, the *intention* of the subject to use this form of memory. A series of studies by Parkinson, Kroll, Parks, and Salzberg (cited in Parks *et al.,* 1972) has defined one experimental condition determining when the choice is made, that is, when the verbal system — an alternative method of storage in these tasks — is occupied to something like its full capacity. This kind of sensory memory is an example of the operation of a strategy, because the subject may or may not use it, but will do so if it is a "smart" thing to do, or his only logical alternative. (Incidentally, "smart" is a useful term in the kind of approach we are employing, because the subject may use strategies that are beyond his or the experimenter's wit to describe verbally). In establishing that the sensory memory is used when the verbal system is otherwise occupied these experiments have gone beyond the description of the plan and have defined a parameter which the planner has considered in opting to use sensory, rather than verbal memory.

We do not believe that anything of a controversial nature has been said up to this stage, yet there are many instances of controversies leading directly from the misclassification of a strategy as a basic process. It seems to us, for example, that much of the arguments over peripheral and central theories of attention might have been avoided had the various workers been content to allow their own formulation the status of strategies; instead there was evidence of a strong incentive to describe The System as an interacting compound of basic processes, whose sequences of operation were determined. Why not instead allow the subject the capacity to choose on the basis of the task he has to perform whether he will operate as if he possessed a peripheral filter or a post-semantic "pertinence" device? When subjects are required to respond to different messages, it obviously makes sense to use the spatial separation of loudspeakers as a cue and so behave in accordance with the Filter Theory (Poulton, 1953, 1956). But when people have been shocked after presentation of certain words, from a particular category it makes sense to monitor the "unattended" channels for these words and others from the same semantic category (Corteen & Wood, 1972). Of course, attenuation theory (Treisman, 1969) can account for both of these results, yet even this theory, ingenious as it is, may represent no more than a compromise, describing the overall effects of various different strategies employed over a group of subjects, or even by a single subject from time to time. It *may* not explain the behavior of one single subject. It is no doubt commendable that scientists pit their wits against natural confusion and find order in it, but when such confusion is the direct result of the operation of different principles, the compromise may not reflect what happens in the individual case.

When one attempts to define a set of conditions under which one would say of a phenomenon "that is the result of a strategy," the major difficulty is distinguishing between the basic process and the very common strategy. A convenient example can be drawn from a number of unpublished findings by one of the authors (Corcoran, 1966, 1967; Corcoran & Weening, 1968) based upon earlier experiments showing that silent letters are difficult to detect in prose. Indicating that one may be dealing with a basic process is a series of experiments in which attempts were made to get rid of the phenomenon and failed. While subjects have been canceling "e"s, high level noise has been presented over headphones, subjects have hummed a tune, recited a nursery rhyme, and shadowed continuous prose; they have been given random words and latterly even pronounceable nonwords as material and none of these measures affect the ratio of probability of missing a silent to a pronounced "e". However, indicating that the process is mediated by a common strategy we have the finding that about one subject in twelve does not show the silent "e" effect, yet is a perfectly adequate reader. More recently there is even evidence to reliably indicate sex differences (Coltheart, Hull, & Slater, 1975). The test seems to be whether subjects *can* perform adequately without employing the process, and this latter test is obviously positive, since some subjects can. Yet such a test is not without difficulties, because the mechanism may be basic in some and strategic in other subjects, since we cannot realistically equate basic processes with genetically determined mechanisms.

Our intention in designing the studies here was to try to discover some conditions that influenced the planner to adopt one strategy rather than another. But this entails two preliminary steps, both of which have been introduced in the preceding paragraphs but must not be made explicit. First, the plan itself must be described because without it we cannot discover why it was adopted as a solution. Second, having described the plan it is necessary to establish whether it is a basic process or a strategy. The test seems to be whether the subject *can* execute the task by means of different plans or whether he has no alternative option. What we did therefore was to establish on the basis of experiments by Egeth, Jonides, and Wall (1972), by Jonides and Gleitman (1972), and by one of our own that subjects in certain conditions "partitioned" their letter and digit stores. (Why this was done will be made clearer subsequently). We then had to discover whether they had no option other than to partition the sets. This was achieved by manipulating task characteristics such that the planner would consider it useful or otherwise to do so.

We chose visual search, because the series of experiments by Egeth and his associates (1972) demonstrated to us (in the frame of mind that we were in) that subjects were changing their strategy in order to cope with the task in a sensible way. In this context these are very illuminating experiments and we begin by describing them in some detail.

II. SOME EXPERIMENTS BY EGETH AND HIS ASSOCIATES

Using a circular display of 3.4° in diameter and 150-sec duration containing 1 to 6 characters around the periphery, Egeth *et al.* (1972, Experiment 1), required subjects to decide whether a display contained all 4s or all Cs ("same" response) or whether the display contained one character which was different — that is, one 4 in Cs or one C in 4s ("different" response). In this and the subsequent two experiments two separate groups of subjects were used: one group had to respond when there was a different character in the display ("presence" responders) and the other when all elements were identical ("absence" responders). (This is an important technique since, by using separate groups of subjects, it is possible to induce separate strategies within a single experiment. It is also possible, as will become evident, to compare performance using presence and absence responders with that when each subject is required to make both presence and absence responses). It was shown that reaction times (RTs) showed no slope, maintaining a level of about 400 msec regardless of the number of items in the display. There was virtually no difference in overall RT between same and different responses (Fig. 1).

To account for these findings requires a parallel scan of the display, by which we mean *only encoding* the elements of the display simultaneously; it requires also that the encoded stimuli find an appropriate internal location indicative of 4 or C; and finally it requires (minimally) that there be a capacity to decide whether one or two locations have been activated.[1]

[1] We assume a single internal location for C, although there may in this instance be six Cs in the display. Evidence for this assumption and evidence that comparions can be made at the level of internal location can be found in an article by Beller (1970) which shows that RTs for same–different judgments are independent of number of elements, provided number of categories remain constant.

In the next experiment, all that changed was instruction. Subjects in the presence group were to respond if there was a 4 and those in the absence group if there was not. The change in instruction allows for a smarter strategy, since now response "present" can be initiated by activation of the internal 4 only, and absence by no activation of the 4. Thus the change of instruction *need* affect results minimally since, given the parallel scan, no increment in RT with display size is to be expected. We might perhaps expect a somewhat lower intercept owing to the fact that one less internal operation needs to be executed and we might also expect some difference to emerge between presence and absence responses, because it may take longer to decide that an internal 4 has not been activated than that it has. However, it would seem that quite a different strategy emerged from the presence responders. Figure 2 shows what might be two parallel lines with the absence RTs at 400 msec as predicted and the presence RTs rather lower as predicted. However, the presence graph has a significant slope of 6.5 msec per item indicating that a parallel scan may not have been used. Instead, it seems that the presence responders saw a smarter way of operating which gained them about 100 msec for each response. This may have been the conversion of the 4 into a visual image that was matched rapidly against the display elements so that delays from more internal processes were abolished. Notice that absence responders might also have used this strategy, responding at failure to obtain a stimulus match, but the problem was presented differently to them, in a manner which suggested that they *do* something when form was *not* present; it did not seemingly occur to them that they might not do something if it was.

In the next experiment subjects were required to look for *any* digit, either in all letter displays or in displays comprising all letters and one digit. In Experiment 3 separate Presence and Absence responders were used and in Experiment 4 the same subjects had to make both responses. The results of Experiment 3 (and the early trials of Experiment 4) produced a variation in behavior which had not previously occurred and that indicates a further potential strategy. Presence

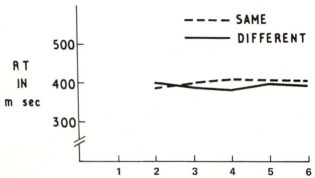

FIG. 1   Reaction time in a same–different task. (From Egeth, Jonides & Wall, 1972, Experiment 1.)

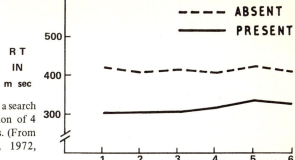

FIG. 2 Reaction times in a search task involving the detection of 4 among a background of Cs. (From Egeth, Jonides & Wall, 1972, Experiment 2.)

responders showed a flat function at about 400 msec, whereas absence respond-ers showed an increased intercept and a steep slope (Fig. 3). A careful examina-tion of the other task demands suggest a further search strategy of some importance. For the present we will limit discussion to Experiment 3.

Theoretically Experiment 3 required a more complicated organization of the internal locations into letter and digit categories. After the scan, either certain locations in the letter store will be activated (at locations representative of the actual letters in the display) or *one* of nine locations in the digit store and one to five locations in the letter store will be activated. The subject now has simply to decide whether the digit category has been activated *at any location*. Therefore, again we would expect, given the parallel scan, that there would be no slope for presence or absence, since the task (given organization of the internal locations into categories) is identical with Experiment 1. However, yet another pattern emerged, in which presence RTs showed no slope with the intercept at 400 msec, while the absence graph showed a higher intercept and a strong slope. In Experiment 2 we saw better performance resulting from a strategy change, whereas in Experiment 3 we see poorer performance, when logically it seems that absence responders need not have shown the large increments in RT. Can these subjects have been behaving optimally? What was smart about the strategy change?

As we saw earlier, subjects simply had to decide whether the digit *category* was activated, but imagine the consequences of *not* noting an activation within the digit store. Can it be concluded that no digit was present in the display? Clearly, if the parallel examination is known to be perfect then this can be concluded, but suppose there is some doubt. While the presence of an item in store is pretty strong evidence that it is present in the display, its absence still leaves some doubt about its absence in the display. To illustrate the latter point, imagine you are searching for a sock in a chest of drawers and you are in something of a hurry. The first drawer is examined briskly and on failure you go on to the next drawer, and so on. Suppose having examined all the drawers the sock has still remained undetected, you will now go back to the first drawer and examine it more closely, followed by the next, and so on. Notice that failure to find the

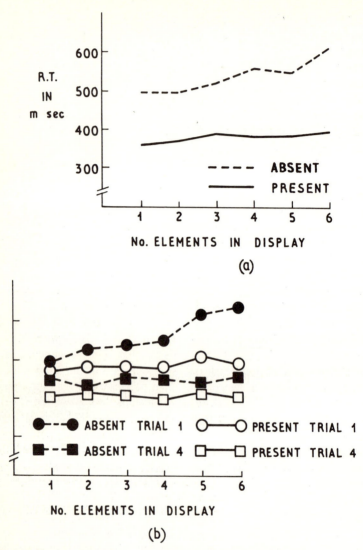

FIG. 3 (a) Reaction times in a search task involving the search for any digit in letter backgrounds. (From Egeth, Jonides & Wall, 1972, Experiment 3.) (b) Effects of practice on the digit search task. (From Egeth, Jonides & Wall, 1972, Experiment 4.)

item after the first brief scan was not sufficient evidence to conclude that it was not there, whereas finding it *is* sufficient evidence that it is there. Egeth (Egeth *et al.,* 1972) refers to this as a failure to confirm the null hypothesis. In Experiment 3, then, it is suggested that on failing to note activation of the digit store the subjects rechecked the physical display item by item before concluding that the digit was not present. There was no need to recheck when the item was found to be present, only in its absence. (Bamber, 1972 has described a similar strategy). In Experiment 4 the task was repeated over four trials, each subject being required to make both presence and absence responses. By the fourth trial the recheck strategy appears to be discarded (presumably on the basis of accumulated evidence that such a procedure was superfluous, since on relatively few trials was it discovered that an item had been misclassified). The end result was that both presence and absence RT showed a flat function. So subjects did eventually get smart, and were rightly being careful in the early trials.

We saw in Egeth's latter experiments that subjects seemed to have partitioned the internal representations of the characters into separate letter and digit categories, so that they could examine a total category rather than its specific contents. In the experiment by Jonides and Gleitman (1972) there is further evidence for such partitioning.[2]

The targets were the letters A, Z, and O, pronounced "oh," and the digits 2, 4, and 0, pronounced "zero." In the display "zero" and "oh" were physically identical. Before each trial a target was specified auditorily and this was followed by one of four kinds of displays — all letter, all digits, one letter in digits, and one digit in letters. Separate presence and absence responders were used. This design leads to two main conditions: (1) target and background of the same category, for example, looking for a letter in a background of letters; and target of a different category to background, for example, looking for a digit in a background of letters. The equal probabilities of target present and absent makes four conditions in all, each of which was sampled at set sizes of 2, 4, or 6.

The findings are shown in Fig. 4. On the left, Fig. 4a, are the overall findings; and on the right, Fig. 4b, the results when analyzed separately for the character O. The remarkable similarity between these figures indicates that O was treated as a letter when named "oh" and as a digit when specified as the target "zero." Two other features in the figures are of interest, one is the absence of a slope in the different category condition and the other the relative slopes for presence and absence responders in the same category conditions.

These results can be interpreted by invoking the principles that seem to have emerged from Egeth's *et al.* (1972) experiments. A likely interpretation is as follows:

1. On presentation of the target, the latter is stored either in the letter or the digit category.

2. On presentation of the display, items are scanned in parallel and stored in their appropriate locations. At the storage level either one or two categories contain items. Now, whereas it was possible in Egeth's Experiments 3 and 4 to

---

[2] We (and others we know of) have failed to replicate this experiment exactly, although some subjects seem to follow the pattern. It is necessary for this discussion only that some subjects conform, since we are describing strategies which are likely to show variations between subjects.

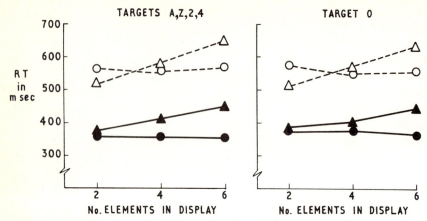

FIG. 4   Search for targets embedded in backgrounds of same or different category from the target. •, Target present, different category; ▲, target present, same category; ○, target absent, different category; △, target absent, same category. (From Jonides & Gleitman, 1972.)

determine simply whether the digit category contained any item, in this experiment it is necessary to discover which items are there, because the target set is one of six possibilities, although there is only one specified target per trial.

3. When the target and background are of the same category, only one store will contain items, and it will be necessary to examine these items for identity with the target. If the target is present, the most reasonable strategy is to self-terminate; when it is absent, of course, the store will have to be exhaustively examined. It is well known (Sternberg, 1966, 1975) that such a strategy should result in a slope value for the absence condition, twice that for presence. This is clear in the data.

4. When target and background are from different categories and the target is present, one store will contain the background items and the other the target plus a replication of the target from the display.[3] In this case the stored target has to be compared with only one item *irrespective of the size of the display*. Therefore there will be no slope in the different category condition; this too is obvious in the data.

5. Finally, when "zero" is specified as the target, it is stored in the digit category but stored in the letter category when called "oh" – thus precisely the same results will be expected; this is also shown in the data.

From these intriguing experiments, we emerge with the hypothesis that subjects can partition their letter and digit stores such that they need not examine

[3] One might assume that the item from the display reactivates the location taken by the target (Baddeley & Ecob, 1973; Corballis *et al.,* 1972). The precise form of the comparison is of no direct concern, as will be clear from the text.

items which reside in a category different from the target. (This interpretation is similar to that advanced by Brand, 1971, and Ingling, 1972.) As yet we have no evidence that this partitioning is strategic: the test is whether we can make partitioning appear when it is useful and disappear when it is not. Second, assuming that this test indicates a strategy we must discover why partitioning is chosen, that is, what parameter in the task situation influenced the planner to partition the letter and digit stores. The first experiment took the very necessary precaution of demonstrating partitioning with the use of a somewhat different methodology in our own laboratory.

III. EXPERIMENT I

A. Method

Displays comprised four characters arranged in a square of visual angle 20° approximately, which were presented for 150 msec over a Cambridge tachistoscope fitted with a Forth digital timer. The display was preceded by a fixation point at the center of the square. Prior to the fixation period one of eight targets was presented verbally; these were A, T, C, S, 4, 7, 3, or 8. It will be noted that the targets are divisible into letter and digit categories and by stimulus features into straight line and curved shapes. Background items were always letters and comprised either all straight line or all curved characters. The straight line backgrounds were chosen from H, N, L, F, and K and the curved backgrounds from O, Q, U, G, and B.

Eight conditions were specified from the three factors:

1. Target and background of same or different categories, that is, either letter target in letter background or digit target in letter background.

2. Target and background of similar or dissimilar physical appearance, that is, straight line target in straight line background, curved target in curved background, straight line target in curved background, or curved target in straight line background.

3. Presence or absence of the target in the display.

One hundred and twenty-eight different cards were used in order to control for position of the target in the display in addition to the factors listed above. At each presentation the subject searched for the presence or absence of the target character and made a two-choice response to indicate whether the target was or was not present. Reaction times were measured from display onset. Half the subjects responded Present with the prefered hand (and Absent with the non-prefered hand) and a half operated with the reverse instruction. Each of the eight conditions were repeated sixteen times by different displays, that were

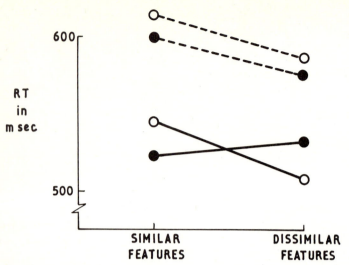

FIG. 5 Experiment I. Interaction between feature similarity and category identity in a search task. ○, Same category: dashed line – target absent. Solid line – target present. ●, Different Category: dashed line – target absent; solid line – target present.

presented in a different order, determined at random for each subject. Subjects were six undergraduates of the University of Glasgow.[4]

B. Results

Error rates were very low, at less than 1%, but RTs were recorded only for correct responses. Median RTs were recorded for each subject under each condition. Figure 5 shows the mean of the medians; each point represents the mean of a maximum of 96 readings.

A three factor repeated-measures analysis of variance was conducted on the data. The following three comparisons were reliable; for all others, F values were exceedingly small (ranging from .097 to 1.096). Physical similarity between target and background increased RT (F = 7.511, df = 1, 5, p < .05). The presence of the target in the display was associated with faster RTs than absence (F = 18.580, df = 1, 5, p < .01). The triple order interaction categories X features X presentation was significant (F = 7.569, df = 1, 5, p < .05). This latter effect is shown in the different category/present condition in Fig. 5, which does not show the drop in RT from similar to dissimilar features, characteristic of the other three plots. All subjects show a greater decrease from similar to dissimilar features in the same category/present condition than in the different category/ present condition. The largest nonsignificant F was for categories, indicating that

[4] This experiment was conducted as a laboratory project by Jean Barclay and Lorna Johnstone under the supervision of the authors.

RT for same categories was nonsignificantly larger than RT for different categories.

C. Discussion

The results are compatible with the hypothesis that in this experiment digits and letters were partitioned into separate categories. This conclusion is based essentially upon the finding that physical similarity affects RT when target and background are from the same category, but not when target and background categories are different. This specific prediction was made prior to the experiment and was based upon the following reasoning.

It is known that physical similarity affects the time taken to differentiate target from background, when the items are taken from the same category (e.g., Rabbitt, 1967). However, if target and background are stored separately — that is, when they are of a different category, the target does not have to be compared with the background items, which reside in a different store. Therefore, there will be no effect of physical similarity. We are not sure why this effect was restricted to presence responses, but assume that a recheck across stores may have been made as a result of failure to find a target. The prediction was to some degree counterintuitive. One would expect A to be discriminated less rapidly from H than C from H, which is the case. Thus one would also expect a 4 and H discrimination to take longer than a 3 and H, but this does not occur. We therefore consider that the results favor the partitioning hypothesis.

It is now necessary to show that partitioning occurs only when it is a potentially useful tactic.

IV. EXPERIMENT II

Experiment II comprised four separate sub-experiments, each conducted identically on independent groups of subjects, but using different pairs of characters. The design of each sub-experiment was identical with Egeth's *et al.* (1972) Experiment 1, except that subjects made both same and different responses and the visual angle subtended by the display was slightly less.

A. Method

Stimulus materials were constructed by photographing yellow "Teazlegraph" upper-case letters (SB357) and numerals (SB35100), all 5 cm in height mounted on dark blue "Velcro." This resulted in a negative with sharply defined black characters on a transparent ground. Negatives were fixed and mounted directly in 24 X 36 mm slide mounts.

The experiment comprised four independent subgroups differentiated by the use of different test characters: (1) Cs and 4s, (2) Cs and 6s, (3) Cs and 4s, and

(4) Cs and Gs. Within any *one* subgroup 120 slides were employed, divided into 5 array sizes with 2 to 6 characters, respectively, displayed in a circular pattern with 10 locations $36°$ apart and presenting a visual angle of $2°$ across the diameter when displayed in a Scientific Prototype 3-Channel Automatic Tachistoscope type GB. The character height presented a visual angle of $.214°$. The location of the characters was randomly generated with the following constraints:

1. All locations should be used equally often.
2. In the different conditions the single discrepant character should appear equally often at all locations.
3. One character should always appear diametrically opposite a discrepant element; thus, in the two-character condition elements are all diametrically opposite.
4. Not more than three adjacent locations might be filled on any one stimulus.

Each subject participated in two sessions (2 blocks of 60). In the first session all subjects received the 120 slides in the same random order; this was used as a

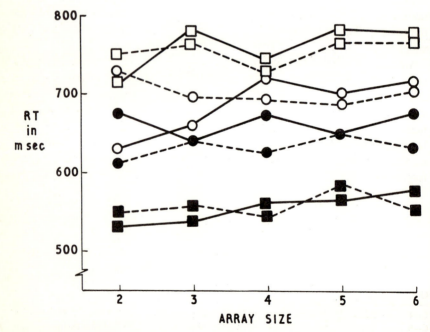

FIG. 6   Experiment II. Same–different tasks using characters with and without categorical identity and feature similarity. □———□: C, G same; □– – –□: C, G different; ○———○: C, 6 same; ○– – –○: C, 6 different; ●———●: C, 4 same; ●– – –●: C, 4 different; ■———■: C, A same; ■– – –■: C, A different.

practice session and to provide data for incorrect responses in the test session. In the second session all subjects received the 120 slides in a different random order. Stimuli were exposed for 150 msec at 10-second intervals, the noise of the slide changer being used as a cue, 3 seconds before presentation. Between presentations a lighted field with central fixation spot was present.

The subjects who had been instructed to respond "as accurately and as quickly as possible," intimated their decision by means of two separate hand held buttons marked "same" or "different," connected to a Forth digital timer. Within any one section response bias was balanced across the subjects' favored and unfavored hands. All subjects were required to respond on every trial, and received feedback as to accuracy but not speed after every trial. Midway through each session the subjects were permitted a short break while test blocks were changed. Thirty-two undergraduate students (17 female, 15 male) were paid to participate in each of two 30-minute sessions. Eight subjects were used in each of the four subgroups.

B. Results

Median scores were calculated from correct responses from each subject under each condition. Figure 6 shows the mean of the medians and each point is based upon a maximum of 96 readings; error rates are presented in Table 1. The only outstanding feature in this table is the high error rate for the C–G condition, which is to be expected.

An analysis of variance was conducted on the RT data comparing subgroups, array size and same–different responses. The analysis revealed that subgroups differed on overall performance ($F = 3.923, 3, 28, p < .025$). There was a significant effect of array size over all the groups; this was a mere 7 msec per item on average ($F = 3.559, 4, 112, p < .01$). A significant interaction emerged between array size and same–different response, indicating that same responses increased more as a function of number of items displayed than different responses ($F = 3.157, 4, 112, p < .025$). Finally, the latter interaction was not

TABLE 1
Experiment II. Percentage Errors at Each Array Size

G P	Same					Different					Means
	2	3	4	5	6	2	3	4	5	6	
C–4	6.25	8.30	10.42	8.30	8.30	7.29	9.38	6.25	4.17	5.21	7.39
C–6	0.0	6.25	8.30	9.30	10.42	8.30	4.17	12.50	0.0	4.17	6.34
C–A	5.21	4.17	6.25	7.29	3.13	9.38	5.21	4.17	5.21	3.13	5.32
C–G	14.58	10.42	16.67	20.83	19.79	9.38	6.25	12.50	10.42	16.67	13.75
Means	6.51	7.29	10.41	11.43	10.41	8.59	6.25	8.86	4.95	7.30	

uniform over groups, although the effect was small, a significant triple-order interaction was also observed ($F = 1.62, 12, p < .05$). Of special concern was the result of a comparison between the C–6 and C–4 groups, which indicated that these groups were reliably different ($F = 5.707, 4, p < .01$).

C. Discussion

The strategic advantage of partitioning letters and digits is simply that given a target of one category, the subject need not examine the contents of the store of a different category. When he expects to receive more than two different characters, partitioning has an advantage, because the number of characters exceeds number of categories. In this experiment only two characters were used (per sub-experiment) and therefore partitioning would not appear to be useful. However, if subjects had no option other than to partition then the rate at which two characters are distinguished will depend upon whether or not they are of the same category, as in Experiment I. Thus, C and 4 will not be any easier to distinguish than C and 6. If, on the other hand, it is not considered worthwhile to partition the categories, then comparisons between categories will occur, and the RTs will be a function of physical similarity between characters, and independent of their category. This latter expectation was confirmed. Specifically, the C–4 group was faster than C–6 and in general overall RT depended upon physical similarity between pairs. The significant (if shallow) slope in our data does not confirm the Egeth *et al.* (1972) findings. This may be due to the greater number of subjects in our study or it may reflect the changes in procedure we adopted, of which the use of each subject as a same and different responder was the most blatant.[5]

Of some interest was the finding that same response increased more with array size than different responses, indeed the latter appear to show no slope at all. In discussing the Egeth *et al.* (1972) contrary findings it was suggested that the elements were encoded in parallel; at the time the possibility that encoding rates for each identical element might vary was not advanced. Such a variation would tend to result in an increase in the slope of the same responses, because the decision "same" could not be made until *all* items have been encoded and the larger the number of items the higher the probability of a long encoding time (Sternberg, 1966). The different responses can be initiated as soon as there is evidence that any two characters have different codes; thus array size will not affect these RTs.

These latter considerations are (fortunately) irrelevant to the main purpose of the experiment, which we believe demonstrated that partitioning of the letters and digits into separate categories did not occur.

---

[5] Other than chance overall differences in speed of reaction between subjects we find no reason why the C–4 data were slower than C–A, since the pairs seem equally discriminable.

V. EXPERIMENT III

In the first experiment we expected partitioning to occur, because it would be a useful device; in the second experiment we introduced a situation in which partitioning was not particularly useful and found evidence that it did not occur. In this final experiment, we wished to introduce it again by arranging that the number of different characters exceeded two.

A. Method

Stimulus materials were constructed in a fashion identical to Experiment II, except in the specific characters used.

The task involved searching for one of four targets, when target and background were of the same or of a different category and when the stimulus features of the target were similar or dissimilar to the background. Thus, ideally, straight and curved letter targets and straight and curved digit targets should be displayed in straight and curved letter, and straight and curved digit backgrounds. Unfortunately, there are insufficient unambiguously straight line digits to balance the design. Accordingly, the design shown in Table 2 was adopted. This design ignores possible differences between different specific letters, for example, that it may be more difficult to discriminate C embedded in a background of curved letters than A in a background of straight letters. In fact, a subsequent examination of RTs showed that there were differences, but these were nonsignificant. However, it allows balance between the following designated target to background relationships: same category and similar features

TABLE 2
Design of Experiment III

Target	Background	Target/background relationship[a]
	Curved letters	SC/SF
C	Straight letters	SC/DF
	Curved digits	DC/SF
	Curved letters	SC/DF
A	Straight letters	SC/SF
	Curved digits	DC/DF
	Curved letters	DC/SF
6	Straight letters	DC/DF
	Curved digits	SC/SF
	Curved letters	DC/DF
4	Straight letters	DC/SF
	Curved digits	SC/DF

[a]S = same, D = different, C = category, F = feature.

(SC/SF); same category and dissimilar features (SC/DF), different category and similar features (SD/SF), and different category and dissimilar features (DC/DF).

Array size was varied such that either 2, 4, or 6 characters appeared. Targets were chosen from C, A, 6, and 4. Whether a target was present or absent, the background never contained a potential target, for example when C was the target, A, 6, and 4 were prohibited from the display. Nontarget characters were chosen from G, S, B, D, P, J, the curved letter set; from T, K, X, E, V, H, the straight letter set; and from 3, 8, 9, 2, 5, 0, the curved digit set. Reference to Table 2 will indicate how the four target to background relationships were equalized across the experiment.

Location of targets in the array were chosen at random with the following constraints: (1) all locations around the periphery were used equally often; (2) targets appeared at all locations equally often; (3) there were no repetitions of target or background letters within a slide, and (4) no more than three adjacent elements occurred. Altogether 432 different slides were prepared and presented to twelve undergraduate and graduate subjects, over one practice session and two experimental sessions.

The same apparatus and exposures were employed as in Experiment II. A target was specified verbally before each trial; this was followed by an auditory cue, a fixation field with the spot at the center of the to-be-exposed display, followed after 3 seconds by the display itself. Subjects pressed one of two hand-held buttons to indicate presence or absence of the target. The preferred hand was used by half the subjects to indicate presence and by half to signal absence. Errors were fed back to the subject on each trial. The usual speed/accuracy instructions were given.

B. Results

The errors recorded under each condition are shown in Table 3 as percentages. Notable are the high rates in those conditions in which the features of the target correspond to the background. Median RTs were recorded for each subject

TABLE 3
Experiment III. Percentage Errors at Each Array Size

Category/Feature Relation[a]	Present			Absent			
	2	4	6	2	4	6	Means
SC/SF	11.1	11.2	12.5	3.7	11.6	22.2	12.05
SC/DF	8.3	5.6	8.8	6	3.2	6.5	6.70
DC/SF	10.7	9.7	12.7	6.9	7.9	16.7	10.77
DC/DF	6.5	10.7	6.9	5.6	5.6	7.4	7.12
Means	9.15	9.30	10.23	5.55	7.08	13.20	

[a] S = same, D = different, C = category, F = feature.

TABLE 4
Experiment III. ANOVA for Presence Data

Source	df	MS	F	p
A^a	1	57.41	0.074	NS
B^b	1	45138.53	19.656	~ 0.001
C^c	2	33159.465	21.356	< 0.0005
A × B	1	1541.24	0.905	NS
A × C	2	3386.77	2.304	NS
B × C	2	1853.61	1.258	NS
A × B × C	2	2039.755	1.2193	NS
A × C × S^d	11	1702.691	–	–
B × C × S	22	1470.027	–	–
A × S	11	770.936	–	–
B × S	11	2296.571	–	–
C × S	22	1554.808	–	–
A × B × C × S	22	1473.511	–	–
S	22	1672.780	–	–
T	143	269537.95	–	–

[a]Category.
[b]Feature.
[c]Array size.
[d]Subjects.

TABLE 5
Experiment III. ANOVA for Absence Data

Source	df	MS	F	p
A^a	1	3140.69	3.044	NS
B^b	1	173868.15	10.548	< 0.01
C^c	2	261653.075	33.738	< 0.0005
S^d	11	410826.6245	–	–
A × B	1	6414.68	2.0539	NS
A × C	2	5229.14	3.9773	< 0.05
B × C	2	23421.61	6.6648	< 0.01
A × B × C	2	3704.395	2.7u7	< 0.1 (NS)
A × S	11	1031.56	–	–
B × S	11	16483.27	–	–
C × S	22	7755.367	–	–
A × B × S	11	3123.09	–	–
A × C × S	22	1314.7268	–	–
B × C × S	22	3514.205	–	–
A × B × C × S	22	1328.82	–	–

[a]Category.
[b]Feature.
[c]Array size.
[d]Subjects.

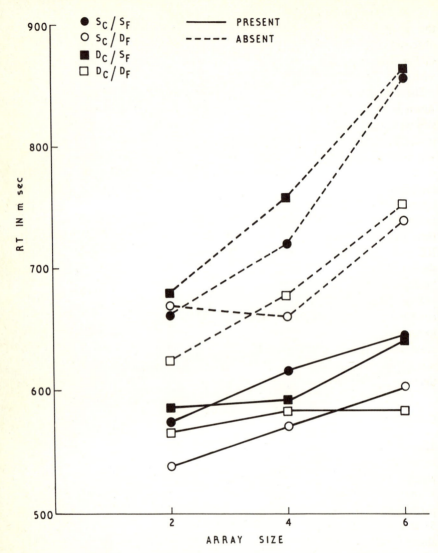

FIG. 7 Experiment III. Search for targets with category and feature similarities to the background elements.

under each of the 24 conditions for each array size. Two separate 3-treatments-by-subjects analyses of variance were conducted on these data (Tables 4 and 5), one for the presence data and one for the absence data (Fig. 7). Within the presence data two main effects were found to be significant. These were (1) similarity of target and background features (referred to as "Feature" in Table 4) in which feature similarity resulted in longer RTs than dissimilarity ($F = 19.656, 1, 11, p < .001$), (2) an increase in RT with the number of elements in the array $(F = 21.356, 2.22, p < .0005)$. No overall category effect was observed, and there were no significant interactions within the data. Inspection of Fig. 7 indicates that the different categories did appear to show less increase with array size than same categories, but this interaction was non-significant.

The category effect was also non-significant for the absence data (Table 5). Again both feature correspondence between target and background and array size were significant variables $(F = 10.548, 1, 11, p < .01$; and $F = 33.738, 2, 22, p < .0005$, respectively). In addition two significant interactions emerged. One was a barely significant category and array-size interaction $(F = 3.9773, 2, 22, p < .05)$. This interaction can be seen in Fig. 7, which shows decidedly nonlinear increases in RT with array size within the same category/absence data. The other interaction was a feature X array-size effect, $(F = 6.6648, 2, 22, p < .01)$ indicated in Fig. 7 by the lesser slopes for the different feature/absence plots than for same feature/absence. Both interactions appear to be largely due to long RT in the SC/DF plot at an array size of 2. Seven out of the twelve subjects showed longer RTs in this latter condition than at an array size of 4, so the "deliquent" datum point cannot be disregarded.

A third analysis of variance was conducted between presence and absence data comparing presence/absence with array size. Absence RTs were found to be longer than presence $(F = 47.95, 1, 11, p < .0005)$. Array size across both presence and absence was also significant $(F = 37.56, 2, 22, p < .0005)$ and there was a significant interaction term $(F = 19.023, 2, 22, p < .0005)$ indicating that the slope of the absence data exceeded that for presence.

C. Discussion

The results of Experiment III were clearly contrary to those expected. The experiment was designed to include those factors which would provide the planner with reasons for choosing the partitioning strategy. But for the category X array-size interaction within the absence data, there is no reliable evidence of partitioning. The latter interaction was marginally significant $(p < .05$, see Table 5) and as previously mentioned could be largely attributable to the SC/DF/ absent datum point at an array size of 2. We cannot account for this interaction. Also, within the Absence data, although category was not statistically significant as a single factor, different categories take on the whole longer to process than same categories.

In retrospect, it is possible to present some reasons why the planner chose not to partition. First, for array sizes of two items, partitioning is probably disadvantageous; some unknown period of time must be used up in the partitioning process, and this time might better be spent in examining simply for feature correspondence between target and items in the array. Since these trials amounted to one-third of those presented, then subjects might be tempted to generalize this strategy across stimuli with larger arrays. A second factor which might influence the planner was the number of actual targets used. In Experiment I there were altogether eight targets, two representatives of each category identity and feature similarity. In this experiment, however, there were only four possible targets. With the larger potential target population it is more likely, after the presentation of the target and prior to the exposure of the array, that the target would be classified as being a letter or a digit and of course such a classification is essential for partitioning to work. With the smaller target set such cognitive classification might have been seen as advantageous. Third, the background set contained letters on two-thirds of the trials and digits on only one-third. Thus partitioning of the search set is less "informative" than it would be with equiprobable digit and letter sets. In combination, it seems at least plausible that these three factors of the experimental situation persuaded the planner to adopt a simple feature-matching strategy for all presentations. Yet there are some indications in the presence data to suggest that the category of the target and background *was* considered to some extent. Taking the DC/DF data alone, a simple array size X subjects analysis of variance was conducted which was nonsignificant, indicating that the overall significant array-size effect did not apply to the DC/DF condition. Also on the basis of a simple measure of the slopes for DC/DF and DC/SF conditions, for each subject, it was evident that the latter exceeded the former in ten out of twelve comparisons. The specific expectations in the present experiment were that DC/DF and DC/SF data would be indiscriminable in overall RT and in terms of their slopes which we expected to be zero. What we do seem to have is that the DC/DF condition *only* conformed to the prediction. Again we can offer no explanation of this finding.

That feature matching between target and items in the array occurred seems well established in the data. Strong feature effects were evident in both presence and absence data (Tables 4 and 5, Fig. 7).

The feature effect itself is of some importance, since it argues strongly for the operation described by the question: "Is this (are there) character(s) the target?" rather than: "What is this character?" It is of interest that the feature effect persisted in the Absence search. This point will be taken up again subsequently.

That the response "absent" takes longer than "present" is well illustrated in Fig. 7. What is also clear is that the slopes for absence exceed those for presence. Due to the essential linearity of the presence data, it is possible to estimate the slope quite accurately at 12–13 msec per item. The zero intercept is at 540 msec, and, since the target is presented before the display, the intercept is probably a measure of pure response time. The absence data, particularly that for same category (SC) appears nonlinear and intercept values are therefore more difficult to estimate, and could lie anywhere between 550 and 640 msec. Slopes for the absence data based upon the linear assumption are approximately 40 msec per item, between three and four times that for presence.

The preceding estimates taken in conjunction with the feature effects, and the lack of a category effect (partitioning) referred to previously, are generally supportive of the following broad description of the manner in which the task was conducted. After verbal presentation of the target, it is converted into a visual image, but is not categorized into digit or letter for the reason advanced earlier. The display is examined to discover whether the items conform to the visual representation of the target. Thus the display is not categorized into letter or digit backgrounds. Whether this search is exhaustive or self-terminating is not entirely clear, since the slope differences between presence and absence do not favor either alternatives. On failure to find the target, a short time elapses. This can be estimated by the difference between the intercepts for Presence and absence — between 10 and 100 msec approximately. During this period the subject prepares to recheck the display. Rechecking the display for absence of the target involves a process similar to the presence search, since the feature effect remains clear within the absence data. (If the items were actually named, that is, the question "What is this character?" asked, then the feature effect would be abolished or at least substantially reduced.) One final point. Since the display was present for 150 msec, and since total RT seems to require about 540 msec as a response component, all datum points above about 690 msec are the result of search among iconically stored items. This perhaps accounts for the slight increase in slope between 4- and 6-item arrays for the absence data. (The fast exposure field in this experiment was white and of the same intensity as the background exposure field. The items were black and so iconic storage should be reasonably good. In fact one subject characteristically took two seconds over some responses with few errors.)

VI. CONCLUSION

In this chapter we have examined very closely the results of four experiments by Egeth and his associates and three of our own — seven tasks that have much in common in their methods, materials, and instructions. We have emerged with as many different descriptions of the performance as there were experiments. One of these strategies, the partitioning of letter and digit stores, we caused to appear in Experiment I, and disappear in Experiment II. When we generated a task that seemed to optimize upon the conditions which would, we thought, favor partitioning, (Experiment III), by increasing the effect of numbers of characters in the display, the predicted effect did not occur. But we had failed to note in advance the presence of other task factors that would influence the planner to adopt the more straightforward strategy of matching the physical features of the target across those of the array, whether or not the array contained items of a different category.

We might easily have been discouraged had we been attempting to discover how the search system operates, that is, to formulate *a* model which would account for the data across all the experiments. But this was not our intention.

Our intention, which may now be clearer to the reader, was to try to understand the factors which the planner took into account in choosing the appropriate strategy for the task. This meant taking a fresh look at each task, and formulating descriptions of the plans that seemed to be followed in the execution of that particular task and discovering the *reasons* why the plan was adopted.

Only when separate groups of subjects are used is the theorist quite free to adopt the "fresh-look" technique, that is, to examine each task independently without concerning himself with carry-over effects from prior conditions. Within-subject designs are, as Poulton (1975) has pointed out, subject to many unwanted effects. Only if the behavior is mediated by basic processes can one be certain that subjects are not steered into the use of plans more appropriate to prior conditions than the one under examination. It was surely the experimentally induced restriction on the planner that caused Luchins (1942) to entitle his paper "*Mechanisation* in problem solving."[6]

It is questionable that since the techniques of the cognitive psychologist have not developed sufficiently to identitify plans inequivocally, we are jumping the gun in attempting to discover the decision parameters of the planner. This, of course, may be so. However, we hope that our investigation has shown that such problems are not intractible.

ACKNOWLEDGMENTS

The authors are grateful to Dr. A. J. Sanford for many critical discussions during the preparation of this manuscript.

REFERENCES

Averbach, E., & Coriell, A. S. Short term memory in vision. *Bell System Technical Journal*, 1961, **40**, 309–328.

Baddeley, A. D., & Ecob, J. R. Reaction time and short term memory: Implications of repetition effects for the high speed exhaustive scan hypothesis. *Quarterly Journal of Experimental Psychology*, 1973, **25**, 229–240.

Bamber, D. Reaction times and error rates for judging nominal identity of letter strings. *Perception & Psychophysics*, 1972, **12**, 321–326.

Beller, H. K. Parallel and serial stages in matching. *Journal of Experimental Psychology*, 1970, **84**, 213–219.

Brand, J. Classification without identification in visual search. *Quarterly Journal of Experimental Psychology*, 1971, **23**, 178–186.

Coltheart, M., Hull, L., & Slater, D. Sex differences in imagery and reading. *Nature*, 1975, **253**, 438–440.

Corballis, M. C., Kirby, J., & Miller, A. Access to elements of a memorised list. *Journal of Experimental Psychology*, 1972, **94**, 185–190.

[6] The italics are ours.

Corcoran, D. W. J. An acoustic factor in letter cancellation. *Nature,* 1966, **210**, 658.

Corcoran, D. W. J. Acoustic factors in proof reading. *Nature,* 1967, **214**, 851.

Corcoran, D. W. J., & Weening, D. L. Acoustic factors in visual search. *Quarterly Journal of Experimental Psychology,* 1968, **20**, 83–85.

Corteen, R. S., & Wood, B. Automatic responses to shock-associated words in an unattended channel. *Journal of Experimental Psychology,* 1972, **94**, 308–313.

Egeth, H., Jonides, J., & Wall, S. Parallel processing of multielement displays. *Cognitive Psychology,* 1972, **3**, 674–698.

Eriksen, C. W., & Collins, J. F. Some temporal characteristics of visual pattern perception. *Journal of Experimental Psychology,* 1967, **74**, 478–484.

Haber, R. N., & Standing, L. G. Direct measures of short-term visual storage. *Quarterly Journal of Experimental Psychology,* 1969, **21**, 43–54.

Ingling, N. W. Categorization: A mechanism for rapid information processing. *Journal of Experimental Psychology,* 1972, **94**, 239–243.

Jonides, J., & Gleitman, H. A conceptual category effect in visual search: O as letter or as digit. *Perception & Psychophysics,* 1972, **12**, 457–460.

Luchins, A. S. Mechanisation in problem solving, the effect of Einstelling. *Psychological Monograph,* 1942, **248**, (Whole No.).

Neisser, U., Novick, R., & Lazar, R. Searching for ten targets simultaneously. *Perceptual and Motor Skills,* 1963, **17**, 955–961.

Parks, T. E., Kroll, N. E. A., Salzberg, P. M., & Parkinson, S. R. Persistence of visual memory as indicated by decision time in a matching task. *Journal of Experimental Psychology,* 1972, **92**, 437–438.

Posner, M. I., Boies, S. J., Eichelman, W. H., & Taylor, R. L. Retention of visual and name codes of single letters. *Journal of Experimental Psychology,* 1969, **79**, (Monograph Supplement 1) 1–16.

Poulton, E. C. Two-channel listening. *Journal of Experimental Psychology,* 1953, **46**, 91–96.

Poulton, E. C. Listening to overlapping calls. *Journal of Experimental Psychology,* 1956, **52**, 334–339.

Poulton, E. C. Range effects in experiments on people. *American Journal of Psychology,* 1975, **88**, 3–32.

Rabbitt, P. M. A. Learning to ignore irrelevant information. *American Journal of Psychology,* 1967, **80**, 1–13.

Shaffer, H. High speed typing. *New Behaviour,* 1975, July, 51–53.

Sperling, G. The information available in brief visual presentations. *Psychological Monographs,* 1960, **74**, (11, Whole No. 498).

Sternberg, S. High speed scanning in human memory. *Science,* 1966, **153**, 652–654.

Sternberg, S. Memory scanning: New findings and current controversies. *Quarterly Journal of Experimental Psychology,* 1975, **27**, 1–32.

Treisman, A. Strategies and models of selective attention. *Psychological Review,* 1969, **76**,

20

Toward a Unitary Model for Selective Attention, Memory Scanning, and Visual Search

Richard M. Shiffrin
Walter Schneider

Department of Psychology
Indiana University
Bloomington, Indiana, United States

ABSTRACT

A series of visual search experiments was carried out in order to verify the commonality of short-term search processes and selective attention. Experiment I used a multiple frame procedure and accuracy as a measure. It varied the relation of the target set to the distractor set, memory-set size, and frame size. To reach a given accuracy level, the presentation time per frame varied from 40 to 800 msec (or more) across conditions. The data showed evidence for slow serial search, termed *controlled search*, when the target and distractor sets varied from trial to trial, and fast efficient parallel search, termed *automatic search,* when the target and distractor sets were fixed from trial to trial. Experiment II used a single frame procedure and latency as a measure. Virtually all the accuracy effects of Experiment I were found in the latency results of Experiment II, and the two experiments were linked together. Experiment III was like Experiment I but presented more than one target per trial. The results qualitatively distinguished automatic from controlled search. First steps were taken toward a search model for selective attention.

I. INTRODUCTION

In *Attention and Performance V* we presented a series of studies showing that subjects can, in carefully controlled situations, divide their attention among multiple inputs without decrement compared to single input control conditions

413

(Shiffrin, 1975). These studies examined inputs in the visual, auditory, and tactile modalities, and all three modalities at once. To obtain the basic effects, it was necessary to reduce as far as possible the subjects' use of slow control processes in active short-term memory. As a result, we suggested that the locus of selective attention lay in search and decision processes within short-term memory, subsequent to the completion of automatic, systemic processing. Critics pointed out at the time, quite appropriately, that is is a long step from such a conclusion to an actual model for selective attention. In this chapter, therefore, we briefly review some recent studies whose goals are virtually the reverse of the earlier ones: an attempt is made to produce the largest attention effects possible. These results are then used to construct a unitary model for selective attention, memory scanning, and visual research.

Note that in this chapter, on account of length limitations, we can present only a sketchy account of the studies, procedures, and results. The theory, also, is summarized rather than presented in full detail. Finally, we must apologize to all the previous researchers whose earlier results and theories cannot be reviewed here. For a more thorough exposition of these matters, please see Schneider (1975), Schneider and Shiffrin (in press), or Shiffrin and Schneider (in press).

II. THE ACCURACY OF VISUAL SEARCH AND THE RELATION TO SELECTIVE ATTENTION

In order to allow the greatest possible scope for the occurence of short-term search and decision processes, as well as those of selective attention, a visual search paradigm was adopted. The basic paradigm is a variant and extension of that utilized by Sperling, Budiansky, Spivak, and Johnson (1971); it is illustrated in Fig. 1. Four elements are presented simultaneously on a cathode-ray-tube screen controlled by a PDP-8e computer. The elements are arranged in a square around a central fixation dot, and their joint presentation for a brief period of time is termed a *frame*.[1] A trial consists of the presentation of 20 frames in immediate succession. The elements presented can be characters (i.e., digits or consonants) or random dot masks. The time from onset of one frame to onset of the next is termed the *frame time*. The frame is displayed for all but the first 15 msec of the frame time, and no character or mask is ever presented in the same screen position in two successive frames.

---

[1] A brief note on procedures and results: There were six extremely highly practiced subjects, each of whom took part in all the conditions and experiments (except the reversal experiment, Fig. 15). Enormous numbers of trials were collected so that all the results discussed are highly significant statistically. The stimuli were plotted so as to appear continuous and were highly discriminable. They subtended about .5 degree visual angle and there was about 1 degree between characters.

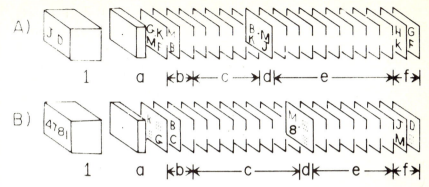

FIG. 1 Two examples of a positive trial in the twenty-frame search paradigm. (A) Varied mapping (VM), memory-set size = 2(J, D); frame size = 4. (B) Consistent mapping (CM), memory-set size = 4 (4, 7, 8, 1); frame size = 2. 1: presentation of memory set; a: fixation dot goes on for .5 sec when subject starts trial; b: three dummy frames which never contain target; c: distractor frames; d: target frame; e: distractor frames; f: dummy frames which never contain target. Frame time is varied across conditions.

The subject's task requires the detection of one of several targets (the *memory set*) presented in advance of each trial. Either no target ($p = .5$) or one target ($p = .5$) is presented on a given trial, in any frame from 4 through 17. The subject presses a key when he thinks he detects a target, or presses a different key at trial's end if he does not detect a target. The frame time was kept constant across the 20 frames of each trial, and the basic dependent variable was the psychometric function relating accuracy to frame time for each condition.

Three basic independent variables were manipulated. In order to explore the connection between selective attention and visual search, the number of characters in each frame was varied from one to four. This variable is denoted *frame size* (abbreviated F) and was held constant during all 20 frames making up a trial. When frame size was less than four, all noncharacter positions were filled by masks. Character positions were chosen randomly for each frame, subject only to certain constraints such as "no repeated elements in successive frames in the same display positions."

In order to explore the connection between selective attention and memory scanning, the number of possible targets presented in advance of the trial was varied from one to four. This variable is denoted *memory set size* (abbreviated M). A different memory set was presented in advance of each trial.

Finally, and most important, the relationship between the targets and the distractors was varied. We were convinced that two fundamentally different types of processing exist, one type in which the detection and location of a target is a fast, efficient, automatic process, part of systemic processing, not making demands upon the decision system in short-term memory; and a second type in which the targets must be detected and located through a "slow," laborious, inefficient search and decision process through much of the contents of short-term memory. In order to contrast these types of processing, we utilized a *consistent-mapping* and a *varied-mapping* condition. The consistent-mapping condition requires the subject to detect a digit target(s) in frames of letter distractors, or a letter target(s) in frames of digit distractors. The varied-mapping condition requires the subject to detect a digit target(s) in frames of digit distractors, or a letter target(s) in frames of letter distractors. Note that the consistent-mapping condition keeps the targets and distractors disjoint over trials — no target is ever a distractor and vice versa. Targets and distractors are mixed from trial to trial in the varied-mapping condition. We refer to the consistent-mapping condition as *CM search* and the varied-mapping condition as *VM search*.[2]

Altogether then, there were 12 conditions: 2 distractor conditions (CM or VM) $\times$ 2 memory-set sizes (1 or 4) $\times$ 3 frame sizes (1, 2, or 4). Each subject ran for a long block of trials in each condition at each frame time before switching to the next time or condition. Subjects whose CM task utilized digit targets saw only letters in their VM conditions (and vice versa). Frame times were chosen so the probability of correct detection or rejection varied from about .60 to 1.0. The first question to be answered, of course, is whether the speed at which frames are presented to reach a given accuracy level will vary at all across conditions.

The results of Experiment I are shown in Fig. 2. Frame times varied so greatly among conditions, it was necessary to graph the results in two panels, using different scalings. In the *VM* conditions frame time for a given accuracy level depended strongly upon the memory-set size (M) and the frame size (F), ranging from 120 msec (for an accuracy of 80%) for the $M = 1$, $F=1$ condition to 800 msec (for an accuracy of 70%) for the $M = 4$, $F=4$ condition. Thus, there is an enormous "selective attention" effect, such that greater numbers of targets in memory, or items per frame, yield great reductions in the speed at which frames can be presented to reach a given level of accuracy. In the VM condition, false alarms are always quite low, so that most errors are failures to detect presented targets, rather than detections when no target is present. Note that frame time to reach a given accuracy level is monotonically related to the product of memory-set size and frame size.

The CM conditions show a strikingly altered pattern of results. First, CM performance is much better than VM performance: even the most difficult

---

[2] It might seem more appropriate to call these conditions *categorical* and *noncategorical* search, considering that in CM search the targets and distractors form separate categories. However, it is possible to maintain a categorical distinction between targets and distractors in a VM search task also (say, if the target and distractor categories are switched from trial to trial). Later results from our studies (not reported here) have convinced us that the consistency of the mapping from trial to trial is the factor of primary importance in causing the differences between our VM and CM conditions.

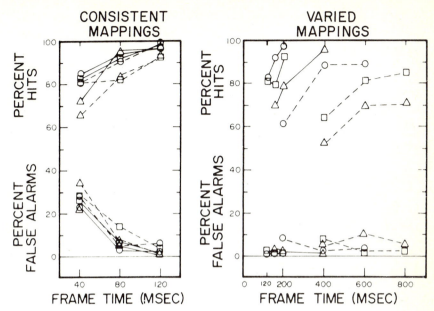

FIG. 2 Experiment I. Hits and false alarms as a function of frame time for each of the 12 conditions. Three frame times were utilized for each condition. ○, frame size = 1; □, frame size = 2; △, frame size = 4; solid line, memory-set size = 1; dashed line, memory-set size = 4.

combinations of frame size and memory-set size, at 80 msec frame time, show performance equivalent or better to that at 120 msec frame time of the easiest VM conditions. Second, there is almost no effect of frame size and only a small effect of memory-set size. Thus, attention may be successfully divided in this condition. Finally, there is a large increase in false alarms (detections when no target was present) at frame times of 80 and especially 40 msec.

The results of Experiment I suggest the operation of two rather different detection processes. In the VM condition, the targets from some trials are distractors on other trials, and vice versa. Thus, no useful mapping of stimuli to responses, or stimuli to categories, can be learned. In such a case, a target(s) will not "stand out" with respect to the distractors, and must be found through a slow, possibly serial, item-by-item comparison of all presented items to all targets in memory. We term this process *controlled search.* Even if the comparison process proceeds as fast as that found by Sternberg (1966), 40 msec per comparison, it should be clear that large frame times would be needed to complete all comparisons in the conditions with large frame and memory-set sizes. For example, 100% detection when $F = 4$ and $M = 4$ would require an approximate frame time of $4 \times 4 \times 40$ msec = 640 msec. In this serial model, detection would fail whenever a new frame was presented before the search of the previous frame (which contained the target) proceeded far enough to reach the target and match it to memory. If we equate a failure to detect with a failure to divide attention, then this view suggests that the failure to divide attention is due to the limited rate of the search of short-term memory.

A rather different detection process appears to operate in the CM condition. In these conditions, no target ever appears as a distractor, and vice versa. Under such conditions a mapping of stimuli to an internal detection or attention response can be learned in long-term memory. Of course, since we used already-learned categories of numbers and letters as targets and distractors, the mapping would be learned very quickly (and this seemed to be the case — most subjects learned within one session to adopt a "fast" processing mode for the CM condition). In these conditions an automatic response to a target can be learned: the subject can simply wait for the occurrence of one of the learned detection responses, check the detected item, then respond. In effect, the target is always matched or scanned first, before any distractors. We call this detection process *automatic search*. The only limitation on the speed at which frames may be presented should be perceptual: at fast enough presentation rates, the individual characters will not be fully processed and some characters will be confused with others. Indeed, as the frame time approaches 40 msec, the false alarm rate climbs greatly in all conditions. Finally, if detections are again equated with the ability to divide attention, then the ability to divide attention in the *CM* condition may be ascribed to the high efficiency of the search process.[3]

Several experiments (that are not reported here) were performed to rule out certain alternative explanations of the findings. Two experiments demonstrated that the differing performance levels among the VM conditions were not due to the varying number of masks in the various conditions. Although it could have been argued that targets adjacent to masks, or targets preceded and followed by masks, were easier to detect than targets adjacent to characters, or targets preceded and followed by characters, the results showed the temporal and lateral masking effects of masks and characters to be roughly equivalent.

Another experiment was carried out to test the level of processing given to the characters in the various conditions. In order to demonstrate that the frame times in the VM condition were long enough that all characters were completely processed and entered into short-term memory, an experiment was carried out in which the subject was asked to report all the items in a given frame in their correct position. Five frames were presented (Fig. 4), the first two and last one consisting of masks only and the central frame containing four characters to be reported. The results are shown in Fig. 3 for several frame times, and for digits and consonants separately. From 80 msec up, report of all four characters is essentially perfect. Certainly then, at frame times in the VM condition ranging from 120 to 800 msec, the characters must be fully perceived.

---

[3] The CM results on accuracy may be compared to related results by Sperling, Budiansky, Spivak, and Johnson (1971) and Neisser (1974).

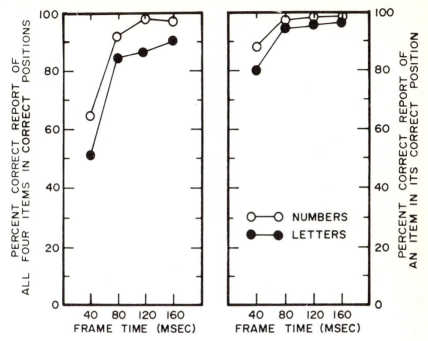

FIG. 3 A single frame experiment, with pre- and postmasking, requiring whole report of the four characters presented. Percentage correct report is given for numbers and letters (separate conditions) as a function of frame time.

The implication is that detection failures arise from failures of (and limitations of) the short-term search processes.

III. THE LATENCY OF SHORT-TERM SEARCH AND THE RELATION TO SELECTIVE ATTENTION

These experiments notwithstanding, the link between the results of Experiment I and short-term search processes remains somewhat tenuous. We therefore attempted to verify a direct relationship between the accuracy results of Experiment I and the latency results of short-term search studies. A sample procedure from Experiment II is depicted in Fig. 4. Five frames were presented on each trial, preceded by a memory set. The first two and last two frames contained masks only. The middle frame contained targets, distractors, and masks. The subject was given instructions to maintain high accuracy, but to give one of two responses as quickly as possible, indicating whether any item from the memory set appeared in the display. Memory-set sizes were 1, 2, and 4, frame sizes were 1, 2, and 4, and the mapping of targets to responses was consistent or varied as

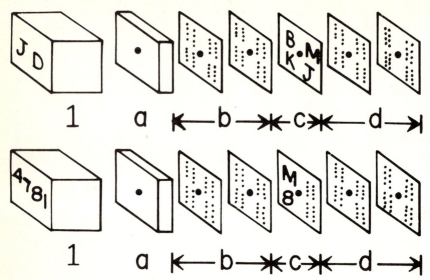

FIG. 4 Two examples of a positive trial in Experiment II. Upper: varied mapping, memory-set size = 2 (J, D); frame size = 4. Lower: consistent mapping, memory-set size = 4 (4, 7, 8, 1); frame size = 2. 1: presentation of memory set; a: fixation dot goes on for .5 sec when subject starts trial; b: two frames of masks; c: target frame; d: two postmask frames. Frame time - 160 msec for each of the last five frames.

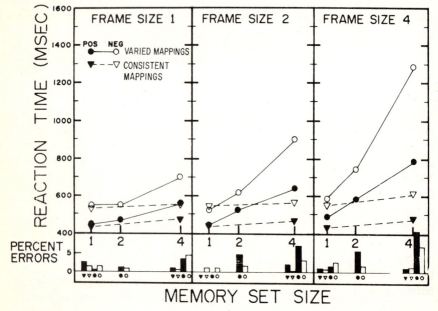

FIG. 5 Data from Experiment II. Reaction time for correct responses and percentage errors as a function of memory-set size, for all conditions.

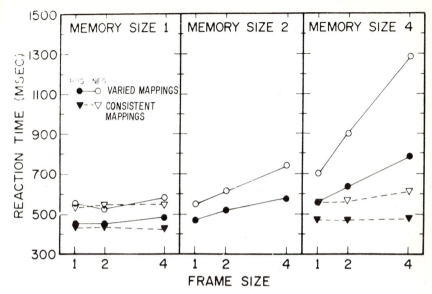

FIG. 6 Data from Experiment II. Reaction time for correct responses as a function of frame size, for all conditions.

in Experiment I; (note that $M = 2$ was not examined in the CM condition). The frame time in all conditions was 160 msec. This frame time is much lower than that needed in Experiment I in many of the conditions, but performance was expected to be accurate nonetheless because the target frame is not followed by any additional frames requiring processing. To produce high accuracy, the subject need only retain in short-term memory the memory set and the (up to four) display letters during his search.

The results are shown in Fig. 5, which gives the reaction time for correct responses for the various conditions. The varied mapping condition is usually termed *varied set* and the consistent mapping condition is usually called *fixed set* in the search literature (see Sternberg, 1966). We see that there is virtually no difference in latency as the memory-set size and/or frame-size increases for the VM condition. For the VM conditions, the functions are reasonably linear and, for the larger values of memory-set size and frame size, the slope of the negative functions (target not present) is just about double that of the positive functions (target present). Such results would seem to indicate serial search in the VM conditions, and direct access minimal search in the CM condition, that is, what has been previously termed controlled and automatic search respectively. For the VM conditions, the 2:1 slope ratios would seem to indicate that the search terminates when the target is found.

---

[4] The flat functions in the CM conditions may be compared to similar results found by Egeth, Jonides, and Wall (1972), Sperling, *et. al.* (1971), and others.

Figure 6 shows the same data graphed as a function of frame size. Much the same pattern is seen, although in the VM condition the frame-size slopes are near zero when memory-set size is one; more will be said about this finding later. Briggs and Johnsen (1973) carried out a very similar experiment to ours; however, their CM conditions did not use digits and consonants, but instead used two disjoint subsets of letters. Figures 7 and 8 show the data from their experiment graphed in the same fashion as those from our experiment. The results are strikingly similar in all respects, although the CM set size functions are not as flat as those from our study, probably because more sessions of training would be needed to give the disjoint subsets of Briggs and Johnsen's experiment the already-learned distinctiveness of digits and letters in our experiment.

We now wish to examine more closely the nature of controlled search in the VM conditions. First, what is the relationship between reaction time and the total number of comparisons to be made, that is, the product of the memory-set size and frame size? Figures 9 and 10 give the appropriate graphs of reaction time as a function of the product of memory-set size and frame size both for our experiment and Briggs and Johnsen's experiment. To a rough approximation, the data from both experiments appear to be amenable to an interpretation of serial terminating search with a search rate of about 50–60 msec per comparison. (However, as seen in Fig. 5–8, the detailed breakdown of the data may indicate a tendency toward parallel, exhaustive search when the memory-set size is one.)

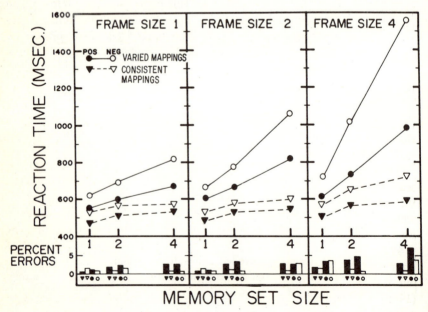

FIG. 7 Data taken from Briggs and Johnsen (1973). Reaction time for correct responses and percentage errors as a function of memory-set-size, for all conditions.

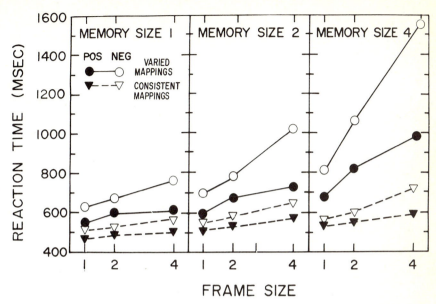

FIG. 8 Data taken from Briggs and Johnsen (1973). Reaction time as a function of frame size, for all conditions.

According to Sternberg's (1969, 1975) hypothesis, exhaustive scanning might be more efficient, on the average, than terminating scanning, if in order to terminate it were necessary to add an appreciable decision time to each comparison. The time lost on positive trials due to searching exhaustively would be more than countered by the time gained through having to make only a single decision at the conclusion of the series of comparisons. If this hypothesis were true, then one would expect the time for a single comparison to be longer when search is of the terminating variety than when search is exhaustive. Indeed, in both sets of data (Figs. 9 and 10) the estimated time per comparison (estimated from the slopes of the reaction time functions) is larger than in the studies that indicate exhaustive search.

One might ask why search should ever revert to termination if exhaustive scanning is more efficient. There are several plausible hypotheses, but perhaps the simplest is that subjects given speeded response instructions may be unwilling to wait as long as 1.5 seconds on every trial before responding. Indeed, we found that our subjects required extensive training and instructions in the M = 4, F = 4 condition before they would respond slow enough to reduce their error rates to acceptable levels. This may account for the discrepancies between our results and other results in the literature. Sternberg (1967), Nickerson (1966), and Scarborough and Scarborough (1975), for example, carried out experiments in which the error rates in the more difficult conditions were not as well controlled and rose to 20% or higher in some cases. As Pachella (1974) has

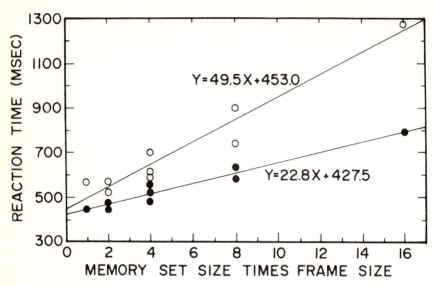

FIG. 9 Experiment II. Reaction time as a function of memory-set size times frame size, for negative trials (open circles) and positive trials (solid circles). The best fitting lines are depicted.

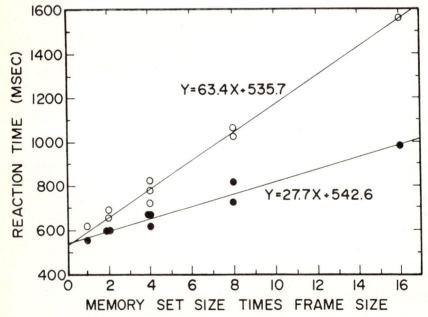

FIG. 10 Data taken from Briggs and Johnsen (1973). Reaction time as a function of memory-set size times frame size for negative trials (open circles) and positive trials (solid circles). The best fitting lines are depicted.

shown, subjects can increase their speed at the expense of errors so that it is difficult to interpret reaction time data in the face of wide variations in error rate. As seen in Figs. 5 and 7 however, the variations in error rates in the present experiments were kept under reasonable control.

Figures 9 and 10 show one other important effect. Frame size and memory-set size can covary so as to keep the total number of comparisons constant. In all instances where such constancy occurs, the reaction is slower, the larger is the memory-set size. This fact strongly suggests that the search process compared all visual items in the display against one memory-set item before turning to the next memory-set item and beginning again. If the change from one memory-set item to the next took some time in addition to the basic comparison time, then for a fixed number of total comparisons, reaction time would be slower the larger is the memory-set size.[5]

IV. THE RELATION BETWEEN SEARCH EXPERIMENTS USING ACCURACY AND LATENCY MEASURES

The main goal in carrying out Experiment II was the derivation of a link to the accuracy results of Experiment I. In virtually every case the frame time in Experiment I (to reach a given accuracy level) is monotonically related to the reaction times of Experiment II. Can a more direct quantitative link be found? If a serial search with identical characteristics is assumed to be operating in the VM conditions in both Experiments I and II, then it should be possible to link quantitatively the frame time in Experiment I to the reaction time for the comparable condition in Experiment II. Figure 11 graphs the negative reaction time for each condition in Experiment II against the estimated frame time required to reach 70% accuracy (hit rates) for the same condition in Experiment I. The assumption of serial search implies that subjects will obtain 70% hits if they finish 70% of all possible comparisons before each new frame begins. Thus, the time to finish all comparisons in Experiment I should be 10/7 of the time required to reach 70% hits. Since the time required to finish all comparisons in Experiment I should differ only by a constant base time from the negative reaction time in Experiment II, we expect the points in Fig. 11 to fall along a line with slope of 10/7. As seen in Fig. 11, a line of slope 10/7 is not highly discrepant from the data, though there are some deviations. A similar plot is shown in Fig. 12 for the positive data from Experiment II, assuming that a serial terminating search is being used. Because termination reduces the negative slope by a factor of two, the predicted relationship in Fig. 12 must have a slope of 5/7 (rather than 10/7). Again the predicted line is not far from the data.

[5] Indeed both sets of data were fit quite well by a serial terminating model assuming a basic comparison time, μ, and a time, δ, to access each new memory element. For our data, $\hat{\mu} = 42$, $\hat{\delta} = 40$; for Briggs and Johnsen (1973), $\hat{\mu} = 57$, $\hat{\delta} = 27$.

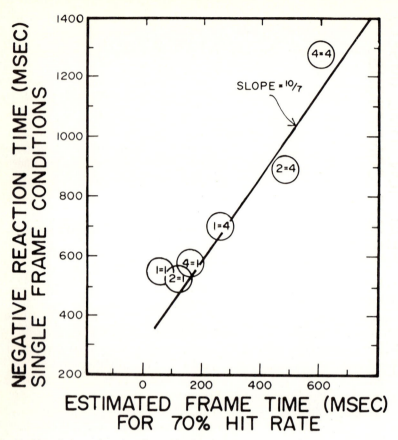

FIG. 11   Negative reaction time for each VM condition from Experiment II graphed as a function of estimated frame time to reach 70% hit rate for that condition in Experiment I. The line of slope 10/7 is predicted by a serial search model with no variance in comparison time (see text).

The data in Figs. 11 and 12 suggest that the search process giving rise to the reaction time results of Experiment II may also be responsible for the accuracy and attention results seen in Experiment I. However, our attempt to relate the data quantitatively fails in certain respects. First, there is a discrepancy between the $M = 1$ conditions in the two experiments. When $M = 1$, frame size does not affect reaction time in Experiment II, but does affect frame time in Experiment I. In order to explore this finding, another experiment (for which space limitations preclude description) examined the relation of error variations to reaction time. It was found that reaction time could only be held constant as a function of frame time at the expense of a small increase in false alarms (and misses). While these error differences were acceptable when only one frame was presented, they could not be tolerated when 20 frames were presented. For example, a correct

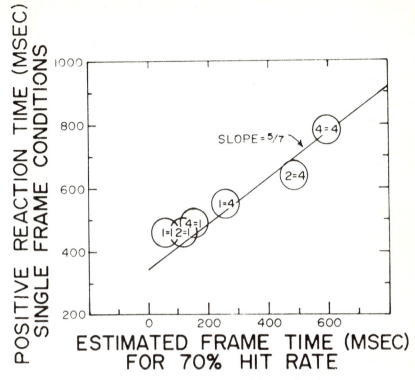

POSITIVE REACTION TIME (MSEC)
SINGLE FRAME CONDITIONS

ESTIMATED FRAME TIME (MSEC)
FOR 70% HIT RATE

FIG. 12   Same as Fig. 11, but for positive reaction times.

rejection rate of 95% for one frame would, if maintained for 20 frames, result in a false alarm probability of 64%, which is clearly unacceptable. Thus, it seems likely that the multiple frame procedure of Experiment 1 forces subjects to relinquish strategies in which search speed is gained at the expense of false alarms.

The second main problem involved in relating the data from the two experiments involves the shapes of the psychometric functions in Fig. 2. If the hypothesis of strict serial scanning at 50–60 msec per comparison is accepted, the psychometric functions should be linear, and in general have smaller ranges than those shown in Fig. 2. Part of the problem of wide ranging psychometric functions may be due to fatigue. We found, for example, that subjects could not raise their accuracy in the $M = 4$, $F = 4$ conditions above about 75% at frame times ranging up to 2 seconds per frame. Subject reports indicated that poor performance at these long durations was due to fatigue; blinking, eye movements, memory loss, and other factors reduced performance when trials lasted 20 or more seconds each. Fatigue, however, is unlikely to account for the shapes of the psychometric functions when frame time is low. For example, when $F = 1$, $M = 1$, accuracy is only 80% at 120 msec frame time and reaches 100% at 200 msec frame time. Yet a search rate of 60 msec per comparison suggests that performance would be perfect at a frame time of 60 msec when only one comparison is needed per frame. Even were some "ready" time needed at the start of each frame before the comparison begins, one would expect the range of the psychometric function to cover only 60 msec of frametime, but this is clearly not the case.

The obvious change in the search model to be applied to Experiment I is the introduction of the assumption that each comparison and each memory access takes an amount of time distributed as an independent random variable, with a mean of μ msec per comparison, a mean of δ msec per each memory access, and variances V_1 and V_2. The parameters μ and δ may be estimated from the Experiment II reaction time data and then V_1 and V_2 would be chosen to fit the accuracy data of Experiment I. The assumption of variability in comparison time can explain why the $M = 1$, $F = 1$ condition requires such long frame times for high accuracy, and why the psychometric functions have such a wide range. We are now fitting such a model to the data of Experiments I and II. Note of course that the predictions for the mean reaction times of Experiment II depend only . upon the mean, and not the variance, of the hypothesized comparison-time and access-time distributions.

As a preliminary test we decided to see whether the data from Experiment I could be predicted from the data of Experiment II, if the approximating assumptions were made that memory access time was negligible and that the time per comparison was distributed as a random variable. Figure 13 shows predictions for the VM data of Experiment I in which each comparison was assumed to be an independent random variable with a mean of 50 msec (taken from Experiment II) and with a standard deviation, σ, to be estimated. The assumption we made was that an item would be detected if and only if the search process reached the target and completed matching before the frame-time was exceeded. We assumed that the search order was random. It proved necessary, in order to fit the results, to adopt one value of σ, 70 msec, for the $M = 1$ conditions, and another value of σ, 16 msec, for the $M = 4$ conditions. (This two-factor approach might reflect the ignored access time variable; each time the search process cycles through the display and picks up the next item in the memory set, the time to find the next memory item might be highly variable.) The predictions in Fig. 13 are derived from the admittedly approximate assumption that the resultant distribution of the time to complete n comparisons is normally distributed.[6]

---

[6] We used the equation:

$$P(\text{Hit}|n, t_F) = \frac{1}{n} \sum_{i=1}^{n} \text{GAU}\left(\frac{t_F - i(50)}{\sqrt{i}\,\sigma}\middle| 0, 1\right)$$

where n = total number of possible comparisons = $M \times F$, t_f = frame time, σ = standard deviation of the comparison time (to be estimated), and GAU = standard normal distribution function.

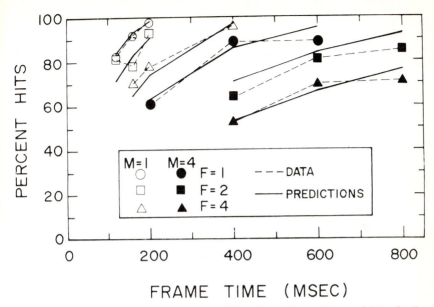

FIG. 13 Predictions for the VM conditions of Experiment I, assuming a serial terminating search model with a mean time per comparison of 50 msec. The $M = 1$ and $M = 4$ curves are predicted assuming standard deviations of the comparison time of 70 and 160 msec, respectively.

The fact that the predictions are in close agreement with the data in Fig. 13 is to be regarded only as a demonstration that the general approach has potential value, and that the data of Experiment I may be quantitatively linked to those of Experiment II. Detailed models of the data from both experiments are currently being explored.

It seems not unreasonable, then, to conclude that the accuracy results in the VM conditions of Experiment I are the result of the controlled, perhaps serial, search processes seen in the latency data of Experiment II. Can the same be said for the CM conditions? In one sense the answer is yes — the frame times for the CM conditions of Experiment I vary very little across memory-set and frame sizes, and the reaction times for the comparable conditions in Experiment II show very little effect of memory-set and frame size. However, in Experiment I, the frame times for any of the CM conditions are always much smaller than any of the frame times for the VM conditions. In Experiment II, the reaction times for the CM conditions are about the same as those for the easier conditions in the VM cases. Thus the shift to the CM conditions results in an overall gain in Experiment I larger than that seen in Experiment II. There are several possible hypotheses to account for this difference between the two experiments. The most likely hypothesis involves the differences in the nature of the two search processes. The reaction time results suggest that automatic search takes at least as long as the easiest controlled search. Supposing this to be true, one would still expect automatic search to be superior in all cases in Experiment 1 if automatic search occurred in parallel across frames as well as within frames. Thus in Experiment 1, the necessary frame time for high performance in automatic search would depend only upon physical factors like lateral and temporal masking, and would not depend upon the completion time for automatic search. On the other hand, controlled search being serial in nature, successive frames would have to be delayed until the search of prior frames was completed.

We next ask just what sort of search process occurs in the CM conditions. This automatic search is obviously very fast and efficient; going further, we would like to suggest that it is qualitatively different than that used in the VM conditions, not just faster. Part of the evidence for this contention is the fact that set sizes have such a small effect on accuracy or latency in the CM conditions. This evidence is not conclusive, however, because some small differences remain. Stronger evidence is seen in Experiment III below.

V. ACCURACY OF SEARCH FOR MULTIPLY PRESENTED TARGETS

The results from Experiments I and II suggest that many deficits in divided attention may be due to limitations on controlled search through short-term memory, but both experiments presented at most one target per trial. A number of results in the attention literature suggests that an additional attentional deficit arises when two targets are presented simultaneously (e.g., see Moray, 1975; Sorkin & Pohlmann, 1973). In our view, the search and decision process may be slowed down when a target appears and the subject is required either to note this fact or to respond. In order to examine the effects of the temporal relation of multiply presented targets, and to examine the interaction of multiple target effects with the VM and CM conditions, we carried out Experiment III.

Experiment III utilized a 20-frame procedure just like that in Experiment I, except that the subject knew that multiple targets might be present and was required to note these as they occurred and respond with the number detected at the end of the trial. In fact, there were, across trials, 25% no targets, 25% one target, and 50% two targets. When two targets were presented, one half of the time they were not identical to each other (NI, for not identical), and one half of the time they were identical to each other (II, for identical items); the two targets were on 1/4 of the trials in the same frame; on 1/4 of the trials in successive frames; on 1/4 of the trials one frame removed; and on 1/4 of the trials three frames removed. The two targets were always in different display positions. Memory-set size was set equal to two and frame size was set equal to two. In VM blocks, frame time was set to 200 msec, and in CM blocks, frame time was set to 80 msec. These frame times were chosen to produce intermediate accuracy levels.

The results are shown in Fig. 14 in their most easily interpreted form. The figure shows the estimated probability that the subject correctly detected one target when one was presented, or both targets when two were presented, for each condition. (The leftmost data point is the observed percentage "zero" responses when "zero" targets were present.) The probabilities are estimates because a simple nonparametric correction for guesses and false alarms has been carried out upon the raw data.[7]

Consider first the VM results. Note to begin with that the probability of detecting a single target, when squared, is about equal to the probability of detecting both targets at a spacing of 4 (the same is true for the CM condition). This indicates that at long spacings the targets are probably being detected independently. Also confirming this hypothesis is the fact that at long spacings the II and NI doubles do not differ. At shorter lags, however, large effects appear. Consider the II doubles. When both targets are in the same frame, they are detected quite well, about as well as at a long spacing. However, a target in the immediately following frame is often missed, even though it is the same target as that just detected. This inhibition probably reflects the slowing down of the search due to some time used up by the decision process which counts detections. It is particularly interesting that the decrement does not occur until the succeeding frame, however. The literature on multiple targets indicates that a decrement occurs when targets are presented simultaneously but the time course of the decrement has seldom been examined. Apparently, the decrement is largest in the VM conditions if there is a delay (of about 200 msec) between the presentation of the two targets.

The VM NI results show a larger decremental effect covering a longer time period than the decrement for II. There is a decrement in the same frame and also at a spacing of 2, although the largest decrement occurs for the spacing of 1.

[7] Let S_{ij} be the real detection of i targets out of j presented ($i \leq j$). Let R_{ij} be the report of i targets given j presented. Let $R_k | S_i$ be the report of k targets given i detected ($k \geq i$). Then

$$P(R_{kj}) = \sum_{i=0}^{j} P(R_k | S_i) P(S_{ij}).$$

We assume $P(S_{00}) = 1$. Simple calculations then show

$$P(S_{01}) = P(R_{01})/P(R_{00});$$

$$P(R_1 | S_1) = \frac{P(R_{11}) - P(R_{10})P(S_{01})}{1 - P(S_{01})}$$

$$P(S_{02}) = P(R_{02})/P(R_{00});$$

$$P(S_{12}) = \frac{P(R_{12}) - P(R_{10})P(S_{02})}{P(R_1 | S_1)};$$

$$P(S_{22}) = 1 - P(S_{02}) - P(S_{12}).$$

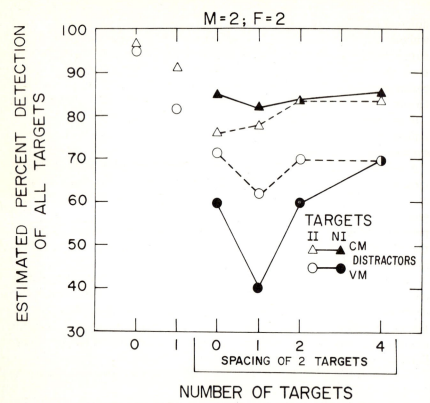

FIG. 14 Experiment III. Probabilities of correctly detecting one target when one was presented, or two targets when two were presented, for each condition. The data shown have been adjusted to remove effects of guessing and false alarms. $F = 2$, $M = 2$; frame time = 80 msec for CM condition and 200 msec for VM condition.

One can explain this pattern of results by assuming that there are two effects of target detection: (1) a certain amount of decision time is lost; and (2) the *order* of search is altered for a few frames so as to compare first the target already found. These two effects would of course be opposed in the II condition so that it would not be surprising to find, in the II condition, an increment, rather than a decrement, at certain spacings. In one of the later experiments in which $M = 2$ and $F = 4$, (not reported here) such an increment was found at a spacing of 2 before a reversion to independent processing was found at a spacing of 4.

Turning to the CM conditions, a radically different pattern of results is found. First of all, NI instances are better than II, the reverse of the pattern for the VM conditions. Second, there is no decrement for NI targets at any spacing, but a decrement for II targets primarily at a spacing of zero (same frame). In the CM condition, apparently, each target has an automatic learned "attention" response which can occur in parallel without inhibition. However, two identical targets in different spatial locations cannot both be detected in close temporal proximity without decrement. Perhaps attention responses occur automatically to all CM targets, but a controlled search must then be carried out to make decisions based upon characteristics internal to the automatically determined target set. In the pesent case some counting mechanism might lose track of multiple identical targets.

In any event, the differing pattern of results for the CM and VM conditions is a finding of great importance. This pattern indicates that what we have called *automatic* and *controlled* search are qualitatively different search processes.

A series of additional studies explored further the detection of multiple targets. We have examined the $M = 2, F = 4$ and $M = 4, F = 2$ conditions. In these cases the CM results are similar to those already shown, while the VM results are generally similar in shape but show greatly reduced accuracy. We have also presented the $M = 2, F = 4$ condition, with one diagonal of the display known by the subject to be irrelevant (i.e., to contain no targets). In this case, performance is virtually identical in both distractor conditions to that seen when $M = 2, F = 2$. All of the results appear compatible with the view that a controlled, perhaps serial, search process is operating in the VM conditions, and an automatic detection process is operating in the CM conditions. However, when multiple targets are presented in CM tasks, either a controlled search must be used to examine the automatically attended subset of targets, or some other process limits performance.

VI. THE DEVELOPMENT OF AUTOMATIC SEARCH, PERCEPTUAL LEARNING, AND CATEGORIZATION

The large qualitative and quantitative differences between the VM and CM conditions raise a number of interesting questions regarding both the nature of the processing in the two cases and the learning process through which the fast efficient processing mode is developed. We regard the automatic processing seen in our digit-consonant (CM) conditions to be producible for any arbitrary set of characters by extensive training with consistent mapping. This hypothesis is supported by results reviewed by Simpson (1972) and Teichner and Krebs (1974), and by the results of Briggs and Johnsen (1973), showing that the set-size functions flatten and become curvilinear with extended CM practice, for memory scanning, visual search, or hybrids of the two. In order to explore the learning process further we carried out a series of experiments designed to watch the course of development of the automatic search mode. The general procedure was to choose two arbitrary character sets, then place a subject in one of the difficult conditions (say, $M = 4, F = 2$) in the multiple frame experiment, but use a frame time close to that for the CM conditions. The target and distractor sets were then fixed over a long series of trials until performance approached that of the CM conditions. Figure 15 shows the results when the two sets were consonants from the first and second half of the alphabet. The subjects began training with a frame time of 200 msec. The false alarms started at a level of about 10% and dropped during initial training. As the figure shows, the hit rate rose over 1500 trials of training to above 90%. Then the subjects were switched to a frame time of 120 msec and their hit rate dropped only to 80%; that is, their performance was beginning to approach that seen for digits in consonants (or vice versa: the CM conditions of Experiment I). At this point, after 2100 trials, the subjects were asked to perform the reverse task on the same categories. The former targets now became distractors, and vice versa. As shown in the figure, there was an enormous difficulty in making the reversal. Despite having had the training on distinguishing the top and bottom of the alphabet, perfor-

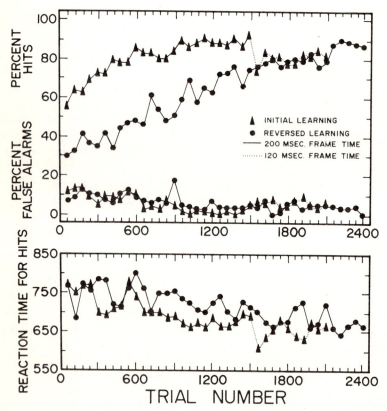

FIG. 15. Initial learning and reversed learning for target and distractor sets taken from the first and second half of the alphabet. $M = 4$, $F = 2$, and frame times are shown. Percentage hits are graphed as a function of trial number. After 2100 trials the target and distractor sets were switched with each other.

mance was much lower on the reversed task than even that during initial
learning.

The reversal learning results suggest to us that there are two components to the
perceptual learning seen. One component is the development of a categorization
such that the various targets are learned as a group. Second, there is a learned
"attention" response such that the members of a target category and the
category itself acquire the ability to "interrupt" the short-term search and direct
the search to themselves at once. As this automatic response becomes learned it
becomes harder and harder to ignore, and takes increasingly long to unlearn.
Thus, after reversal, the former targets, now distractors, continue to be given
attention automatically and thereby harm detection of the former distractors,
now targets.

We have carried out a number of studies designed to explore further these
mechanisms of attentional learning. We have learned that two arbitrary sets that
are highly visually confusable with each other can be used as targets and
distractors and trained to the point at which detection will become fast and
efficient, but the rate of development of perceptual learning in such a case is
much slower than for sets of characters which are less visually confusable.
Finally, we took our subjects who were highly trained in the multiple frame
tasks and reversed them: if in the CM conditions they had been searching for
digits in consonants, they now searched for consonants in digits, and vice versa.
If in the VM condition they had been searching for consonants in consonants,
they now searched for digits in digits, and vice versa. After reversal, subjects
showed a hugh performance decrement in the CM conditions, but no performance change in the VM conditions.

VII. THE IMPLICATION OF SEARCH EXPERIMENTS
FOR SELECTIVE ATTENTION

It is not possible to review the attention literature in this chapter but a few
general comments are in order. It is convenient to classify attention experiments
into two classes: *divided attention* experiments, in which deficits occur when
attention to multiple inputs is required; and *focused attention* experiments, in
which performance is harmed by an inability to exclude from consideration
inputs known (in advance) to be irrelevant. Divided attention experiments may
further be subdivided into accuracy and latency experiments, and accuracy
experiments may be broken into two further groups; those utilizing near-
threshold stimuli, and those utilizing stimuli well above threshold.

Divided attention experiments utilizing near-threshold stimuli generally show
attentional deficits because the presented information decays so quickly from
short-term memory that the short-term search process does not have time to

complete the necessary retrieval and decisions (e.g., Eijkman & Vendrik, 1965). Sometimes a decision related to the detection of one target will use up search time so that forgetting will occur and preclude detection of a simultaneously presented target (e.g., Sorkin & Pohlman, 1973). A deficit can also occur due to forgetting when the subject is told which input is relevant, but not until some time after presentation (e.g., Taylor, Lindsay, & Forbes, 1967).

Accuracy experiments using above-threshold stimuli (like that in the VM condition of Experiment I in this chapter) usually present a rapid sequence of stimuli. In such a case, deficits occur when the next stimulus appears before the search process has time to finish examination of the preceding stimuli (e.g., Treisman & Riley, 1969). The deficits can be removed if the search process is of the fast, automatic rather than slow, serial mode (e.g., Lawson, 1966; Treisman & Riley, 1969), though the deficits may remain if multiple simultaneous targets are presented (see Moray, 1975).

Latency experiments can of course reveal slowed responses whenever multiple inputs are used and search is of the controlled variety (e.g., Sternberg, 1966), but attentional deficits can disappear when search is in fast, parallel, automatic mode (e.g., Egeth, Jonides, & Wall, 1972).

Finally, focused attention experiments reveal a reversal of the roles of automatic and controlled search. Ignoring stimuli should be easy when controlled search is being used, but automatic responses that occur whenever a stimulus occurs, responses that enable automatic search to achieve its efficiency, can result in deficits when the task requires these stimuli to be ignored (e.g., Eriksen & Eriksen, 1974).

Virtually all of these processes have been demonstrated in the series of experiments reported in this chapter, and they have been linked together via the mechanisms of short-term search. We believe that the attention literature can be organized along the lines outlined, but any extensive treatment of the vast attention literature must await another paper.[8]

VIII.   CONCLUSIONS

Short-term search can be of two major qualitatively different types, a fast, efficient parallel process, termed automatic search, which is not highly affected by the number of characters in memory nor by the number of characters presented, and a slower, possibly serial process, termed controlled search, which must take time to compare each memory set item to each display item in turn.

[8] For a slightly more extensive review of the literature, see Shiffrin (1976) and Schneider (1975).

The development of the automatic search mode depends upon the learning of an "attention" response (perhaps facilitated by an already learned categorization) which controls the order of search, and directs attention automatically to relevant targets. Training in a search task using consistent, unchanging target and distractor sets will lead to the development of the automatic search mode, but only for the target set, not the distractor set.

Controlled search can be of two main types: exhaustive or terminating. Exhaustive search will tend to occur when the tasks are simple and the average reaction time will be very fast; terminating search (at a slower rate per comparison than exhaustive search) will tend to occur in complex tasks requiring large numbers of comparisons, tasks in which an exhaustive search would lead to slow reaction times on all trials.

In tasks requiring controlled search for memory sets of size larger than one, through visual displays of size larger than one, the subject will tend to search through the entire visual display for each memory element in turn; in addition to the basic comparison time, some time is needed to locate each new memory item.

A large class of selective attention results is due to the limitations upon short-term search. Attentional deficits will tend to appear when controlled search must be used and the task does not allow sufficient time to complete the search. In such cases, focused attention instructions or manipulations will allow a more efficient order of search to be adopted. The limitation on available search time can arise because short-term memory decays quickly (usually in tasks using near-threshold stimuli) or because new stimuli are presented which require processing (usually in tasks utilizing above-threshold stimuli).

Decisions themselves take time and processing capacity, so that detection of one target can cause another target in close temporal proximity to be missed. However, the deleterious effects of multiple targets are quite different depending upon whether the subject is in automatic or controlled search mode. In automatic mode identical targets inhibit one another, while in controlled mode, different targets inhibit one another. Also the time course of the inhibition differs in the two cases.

Search and/or attention tasks using accuracy measures can be qualitatively and quantitatively linked to search and/or attention tasks using latency measures, through the simple requirement that a target will be found only when there is time for the search process to locate it.

Although the research reported in this chapter is still in progress, and the models are still undergoing development and testing, we hope that a groundwork has been laid for a common theory of selective attention and short-term search processes. It is hoped further that the evidence presented in this chapter shows that memory scanning, visual search, and selective attention are manifestations of the same basic mechanisms.

ACKNOWLEDGMENTS

This research was supported by Public Health Service Grant 12717 to the first author. A more extensive treatment of the results in this paper may be found in Schneider, 1975, Schneider and Shiffrin (in press), and Shiffrin and Schneider (in press).

REFERENCES

Briggs, G. E., & Johnsen, A. M. On the nature of central processing in choice reactions. *Memory & Cognition*, 1973, **1**, 91–100.

Egeth, H., Jonides, J., & Wall, S. Parallel processing of multielement displays. *Cognitive Psychology*, 1972, **3**, 674–698.

Eijkman, E., & Vendrik, A. J. H. Can a sensory system be specified by its internal noise? *Journal of the Acoustical Society of America*, 1965, **37**, 1102–1109.

Eriksen, B. A., & Eriksen, C. W. Effects of noise letters upon identification of target in nonsearch tasks. *Perception & Psychophysics*, 1974, **16**, 143–149.

Lawson, E. A. Decisions concerning the rejected channel. *Quarterly Journal of Experimental Psychology*, 1966, **18**, 260–265.

Moray, N. A data base for theories of selective listening. In P. M. A. Rabbit & S. Dornic (Eds.), *Attention and performance V*. London: Academic Press, 1975.

Neisser, U. Practiced card sorting for multiple targets. *Memory & Cognition*, 1974, **2**, 781–785.

Nickerson, R. S. Response times with memory-dependent decision task. *Journal of Experimental Psychology*, 1966, **72**, 761–769.

Pachella, R. G. The interpretation of reaction time in information processing research. In B. H. Kantowitz (Ed.), *Human information processing: Tutorials in performance and cognition*. Hillsdale, N.J.: Lawrence Erlbaum Associates, 1974.

Scarborough, D. L., & Scarborough, H. Encoding and memory processes for visual displays. In P. M. A. Rabbit & S. Dornic (Eds.), *Attention and performance V*. London: Academic Press, 1975.

Schneider, W. Memory scanning, visual search, and selective attention: Three components of one process. Doctoral dissertation, Indiana University, Bloomington, 1975.

Schneider, W., & Shiffrin, R. M. Controlled and automatic human information processing: I. Detection, search, and attention. *Psychological Review*, in press, 1977.

Shiffrin, R. M. The locus and role of attention in memory systems. In P. M. A. Rabbit and S. Dornic (Eds.), *Attention and performance V*. London: Academic Press, 1975.

Shiffrin, R. M. Capacity limitations in information processing, attention, and memory. In W. K. Estes (Ed.), *Handbook of learning and cognitive processes, Vol. IV: Memory processes*. Hillsdale, N.J.: Lawrence Erlbaum Associates, 1976.

Shiffrin, R. M., & Schneider, W. Controlled and automatic human information processing: II. Perceptual learning, automatic attending, and a general theory. *Psychological Review*, in press, 1977.

Simpson, P. J. High-speed memory scanning: Stability and generality. *Journal of Experimental Psychology*, 1972, **96**, 239–246.

Sorkin, R. D., & Pohlman, L. D. Some models of observed behavior in two-channel auditory signal detection. *Perception & Psychophysics*, 1973, **14**, 101–109.

Sperling, G., Budiansky, J., Spivak, J. G., & Johnson, M. C. Extremely rapid visual search: The maximum rate of scanning letters for the presence of a numeral. *Science*, 1971, **174**, 307–311.

Sternberg, S. High-speed scanning in human memory. *Science,* 1966, **153,** 625–654.

Sternberg, S. Scanning a persisting visual image versus a memorized list. Paper presented at the annual meeting of the Eastern Psychological Association, 1967.

Sternberg, S. Memory scanning: Mental processes revealed by reaction-time experiments. *American Scientist,* 1969, **57,** 421–457.

Sternberg, S. Memory scanning: New findings and current controversies. *Quarterly Journal of Experimental Psychology,* 1975, **27,** 1–32.

Taylor, M., Lindsay, P., & Forbes, S. Quantification of shared capacity processing in auditory and visual discrimination. In A. Sanders (Ed.), *Attention and performance I.* Amsterdam: North-Holland Publ., 1967.

Teichner, W. J., & Krebs, M. J. Visual search for simple targets. *Psychological Bulletin,* 1974, **81,** 15–28.

Treisman, A. M., & Riley, J. G. A. Is selective attention selective perception or selective response? A further test. *Journal of Experimental Psychology,* 1969, **79,** 27–34.

21
Memory Control of
Visual Search[1]

Wolfgang Prinz[2]

*Psychologisches Institut der Ruhr-Universität
Bochum, Germany*

ABSTRACT

Models of the memory control of continuous visual search are discussed at three levels of analysis. At the *sample level* there are two rival views concerning the nature of the memory representation that enters the comparison between stimulus information and memory information: memory control of search can be exerted by a memory representation of the target(s) or of the nontarget(s) (target control versus context control). At the *trial level* two principal modes of temporal organization of subsequent sample analyses are distinguished: a one-process structure consisting of a chain of equivalent sample analyses and a two-process structure with an additional check at the end of the trial (scan-alone versus scan-and-check). At the *level of training sessions,* a model with three stages of practice is proposed. According to the model the search is under exclusive target control in Stage I and under exclusive context control in Stage III (scan-alone mode in both cases). Stage II mediates the transition from Stages I to III by means of a scan-and-check mode of processing, with the scan under context control and the check under target control. Evidence from a training experiment suggests that, within the range of task complexity employed, Stage I processing is restricted to the very first trials of the training period. Even the transition from Stage II to III can only be observed when the context is rather complex. It is concluded that search can be conducted under context control even without much practice.

---

[1] The experiment in Section III of this chapter was conducted by M. Junghoefer as part of his Diplom-Arbeit. The program for the generation of stimulus lists was written by D. Ataian.

[2] Now at the University of Bielefeld.

I. INTRODUCTION

A. The Nature of Search

Overt searching behavior seems to be a stimulus-controlled activity. At a descriptive level of analysis, there is no need for referring to memory control of the search process. Memory control comes into play at a functional level of analysis. When asked to explain a subject's behavior in an overt search task — or even to model it by constructing a machine that can search — we must regard the main components of overt search behavior (i.e., the eyes and the motor systems that control the orienting movements, and the target detection response as well) as afferent and efferent parts of the periphery of a central processing unit. The processor controls the overt search behavior by testing the input for the presence or absence of some predefined critical attribute(s) or some conjunctions thereof. This must be done by comparing an internal representation of the stimulus with a stored representation of the critical attribute(s). The central processor can be conceived as a device that comprises three parts (Fig. 1): a comparator (C), a stimulus representation (SR) and a memory representation (MR).

The flow chart in Fig. 1 gives an idea of how the machine could operate under conditions of discontinuous stimulus sampling. This principle of operation is of special interest since it seems to correspond to the discontinuous mode of information intake in the human visual system. So the chart can be read as a preliminary representation of human visual search if the operation of taking a new sample is interpreted as triggering a saccadic movement (Prinz & Ataian, 1973).

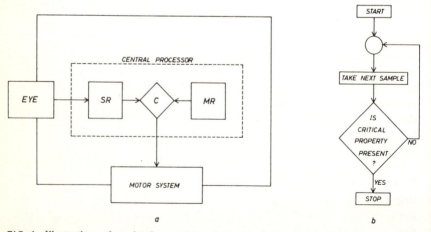

FIG. 1   Illustration of a simple searching device. a: basic structural equipment (SR = stimulus representation; MR = memory representation; C = comparator); b: flow chart of a search with discontinuous stimulus sampling.

B. The Search Experiment

The role of the memory representations that enter the comparator is to provide standards against which the stimulus samples – or their internal representations – are to be matched. How the search is controlled by memory information can be analyzed by means of measurements of SR–MR comparison times that are obtained in the same stimulus stimulation under conditions that differ in their memory load. Measurements of the comparison times cannot be obtained directly. This is because time and error scores are recorded at the level of search trials (i.e., chains of sample analyses that lead to a finding response) and not at sample level. One attack on this problem is to replace subject-controlled sampling behavior by very brief presentation of experimenter-controlled samples. This method for measuring time per sample (without eye-movement time) has been employed in experiments using discretely presented displays (cf. Estes & Taylor, 1966). Another method is provided by the statistical decomposition of search times as proposed by Neisser (1963, 1967). As Neisser has pointed out, it leads to an estimate of the processing time for an arbitrary section of the stimulus list (time per item, time per row), which is unaffected by motor response time: decision time without reaction time.

Neisser's method makes use of the same logic as Sternberg's well-known procedure for separating preprocessing and processing of information and measuring the time needed to perform these operations (Sternberg, 1967). The method can be applied to search time data from tasks with a linear arrangement of the search field (rows or columns of symbols) and with just one target symbol per row or column. Time per trial (= time that elapses between the start of the search and the finding response) is plotted over the position of the target in the linear field. The data from several trials are combined and plotted over target position. The regression function estimates two parameters of the underlying linear model, slope and intercept. The slope constant represents the subject's mean scanning rate. Its dimension is time per position unit. For the fictitious case of a direct correspondence between samples and position units the slope represents a direct measure of the wanted quantity "time per sample." It is unaffected by the time needed for those component processes of the search trial that are independent of the target position. The slope reflects the mean time for just one run through the loop of the chart in Fig. 1b, whereas the intercept is the sum of all time components outside the loop.

Some objections can be raised against this interpretation of the slope constant. First, the size of the functional sample is unknown. It could be both, smaller or larger than one position unit. Second, the slope could represent the time for simultaneous processing of items from different locations (samples) instead of time per sample if overlap of processing is assumed according to the model advanced by Sternberg and Scarborough (1969). Third, the slope comprises both, comparison times and eye movement times. Sperling, Budiansky, Spivak

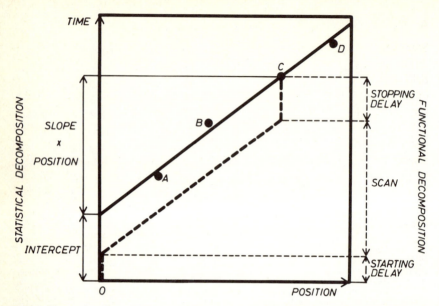

FIG. 2 Regression line relating search time to target position (solid thick line). The decomposition of search time in Observation C is shown. Solid lines: "statistical" decomposition (two time components). Broken lines: "functional" decomposition (three-component processes).

and Johnson (1971) have even argued that the rate of eye movements is the limiting factor in search — rather than the rate of information processing. These objections lead to the conclusion that the slope is not a direct measure of the time per sample. It is rather a "convenient fiction" (Neisser's term) for comparing scanning rates that are obtained under different task conditions.

Any component process that occurs just once in each trial will contribute to the intercept. This is especially true for all activities which have to do with starting and stopping the trial. Starting and stopping time should be independent of the target position. Figure 2 summarizes the statistical decomposition of search time into two parts and the corresponding functional decomposition into three components.

II.   MODELS OF MEMORY CONTROL OF SEARCH

Which memory representations are used in the control of search and how are they applied? This question can be raised at three different levels. At the first level it is concerned with the microstructure of the comparison process in each *sample.* At the second level it inquires about the structure of the search *trial.* At the third level it deals with changes in the mode of memory control in the course of *extended practice.*

A. Memory Control in Sample Analysis

Searching involves perceptual learning since it presupposes the detection of differences between the target object and the irrelevant context objects in the field. The distinguishing attributes are usually thought to result from some kind of natural selection from a lower-order list of standard features, with discriminatory power as the main criterion for survival (cf. Gibson, 1969, pp. 77 ff., 168 ff.). To the degree an attribute is distinguishing (with respect to its value for a discrimination task) it is said to be valid or criterial or even defining (with respect to an identification task). A distinguishing attribute (say, the roundness of the target symbol G in a search task) represents but one of the values of a two-valued dimension. Its discriminatory power is based on the existence of a complementary value (the jaggedness of the context letters K, X, W, Z). But this does not imply that both values of the dimension are functionally equivalent and that the subject controls his search by memory representations of both the target and the context symbols. Dimensions of difference between target and nontarget stimuli can be used to perform discriminations along them (dimensional discrimination). They can also be used to build an appropriate memory representation that serves for rapid identification of the members of one of the two stimulus classes involved (attribute detection). As has been shown elsewhere there is much evidence in favor of the attribute detection view (cf. Prinz & Scheerer-Neumann, 1974). According to this principle, a memory representation is needed for only one of the two stimulus categories. Which of both memory codes is used for the control of search: the memory representation of the target or of the nontarget category?

1. Target Control

Since searching is directed at detecting a target, it seems to be natural to assume that it is conducted under the control of a memory representation of the target. This logic is incorporated in most theories of visual search. Many discussions of memory control are concerned with the temporal organization of memory interrogation in disjunctive search tasks, that is, with whether the memory representations of multiple targets enter the comparator serially or simultaneously, without questioning whether the search is under target control at all (Kaplan & Carvellas, 1965; Kaplan, Carvellas & Metlay, 1966; Neisser, 1974; Neisser, Novick, & Lazar, 1963; Shurtleff & Marsetta, 1968; Ueno, 1968).

The principle of target control of sample analysis is illustrated in Fig. 3a. The comparator makes use of representation(s) of the target(s). It works as a target detector (recognizer, demon). As long as no target appears in the stimulus, the detector is silent and stimulus sampling goes on. When a match occurs between the stimulus representation and the memory representation of the target, the detector is activated. Sampling is interrupted and an overt finding response is triggered.

Though this model is extremely plausible it meets with two difficulties when its implications are examined in detail. The first difficulty is related to the

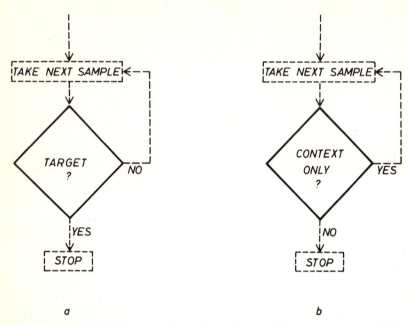

FIG. 3   Operation of the comparator under target control (a) and context control (b).

control of the sampling operation. According to this model, the sampling response (a saccadic movement) can only be triggered by default, that is, after failing to find evidence in favor of a finding response (cf. Neisser, 1964, p. 2). It is usually assumed that responses which are based on decisions by default can only be triggered at the end of some waiting interval. If errors are to be avoided the waiting time criterion must be set at a value greater than the mean time for responses based on decisions by positive evidence (cf. Nickerson's counter-and-clock model, 1969). Thus, according to this reasoning, a decision by default (leading to the sampling response) should take more time than a decision by positive evidence (leading to the finding response). This type of search control would seem to be rather uneconomical, especially since the sampling response must be triggered much more frequently than the finding response.

The second difficulty concerns a restriction of what can be learned to improve the search. When the search is under target control, the subject cannot alter the size of the units of comparison. This is because with this mode of memory control, the critical property is defined at the symbol level. Clusters of symbols cannot enter the comparator since they cannot be compared with stored representations of target symbols. Even if many symbols are included in one sample (as defined by an eye fixation) each of them must be compared individually to the target representations. According to this view, the large improvement that search performance undergoes with practice cannot be explained by the assumption that the subject learns to make use of higher order units of processing.

2. Context Control

Neisser has presented two different theories of search control. The target control model is the first of them (Neisser, 1967, p. 71 ff.). The second model is introduced in a later chapter of the same book. According to this model, search is under the control of recognizers that are not sensitive to individual symbols but to larger portions of the display. Though Neisser is not very explicit about how these recognizers control the search, he obviously assumes that the target is detected by default. The recognizers of Model II are not watching for the target as a target. Thy detect it in the same way as one detects a flash of light: as an event that does not fit into the subject's model of his present environment — and thus attracts his attention (Neisser, 1967, p. 99 f.).

This type of model implies that the search is performed under control of a memory representation of the context. When the search is controlled by a context representation, both of the above difficulties are avoided. As is illustrated in Fig. 3b, with context control the sampling response is triggered by a match between stimulus information and memory information — at the cost of triggering the detection response by a mismatch, of course. This mode of operation has two important implications. First, it displaces the problem of decision by default from the control over the (frequent) sampling response to the control over the (infrequent) detection response (which implies that the weakness of a decision by default can easily be compensated by some additional processing as is discussed in the next section of this chapter.

Second, it allows for comparisons at the level of clusters of symbols (and therefore gives opportunity for improving search speed by enlargement of the units of comparison). When the critical event that leads to detection is defined as a mismatch, the size of the units of comparison is no longer restricted to the symbol level. It will be limited by factors which are related to the visual structure of the context, because the ease of building a valid and distinguishing recognizer for larger portions of the display will depend on its internal homogeneity. But there is no limitation in principle. As far as the visual structure of the field permits, the subject's units of comparison can comprise increasingly larger portions of the field. One should note that learning to increase the size of the units of comparison is a possible but not a necessary implication of context control. Even if comparisons are performed at symbol level, context control can avoid the problem of triggering the sampling response by default.

There is now much evidence in favor of the concept of context control.

1. Neisser (1967, p. 100) observed that subjects who were trained on a disjunctive search task with multiple targets often reported that they stopped scanning without knowing which of the possible targets was present. This could imply that the target is not detected as a target, but as a non-context signal.

2. A similar line of reasoning has lead Neisser and Lazar (1964) to test subjects' ability to search for ill-defined targets. Their results are suggestive — though not conclusive — of an explanation in terms of context control. They

argue that a subject could detect ill-defined targets (novel targets, as they say) by failing to match them against a set of expected stimuli.

3. This explanation is supported by subjects' ability to detect targets they are not instructed to look for: when, after some practice, a search list is presented that contains the same context as usual but different targets, the subject will usually detect them. This observation was first made incidentally in our laboratory when wrong lists were presented by mistake. We are still engaged in a systematic study of this effect by means of a *hurdling technique*. In this paradigm, subjects are first given some training in a usual search task of the Neisser type. After some practice, slightly different lists are presented to them. The new lists are identical to the previous ones, except for the insertion of one or two new signals (*hurdles*) that did not appear in the context before. Though the task is untrained, subjects usually detect the hurdles on their very first occurrance (see Prinz, Tweer, & Feige, 1974, for a description of the method). Recent experiments (Prinz, 1976) suggest that there need not be much practice on the context before hurdles can be detected.

4. Context control of search has also been substantiated in transfer experiments with a card sorting technique conducted by Rabbitt (1967). He stated that a large portion of what a subject learns in a (search-like) card sorting task is related to the irrelevant items in the display and that the specificity of the cues that are used increases with practice. Rabbitt also found that the visual structure of the stimulus material is a very critical factor in the prediction of the degree of transfer.

5. A transfer paradigm was also applied by Prinz and Ataian (1973). They found that the scanning rate in a transfer task A/B ($=T/C$ where T = target category; C = context category) was superior for subjects who had been trained with a same-context task (A/B or C/B) as compared to subjects with practice in a different-context task (A/D or C/D). This superiority could be observed for both, same-target practice (A/B versus A/D) and different-target practice (C/B versus C/D). Though the degree of context-based transfer depended heavily on the visual structure of the search lists involved, the finding supports the concept of search control by a memory representation of the context.

6. Gordon (1968) has presented evidence in favor of the view that context related comparisons are carried out at the level of strings of symbols. He studied the relation of search speed to the size of the alphabet from which the context is constructed. Because search speed in complex-context tasks was not predictable from simple-context tasks, Gordon argued that context processing is not related to individual symbols but to strings of symbols.

3. Target Control Versus Context Control

We should not ask whether search is under target control or context control, but rather under which conditions each mode of processing is prevalent. Degree of specific practice could be a critical factor: without practice, a subject will be forced to operate under target control since he has not yet become familiar with the context. Practice will then increasingly favor context control since the subject becomes acquainted with the context more and more — first at the symbol level and then at the level of clusters of symbols after extended practice. The relative importance of both modes of control could also depend on the relative degree of complexity of the target set and the context set. When there are few relevant and many irrelevant symbols, target control could be more efficient than context control. Context control could be more likely to occur with many relevant and few irrelevant symbols. Assuming such relationships presupposes that, in principle, a subject has both control strategies at his disposal. Which of them is activated is contingent upon the actual task requirements.

B.   Structure of Processing on a Trial

1.   "Scan-alone"

In the case of target control there is no specific problem with integrating successive sample analyses in a trial. A subject will take a new sample when the last one has not led to a target match within some critical time limit. The resulting structure of the trial can be described as a chain of equivalent links (*scan-alone*). When the target is detected, no further link is added. The chain structure is mirrored in the flow chart in Fig. 1 (with target presence as the critical property). In the case of context control the chain structure model can also be applied (with partial context absence as the critical property). It then implies that the overt finding-and-stopping response is triggered by default.

2.   "Scan-and-check"

There are, however, some reasons to doubt this view. It could be argued that the scan-alone mode of processing changes into a *scan-and-check* mode after some practice, with the scan under context control and the check under target control. The scan would result in the detection of a critical location in the display. The check would test whether or not that location contains a target.

Neisser noted that skilled subjects (who can be assumed to operate under some degree of context control) often report on two distinct activities in relation to finding the target. One of them is detecting a critical location in the display. The other activity is rechecking which of several targets is contained in the sample. Detection results from what Neisser (1967, p. 100) calls a preattentive mode of operation, whereas rechecking needs focal attention.

Beller (1968) has put forward similar ideas. He distinguished two modes of information processing: "preattentive" and "focal attentive." In a search task the preattentive processing pertains to the irrelevant signals. It serves to elicit attention. When the focal attention mode of processing is switched on, object identification is possible. This two-process view was suggested by the finding that irrelevant processing times are shorter than relevant processing times.

Direct evidence for a check under target control was observed in a study by Sternberg and Scarborough (1969). They found in a simulated search experiment that the time that elapses between the presentation of a target containing sample and the overt finding response is linearly related to the size of the target category. This implies that at least the analysis of the target sample is under control of memory representations of the target(s). (From this result, no direct inferences regarding the processing of nontarget samples can be drawn. The authors argued that the same mode of processing could be applied to all earlier samples, with overlap of processing for subsequent samples. This is only a possible, not a necessary, conclusion).

As was pointed out by Prinz and Ataian (1973) the "preattentive" appearance of the scanning phase of a trial could be due to the context control of that phase. In the same way the "focal" nature of the check could be related to the target control which was postulated for that phase. The scan leads to target detection whereas the check leads to target identification. If the overt response were contingent upon both, detection and check for target identity, search time would include the time for the check. As the check usually occurs just once in each trial, checking time would enter into the intercept of the search function without affecting its slope. According to this reasoning, the authors predicted that transfer to a task with a new target category should affect the intercept of the search function involved. This prediction was basically confirmed.

A comment should be added regarding the notion of preattentiveness. This term can be defined at two levels: descriptive and explanatory. In a descriptive sense the preattentive phase of search is preattentive because it leads to the elicitation of a focal attentive response. At the explanatory level two types of theories have been put forward in order to model how preattentive processing differs from focal-attentive processing. Some writers have postulated differences in the *depth of processing* between the preattentive and the attentive stages of search (Beller, 1968; Neisser, 1967; Snyder, 1972). Other authors have proposed to assume a difference in the *mode of memory control* instead (Prinz & Ataian, 1973). According to this explanation, the preattentive character of the scan would result from the operation of recognizers operating on rather large sections of the display that permit a high degree of automaticity. When taken in this way the preattentive control of search by a memory representation of the context has much in common with the logic of Sokolov's (1963) concept of the neuronal model of the stimulus and its relation to the orienting response: as long as the actual stimulus (sample from the display) matches the corresponding neuronal model (memory code of the context), no orienting reaction can be observed (= preattentive mode). "An orienting reaction (= focal attentive response) develops at the moment when the stimulus administered ceases to coincide with a neuronal model . . ." (p. 287).

C. Changes of Search Control with Practice

As has been shown in several multiple-target experiments the influence of the size of the target set on search speed is drastically reduced with practice. Neisser's finding that subjects can learn to search for ten targets as rapidly as for one has never been exactly replicated (Neisser, Novick, & Lazar, 1963). But it has frequently been approximated in training experiments where extensive practice was provided. Several modifications of Neisser's initial parallel processing model and some alternatives to it have been suggested.

Kaplan and Carvellas (1965) suggested that practice appears to transform the initial condition of sequential search into the terminal condition of simultaneous search (where sequential search means: sample analysis by sequential memory search among the memory representations of the target category). This view implies that practice brings about a change in the structure of the target-related memory search that is performed within each sample analysis.

Graboi (1971) has refuted this interpretation. He summarized the result of his training experiment by saying that search for unfamiliar targets yields data like those of Sternberg (1967), whereas after extended practice with specific targets the data look most similar to those of Neisser. Graboi (1971) did not dwell on these similarities but on the discrepancies. A closer look revealed that there was neither evidence in favor of a serial memory search without specific practice nor of a parallel mode of processing with specific practice. He refused the view that practice serves to change the temporal organization of some target-related memory search. He favored another explanatory principle that had first been suggested by Neisser (1967, p. 71). It assumes that practice operates to enhance the efficiency of memory representations of the targets, without affecting the organization of the memory comparisons at all. For the unpracticed searcher, a many-target task will be more difficult than a one-target task since the mere chance of detecting valid and distinguishing attributes will decrease as the complexity of the target category increases. This is because increasing the target category (with context category constant) tends to increase the number of attributes that are shared by some targets and some nontargets and thus to reduce the number of attributes that can be used to distinguish between both categories. When specific practice improves the efficiency of the memory codes, the absolute difference between both tasks will become smaller (no matter whether the processing is serial or parallel). But due to the inverse relationship between the number of the targets and the ease of detecting the defining attributes of the target category, it will never go to zero.

Several writers have suggested that search performance cannot be analyzed without considering error rates. Wattenbarger (1968) found that subjects could only search equally rapidly for one and many targets if stress on accuracy was low. Similar conclusions were drawn from an experiment by Kristofferson (1972). In this study, error rates were low and the difference in search speeds between single target and multiple target conditions did not disappear even after 25 days of practice. Yonas and Pittenger (1973) recorded the error rates for each member of a multiple target set and compared them with error rates obtained for the same characters in single target conditions. Though the overall error rates were approximately equivalent in both conditions, detection accuracy for the most difficult target tended to be lower in the multiple target task as compared to the single target task. Since the search rate was roughly the same in these two tasks this could imply that subjects maintain a certain speed level in both tasks, at the cost of a loss in accuracy in the more difficult task. Neisser (1974) found similar results in a card sorting experiment. These findings join in the conclusion that implications of search rates for models of search cannot be discussed without reference to accuracy data.

Sternberg and Scarborough (1969) put forward the idea that the simultaneous appearance of a many target search could be due to a serial memory search (among the memory representations of the targets) for several items (samples) simultaneously. The model works well for simulated search where stimulus sampling is experimenter controlled. But it is hard to see how it can account for search tasks with subject-controlled sampling. Given that a subject has a capacity for testing n stimuli in parallel against one memory representation it is reasonable to assume that he samples these stimuli simultaneously if they are all available at the same time. If he does so, his search rate cannot be independent of the number of targets since he cannot take a new sample before the old one has been matched against all target representations. The overlap hypothesis seems only to work in situations in which the rate of stimulus presentation is beyond the subject's capacity for simultaneous sampling.

Another way of improving the efficiency of search is suggested by the distinction of target control and memory control. As indicated above, practice could change the memory control of search by passing from target control to context control. Efficiency will be improved because the size of the units of comparison could be enlarged with context control. Figure 4 illustrates a theory of search control that distinguishes three stages of practice. It predicts a gradual improvement of search speed resulting from a qualitative change in the mode of sample analyses. This is warranted by the assumption of concomitant changes in the structure of the search trial. The theory assumes that a subject starts his search under exclusive target control (Stage I). This is postulated on a priori grounds since the instruction enumerates the targets without designating the nontargets. After some practice, representations of the nontargets can be formed. They are used in the search, though not exclusively. As was outlined above, it is reasonable to assume that the overt stopping response remains under target control for some time. This leads to the scan-and-check procedure illustrated in the chart for Stage II. It can be read in one of two ways. When the broken arrow is disregarded it represents the scan-and-check as was outlined in the above section on trial structure: there is just one check per trial. This is the

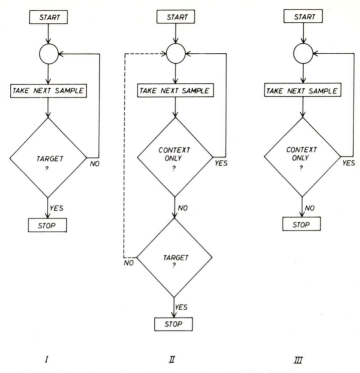

FIG. 4 Three stages of practice in search control. For details, see text.

final state of Stage II. When the dotted arrow is included, the chart represents the state of transition from Stage I to Stage II: depending upon the degree of efficiency of the context representation that is being established, the subject will mix small and big loops in his trials. When efficiency increases the proportion of big loops will decrease and finally be reduced to but one final checking step. Stage II can then pass into Stage III. This would occur when the memory codes for context control have attained perfect efficiency. This criterion is fulfilled when each location of the display that leads to a context mismatch does contain a target (perfect distinctiveness; no errors of commission) and when each location that contains a target leads to a context mismatch (perfect validity; no errors of omission).

What are the implications of this theory regarding the influence of the size of the target set on search speed at different stages of practice? In Stage I, the set size should clearly affect the slope of the search function, since it mirrors the rate of the scan under target control. When the scan is a mixture of sample analyses under target and context control, the effect of the target set size should be reduced. The final states of Stages II and III are equivalent as far as the scanning phase of the search trial is concerned. Though exclusive context control seems to imply independence of the scanning rate from the size of the target set, some residual effect must be predicted even for these stages. This is because the previously mentioned argument in relation to memory representations of the target must also be applied to the representation of the context: the larger the target set the smaller the number of valid and distinctive attributes that can be used for a functional definition of the nontarget category. So far the theory explains known effects. It also predicts new effects which are related to the intercept of the search function. The intercept should not be affected by target set size in Stages I and III. During these stages it only comprises the delay time at starting and stopping the trial. But there must be a stage of transition between the initial and the final stage in which target-related processing (which is assumed to be affected by alphabet size) is confined to the check that occurs just once on a trial. This should be reflected in a transient effect of target-set size on the intercept of the search function.

III.   EVIDENCE FROM A TRAINING EXPERIMENT

A. Purpose

The following experiment was run in order to learn how the slopes and the intercepts of search functions develop over extended practice with few and with many targets. In addition to the size of the target set and the degree of specific practice, context complexity was introduced as the third experimental variable. It was added in order to learn whether the complexity of the display determines how rapidly subjects can pass through the three postulated stages. It was expected that the final stage would be attained earlier with (relatively) homogeneous lists as compared to (relatively) complex or heterogeneous lists. This was predicted because the ease of establishing an efficient memory code of the context should vary inversely with context complexity.

B. Procedure

1. Stimulus Materials

Search lists were generated by a computer and printed on a teleprinter (Siemens T 100, with upper case letters). The program produced lists that contain 64 (rows) × 8 (columns) = 512 symbols. Each list contained one target at a randomly selected position. The rules for the generation of the lists have been described in detail by Prinz and Ataian (1973; see also for sample letters, p. 273). For the present experiment the program was modified to allow for the generation of lists with variable size of both target and context set. All nontargets appeared about equally often within the set of lists prepared for each stimulus condition (see the following).

2. Apparatus

The apparatus for the presentation of search lists has been described elsewhere (Prinz, Hartlich, & Lahmeyer, 1972). Search times were recorded to the nearest .01 sec).

3. Task

Each subject took part in 3 conditions within each of 20 sessions. The conditions differed with respect to the size and the content of the target category, but they did not differ with respect to the context. In the 3 conditions the subject was to search for 2, 4, or 8 targets, respectively (conditions T2, T4, T8). The target sets did not overlap. Nesting of conditions was avoided because with nested conditions, the subject could search for the most complex target category all the time, thereby scanning with the same speed in all conditions (this would be a possible explanation for the parallel search in the 10-target experiment by Neisser et al. (1963; cf. Kristofferson, Groen, & Kristofferson, 1973)). For each subject, the composition of each target set was kept constant over the 20 sessions. The conditions were presented in blocks, with the order of blocks balanced over sessions. As a period of 1 hour was regarded to be the upper time limit for an experimental session, a block was initially not limited by a certain number of trials, but by a period of 20 minutes. This criterion was applied until the subject searched at a rate of approximately 20 successful trials per block. When he reached this criterion, the limit of 20 minutes was replaced by a limit of 20 target detections. Note that the number of successful detections is smaller than the number of trials actually performed, since warm-up trials (1 per block) and trials with failure of detection are not included. Those subjects that were run in C5 (simple context) reached this criterion about Sessions 5 and 6. For the subjects in C10 this occurred much later in the course of practice – if at all. As far as possible, sessions were arranged at the same time on consecutive days.

4. Subjects and design

Subjects were 6 students of psychology who took part in the experiment in partial fulfillment of a curriculum requirement. Each subject was assigned to one of the two levels of context set size. The "homogeneous" context (subjects 1–3) was made up from 5 symbols (G J N U Y), the "heterogeneous" context (subjects 4–6) from 10 symbols (C G J K N S U W X Y) (Conditions C5 and C10). The composition of the target sets was as follows:

Subjects	T2	T4	T8
1, 4	AD	EOPT	BFHLQRVZ
2, 5	DO	BEPT	AFHLQRVZ
3, 6	AO	BDPT	EFHLQRVZ

5. Data Analysis

For each block the slope and the zero intercept of the search function were computed. Sixty search functions (20 sessions × 3 target conditions) were thus obtained for each subject. The resulting estimates of slope and intercept were classified according to the factors C (context-set size), T (target-set size), and P (practice sessions) and subjected to analysis of variance (with C between, and with T and P within subjects). As error variance was reduced drastically with practice, the data from the beginning and the end of the experiment had to be processed separately, yielding two analyses for the slopes and two other ones for the intercepts.

C. Results

The effects of T and C on the slope of the search function in the first five and the last five practice sessions are depicted in Fig. 5. It can be seen that the final speed of scanning is about six times the initial speed. It is also obvious that the effect of the factors T and C decreases heavily with practice. For the first five sessions of practice both T and C are significant sources of variation ($F = 48,11$, $df = 2/8$, $p < 0.001$; and $F = 10,54$, $df = 1/4$, $p < 0.05$ for T and C, respectively). P is a significant factor, too ($F = 20,46$, $df = 4/16$, $p < 0.001$), but it does not interact with T or C. In the last five sessions of practice the between-subject factor C becomes insignificant. But target-set size is still a very potent predictor of the scanning rate ($F = 25,05$, $df = 2/8$, $p < 0.001$). As the curves indicate, this small but reliable effect can be observed in both context conditions. P remains a highly significant source of variation even after 16 days of practice ($F = 10.71$, $df = 4/16$, $p < 0.001$). This is due to a decrease in mean scanning rate from .128 to .091 seconds per item that still occurs between Sessions 17 and 20.

So far the results replicate the usual finding that practice serves (1) to speed up the scan very drastically and (2) to reduce heavily the effect of target set size — without, however, affecting its statistical reliability. These findings are inconclusive since they can be explained by many classes of models. Yet another finding supports the view that practice serves to improve the efficiency of the analyzers involved. As is indicated in Fig. 6 the effects of T and C are not independent. Their interaction ($T \times C$) just fails to reach the level of significance in the above analyses ($p \approx 0.07$ in both cases), but it is clearly reliable in the Practice Sessions 6–15. This interaction seems to imply that both factors are operating at the same stage of processing. This is to be expected under the hypothesis of improvement of analyzer efficiency. Whether an analyzer recognizes targets or nontargets, its efficiency must depend on the feature relations of both categories. An analyzer for a complex category will be more affected by an

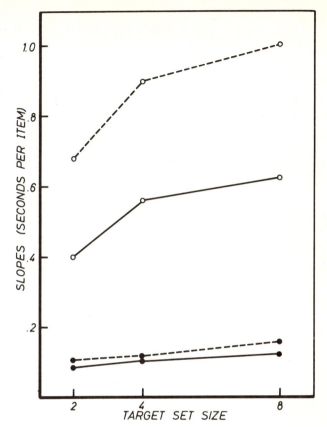

FIG. 5 Time per item (row of eight symbols) over target set size for Sessions 1–5 (open circles) and 16–20 (solid circles). Solid lines: condition C5; broken lines: C10.

increase of the alphabet size of the complementary category than an analyzer for a simple category.

Figure 6 shows the effects of T and C on the intercept of the search functions for the first five and the last five sessions. The intercept decreases from the early to the late sessions. For Group C10 the decrease seems to be larger than for Group C5, but this interaction cannot be tested in the present form of analysis. In the last 5 sessions the intercept is neither affected by T nor by C nor by their interaction ($F < 1$ in all cases). This picture is quite different for the first days of practice. For these data, T and $T \times C$ are significant sources of variation ($F = 7,8$ and $7,11$, $df = 2/8$, and $p < 0.05$ in both cases). C is insiginficant ($F < 1$). As is evidenced by a decomposition into simple main effects the influence of T on the intercept is reliable under condition C10 ($F = 13,93$ with $df = 2/8$, $p < 0.01$), but not under condition C5 ($F < 1$). But even for the C10 group the intercepts

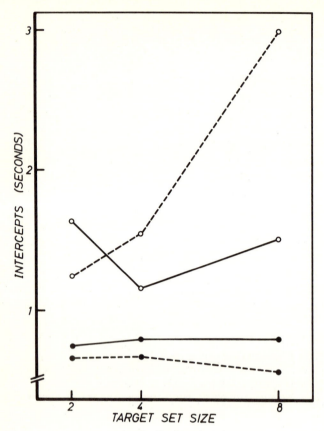

FIG. 6 Intercepts over target set size for Sessions 1–5 (upper curves) and 16–20 (lower curves). Same coding as in Fig. 5.

become virtually independent of target set size after 5–7 sessions of practice (the curves for Sessions 6–10 are as flat as those for sessions 16–20). It must be concluded that target set size can affect the intercept in the very early stages of practice, provided that the context is not too simple.

The error rates (errors of omission) differed markedly between conditions C5 and C10. In the C5 condition they were low (3,4% in the first five and 0,8% in the last five sessions) and did not covary with T. In the C10 condition they were much higher and positively related to the T conditions. In the first five sessions they were 11.5, 20.4, and 29.0% for T2, T4, and T8. In the last five sessions the corresponding values were 14.8, 4.8, and 18.5%. Overt errors of omission were too infrequent for an analysis (less than 0, 4%). The pattern of omissions seems to suggest that subjects' overall accuracy criterion went down with increasing complexity of the target category in the C10 condition. This rules out a possible explanation of the effects of T on the slopes in terms of speed—accuracy trade off. Increasing the complexity of the target set deteriorates both slopes and omission errors at the same time.

D. Discussion

An account of these results in terms of the above outlined three-stage theory of practice could be given as follows. For the heterogeneous lists two functional stages are observed instead of the expected three. Performance in the early sessions reflects the scan-and-check mode of search control which is represented in the model for Stage II. Performance in the late sessions reflects processing according to the Stage-III model (efficient context control). For the homogeneous lists processing corresponds to this latter model from the beginning. According to this view the initial stages of practice cannot be inferred from the present data, because they are confined to the initial trials in the first session. In these very first trials the search must be target controlled by definition (Stage I of the model). During these trials a memory representation of the context is established. Within the range of context complexity that was employed in the present experiment, this memory code attains a considerable degree of efficiency within a few trials. When the lists are simple, the efficiency of the code is virtually perfect after this small amount of practice, and the subject can run the total trial under exclusive context control. When the lists are complex, an additional check is needed for some time for the control of the overt stopping response. It drops out when further practice has improved the distinctiveness of the context code to a sufficient degree of efficiency. Thus the transition from Stage II to Stage III comes later for the complex lists.

This interpretation of the results suggests the conclusion that the search is conducted under context control from the beginning — perhaps with the exception of the very first trials. Contrary to our expectations the transition from Stage I to Stage II seems to be accomplished rather easily within the present range of task complexity. The previous reasoning concerning different mixtures of small and big loops in the stage of transition from Stage I to II is not needed since this step must have occurred in a few trials. Perhaps Stage I could be more clearly demonstrated with more complex tasks.

Three explanations can be offered for the disappearance of the effect of target set size on the intercept with practice: (1) the extra check process simply drops out; (2) it remains, but due to practice it becomes independent of the target set size; (3) it remains, but it ceases to affect search time, because the control over the triggering of the overt stopping response passes from the check to the scan. The second explanation can be disregarded since it cannot account for the dependence of the target set size effect on the complexity of the context. A decision between the remaining two explanations cannot be reached with the present data. Both alternatives attribute the disappearance of the effect with practice to the growth of efficiency of the memory code of the context.

IV. CONCLUSION

The summary of the results in terms of the three-stage model of practice can only be tentative. In this experiment there is no direct evidence for context control during the scan. There is evidence for an extra check occuring once per trial in the initial stage of practice with a rather complex context. The occurrence of the target check suggests that a different mode of processing is applied during the scan. In principle, this could be both context control or a fast, superficial version of target control. Converging operations are needed in order to substantiate the view that the scan is under context control. One of them is the use of hurdles as described (see Prinz, Tweer, & Feige, 1974). Recent experiments (Prinz, 1976) showed that hurdles which are interspersed among the context symbols are detected at their very first occurrence in the first session. This could indicate that the search is conducted under context control virtually from the beginning, thus corroborating the above tentative conclusions.

These considerations lead us to remodify the modified model presented in the discussion by Prinz and Ataian (1973). They introduced, as a modification of their initial reasoning, an operation that was called a test for internal consistency (of a sample). This operation was to account for a lack of context-based transfer in the scan for two of the four stimulus lists of their experiment (i.e., subjects who had practiced with the same context before did not scan faster as compared to subjects with different-context practice). These findings suggest that this additional operation need not be postulated. Lack of context transfer can also be explained by the assumption that, with "easy" lists, an efficient memory representation of the context can be established so readily that specific pretraining on the same context does not give any lead as compared to different-context practice. Such rapid establishment of a memory representation was not taken into consideration by Prinz and Ataian (1973), because they had assumed that context control of search could only occur after a high degree of specific practice. Since this view must be questioned now, their memory-independent test for sample consistency should be replaced by memory-dependent sample analyses under the control of a readily established memory representation of the context.

ACKNOWLEDGMENTS

Program development was supported by Grant Pr 118/1-2 from the Deutsche Forschungs-gemeinschaft to the present author.

REFERENCES

Beller, H. K. *Stages of processing in visual search.* Unpublished Doctoral Dissertation, Brandeis University, 1968.

Estes, W. K., & Taylor, H. A. Visual detection in relation to display size and redundancy of critical elements. *Perception & Psychophysics,* 1966, **1,** 9–16.

Gibson, E. J. *Principles of perceptual learning and development.* New York: Appleton-Century-Crofts, 1969.

Gordon, I. E. Interactions between items in visual serach. *Journal of Experimental Psychology,* 1968, **76,** 348–355.

Graboi, D. Searching for targets: The effects of specific practice. *Perception & Psychophysics,* 1971, **10,** 300–304.

Kaplan, I. T., & Carvellas, T. Scanning for multiple targets. *Perceptual and Motor Skills,* 1965, **21,** 239–243.

Kaplan, I. T., Carvellas, T., & Metlay, W. Visual search and immediate memory. *Journal of Experimental Psychology,* 1966, **71,** 488–493.

Kristofferson, M. W. Types and frequency of errors in visual serach. *Perception & Psychophysics,* 1972, **11,** 325–328.

Kristofferson, M. W., Groen, M., & Kristofferson, A. B. When visual search functions look like item recognition functions. *Perception & Psychophysics,* 1973, **14,** 186–192.

Neisser, U. Decision-time without reaction time: Experiments in visual scanning. *American Journal of Psychology,* 1963, **76,** 376–385.

Neisser, U. Experiments in visual search and their theoretical implications. Paper presented at the annual meeting of the Psychonomic Society, October 1964.

Neisser, U. *Cognitive psychology.* New York: Appleton-Century-Crofts, 1967.

Neisser, U. Practiced card sorting for multiple targets. *Memory & Cognition,* 1974, **2,** 781–785.

Neisser, U., & Lazar, R. Searching for novel targets. *Perceptual and Motor Skills,* 1964, **19,** 427–432.

Neisser, U., Novick, R., & Lazar, R. Searching for ten targets simultaneously. *Perceptual and Motor Skills,* 1963, **17,** 955–961.

Nickerson, R. S. 'Same'–'Different' response times: A model and a preliminary test. In W. G. Koster (Ed.), *Attention & Performance II.* Amsterdam: North-Holland Publ., 1969. Pp. 257–275.

Prinz, W., & Ataian, D. Two components and two stages in search performance: A case study in visual search. *Acta Psychologica,* 1973, **37,** 218–242.

Prinz, W., Hartlich, S., & Lahmeyer, W. Nicht-visueller Transfer in einer visuellen Suchaufgabe. *Psychologische Forschung,* 1972, **35,** 218–242.

Prinz, W., & Scheerer-Neumann, G. Component processes in multiattribute stimulus classification. *Psychological Research,* 1974, **37,** 25–50.

Prinz, W., Tweer, R., & Feige, R. Context control of search behavior: Evidence from a 'hurdling' technique. *Acta Psychologica,* 1974, **38,** 73–80.

Prinz, W. Development of Context Control in a Visual Search Task. Paper presented at the 1st Scandinavian Symposium on Attention and Performance. Uppsala, Sweden, 1976.

Rabbitt, P. M. Learning to ignore irrelevant information. *American Journal of Psychology,* 1967, **80,** 1–13.

Shurtleff, D. A., & Marsetta, M. Y. Visual search in a latter canceling task reexamined. *Journal of Experimental Psychology,* 1968, **77,** 19–23.

Snyder, Ch. R. R. Selection, inspection and naming in visual search. *Journal of Experimental Psychology,* 1972, **92,** 428–431.

Sokolov, Y. N. *Perception and the conditioned reflex.* London: Pergamon Press, 1963.

Sperling, G., Budiansky, J., Spivak, J. G., & Johnson, M. C. Extremely rapid visual search: The maximum rate of scanning letters for the presence of a numeral. *Science,* 1971, **174,** 307–311.

Sternberg, S. Two operations in character recognition: Some evidence from reaction time measurements. *Perception & Psychophysics,* 1967, **2,** 45–53.

Sternberg, S., & Scarborough, D. L. Parallel testing of stimuli in visual search. In *Visual Information processing and Control of Motor Activity.* Bulgarian Academy of Sciences, Sofia, 1969. Pp. 179–188.

Ueno, T. Visual search time based on stochastic serial and parallel processings. *Perception & Psychophysics,* 1968, **3,** 229–232.

Wattenbarger, B. L. Speed and accuracy set in visual search performance. Paper presented at the meeting of Mid-Western Psychological Association, Chicago, 1968.

Yonas, A., & Pittenger, J. Searching for many targets: An analysis of speed and accuracy. *Perception & Psychophsysics,* 1973, **13,** 513–516.

22

The Place of the Concept of Activation in Human Information Processing Theory: An Integrative Approach

Peter Hamilton

Department of Psychology, University of Stirling
Stirling, Scotland

Bob Hockey

Department of Psychology, Durham University
Durham, England

Mike Rejman

Department of Psychology, University of Stirling
Stirling, Scotland

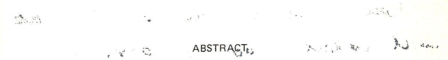

ABSTRACT

Effects on several component processes of human performance due to the action of mild noise-induced stress are outlined. These include changes in attentional disposition, information transformation rate, primary memory capacity, and response bias in a choice task. It is shown that performance of a complex multicomponent skill, here called closed-system thinking, is affected by noise in directions predictable from a knowledge of the stressor's effects on individual components. On the basis of these, and relevant physiological data we argue that changes in state due to stressors are more realistically seen as vector rather than scalar quantities, having "direction" as well as magnitude. Such an assumption involves activation processes quite intimately in the ongoing control of cognitive operations. A conceptual model of the control hierarchy is presented, incorporating a "state selection" operation based on short-term processing goals, and a "state acquisition" operation based on operant control of an "executive" response. Data bearing on the model are presented and discussed.

I. ACTIVATION STATES AND COMPONENTS
OF HUMAN PERFORMANCE

The physiological state of the organism may be indexed by the functional level of a wide range of autonomic and central nervous system variables. Intercorrelation between the functional levels found in a variety of situations is quite low, and indeed the direction of relative movement may be found to vary as a function of the activity in progress (Lacey, 1967). Under these circumstances caution demands that we conceive of the organism at any moment as being in one of many possible *activation states* representing points in a notional multi-dimensional space, rather than as being at some level on a single dimension ranging from low to high activation. Such a concept is implicit in much recent work (Broadbent, 1971; Kahneman, 1973; Pribram & McGuinness, 1975).

Different patterns of autonomic activity seem to be associated with different types of cognitive function. In tasks involving acceptance of environmental input heart rate typically decelerates while pupil diameter increases. When information is being transformed or output heart rate accelerates though pupil diameter still shows an increase (Lacey, 1967). One must suppose that the particular physiological configuration observed is appropriate to the type of information processing in progress. Kahneman (1973) has reviewed the literature on these points.

The idea that a particular state of physiological balance may be injurious to some and beneficial to other aspects of information processing suggests that a rethinking of accepted rules governing the relationship between activation and performance is required. These rules are enshrined in the Yerkes–Dodson law, originally developed in the field of animal discrimination learning. The law describes an inverted U-shaped relationship between performance of a task and activation level, such that performance rises to an optimum as activation level rises, then subsequently declines. Furthermore, the optimal levels of activation for "simple" tasks are higher than those for "complex" tasks. There is a good deal of empirical support for the law, gained by use of diverse stressors on a wide range of laboratory tasks. A few attempts have been made, and these are mentioned subsequently, to say exactly *why* processing efficiency should relate to activation in this way, and to impart some psychological meaning to the terms simplicity and complexity. These attempts indicate fairly clearly that explanation in terms of a single pervasive central process is extremely unlikely. Kahneman (1973) notes that manipulations of activation have yielded effects on long-term memory, short-term memory, attention distribution, stimulus discrimination, and speed–accuracy tradeoff. Broadbent (1971) warns that the type of breakdown under stress in terms of errors, loss of speed and so on, varies from stressor to stressor, thus ". . . it is clear that one must examine the possibility that different stresses are affecting different mechanisms" (p. 405).

Assume for the moment that the above is true. It would then seem that the effects of a given activation state on performance would depend precisely on the functional level of various processing mechanisms set by that state *and the extent to which each of these must be deployed in performance of the task.* One is then forced to the position of considering the interaction between the quality of the particular state (rather than activation level) and the quality of task demand (rather than level of complexity). In such circumstances the relationship between state variables and cognitive efficiency is likely to be much more complex and intimate than established theory would hold. The concept of activation as a "volume" control for information flow would inevitably cease to be even a useful metaphor.

It was in pursuit of these ideas that the following set of experiments was devised. We have taken two activation states: that prevailing in a "normal" test situation and that produced by the introduction of a moderate level of white noise. The aim is to assess the nature of changes that take place in various component processes of performance such as attention and memory, in tasks that are heavily dependent on these components. Following this exercise we examine the effect of the state change on tasks embodying different weightings of these components to assess the extent to which overall efficiency shifts reflect the quality of change in the individual components. Although we have, in the main, restricted our analysis to a single stressor, noise, the implications for the activation concept in general are quite apparent. It would be quite out of place, in this chapter, to present a review of the effects of noise, let alone those of stress in general, on human performance. All we can do, in the space available is to make reference to the more widely accepted conclusions, where the argument demands it.

At the outset we should say that having borrowed the principle of activation state (as opposed to level) from physiology we feel no need to base subsequent work on consideration of physiological detail. It is sufficient to postulate that the functional levels of various behavioral processes can at any time be mapped on to a corresponding physiological pattern. From that point on the onus is on the researcher to show that unique patterns of component function can be observed, and that they reflect in a meaningful way on performance of tasks in which a number of such functions are employed.

A.   The Relative Strength of Reaction Potentials

Changes in activation state are commonly accompanied by shifts in the disposition of attention over competing sources in the experiment (Easterbrook, 1959; Hockey, 1970). Noise, for instance, appears to cause an increase in scanning of sources of high relevance or priority. A possible explanation is that differences between the "reaction potentials" determining scanning response allocation are disturbed by state changes. The resulting shift in input selection bias may, thus, be mirrored by changes in output selection bias. If so this would indicate that some central process common to the two is the source of the effect.

In a normal monitoring situation two factors determine the scanning frequency of different sources. These are the relative probability that particular sources will yield critical information, and the probability that there *is* critical information in the space being scanned (Hamilton, 1969). When many of the subject's sampling responses are "irrelevant," because of a low rate of information input, sampling may be devoted equally to all sources in spite of large differences in their relative probabilities of yielding information. Sampling is said to be less *selective* when information flow is low. It is in this situation that effects of noise are observable. Hockey (1973) showed that increased sampling of high signal probability sources resulted from noise administration, but the rate of signal input was such that *the probability of no signal existing in the system at the time of scanning was quite high.* On the other hand, little is known about the effects of noise when irrelevant outcomes are nonexistent, that is, when the probability that there is usable information in the system is unity. The monitoring behavior of subjects in a normal state seems to be closely mirrored by the output of operant responses in a prediction situation. Where an outcome always follows a prediction, guessing is seen to match the relative probability of outcomes. If sometimes an "irrelevant" outcome not within the prediction set appears, its effect is to reduce discrimination between outcomes of differing probability (Greeno, 1962). There is no evidence that noise affects response bias in the former situation (Broadbent, 1971), but by analogy with the monitoring experiment we should expect to detect some change when irrelevant outcomes are introduced. This hypothesis is tested here in the context of a prediction situation similar to that used by Greeno (1962). The subject is required to guess on each trial which of two events will occur and is subsequently informed of outcome. Changes in output response bias can be inferred from observed guessing frequencies. In the present task, the relative probability of events to be predicted is varied, although the absolute difference between probabilities is held constant. The probability of an irrelevant outcome is also varied. We would predict on the basis of the previously mentioned attention research that: (1) where irrelevance of outcome is high the frequency of response to high probability events will be below that predicted by a probability matching hypothesis; and (2) responses to the high probability source will increase in noise, at least where irrelevance is high.

1. Experiment I

Performance in quiet (50 dB background) and white noise (85 dB) was measured in a guessing situation. On each trial subjects guessed which of two lights, red or green, was to be illuminated. In some conditions of the experiment a guess was followed by an irrelevant event — the occurrence of either a white light or both red and green lights on the display. Ten groups of ten subjects performed the task, five groups in noise and five in quiet. Each of the five groups in a given stress condition dealt with a different set of event probabilities. These are shown in Table 1.

As can be seen the absolute difference between p_{red} and p_{green} is held at .4 throughout. Subjects in all groups were told that occasionally the computer generating the outcomes might malfunction and throw up a white light or both red and green lights. Such events were to be ignored. Responses to the high probability (red) light were accumulated on counters, with totals noted after the completion of each 40 "real" (i.e., red or green alone) events. Testing continued until each group had experienced 280 such events (7 blocks of trials).

The probability of response to the red light over the last three trial blocks for all ten groups is shown in Fig. 1.

The data were collapsed over types of irrelevant event to give an overall impression of the effect of irrelevance in the situation. This is shown for all learning trials in Fig. 2. At the asymptote, the general picture is that responses to the red light occur with about equal frequency for all event schedules in quiet. There appears to be an interaction between noise and conditions such that increase in "red" responses occur when irrelevant event outcome is high, but decrease when it is zero. The observed change in responding at high irrelevance levels thus takes the same form as that found in attention tasks. In spite of the coherence of the picture the statistical evidence is rather weak. Error estimates are enlarged by the few subjects in each group who adopt formal optimization strategies and an overall F test indicates that the expected interaction between noise and probability conditions is not significant. However, since we have predicted that an increase of irrelevance of any kind will lead to an increased tendency for noise to be associated with high probability responses, a planned comparison is the more appropriate procedure. A comparison of the difference between the .7, .3 and the average of the two .5, .1, .4 conditions for noise and quiet does in fact achieve significance ($F = 3.95$, $df = 1, 90$, $p = .05$), in accordance with this prediction.

These data *do* cast some doubt on the assertion by Broadbent (1971) that noise affects only stimulus selection processes. If an appropriate one-to-many

TABLE 1
Event Probatilities in the Prediction Experiment

Condition	Probabilities presented			
	White	Red	Green	Red and green
1	.4	.5	.1	0
2	.2	.6	.2	0
3	0	.7	.3	0
4	0	.6	.2	.2
5	0	.5	.1	.4

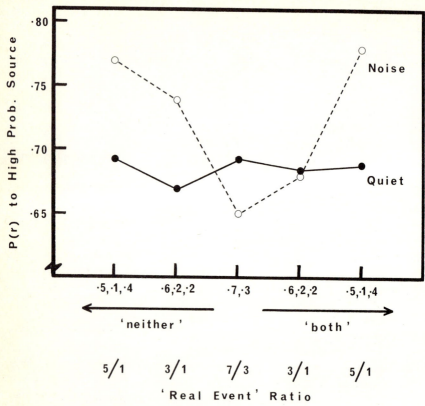

FIG. 1 Mean prediction probability for the most frequent event over the final 120 "real" events, in quiet and noise. In the conditions labeled "neither," a white light was the irrelevant event. In those labeled "both," there was simultaneous presentation of red and green lights.

mapping situation can be found we believe that a distinct change in operant response bias will be observed.

Within the present paradigm we *can* exclude the possibility that any difference observed in the main experiment is due either to change in the perception of probabilities within an event sequence, or to ability to generate responses from a known set of probabilities.

2. Experiment II

The aim was to determine the accuracy of perception of probabilities as a function of noise and event schedule. Subjects were exposed to a rapidly flashed series of signal events of the type used in Experiment I. They were subsequently asked to assess the relative probabilities of these events. Over six trials, the probabilities used were either $p_{red} = .7$, $p_{green} = .3$, $p_{white} = .0$; or $p_{red} = .5$,

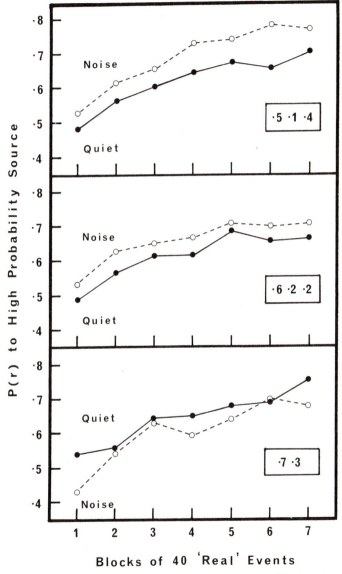

FIG. 2 Learning curves for three levels of irrelevant event probability in quiet and noise. Data for "red and green" and "white" irrelevant events are combined.

TABLE 2
Mean Reported Probabilities of Events Following a
300-Event Sequence

Probability reported	Probability presented					
	Red .7	Green .3	White 0	Red .5	Green .1	White .4
Quiet	.71	.29	–	.46	.13	.41
Noise	.69	.31	–	.47	.15	.38

p_{green} = .1, p_{white} = .4. These schedules alternated three times. There were three hundred events in each trial. Seventeen subjects performed in quiet, fourteen in noise.

The results are shown in Table 2, and indicate that perceived frequencies are accurate in all conditions.

3. Experiment III

Here the design used was as in Experiment II, but instead of being asked for a statement of relative probability on each trial subjects were asked to generate a two-hundred event series typical of the schedule they had just seen. Nineteen subjects performed in quiet, sixteen in noise. The mean relative frequencies of response are shown in Table 3. Here again performance is quite accurate and there is no appreciable difference in accuracy over conditions. The subjects' ability to perceive and reproduce probabilities is unaffected by noise or event schedule.

Shifts in the relative frequency of competing operant responses are thus attributable to changes in the potentiation of these responses in the prediction situation alone. The element of gain consequent to a correct choice is therefore probably a key factor in the task. Broadbent (1965) suggested that a fundamental effect of treatments which change the organism's state is to alter the overall gain factor, or tendency to action within the task. A model by Broen and Storms

TABLE 3
Mean Event Probabilities Generated in a 200-Response
Sequence Following Exposure to a Sample Sequence

Probabilities generated	Probability in sample					
	Red .7	Green .3	White 0	Red .5	Green .1	White .4
Quiet	.7	.30	–	.52	.13	.35
Noise	.69	.31	–	.50	.13	.37

(1961) of this process in fact predicts the form of the data seen in Experiment I if we assume that the overall gain factor is low when many responses are irrelevant. On the face of it then, the first element in our picture of the "noise state" is an alteration in the function of a central selective process governing both intake and output procedures.

B. Primary Memory Processes

1. Experiment IV

One of the reasons for favoring a "state" theory of activation rather than one based on a single energic dimension is that the brain's metabolism apparently does not vary as a function of the "violence" of its activity (Pribram & McGuinness, 1975). We can simply say that measured improvements in efficiency in performance of one task are obtained at the expense of a sacrifice in potential to perform another. If attention and response dispositions change under noise, in what kinds of task will the implied tradeoff show up? Broadbent (1965) suggests that the relative strength of competing responses at a point in time may be determined as follows — ". . . that the organism maintains a store of the expected value of each possible response . . . One point of some interest is the decay of the store with each successive response. The severity of this decay will determine the extent to which the remote, rather than the recent, past will determine the value in store . . ." (p. 155). One may suppose that organisms which are determined in their behavior entirely by the remote past or by nothing in the past are either very slow learners or nonlearners. Broadbent's suggestion implies that a balance is struck between some overview of task requirement and the effect of immediately past events on one's current behavior. This idea of modification of present action by recent past leads us directly to consider the role of primary memory in ongoing action. It may be that subjects operating in noise are *less* subject to the consequences of their immediate past behavior and more liable to comply with long-standing task demands. There is certainly a considerable literature implicating noise in a shift in the balance between short- and long-term memory (e.g., Hamilton, Hockey, & Quinn, 1972; McLean, 1969). Most of this literature classifies short-term memory as recall elicited some minutes after the input of a list of stimuli. There is however some evidence that changes in recall of the order of seconds after delivery of a stimulus can be observed with change in state. Hamilton, Wilkinson, and Edwards (1972) showed that recall in a test of auditory running memory span *improved* over four days of partial sleep deprivation, while performance of tests of processing ability was degraded. The same sort of test is used here to examine the rate of decay in primary memory as a function of noise administration. In this case visual presentation is of course necessary. Running memory is tested by presenting the subject with long sequences of stimuli of indeterminate length. At some point the sequence is interrupted and the subject is asked to report the last few items presented. With relatively long series of inputs this technique provides a good measure of the "echoic past" of the subject, free from primacy effects. In this experiment the subject was asked to recall what he could of the last eight stimuli he saw. These were random consonants, delivered at rates of .56, 1.1, 1.67, and 3.3 items per second. The average length of list was about 30 items, with a minimum of 18. When listening was interrupted subjects were required to write in an 8-box matrix the items seen just prior to interruption, in the order in which they were seen.

Two groups of twelve subjects performed the task under either ambient quiet conditions or 85 dB noise. After practice they ran for 160 trials, 40 of each input rate presented in balanced blocks of 20 trials. Testing was carried out in groups, and the consonants were presented sequentially on a closed-circuit television screen. Recall was scored on a strict order criterion. The results are shown in Fig. 3.

Visually, the results are quite arresting. In each rate condition recall under noise is better for recently heard items, but shows a faster fade-off. At about five items back a "noise listener" is always worse off that a quiet listener. In noise, subjects appear to have high initial acquisition strength for each item — but a higher loss rate. This has all the characteristics of a "knock-down" store in which acquisition strength of new input reflects negatively on items held. We may say then that noise stress increases acquisition strength of incoming stimuli — and suffers the consequences in terms of the time old stimuli remain accessible. Is

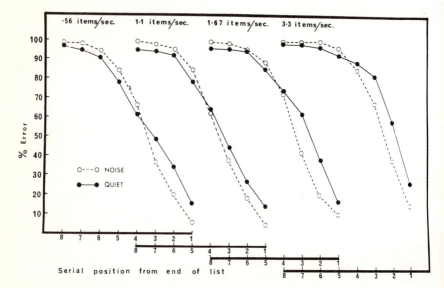

FIG. 3   Errors in running memory span as a function of stimulus-input rate, serial position, and noise.

this tradeoff between short-term "hold" and acquisition strength adaptive in any respect?

The changes in attentional distribution and reaction potential discussed earlier were put down to an increased tendency to action on behalf of the subject. In such a state one would imagine that the organism is geared to react quickly to events occurring around it. A high capacity holding memory is a facility that may be indispensable for internalized operations such as reasoning, but might well be a hindrance when the time comes for action. We noted earlier a rather unusual finding – that running memory improves in sleep deprived states, while processing efficiency declines. It may be that the capacity of the brain to store in the short term trades off against ability to process quickly. Some early experiments cited by Broadbent (1958) indicate that this is indeed the case. These were conducted on tests of continuous five-choice reaction time. In this task a subject places a stylus on a disk related to a given light. On contact, a new light appears and he must move there. In performance of this task occasional long gaps between responses appear – the subject "freezes." In sleep deprived states (where running span is relatively efficient) these gaps increase in frequency. In some way the subject becomes totally insensitive to input, or totally unable to act on it. It may require an inversion of accepted thinking to find a cause for this effect. Ordinarily we stress ability to store as a virtue – it is a quality we assume to contribute toward operational efficiency. But in speeded operations excessive storage of information in primary memory can only provide a mounting noise background for new input – and a cessation of activities is guaranteed. An adequate rate of clearance of working store is a prerequisite of efficient throughput – and that may be the reason for inefficient throughput in sleep-deprived states. Noise may sometimes decrease the number of these gaps in continuous activity (Wilkinson, 1964), so that a high rate of loss from store seems adaptive in this respect. The state induced by noise appears in effect to be conductive to fast continuous information processing, at the expense of a reduced short-term store.

From that previously cited it follows that measures of throughput of information should improve under administration of noise. But here there is a difficulty. Some measures of information throughput taken in the laboratory stress the subject to the maximum of his resources for short periods of time. These take the form "How many of these can you do in a minute?". Other measures require the subject to marshal his resources at a particular point in time, as in a prewarned choice reaction time experiment. If he is able to marshal maximum resources in the short run, how is the change in performance due to extraneous noise to be measured? To the extent that he perceives the experimenter's criterion to be based on some measure of processing rate he will devote resources to satisfaction of that criterion. Norman and Bobrow's (1975) distinction between resource- and data-limited processes is important here. A task is resource limited if an increase in the application of processing resources to it results in improved performance. It is data limited when performance is independent of change in allocated resources over a given range. As these authors point out, after Thomas (1973), subjects may tend normally to work at the boundary between these two conditions. An increased allocation of resource after the point of data limitation leads only to more error-free processing with longer processing times or to faster performance at a cost in error rate. It is impossible to confirm our suspicions about increased rate of throughput if the increased source allocation we postulate in noise takes the subject to the point where he acts as his own source of data limitation. What evidence there is shows that he does exactly this. Noise may reduce the incidence of gaps in a five-choice task but it has the effect of increasing choice errors for a very small gain in operating rate.

The implication that rate of processing is increased in noise is thus difficult to examine in any simple way. It may be pointed out that, despite the general lack of convincing effects of noise in early studies (Broadbent, 1957), there are a number of results that fall into line with the general picture we have been painting. Occasional improvements in performance are found, which tend to be associated with tasks involving a strong component of speed (clerical speed, mental arithmetic, and so on), although an increase in rate of work may be accompanied by increased errors (e.g., Wilbanks, Webb, & Tolhurst, 1956). For the reasons already outlined, however, such results are rare. Subjects are normally able to operate for the brief duration of the tasks in most of these early studies at a level of resource allocation which is adequate to meet the demands of the situation. The obvious solution to this problem is to "destress" the testing situation by prolonging the set work period (this could have the effect of reducing resource allocation to a point below that at which performance ceases to be resource limited, in Norman and Bobrow's terms). The data available on processing rate are thus quite equivocal, and though we are trying to find situations in which the subject *can* benefit from the imposition of this stress in spite of his own efforts to allocate resources we can as yet report no remarkable success.[1]

In sum, when we put noise stress on a normal subject we expect the following pattern to emerge:

1. The deployment of attention over competing sources in the task will change; and sources which have a high probability of yielding information relevant to the task criterion will be favored. The same effect may be obtained

---

[1] Since these comments were written we have observed a marked beneficial effect of noise on the alphabet processing task used in Experiment V. There was no storage load, and subjects simply worked their way through lists of random length transformations ($J + 2$, $N + 5$, and so on). Work time was about 40 minutes and subjects alternated three-minute periods in noise and quiet. The beneficial effect of noise increases over time, as quiet performance gets progressively slower.

with competing output responses. The consequences for performance cannot be known independently of a task specification and knowledge of the scoring criterion.

2. The holding capacity of primary memory will diminish, although immediate input will be more strongly registered.

3. The conditions required for an increase in processing rate will exist, but choice of tasks which are data limited in operation will lead only to speed–accuracy tradeoffs.

We hope then that we have been able to provide a crude map of the state induced by a single stressor. However, it should be even more clear that, given the complex nature of this state, any analysis of its effects will depend very precisely on the nature of the test chosen. If there are other states (including the normal state) that display different balances between these diverse functions, then the aim of measuring human performance is surely better served by detailed attention to the qualitive change in component processes, a proper skepticism about efficiency criteria, and a thorough understanding of the demands of the task selected than by complacent acceptance of the mystiques of "task complexity." We now attempt to devise a series of tasks that rely to varying degress on the component processes we have previously discussed. Response strength shifts, insofar as they affect scanning and output, we admit we have failed to include. But it *is* possible to devise a task that does demand varying emphasis on throughput processing and holding capacity. It is described in Experiment V.

C. Closed System Thinking

1. Experiment V

In tests of closed system thinking the required output is obtained by a series of transformations on the input. Mental arithmetic is a case in point. No information reduction or creation is involved. If we ask a subject to "give the third letter after B in the alphabet" the answer is implicit in the instruction and the input B. Time to produce the answer E is to some extent a measure of time required to access long term store and make the B–C–D–E transition. By varying the size of transition demanded (1, 2, 3, or 4 letters) we can measure transition rate. In many closed-system tasks however we require to hold information temporarily while new transformations are performed (e.g., multiply 367 by 8 in your head). This storage requirement can be manipulated by requiring the subject to hold a variable number of outputs in store while producing new ones.

In the task used here subjects were required to make forward transition of variable length from a given letter in the alphabet (e.g., B + 1, 2, 3, or 4). On some occasions letters were presented in groups (BS, JMF, RLCJ, and so on) and no output was allowed until the whole group had been transformed. Results of early transformations had thus to be held until the final transformation was

TABLE 4
Storage and Process Conditions in the Closed-System Thinking Task, with Examples of
the Task Performed

Storage instruction	Add 1 Stimulus	Add 1 Response	Add 2	Add 3	Add 4 Stimulus	Add 4 Response
			Process instruction			
Store 0	F	G	–	–	F	J
Store 1	–	–	–	–	–	–
Store 2	–	–	–	–	–	–
Store 3	FBRJ	GCSK	–	–	FBRJ	JFVN

complete. Varying both transformation requirements and storage load we can create a range of tasks from those requiring pure processing power to those which require a subtle balance between maintaining store and processing new input. Transition length and storage load were varied in a 4 X 4 matrix which is shown in Table 4 above. All sixteen tasks were performed by all subjects in a balanced design. Twelve subjects performed in noise, and twelve in quiet. Letters of the alphabet were presented on sheets of paper arranged as columns of single letters, columns of groups of two, and so on. The subject was required to work down these columns, performing a prearranged transformation. On sheets upon which letters were grouped he was instructed to issue his response as a single unit rather than transform and output each letter in the group separately. Work on

TABLE 5
Mean Time Per Item Output in Quiet and Noise for 16
Process/Storage Conditions (Noise Scores are in
Brackets)

Storage load	Process level 1	Process level 2	Process level 3	Process level 4
0	1.2	2.1	2.9	3.4
	(1.3)	(1.9)	(2.5)	(3.0)
1	2.0	2.8	4.8	5.9
	(1.9)	(3.2)	(4.7)	(5.5)
2	2.3	3.8	5.6	6.9
	(2.4)	(4.4)	(6.6)	(7.3)
3	2.8	4.7	6.9	7.9
	(2.9)	(5.9)	(7.6)	(9.2)

each sheet was terminated before all items had been transformed, and time at task measured. Time at work was then converted to time per letter output for each work sheet.

The results, in terms of time per letter output are shown in Table 5. It is very difficult to picture the effect of noise from the table, since the effects of increased storage and processing requirement are so massive. In Fig. 4 mean noise times for each condition are expressed as a percentage of the correspond-

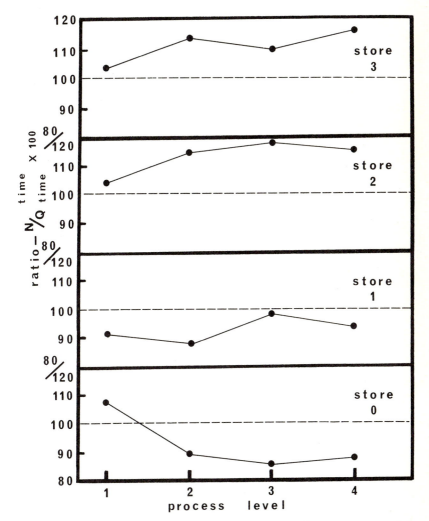

FIG. 4 Closed-system thinking performance in noise expressed as a percentage of time taken under quiet conditions. The four panels depict different storage levels.

ing quiet times. The figure indicates that where storage load is nil there is a slight benefit to be had from noise administration. On the other hand, at high storage levels noise performance seems to be worse than that in quiet.

Over the range of storage loads the noise effect is manifest as an increase in the rate of change of performance efficiency. To test this we assume a linear fit through points generated by increasing processing requirement at each storage level. This yields four lines for each subject, and their rate of change of slope may be measured to give an index of disparity between zero and high storage loads as a function of processing load. The rate of change is higher for noise groups than for quiet (Mann–Whitney $U = 19, p < 0.002$).

It is essential to note that the above index is one of within-group *variance*. As we have shown, fairly large scale experiments are required to demonstrate consistent directional effects of stress on *component* functions. Where a tradeoff in the relative efficiency of components is indicated (as here), and if tests with graded weightings on each component are employed, effects are more easily identified. Given that subjects do start from different "normal" states they are likely to show differing consequences of the tradeoff. For some, a major improvement in processing rate may result, while for others a loss of holding capacity may be quite critical. In each case the differential between conditions will increase but the direction of change may vary, and result in no systematic overall effect. This principal may be important for future work along these lines.

The data from this experiment comply in form to the Yerkes–Dodson law in that difficult tasks tend to suffer under stress, while easy ones tend to benefit. Yet it is easier to argue that deterioration stems from a change in the relationship between storage and processing power than to use accepted explanations of the Yerkes–Dodson effect. Most common among these are an analysis of decrement in discrimination behavior in terms of changes in competing response strengths (Broadbent, 1965) and an attentional explanation by Easterbrook (1959) based on narrowing of cue usage in activated states. The law thus seems to be an entirely general one, reflecting some fundamental property of the system which is observed in different forms depending on task demands and state of the organism.

To sum up Section I of this chapter, we have attempted to describe in some detail the cognitive consequences of the activation state produced by noise. It should be clear that this exercise may, as easily, be carried out with other states, such as those produced by sleep deprivation or alcohol. Any arguments we have used depend less on the specific findings from our noise experiments than on the general principle that effects of stressors are best seen as changes in pattern of functioning of the component processes involved in the behavior being examined. The indications are that there is a quite characteristic "shape" to behavior in the presence of noise, over and above any considerations of efficiency of performance. Section II is an altogether more tentative affair, in which we examine the consequences of the idea that "voluntary" selective control of activation state is possible.

II. THE CONTROL OF ACTIVATION STATE

In brief experiments it is notoriously difficult to demonstrate effects of stress on efficiency (Broadbent, 1958). Changes in behavior begin to appear only after a period of some time at work in noise experiments, and in remarkable demonstration of the ability of the subject to override stress, Wilkinson (1964) showed that subjects were able to withstand prolonged sleep deprivation if the task allotted was personally interesting to them. Rather than viewing it as a hindrance to our research efforts, it is important that we incorporate this facility for control into our view of the system. The theory of physiological stress (Selye, 1957) has done remarkably well with the concept of homeostasis, but a straightforward view of systemic balance will not suffice for psychological purposes.

Our argument goes as follows: stressors applied to the subject place him in a particular state of cognitive balance. He can resist such a process in the short-term to maintain an optimum state for any task imposed on him. If the demands of the task are consonant with his state there is no need for "resistance." This point is well illustrated in the apparent conflict between the findings of Corcoran (1964) and Malmo and Surwillo (1960). Corcoran took physiological measures from sleep-deprived subjects engaged in a vigilance task (a passive type of behavior) and concluded that they showed signs of "de-arousal." Malmo and Surwillo required their similarly stressed subjects to perform a speeded task with aversive feedback for poor performance, and observed all the signs of high arousal. Presumably in the latter case some effort had to be marshaled to override the effects of the stressor. At the same time it is unlikely that the subject in a normal or "equilibrium" state will find that state optimal for many of the tasks which he is set, and must move *from* the norm to cope with the demand. In short, psychological stress may only be definable in terms of the discrepancy between *required* state and *current* state. A subject is not stressed by sleep deprivation if he is allowed to go to sleep!

It appears likely, then, that the organism can achieve controlled transitions between different activation states, in compliance with current demands of his situation. But it is difficult to proceed from this assumption unless we can attempt a description of such a control system in four main areas.

A. The Primary Dimensions of "Activation Space"

Kahneman (1973), in his review of this topic, indicates that two or perhaps three states of arousal ought to be distinguished. The major two are states associated with first, alerted intake of information, and second, a general effort toward action. The third, a "state of relaxed acceptance of external stimulation," we might all subjectively identify with as the kind of ruminative mental activity which occurs when we are quite passive. As he points out, the state normally observed appears to be some functional mix of these types. (Some interesting data on this point are currently being collected by a research student at Stirling, Liz Russ.) Subject's heart rate is measured as they carry out the closed-system thinking task previously described. They verbalize as they work. In some conditions a simple stream of "+4" transitions is performed, and the heart rate profile for these is compared with that obtained when the subjects have to accumulate data in store for final report as a group. Heart rate is suppressed as store accumulates, indicating a progressive change in state. This is perhaps an example of Kahneman's "inhibitory tendency," a feature of the alert state.

Pribram and McGuinness (1975) effect a more discrete separation of the physiological systems involved in this area. *Arousal* is a process determined by phasic response of the system to input, and is primarily concerned in sensory and encoding processes. *Activation* is a process concerned with readiness to respond. Coordinating control of these processes is achieved by a separate control system, the coordinating activity demanding *effort*.

The activation state of the subject, as we have used the term, is thus likely to be defined by variation on at least two major dimensions. We have implied in our argument here that points in the space delineated by these dimensions are appropriate to different types of cognitive function.

B. Operational Characteristics of the Control Process

If state selection procedures are to act as an aid to the efficiency of information processing, clearly they must be amenable to control in the very short run. The data available, in fact, imply that the attainment of a selected state is a fairly slow process. From contingent negative variation studies (Tecce, 1972) and from a determination of the point of minimum reaction time following a warning (Posner & Boies, 1971), the time taken to move to a state of receptive alertness is about 500 msec. When phasic changes must be continuously managed in time, even slower rates of change are indicated. Hamilton and Hockey (1974) delivered nine-item lists to subjects are various rates, and subjects were required to actively listen only for those items at critical positions 2, 4, 6, and 8 in the series. Appreciable benefits from this opportunity to "phase" listening only appear when critical items are separated by about one second. Such operations are far too slow to be considered an integral part of the information processing operations seen in skilled performance, so that the involvement of state selection in information processing must be a limited one. It is probably limited to those activities in which individual stages of a processing sequence take appreciable amounts of time and optimization of state is a viable strategy. Where behavior is habitual, and stimulus–response compatibility high, action is freed from this more gross control procedure.

C. The Output of the Control Process

Nothing so far has been said about how state changes fit into the hierarchy of control. Since the relative potential of competing behaviors is changed, we suggest that state change reflects through a hierarchy of the type shown, as follows:

Source of change	Tendency to action	Task set	Competing component processes	Competing information sources or outputs	
		increased → versus decreased	p_1 versus p_2	→ S_a versus S_b	→ selected
	increased → versus decreased				
noise → stress state			. . . . p_n	. . . . S_n	

Some principles of operation in such a scheme are known, and are briefly outlined here.

First, potentiation of a detailed action at the right of the hierarchy can proceed in parallel with the general changes at the left. Posner and Boies (1971) report that encoding of a stimulus to be later matched and the buildup of phasic alertness in a warning interval occur together in time without loss. Using a choice reaction-time task with biased signal probabilities and variable foreperiod, Allan White at Durham (personal communication, 1975) has shown a steadily increasing discrepancy between RTs to high and low probability sources as preparation proceeds, selectivity reaching an optimum at a foreperiod duration of 500 msec.

Second, the degree of bias to any element at a given level reflects on the potential of its competitors. Ninio and Kahneman (1973) show that subjects are able to control bias between dichotic lists of words to give high efficiency on one list, or equal but degraded performance on both. In the same sense, reaction time to a probe stimulus is lengthened as a function of its proximity to the onset and execution phases of a primary task response (Posner & Boies, 1971).

Third, where competing tasks employ elements in common they may both benefit from a bias to those elements. This can be illustrated in the phasic listening task of Hamilton and Hockey (1974). Tones to be detected are inserted in the sequence at various points on a number of trials, and detection reports taken after the trial. Detection efficiency cycles in time with phasic listening, and is highest just before onset of a critical item. The performance observed is shown in Fig. 5. Preparation to listen for the critical input clearly modulates receptiveness for the detection probe. The above data indicate that state selection is the first step in a process that ensures detailed preparation for an anticipated stimulus, or maximal priming of a probable response. If there is a

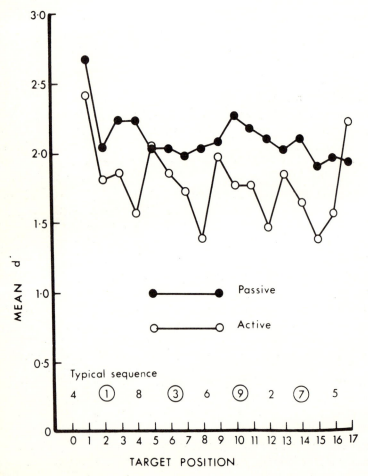

FIG. 5 Detection efficiency (d') as a function of detection probe location in a phasic listening task (○). Performance may be compared with passive listening (●) in which the subject must process all inputs.

state which corresponds to internalized thinking one would imagine that it too is geared to the isolation of particular themes in awareness (James, 1890). Some rationale for the differential priming of elements at each level of the hierarchy has been provided by other workers. Treisman's (1960) concept of dictionary units may be appropriate. In our case overall task goals and current conditions may adjust the firing threshold on certain elements so that they are more easily activated. On Deutsch and Deutsch's (1963) "priority" formulation they might be partially activated by current goals and thus in a position of possible ascendancy. The degree of dominance of a particular set of elements may be determined at a very basic level of control. It has been shown that the noise state is one determinant, so it is clear that very fundamental changes in the organism will serve to adjust the relative strengths of competing behaviors.

D. The Ultimate Level of Control

Once task demands specify the direction of bias we need an executive process which can vary its degree. Any movement of the organism from a state of neutral balance to one which favors a given type of processing presumably requires some effort. Pribram & McGuinness (1975) attribute this work to the hippocampus, interference with which ". . . reduces the organism to a state in which the more effort demanding relationships between perception and action . . . are relinquished for more primitive relationships in which either input or output captures an aspect of the behaviour of the organism without the coordinating intervention of central control operations" (p. 129). Such a process would fulfill our present requirements. Although Kahneman (1973) specifically warns against such generalization, it seems to us useful conceptually to imagine the process as akin to an orienting reaction, issued as an operant response to "capture" currently wanted behaviors. For lack of ingenuity it is termed the *executive* response.

In Fig. 6 we attempt to outline the kind of control system that would have the characteristics discussed above. The scheme has, for simplicity's sake, been confined to two activation states appropriate to reception of stimuli and ensuing action. The following rules apply to operations within this framework:

1. Inputs to the system may arrive while it is in any state, at any level. Efficiency of action will depend on the "distance" between optimal and present position, and on the directness of stimulus response mapping.

2. Outputs from the system may occur while it is in any state, at any level, and efficiency will be determined as for stimulus reception. These rules allow the organism to carry out automatized operations free of the requirement of state selection and effort expenditure.

3. Where input does not map directly on to output, the organism moves to a state (receive) appropriate to handling and classifying it. Where the categorized

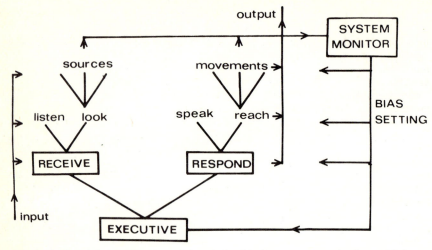

FIG. 6   A pictorial representation of the relationship between state selection and information processing.

input does not map directly to a response, the organism changes state with a view to optimizing response selection (respond). Both of these rules imply that all levels of a given hierachy are primed to effect isolation of appropriate elements.

4. All ongoing operations are monitored with reference to current processing plans; in addition the monitoring process is permanently biased to operate on novel events, whether externally or internally generated.

5. The output of the monitoring operation sets the bias on competing elements in the hierarchy.

6. The monitor can command an "executive response" at the cost of some effort. This acts to increase the discrepancy between elements to which the system is biased and others in competition.

A scheme of this complexity is not demanded by the data at our disposal. But there are signs that psychology has been poorly served by the principle of parsimony in this area. The accepted mapping of the hardware/software distinction on to some body/mind dichotomy seems unjustified. The state of the hardware itself is programmable, and physiological state appears to be irretrievably bound up with cognitive efficiency. While we make no claim for the detail of our speculation we would follow Kahneman in arguing for a move away from "passive-machine" theories of function to those involving active and effortful participation of the whole organism.

ACKNOWLEDGMENTS

The authors are indebted to the Medical Research Council for financial support in this work.

REFERENCES

Broadbent, D. E. Effects of noise on behavior. In C. M. Harris (Ed.), *Handbood of noise control*. New York: McGraw-Hill, 1957.

Broadbent, D. E. *Perception and communication*. London: Pergamon Press, 1958.

Broadbent, D. E. A reformulation of the Yerkes–Dodson Law. *British Journal of Mathematical and Statistical Psychology*, 1965, **18**, 145–157.

Broadbent, D. E. *Decision and stress*. London: Academic Press, 1971.

Broen, W. E., & Storms, L. H. A reaction potential ceiling and response decrements in complex situations. *Psychological Review*, 1961, **68**, 405–415.

Corcoran, D. W. J. Changes in heart rate and performance as a result of loss of sleep. *British Journal of Psychology*, 1964, **55**, 307–314.

Deutsch, J. A., & Deutsch, D. Attention: Some theoretical considerations. *Psychological Review*, 1963, **70**, 80–90.

Easterbrook, J. A. The effect of emotion on cue utilization and the organization of behavior. *Psychological Review*, 1959, **66**, 183–201.

Greeno, J. G. Effects of non-reinforcement trials in two-choice learning with non-contingent reinforcement. *Journal of Experimental Psychology*, 1962, **64**, 373–379.

Hamilton, P. Selective attention in multi-source monitoring tasks. *Journal of Experimental Psychology*, 1969, **82**, 34–37.

Hamilton, P., & Hockey, G. R. J. Active selection of items to be remembered: The role of timing. *Cognitive Psychology*, 1974, **6**, 61–83.

Hamilton, P., Hockey, G. R. J., & Quinn, J. G. Information selection, arousal and memory. *British Journal of Psychology*, 1972, **63**, 181–189.

Hamilton, P., Wilkinson, R. T., & Edwards, R. A study of four days' partial sleep deprivation. In W. P. Colquhoun (Ed.), *Aspects of human efficiency*. London: English Universities Press, 1972.

Hockey, G. R. J. Effects of loud noise on attentional selectivity. *Quarterly Journal of Experimental Psychology*, 1970, **22**, 37–42.

Hockey, G. R. J. Changes in information-selection patterns in multisource monitoring as a function of induced arousal shifts. *Journal of Experimental Psychology*, 1973, **101**, 35–42.

James, W. *The principles of psychology*, New York: Holt, 1890.

Kahneman, D. *Attention and effort*. Englewood Cliffs, N.J.: Prentice-Hall, 1973.

Lacey, J. I. Somatic response patterning and stress: Some revisions of activation theory. In M. H. Appley & R. Trumbell (Eds.), *Psychological stress*. New York: Appleton-Century-Crofts, 1967.

McLean, P. D. Induced arousal and time of recall as determinants of paired-associate recall. *British Journal of Psychology*, 1969, **60**, 57–62.

Malmo, R. B., & Surwillo, W. W. Sleep deprivation: Changes in performance and physiological indicants of activation. *Psychological Monographs*, 1960, **74** (Whole No. 502).

Ninio, A., & Kahneman, D. Reaction time in focused and divided attention. *Journal of Experimental Psychology*, 1973, **84**, 394–399.

Norman, D. A., & Bobrow, D. G. On data limited and resource limited processes. *Cognitive Psychology*, 1975, **7**, 44–64.

Posner, M. I., & Boies, S. J. Components of attention. *Psychological Review*, 1971, **78**, 391–408.

Pribram, K. H., & McGuinness, D. Arousal, activation and effort in the control of attention. *Psychological Review*, 1975, **82**, 116–149.

Selye, H. *The stress of life*. London: Longmans, 1957.

Tecce, J. J. Contingent negative variation (CNV) and psychological processes in man. *Psychological Bulletin*, 1972, **77**, 73–108.

Thomas, E. A. C. On expectancy and the speed and accuracy of responses. In S. Kornblum (Ed.), *Attention and performance IV*. New York: Academic Press, 1973.

Treisman, A. M. Contextual cues in selective listening. *Quarterly Journal of Experimental Psychology,* 1960, **12**, 242–248.

Wilbanks, W. A., Webb, W. B., & Tolhurst, G. C. *A study of intellectual capacity in a noisy environment*. (United States Navy School of Aviation Medicine Research Report No. NM001104100 Report No. 1). 1956.

Wilkinson, R. T. Effects of up to 60 hours' sleep deprivation on different types of work. *Ergonomics,* 1964, **7**, 175–186.

Part IV

PROCESSING WORDS AND READING

23
General Shape and Local Detail in Word Perception

D. E. Broadbent
M. H. P. Broadbent

Department of Experimental Psychology
Oxford University
Oxford, England

ABSTRACT

Different methods of assessing word perception degrade different parts of the information in the original stimulus; in particular the brief exposures used in a tachistoscope have different effects on receptors sensitive to high spatial frequencies and upon receptors for low spatial frequencies. In a first experiment, common and rare words, each with predictable and unpredictable letter sequences, were exposed masked by visual noise which had been high-pass or low-pass filtered. With rare words, there was an interaction between the nature of the masking noise and the predictability of the letter sequence. This encouraged a further experiment in which neutral and unpleasant words were presented after removal of alternate letters, as if masked by relatively low frequencies. These words have previously shown an effect of emotionality in a tachistoscope, but not when presented defocused. In the version with alternate letters missing, the unpleasant words were less frequently identified by subjects. Further analyses, and two more experiments, showed that the effect of emotionality was not that of a constant bias against unpleasant words: it appeared to be rather an increased variance on such words, causing them to be chosen more when evidence pointed toward them and less when evidence pointed against them. These results have methodological implications, but also confirm that some important information about words comes from their general shape rather than detail; finally, they show that it is not necessary, in order to explain the effect of word emotionality, to suppose any system feeding back from partial identification of words in order to cut down incoming evidence.

I. INTRODUCTION

If we draw a horizontal line across the visual field, the brightness of each point on the line can vary from a very low to a high value. A plot of the variation of brightness with spatial distance across the field will produce a complex wave, just as a similar wave can be produced by plotting the sound pressure of a spoken utterance. In the latter case, of course, we would plot sound pressure level against time, while in the case of brightness we use space, but in both cases it is possible in principle to regard the wave as the sum of a number of simple waves differing in frequency, amplitude, and phase. If we deliberately construct a visual stimulus in which brightness varies according to such a simple sine wave in the horizontal dimension, it will be seen as a series of vertical stripes, whose spacing and sharpness depends upon the frequency. Using such stimuli, a number of effects can be demonstrated. In particular, a grating of one frequency can be detected just as well in the presence of another frequency an octave higher; but following exposure to one frequency, the threshold for that frequency is raised while higher and lower frequencies are much less affected. There is also physiological evidence that individual cells are active primarily to particular spatial frequencies. A number of lines of evidence on such points are reviewed by Campbell (1974).

The relevance of this line of research to word recognition is that experiments on high-frequency stimuli show rather different results from those on low-frequency stimuli. Perhaps the most important point is that the time characteristics are different. It has been shown by Tolhurst (1975) and by Nachmias (1967) that the duration of exposure of a stimulus makes a difference to the detectability of a high-frequency grating over a fairly large range, but to a low-frequency stimulus only over the shorter time durations. Tachistoscopic exposures, therefore, are losing some kinds of information at relatively large values, and degrading other kinds of information at relatively short values.

Another form of asymmetry between high and low spatial frequencies has been shown by Henning, Hertz, and Broadbent (1975), by presenting a cluster of three relatively high frequencies, so chosen that the resulting wave form was that of a carrier wave modulated in amplitude at a relatively low frequency. On looking at such a stimulus, one can see a repetition at a fairly wide spacing, as one would if a low frequency were present. This apparent low frequency masks and is masked by simple gratings of the same apparent frequency. We have already noted that a simple high frequency cannot be masked by a simple low frequency: and there is therefore an asymmetry between the results, such that any explanation of the effects in terms of nonlinearity would have to suppose that the high frequency system showed a departure from linearity substantially greater than that found in the low-frequency system. For this and other reasons, Henning, Hertz, and Broadbent (1975) suggested that the most plausible explanation was that a system capable of detecting low frequencies, and extending over a substantial area of the visual field, was fed by more localized systems detecting high frequencies. In a more general vein, such a mechanism has been linked by Broadbent (1975) to the general psychological problem of linking together features that are characteristic of the same object or source of stimulation. These problems are raised also by Treisman, Sykes and Gelade and by Kahneman and Henik, (in this volume), and it is clear that there is a functional need for a mechanism in which detailed features are nested within broader characteristics of spatial location and timing, so that they are linked together. One cannot assume that information concerned with the linkage will behave in the same way as information concerned with elements to be linked.

From a methodological point of view, we need therefore to establish whether degradation of the kind which loses detailed information is the same in its effects as degradation which preserves some detail but loses broader characteristics of the word. The first experiment had this aim.

II. EXPERIMENT I: WORD PROBABILITY, LETTER DIAGRAM PREDICTABILITY, AND NOISE MASKING

Following an earlier report by Owsowitz (1963), a curious interaction in tachistoscopic perception was found by Broadbent and Gregory (1968). In general, sequences of letters which are frequent in the language and therefore have a high score of predictability are easier to perceive (Baddeley, 1964). With rare words, however, an unlikely sequence of letters actually improves intelligibility. More recently, Broadbent and Gregory (1971) have counted the number of words in the language closely similar to each of the stimulus words they employed in the earlier paper, and found that rare words with unpredictable letter sequences also have very few words in the language which are of the same length and start with the same two letters. Since therefore there are fewer possible errors, it seems plausible that these words would be easier to see. In a similar vein Rumelhart and Siple (1974) have simulated the effect by supposing that the detection of certain segments of letters in the unpredictable sequences succeeds more perfectly in distinguishing by Bayesian computation between the alternative possibilities. The original results rest however upon tachistoscopic exposures in which, as already indicated, it is unknown what type of information has been lost from the presentation.

A. Method

Forty words (those published by Broadbent and Gregory, 1968, as being presented to their Groups 1 and 3) were printed in lower case on standard 2 × 2 slides, and projected on a screen so that each five-letter word was approximately 10 in. long. Superimposed on the same screen was the image produced by an overhead projector from a transparency of visual noise. In the latter, every point in a vertical plane possessed the same brightness, but in the horizontal plane the brightness varied according to a computer generated signal which was originally of wide band noise, but which had been high-pass filtered on some trials and low-pass filtered on others, so that the noise was confined to the upper or lower part of the spatial-frequency spectrum. Cutoff frequency for the high-pass and low-pass filters corresponded to 1.89 cycles per inch on the ultimate projection screen. Remembering the spaces between letters, each letter had a width of about .5 in., and the effect, therefore, was that in the high-frequency noise every letter of the word was degraded to some extent, having at least two vertical lines drawn through it. In the low-frequency noise, this was the upper limit of variation within a letter, and the visible impression was rather that some letters were removed altogether while others remained intact. For each kind of noise, four different photographic samples of computer output were used: as words were always projected in the same location on the screen, and as each sample of noise was always projected in the same position, the same regions of maximal interference occurred each time a noise was employed.

Subjects were tested in groups, seated between eight and twelve feet from the screen. Broadly speaking, this means that our borderline between high- and low-frequency noise occurs about four cycles per degree.

For each session, the procedure was as follows. As each session was widely spaced in time, and illumination levels might change, before each session the relative brightness of the two projectors was adjusted by adding neutral density filters until the difficulty level was approximately correct as verified on discarded experimental subjects. For this reason and because no attempt was made to equalize total noise power, main effects of differences between noise spectra would be meaningless.

In the main session each sequence of four words was made up of two AA words from those previously used, and two with occurrences between five and twenty-five per million. Within each class, one word had high letter digram predictability and one low. Before each word was projected, the experimenter inserted a new noise slide, but kept to the high-frequency noises for one group of four words and the low-frequency noises for the next group of four words. Thus the same noise did not occur again to the same subject until seven other presentations had intervened. Half the subjects started with the high-pass noise and half with the low and the sequence of words was the same for all subjects: thus the same words were masked by both noises, but on different subjects. The word was observed for five seconds, after which a written response was obtained.

B. Results

The percentage of correct responses is shown in Table 1. The most obvious feature of the table is the higher level of performance with low-frequency noise, but as already indicated the mean noise power was not controlled and no

TABLE 1
Percentage Correct for Words Masked by High- and Low-Frequency Noise

	Common words		Rare words	
	High-frequency noise	Low-frequency noise	High-frequency noise	Low-frequency noise
Letters predictable	37.1	60.9	25.7[a]	60.0[b]
Unpredictable	38.1	64.7	41.9[c]	53.3[d]

[abcd]Interaction shown gives $p < .01$.
[ac]differs $p < .02$.

emphasis should therefore be put upon this. The important features of the results lie in comparisons within a noise: for common words, the predictability of the letter sequence made little difference in either case, there being an insignificant advantage for the unlikely sequences of letters. With rare words, however, letter predictability had quite different effects depending upon the noise present: for a high-frequency noise the predictable sequences of letters were harder to see, whereas for a low-frequency noise the difference was slight and in the opposite direction. The interaction was highly significant $p < .01$, and the advantage of the unpredictable sequences with high frequency noise was also significant $p < .02$. Thus the result found in the tachistoscope appears only when the word is masked with high-frequency noise, not when it is masked with low-frequency noise.

From the point of view of common sense, this is not altogether surprising; a word masked by low frequency may give very high information about one letter but not about its neighbor, and this may cause the received sensory evidence to point toward probable letter sequences rather than rare ones. Conversely a high-frequency noise will allow detection only of fragments chosen from a number of different letters, as in the theory developed by Rumelhart and Siple (1974), and this evidence will be consistent only with a relatively small number of possible words when the letter sequence is an unusual one. The high-frequency noise allows digram and word shape information to pass through more readily than the low-frequency noise does. The experiment therefore establishes the methodological point which it was intended to examine.

III. EXPERIMENT II: EMOTIONAL WORDS
WITH LETTERS DELETED

The methodological point then leads on to a more empirical one. Broadbent and Gregory (1967) reported a difference in correct perception through noise of spoken words which were highly unpleasant and neutral, as rated by a panel of judges similar to the experimental subjects. The puzzling feature of the results was that misperceptions were also collected and rated for emotional quality, and it appeared that there was no response bias against unpleasant words. When presented with an unpleasant word, such as "blood," a subject was less likely to hear it correctly, but as likely to produce an unpleasant misperception, such as "death," as any neutral misperception of the same probability in the language. The result could not therefore be accounted for in terms of an average response bias, as can the general effect of word frequency (Broadbent, 1967). In attempts to unravel the explanation for this fact, a series of visual experiments were begun that have not as yet been reported in detail, but are outlined by Broadbent (1973). Briefly, the same words used in the original experiment, and a fresh series of five-letter words, failed to show any difference between "neutral" and "bad" words when presented for lengthy inspection in a blurred form, by defocusing the projector. The same words did, however, show a difference between neutral and bad words if presented in a tachistoscope. At that point, the most plausible explanation seemed to be that, during the process of recognition, the partial arousal of processes connected with semantically unpleasant words would produce by some feedback loop a change in the intake of fresh sensory information. (Compare this to the results of Allport in this volume.) This in turn would make little difference to the ultimate recognition if the word was visible for a long time, but might be important if the word was exposed only briefly.

However, the blurring of a word by throwing it out of focus is, broadly speaking, equivalent to removal of high frequencies; whereas we have already seen that tachistoscopic exposure, at short durations, may also remove low-frequency information. The possibility arose that the difference between the two techniques lay, not in the time for which the sensory evidence was presented, but rather in the kind of evidence which was provided. As already noted, the perception of a word through low-frequency noise leaves some letters unaffected while others are seen quite clearly. A simple and effective technique for producing the same result is simple to type a list of words, from which alternate letters have been deleted, and to ask the subject to name a word which fits the surviving letters. An incidental advantage of this technique, as opposed to tachistoscopic exposure or defocusing, is that one can identify perfectly the sensory information to which the subject is acting, and also the possible words in the language which could be consistent with that information. This therefore allows a closer examination of the nature of any response bias.

The technique has already been used by Broadbent and Broadbent (1975) to show that different words consistent with a particular stimulus do not have equal chances of being chosen by the subject. Subjects tend rather to choose those words for which the missing letters are highly probable, given the letters detected, and there is therefore more evidence in favor of some words than others. The argument of their paper was that the sensory evidence in favor of a particular word combines multiplicatively with a bias factor derived from probability in the language, to determine the overall chance of response, and a similar analysis would also be possible for emotional quality. Accordingly, Experiment II compared the probability of identification of neutral or bad words from which alternate letters had been omitted.

A. Method

One group of 37 subjects, all members of the housewife panel of Applied Psychology Unit, Cambridge (and therefore of the same type as those who originally rated the words), received the 15 neutral and 15 bad words of AA category, published by Broadbent and Gregory (1967). There were four different subgroups, in order that each word could be presented to half the subjects with the first and other odd letters present and to the other subjects with the second and other even letters present. In each category, the word occurred in one group following a neutral word on the list and in the other group following a bad word. All 30 words were typed on the same sheet, with alternate words starting with an odd and with an even letter. The instructions were to choose a word which fitted the letters given, with the example that "s-e-p" could be "sleep." A second group of 37 subjects received 48 words of frequency 10–49 occurrences per million, and each of 5 letters, making up the lists used in the experiments reported by Broadbent (1973). As these words have not previously been published, they are given in Table 2. Once again there were four subgroups for the same reasons as previously. A search was also made through the Thorndike and Lorge count to determine the number of possible words in the language consistent with each fragmentary stimulus, in each frequency category, for the case in which the odd numbered letters were provided.

B. Results

The results are presented in Table 3. The most satisfactory comparison is that on the AA words, for which the number of alternative words that might have been chosen is the same whether the original target word was neutral or unpleasant.

TABLE 2

The Rare (10–49) Words Used in Experiment II

Bad			Neutral		
abuse	drown	mourn	abide	daisy	miner
agony	exile	noisy	ankle	drawn	newly
bleed	fatal	panic	blend	entry	pilot
bully	fever	pinch	broom	feast	plank
cheat	fraud	skunk	chart	flake	sauce
crash	grief	sneer	chase	friar	sheer
curse	groan	sting	clasp	gleam	shrub
dirty	guilt	thief	curve	graze	thumb

TABLE 3
Performance on Unpleasant Words with Alternate
Letters Missing

	Common words		Rare words	
	Neutral	Bad	Neutral	Bad
Correct	29.6	21.0	20.1	27.4
Possible				
alternatives	78	79	56	38
Omissions	1.59	1.87	14.5	20.6

As will be seen, the neutral targets were chosen substantially more often than the unpleasant ones, and this is highly significant across subjects, 25 people showing the effect while only 4 reversed it. No differences in letter predictability or other accidental features could be detected between the neutral words, on the one hand, and the unpleasant ones, on the other. The sample of uncommon words was less satisfactory, because the unpleasant target words leave many fewer other words consistent with the surviving letters. As might be expected, there is a clear relationship between the number of words consistent with the stimulus given, and the probability of choice of a target word, so that it is scarcely surprising that the effect on correct choices of a target word reverses with this sample of words, the bad words being chosen more often than the neutral. Possibly more important with these rare words is a count of the number of completely blank responses, in which the subject could think of no word fitting the letters provided. This happened substantially more frequently when the target word was unpleasant, and the difference is comfortably significant $p <$ .001. It should be noted that this is not a consequence of the smaller number of possible words for these targets, since correlation across the neutral targets between the number of blank responses and the number of alternative words shows a small and quite insignificant correlation in the wrong direction. There is therefore some sort of change, for both samples of words, suggestive of a block or failure to retrieve the unpleasant target words.

We can now examine the question of bias for or against a particular word, as compared with the other alternative words consistent with a stimulus. For each word we can count the number of other words that might have been chosen rather than the target, and thus obtain the ratio of nontarget to target alternatives. We can also count the number of subjects who gave one of these other words, and the number who gave the target. Then if, for example, there were one target and one other possible word, and if only 10% of the subjects gave the target and 90% the other, one can count this as a case in which there was a bias against the target word. In general, if the ratio of nontarget to target words is greater than the ratio of subjects choosing each type of word, we can count the word as one in which there is a bias toward the target, while the opposite is true where there is a bias against it. Table 4 shows the number of words for which each is true, for bad and for neutral targets. It can be seen that there is a possible slight bias in favor of targets rather than other words, although not large enough to be significant on these data. (If genuine, this preference for the target words would probably result from the control of predictability of letter sequences, which might well make the targets more frequently chosen than a truly random selection of words would be.) However, there is no indication whatever of any difference between neutral and bad targets in terms of degree of bias.

This relationship is curious, and may take a little understanding; to repeat, when the target is unpleasant it gives rise to different behavior than when the target is neutral. Nevertheless, between the alternative words possible for a given stimulus, there is no bias against the bad word.

Another way of putting this is that, if one had chosen neutral targets which gave the same sequence of surviving letters as bad targets, they would have given the same results as for bad targets: If we start with the target "broad" and delete the even numbered letters, we obtain a stimulus which might have come from the target "blood." According to our results targets such as "broad" would (like bad targets) have shown fewer correct choices if they were common words, and more omissions if they were rare ones.

Such a result is quite consistent with the earlier acoustic and tachistoscopic studies: fewer correct perceptions and yet no sign of a bias on erroneous responses. In this case, however, one cannot interpret the result in terms of a shutting off of sensory information, since that information is clearly and permanently present. It might fail to be utilized, and in general terms this pattern of results must imply, since there is no bias against bad words, that there must be an increased variance associated with the decisions concerning them. If on some occasions bad words had a lower probability of being chosen, and this was balanced by other occasions on which they had too high a probability, then

TABLE 4
Bias between Possible Words with Alternate Letters
Missing

	Stimuli for which	
	$x < y$	$y < x$
Bad targets	13	9
Neutral targets	14	8

$$x = \frac{1 (= \text{number of target words})}{\text{number of nontarget alternatives}} .$$

$$y = \frac{\text{number of subs choosing target}}{\text{number choosing alternatives}} .$$

there would on average be no bias against them. There might nevertheless be fewer choices of the target in such decisions than there would in decisions involving only neutral words, for the same reason as the reduction in d' found in signal detection tasks if bias varies from trial to trial. There are various ways in which such increased variance might apply to emotional words, and Experiment III was designed to examine some of these.

IV. EXPERIMENT III: AFTEREFFECTS OF EMOTIONAL WORDS

It is extremely plausible that detection of one word may affect biases toward or against the detection of other words, associated with the original word. This is shown for example in the experiments of Meyer, Schvaneveldt, and Ruddy (1975). It is also possible that this kind of interaction may occur even if a stimulus is presented, to which no response is made, as is discussed by Allport (in this volume). Applied to the present problem this means that a subject might be biased in favor of unpleasant words when he has just perceived such a word, but against them when he has perceived a neutral word. It is also conceivable that he might be influenced by a sequence of letters consistent with an unpleasant word, even though he chose a perfectly neutral one. Although the previous experiment was controlled for the order in which words occurred in the list, the presence of all the words on the same sheet of paper made it doubtful whether the subjects had really looked at them in the order suggested. The present experiment was aimed specifically at comparing the number of choices of unpleasant targets when there were different immediately preceding events.

A. Method

Twenty neutral and 20 unpleasant words were selected from among those used in Experiment III, and were presented in every case with the second and fourth letter deleted and replaced by a hyphen. Each word was typed on a separate sheet of a booklet, so that the subject could go through them only in the prescribed order: there were in fact two types of booklet, in both of which the neutral words occupied the same pages. The unpleasant words were counterbalanced so that each word occurred in one booklet preceded by a stimulus derived from a neutral target, and in the other booklet preceded by a stimulus derived from an unpleasant target. In each booklet there were two occasions when an unpleasant word was followed, as well as preceded, by neutral words, two occasions in which groups of three unpleasant words occurred as a sequence, and the remaining twelve unpleasant words occurred in pairs. Twenty-six subjects from the Oxford housewife panel filled in one booklet, and 27 the other.

B. Results

We may compare the proportion of unpleasant target words that were chosen under each of three conditions. The first, 0.30, was the case in which the target was preceded by a neutral word. When, however, the preceding target was an unpleasant word, one can separate cases in which the preceding target had in fact been chosen, and cases in which it had not. Thus we can examine the possibility either that a preceding response primes a succeeding one of the same type, or that a stimulus consistent with an unpleasant word primes such responses even when it is not recognized. In fact, the corresponding proportions are 0.34 and 0.24, respectively. The differences are extremely small and quite insignificant: with this type of technique, there does not seem to be any priming sufficient to produce the variance we are seeking.

Another possible source of variance lies in consistent differences between subjects. If some people have a consistent bias toward unpleasant words, and others against them, we would get a suitable increase in variance. This need not be a permanent characteristic of the individual, but might merely reflect a gloomy or cheerful mood on the day of the experiment. In fact one can correlate the number of unpleasant targets chosen by each individual under the three conditions. There is a correlation of 0.26 between the two conditions in which the preceding response is a neutral word, and this is comfortably significant $p < .02$. There is no corresponding correlation (< 0.10) involving the condition in which the preceding response was unpleasant; this may merely reflect the smaller amount of data in that case, or just possibly it might represent a second dimension of individual variability. There is in any case some evidence for variability between individual subjects in degree of bias, but the magnitude of the correlation is small, and it seems doubtful that it would be sufficient to explain the size of the effect found in Experiment II. We must therefore look for a further source of variance.

V. EXPERIMENT IV: THE EFFECTS OF VARYING THE AMOUNT OF INFORMATION

One possible source of variance in decisions involving unpleasant words may be found by thinking again about the theoretical basis for any differences. Given inadequate evidence for deciding between two words, it is reasonable to suppose that the perceptual system will choose one of them with a probability increasing as some function of the expected value of doing so. For any pair of words A and B, if

p = probability of A rather than B
$1 - p$ = probability of B rather than A
G = amount of gain for a correct choice
L = amount of loss for an error

then the difference in the expected value in favor of A is given by $(2p - 1)(G + L)$. Thus if the probability of choosing one word is greater than choosing another, a mechanism which chooses that word more frequently will be adaptive. A constant bias in favor of probable words is therefore a plausible part of any theory.

In the case of unpleasant words, the reason for any bias is presumably motivational, and based on the possibility that the choice of an unpleasant word represents an unpleasant event to the person choosing it. It is by no means evident however that the bias would be constant in this case; it would indeed be so if the choice of a bad word was *always* a negative event. The use of an unpleasant word may be especially negative when it is incorrect and unnecessary and yet especially rewarding when it corresponds to an objective stimulus in the outside world. One may dislike contemplating fog or pain when there is no need to do so: but it may be very rewarding indeed to hear correctly a radio announcement that "there is fog on the highway tonight" or to read the instruction "If pain persists, consult your doctor." It might therefore be more appropriate to consider unpleasant words as being stimuli in which the stakes are higher, both the penalty for inappropriate use and the reward for correct perception being greater by a factor X. In that case, the difference between words A and B in expected value, where one of them is unpleasant, becomes $(2p - 1)(G + L)X$. For a given difference in probability the difference in expected value is greater than it would be for neutral words, and the difference in bias might also be expected to be greater. Whether the difference favors or opposes the unpleasant word will, however, depend on the value of p; if $2p < 1$, the bias will favor word B, but if $2p > 1$, it will favor word A.

Furthermore, suppose the amount of sensory evidence is reduced, so that other words become possible. This will reduce both p and $1 - p$ in the same proportion, and therefore the difference in expected value. Because of the factor X, the absolute reduction in the difference will be greater than it would for a pair of neutral words. Consequently, it would be reasonable for the bias affecting emotional words to be more extreme at high levels of evidence than at low levels.

A number of minor features of the earlier experiments is consistent with such a view. This is the point at which we should emphasize that the significance of the result of Experiment II is tested against subjects, and not words: we can only assert that a repetition of the experiment with fresh subjects but the same words would give the same result, and not that a fresh sample of words would do so. Examining the individual words, it is easy to find cases of unpleasant words with predictable letter sequences, and few alternatives, which are readily detected. However, it would be easy to analyze motivational factors in some other way to produce quite different predictions. A fresh experiment was therefore performed to shed light deliberately on the effect of increasing and decreasing the evidence concerning a word.

A. Method

Twenty-four unpleasant five-letter words were selected such that each had one neutral word identical with it in the first letter and in every other letter except one. By deleting this one crucial letter, a stimulus was therefore obtained consistent with one neutral and one unpleasant word, but with very few others. By deleting another letter, a stimulus consistent with a larger variety of words was obtained; and by deleting a third letter a stimulus derived from each of the 24 pairs of targets, a third of the stimuli having only one letter deleted, a third two, and a third three deletions. The different kinds of stimulus were typed on the same sheet in intermingled order. Thirty-nine subjects from the Oxford subject panel were tested, divided into three subgroups so that the target pairs given with only one deletion to one subgroup could be presented with two deletions to a second subgroup and with three deletions to a third. Within each target pair, an attempt was made to ensure that the neutral word was similar to the unpleasant one both in probability in the language, and in predictability of the letter sequence. In fact it was impossible to avoid quite large discrepancies on individual pairs. There were cases of letter predictabilities differing by up to 21, and cases of an AA word being paired with a word occurring less than twenty times per million. These discrepancies, however, were not systematically in favor of either class of targets; in a slight majority of cases letter predictability favored the bad words and in a slight majority the probability of the neutral word was higher than that of the unpleasant one. Furthermore, the two differences were in opposite directions for the majority of pairs: there were only six cases in which one word had the advantage both in probability and in letter predictability.

B. Results

The interest of the experiment lies in the relative number of choices of the neutral target, and the unpleasant target, at each of the three levels of evidence. There are marked biases on the individual pairs, which sometimes favor the neutral word and sometimes the unpleasant one. Out of the 13 subjects who received each stimulus at the middle level of evidence, the choices on individual pairs ranged from 10 subjects choosing the neutral alternative to 9 subjects choosing the unpleasant one. These differences are at least in part related to the differences in predictability between the targets in each pair: there is a highly significant correlation between the difference in predictability for each pair and the ratio of the number of choices of one possible target over the other. The theoretical analysis we gave earlier would predict that, whatever the bias between the two words, it should not remain independent of the amount of evidence provided, but rather should increase as more and more of the other possible words are eliminated.

TABLE 5
Bias between Neutral and Bad words[a]

	1 letter missing	3 letters missing
Bias toward word showing advantage with 2 letters missing	2.76	1.34
Bias toward bad word	1.65	1.47

[a]The score given is the geometric mean, across stimuli, of the ratio of number of subjects choosing one word to the number choosing the other.

Table 5 shows the bias at the highest and lowest levels of evidence, the direction of the bias for each pair of targets being that found at the middle level. The choice of direction is therefore independent of the data used for analysis. It is clear that the bias increases steeply as the amount of evidence increases; out of the 22 pairs showing a change of bias, 19 showed an increase, so that the effect is very highly significant tested against words. For comparative purposes, the bias toward bad words is also shown; it does not change significantly as the evidence increases.

It is clear, therefore, that our conjecture is confirmed; the relative choice between a neutral and an unpleasant word may go either way depending on the letter probability, but as the sensory evidence increases the size of the bias increases. More remotely, this result is consistent with the conception that emotional words are ones carrying a higher stake, with greater rewards for correct perceptions as well as penalties for error. If this is so, the greater variance in decisions involving emotional words, which is needed to explain their poorer perception with no constant bias against them, is a variance between words rather than between people or between momentary situations.

VI. CONCLUSION

Although we have been discussing interconnected topics in word recognition, there are admittedly several distinguishable strands. First, there is the methodological point that different frequencies of masking noise produce different results, and that therefore some important information is based on relations between widely spaced events in the visual field such as word shape, while other information comes from concentrated detail. The conclusion is put in these terms because, for our purposes, we need not assume a perfect Fourier analysis extending over the entire scene; the existence of receptive systems designed to detect broad bars or regions on the one hand, and fine lines or details on the other, would leave our central point untouched (Macleod & Rosenfeld, 1974). We are emphasizing merely that detail reception alone is not enough.

Second, our evidence is that techniques involving loss of the broad or shape information make it easier to demonstrate the puzzling effect of word emotionality. We cannot, on these data, say whether this is because of some semiphysiological connection of emotionality with general shape and with local detail systems, or whether it is due to the statistical properties of written language. The latter might, for example, provide quite different distributions of "possible" words for detail and for shape information on the same target.

Third, we can now confirm more precisely that poor performance at identifying a "correct" or "target" word, when it is emotional, need not go with a steady bias against such words. This must imply some source of greater variance in decisions involving these words.

Fourth, we have found no evidence that this variance results from changes in priming, and we do not need, for these results, any feedback from semantic analysis to change the perceptual process before a word has been identified. On the contrary, the differences between one emotional word and another seem to provide the source of variance we are seeking, and to suggest that such words are especially prone to be seen when evidence points toward them or to fail to be seen when it points against them, rather than having a steady bias against them.

ACKNOWLEDGMENTS

In Experiment I, the very major contribution of preparing and calibrating the visual noise was entirely due to G. B. Henning, now of Oxford. The photographic work was carried out by D. C. V. Simmonds of the Applied Psychology Unit Cambridge. The authors are employed by, and their research is supported by, the Medical Research Council.

REFERENCES

Baddeley, A. D. Immediate memory and the "perception" of letter sequences. *Quarterly Journal of Experimental Psychology,* 1964, **16**, 364–367.
Broadbent, D. E. The word-frequency effect and response bias. *Psychological Review,* 1967, **74**, 1–15.
Broadbent, D. E. *In defence of empirical psychology,* London: Methuen, 1973.
Broadbent, D. E. Waves in the eye and ear. *Journal of Sound and Vibration,* 1975, **41**, 113–125.
Broadbent, D. E., & Broadbent, M. H. P. Some further data concerning the word-frequency effect. *Journal of Experimental Psychology: General,* 1975, **104**, 297–308.
Broadbent, D. E., & Gregory, M. H. P. The perception of emotionally toned words. *Nature,* 1967, **215**, 581–584.
Broadbent, D. E., & Gregory, M. H. P. Visual perception of words differing in letter digram frequency. *Journal of Verbal Learning and Verbal Behaviour,* 1968, **7**, 569–571.
Broadbent, D. E., & Gregory, M. H. P. Effects on tachistoscopic perception from independent variation of word probability and of letter probability. *Acta Psychologica,* 1971, **35**, 1–14.
Campbell, F. W. The transmission of spatial information through the visual system. In F. O.

Schmitt & F. G. Worden (Eds.), *The neurosciences third study program.* Cambridge, Mass.: MIT Press, 1974.

Henning, G. B., Hertz, B. G., & Broadbent, D. E. Some experiments bearing on the hypothesis that the visual system analyses spatial patterns in independent bands of spatial frequency. *Vision Research,* 1975, **15,** 887–897.

Macleod, I. D. G., & Rosenfeld, A. The visibility of gratings: Spatial frequency channels or bar-detecting units? *Vision Research,* 1974, **14,** 909–915.

Meyer, D. E., Schvaneveldt, R. W., & Ruddy, M. G. Loci of contextual effects on word recognition. In P. M. A. Rabbitt & S. Dornic (Eds.), *Attention and performance V.* London: Academic Press, 1975.

Nachmias, J. Effect of exposure duration on the visual contrast sensitivity with square-wave gratings. *Journal of the Optical Society of America,* 1967, **57,** 421–427.

Owsowitz, S. E. The effects of word familiarity and letter structure familiarity on the perception of words. *Rand Corporation Publications* No. P-2820, 1963.

Rumelhart, D., & Siple, P. Process of recognizing tachistoscopically presented words. *Psychological Review,* 1974, **81,** 99–118.

Tolhurst, D. J. Reaction times in the detection of gratings by human observers: A probabilistic mechanism. *Vision Research,* 1975, **15,** 1143–1149.

24
On Knowing the Meaning of Words We Are Unable to Report: The Effects of Visual Masking

D. A. Allport

Department of Psychology
Reading University
Reading, England

ABSTRACT

The errors generated by normal adults in attempting to read arrays of unrelated words, followed at brief delays by a graphemic pattern mask, are compared with the types of reading error produced, even with unlimited viewing time, by brain-damaged phonemic dyslexics. Among other findings, the discovery of semantically related reading errors (e.g., "blues" → "jazz") under pattern masking leads to a reconsideration of the relation between processes involved in conscious perception or explicit report of a word's identity and processes sufficient for a reader to be influenced by a word's meaning. In one experiment subjects were found able to report, selectively, words belonging to a prespecified semantic category, under conditions of masking such that only one word could be reported, on average, from each multiword array. In another experiment, the accuracy of report of a target word was facilitated by the presence of an associatively related word whose identity or even presence subjects were unable to report. Implications of these results are described in terms of an outline model for pattern masking and visual word recognition.

I. INTRODUCTION

In this chapter I am concerned, at one level, with a well-known and readily reproducible laboratory phenomenon. More fundamentally, I am concerned with the mechanisms of reading and of reading for meaning. At a further remove, it is one small part of a search for what it is that makes conscious mental processes conscious.

The phenomenon with which I am concerned is that whereby a scrambled array of graphemes, following a few tens of milliseconds after a previous graphemic stimulus, reduces the span of immediate, explicit report regarding the identity of the preceding items.

In the absence of an aftercoming masking stimulus, subjects cannot recall much above four or five unrelated letters or similar items from a briefly presented visual display, a limitation which has come to be labeled the *span of immediate visual memory* (Sperling, 1960). Subspan arrays, however (that is, typically, arrays of four items or less), can be recalled without error, independently of exposure duration, at least down to durations of a few milliseconds. Prolonging the exposure time of the display increases only very slowly the number of items that can be reported beyond the span, the increase occurring at about the rate of articulatory rehearsal (e.g., Mackworth, 1962, 1963; Sperling & Speelman, 1970). The situation is dramatically altered if the same display is succeeded, in the same retinal location, by an array of densely distributed letters, or letter fragments (a *pattern mask*). Accuracy of report of the target letters is now critically dependent on the stimulus onset asynchrony (SOA) between the target stimulus and the pattern mask (Turvey, 1973), increasing by one item correctly named for every 10 to 30 msec of SOA, up to the span of around four items (e.g., Sperling, 1963, 1967; Allport, 1968, 1971; Merikle, Coltheart, & Lowe, 1971). This very rapid, initial rate of gain of nameable information with increasing SOA, up to about four items, is referred to here as the *masking interval function*. Above the span, the rate of gain is very much slower, and is again limited approximately to the rate of subvocal rehearsal (idem).

One question, which I believe is a fundamental one, and which has still not been answered satisfactorily, is: *What limits the masking interval function,* between SOAs at which at least one item can be reported on at least some trials, up to SOAs at which the subject can identify three or four items?

Where none of the items in a pattern-masked array can be identified correctly, it might be possible to argue that this is because the visual information has been degraded comprehensively by contrast summation with the pattern mask (e.g., Neisser, 1967). However, when at least some items can be identified — provided these stimuli were not specially privileged by virtue of their position on the retina — this interpretation becomes distinctly less plausible as an explanation for the inability to report the remainder. In an information-processing as well as in a logical sense it appears that some item or items have been *selected* for priority of reporting. What is the mechanism of selection, and at what stage of processing does it occur? To what extent, other than by fixation changes, is it under the subject's control?

Introspectively, the situation is noticeably paradoxical. In some sense the subject is aware of the presence of other items in the array; yet he is unable to name them. In this it is reminiscent of the experience described by subjects attempting to report from a conventionally supraspan array, without pattern masking (Sperling, 1960). Only now depending on SOA, the occurrence of the pattern mask has reduced the magical number four or five – the span of immediate visual memory found in the absence of pattern-masking – to the magical numbers three, two, one, or zero.

In some experiments carried out a few years ago I showed that the masking interval function was essentially the same (at around 15 or 20 msec per *word*) for unrelated consonants as it was for arrays of unrelated common words of three to six letters in length (Allport, 1973). This result seems to imply that the masking function does not simply reflect a capacity limit in the processing of visual or graphemic features (e.g., Rumelhart, 1970). The result is also difficult to reconcile with the idea that the masking interval function represents the rate of encoding of purely visual features into a posticonic short-term visual memory, not vulnerable to masking (Coltheart, 1972). While word frequency has a substantial effect, no significant difference was found between the performance for single-morpheme words of one or two syllables (Allport, 1973). Moreover, stimuli which require to be "named" rather than "read" (Fraisse, 1964), such as Landolt Cs, yield a substantially less steep masking interval function, and a lower span (Allport, 1968). This reduction in the rate of gain of information is not due to the size of critical features, although severe size reduction (or, possibly, critical information carried by very high spatial frequencies; see Broadbent, this volume) can reduce the slope of the masking interval function still further (Allport, 1968, Experiment 2). Taken together, these results suggest that visual pattern masking of words or letters imposes a limit not primarily on the amount or complexity of visual or phonological encoding per unit time before the arrival of the mask, but rather on *lexical* encoding, that is, essentially on the number of names needed in the subject's report. The information gained appears moreover to be unaffected by concurrent implicit speech (Henderson, 1972; Scarborough, 1972; Scarborough & Scarborough, 1975), a result that has also been observed in normal, silent reading of prose (e.g., Hardyck & Petrinovich, 1969).

The currently most widely accepted interpretation of pattern masking (e.g., Sperling, 1963, 1967; Turvey, 1973) is that visual feature information from the target stimulus is erased, or replaced, by features present in the pattern mask. According to this view, identity of items in the target stimulus will not subsequently be recoverable unless they have already been encoded in some suitably mnemonic form before the arrival of the pattern mask. While theorists differ about what the mask-free form of representation might be – visual, phonemic, articulatory, or in some more abstract linguistic or symbolic code – almost all assume that, prior to the critical stage of encoding revealed by the masking interval function, the stimulus information is available solely in visual or *iconic* form. In other words the common assumption is that the masking interval function is limited by the rate at which visual stimulus information can address a higher level representation.

The contention of this chapter is that, while this account is partially true, it is in a sense upside down. I will seek to present evidence that masked stimuli, that is, stimuli whose identity is not recoverable in the subject's report, have nonetheless already accessed the linguistic/semantic system. The limitation on the subject's explicit report imposed by the pattern mask is then essentially in getting this semantic information back into contact with the visual code.

An additional, a priori assumption in the currently accepted interpretation of visual pattern masking is that we have to do with a linear sequence of processing stages, driven by the stimulus from the "bottom up." The theoretical orientation of this chapter, on the contrary, is toward a processing organization in which many different processing "specialists," in the sense used by Winograd (1972), operate in parallel, within different processing domains (phonemic, syntactic, semantic, pictorial, . . .) on the same visual input data. If so, the results computed by the different specialists must then be recombined – in Pribram's phrase, the stimulus must be *re*membered – before it can form part of an integrated perceptual event (cf. Treisman, this volume). The principal conclusion toward which I argue in this chapter is that the critical limitation imposed by pattern masking, and reflected in the masking interval function, is also located at this final stage of perceptual integration.

To this end I present first some evidence concerning the qualitative nature of errors people make in reading pattern-masked multiword arrays. Specifically, I seek to argue that the effect of the pattern mask is to mimic, transiently, the condition of the brain-damaged phonemic dyslexic. Second, I describe two further experiments exploring some of the ways in which a subject may be influenced by, and select among, the meanings of pattern-masked words whose identity he is otherwise unable to report. Finally, on the basis of this and other evidence I will outline a preliminary processing model for pattern masking and visual word recognition.

II. PHONEMIC DYSLEXIA

This is the term adopted by Shallice and Warrington (1975) to denote a relatively rare form of acquired dyslexia. The "purest" clinical example of the syndrome studied in any detail, subject G.R., has been lucidly described in a series of publications by Marshall and Newcombe (1966, 1973; Marshall, Newcombe, & Marshall, 1970). The cardinal symptom is a disability (in G.R. the total inability) to pronounce orthographically regular nonwords (RNWs) or nonsense syllables or to name individual letters presented visually. Associated with this is the production of semantically related or paralexic errors, in attempting to read isolated words with unlimited viewing time. Shown the word BUSH, for example, the subject may read it as "tree," or LIBERTY as "freedom." In reading nouns, up to 69% of G.R.'s error responses are identifiable as semantically related to the target word. Many of these paralexic responses also preserve some degree of visual similarity to the target word. The proportion of paralexic errors is smaller for adjectives and verbs, as is the proportion of correct responses. G.R. is effectively unable to read any function words. Third, essentially none of G.R.'s error responses are words which sound like — rather than look like or have the same meaning as — the target word; that is, he does not produce *phonemic* errors. Finally, his speech, though *telegrammatic* (i.e., with some loss of function words) is coherent; he can repeat without error individual words spoken to him, and can name objects appropriately; that is, his word production is not specifically impaired. Marshall and Newcombe (1973) therefore proposed that the left tempero-parietal lesion suffered in G.R. had effectively destroyed the cerebral mechanisms responsible for converting regular grapheme strings (words and RNWs) to a phonemic representation. A similar proposal in respect of a patient with a qualitatively identical pattern of disabilities has been put forward by Shallice and Warrington (1975). Other similar cases have been described by Low (1931) and Böttcher (1974). If their interpretation is correct, then on the evidence of paralexic errors in these patients it must follow that they have some means of access to the semantic system for visually presented words that does not require mediation by a phonemic code. It is implausible that such patients should have acquired since their injury a specific visual—semantic route which is not also available in normal subjects. The existence of a direct visual route in word recognition has been argued elsewhere by Bower (1970), Morton (1970), Baron (1973, this volume), and others.

III. ERROR RESPONSES OF NORMAL SUBJECTS IN PATTERN MASKING

Under ordinary viewing conditions, normal adult readers do not make paralexic errors in reading aloud isolated words, although these errors do occur in both adults and children in reading connected prose (Kolers, 1970; Marcel, 1974a; Weber, 1968). The principal impetus to this research was the discovery that normal subjects (local housewives and undergraduate students) attempting to read arrays of unrelated English words, followed at brief SOAs by a graphemic pattern mask, also produce error responses that are semantically related to the target word. The word *blues,* for example, was reported as *jazz, kind* as *nice, blue* as *brown, deal* as *ace, drink* as *wine.* Further examples of this kind of error are illustrated in Table 1. In a number of experiments conducted by the writer, employing arrays of between two and four unrelated content words, typically 6% to 9% of all whole-word error responses could be classified, by a relatively cautious criterion, as semantically related to the target words. Of these, about one-quarter also had two or more letters in common with the target word, as for example *dust* read as *dirt.* If "derivational" or morphemic errors are included

TABLE 1
Semantic (Paralexic) Errors (Examples)

bar → beer	fuzz → haze (2)	pot → jug
brim → bank	glove → coat	psalm → sound
cage → catch	hole → false	rod → rail
calf → lamb	ice → gel	rut → lust
cat → dog	jet → air	sea → sail
clip → cut (2)	lamb → babe	sheep → goat
coke → coal	lens → clear	sprig → wood
coal → pick	lint → clean	sow → pig
colt → foal	log → book	slum → drab
cork → light	mast → sail	stain → paint
cup → sip	mesh → net	stall → shop
forge → torch	pen → nib	swine → pig
fork → dig	pie → tart	vent → tap

cow → calf . . . veal . . . yak	gilt → cross . . . frame
gin → trap . . . bottle	leash → latch . . . line
lug → peg . . . wedge	urn → ash . . . grate
wick → lamp . . . tape	zip → slit . . . quick

under semantic errors, for example, *sleep → asleep, saw → see, army → arms,* the average proportion of such error responses increases to nearly 20%. Their incidence varies considerably among individual subjects. Error responses obtained from one subject, a graduate student, in an experiment involving two-word stimulus arrays, included more than 25% of nonderivational paralexic responses (Table 2). As with the paralexic responses generated by G.R., no antonym responses have been found so far in the protocols of normal subjects.

These data for normal subjects under conditions of pattern masking may be compared with the incidence of paralexic errors in the phonemic dyslexic patient described recently by Shallice and Warrington (1975). By a relatively lax criterion, allowing *vehicle → vintage,* for example, as a semantically related response, 4% of this subject's reading errors, or about 2% by a more cautious criterion, could be described as purely semantic, nonderivational errors, while a further 10% were mixed semantic–visual errors (e.g., *lose → stole*).

The discovery of paralexic errors in normal subjects, under conditions of severe pattern masking, raises the possibility that the pattern mask, in reproducing one of the effects of phonemic dyslexia, also mimics the cause. That is, the effect of a grapheme pattern mask may be selectively to interrupt or preempt the operation of the grapheme -phoneme translation process. In the protocols of normal subjects attempting to read pattern-masked arrays of words there is a striking absence of identifiable *phonemic,* as distinct from visual, confusion errors, again as is the case with the phonemic dyslexics. This contrasts with the preponderance of this type of error in the recall of supraspan lists of visually presented letters (e.g., Conrad, 1964; Sperling & Speelman, 1970), and

TABLE 2
Paralexic Errors Generated by One Subject[a]

bread	→ butter	clip	→ tweezer
chive	→ shallot	nail	→ pencil
curds	→ cheese	paddle	→ spade
curry	→ brew	pin	→ screw
icing	→ cake	probe	→ spear
lard	→ cheese	scissors	→ chisel
peas	→ berry	tongs	→ prong
spice	→ chutney		
stew	→ mash		
sweet	→ coffee(?)		
pudding	→ mash		

[a]Sixty trials with two-word displays (120 words); 65 error responses, 17 semantic (26%).

with the relatively small proportion of visual confusion errors in that task (Laughery & Harris, 1970).

One more, very distinctive category of error responses found in reading pattern-masked multiword arrays should be mentioned here. In a large proportion of error responses it is immediately apparent that, while two or more letters of a stimulus word have been correctly identified, the error consists in substituting or inserting into the correct letter sequence one or more letters from another word (or words) in the array. This is referred to here as a *segmentation error*. The most striking feature of these segmentation errors is that, in the great majority of cases the substituted letter, or letter cluster, is derived from a *corresponding* letter position in another word in the array. They are described in greater detail later in this chapter, in relation to Experiment IB. Examples can be found in Table 6. The remaining error responses represent, most often, simple omission of letters; they also include inversion of the letter sequence within a word, and intrusion of letters not present in the array.

The existence of semantic confusion errors in reading pattern-masked arrays of words, as in phonemic dyslexia, is strong evidence that at least some stimulus words which could not be correctly reproduced in the subject's report must nevertheless have gained contact with semantic or lexical memory. Considerable recent support has been forthcoming for the notion of nonselective, parallel access to the internal lexicon, at least in the absence of pattern masking (e.g., Kantowitz, 1974; Keele, 1973; Norman, 1968; Shiffrin & Geisler, 1973). Evidence to this effect in the case of simultaneous *auditory,* or bimodal, word stimuli has been found in a variety of experimental paradigms (e.g., Corteen & Dunn, 1974; Lewis, 1972; Mackay, 1973). It may well be that all visually presented words, even though followed by a graphemic pattern mask, gain access to semantic memory. Wickens (1972) has presented evidence compatible with the interpretation that the subject has partial knowledge about word meaning, in terms of comparisons on semantic differentials, under conditions of pattern masking in which he is apparently unable to identify the word. Recently Marcel (1974b) has extended these results in a very beautiful series of experiments. These show that, even under extremely stringent criteria for the subject's inability, due to pattern masking, to report a word's identity or presence, semantic attributes of the word still affect (1) the latency of color identification (Stroop effect) and (2) the latency of a subsequent lexical decision (Meyer effect). Cumming (1972) has also shown, in a brilliant sequence of experiments, that (letter versus digit) category information derived from stimuli which are phonomenally totally suppressed under conditions of optimal metacontrast can nevertheless be used to control a rapid binary response. Evidence referred to in the Introduction showed that the limiting process in visual word recognition under grapheme pattern masking is not the amount of visual feature information to be encoded, but depends rather on the number of mnemonic units or names needed in the subject's report. At least at or above SOAs at which one word can be reliably reported from a multiword array, the masking interval function appears to be resource limited, rather than data limited (Norman & Bobrow, 1975). The evidence here reviewed suggests that the resource-limited process responsible for the masking interval function is located at a stage *subsequent* to stimulus access to lexical or semantic memory. The two experiments which follow examine this hypothesis further.

IV. EXPERIMENT I

If the limiting process responsible for the masking interval function occurs before access to an internal lexicon, there should be no possibility of selecting items for priority of reporting in terms of *semantic* categories. This experiment required subjects selectively to report words belonging to a particular category ("Animals") under conditions of pattern masking such that only one word, on average, could be correctly identified from any one four-word array.

Those parts of the Method common to both Experiment IA and IB are described first.

1. Method

Word Population. The English names of familiar, four legged animals were collected as follows. All were monosyllables, of three to five letters in length. They were further subdivided into three ranges of word frequency, 1—5, 6—10, and 11—150 occurrences per million (Kucera & Francis, 1967). These will be referred to as "Animal" (A) words of low, medium, and high frequency, respectively. A second, and much larger pool was composed of nouns, also monosyllables of three to five letters, denoting nonliving perceptible objects or substances: "Nonanimal" (NA) words. Each A word was then carefully matched, in terms of word frequency and number of letters, with three NA words, such that, in each resulting array of four words, at least one NA word was of higher frequency of occurrence than the A word in that array. Word frequency within any array was matched to ± 2 for low- and medium-frequency groups, ± 5 for high-frequency groups.

To each of these Animal-word arrays (one A-word, three NA-words) a second array of four NA words was then similarly matched for word frequency and length. These will be referred to as Nonanimal arrays. The resulting mean word frequencies in each category are shown in Table 3. (Word frequencies were also calculated to include the frequencies of derivational noun forms (possessives, plurals) of the words. In nearly all cases the relative frequencies of Animal and Nonanimal words remained unchanged, although of course their absolute values increased. Word groups which did not meet this criterion were rejected).

Stimulus Arrays. Words within each group were assigned randomly to one of four array positions (upper left, upper right, lower left, lower right), with the constraint that, within each frequency range, the A words occurred equally often in each of the four positions. The words were printed in lower-case black Letraset (Type Helvetica Medium 726) on 126 X 180 mm white cards. The letters were 5 mm high with a strokewidth of 1 mm. The words were spaced 40 mm center to center horizontally, and 24 mm vertically, leaving a rectangular blank space of approximately 20 X 20 mm in the center of the card, such that, as seen in the mirror tachistoscope (Experiment IB), the most proximal letter of each word was .5° of visual angle from the center point. The whole array occupied a horizontal extent of approximately 3°.

The pattern mask was composed of black Letraset letters and letter fragments, in the same typeface as the words, distributed semirandomly, in all orientations, and in such a way as to form a uniform 40% density of black-to-white surface over the whole stimulus field.

TABLE 3
Mean Word Frequencies

	Word group		
	A		NA
Frequency range	Animal names	Nonanimal names	(Nonanimal names)
Low (1−5)	2.6	2.9	3.0
Medium (6−10)	7.4	7.8	7.5
High (11−150)	25.7	27.6	27.6

Note: From Kucera and Francis, 1967.

Stimulus Sequence. At the start of each trial, after a "ready" signal by the experimenter, a blank field containing a small central fixation cross appeared for 2.0 sec. At offset this was immediately replaced by a four-word array, followed in turn by the pattern mask, which stayed on until the start of the next trial. The background luminance of all three fields was equal.

Subject's Task. There were two conditions of report, Selective and Nonselective. In both conditions the task was to write down as many words or letters as possible following each exposure. Under the Selective condition, subjects knew, in addition, that each array would contain the name of a four-legged animal. Their primary task was then to report the Animal name, but they were also to write down any other words or letters they could. Besides the animal words they were informed that all the other stimulus words would be the names of nonliving things or substances. In the Nonselective condition the task was simply to report as many words or letters as possible. The experimental groups served under both Selective and Nonselective conditions. The control group served only under the nonselective condition. They were informed that the words were all names of perceptible things or substances, both living and nonliving. They were presented with both Animal and Nonanimal arrays, in random sequence. Subjects were reminded frequently of the importance of fixating the center cross of the adapting field at the start of each trial.

Essentially two replications of the experiment were performed within Experiment IA, using a three-field projection tachistoscope, and a group testing procedure, with student subjects. In a third replication (Experiment IB) nonstudent subjects (housewives) were tested individually on a Scientific Prototype GB Mirror Tachistoscope.

A. Experiment IA

1. Method

Subjects. The subjects were 49 first- and second-year students of psychology at Reading University. They were paid for their participation.

Apparatus. Experiment IA was performed by means of a three-field projection tachistoscope. Three DAF slide projectors were modified by AIM Biosciences with electromechanical shutters fitted in the focal plane of the projection beam. The shutters were activated by a four-stage Digitimer, accurate to ±.1 msec. Rise and fall time of the shutters in each projection beam was completed within 2.5 msec. The stimuli were front projected onto a white canvas screen 3 ft × 4 ft and were viewed binocularly by the subjects from 20 to 36 ft. Total visual angle subtended by the four-word array ranged from 2.3° to 3.4° horizontally, and 1.0° to 1.3° vertically, depending on viewing distance. Ambient room illumination was just sufficient for subjects to record their responses in response booklets without difficulty.

At the start of each trial, after a "Ready" signal from the experimenter, the fixation field appeared for 2.0 sec, followed immediately by the four-word array, and in turn, by the pattern mask which then stayed on until the next trial.

Procedure. The experiment was run in two sessions, the first for practice and the second for gathering the experimental data. In the course of the practice session, experimental subjects were divided into two groups of "fast" and "slow" performers, respectively, under Nonselective reporting. Performance in this session enabled an SOA to be established for each group yielding a hit rate (HR) of approximately 25%, that is, on average one word from a four-word array correctly reported per trial. SOA was 50 msec for the fast group (Group 1, N = 13), 70 msec for the slow group (Group 2, N = 19). Experimental Group subjects also had just 12 practice trials of Selective Animal-name report. The experimental session consisted, after a few warm-up trials, of four blocks of 12 trials each, Block 1 under Nonselective instructions, Blocks 2 and 3 under Selective instructions, and Block 4 again under Nonselective instructions. Arrays of high-, medium-, and low-frequency words occurred in a randomized sequence within each block.

The control group (N = 17) was not informed about the Selective report condition. Control subjects performed the whole experiment under Nonselective reporting at 70 msec SOA with Animal and Nonanimal arrays presented in a randomized sequence.

2. Results

The principal results are shown in Table 4. The data were subjected to a series of analyses of variance. The results for the control group (bottom panel of Table 4) are the simplest to describe and are summarized first. There was a significant effect of word frequency (F = 6.05, df = 2,32, $p < 0.01$), but no significant difference in the accuracy of reporting A or NA words ($F < 1.0$) and no significant interactions. We may therefore safely conclude that there is no intrinsic superiority of reporting Animal words, in the absence of Selective report instructions.

The two experimental groups, on the other hand, exhibit a very substantial superiority in the accuracy of reporting A over NA words: Group 1, F = 31.9, df = 2,24, $p < .01$; Group 2, F = 15.2, df = 2,36, $p < .01$. The effect of word frequency is reliable, $p < 0.01$ in both cases, as is the interaction between report category and word frequency. Multiple planned comparisons between the accuracy of naming Animal words in Selective report versus overall accuracy in the Nonselective condition (Column 1 versus Column 3 in Table 4) constitute the most obviously critical contrast, in demonstrating a selective report superiority. They revealed that a semantic selection effect was present in Group 1 data at all three word frequencies: low frequency, t = 2.06, df = 24, $p < .05$; medium frequency, t = 3.01, df = 24, $p < .01$; high frequency, t = 5.18, df = 24, $p <$

TABLE 4
Experiment IA: Selective Report by Semantic Category: Percentage Words Correct

		Selective report condition		Nonselective
	Word frequency	(1) Animal names	(2) Nonanimal	(3) (Nonanimal)
Experimental group 1 (50-msec SOA)	Low (1–5)	27.9	15.1	20.5
	Medium (6–10)	26.2	19.5	26.2
	High (11–150)	45.2	26 9	25.8
		(1)	(2)	(3)
Experimental group 2 (70-msec SOA)	Low (1–5)	24.3	14.3	22.3
	Medium (6–10)	35.5	18.7	26.9
	High (11–150)	45.5	26.4	26.8
		(Nonselective report)		
		(1)	(2)	(3)
Control group (70-msec SOA)	Low (1–5)	23.3	17.5	20.4
	Medium (6–10)	26.6	25.6	26.0
	High (11–150)	30.1	28.7	29.7

0.001. In Group 2, the contrast was significant only at the high word frequency, $t = 3.67, df = 36, p < .001$.

Table 4 suggests that the Selective advantage in favor of A words has been gained, in part, at the cost of a reduction in the accuracy of naming NA words from the same arrays. This is not a simple tradeoff, however. Multiple comparisons of Column 2 versus Column 3 in Table 4 show a significant reduction in NA words under Selective report at low word frequencies, when the Selective report effect is smallest, (Group 1, $t = 2.97, df = 12, p < .02$; Group 2, $t = 4.14, df = 18, p < .001$, and at medium word frequency, Group 1, $t = 3.66, df = 12, p < .01$; Group 2, $t = 4.54, df = 18, p < .001$), but there is *no* reduction in HR for NA words at high word frequency, where the Selective advantage is greatest. (Note: the HR for A words relates to only one word in four of every display, and, though high, is insufficient to raise the combined HR for all words in Selective report significantly above the overall HR in Nonselective report).

B.   Experiment 1B.

This was a replication of Experiment IA on a different subject population and with a number of minor procedural variations.

1.   *Method*

Subjects were 16 housewives from the Reading University subject panel, recruited via a newspaper advertisement, and paid at the rate of 40 pence per hour. Each subject was tested individually, over two sessions, using a Scientific

Prototype, Model GB, three-field mirror tachistoscope. The masking SOA to be used in the experiment was titrated for each subject individually during the practice session, to achieve an average HR of approximately 25%, that is, an average of one word correct per exposure. Critical masking SOA for individual subjects ranged from 50 to 180 msec, median 80 msec.

In the experimental session, successive blocks of 12 trials were performed at each word frequency, and under Selective and Nonselective conditions of reporting. (All subjects encountered the medium word-frequency range in the first two experimental blocks. In a few cases, subjects' performance in these blocks was better than the required one word per trial, and SOA for these subjects was accordingly reduced by 10 or 20 msec prior to completing the remainder of the experiment. For this reason comparisons of the absolute level of HR between words of medium frequency versus the other two frequency ranges are unreliable). The order of trial blocks in the remainder of the experiment was counterbalanced over the 16 subjects. On each trial, when ready and fixating the cross in the center of the stimulus field, subjects triggered presentation of the word arrays by pressing a microswitch. They said aloud their replies and then wrote them down in a response booklet.

2. Results

Figure 1 shows the proportion of trials on which 0, 1, 2, 3, or 4 words were correctly reported. In 77% of trials subjects correctly identified not more than one of the stimulus words. In less than 2% of trials were they able to report more than two words from an array. Table 5 shows the percentage of words correctly reported, within each word-frequency range, under Selective and Nonselective report. Analyses of variance were carried out both across subjects and across individual words. Across words the principal contrast between Selective A-word and Nonselective (NA-word) report was highly significant ($F = 15.93, df = 1,146, p < .001$). The effect of word frequency was also reliable ($F = 4.48, df = 2,146, p < .025$). Analyzed across subjects the Selective report effect was again significant ($F = 18.93, df = 1,15, p < .01$), as was word frequency ($F = 4.04, df = 2,30, p < .05$). The numerical results therefore replicate very closely the outcome of Experiment IA. In addition a number of more detailed analyses were carried out on the data of Experiment IB.

Conjoint Frequency. The size of the Selective report superiority for each Animal name was calculated, as the HR for that word minus the average HR for words of that frequency and in the same position on the array, under Nonselective reporting. These differences were ranked. Estimates of the salience of these A words as members of the category of four-legged animals were then derived from their ranked frequency of occurrence (*conjoint frequency*) in category production norms for British subjects (Brown, 1972). There was a small, but significant correlation between conjoint frequency and selective report superiority, $\rho = .361, p < .05$.

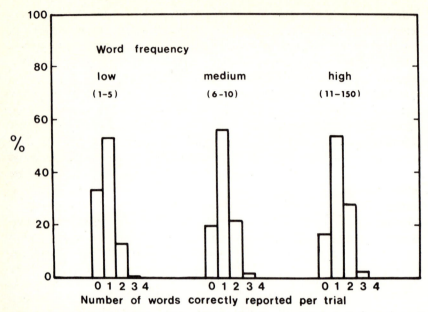

FIG. 1 Percentage of trials in which subjects correctly reported 0, 1, 2, 3, or 4 words (Experiment IB).

Position in Array. There was a marked bias in favor of the upper word positions (F = 213.24, df = 1,146, p < .001), but no consistent difference in the accuracy of identifying words in the right or left visual fields, at least in the Nonselective condition. In the Selective condition, however, there was a marked right-visual-field (RVF) superiority in the ratio of at least 2:1 as between the two lower quadrants only. The response sheets indicated four positions for each stimulus array, and subjects were asked to write their responses in the appropriate position, wherever possible, but if necessary to guess the position. Of all correctly identified whole words 10.2% were reported in the incorrect quadrant.

TABLE 5
Experiment IB: Selective Report by Semantic Category
Percentage Words Correct

Housewife subjects	Report condition		
	Selective		Nonselective
Word frequency	(1) Animal names	(2) Nonanimal	(3) (Nonanimal)
Low (1–5)	30.1	14.0	22.5
Medium (6–10)	39.4	18.1	29.6
High (11–150)	43.6	24.2	28.1

Segmentation Errors. In the sample of 737 error responses of three or more letters in length obtained in Experiment IB, 52% were identifiable as segmentation errors. Some examples are shown in Table 6. Segmenting all stimulus words into an initial consonant or consonant cluster, a vowel or vowel group, and a terminal consonant or consonant cluster — including silent "e"s — it turns out that 79.4% of segmentation errors contain only letters found in corresponding segments of another word or words in the same array. Examples of segmentation errors (SEs) from noncorresponding segmental loci are shown in Table 6c. Of segmentation errors, 11.5% combined letters from three or even four different words in the array, yet in the majority of these cases too the substituted letters were derived from corresponding segmental loci. In those responses combining letters from just two words of any array, 47% of substitutions occurred between vertically adjacent word pairs, 40% between horizontal pairs, and the remaining 13% between diagonal pairs. Eleven percent involved the insertion of an *additional* letter, for example: *rim gag → grim; lens calf → leans.* (Words on the left of

TABLE 6
Segmentation Errors (Examples)

(1)	rust	zinc	→	rest . . . runt . . . zip . . .			
	vent	ramp		vest . . . vamp . . .			
	gin	rod	→	gig . . . (ig) . . . rig . . . gid . . . gun . . .			
	rug	tie					
	spray	stall	→	stray . . . shall . . .			
	guest	sheep		shell . . .			
	tab	cud	→	cab(2) . . . tag . . . cub . . . tub . . .			
	bib	bog		bug . . . tib . . .			
	sock	tack	→	sack(3) . . . soap . . . soak			
	wick	hoop		sick . . . tap . . .			
(b)	. . .	. . .		. . . glove	→	glade . . .	
	cake	lawn	→ lake	. . . spade			
	flag	rope	→	flake . . .	mast . . .	→	map . . .
	bull	rake		rape . . .	prop . . .		
	slum	dock	→ duck(4)	. . . wolf	→	waif	
	. . .	. . .		. . . nail			
(c)	. . .	. . .		. . . brew	→	refuse	
	goat	slab	→ stab . . .	. . . fuse			
	cab	hut	→ but . . .	junk . . .	→	jungle . . .	
	. . .	. . .		glen . . .			

Note: Words on left of arrow are in stimulus array; on the right of arrow, the subjects' responses the arrow occurred in the stimulus array; words to the right of the arrow are the subject's response.) The remainder (89%) represent direct substitutions of one letter or letter group for another. In the error data generated by Experiment IB, 31.2% are substitutions of one or more letters between the *initial* letter groups of two words; 36.2% are substitutions between *vowels* or vowel groups; and the remainder, 32.6%, involve substitutions within *terminal* letter groups. A pattern of substitutions which only very rarely occurred was for the initial letter of a word on the right of fixation to be substituted for the terminal letter of a word on the left, or a terminal letter of a word on the left to replace the initial letter of a word on the right (see Table 6(c) for an example), even though a substitution of this sort would involve a minimal spatial disarrangement of graphemes. The fact that the substituted or inserted letter is at least as often a medial vowel as an end letter, despite greater lateral masking suffered by the inner letters (Bouma, 1970), is additional indication that these error responses do not represent simply random concatenations of the most visible letters in the display. Evidently the effect of pattern masking more readily disturbs information about the gross position within the array of word constituents (letters and letter groups) than information about the structural or segmental loci of graphemes within a word, even though the former involves displacement over a much larger visual angle and to a different quadrant of the visual field.

These results, in particular the discovery that letter substitutions, in 70–80% of cases, occur only between letters occupying corresponding segmental loci in two or more stimulus words, imply that a considerable amount of structural parsing or segmentation has already been carried out on more than one word in the array – on some occasions, at least, on all four words – including words of which the subject is unable explicitly to report any other constituents aside from those letters occurring as substitution errors in another word.

Semantic (Paralexic) Errors. A total of 658 error responses obtained in Experiment IB were English words. Of these, 40 (i.e., 6.1%) could be classified by a relatively cautious criterion, as semantically related to the stimulus word (excluding "derivational" errors). Three subjects produced no clear semantic errors, while for another three 10% and for one subject 15% of her whole word error responses could be so classified.

C. Discussion

The immediate conclusion to be drawn from Experiment I is that, under conditions of severe pattern masking of subspan arrays of words, subjects can selectively favor naming of words within a given semantic category. (The result has been demonstrated, at least, for the category of four-legged animals, or what amounted to the same thing in this experiment, living things. Some caution should no doubt be exercized until the phenomenon can be demonstrated using other populations of words and other categories.) This result implies either that the level of representation reached by the unreported (that is, masked) words is one at which the discrimination of semantic categories is possible, or at least that the "selection" process itself occurs at such a level. It is therefore in agreement with the hypothesis suggested earlier by the occurrence of semantic confusion errors under pattern masking. The outcome appears to conflict with the commonly made assumption, referred to in the Introduction, that prior to the critical stage of encoding revealed by the masking interval function the stimulus information is available solely in visual, or iconic, form. Further implications of the data from Experiment I are considered subsequently.

V. EXPERIMENT II

While the results of Experiment I clearly favor this interpretation, it is obviously essential that the cardinal proposition of this chapter, that access to the semantic system is obtained in parallel by pattern-masked words, under conditions in which they nevertheless cannot be reported, be subjected to some more direct test. The question addressed by Experiment II is simple. Under conditions of pattern masking in which one of two stimulus words is effectively *never* available for report, will variations in its semantic relatedness to a second word affect the accuracy with which the second word can be identified?

A. Method

1. Stimuli

Target words in black lower-case pica type were presented centrally on a white screen, by means of a three-channel projection tachistoscope. In some experimental conditions (see below) a second, distractor word was presented, also in lower case, directly above the target word and separated from it by double spacing, that is, by approximately $1°$ of visual angle. The target word was preceded by an adapting field containing two short vertical bars, serving as fixation indicators, one letter space right and left of the location of the target word. At offset (SOA = 20 msec), target and distractor words were immediately replaced by a pattern mask of equal background luminance consisting of letters in the same typeface as the target words, distributed densely and randomly, in all orientations, over the entire area of the display.

2. Word Populations

Word pairs were drawn from word-association norms (Postman and Keppel, 1970) to conform to two different conditions of association: (1) two-way associates, in which each member of the pair was the highest-ranking associate of the other word; (2) one-way associates, in which the first word appeared as an associative response to the second in at least 30% of responses, while the second word occurred as an associate of the first in fewer than 10% of responses. Words were from 3 to 6 letters in length, and of either one or two syllables. Words with a frequency of less than 10 (Kucera & Francis, 1967) were excluded.

In each word pair, one word was designated as the target word (T), while the other served as the associated distractor (A). From the above associative pairs, three sets of word pairs were constructed: (1) two-way associates (A ↔ T); (2) one-way associates, with the target word as the response term (A → T); and (3) one-way associates, with the target word as the stimulus term (A ← T). Subsets of 12 word pairs from each of the above conditions were prepared, such that word frequency and letter and syllable length of the target words could be exactly matched across all three conditions. A words were also matched for letter length across each condition. There was an equal ratio of A words higher or lower in word frequency than their corresponding T words within each condition.

Two further sets of 12 T words were selected from the word-frequency norms to exactly match the preceding target words in both frequency and number of letters. To one of these sets was added a set of distractor words (U), unrelated by association or meaning to their respective target words, and again matched in frequency and number of letters to the A words in the preceding conditions to form a fifth condition (U–T). The other set of target words was presented without any distractor words, and served as a baseline condition (T).

3. Subjects

The subjects were 27 second-year psychology students at Reading University. They participated as part of a laboratory course requirement.

4. Procedure

Subjects were instructed that, on each trial, one word would appear briefly on the screen, between the bar markers, to be followed by a pattern mask. Their task was to write down the target word, or any letters in it they could, following each trial, and to guess when they were unsure. They were asked to try to write down at least some letters on every trial. They were told that on some trials there would be a second word immediately above the target word, but that it was to be ignored. Great emphasis was laid on the importance of fixating between the bar markers before each stimulus exposure. Each subject then performed 25 practice trials with only a single target word presented on each occasion. The first few trials were presented at a longer exposure to acquaint the subjects with details of the stimulus arrangements; the last 12 trials were run at 20 msec SOA.

The subjects then performed 60 experimental trials, 12 in each target-word condition, in a randomized order. Each trial commenced with the experimenter saying "Ready . . . now." On the word "now," the adapting field, containing the fixation markers, appeared for 2.0 sec, followed by the target (and distractor) word(s) for 20 msec and succeeded in turn by the pattern mask, which remained until the initiation of the next trial.

B. Results

The mean percentage of target words correctly reported in each condition is shown in Table 7. The data were subjected to a Friedman's two-way analysis of variance, yielding a significant main effect of the different conditions ($p < .01$), and to subsequent Wilcoxons, computed both across subjects and across individual target words. Computed across individual words, HRs in each condition were significantly different from every other condition ($p < .01$), with the sole exception of the contrast between the two one-way Associated distractor conditions, (A → T) versus (A ← T), which did not differ significantly from each other. Computed across subjects, the HR differences between each of the conditions were significant individually at $p < .01$, except for the following contrasts: (1) between (A ↔ T) and (A← T) which was significant at $p < .05$; (2) between (A ↔ T) and the baseline condition (T), and the two remaining contrasts within the Associated distractor conditions, that is, (A ← T) versus (A → T) and (A ↔ T) versus (A → T), which were not significant.

Excluding trials on which no response of any sort was recorded, the remaining error responses were classified exhaustively as follows:

1. visual errors (that is, with at least some letters in common with the target word but excluding Examples 2, 3, and 4 below, 48.5%;
2. derivational errors (like, "scared" → "scare"), 9.4%;
3. semantic, nonderivational, errors, 7.8%;
4. phonemic errors (like "screw" → "kew"(?)), 0.9%;
5. other (no letters in common with target word), 33.4%.

The incidence of nonderivational, semantic errors varied slightly over the experimental conditions: most frequent in (A ↔ T) and (A → T), slightly fewer in (A ← T) and (U−T), and essentially absent in the single-word baseline condition (T).

TABLE 7
Experiment II

Stimulus condition	T^c	U^a T^c	A^b ↕ T^c	A^b ↓ T^c	A^b ↑ T^c
Percentage correct	69.4	50.6	64.5	59.6	57.7

[a]Unassociated.
[b]Associated distractor.
[c]Target word.

Segmentation errors, the predominant error type in Experiment I in which all words were equidistant from the fovea and of equal task priority, were rare or absent in Experiment II.

C. Discussion

Three main aspects of these results can be summarized as follows. First, the presence of an unrelated distractor word reduces HR on the target word by about 20%, as compared with no distractor word present. A somewhat similar effect has been found in reporting supraspan arrays of letters or digits, where the codability of the distractor items has a marked effect (Butler, 1974; Mewhort, 1967). Second, an associative (semantic) relationship between target and distractor words reverses or antagonizes the first effect. This facilitatory effect of semantic relatedness is thus in the opposite direction to that found in the Stroop color—word phenomenon (Dyer, 1973), and suggests, therefore, that they depend on different mechanisms. Third, while there was an apparently reliable superiority of the two-way Associated word pairs (T ↔ A) over the two other, one-way Associated conditions, there was no significant difference in HR between the two latter conditions due to the direction of association.

In sum, there was a clear semantic facilitation effect due to the (parafoveal) distractor word, under conditions of pattern masking at which the target word itself, presented centrally on the fovea, could be identified correctly on little over half of all trials. Questioned at the end of the experiment, subjects insisted that on no trials had they been aware even that a second word or letter string had been presented. (On just three occasions, out of a total of 1,640 trials, however, subjects in fact reported the distractor rather than the target word. All three instances occurred in the (A ← T) condition). The experiment would clearly be strengthened by the inclusion of a control condition in which the subjects attempted explicitly to report both the target and the (parafoveal) distractor words. Because of the evident difficulty of controlling the subject's fixation strategies in such a task, however, this condition is not included in the present experiment. However, given (1) the relatively low level of HR even on the target items, despite their advantage in terms of retinal location and task variables, (2) the extremely low rate of explicit intrusions from the distractor words — completely absent in condition (A ↔ T) showing the strongest facilitation effect, f and (3) the subjects' introspective reports, it must be extremely unlikely that any significant number of distractor words could be explicitly identified at this pattern-masking SOA, at least without a corresponding decrease in the accuracy of report of the (foveal) target words.

The experiment is therefore taken as giving strong support to the hypothesis that (at least) two stimulus words can gain contact simultaneously with the lexicon/semantic system, under conditions of pattern masking in which there is an essentially zero probability of both words being consciously perceived and/or appearing together correctly in the subject's overt report. A possibly related phenomenon has been described by Bradshaw (1974). A peripherally presented word, briefly exposed without a pattern mask, can influence the semantic interpretation of a centrally presented homograph, even when the disambiguating, peripheral word apparently could not be explicitly reported.

VI. GENERAL DISCUSSION

I set out, in this chapter, to consider the question of what is the limiting process responsible for the masking interval function. The evidence which has been presented converges toward the conclusion that one (at least) of the limiting resources in reading pattern-masked multiword arrays is located at a stage *subsequent* to stimulus access to the semantic system. The question naturally arises, therefore, as to what the function of this apparently critical "post-semantic" stage of processing might be. To put this question another way: granted that pattern-masked words access the lexicon/semantic system, then why, or how, does the pattern mask prevent this lexical information from becoming available to conscious experience or for explicit word production? Why are the words not seen, and why can they not be named?

Thus far, the most consistent and best developed general theory of naming and word recognition is Morton's *logogen* model (Morton, 1968, 1970; Seymour, 1973). In that model, outputs from the logogen system take the form of abstract, morphemic units which become available one at a time for conversion to a potential articulatory response. However, the model lacks a specific mechanism for relating particular logogen outputs to the particular stimuli that evoked them. In particular where more than one word, or nameable item, is presented at the same time, a mechanism is clearly required to integrate appropriately the nominal identities of the items — their logogen outputs — with their other physical attributes — location, color, size, etc. In experiment IB, when subjects could correctly identify a word, on 90% of occasions they could also assign it to the correct location in the visual array. In the Stroop word—color naming task, subjects can, in fact, respond in terms of the "correct" name, as defined by the stimulus attributes from which it was derived. A passive "threshold" mechanism would not be sufficient to resolve cases of competition between potential word responses, as in the Stroop task, where the strongest or earliest available response may not necessarily be the one that is selected. A model of the naming process should be able to account for performances such as these, as well as for the phenomenology of visual word perception. (What one *perceives*, at least in my experience, is not a disembodied name but a printed word having a given position, size, etc., in the visual field and, usually, having some meaning.)

Given a specialized linguistic mechanism concerned uniquely with the lexical identity of word stimuli regardless of their "precategorical" stimulus attributes, that is, a logogen system, performance and phenomenology alike call for the integration of information from both the logogen system and the mechanisms responsible for the analysis of visual form and location. Presumably the results of the grapheme—phoneme conversion process, and of any other functionally separable specialists which can contribute to episodic memory, must likewise be able to converge in its construction. This convergence and integration of outputs from the different perceptual specialists should then represent the interface between the multiplicity of automatic or "systemic" processing (Shiffrin, 1975) and the contents of conscious perception and episodic memory. The hypothesis here proposed is that this same process of integration between the results of linguistic and visual specialists is responsible for the masking interval function.

In any complex cognitive system in which specialized "knowledge sources" contribute from within different domains or levels of knowledge, the problem inevitably arises as to how these separate specialists are to communicate with each other. This turns out to be a much harder and more crucial problem in the design of intelligent systems that many people originally realized (see Winston, 1975). The apparently simplest solution, that of a fixed, linear sequence of hierarchically ordered processing stages, has been found generally to be unworkable in other than rigidly and extremely simplified cognitive contexts, and has been largely replaced in current AI efforts by a more interactive, "heterarchical" processing organization (Minsky & Papert, 1972). A particularly interesting example is provided by the speech understanding system known as Hearsay II, being developed at Carnegie—Mellon University (Lesser, Fennell, Erman, & Reddy, 1974; Reddy & Newell, 1975). In this system separate knowledge sources operating at phonemic, syllabic, lexical, syntactic, and conceptual levels communicate via a single, centralized data structure ("blackboard") in which hypotheses at any of these levels, regarding the current speech input, can be proposed, strengthened, vetoed, or modified, in principle, by any of the contributing knowledge sources. Rumelhart (this volume), puts forward the system structure of Hearsay II as the framework also for a psychological model of the reading process. My immediate concern, in this chapter, has been to argue for the psychological necessity of *some* postsemantic process of perceptual integration (and its contribution to the masking interval function). The evidence which has been reviewed, however, does suggest a number of general features of processing organization, which I shall attempt to summarize in the form of a preliminary model for pattern masking and word recognition.

VII. OUTLINE MODEL FOR THE PERCEPTION
OF PRINTED WORDS

Graphemic information is processed asynchronously and independently (illustrated schematically in Fig. 2) in at least three parallel systems:

1. The dominant, and of course ontogenetically primary process is a purely visual, nonlinguistic analysis of word or letter shapes as two-dimensional pic-

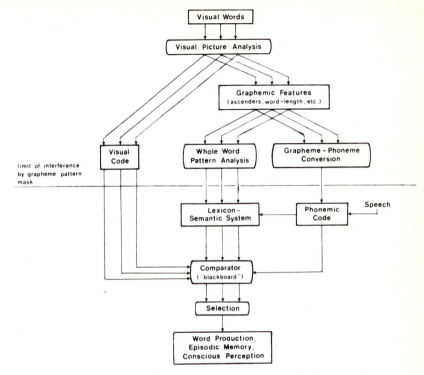

FIG. 2   Diagram of outline model for the perception of printed words.

tures. The output of this system is called here a *visual code* (without prejudice to previous uses of the term), and should probably include a description of "where is it?" as well as "what is it?". The visual code is not immediately open to awareness. (The process of visual picture analysis itself obviously requires access to real-world knowledge or LTM. In the interests of a limited exposition, many such essential components beyond the immediate purview of this chapter have been omitted from Fig. 2.)

2. The second processing system, labeled Whole-Word Pattern Analysis, serves the recognition of (at least) single-morpheme content words, enabling direct visual access, *in parallel*, to the lexicon/semantic system. This pathway is presumably homologous with the mechanism involved in reading Chinese, or Japanese Kanji, characters (see Carroll, 1972; Kaiho, 1975; Martin, 1972; see also Murrell & Morton, 1974). There is some neurological evidence that these are predominantly right-hemisphere functions. The mechanisms responsible for Systems 1 and 2 are not necessarily functionally distinct, at least in their early stages. The *products* of the two systems, however, are clearly distinct in that this second system has direct access to linguistic categories, while the former has not.

3. The third processing system concerned with grapheme information is specialized for the application of grapheme–phoneme conversion rules

(Venezky, 1970) applied to both words and RNWs. The resulting phonemic codes become available sequentially, word-by-word or, possibly, syllable-by-syllable. By contrast, on the evidence of segmentation errors (Experiment I), the early stages of grapheme–phoneme conversion, including the parsing of something like Vocalic Centre Groups (VCGs) (Smith & Spoehr, 1974), are frequently begun on two or more words of an array at the same time. The resulting phonemic code also has access to the internal lexicon (Coltheart, Davelaar, Jonasson, & Besner, this volume).

The component labeled "lexicon" in Fig. 2 is intended to include semantic, and possibly syntactic, as well as lexical specialists, whose operation proceeds automatically without attentional control. It thus corresponds to the combined logogen and semantic systems in Morton's (1970) model of word recognition, with the important difference that, in this model, lexicon outputs can become available simultaneously.

(The contribution of syntactic processing has yet to be explored. It is possible that in the absence of a syntactically structured input – as in the experiments described here with arrays of unrelated words – the whole-word visual route to the lexicon is unable to handle function words or bound morphemes. The specific difficulty of phonemic dyslexics in reading function words, and the high incidence of derivational errors both in phonemic dyslexics and in normal subjects reading pattern-masked word arrays, suggests that there is some functional separation between processing these syntactically important elements and processing lexical root or single-morpheme content words.)

Outputs of all three processing systems, visual code, phonemic code, and lexicon are generated in parallel, asynchronously, and without attentional control. Taken together, they correspond to what Shiffrin and Geisler (1973) identified as the iconic phase of the perceptual process. Lexicon outputs, ex hypothesi, take the form of abstract morphemic units, whose specification is capable of addressing, without capacity limitations, their corresponding visual or phonemic codes. That is, *with further processing,* these specifications can be translated into a description of the sound pattern or the visual appearance of the root word. Without further translation they can also be compared against the visual and/or phonemic codes generated by the immediately preceding sensory input. Conscious perception of a word (rather than a row of black squiggles) as present in a visual array is contingent on the outcome of this comparison process. That is, unless matched with a lexical (or syllabic) code, the visually complex contours in a word array cannot be economically described by the visual code alone and will exceed the capacity of working memory. Consequently, though the subject may perceive the presence of complex, letter-like forms, their details will be almost instantaneously forgotten. On the other hand a *lexicon* output alone, in the absence of either an appropriate visual or phonemic code, and more particularly in the presence of an inappropriate visual code (for example, resulting from the pattern mask), will be vetoed by the comparator. The word is not "seen." This is the situation, in terms of the model, in the case of pattern-masked multiword arrays. The masking interval function is thus limited, according to this hypothesis, by the rate at which the comparison process between visual and lexical codes can occur, that is, ultimately, by the rate of perceptual integration.

To recapitulate, according to this model the effect of a graphemic pattern mask is twofold. (1) It interrupts, or preempts, the relatively slow process of grapheme–phoneme (or grapheme–syllable) conversion. At short masking SOAs this route is therefore wholly unavailable for the control of particular word outputs. (2) The pattern mask also disrupts information represented in the visual code. Only those potential outputs from the lexicon/semantic system which have already been correlated with appropriate visual code information, before the arrival of the pattern mask, can control perceptual reports. Partial or incomplete matchings between visual code and lexical outputs, interrupted by the pattern mask, may, if the subject is willing to "guess," result in semantic confusion errors. This interpretation implies that phonemic dyslexics, such as G.R., who also produce a high proportion of semantic errors, also suffer some disturbance of visual code, as well as of grapheme–phoneme conversion.

The process of word production, either in speech or writing, appears to be basically sequential in nature, at least within either principal output mode. Since phonemically or visually coded words can become available simultaneously, a further selection process is indicated before final command of one or other word-production system can be obtained. Delays imposed by competition for the comparison (or selection) stage are presumably reflected in different versions of the Stroop situation. (This discussion is limited to word production within just one mode – speech or script. The possibility of simultaneous, independent output streams in different production modes need not concern us directly. Suffice it to say that the speech production mode can be directly addressed via a phonemic code (see Chistovich *et al.,* 1962) while graphic production is directly addressed via the visual code. Truly simultaneous, independent output streams *in different production modes* are apparently possible when both involve *direct* (or possibly "ideo-motor compatible") input–output addressing (cf. Allport, Antonis, & Reynolds, 1972; Greenwald, 1972; Tierney, 1973; Shaffer, 1975).)

Breakdown of the veto or interdiction mechanism in the comparator would presumably result in hallucinatory experiences of words whose lexicon units had been activated by semantically controlled "spreading excitation" in the absence of immediate stimulation. Rapid reading for meaning, on the other hand, where the aim is evidently not to perceive the identity of individual words but rather to engage in "externally guided thinking" (Neisser, 1967), may specifically depend on the deliberate inactivation of the comparator stage, enabling controlled "hallucination" of the meaning of a text in the absence of any conscious visual experience of the printed words.

ACKNOWLEDGMENTS

The motivation for Experiments I and II, and the resulting theoretical interpretation, was prompted initially by the beautiful series of experiments, referred to in the text, by A. J. Marcel (1974b). The preparation of this paper has benefited from conversations with many friends and colleagues. I am particularly indebted to Max Coltheart, Tony Marcel, Ian Dennis, Tim Shallice, and Derek Besner. I also gratefully acknowledge the assistance of Jackie Daykin, Sian Jones, Eileen Davelaar, and Rhona Stainthorp in the preparation, data collection, and analysis of these experiments.

REFERENCES

Allport, D. A. The rate of assimilation of visual information. *Psychonomic Science,* 1968, **12,** 231–232.

Allport, D. A. Parallel encoding within and between elementary stimulus dimensions. *Perception & Psychophysics,* 1971, **10,** 104–108.

Allport, D. A. Word recognition and the recognition buffer. Paper presented to Experimental Psychology Society, London, January 1973.

Allport, D. A., Antonis, B., & Reynolds, P. On the division of attention: A disproof of the single-channel hypothesis. *Quarterly Journal of Experimental Psychology,* 1972, **24,** 225–235.

Baron, J. Phonemic stage not necessary for reading. *Quarterly Journal of Experimental Psychology,* 1973, **25,** 241–246.

Baron, J. What we might know about orthographic rules. This volume.

Böttcher, R. Zur Rolle von graphischen und semantisch-syntaktischen Faktoren beim Wortlesen. *Zeitschrift für Psychologie,* 1974, **182,** 40–67.

Bouma, H. Interaction effects in parafoveal letter recognition. *Nature,* 1970, **225,** 177–8.

Bower, T. G. R. Reading by eye. In H. Levin & J. Williams (Eds.), *Basic studies on reading.* New York: Basic Books, 1970.

Bradshaw, J. L. Peripherally presented and unreported words may bias the perceived meaning of a centrally fixated homograph. *Journal of Experimental Psychology,* 1974, **103,** 1200–1202.

Broadbent, D. E. General shape and local detail in word perception. This volume.

Brown, W. P. Studies in word listing: Some norms and their reliability. *The Irish Journal of Psychology,* 1972, **3,** 117–159.

Butler, B. The limits of selective attention in tachistoscopic recognition. *Canadian Journal of Psychology,* 1974, **28,** 199–213.

Carroll, J. B. The case for ideographic writing. In J. F. Kavanagh & I. G. Mattingley (Eds.), *Language by ear and by eye.* Cambridge: MIT Press, 1972.

Chistovich, L. A., Klass, Y. A., & Kuźmin, Y. I. [The process of speech sound discrimination.] *Voprosi psikhologii,* 1962, 8 (6), 26–39 (Research Translation ETR 63-10). Bedford Mass.: Air Force Cambridge Research Laboratories, 1963.

Coltheart, M. Visual information processing. In P. C. Dodwell (Ed.), *New horizons in psychology 2.* London: Penguin Books, 1972.

Coltheart, M. Davelaar, E., Jonasson, J., & Besner, D. Access to the internal lexicon. This volume.

Conrad, R. Acoustic confusions in immediate memory. *British Journal of Psychology,* 1964, **55,** 75–83.

Corteen, R. S., & Dunn, D. Shock-associated words in a nonattended message: A test for momentary awareness. *Journal of Experimental Psychology*, 1974, **102**, 1143–1144.

Cumming, G. A. Visual perception and metacontrast at rapid input rates. Unpublished doctoral dissertation, Oxford University, 1972.

Dyer, F. N. The Stroop phenomenon. *Memory and Cognition*, 1973, **1**, 106–120.

Fraisse, P. Le temps de réaction verbale. I: Dénomination et Lecture. *Année Psychologique*, 1964, **64**, 21–46.

Greenwald, A. G. On doing two things at once: Time sharing as a function of ideomotor compatibility. *Journal of Experimental Psychology*, 1972, **94**, 52–57.

Hardyck, C. D., & Petrinovich, L. F. Treatment of subvocal speech during reading. *Journal of Reading*, 1969, **12**, 1–11.

Henderson, L. Visual and verbal codes: Spatial information survives the icon. *Quarterly Journal of Experimental Psychology*, 1972, **24**, 439–447.

Kaiho, H. [Semantic information processing of Chinese characters.] *Journal of Gakugei Tokushima University* (Educational Science), 1975, in press.

Kantowitz, B. H. Double stimulation. In B. H. Kantowitz (Ed.), *Human information-processing: Tutorials in performance and cognition.* Hillsdale, N.J.: Lawrence Erlbaum Associates, 1974.

Keele, S. W. *Attention and human performance.* Pacific Palisades, Cal.: Goodyear, 1973.

Kolers, P. Three stages of reading. In H. Levin & J. Williams (Eds.), *Basic studies on reading.* New York: Basic Books, 1970.

Kucera, H., & Francis, W. N. Computational analysis of present-day American English. Providence, R.I.: Brown University Press, 1967.

Laughery, K. R., & Harris, G. J. Visual and auditory intrusion errors in short-term memory. *Journal of Experimental Psychology*, 1970, **83**, 101–106.

Lesser, V. R., Fennell, R. D., Erman, L. D., & Reddy, D. R. Organization of the Hearsay II speech understanding system. IEEE Symposium on Speech Recognition, Carnegie-Mellon University, Pittsburgh, April 1974.

Lewis, J. L. Semantic processing with bisensory stimulation. *Journal of Experimental Psychology*, 1972, **96**, 455–457.

Low, A. A. A case of agrammatism in the English language. *Archives of Neurology and Psychiatry*, 1931, **25**, 556–597.

Mackay, D. G. Aspects of the theory of comprehension, memory and attention. *Quarterly Journal of Experimental Psychology*, 1973, **25**, 22–40.

Mackworth, J. F. The visual image and the memory trace. *Canadian Journal of Psychology*, 1962, **16**, 55–59.

Mackworth, J. F. The relation between the visual image and the post-perceptual immediate memory. *Journal of Verbal Learning and Verbal Behavior*, 1963, **2**, 75–85.

Marcel, A. J. The effective visual field and the use of context in fast and slow readers of two ages. *British Journal of Psychology*, 1974, **65**, 479–492. (a)

Marcel, A. J. Perception with and without awareness. Paper presented to Meeting of Experimental Psychology Society, Stirling, Scotland, July 1974. (b)

Marshall, J. C., & Newcombe, F. Syntactic and semantic errors in paralexia. *Neuropsychologia*, 1966, **4**, 169–76.

Marshall, J. C., & Newcombe, F. Patterns of paralexia: A psycholinguistic approach. *Journal of Psycholinguistic Research*, 1973, **2**, 175–99.

Marshall, M., Newcombe, F., & Marshall, J. C. The microstructure of word-finding difficulties in a dysphasic subject. In C. B. Flores D'Arcais & W. J. M. Levelt (Eds.), *Advances in Psycholinguistics.* Amsterdam: North-Holland Publ., 1970.

Martin, S. E. Nonalphabetic writing systems: Some observations. In J. F. Kavanagh & I. G. Mattingley (Eds.), *Language by ear and by eye.* Cambridge: MIT Press, 1972.

Merikle, P. M. Coltheart, M., & Lowe, D. G. On the selective effects of a patterned masking stimulus. *Canadian Journal of Psychology,* 1971, **25**, 264–79.

Mewhort, D. J. K. Familiarity of letter-sequences, response uncertainty and the tachisto-scopic recognition experiment. *Canadian Journal of Psychology,* 1967, **21**, 309–321.

Minsky, M., & Papert, S. Progress Report on Artificial Intelligence (Memo 252). Cambridge, Mass.: M.I.T. Artificial Intelligence Laboratory, 1972.

Morton, J. Consideration of grammar and computation in language behavior. In J. C. Catford (Ed.), *Studies in language and language behavior.* Washington, D.C.: U.S. Office of Education, 1968.

Morton, J. A functional model for memory. In D. A. Norman (Ed.), *Models of human memory.* New York: Academic Press, 1970.

Murrell, G. A., & Morton, J. Word recognition and morphemic structure. *Journal of Experimental Psychology,* 1974, **102**, 963–968.

Neisser, U. *Cognitive psychology.* New York: Appleton-Century-Crofts, 1967.

Norman, D. A. Toward a theory of memory and attention. *Psychological Review,* 1968, **75**, 522–36.

Norman, D. A., & Bobrow, D. G. On data-limited and resource-limited processes. *Cognitive Psychology,* 1975, **7**, 44–64.

Postman, L., & Keppel, G. (Eds.), *Norms of word association.* New York: Academic Press, 1970.

Reddy, R., & Newell, A. Knowledge and its representation in a speech understanding system. In L. W. Gregg (Ed.), *Knowledge and cognition.* Potomac, Md.: Lawrence Erlbaum, Associates, 1975.

Rumelhart, D. E. A multicomponent theory of the perception of briefly exposed visual displays. *Journal of Mathematical Psychology,* 1970, **7**, 191–218.

Rumelhart, D. E. Toward an interactive model of reading. This volume.

Scarborough, D. L. Memory for brief visual displays. *Cognitive Psychology,* 1972, **3**, 408–429.

Scarborough, D. L., & Scarborough, H. Encoding and memory processes for visual displays. In P. M. A. Rabbitt & S. Dornic (Eds.), *Attention and performance V.* London: Academic Press, 1975.

Seymour, P. H. K. A model for reading, naming and comparison. *British Journal of Psychology,* 1973, **64**, 35–49.

Shallice, T., & Warrington, E. K. Word recognition in a phonemic dyslexic patient. *Quarterly Journal of Experimental Psychology,* 1975, **27**, 148–160.

Shaffer, L. H. Multiple attention in continuous verbal tasks. In P. M. A. Rabbitt & S. Dornic (Eds.), *Attention and performance V.* London: Academic Press, 1975.

Shiffrin, R. M. The locus and role of attention in memory systems. In P. M. A. Rabbitt & S. Dornic (Eds.), *Attention and performance V.* London: Academic Press, 1975.

Shiffrin, R. M., & Geisler, W. S. Visual recognition in a theory of information processing. In R. Solso (Ed.), *The Loyola Symposium: Contemporary viewpoints in cognitive psychology.* Washington, D.C.: Winston, 1973.

Smith, E. E., & Spoehr, K. T. The perception of printed English: A theoretical perspective. In B. H. Kantowitz (Ed.), *Human information-processing: Tutorials in performance and cognition.* Hillsdale, N.J.: Lawrence Erlbaum Associates, 1974.

Sperling, G. The information available in brief visual presentations. *Psychological Monographs,* 1960, **74**, 1–29.

Sperling, G. A model for visual memory tasks. *Human Factors,* 1963, **5**, 19–31.

Sperling, G. Successive approximations to a model for short-term memory. *Acta Psychologica,* 1967, **27**, 285–292.

Sperling, G., & Speelman, R. Acoustic similarity and auditory short-term memory: Experiments and a model. In D. A. Norman (Ed.), *Models of human memory.* New York: Academic Press, 1970.

Tierney, M. A. Dual task performance. Unpublished B. A. dissertation. University of Reading, 1973.

Treisman, A. Attention and stimulus integration. This volume.

Turvey, M. T. Peripheral and central processes in vision. *Psychological Review,* 1973, **80,** 1–52.

Venezky, R. L. *The structure of English orthography.* The Hague: Mouton, 1970.

Weber, R. M. The study of oral reading errors: A survey of the literature. *Reading Research Quarterly*, 1968, 4, 96–119.

Wickens, D. D. Characteristics of word encoding. In A. W. Melton & E. Martin (Eds.), *Coding processes in human memory.* New York: Wiley, 1972.

Winograd, T. *Understanding natural language.* Edinburgh: University Press, 1972.

Winston, P. H. *The psychology of computer vision.* New York: McGraw-Hill, 1975.

25

Access to the Internal Lexicon

Max Coltheart

Department of Psychology
Birkbeck College
London, England

Eileen Davelaar
Jon Torfi Jonasson
Derek Besner

Department of Psychology
University of Reading
Reading, England

ABSTRACT

In order to understand how a word is read for meaning, we need to know how a reader proceeds from the printed representation of a word to the word's entry in the reader's internal lexicon, where the word's meaning is stored. This raises two principal questions: what is the *code* in which the word is represented when this process, lexical access, is being carried out, and what is the *procedure* by which this representation is used to find the word's entry in the lexicon. The lexical-decision task is a suitable one for the investigation of these questions. Two experiments using this task are reported. In one, it was found that a letter string's similarity to English words influenced the "no" response latency, but not the "yes" response latency, and it is argued that this result favors the view that lexical access is "direct," rather than requiring search. The other experiment showed that a nonword's phonological properties influenced the time taken to say "no" to it. Thus phonological encoding is occurring in these experiments. It remains to be shown, however, that this is any more than an epiphenomenon; neither these findings, nor those of previous investigators, compel us to abandon the view that skilled reading of single words proceeds solely by making use of visual representations of printed words.

I. INTRODUCTION

Treisman (1960, 1961) was the first to propose a theoretical framework for reading and speech perception based upon the concept of an internal lexicon (or "dictionary store," as she termed it). This lexicon consists of all the information a reader or listener has acquired about the words of his language – in particular, information about the meanings, the pronunciations, and the spellings of the words he knows.

The lexicon is made up of subsystems of information, each subsystem characterizing a particular word. These subsystems are lexical entries ("dictionary units," in Treisman's terminology). The lexical entry for any word includes specifications of the meaning of the word, of its pronunciation, and of its spelling.

Within this framework, reading a word for meaning consists of extracting some form of information from a set of ink marks and using this information to reach the word's lexical entry. The successful execution of this process ("lexical access") furnishes the reader with the meaning of the word, since such semantic information is stored as part of the word's lexical entry. Understanding a spoken word is achieved in the same way, except that the information used for lexical access is extracted from an acoustic input.

Speaking and writing can also be interpreted within this framework, though they are more mysterious than understanding speech or reading. During speech, we have in mind meanings which we wish to express by speech; we use *semantic* information to locate the lexical entry for the word we wish to say, and there we find the word's articulatory specifications, allowing us to articulate it (and we also find its spelling there, enabling us to write down what we mean). Thus lexical access can proceed in either direction: the lexicon can be used to tell us the meaning of a word we are looking at or hearing, and also to tell us how to write ‘or utter a word which expresses the meaning we have in mind at that moment.

Treisman also proposed that lexical entries are not isolated and independent – that, instead, the lexicon is an associative network, with facilitatory connections between the lexical entries of semantically related words; this was the way in which she conceptualized context effects. She proposed that, once the lexical entry for a particular word is reached, the associative links between the entry for this word and the entries for semantically related words produce temporary increases in the accessibility of these entries, thereby accelerating the subsequent perception of any of these words. Over a short time course this temporarily increased accessibility declines back to its normal resting level. This idea has been enthusiastically used in recent years – for example, to explain extensions of the Stroop effect (Warren, 1972) or contextual facilitation of lexical decisions (Schvaneveldt & Meyer, 1973).

This is the skeleton of a potential theory of reading and speech perception. The next step is, clearly, to try to put flesh on its bones. (From here on, we will be considering visual word recognition only, though many of the considerations below can be applied to speech perception also.) In particular, what we need is more specific ideas about just how a reader proceeds from the information he extracts from a word stimulus to the corresponding lexical entry. This requires that two questions be answered:

1. What is the access *code*? That is, what is the nature of the information extracted from a printed word for use of lexical access?
2. What is the access *procedure*? That is, how is this stimulus information made use of in order to gain access to the desired lexical entry?

In subsequent pages these will frequently be referred to as Questions 1 and 2.

II. THE ACCESS CODE

This has been a frequently discussed topic amongst students of reading. These discussions have usually taken the form of an advocacy of one or other of two opposing viewpoints: according to one, the access code during reading is phonological; according to the other it is visual.

Proponents of the first viewpoint assert that a printed word is first converted into a corresponding phonological representation (using a system of grapheme–phoneme correspondence rules), and that it is this phonological information which is subsequently used to represent the printed word during the process of lexical access. For example:

In order to read alphabetic writing one must have an ingrained habit of producing the sounds of one's language when one sees the written marks which conventionally represent the phonemes. (Bloomfield, 1942, p. 128)

The printed word is mapped onto a phonemic representation by the reader. (Gough, 1972, p. 337)

The heart of /reading skill/ is surely the process of decoding the written symbols to speech. (Gibson, 1970, p. 139)

Proponents of the second viewpoint assert, on the contrary, that it is purely visual information from the printed word that is used during lexical access: for example, individual letter shapes, multiletter visual features such as the curve repetitions in COOP or the angularity of FEET, overall word shape (especially with lower-case words) or even the Fourier spectrum of the word (see Broadbent, this volume). Some expressions of this viewpoint are:

Reading can be, and for skilled readers often is, a visual process. (Bower, 1970, p. 145)

Reading does not need to proceed by the reader's forming auditory representations of printed words. (Kolers, 1970, p. 115)

> Readers are . . . regarded as "predicting" their way through a passage of text, elimi-
> nating some alternatives in advance on the basis of their knowledge of the redundancy
> of language, and acquiring just enough visual information to eliminate the alternatives
> remaining. (Smith, 1971, p. 230)

This dispute has been experimental as well as theoretical. Various kinds of experimental findings have been offered in support of one or other viewpoint. We would wish to claim that, with perhaps only one exception, these findings are not really relevant to the question of the nature of the lexical access code, and we illustrate this claim with some examples.

A finding commonly cited as evidence for the view that printed words go through an obligatory phonological recoding prior to lexical access is that of Corcoran (1966), who showed that subjects searching through a passage of prose for instances of the letter "e" were more likely to miss the target letter in words where it was not pronounced (such as "mate" or "queue") than in words where it was pronounced ("met" or "queen"). Clearly subjects are at least operating some of the time with a phonological representation of the stimulus in this "visual" search task. However, there is no evidence that lexical access is used in carrying out this task, and so the effect is not necessarily evidence that phonological encoding occurs as a necessary preliminary to lexical access. Even if lexical access *were* occurring, the phonological code being used by the subjects might be generated from the lexical entry, rather than the other way around.

Bower (1970) found that reading aloud was considerably disrupted if the spelling of a prose passage was altered without altering its sound (his material was Greek prose; an English equivalent would be TWO BEE OAR KNOT TOO BEE). He argued that this manipulation should have no effect if the first stage in reading were an obligatory translation into a phonological code. As is subsequently demonstrated, the theory of lexical access suggested by Rubenstein, Lewis, and Rubenstein (1971) would predict Bower's effect, and yet this theory assumes that the first stage in reading *is* an obligatory phonological recording. Therefore Bower's finding is not sufficient to refute such an assumption.

Gough (1972) objected to the view that lexical access during reading proceeds via a phonological recoding, on the ground that this would be too slow, since "M. Stewart, C. T. James and I found that production latency for a three-letter word is in excess of 600 msec" (p. 334). This objection is an irrelevant one, since inertia in peripheral parts of the articulatory apparatus could well introduce very large delays between the time when a phonological code becomes available and the time when it actually begins to be executed. Generation of a phonological code for a printed symbol might be a very fast process.

There is a less obvious but more important reason for discounting Gough's objection; namely, that:

> . . . it is not necessary to equate the output of phonemic recoding with the information
> necessary for pronounciation. That is, phonemic recoding may still be necessary for

lexical search, but may be insufficient for rapid naming. One possibility is that the lexical entry contains stored motor commands, which permit much faster naming than a conversion from phonemes to motor commands. (Forster & Chambers, 1973, p. 633)

We would want to elaborate this point by claiming that, even if lexical access were *always* preceded by an obligatory phonological recoding:

1. There is no reason for assuming that the phonological stimulus representation so produced is in a form immediately executable by articulators.
2. There is no reason to assume that this phonological stimulus representation is accessible to introspection, and
3. There is no reason to assume that this phonological stimulus representation is usable for other cognitive tasks, such as same—different matching or letter search.

Thus a failure to find effects of phonological similarity or syllabic length on same—different matching of words would not count as evidence against a phonological theory of lexical access. Nor would we accept the argument that, if a phonological code is constructed prior to lexical access, subjects should be faster at judging that two words are homophones than judging that they are synonyms.

Tasks involving visual search, naming latency, same—different matching, and so on are therefore open to the objection that they are not necessarily relevant to the question of lexical access; any effects observed in such tasks may be nonlexical (it is possible to pronounce nonwords; therefore it is possible to pronounce words without necessarily using the lexicon) or postlexical (phonological codes can be generated as a consequence of locating a lexical entry), instead of lexical.

One task to which these objections do not apply is word/nonword discrimination or *lexical decision*. One can of course judge that SKRPJK is not an English word without needing to consult one's internal lexicon, and it would be easy to supply a computer with a small set of rules that would enable it to judge that letter strings of this kind are nonwords. However, nonwords like SLINT, PRONK, and MANTINESS are a different matter. There are no rules which could be used to judge that these strings are nonwords. They *could* be English words; they simply happen not to be.

The only way to discover that SLINT is not a word is to establish that it is absent from the internal lexicon. So, if nonwords of this sort (*legal nonwords*) are used, the lexical decision task necessarily requires lexical access, and consequently avoids the objection that subjects might be performing the task nonlexically. We may therefore try to find out whether a visually presented letter string is or is not converted to a phonological representation during the lexical decision task, as a means of investigating the nature of the access code; and this is what Rubenstein *et al.* (1971) did.

Before discussing their work, one objection to the use of the lexical-decision task as a means of studying lexical access will be raised (and not rebutted). Essentially, this objection is that although lexical decisions *are* made via lexical access, the manner in which this access is achieved differs from the way in which it is achieved during reading, and that therefore we cannot learn about how people read by studying how they make lexical decisions. Suppose, for example, a person is reading, and during the analysis of a particular word has established that it has five letters, that it begins with BR-, and that it ends with -BE. This information is sufficient to establish that the word is BRIBE, since no other English word meets these three conditions. So access to the correct lexical entry can be accomplished with only partial analysis of the stimulus – when we are reading. Not, however, when we are making lexical decision; BR-BE could be BREBE, BRABE, BROBE, or BRUBE in a lexical decision experiment. In this experimental situation, then, full analysis of the stimulus is necessary if its lexical entry is to be reached with certainty, whereas partial analysis will often suffice in reading (since the reader is armed with the knowledge that, whatever the word is that he is inspecting, at least it is a word). This argument implies that the time taken to achieve lexical access for a particular word will be less when nonwords cannot occur than when they can, and may be the explanation of an effect observed by Frederiksen and Kroll (1974). They measured naming latencies for visually presented words and legal nonwords, under two conditions: blocked (all items, for one group, were words; for another group, all were nonwords) and randomized (these subjects saw a random sequence of words and nonwords). The same words were used in the two conditions. Naming latencies for words were much lower in the blocked condition (in which the subject could be sure that the letter string was a word before it even appeared, as in reading) than in the randomized condition (where it might be a nonword, as in lexical decesion tasks). Clearly, then, foreknowledge that a letter string is a word can be used to facilitate processing of that string (which in turn implies that at least on some occasions, though not necessarily all, subjects make use of the lexicon in a naming-latency situation).

Although this point ought to be kept in mind when evaluating the theoretical significance of the results of lexical-decision experiments, we do not regard it as necessarily invalidating the lexical-decision task as a source of information concerning lexical access during normal reading, since the difference between the two tasks, according to this argument, is a quantitative one; there is no suggestion that qualitatively different forms of access code, or qualitatively different access procedures, are used in the two tasks.

We have argued, then, that of the tasks which have been used to study the access code during reading, only the lexical decision task is a really suitable one; and so we wish now to consider the first application of this task to the study of the access code, namely, the work of Rubenstein *et al.* (1971).

III. RUBENSTEIN *ET AL.* (1971)

In this experiment two types of words (homophones such as SALE or WEAK, and nonhomophones such as BATH or PINK) and two types of legal nonwords (pseudohomophones such as BURD and GROE, and nonpseudohomophones such as ROLT and SAFT) were used. By pseudohomophone we mean a letter string which is not a word, but which is pronounced exactly the same way as some English word. A random sequence of the four kinds of stimuli was presented, and subjects made a lexical decision about each stimulus. Rubenstein and co-workers found that the "yes" response was slower to homophonic words than to nonhomophonic words, and that the "no" response to pseudohomophones was slower than the "no" response to nonpseudohomophones. To account for their results they developed a detailed model of lexical access.

The theory specifically answers both Questions 1 and 2. It states that the access code is solely phonological, and it states that the access procedure is one of serial search.

According to this model, lexical access is carried out in the following way. A letter string is first converted to its phonological representation. A search for a matching phonological representation then begins through the lexical entries, in order of word frequency, common words first (hence the inverse relationship between word frequency and "yes" latency). When, during this search, a match is detected between the phonological stimulus representation and a phonological lexical entry code, the search stops. The response "yes" cannot yet be made, because the letter string might just *sound* like a word (e.g., BURD), or it might be a homophonic word (it might be WEAK, and the first lexical match might be with the lexical entry for WEEK). So a spelling check is carried out – the correct spelling of the lexical entry is matched against the letter string's actual spelling. If this spelling check succeeds, the correct lexical entry has been found, and the response "yes" can be made. If the spelling check fails, the search must restart, at the point where it stopped. If the letter string is a nonword, there will be an exhaustive search through the lexicon, at the completion of which the response "no" can be made.

This theory predicts the following:

1. It will take longer to say "no" to BURD than to BARP; in both cases, an exhaustive lexical search will be carried out; in addition, for BURD and other such pseudohomophones, there will be the extra time consumed by stopping the search, carrying out the (unsuccessful) spelling check, and restarting the search. This will produce longer "no" latencies for pseudohomophonic nonwords.

2. In the case of *words,* a string will only suffer through being a homophone when it is the *less common* member of a homophone pair. Consider the words WEEK (frequency 1278) and WEAK (frequency 243). Whichever of these two is

actually presented, the lexical search will first stop at WEEK, the more frequent word. If indeed WEEK was presented, the spelling check will succeed and the response "yes" will be made; the existence of another lexical entry with the same phonological code, further down in the lexicon, will have no effect, But if WEAK is presented, there will have been a time-consuming stop, spelling check and restart during the search down to the entry WEAK. So WEAK will suffer by being a homophone, while WEEK will not.

Consequently, Rubenstein and co-workers reanalyzed their "yes" data, and concluded that the homophone effect they had found with words was confined only to those homophones that were the less frequent members of homophone pairs, which is what their theory required.

There are, however, three rather serious problems with the Rubenstein *et al.* (1971) work:

1. Their "yes" effect is not significant using statistical analyses which treat both subjects and words as random effects (Clark, 1973). This means that their conclusion that less frequent homophones have long "yes" times may not be generally true for all subjects and all homophones, it may just be a consequence of one or two aberrant words in the set of homophones they used.

2. Of the 12 homophones they used, 8 were less frequent ones. The non-homophonic control words with which these 8 were compared were not matched with the homophones on word frequency, part of speech or number of letters. All three of these variables affect lexical decision time (see, e.g., Fredriksen & Kroll, 1974; Scarborough & Springer, 1973), and so this confounding is a serious one.

3. Although their "no" effect remains significant when reanalyzed using the methods suggested by Clark (1973), it is not clear that the effect is a phonological one, since no attempt was made to control for the extent to which nonwords were visually similar to words. The nonwords which sounded like English words might also have looked more like English words. Our second experiment suggests that this would slow the "no" response. Thus the interpretation of their "no" effect is unclear.

In view of the theoretical importance of their experiment, then, we decided to carry out an improved version of it, designed to avoid these three problems.

IV. EXPERIMENT I

Twenty students, undergraduage and graduate, 10 of each sex, served as subjects. Letter strings were plotted on a remote oscilloscope under the control of a PDP-12 computer, that also recorded responses, measured RT, and tabulated and analyzed data. A string remained visible until a response was made; there was then an interval of about 2 sec before the next string appeared.

After some practice trials, each subject saw 156 letter strings in a randomized sequence. Of these, 78 were words and 78 were legal nonwords. The subjects were told that 50% of the stimuli would be words and 50% nonwords, and were asked to press the button under their right forefinger if the string was a word, and the button under their left forefinger if it was not. They were asked to make the response as quickly as possible without making more than a few errors.

Of the 78 words, 39 were homophones; each was the less common member of a homophone pair, by a considerable amount (homophone pairs with fairly similar frequencies were avoided). For each of these homophones, a control word was selected, matched with the homophone on Kuceras–Francis frequency, number of letters, number of syllables, and part of speech (including inflections). Thus 39 control words were used.

Of the 78 nonwords, 39 were double pseudohomophones. That is, each sounded exactly like some English homophone (not just some English word). Examples are GRONE or PORZE. The point of this was to magnify the "no" effect, since according to the Rubenstein *et al.* (1971) theory the "no" response will be lengthened still more by two unsuccessful stops and spelling checks than by one. From each of these nonwords, a control nonhomophonic nonword was generated by changing a single letter, for example, BRONE from GRONE, PORCE from PORZE. This was done without altering the pronounceability or syllabic length of the string. We considered that this procedure made it extremely unlikely that there was any difference between the two sets of nonwords in their similarity to English words.

The 156 letter strings, together with the mean RTs of all correct responses to each string, are given in the Appendix. The mean correct RTs and error rates are shown in Table 1.

Consider first the "no" data. All 20 subjects were slower with the pseudohomophones than with the nonpseudohomophones. The size of this effect was significantly greater for the female subjects ($U = 23, p < .05$). Thus it does seem to be the case that a nonword which is pronounced exactly like some English word produces a slower "no" response, and, if our control for visual similarity is adequate, there is therefore evidence that phonological recoding is playing *some* part in the lexical decision task. The possible implications of this result are discussed below.

On the other hand, there is no trace of an effect of homophony on the "yes" response, even though we used 39 less frequent homophones, compared with the 8 used by Rubenstein *et al.* (1971). Since their theory demands that there will be such an effect, it would seem that their theory is wrong.

The theory offers answers to both Questions 1 and 2; if it is wrong, which of these answers is wrong? Is lexical access *not* phonological? This seems unlikely,

TABLE 1
Mean Correct RTs and Percentage Error Rates for Experiment I

Word data	Homophones	Controls	Difference	t	df	p
Subjects	578	573	+5	.63	19	> .50
Stimuli	558	575	−17	1.52	39	> .10
Errors (%)	7.2	4.6				
Nonword data	Pseudohomophones	Controls	Difference	t	df	p
Subjects	658	596	+62	4.76	19	< .001
Stimuli	623	588	+35	2.90	38	< .01
Errors (%)	6.8	3.6				

Min $F' = 4.83$, $df = 1, 55$, $p < .05$.

in view of the nonword effect we obtained. Consequently, we turned our attention to the theory's answer to Question 2. Perhaps lexical access is not a search process (if it were, of course, it would have to be a stupendously fast search). This is the subject of our second experiment.

V. EXPERIMENT II[1]

The subjects were 18 undergraduates at the University of Reading. The apparatus was the same as in Experiment I, as were the instructions and the subject's task (lexical decision).

Define the N of a letter string as the number of different English words that can be produced by changing just one of the letters in the string to another letter, preserving letter positions. In this experiment 39 high-N words and 39 low-N words were used (these words, their N values, and their RTs are listed in the Appendix). These were matched pairwise for Kucera—Francis frequency and number of letters, that is, for any high-N word there was a corresponding low-N word with the same frequency and same number of letters. There were also 40 high-N nonwords and 40 low-N nonwords (also listed in the Appendix), with pairwise matching for number of letters. All nonwords were easily pronounceable. After some practice trials, these 158 letter strings were presented in a random sequence, and the subject made a lexical decision about each one.

What should be the effect of N on RT if lexical access involves the kind of search process proposed by Rubenstein et al. (1971)? There should be no effect, because none of the nonwords look or sound identical to a lexical entry, so all should be dealt with by an uninterrupted exhaustive serial search, whether they

[1] This experiment was suggested by Alan Allport and run as an undergraduate project by Nick Davison.

are high-N or low-N nonwords. None of the words were homophones, so each has a single lexical entry only; whether a word is high N or low N cannot influence the time it takes for the search to reach that word's entry.

The results of this experiment are shown in Table 2. Consider first the "no" data. High-N nonwords yielded significantly slower "no" responses than low-N nonwords. This is inconsistent with the Rubenstein *et al.* (1971) version of a search model. However, with a minor and plausible modification, the search model can be made compatible with the result. We need merely suppose that the time taken to compare an encoded word with a lexical entry depends upon the similarity of the word to the entry — dissimilarity permits a quick rejection, similarity produces a slow one. So the exhaustive search through the lexicon will be slower for high-N nonwords (which are similar to many lexical entries) than for low-N nonwords (which are similar to few); and this is what we found.

This modified search model predicts that there will also be an effect of N on the "yes" response. As the search proceeds down to the desired lexical entry, it will proceed more slowly for high-N words than for low-N words, because more entries will be encountered that are similar to the encoded word when it is a high-N word. So "yes" should be slower for high-N words than for low-N words. This was not so; it is evident from Table 2 that N has no effect whatsoever on the latency of the "yes" response.

We do not see how any model that views lexical access as a serial search procedure can cope with this set of results, and so we will consider an alternative class of models below, namely, those which propose that there is "direct access" or "parallel access" to lexical entries. (It should also be noted that, if lexical access does not involve serial search, then the failure to find an effect of homophony on the "yes" response in Experiment I is not evidence against the view that the access code for the lexicon is phonological; it is only evidence against the joint assertion that the code is phonological and that the procedure is serial search, that is, against the Rubenstein *et al.* (1971) model.)

TABLE 2
Mean Correct RTs and Percentage Error Rates for Experiment II

Word data	High N	Low N	Difference	t	df	p
Subjects	560	563	−3	.32	17	> .50
Stimuli	571	575	−4	.25	38	> .50
Errors (%)	4.1	3.7				
Nonword data	High N	Low N	Difference	t	df	p
Subjects	654	617	+37	3.99	17	< .001
Stimuli	660	619	+41	2.42	78	< .02
Errors (%)	4.8	2.6				

Min $F' = 4.28$, $df = 1, 90$, $p < .05$.

VI. PARALLEL ACCESS TO THE LEXICON

The only detailed realization of this kind of model of lexical access is the logogen model developed by Morton (1968, 1969, 1970). According to this model, each word in the internal lexicon has its own logogen. A logogen is an evidence-collecting device, that is excited by a letter string to varying degrees, depending upon how similar this string is to the word belonging to the logogen. The logogen for TREE collects little evidence from BLED, a lot from FREE, and a maximal amount from TREE. Therefore this logogen is scarcely excited by BLED, considerably excited by FREE, and maximally excited by TREE. Logogens have thresholds: if excitation of a logogen reaches threshold, lexical access has occurred, and the semantic features of the word corresponding to this logogen are made available. Word-frequency effects are explained by postulating that logogen threshold is inversely related to word frequency: so common words do not require much evidence and rare words do. Priming effects are explained by temporary decreases in threshold, which produce temporary increases in accessibility (see Warren, 1972).

If one tries to apply this model to the results of Experiments I and II, there is an immediate major problem: the logogen system cannot say "no." Nonwords do not have logogens. If a nonword is presented, it will excite various logogens to various degress, but none to threshold; so there will be no output from the logogen system. There is no event corresponding to the decision that the string is not a word, and so no event which could be used to trigger the decision "no" in a lexical-decision experiment. The fact that, x msec after stimulus onset, no logogen has yet reached threshold, does not justify a "no" response; maybe a logogen will reach threshold in the next millisecond.

People *can* judge that PRONK is not a word. Can we modify the logogen model in some way that is satisfactory and that explains this ability? One possibility is to use a deadline: a rule may be applied to the logogen system saying "If no logogen has reached threshold by t msec after stimulus onset, decide that none is going to, and respond "no." " If t is greater than the threshold time of the slowest logogen, this rule will produce error-free "no" responding.

This proposal, however, can be promptly refuted, since it cannot explain why the "no" response to CRVSS is much faster than the "no" response to CRUSS (Stanners & Forbach, 1973), that is, why illegal nonwords are rejected faster than legal nonwords. Nor can it explain why, if only legal nonwords are used, low-N nonwords are rejected faster than high-N nonwords (our Experiment II). If all nonwords are rejected because a fixed deadline time has elapsed, there is no way in which the "no" latency can vary with the word likeness of a nonword, as it clearly does.

To cope with this, we need to make the deadline more flexible. Ollman (this volume) has discussed the concept of a variable deadline: in a situation where discriminations are easy, the deadline can be lowered, whereas it is increased in a situation where discriminations are hard. This will not serve our purpose, however, because it only works when the subject knows the difficulty of the discrimination beforehand and so can preset the deadline value. In our Experiment II, high-N and low-N nonwords occurred in a random sequence, so a presetting contingent on N was impossible. We propose instead that the deadline value can be adjusted up or down *during processing.*

This could be accomplished if there were a mechanism which was capable of monitoring the overall level of excitation in the logogens during the period between stimulus onset and the point at which some threshold was reached or the deadline time expired. In this case, matters could be arranged so that the deadline begins at some low value, preset before stimulus onset. At stimulus onset, information begins to flow into the logogen system. Excitation rises at various rates in various logogens. If the overall amount of excitation is rising rather rapidly, the value of the deadline is increased considerably, since in these circumstances, the letter string is probably a word, so "no" is probably the wrong response; if the logogen system is fairly quiescent, the deadline value is not increased, since "no" is likely to be the correct response.[2]

If such adjustments are constantly being made as information from the letter string is flowing into the logogen system, illegal nonwords, which are very unlike words and so do not excite any logogens much, will have a short deadline and so a fast "no," compared to legal nonwords, which are more wordlike and so excite logogens to a greater degree. Furthermore, among legal nonwords, those which are like many words will excite many logogens, while those which are like few words will excite few. Therefore, the deadline time, and hence the "no" latency, will be longer for high-N nonwords than for low-N nonwords, as was found in Experiment II.

What about the effect of N on "yes" latency? The "yes" response is triggered when some logogen has actually reached threshold. A principal determinant of the time which elapses between stimulus onset and the reaching of a threshold is word frequency, since the amount of excitation required for the threshold to be attained is inversely related to word frequency. This time, however, will not be influenced by whether many other logogens are partially excited (as is the case for a high-N word). Therefore the time required to respond "yes" to a word will be strongly affected by the word's frequency, but not affected at all by whether it is a high-N or a low-N word.

This model, then, correctly predicts the pattern of results obtained in Experiment II, namely, that high-N nonwords produce slower "no" responses than low-N nonwords, whereas N has no effect on the latencies of "yes" responses.

It is normally a property of deadline models of this clock-counter variety (Nickerson, 1969, 1971) that "no" latency has to be greater than the slowest

---

[2] This may seem a rather artificial adjunct to the logogen system; but then making lexical decisions is a rather artificial task.

kind of "yes" latency, but this property no longer holds with the variable deadline procedure we are suggesting. The "no" response to illegal nonwords is much faster than the "yes" response to words (e.g., Stanners & Forbach, 1973), but this is quite compatible with the procedure we are proposing; a word is very wordlike, so the deadline is greatly extended compared to what happens when an illegal nonword is being processed.

Some data reported by Frederiksen and Kroll (1974) are of interest here. Theirs was a lexical decision experiment; each nonword was derived by changing one letter in one of the words, which is why a "frequency" can be assigned even to nonwords.

For low-frequency words, "yes" and "no" times are about equal. This must mean that the deadline used to make the "no" response is sometimes exceeded even when the stimulus is a word; so the subject will make an appreciable number of errors with infrequent words, responding "no" and then finding, too late, that a logogen threshold *was* reached eventually. In other words, a riskily low deadline was being used. Such error effects did occur: The percentage of correct "yes" responses is about 75% for Frequency Class 3 and is close to chance (about 57%) for Frequency Class 4, whereas performance is quite good (around 90%) with high-frequency words.

The general answer we wish to give, then, to Question 2 is that access to the lexicon is a parallel procedure. Associated within any lexical entry is an evidence-collecting device that is variably excitable and that has a threshold; the degree to which a letter string excites a lexical entry is proportional to the similarity between the string and the word represented by an entry. The inverse relationship between word frequency and "yes" latency occurs because common words have low thresholds and rare words have high thresholds. The "no" response is made by means of a deadline whose value is adjustable during processing: if the evidence collectors are considerably excited, the deadline value is high, and if they are not it is low.

This logogen-like model, however, does not specify an answer to Question 1, that is, it does not state what is the *nature* of the evidence collected during reading. This might be purely visual evidence. However, if our control for visual similarity in Experiment I was adequate, the results of this experiment indicate: (1) that a word like GRONE produces more overall excitation in the lexicon than a word like BRONE; and (2) that this is not because GRONE is more visually similar to some English words than is BRONE.

In other words, the key factor here is that GRONE has the same pronunciation as an English word; that is why it excites the lexicon more than BRONE; and this implies that at least part of the input to the lexicon is phonological, even when presentation is visual.

If the lexicon dealt *only* with phonological input, GRONE and GROAN could not be discriminated, and a lexical decision would not be possible. Therefore *some* use must be made of visual information; so the answer to Question 1 will consist of a statement defining the precise nature of the interplay between phonological and visual information in the lexicon during reading.

VII. GENERAL DISCUSSION AND CONCLUSION

A rather neglected aspect of the Stroop effect is of considerable relevance to our findings, namely, the use of the Stroop technique to demonstrate phonological encoding. If a subject is asked to name the color in which a word is printed, his naming latency is considerably slowed if the word is a color name different from its ink color (Stroop, 1935). Furthermore, this color-naming latency is increased if the base word, though not a color word, has temporarily been made more accessible — for example, it is harder to name the color of the word AUNT if the word UNCLE has been presented shortly before (Warren, 1972). This Stroop effect is often interpreted in terms of the automaticity of lexical access: a reader cannot prevent a printed word from exciting its lexical entry, so when RED is presented in blue ink, the lexical entry for RED is excited, and then in some way which has never been specified the word "red" interferes with the word "blue" (the correct response). Warren's result shows that the extent of this interference can be manipulated by varying the accessibility of the lexical entry of the base word.

This cannot be the whole story, however, Bakan and Alperson (1967) showed that legal nonwords (DAP, ISH, LAR, FON) produce a larger Stroop effect than illegal nonwords (FJQ, RZQ, VGJ, XFH). None of these stimuli have lexical entries, since none of them are words. We suggest this result should be interpreted in terms of the automaticity of phonological encoding, and of the generation of an articulatory code from the phonological code. When the phonological encoder is operating automatically on an "unpronounceable" sequence such as FJQ, the time required to produce a code is much longer than when it is operating on a pronounceable sequence like FON; so the code is available earlier for pronounceable sequences, and hence will interfere more severely with the phonological code of the color name, intended for generating an articulatory code.

The Stroop effect is not entirely a phonological one; there is also lexical conflict, indicated by Warren's findings, and also by the finding of Bakan and Alperson (1967) that, with pronounceability equated, words generate more Stroop interference than nonwords do. However, our point is that the existence of a phonological Stroop effect suggests strongly that phonological encoding of legal nonwords, and hence of words too, is an automatic and very rapid process. This is evident from the results of Experiment I, since the phonological encoding there was rapid enough to interfere with lexical decisions.[3]

---

[3]See also the finding of Dalrymple-Alford (1972) that color naming is slower if the base word shares phonemes with an incongruent color name (bed, true) than if it does not.

However, what we want to find out is something more ambitious than this: we want to know whether this automatic rapid phonological encoding actually plays a part in reading isolated words for meaning, and this we do not yet know. There are several alternative explanations for our results; some view phonological encoding as essential for lexical access during normal reading, some view it as an optional access method, and some view it as an epiphenomenon which plays no part in normal reading. We hope eventually to be able to adjudicate between these alternatives by means of experiments currently in progress. For the time being, however, we will conclude this chapter by outlining possible interpretations of our results.

The interplay between visual and phonological access routes to the lexicon has been characterized as a race by Meyer and Ruddy (1973). Lexical access on this view is a discrete event like a runner breaking the tape, rather than a continuous incremental process such as increasing logogen excitation. Sometimes the visual route wins the race to the lexical entry; sometimes the phonological route does, in which case a spelling check is carried out and access is confirmed only if this check succeeds (this must be postulated otherwise, on those occasions when the phonological route wins the race, homophones could not be distinguished, and pseudohomophonic nonwords would be judged to be words). Their model, however, is a search model; the "no" response is produced by an exhaustive search, sometimes lengthened by an unsuccessful spelling check with pseudohomophonic nonwords. We have earlier given reasons for rejecting the view that the lexical access procedure is serial search.

Our inclination is to think of the relationship between phonological and visual inputs to the lexicon as one of cooperation, rather than competition. We suppose that the level of excitation of a lexical entry can be raised by appropriate visual input and also by appropriate phonological input, and as this level rises during the process of reading a word, the lexical entry is *summing* phonological and visual evidence. In order to prevent the lexical entry for BIRD from reaching threshold when BURD is presented, it would be necessary to set thresholds when reading high enough that they cannot be reached if the only strong evidence collected is phonological. Alternatively, a spelling check procedure might be used. This theory is compatible with the results of our experiments, but we do not wish to pursue this point here, because we do not consider it a worthwhile procedure to advocate one theory when other, quite different, theories are still viable, and this is the case at present. Our view that lexical access involves the summation of visual and phonological evidence is consistent with our data, makes sense, and might be true; but the data are also compatible with the view that, although visual and phonological access routes to the lexicon do exist, phonological access is so slow that, when a word is presented, its lexical entry is reached and its meaning obtained solely by using visual evidence. Lagging behind is the phonological-input system, which will eventually reach the correct entry; this will be irrelevant for practical purposes because the entry has been reached already. In this case, phonological recoding plays no part in getting from a word to its lexical entry, except for words the reader has heard before but never seen. Nevertheless, the phonological effects evident in Experiment I are predicted by this theory. When a letter string is not a word, if the "no" decision is made by a deadline, the deadline time may be long enough so that phonological input has time to reach the lexicon before the deadline has elapsed; in this case, if the phonological input is that of a word (i.e., if the string is a pseudohomophone), it will be possible for this to delay the "no" response by extending the deadline. Here, phonological effects can only occur with nonwords.

This objection can be raised against various experiments claimed to demonstrate that lexical access is even *sometimes* phonological. For example, Meyer and Ruddy (1973) found that the "no" response to the question "Is this word the name of a fruit?" is slower when the test word is phonologically identical to a fruit name (PAIR) than when it is not (TAIL). We have confirmed this. It does not necessarily mean, however, that phonological input is ever used for lexical access when reading for meaning; if the "no" response in their categorization task is made by means of a deadline applied, not to the whole lexicon, but to the region of fruits in the lexicon, lexical access used for the "yes" response when the item *is* a fruit might be purely visual; the lagging phonological input can only influence behavior when the item is *not* a fruit. On the other hand, if the categorization task is performed by accessing the entry for the target word and inspecting the semantic features therein to determine if the word is the name of a fruit, their result *would* constitute a demonstration that phonological input is sometimes fast enough to contribute to lexical access. We do not know how the categorization task is carried out, though the existence of category-size effects on the "no" response (even when the nonmember is a nonword; see Landauer & Meyer, 1972; Meyer & Ellis, 1970) seems to imply that categorization is achieved by monitoring a category rather than by accessing the lexical entry of the test word. Thus the interpretation of the Meyer and Ruddy (1973) results rests in turn on how we think subjects carry out the categorization task, and we do not know how they do it.

Consequently, we think it is premature to claim that there is any evidence at all which demands acceptance of the view that proceeding from a printed word to the lexical entry for that word ever uses a phonological conversion of the printed characters, even though such conversions are performed by our subjects, quite rapidly, and are transmitted to the lexicon at least eventually. Unequivocal evidence for this view would be obtained by demonstrating that the phonological code for a word is sometimes used in making the "yes" response to that word in a lexical decision or categorization task; such a demonstration remains to be achieved.

VIII. APPENDIX

A. Mean Correct RT (in msec) for Each Letter String in Experiment I

Rarer homophones		Matched control words		Pseudohomophones		Matched control nonwords	
ALOUD	573	ERECT	541	ILE	500	IFE	547
ALTAR	560	ASSET	627	BLOO	553	PLOO	538
BEECH	574	BRUTE	570	BOALED	578	NOALED	599
BOARDER	608	BOOSTER	693	BRUDE	746	TRUDE	691
SELLER	585	HELPER	515	BROOZE	774	DROOZE	611
KERNEL	454	KENNEL	601	BILD	749	RILD	616
URN	626	OWL	545	CHUZE	587	THUZE	555
FLOUR	508	FRAUD	596	KORD	535	KORP	566
GUESSED	566	DRAGGED	572	FRAZE	523	FRUZE	547
HARE	572	HARP	568	GRONE	772	BRONE	660
HAUL	503	CHAT	621	HORL	609	DORL	547
HEAR	534	MEET	517	HELE	572	HEFE	541
HERD	561	JOKE	536	HOAL	730	JOAL	683
HIRE	520	DRAG	607	LAKS	606	GAKS	565
HOUR	536	FOOD	526	LEKE	584	LEBE	517
HYMN	582	HINT	557	MONE	680	MOBE	648
LEASED	504	LAGGED	588	WUN	561	VUN	551
LONE	562	SANE	566	PORZE	599	PORCE	625
MAID	544	BEEF	517	PEESE	512	JEESE	572
MANOR	545	SATIN	566	RIE	624	KIE	566
PACT	610	PULP	646	TAKS	569	KAKS	527
PAWS	601	RATS	528	THROO	584	PHROO	555
SAIL	500	GAZE	578	THROAN	751	PHROAN	776
SCENE	510	PRICE	508	TODE	628	DODE	596
SEA	493	OIL	512	WAID	678	DAID	632
SEAM	572	CAVE	522	WATE	825	WUTE	576
SHORE	530	COAST	565	STAWK	529	STEEK	417
SIGHED	585	SUITED	611	WURLD	569	MURLD	552
SIGHS	581	SHUTS	681	WOAR	683	WOAL	626
STEAL	557	STING	526	FLORE	615	FLURE	583
SUITE	582	SHIRT	501	AHMS	659	AHNS	588
TAUT	559	SMUG	606	BORL	564	BARL	621
TIDE	542	TOMB	615	BAIR	622	JAIR	620
WAIST	555	SHAFT	572	BOR	574	BOL	518
WEAK	541	CURT	747	BRAIK	517	PRAIK	551
WHINE	744	WEAVE	621	GRAIT	722	BRAIT	662
WHOLLY	645	WILDLY	585	SOAL	576	SOAM	698
WITCH	527	TRUCE	607	CORT	645	DORT	565
WOOD	523	WOOP	488	FLOO	582	FROO	516

B. Mean Correct RT (in msec) for Each Letter String in
Experiment II

High-N words			Low-N words			High-N nonwords			Low-N nonwords		
Word	N	RT	Word	N	RT	Nonword	N	RT	Nonword	N	RT
SAME	17	509	KNOW	4	481	BAVE	15	742	BAFT	3	618
HAND	9	483	ONCE	0	579	BRAB	10	651	BLID	1	616
WORD	12	492	FREE	3	486	FAND	11	663	BUCH	4	591
FULL	14	570	ELSE	2	604	FILT	12	723	BUKE	4	630
BILL	18	622	CLUB	3	530	FLAD	11	679	CREM	2	650
SLOW	12	510	NECK	4	576	GARK	10	573	DIRN	3	647
MINE	22	512	JURY	2	557	HAGE	14	577	FRIP	4	565
SEAT	17	614	BUSY	3	536	MIDE	15	631	GRUN	2	602
RARE	18	626	POEM	1	575	MOOK	13	600	JILD	4	585
BARN	13	567	POND	3	619	NUCK	11	682	PLUN	4	634
BOLD	12	545	UGLY	0	607	RAME	21	768	SALN	3	567
SUNG	9	790	DIET	4	571	SARE	27	686	SHUB	4	671
BOOT	13	489	GOWN	4	641	SOLT	15	707	SLET	2	609
CAVE	18	599	AXLE	1	636	TANE	20	588	SPOG	4	614
LASH	13	690	ITCH	2	709	TINK	11	603	SWOD	3	549
SUCK	15	623	AJAR	1	669	TORD	12	560	TRAS	4	556
HOOK	11	563	GULP	3	639	WACE	13	595	TRIN	2	557
CART	15	613	RASP	4	617	WULL	13	608	VOND	4	587
MOLE	17	546	GNAW	1	782	YOLE	13	607	WEGE	2	614
BRAG	9	649	SNOB	2	514	ZALE	12	654	WOLN	1	532
SOUND	7	508	MAJOR	1	507	BATER	10	719	ASPET	3	786
SPACE	6	524	BELOW	0	556	BLANE	8	637	BLICE	2	621
TRIED	6	566	MONTH	1	545	BRACK	8	787	CLUNE	3	588
LOWER	10	540	WRONG	3	554	CHACK	8	616	CRICH	1	651
EIGHT	10	553	PIECE	1	536	CHONE	7	608	DARCE	2	677
SHARE	12	534	SCENE	3	516	CRADE	9	716	FLORT	3	600
WATCH	7	513	COAST	3	633	CRUSS	6	706	GLIME	3	724
GROWN	7	598	MOTOR	1	484	FLACK	8	706	LEPEN	1	640
GRADE	7	581	CROSS	3	537	GIGHT	12	634	PRENT	2	617
SHEEP	6	520	SLEPT	2	565	GLAVE	7	672	RONCH	2	576
PITCH	8	565	STIFF	3	548	GRAFE	7	599	ROTAN	0	621
CLOCK	8	513	FLOOD	2	453	JATED	9	639	SHOLD	1	756
TRICK	7	557	WAIST	2	549	MOUGH	6	656	SKARN	0	632
SPINE	7	555	YACHT	0	603	PRAIN	6	706	SOTCH	2	746
BULLY	9	552	DWARF	0	616	RARED	16	889	STULT	2	511
GREED	7	517	FARCE	1	605	SHART	11	642	STURD	0	673
FATED	11	602	THORN	1	526	SLARE	14	668	THARN	1	620
STANK	9	789	CLOWN	3	609	STABE	6	646	TROCT	2	539
MINER	8	576	DAISY	2	540	STINE	8	653	WARAL	0	598
						STRAT	6	594	WROLK	0	602

ACKNOWLEDGMENTS

This work was supported by grants from the Science Research Council and the Social Science Research Council. We thank Ken Forster and Alan Allport for valuable discussions.

REFERENCES

Bakan, P., & Alperson, B. Pronounceability, attensity, and interference in the color–word test. *American Journal of Psychology*, 1967, **80** 416–420.

Bloomfield, L. Linguistics and reading. *Elementary English,* 1942, **19,** 125–130.

Bower, T. G. R. Reading by eye. In H. Levin & J. P. Williams (Eds.), *Basic studies on reading.* New York: Basic Books, 1970.

Clark, H. H. The language-as-fixed-effect fallacy: A critique of language statistics in psychological research. *Journal of Verbal Learning and Verbal Behavior,* 1973, **12,** 627–635.

Corcoran, D. W. J. An acoustic factor in letter cancellation. *Nature,* 1966, **210,** 658.

Dalrymple-Alford, E. C. Sound similarity and colour–word interference in the Stroop task. *Psychonomic Science,* 1972, **28,** 209–210.

Forster, K. I., & Chambers, S. M. Lexical access and naming time. *Journal of Verbal Learning and Verbal Behavior,* 1973, **12,** 627–635.

Frederiksen, J. R., & Kroll, J. F. Phonemic recoding and lexical search in the perception of letter arrays. Paper presented at meeting of Psychonomic Society, Boston, November 1974.

Gibson, E. W. The ontogeny of reading. *American Psychologist,* 1970, **25,** 136–143.

Gough, P. One second of reading. In J. P. Kavanagh & I. G. Mattingly (Eds.), *Language by eye and by ear.* Cambridge, Mass.: MIT Press, 1972.

Kolers, P. Three stages of reading. In H. Levin & J. P. Williams (Eds.), *Basic studies on reading,* New York: Basic Books, 1970.

Landauer, T. K., & Meyer, D. E. Category size and semantic-memory retrieval. *Journal of Verbal Learning and Verbal Behavior,* 1972, **11,** 539–549.

Meyer, D. E., & Ellis, G. B. Parallel processes in word recognition. Paper presented at meeting of Psychonomic Society, San Antonio, November, 1970.

Meyer, D. E., & Ruddy, M. Lexical memory retrieval based on graphemic and phonemic representations of printed words. Paper presented at meeting of Psychonomic Society, St. Louis, November 1973.

Morton, J. Considerations of grammar and computation in language behavior. In J. C. Catford (Ed.), *Studies in language and language behavior.* Ann Arbor: University of Michigan Press, 1968.

Morton, J. Interaction of information in word recognition. *Psychological Review,* 1969, **76,** 165–178.

Morton, J. A functional model for memory, In D. A. Norman (Ed.), *Models of human memory.* New York: Academic Press, 1970.

Nickerson, R. S. "Same"–"Different" response times: A model and a preliminary test. In W. G. Koster (Ed.), *Attention and performance II.* Amsterdam: North-Holland Publ., 1969.

Nickerson, R. S. "Same"–"Different" response times: A further test of a counter and clock model. *Acta Psychologica,* 1971, **35,** 112–127.

Rubenstein, H. R., Lewis, S. S., & Rubenstein, M. A. Evidence for phonemic recoding in visual word recognition. *Journal of Verbal Learning and Verbal Behavior,* 1971, **10,** 645–657.

Scarborough, D. L., & Springer, L. Noun—verb differences in word recognition. Paper presented at meeting of Psychonomics Society, St. Louis, November 1973.

Schvaneveldt, R. W., & Meyer, D. E. Retrieval and comparison processes in semantic memory. In S. Kornblum (Ed.), *Attention and performance IV*. New York: Academic Press, 1973.

Smith, F. *Understanding reading*. New York: Holt, Rinehart and Winston, 1971.

Stanners, R. F., & Forbach, G. B. Analysis of letter strings in word recognition. *Journal of Experimental Psychology*, 1973, 98, 31—35.

Stroop, J. R. Studies of interference in serial verbal reactions. *Journal of Experimental Psychology*, 1935, **18**, 643—662.

Treisman, A. Contextual cues in selective listening. *Quarterly Journal of Experimental Psychology*, 1960, **12**, 242—248.

Treisman, A. *Attention and speech*. Unpublished doctoral dissertation, Oxford University, 1961.

Warren, R. E. Stimulus encoding and memory. *Journal of Experimental Psychology*, 1972, **94**, 90—100.

26

What We Might Know about Orthographic Rules

Jonathan Baron

Department of Psychology, T3
University of Pennsylvania
Philadelphia, Pennsylvania, United States 19174

ABSTRACT

The rules relating spellings to sounds seem to be useful in adult reading as well as in learning to read. There are three ways people might make use of the existence of rules: the component—correspondence method uses knowledge of letter—sound relations; the analogy method makes inferences based on the changes in whole words; and the similarity method takes over the entire response from a similar word. Evidence for all three methods is found in three studies of adults pronouncing nonsense syllables. The analogy method is most frequently associated with correct answers. The role of analogy in teaching people to read, and in the origin of linguistic rules, is discussed.

I. INTRODUCTION

The rules relating spellings to sounds in Western alphabets place interesting demands on the beginning reader. Many of the rules can be expressed as simple associations between letters and phonemes. But unlike other stimulus—response associations, these cannot be learned separately. It is not only impossible to produce many phonemes in isolation, but it is even impossible to produce a string of them slowly. If we try to pronounce CAT slowly, for example, we might produce something like KUH-A-TUH, but this actually adds two extra phonemes, UH and UH, even if they are whispered. This problem does not exist in languages, such as Japanese, that have systems of writing in which characters represent syllables. In a syllabic orthography the response to a single character can be learned in isolation, and learning to read out loud is largely a matter of producing these associated responses faster and faster.

Many others (e.g., Gibson & Levin, 1975; Gleitman & Rozin, 1973, Rozin & Gleitman, 1977; Savin, 1972) have pointed to the impossibility of pronouncing phonemes in isolation as one of the difficulties in learning to read. My purpose here is to examine some consequences of this difficulty, and then to suggest ways in which it might be overcome. This examination might also shed light on the way we use other rules besides orthographic ones. Before getting into the substance of the issue, I first try to convince the remaining skeptics of the importance of learning to use these orthographic rules (rules relating letters and sounds) in the course of learning to read. I then examine what adults might know about these rules, as a way of our gaining information about what the beginning reader must learn. Finally, I discuss some possible mechanisms for acquiring the rules in the form in which adults know them.

II. WHY THE RULES ARE WORTH LEARNING TO USE

It is important to learn to use the rules relating spellings to sounds because they are used in fluent reading, because they are used by beginning readers, and because once they are learned, a person can figure out most new words without the aid of a teacher.

It is conceivable that our ability to learn associations between visual patterns and names is so great that we could learn the name of each word as a visual pattern, without making any use of the relations between letters and sounds. However, this does not seem to be the case. Brooks and I (Baron, in press; Brooks, 1977) made up a six-letter artificial alphabet, which we used to write six four-letter words. In one condition, the subjects learned to pronounce the words according to the orthography; the same symbol always stood for the same letter. In the other condition, the six printed words were randomly paired with the six spoken words, so that the orthography was no longer useful. Even after four hundred trials with each stimulus, pronouncing the words was faster in the condition with the orthographic relationship. Strawson and I (Baron & Strawson, 1976) showed that this general result can be extended to real words as well. English words which are exceptions to orthographic rules, such as SWORD, take longer to pronounce than words which followed the rules, such as SWEET. Further, we found that subjects differ predictably in the extent to which they rely upon the rules as opposed to rote word-specific associations.

People use the orthographic rules for getting meaning out of words as well as getting sounds. Glenn and I (cited in Baron, in press) induced subjects to learn to produce both a pronounciation and a written squiggle in response to words written in an artificial alphabet. The squiggles were related to the words in the arbitrary way in which meanings are related to words. The subjects practiced producing the sounds and drawing the squiggles simultaneously in response to the artificial words for a few weeks. Then they were asked to draw the squiggles from the artificial words without saying the names aloud. This drawing was done either with or without articulatory interference, which consisted of saying "another, another, . . ." while doing the task. This interference had more of an effect when the relation between artificial words and sounds was orthographic than in another condition in which it was not. This result suggests that some sort of articulatory mediation was used when the orthographic relationship between words and sounds was available. Thus the orthography was useful for mediation even when there was no correspondence between components of each stimulus and components of its response.

In a similar experiment using real words (Baron, in press) I presented subjects with lists of digit names written out as English words (one, two, etc.) and asked them to check off the cases where the digit was larger than the preceding one. This corresponded to the orthographic condition in the experiment done by Glenn and me, since though English words related to their sounds through an orthography, only the meanings, not the sounds, were needed for the task. In the other condition, subjects were given lists of Roman numerals, and again asked to check off those that were larger than the preceding numeral. Without articulatory interference, the task was easier with the English words than the Roman numerals but with interference the task was easier with Roman than English. In fact, the interference had no detectable effect on the Roman numerals at all. (A similar interaction was found using Arabic numerals instead of Roman.) Since the English was harder than the Roman with articulatory interference, we can conclude that when phonemic mediation is not allowed the direct path from English words to meanings is less efficient than that from Roman numeral to meanings. The advantage of English words over Roman numerals without interference thus seems to be due to the value of the orthography in forming an intermediate phonemic code. In sum, in tasks examined so far, the orthography seems to be useful not only in reading words aloud, but also in getting meaning from them.

This evidence that the orthography is useful to the fluent reader is complemented by a great deal of evidence that orthographic rules are if anything *more* important for the beginning reader. Rozin and Gleitman (1977) have recently summarized this evidence, but it is useful to review some of the high points.

One study by Firth (1972) examined correlations between ability to read text aloud in beginning readers and a number of variables that might be basic to learning to read. With intelligence partialed out, the speed of learning to associate names with strings of nonsense forms, essentially the paired-associate condition Brooks and I used (Baron, in press; Brooks, 1976), did not correlate at all with reading ability, but tasks involving sound manipulation did correlate. Other tests measured what the child had learned from his reading instruction.

Among these variables, ability to use context to guess what a word would be had a very low correlation with reading ability, while the ability to pronounce nonsense words had a correlation of over .90. In fact, when intelligence and the ability to pronounce nonsense words were partialed out, all other correlations with reading ability essentially disappeared. The nonsense-word test is about the most direct measure there could be of knowledge of orthographic rules, so it would seem that learning these rules is quite important in the early stages of reading.

Perfetti and Hogaboam (1975) reported a similar result. Children classified as skilled or unskilled comprehenders were timed while pronouncing words and nonwords. The biggest difference between the groups was for nonwords and low-frequency words, again suggesting that "decoding skills" set the limit on reading ability for children. While a number of studies (see Calfee, Venezky, & Chapman, 1969; Gibson & Levin, 1975) suggest that decoding skills are less highly correlated with comprehension in older readers, it seems reasonable to suppose that the factors influencing comprehension in older readers also have less to do with reading per se, and more to do with other aspects of intelligence and language comprehension.

Other evidence suggests that poor readers not only do not know the rules, but they do not even know the principles behind the rules. Rozin, Bressman, and Taft (1974), for example, found that students selected from classes of poor readers in the second grade could not tell which of the printed words MOW— MOTORCYCLE matched up with which spoken word. These readers knew so little about the principles of orthography that they could not even tell that the longer word would most likely have the longer spelling.

Aside from such experimental evidence, there are practical arguments for the importance of learning the rules in the early steps of learning to read. The most convincing of these is the fact that a beginning reader who knows the rules can in essence teach himself to read, without continual feedback from a teacher who tells him the identity of each new word he encounters. Even though the rules in English are far from perfect in their ability to specify a pronounciation uniquely, they are usually good enough, with the help of context.

III.   HOW ADULTS PRONOUNCE NONSENSE WORDS

I have argued that both fluent and beginning readers need some sort of knowledge derived from the correspondences between spellings and sounds, and that this knowledge somehow helps them read. But it is not clear what sort of knowledge this is. In the experiments I report, we have attempted to find out what sort of knowledge is used by asking fluent readers to pronounce nonsense words such as WIRD.

There are three ways a person might deal with such a task. All of these ways could account for the helpfulness of orthographic rules in the experiments I discussed. The most obvious thing the reader might know about rules is that they relate letters to sounds, or perhaps groups of letters to groups of sounds. Each letter in WIRD corresponds to a phoneme, and if the person cannot produce the phonemes on the first try, he can at least listen to see whether the string of phonemes he produces corresponds to the string of letters. Note that to use this mechanism a person needs not be able to state the rules, but he must know them in some sense.

Another way in which a person could exhibit what would pass for knowledge of rules is to find *analogies* between new situations and old ones in which he already knows what to do. To use this method to pronounce new words or nonsense words, a person needs to know only the pronunciations of whole words, plus general strategies for forming analogies. For example, given the nonsense word WIGHT, the person might be reminded of NIGHT. His general strategies for forming analogies would allow him to infer that only the first phoneme need be changed. In principle, he could even infer the nature of the required change from such minimal pairs as NIT and WIT. Thus, he need never rely on knowledge of specific letter-sound correspondences. While words spelled similarly are not always pronounced similarly, they are often enough to make this analogy strategy a useful one. This method of finding analogies, I should note, is a useful one in many other linguistic and nonlinguistic tasks. For example, if you are asked to paraphrase a compound noun such as FOOT-BIRD (a task used by Gleitman & Gleitman, 1970), and if you do not happen to know the "rule" for paraphrasing compound nouns, one thing you can do is form an analogy. By this method, a FOOT-BIRD might well turn out to be "a bird at the bottom of the page" (L. Gleitman, personal communication, 1975). Note that to use the analogy strategy, one does not have to know the orghographic rules beforehand in any direct sense, but the strategy is not useful unless the rules are there to be used. Hence we may speak of using rules without knowing them.

A third method for making it seem as if you know at least some orthographic rules is to respond entirely on the basis of *similarity*. Finding similarities is part of the analogy strategy, but using analogies requires making changes. In using similarities, we simply take over the old response and assign it to the new stimulus. This is like functional fixedness in problem solving. If a child uses a similarity strategy and pronounces CAP as if it were CAT, we might mistakenly credit him with knowledge of the relations between two of the letters and their respective phonemes, when really what he is doing is simply using the form as a whole word. While this strategy usually leads to error, it is occasionally useful. Those of us who learned to read English in the United States, for example, do well to read PREMISS on the basis of similarity with PREMISE, rather than thinking it might be a new word for an early failure or a young girl. Another value of the similarity strategy is that it allows us to read without being greatly slowed down by mispellings. It can even be argued that similarity alone can account for many of the advantages of orthographic systems that I spoke of previously (for details, see Baron, in press; Brooks, 1977).

A. Experiment I

To find out what sort of strategies adults use in pronouncing nonsense words, I asked subjects to go through a list of 35 nonsense words and give the best pronunciation they could, as if each nonsense word was an English word they had never seen before. The list was: CAWS, SAIF, WIGHT, HOUGHT, FRISH, AIT, FIGN, SHUD, PHREND, BLUD, NAL, MAGOR, FOCIAL, TEIGH, KNIF, PEAN, SHUE, GAWN, WIRD, CIP, BIGN, FURD, PUCH, HAMB, DUR, SPOY, PSOAL, GAF, COM, ROTION, CEN, TION, FLOE, CIAL, and CAUF. The subjects were then asked how they did the task, in general. Then they were asked to go through the list again, feeling free to change their mind about the first answer. They were asked to explain why they changed their answer, when they did. We counted as correct any pronunciation that was within the rules as stated by Venezky (1970), or any pronunciation that would be correct by an appropriate analogy with an English word. For example, TEIGH could be pronounced so as to rhyme with either PEA or PAY (in the first case, by analogy with JANET LEIGH). CEN, however, could only be pronounced as if it were SEN, since there is no word in English in which C followed by E is pronounced as if it were K.

First of all, of the 20 subjects (all undergraduate or graduate students), 13 said that they generally used an analogy method to sound out new words, 15 said they used some sort of rules, and only 8 said they used a similarity method. Randomly chosen examples of the kinds of statements made are: "BLUD looks like misspelled BLOOD" (similarity); "first phonetic rule that comes to mind – if it sounded terrible or was hard to pronounce, I changed it" (correspondence); "if it sounded like another word, like ROTION, and MOTION" (analogy); "use rules that you remember; long A or not, silent letter or not" (correspondence); "think of other words – easiest way, it would be another word – WAIF–SAIF, FRISH–FISH" (analogy); "words that should be spelled differently" (similarity). At least subjects report using all three methods for pronouncing new words.

In order to examine which method is better, we can look at the justifications given for changing one's mind about the best pronunciation of a word. Table 1 shows the number of times each type of justification was associated with a correct response or an incorrect response. (Whether the correct response was given first or second made no difference in fact. Also, changes from correct to correct or from incorrect to incorrect were not analyzed, as there were very few.) For example, if a subject said, "I pronounced WIRD as WIRED the first time because it looked like it, and the second time I pronounced it so as to rhyme with BIRD," this was counted as an association between the analogy strategy and the correct answer and between the similarity strategy and the incorrect answer. Clearly, of the three strategies, the analogy strategy is most likely to lead to the right answer, and the similarity strategy is least likely.

TABLE 1
Relation between Strategy and Correctness of Answer
when Subjects Changed Answers: Experiment I

	Analogy	Correspondence	Similarity
Right	7	2	1
Wrong	0	2	11

Examination of individual differences supports this conclusion. Those subjects who said they used the analogy strategy tended to do better than those who did not (3.3 errors per list versus 5.1 on both lists included, $t(18) = 1.43$). Those who used the similarity strategy tended to do worse than those who did not (5.3 errors versus 3.0, $t(18) = 2.03$). And use of the correspondence strategy made little difference (3.7 errors with versus 4.6 without, $t(18) = 0.64$).

Probably we could pick our words in such a way that the similarity strategy would be more useful; given the words we used, it is not surprising that the similarity strategy was so useless. It is also not so surprising that the analogy strategy was so helpful, since we defined some of our correct answers in terms of analogies, and, as I argue subsequently, linguists such as Venezky probably also rely heavily on analogies when they are trying to figure out what the rules are. Still, it is possible to make inappropriate analogies (e.g., DAM is to DAMN as BIG is to BIGN), and the fact that subjects did so so rarely suggests that they knew something about what sort of analogies to make — another point I return to subsequently.

Perhaps the most surprising finding is that the subjects made so many errors. It seems likely from these results that while simple rules may be used quite a bit, our ability to pronounce complex nonsense of the sort used here does not depend heavily on our knowledge of rules, for when we explicitly attempt to apply that knowledge, we are fairly likely to apply it wrongly. The fact that fluent readers do not really know many rules of pronunciation has been previously noted by Calfee, Venezky, and Chapman (1969), who found that many college students did not know the rule governing the pronunciation of C as a function of the following vowel, or the rule relating the sound of a middle vowel to the presence or absence of a final E.

B. Experiment II

If subjects rely heavily on the analogy strategy in producing correct responses, we ought to be able to improve their performance by increasing their reliance on this strategy. Unlike the use of component–correspondence, the analogy strategy can in principle be taught or facilitated without changing any specific knowledge about pronunciations of words or letter groups. All we have to do is to tell the subject that when he is not sure about how to pronounce something, he should try to think of words that contain the part he is not sure about. This is exactly what we did. Using the same nonsense words in the list given above, we asked 30 college-aged subjects to go through the list once and give everything they thought might be a possible pronunciation for each item. The reason for asking for all possible pronunciations was to make sure that any errors, that is, failures to give a correct response as one of the answers, would not be due to the momentary effects of one strategy overriding another (for example, similarity overriding analogy). Then we gave each subject the instructions about finding analogies, previously summarized, and then asked him to go through the list again.

For the 35 items, subjects gave an average of 45.6 responses, total on the first run, and 36.8 on the second, after the analogy instructions. In spite of the decrease in the overall number of responses, the number of items for which one of the answers given was correct increased from 31.8 (9.1% errors) to 33.6 (4.0% errors). This increase was significant across subjects ($t(29)$ = 3.84, $p < .001$) and across stimuli ($t(34)$ = 4.01, $p < .001$). Naturally, the proportion of responses that were correct also increased from 74.8% to 93.5%, as a result of the instructions. The training itself, rather than mere repetition, seemed to be crucial for the improvement, since the amount of improvement (in terms of items with a correct answer) was greater in this experiment than in the first one ($t(48)$ = 3.54, $p < .001$, across subjects), where there was essentially no improvement.

It is of interest to examine the effect of the analogy instructions on certain types of errors. Of particular interest are those that can be ascribed to violation of a simple and ubiquitous rule. One such rule is that which requires that a vowel followed by a consonant cluster and then the end of a word should be pronounced as "short" (e.g., PIN) as opposed to "long" (e.g., PINE). There were seven items in the list requiring a short pronunciation according to this rule, SHUD, BLUD, CIP, HAMB, GAF, COM, and CEN. (Cases in which an error resulted in pronunciation as a real word were eliminated because of the possibility that these errors could be due to use of a similarity strategy.) Use of the long pronunciation decreased as a result of the training, from a mean of 6.0 errors per item to 1.3 (out of 30 subjects, $t(6)$ = 5.13, $p < .005$, across stimuli). Another rule that could be examined specified that C should be pronounced as S when followed by E or I, and as K when followed by A, O, or U. For the five items for which this rule applied (CIP, COM, CEN, CIAL, and CAUf), 8.4 errors per item were made before training. 2.0 after ($t(4)$ = 4.24, $p < .005$). A third type of error involves the production of phonologically illegal sequences, pronouncing both the K and N in KNIF, the G and N in BIGN, the P and S in PSOAL, and the M and B in HAMB. These errors decreased from 3.5 to .5 per item as a result of training ($t(3)$ = 2.78, $p < .05$). While all of these results support the argument that analogy instructions make subjects act as if they knew the rules better, the last result concerning illegal sequences is of particular interest because these errors could only arise as a result of overapplication of a component—correspondence strategy. Their existence thus provides evidence of the use of this strategy, and their virtual disappearance after training argues for the superiority of the analogy strategy for these cases.

C. Experiment III

One interesting property of the analogy strategy, as opposed to the component—correspondence strategy, is that a "rule" need not have been previously "productive" in order to be psychologically real. Because of this property, the analogy strategy can be used to invent new rules that "make sense" in terms of what we already know. (Bar-Adon, 1964/1971, has, in fact, found some illustrations of this use of analogies in historical changes in Hebrew grammar.) When we ordinarily speak of rules in language, we usually require that a rule account for a number of instances — surely more than one — in order to count it as a real rule. To drop this requirement would lead us into saying that every time we learn a single word and its pronunciation, we also learn a large number of rules, each rule corresponding to a *potential* regularity uniting this new word and others that we have not yet learned. For example, suppose I tell you that LB is pronounced "pound," and then ask you how to pronounce LP. And say you tell me that LP must be pronounced "pount" because T is to D as P is to B, according to their distinctive features. In this case, I would have to credit you with having learned the "rule": pronounce L as "poun" and then change labials to dentals. In other words, if we credit people with *having learned* rules every time they discover analogies, we would have to credit them with having learned an enormous number of rules. Thus, the restriction that rules must account for a number of instances people already know in order for us to call them rules is a reasonable restriction. To pick another example closer to home, it seems unreasonable to say that we have learned a rule that final EIGH may correspond to EE as in LEE since (JANET) LEIGH is the only word in English which this correspondence is present. However, such an extension from a single case would be perfectly natural using an analogy strategy.

Thus, if people use analogies rather than rules in the true sense, it ought to be possible to show that they will use analogies with real words even when there is only one word in the language for which a particular analogy is appropriate. We were encouraged by several instances in the last experiment in which words were pronounced by such analogies with "one of a kind": TEIGH by analogy with LEIGH, and SAIF with SAID. To do a more systematic test, we made up a list of 16 nonsense words so that this one-of-a-kind strategy could be used for every word in the list, and so that the pronunciation generated this way would be an exception to the rules. The list was YAID, YOUGH, YEEN, YAUGH, YOUCH, YONGUE, YIEND, YONE, YEART, YORD, YOPY, YOTH, YONT, YOES, YASH, and YAVE. Ten subjects were told to give all possible pronunciations of each item and then to tell us which was the best for each item.

Responses were classified according to whether they were based on the one-of-a-kind strategy (e.g., YAID, rhyming with SAID) other legal pronunciations, or errors. Or all the responses given, 78 were based on a one-of-a-kind analogy, 133 otherwise correct, and 46 errors. Of the responses considered "best," 29% were one-of-a-kind, 67% otherwise correct, and 4% errors. The number of one-of-a-kind responses thus exceeded the number of errors for the responses taken together (across stimuli, $t(15) = 2.36, p < .02$; across subjects, $t(9) = 3.49, p < .01$) and for the responses considered "best" (across stimuli, $t(15) = 3.38, p < .01$; across subjects, $t(9) = 5.85, p < .001$).

Of particular interest are those four stimuli (YAUGH, YONGUE, YEART, and YOPY) for which there is only one analogy based on everything following the Y (and for which the use of this analogy yields an irregular pronunciation, as is true for all items). For these stimuli, the analogy response was more frequently given than other legal responses (78% of subjects versus 53% averaged across stimuli) and more frequently indicated to be best (68% versus 25% of subjects, with the one-of-a-kind response at least as frequent for all four items). The only other item for which the one-of-a-kind response was more frequent than the regular response was YOTH, where the word BOTH is much more frequent than any of the regular words following the same pattern (MOTH, CLOTH, BROTH, and SLOTH). This study as a whole thus provides clear evidence of the use of the analogy strategy, and strongly suggestive evidence that this strategy often wins out over direct application of rules.

IV. OTHER EVIDENCE FOR THE ANALOGY STRATEGY

It may be of interest to compare these results with those concerning "implicit learning" of concepts or rules (Brooks, 1974; Reber, 1976). Such experiments have usually presented subjects with two types of items following different structural principles. In one such experiment, Brooks (1974) used strings of letters such as VVTRXRR or MRRMRV, and asked subjects to learn associations between each string and the name of an animal or a city. For example, the first string was associated with the response "Paris." In the basic condition, strings made up according to one rule were associated with cities, and strings made up according to another rule were associated with animals. The subjects were not told about the rules during the rote learning of the paired associates, but afterward they were given cards with new strings, which they were to classify as animals, cities, or neither. Evidence for "implicit learning" is the fact that subjects could classify the new strings above chance. ("Chance" was determined by asking new subjects to sort the cards into piles on the basis of similarity, that is, to put the cards together that seemed to go together, and then assigning "animal," "city," or "neither" to the three piles so that the subject got the highest "score.") When subjects were simply told to discover the rule, they performed no better than chance on a transfer test.

On the basis of these results so far, we might claim that subjects learned rules only when they were not looking for them. However, it is not clear that rules were learned at all during the training phase of the experiment. It might be that all the subjects learned were particular instances, and that they classified new cases in the transfer test on the basis of similarity with old ones. Thus, the implicit condition worked better than the explicit one not because the subject was *not* looking for the rules, but rather because he *was* memorizing specific instances.

To test this possibility, Brooks (1974) associated strings made up according to one rule with New World cities *and* animals (e.g., Boston, moose) and Old World cities and animals (e.g., Pairs, tiger). Thus, even if the subjects had looked for a relation between the two obvious response categories, animals and cities, and rules during training, they would not have found one. No subject noticed the division into New and Old World until he was asked to sort new cards based on this distinction. The interesting result was that performance at sorting new instances into New World and Old World in this condition was just as good as performance in the animal versus city condition. Previous knowledge of the possibility of learning a rule is thus of no help. What seems to be important in this case is nothing more than the opportunity to memorize instances, and the ability to use one's memory of instances at the time of generalizing the rule.

Of course, these experiments concern "concept learning" rather than "rule learning" in the sense in which we are discussing it here. The difference is that in Brooks' test conditions, the similarity strategy is always appropriate, since there are only three possible responses, and there is no such thing as a possible analogy strategy. Otherwise, the results fit together well with those of the one-of-a-kind experiment. While I do not mean to deny the possibility that adults learn to apply real rules (as they obviously do in "concept formation" tasks), I would argue that a substantial part of our ability to pronounce new words, at least, is based on rote memory of words we have already learned, plus knowledge of the general strategy of finding and using analogies. Further, it seems that the analogy strategy is not used automatically to its full extent, but rather the extent of its use is easily modified by training.

A brief digression: If the rules are only used at the time of transfer, one might ask, why do they seem to help us remember things? Answer: Because the analogy strategy can be used at the time of recall — perhaps even very quickly and unconsciously — to help strengthen weak memories or reconstruct missing parts, thus placing fewer demands on rote memory.

V. ANALOGY AS A TEACHING METHOD

Is the analogy strategy useful in teaching children to read? One experiment (reported in Baron, in press) suggests that it is. Four-year-olds learned two words, such as TAX and TIN, at a time. Every other pair of words was related to the previous pair; for example, AX and IN could follow TAX and TIN. This relation made an analogy strategy useful in learning the second pair. The difference between the number of errors made in learning the first pair and the number made in learning the second can thus serve as a measure of the use of the analogy strategy. By this measure, use of the strategy increased substantially and significantly over 12 pairs. This finding, in combination with others (Baron, in press), indicates that young children can learn the strategy of making use of similarities between new words and old ones, the essence of the analogy strategy.

In sum, it seems that the analogy strategy is an easy one for children to acquire as well as for adults to use. Of course, this experiment says nothing about the relative usefulness of different strategies in the long run. I am only trying to argue here that the analogy strategy is one that can be used, and that it can be taught as a general strategy. I also think that the long-run effectiveness of teaching children to read in this way is something that should be examined more closely.

The analogy strategy makes an inference that similarity in print implies similarity in sound. This is a consequence of the existence of rules, but we need know nothing about rules in order to use this strategy. Of course, this general principle does not always work, but it does work surprisingly often, perhaps even often enough to get the reader close enough to use context to figure out which of several possible analogies apply. (Another way to avoid the problem of false analogies is to find several analogies for each new word. False analogies lead to inconsistent pronunciations if this is done. However, full reliance on such a method seems inconsistent with the results of Experiment III.)

For most practical purposes the analogy strategy allows people to learn the rules of correspondence between letters and phonemes without ever having to produce the phonemes in isolation. When I previously spoke of taking part of the sound of one word and adding it to the sound of another (e.g., WIT and NIGHT, to get WIGHT), I did not imply that the sound ever had to be produced in isolation. The entire strategy can be thought of as replacing and combining sounds; it never requires taking sounds away and producing what is left (at least to the point at which all is left is a single phoneme). Thus, the use of the analogy strategy is one possible solution to the problem I posed at the very beginning. It is in fact possible to teach people to use the rules without ever teaching individual letter–sound associations.

I should note that there are other ways to overcome this problem besides the analogy strategy. One is the traditional phonics method, in which the child is taught a mnemonic syllable (phonic = phonemic mnemonic!) for each letter. Then he is taught to "blend" the syllables to produce a smooth word. Most likely, this method was invented by people who thought that phonemes could in fact be pronounced in isolation, and that blending was essentially a process of speeding up, just the way one learns to play arpeggios on the piano by first playing them note by note and gradually increasing the speed.

Even though this idea is surely wrong, there may be some good intuitions behind the use of phonics after all. For one thing, the analogy method as used by adults depends upon memorizing a large stock of examples. In our experiment on the use of the analogy method in children, we made the task easy for them by using only a few words at a time. Without doing this, the task may be much harder. The use of phonics can lighten the memory load of having to remember all of the words that might form the basis of analogies. The learner need only remember sounds corresponding to each of the letters of the alphabet.

But what about blending? The difficulty of blending is not only apparent in beginning readers, but also in adults who learn new alphabets. Anderson and Brooks (cited in Brooks, in press) taught adults an artificial alphabet representing only sounds such as SS, SH, RR, and OO, that is, without stop consonants. Subjects practiced producing the individual sounds in response to the letters and then were tested at sounding out words written in the alphabet. They took so long to sound out the words that they were faster at "sounding out" the letters in a word than at pronouncing the whole word. Blending is thus a problem even when the sounds seem to be pronounceable in isolation, although it is not clear that S produced in isolation is motorically or psychologically identical to S preceding a vowel.

Although I have no evidence, I would argue that in principle the problems of learning to blend could be solved by extending the analogy strategy. In the simplest case, consider the child who has learned NUH as a phonic for N, GUH for G, and the word NO. Given the word GO, with this knowledge he can use the simple analogy, NUH is to NO as GUH is to GO, as a way of figuring out the new word. Use of the phonics method involves replacing the UH with the other sounds of a word, just as the analogy strategy often involves replacing part of a word with part of another word, often a large part. Since the analogy and the phonics strategy contain this common component, replacing parts, we might well expect that teaching the child one of these methods would facilitate his learning the other (Baron, 1973), especially if the relation between them were made apparent.

Of course, things get a bit more complicated when the phonics method is applied to two parts of a word at once. Conceivably, the method could be applied in steps (BUH-A-DUH, BA-DUH, BAD), which may even be done simultaneously. Alternatively, children could be taught to read using sequences of words in which each new word was familiar except for one new letter.

There is a third way of overcoming the problem posed initially. This involves teaching the child to abstract his own rules for component correspondences. Once a child had the appropriate learning set, we could then simply present him with words and their pronunciations, and he would discover the rules by a process of trial and error, more or less the way a linguist discovers rules by examining words and their pronunciations. But unlike the linguist, the learner would not simply write the rules down, but would translate them into mental subroutines for producing the appropriate phonemes in response to strings of letters. There is little evidence that such a process can work. But even if it could, there is reason to think that the analogy strategy would still be helpful. For once our little linguist had proposed a potential rule, it would be efficient for him to check it by thinking of other examples where it might apply. Given the word PSYCHOLOGY, for example, he might propose a rule to the effect that P should be pronounced as S. This rule could be rejected fairly quickly, in its simple form, be recalling from memory words that contain P, and checking them to see whether they have an S sound in the pronunciations. This checking strategy is not the same as the analogy strategy, but it does share one component with the analogy strategy as it is used by adults. Both strategies require that words be recalled from memory according to properties they possess. In pronouncing FIGN, for example, it might help to be able to retrieve words that end with IGN. Similarly, in testing a rule, it helps to be able to recall words that contain whatever unit the rule applies to. Again, if this "learner-as-linguist" strategy existed, it might be acquired more easily if the analogy strategy had been taught first. In this context, I should note that the ability to retrieve from memory according to a specified property, and then modify what one has retrieve so that it fits the situation at hand, is surely useful in many other situations besides this one.

Note also that a similar sort of generate-a-rule-and-test-it procedure can be used to discover rules for *finding* analogies. One useful rule, for example, might be to divide a word into its initial consonant-cluster and the rest, and then look in memory for words containing each part. This rule can be tested by finding out whether it leads to consistent analogies. The rarity of inappropriate analogies suggests that adults, at least, have learned such parsing rules.

Up to now, all the possibilities I have discussed require the formation of learning sets, learning sets for forming analogies, for using phonics, or for generating and testing proposed rules. In essence, these methods address the traditional educational problem of teaching for transfer, but in doing so they change the question. Rather than asking how we can teach the rules *for* transfer, we have been asking how we can teach the learner *to* transfer the rules. If transfer skills can be taught, and if teaching transfer skills facilitates transfer of these skills to new situations, teaching people to transfer may be a very important educational goal indeed, of importance beyond the teaching of reading or even other language skills. This possibility makes me partial to the idea that learning to read is part of this more general process of intellectual development.

But this need not be the case. It is also possible that no learning set is required. Perhaps orthographic rules can be learned incidentally as a mere by-product of memorizing associations between printed words and their corresponding sounds. While this is surely a possibility, I would argue that all the evidence I have presented weighs against this idea. For one thing, there are many rules that adults have not learned. For another, for both adults and children, there are other more active strategies that seem to work better than such an incidental learning mechanism, even it is existed. Finally, there is the Brooks (1974) experiment in which people learned as much about a rule when the category it concerned was completely unforseen than when it was not (New versus Old World). It is hard to imagine an incidental learning mechanism that could discover a rule under such conditions.

If my argument is correct, we cannot expect children simply to "pick up" the correspondences between spellings and sounds by practice or drill at learning associations between printed and spoken words. We must first make sure that they have the learning sets required to make use of this information, whether these sets involve finding analogies at the time of encountering new words (or when trying to recall the pronunciations of old ones), or using phonics, or playing linguist by discovering the rules and then turning them into mental computer programs. Further, since many children have trouble learning orthographic rules, it would seem that acquisition of these learning sets is not the automatic result of whatever education children receive outside of school.

There is another implication of the argument I have been trying to make. If this argument can be extended to other linguistic skills, it would seem that linguistic rules can have a different sort of psychological reality than that we usually imagine, perhaps along with the usual kind. The psychological representation of linguistic rules might be more similar to the kinds of paradigms that used to be used in teaching conjugations and declensions than to the rules for rewriting and transformation as written by modern linguists. The paradigms, or examples, as vague as they may be in our heads, may act as the basis for analogies. Further, it might be possible to trace the general regularity in human languages to our propensity to form analogies from single instances, thus creating new rules. In this way, much of our capacity for language may be seen as a consequence of our intelligence, which in turn can be seen in large part as an ability to use old knowledge for new purposes.

ACKNOWLEDGMENTS

The ideas presented in this paper were influenced by discussions with Lee Brooks. Debby Kemler made helpful comments on a draft. Donna Ducanis provided able assistance in the research. The research was supported by a grant from the National Science Foundation (U.S.A.).

REFERENCES

Bar-Adon, A. "Analogy" and analogic change as reflected in comtemporary Hebrew. In A. Bar-Adon &. W. F. Leopold (Eds.), *Child language, a book of readings.* Englewood Cliffs, N.J.: Prentice Hall, 1971. (Originally published 1964)

Baron, J. Semantic components and conceptual development, *Cognition,* 1973, **2**, 299–317.

Baron, J. Mechanisms for pronouncing printed words: Use and acquisition. In D. LaBerge & S. J. Samuels (Eds.), *Basic processes in reading: Perception and comprehension.* Hillsdale, N.J.: Lawrence Erlbaum Associates, in press.

Baron, J., & Strawson, C. Use of orthographic and word-specific knowledge in reading words aloud. *Journal of Experimental Psychology,* 1976, in press.

Brooks, L. R. Implicit learning and rule statements in rule-learning experiments. Paper presented at the Meetings of the Psychonomic Society, Boston, November 1974.

Brooks, L. R. Visual pattern in fluent word identification. In A. Reber & D. Scarborough (Eds.), *Toward a psychology of reading: The proceedings of the CUNY conferences.* Hillsdale, N.J.: Lawrence Erlbaum Associates, 1977.

Calfee, R., Venezky, R., & Chapman, R. *Pronunciation of synthetic words with predictable and unpredictable letter-sound correspondence* (Wisconsin Research and Development Center for Cognitive Learning, Technical Report No. 71). Madison, Wisconsin, 1969.

Firth, I. *Components of reading disability.* Unpublished doctoral dissertation, University of New South Wales, 1972.

Gibson, E. J., & Levin, H. *The psychology of reading.* Cambridge, Mass.: MIT Press, 1975.

Gleitman, H., & Gleitman, L. *Phrase and paraphrase: Some innovative uses of language.* New York: Norton, 1970.

Gleitman, L. R., & Rozin, P. Teaching reading by the use of a syllabary. *Reading Research Quarterly,* 1973, **8,** 447–483.

Perfetti, C. A., & Hogaboam, T. Relationship between single word decoding and reading comprehension skill. *Journal of Educational Psychology,* 1975, **67,** 461–469.

Reber, A. Implicit learning of synthetic languages: The role of instructional set. *Journal of Experimental Psychology: Human Learning and Memory,* 1976, **2,** 88–94.

Rozen, P., Bressman, B., & Taft, M. Do children understand the basic relationship between speech and writing? The Mow-Motorcycle test. *Journal of Reading Behavior,* 1974, **6,** 327–334.

Rozin, P., & Gleitman, L. The structure and acquisition of reading. II. The reading process and the acquisition of the alphabetic principle. In A. S. Reber & D. Scarborough (Eds.), *Toward a psychology of reading: The proceedings of the CUNY conferences.* Hillsdale, N.J.: Lawrence Erlbaum Associates, 1977.

Savin, H. B. What the child knows about speech when he starts to learn to read. In J. F. Kavanagh & I. G. Mattingly (Eds.), *Language by ear and by eye: The relationships between speech and reading.* Cambridge, Mass.: MIT Press, 1972.

Venezky, R. L. *The structure of English orthography.* The Hague: Mouton, 1970.

27
Toward an Interactive Model of Reading

David E. Rumelhart

Department of Psychology
University of California, San Diego
La Jolla, California, United States

ABSTRACT

The purpose of this chapter is to develop a formalism within which psychologists can develop detailed information processing models of the reading process. I argue that such a formalism is necessary because the usual formalisms tend to lead most naturally to bottom-up, serial, stage-by-stage models of reading. Moreover, I argue that there is a good deal of evidence suggesting that reading is best characterized as a process of applying simultaneous constraints at all levels and thereby coming up with the most probable interpretation of the input string. Although it is probably not impossible to use the usual flow chart formalisms to represent such models (have arrows pointing back from higher levels to lower levels) it is not especially natural and when carried to the extreme of a completely interacting system is not very informative (two way arrows between every pair of levels). I suggest that the formalisms designed for parallel computing applications are the best substitutions. Finally, I develop a model based on HEARSAY II and GSP and argue that such a model has many very promising features.

I. INTRODUCTION

Reading is the process of understanding written language. It begins with a flutter of patterns on the retina and ends (when successful) with a definite idea about the author's intended message. Thus, reading is at once a "perceptual" and a "cognitive" process. It is a process which bridges and blurs these two traditional distinctions. Moreover, a skilled reader must be able to make use of sensory, syntactic, semantic, and pragmatic information to accomplish his task. These various sources of information appear to interact in many complex ways during the process of reading. A theorist faced with the task of accounting for reading must devise a formalism rich enough to represent all of these different kinds of information and their interactions.

The study of reading was a central concern of early psychologists (see Huey, 1908). Now, after years of dormancy, reading has again become a central concern for many psychologists. It would seem that the advent of the information-processing approach to psychology has given both experimentalists and theorists paradigms within which to study the reading process. The formalisms of information processing, the flow charts, notions of information flow, etc., have served as useful vehicles for the development of first approximation models of the reading process. Unfortunately, the most familiar information-processing formalisms apply most naturally to models assuming a series of noninteracting stages of processing or (at best) a set of independent parallel processing units. There are many results in the reading literature that appear to call for highly interactive parallel processing units. It is my suspicion that the serial, noninteracting models have been developed not so much due to an abiding belief that interactions do not take place, but rather because the appropriate formalisms have not been available. It is the purpose of this chapter to adapt a formalism developed in the context of parallel computation to the specification of a model for reading and then show that such a model can account in a convenient way for those aspects of reading that appear puzzling in the context of more linear stage-oriented models. No claim is made about the adequacy of the particular model developed. The primary claim is that this richer formalism will allow for the specification of more detailed models. These will be able to characterize aspects of the reading process which are difficult or impossible to characterize within the more familiar information-processing formulations.

I will first review two recent models of the reading process. Then, I will discuss some of the empirical evidence that is not conveniently accounted for by these models or their natural extensions. Finally, I will develop a reading model which makes use of a formalism allowing highly interactive parallel processing units, and then show that this model offers a reasonable account of the problematic results of Section III.

II. CURRENT MODELS OF READING

A. Gough's Model

Gough (1972) has proposed a model of reading that is remarkable in the degree to which it attempts to give a complete information-processing account of the reading process. Gough attempts to pin down as completely as possible the events that occur during the first second of reading. A schematic diagram, representing the flow of information during the reading process is shown in Fig. 1. According to Gough's model, graphemic information enters the visual system and is registered in an *icon* which holds it briefly while it is scanned and operated on by a *pattern recognition* device. This device identifies the letters of the input string. These letters are then read into a *character register* which holds them while a *decoder* (with the aid of a *code book*) converts the character strings into their underlying *phonemic* representation. The phonemic representation of the original character string serves as input to a *librarian* which matches up these phonemic strings against the *lexicon* and feeds the resulting lexical entries into *primary memory*. The four or five lexical items held in primary memory at any one time, serve as input to a magical system (dubbed *Merlin*) which somehow applies its knowledge of the syntax and semantics to determine the deep structure (or perhaps the meaning?) of the input. This deep structure is then forwarded to its final memory register *TPWSGWTAU* (the place where sentences go when they are understood). When all inputs of the text have found their final resting place in TPWSGWTAU, the text has been read and the reading is complete.

I do not want to discuss the merits or demerits of Gough's particular model at this point. Instead, I point to the general form of the model. For Gough, reading consists of a sequentially ordered set of transformations. The input signal is first registered in the icon and then transformed from a character level representation to phonemic representation, lexical level representation and finally to deep structural representation. Thus, the input is sequentially transformed from low-level sensory information into ever higher-level encodings. Note, however, that the information flow is totally "bottom up." That is, the information is initiated with the sensory signal and no higher level of processing can effect any lower level. The reading process is strict letter-by-letter, word-by-word analysis of the input string. There is no provision for interaction within the system. The processing at any level can directly effect only the immediately higher level.

B.   LaBerge—Samuels Model

In another recent paper, LaBerge and Samuels (1974) have developed an equally detailed (though somewhat more perceptually oriented) model of the reading process. Figure 2 gives a schematic representation of their model. The basic model consists of three memory systems holding three different representations of the input string. The Visual Memory System holds visually based representations of the features, letters, spelling groups, words, and word clusters. The Phonological Memory System holds phonological representations of spelling groups, words, and word groups. Finally, the Semantic Memory System holds the semantic representation of the words, word groups, and sentences that are read. The reading process begins with the registration of the visual signal on the sensory surface. The information is then analyzed by a set of specialized *feature*

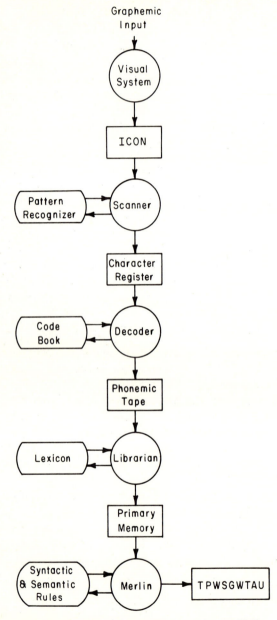

FIG. 1   Gough's reading model. (After Gough, 1972.)

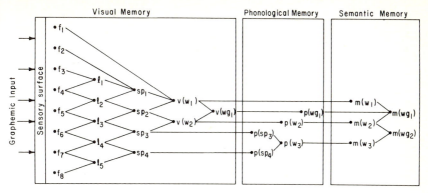

FIG. 2   Reading in the LaBerge–Samuels model. (After LaBerge and Samuels, 1974.)

detectors which extract information about lines, angles, intersections, etc., from the physical stimulus. Most of these feature detectors, f_i, feed directly into letter codes, l_i. Thus, the activation of letter codes results naturally from the convergence of a set of feature detectors. These letter codes feed into spelling pattern codes, sp_i, which in turn feed into visual word codes, $v(w_i)$. Some features (e.g., f_2) map directly into spelling pattern codes and others (f_1) directly into visual word codes. Such features are sensitive to the over all configuration of the words and spelling patterns. There are a number of routes whereby words can be mapped into meanings:

1. Visual word codes can feed directly into word meaning codes $m(w_i)$. This route would be necessary for the discrimination of such homophonous word pairs as "pear" and "pair" or "chute" and "shoot."

2. The visual word codes can pass through a phonological word code, $p(w_i)$ and then into a word meaning code. This is perhaps the ordinary route of analysis within the LaBerge–Samuels model.

3. The model also allows for word groups, such as "time out," to be analyzed into visual word group codes, $v(wg_i)$, from these into phonetic word group codes, $p(wg_i)$, and finally into group meanings, $m(wg_i)$.

4. When a word has not been learned as a visual stimulus, information can be translated directly from visual spelling patterns into phonological spelling patterns, $p(sp_i)$, from these into phonological word codes and finally into word meaning codes. In addition, word meaning codes feed into word group meaning codes.

Ultimately, when the entire set of inputs have been presented, a set of word group meanings will emerge and the reader will be said to have understood the input.[1]

---

[1] LaBerge and Samuels were particularly interested in the role of attention and the notion of automaticity in reading. I have also omitted discussion of episodic memory since neither of these aspects of their model is relevant to my point here.

Again, I do not want to discuss the particular merits or demerits of the LaBerge—Samuels model. Rather, I again point out the general form of the model and suggest that it takes that form, at least to some extent, because of the formalisms used to represent the ideas. The LaBerge—Samuels model, like the Gough model, is a strictly bottom-up process.[2] Although there are alternative routes, the basic sequence is from features to letters, to spelling patterns, to visual word representations to phonological word representations to word meanings to word group meanings. A series of stages, each corresponding to a level of analysis in which no higher level can in any way modify or change the analysis at a lower level. The LaBerge—Samuels model (unlike the Gough model) does allow certain stages to be bypassed. This allows multiple paths of analysis and alleviates some of the empirical problems of the Gough model. Nevertheless, there are a number of results in the literature that are difficult to account for with either model. I turn now to a discussion of a number of these problems.

III. PROBLEMATIC RESULTS

All of the results discussed in this section have one characteristic in common. In each case it appears that the apprehension of information at one level of analysis is partially determined by higher levels of analysis. By and large, such results are very difficult to incorporate in a processing model which assumes that information flows strictly from lower to higher levels. I will begin with a discussion of the effects of orthographic structure on the perception of letters, proceed to a discussion of the effects of syntax on word perception, then to the effects of semantics on word and syntax perception and finally to the effects of general pragmatic factors on the perception of meanings.[3]

A. The Perceptions of Letters Often Depend on the Surrounding Letters

The literature on reading abounds with evidence on this point. Perhaps the most difficult of these results for a purely bottom-up model to account for are the well-known context effects illustrated in Fig. 3 (after Nash-Weber, 1975). Here we see an ambiguous symbol, *ℓℓ* , which is interpreted as a W in one context

---

[2] Actually the aforementioned attention mechanism of the LaBerge—Samuels model offers *some* top-down capacity. However, within their model it is limited and serves to speed up certain weak bottom-up paths.

[3] I use the term *perception* rather freely here. In general, it is my opinion that the distinction between the perceptual and conceptual aspects of reading is not that useful. As I will suggest later, there appears to be a continuity between what has been called perception and what has been called comprehension. My use of the term perception in the present context is simply the use of the one term to cover the entire process.

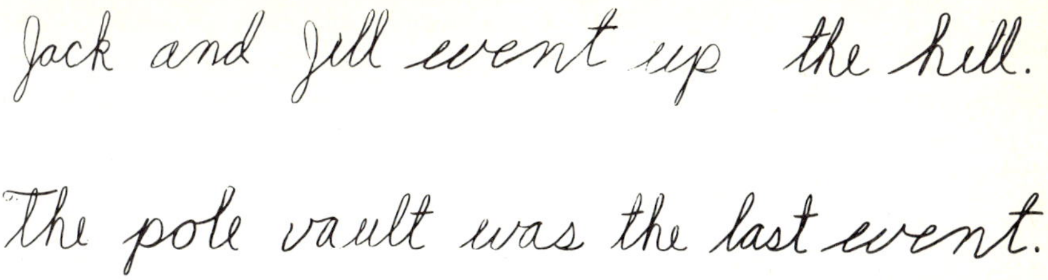

Jack and Jill event up the hill.

The pole vault was the last event.

FIG. 3 The dependence of letter perception of context. (After Nash-Weber, 1975.)

and interpreted as an E followed by a V in another context. It would appear that our interpretation of the sentence has determined our perception of the ambiguous symbol.

The problem with results such as these stems from the fact that we appear to have "word-level" or "phrase-level" perceptions determining our perceptions at the letter level, a higher-level perception affecting a lower-level one. These results can be accounted for by bottom-up models, but only at some cost. No final decision can be made at the letter level. Either a set of alternative possibilities must be passed on, or the direct feature information must be sent to the higher levels. In either of these cases the notion that letter perception preceeds word perception becomes suspect. Word and letter perception occur simultaneously.

Perhaps the strongest objection to a demonstration like this one is that it is very unusual to find such ambiguous letters and that the norm involves characters which are perfectly discriminable. Although this may be true of printed text, it is not true of handwriting. Characters can often be interpreted only with reference to their context. Yet, I would not want to argue that the reading process is essentially different for handwritten than for printed material.

There are many other results which appear to call for this same conclusion. For example, more letters can be apprehended per unit time when a word is presented than when a string of unrelated letters is presented (Huey, 1908/1968). Letter strings formed either deleting a letter of a word or replacing one or two of the letters of the word is often clearly perceived as the original word (Pillsbury, 1897). Even when great care is taken to control for guessing, a letter is more accurately perceived when it is part of a word than when it is among a set of unrelated letters (Reicher, 1969). All of these results appear to argue strongly that letter perceptions are facilitated by being in words. Word-level perceptions effect letter-level perceptions. Here again, the only way that the types of models under consideration can account for these effects is to suppose that partial letter information is somehow preserved and the additional constraints of the word level is brought to bear on the partial letter information.

It is of some interest that these effects can be observed in letter strings which are not words, but which are similar to words in important ways. For example, the more the sequential transition probabilities among letters in a string approximate those of English, the more letters can be perceived per unit time (Miller,

Bruner, & Postman, 1954). Similarly, even when guessing is controlled (as in the Reicher, 1969, experiment), letters embedded in orthographically regular strings are more accurately perceived than those embedded among orthographically irregular strings (McClelland & Johnston, in preparation). Thus, not only is a letter embedded in a word easier to see, but merely being a part of an orthographically well-formed string aids perception virtually as much. This suggests that orthographic knowledge plays a role nearly as strong as lexical knowledge in the perception of strings of letters.

Not only does orthographic structure have a positive effect on the perception of letters embedded in an orthographically regular string, but our apprehension of orthographically irregular strings is often distorted to allow us to perceive the string as being orthographically regular. This point is nicely illustrated in a recent experiment carried out in our laboratory by Albert Stevens. In this experiment subjects were presented with letter strings consisting of two consonants (i.e., an initial consonant cluster designated CC_i) followed by two vowels (a vowel cluster, designated VC) followed by two more consonants (a final consonant cluster CC_f). The initial consonant cluster was constructed from pairs of consonants that can occur at the beginning of English words in only one order (e.g., English words can begin with "pr," but not "rp"). Similarly the vowel cluster used occur as dipthongs in English in one order but not in the other (e.g., "ai" but not "ia"). The final consonant clusters were similarly chosen so that they occur at the end of English words in one order, but not the other (e.g., "ck" but not "kc"). Strings were then constructed in which each letter cluster was either in its legal or illegal order. Table 1 illustrates several examples of the various types of letter strings.

Subjects were given tachistoscopic presentations of the various letter strings and asked to name the letters they observed. Of particular interest are the times when they were presented illegal strings, but made them legal by transposing the letter pair in their reports. Figure 4 illustrates the comparison of interest. The figure compares the percentage of times an illegally ordered letter cluster is

TABLE 1
Examples of Legal and Illegal Letter Strings

| | CC_i | | | |
| | Legal VC | | Illegal VC | |
CC_f	Legal	Illegal	Legal	Illegal
legal	praick	priack	rpaick	rpiack
	stourt	stuort	tsourt	tsuort
illegal	praikc	priakc	rpaikc	rpiakc
	stoutr	stuotr	tsoutr	tsuotr

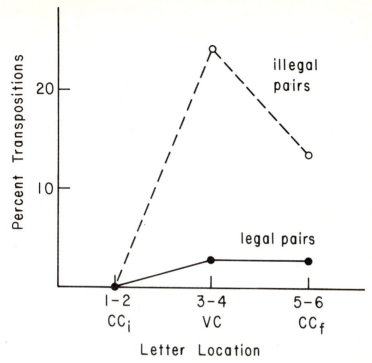

FIG. 4   Transpositions as a function of letter location.

transposed into a legal cluster with the number of times a legal letter cluster is transposed into an illegal one. The results show that although initial consonant clusters are never transposed, illegal vowel clusters are transposed almost 25% of the time as compared to only about 3% transposition for the legal vowel clusters. Similarly final consonant clusters are transposed almost 14% of the time when they are illegal, but only about 3% of the time when they are legal. These results show clearly the effect that orthographic structure has on our perception of letter strings. The perception of a certain letter in a certain position depends on what we perceive in adjacent positions as well as on the sensory evidence we have available about that position in the string.

To summarize, then, it appears that no model which supposes that we first perceive the letters in a stimulus and then put them together into higher-order units can be correct. However, models like the Gough model and the LaBerge–Samuels model can survive such results if they assume that partial information is somehow forwarded to the higher levels of analysis and that the final decision as to which letters were present is delayed until this further processing has been accomplished.

Whereas it is not too difficult to see how, say, the LaBerge–Samuels model could account for the effects of orthographic structure on letter perception, it is somewhat more difficult to see how the effects of syntax and semantics can be mediated within such a model. I now turn to evidence for syntactic effects in reading.

B. Our Perception of Words Depends on the Syntactic Environment in Which We Encounter the Words

Perhaps the best evidence for syntactic effects on the level of word perception comes from an analysis of oral reading errors. The most common error in oral reading is the substitution error — when an incorrect word is simply substituted for the correct one. If syntax had no effect on the perception of words, we would expect that reading errors should be determined by visual similarity and not by part of speech. However, there is a strong tendency for a reading error to be of the same part of speech as the word for which it was substituted. Thus, for example, Kolers (1970) reported that nearly 70% of the substitution errors made by adult readers on geometrically transformed text were of the same part of speech as the correct word. By chance, one would expect only about 18% of the errors should be of the correct part of speech.

In another study, Weber (1970) analyzed reading errors by first graders and found that over 90% of the errors made were grammatically consistent with the sentence to the point of the error. Although it is not clear what percentage to expect under assumptions of random guessing, it is obviously much lower than 90% in most texts. One might argue that these results and those of Kolers occur because words in the same syntactic class are more similar to each other than they are to words outside of that class. It is interesting to note in this regard that in the Weber study, the ungrammatical errors were significantly more similar to the correct word than were the grammatical words—at least an indication that this is a syntactic effect and not a visual one.

In another experiment carried out by Stevens and Rumelhart (1975) with adult readers an oral reading task showed that about 98% of the substitution errors that were recognizable as words were grammatical. Moreover, nearly 80% of the time the substituted words were of the same syntactic class as the class most frequently predicted at that part in a cloze experiment. Once again, it appears that we have a case of grammatical knowledge helping to determine the word read.

In addition, in an important experiment, Miller and Isard (1963) compared perceptibility of spoken words under conditions in which normal syntactic structure was violated with the case in which syntactic structure was intact. They found that many more words could be reported when the sentences were syntactically normal. Although I do not know of a similar study with written materials, it is doubtless that similar results would occur — another case of a higher level of processing determining the perceptibility of units at a lower level.

It is difficult to see exactly how the models under discussion would deal with results such as these. In the Gough model syntactic processing occurs only very late in the processing sequence – after information has entered short-term memory. It seems unlikely that he would want to assume that partial information is preserved that far in the process. It is not clear just where syntax should be put in the LaBerge–Samuels model. It is particularly difficult to represent productive syntactic rules of the sort linguists suggest in the LaBerge–Samuels formalism. As I will discuss subsequently, it would appear to be essential to be able to represent systems of rules to account for such results.

C. Our Perception of Words Depends on the Semantic Environment in Which We Encounter the Words

It is even more difficult to incorporate a mechanism for semantic effects on the word recognition process into a purely bottom-up model than it is to incorporate a mechanism for syntactic effects. There have recently been a number of studies which provide very nice demonstrations of semantic effects on word recognition.

In a series of experiments Meyer, Schvaneveldt, and Ruddy (Meyer & Schvaneveldt, 1971; Meyer, Schvaneveldt, & Ruddy, 1972; Meyer, Schvaneveldt, & Ruddy, 1974; Ruddy, Meyer, & Schvaneveldt, 1973; Schvaneveldt & Meyer, 1973) have reported convincing evidence of semantic effects on word recognition. The basic procedure in these experiments involved measuring reaction times to come to a lexical decision about a pair of words. The basic result is that the decision can be made much faster when the pair of words are semantically related (such as BREAD–BUTTER or DOCTOR–NURSE) than when they are unrelated (such as BREAD–DOCTOR and NURSE–BUTTER). The most plausible account of these results would seem to be that the process of perceiving the first word somehow allows us to process the second word more quickly just in case it is a semantically related word. Thus, we again have the processing at the semantic level modifying our processing at the word level.

In a series of experiments recently carried out in our laboratory Graboi (1974) demonstrated this same general effect using quite a different method. In one of his experiments Graboi employed a variation of Neisser's search procedure. First subjects were trained to search for occurrence of any one of five target words among a list of semantically unrelated nontargets. Half of the subjects searched for any one of the words labeled Experimental Target Set (see Table 2) scattered among lists constructed from the Unassociated Nontargets. The other half of the subjects searched for the words labeled Control Target Set against the same background. Notice that neither target set is semantically related to the nontarget background in which it is searched for. After 14 hours of training, the experimental group was searching their lists at a rate of 182.2 msec per word. The control group scanned at a rate of 180.0 msec per word. On the fifteenth hour of practice, the background lists were changed. Both groups now search for their targets against the Associated Nontarget background. Now the experi-

TABLE 2

Alternative Stimuli in the Target and Nontarget Sets

A. Associated Nontargets

WORM CHICK NESTS ROBIN CHIRP WINGS FLY EAGLE PARROT SONG
BLACK GRAY PURPLE BROWN GOLD BLUE RED YELLOW GREEN PAINT
SAVE SPEND COINS DIME BANK SILVER DOLLAR CASH PENNY PEARL
BOOKS SCHOOL READ CLASS WRITE TEACH EXAM NOTES GRADE STUDY
ORANGE NUTS GRAPE SWEET PLUM APPLE PEACH PEAR FRESH LEMON

B. Unassociated Nontargets

HUG PEN SLEEP NIGHT BRIDGE STAPLE LAMP RULER LEADER ROAR
SUNNY PLACE CORNER ALBUM ABOUT RATE WEEK POINT SWITCH ANKLE
TOWN DIAL SPOON TOWEL SHEET STOVE CRUST BRUSH GLASS ROAD
WHICH AFTER PASS STORY SIGN CHURCH MURAL PHONE BOOTH CARD
STREET MOTOR RADIO KNOB PLUG DRIVE LINE TASK PRINT SHIFT

Experiment-
al target
set

BIRD :
COLOR :
MONEY :
LEARN :
FRUIT :

Control
target
set

: ROCK
: CHAIR
: HOUSE
: SPORT
: CLOUD

mental group was searching for its targets against a background of nontargets, all semantically associated with the target set. The control group was also switched, but the Associated Nontargets were not semantically related to the control target set. After the change we find that the control group scans against the new background at about the same rate as they scanned the old one — 179 msec per word scanned. The experimental group, however, scanning through words semantically related to the target set was slowed to a rate of 197.4 msec per word.

One might suppose that the subjects in the experimental group were just surprised to see related words in the background and a few long pauses accounted for the entire difference. However, on this account one would expect the difference soon to disappear. But this did not happen. Through five additional hours of searching (they searched through 2000 words during one hour session) the difference between the control and experimental subjects remained at about 20 msec per word. It would thus appear that even when searching for particular words our expectations are based on meaning as well as visual form.

Using still another experimental procedure, Tulving and Gold (1963) and Tulving, Mandler, and Baumal (1964) both found that the prior presentation of a sentence context lowers the threshold at which a tachistoscopically presented word can be recognized.

Again we have a case of a higher level of processing (meaning) apparently effecting our ability to process at a lower level (the word level). Notice, moreover, that semantic relatedness can either make our processing more efficient (as with the Meyer *et al.* (1974) and Tulving & Gold (1963) experiments) or it can interfere with our processing (as with the Graboi (1974) experiment). It is again difficult to see how a strictly bottom-up, stage-by-stage processing model can account for results such as these.

D. Our Perception of Syntax Depends on the Semantic Context in Which the String Appears

Although neither Gough nor LaBerge and Samuels have attempted to specify their models much beyond the level of words, a complete model of reading must, of course, account for the way semantics effects our apprehension of the syntax of a sentence we are reading. Experiments at this level are few and far between, but there are numerous examples which seem rather compelling on this general point.

Perhaps the most commonly observed effect of this sort involves the semantic disambiguation of syntactically ambiguous sentences. Consider the following sentences:

(1) a. They are eating apples.

    b. The children are eating apples.

    c. The juicy red ones are eating apples.

At the syntactic level all three sentences allow for at least two readings:

1. The reading in which the thing referred to by the first noun phrase is performing the act of eating some apples.
2. The reading in which the things referred to by the first noun phrase is said to be a member of the class of "eating apples."

However, at a semantic level only the first one remains ambiguous – even it would be disambiguated if we had some notion as to the referent of *they*.

Schank (1973) has given a number of similar examples. Consider, for example:

(2) a. I saw the Grand Canyon flying to New York.

   b. I saw the Grand Canyon *while I was* flying to New York.

   c. I saw the Grand Canyon *which was* flying to New York.

Most readers immediately interpret Sentence (2a) as meaning the same as (2b) rather than Sentence (2c) simply on the grounds that it is semantically anomalous to imagine the Grand Canyon actually flying. On the other hand Sentence (3a) is ordinarily interpreted to mean the same as Sentence (3c) rather than Sentence (3b):

(3) a. I saw the cattle grazing in the field.

   b. I saw the cattle *while I was* grazing in the field.

   c. I saw the cattle *that were* grazing in the field.

In Examples (1), (2) and (3) semantics play the determining role as to which surface structure we apprehend. Thus, just as orthographic structure effects our ability to perceive letters and syntax and semantics effects our perception of words, so too does semantics effect our apprehension of syntax.

E. Our Interpretation of the Meaning of What We Read Depends on the General Context in Which We Encounter the Text

Just as the appropriate interpretation of our ambiguous symbol, *ƚʊ* , was determined by the sentence in which it was embedded, so too it often happens that the *meaning* of a word is dependent on the words surrounding it. Consider, for example, the following sentences:

(4) a. The statistician could be certain that the difference was significant *since all of the figures on the right hand side of the table were larger than any of those on the left.*

   b. The craftsman was certainly justified in charging more for the carvings on the right *since all of the figures on the right hand side of the table were larger than any of those on the left.*

Here our interpretation of the second clause is thus quite different depending on the nature of the first clause. In Sentence (4a) for example, the term *figure* is readily interpreted as being a number, the term *table* a place for writing numbers, and the relation *larger* can properly be interpreted to mean >. In Sentence (4b) on the other hand, the term *figure* presumably refers to a small statue, the term *table* refers to a physical object with a flat top used for setting things on, and the relation *larger* clearly means something like *of greater volume*. Here we have a case in which no determination about the meaning of these individual words can be made without consideration of the entire sentence. Thus, no decision can be made about the meaning of a word without consideration of the meaning of the entire sentence in which the word appears.

Not only is the interpretation of individual words dependent on the sentential context in which they are found, but the meaning of entire sentences are dependent on the general context in which they appear. The following example from Bransford and Johnson (1973) is a case in point:

(5)   Watching a Peace March from the 40th Floor

The view was breathtaking. From the window one could see the crowd below. Everything looked extremely small from such a distance, but the colorful costumes could still be seen. Everyone seemed to be moving in the same direction in an orderly fashion and there seemed to be little children as well as adults. The landing was gentle, and luckily the atmosphere was such that so special suits had to be worn. At first there was a great deal of activity. Later, when the speeches started, the crowd quieted down. The man with the television camera took many shots of the setting and the crowd. Everyone was very friendly and seemed glad when the music started. (p. 412)

In this passage, the sentence beginning "The landing was gentle . . ." appears to make no sense. No clear meaning can be assigned to it in this context. As such, when subjects are given the passage and later asked to recall it very few subjects remembered the anomalous sentence. On the other hand, when the passage was entitled *A Space Trip to an Inhabited Planet* the entire passage was given quite a different interpretation. In this case the anomalous sentence fits into the general interpretation of the paragraph very well. Subjects given the *Space Trip* title recalled the critical sentence three times as often as those given the *Peace March* title. Many other examples could be given. The dependence of meaning on context would appear to be the norm rather than the exception in reading.

To summarize, these results taken together appear to support the view that our apprehension of information at one level of analysis can often depend on our apprehension of information at a higher level. How can this be? Surely we cannot first perceive the meaning of what we read and only later discover what the sentences, words or letters were that mediated the meaning. To paraphrase a remark attributed to Gough (cited in Brewer, 1972): It is difficult to "see how the syntax [or semantics for that matter] can go out and mess around with the print" (p. 360). The problem I believe, arises from the linear stage formalism that has served so well. The answer, I suspect, comes by presuming that all of these knowledge sources apply simultaneously and that our perceptions are the product of the simultaneous interactions among all of them.

IV. AN INTERACTIVE MODEL

Perhaps the most natural information-processing representation of the theoretical ideas suggested in the previous section is illustrated in Fig. 5. The figure illustrates the assumption that graphemic information enters the system and is registered in a visual information store (VIS). A feature extraction device is then assumed to operate on this information extracting the critical features from the VIS. These features serve as the sensory input to a pattern synthesizer. In addition to this sensory information, the pattern synthesizer has available nonsensory information about the orthographic structure of the language (including information about the probability of various strings of characters), information about lexical items in the language, information about the syntactic possibilities (and probabilities), information about the semantics of the language and information about the current contextual situation (pragmatic information). The pattern synthesizer, then, uses all of this information to produce a "most probable interpretation" of the graphemic input. Thus, all of the various sources of knowledge, both sensory and nonsensory, come together at one place and the reading process is the product of the simultaneous joint application of all the knowledge sources.

Although the model previously outlined may, in fact, be an accurate representation of the reading process, it is of very little help as a model of reading. It is one thing to suggest that all of these different information sources interact (as many writers have), but quite another to specify a psychologically plausible hypothesis about how they interact. It is thus clear why serious theorists who

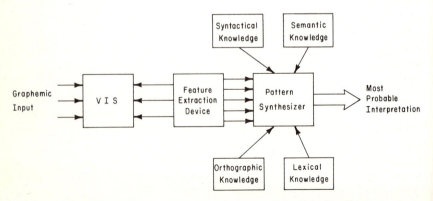

FIG. 5   A stage representation of an interactive model of reading.

have attempted to develop detailed models of the reading process (e.g., Gough, 1972; LaBerge & Samuels, 1974) have stayed away from a formulation of the sort illustrated in Fig. 5. All that is interesting in the model takes place in the box labeled "Pattern Synthesizer." The flow chart does little more than list the relevant variables. We need a representation for the operation of the pattern synthesizer itself. To represent that, we must develop a means of representing the operation of a set of parallel interacting processes.

Flow charts are best suited to represent the simple serial flow of information. They are badly suited for the representation of a set of parallel highly interactive processes. However, with the advent of the parallel computer (at least as a conceptual device), computer scientists have begun to develop formalisms for the representation of parallel processes. It is interesting that the major problem in each case seems to have been the representation of the lines of communication among the otherwise independent processes.

Of the several different systems of communication that have been proposed, two were developed in the context of language processing by computer and seem to be most promising as a formalism for the development of a reading model. One of these was developed by Kaplan (1973) and is called the General Syntactic Processor (GSP). The second was developed by Reddy and his associates at Carnegie – Mellon University (see Lesser, Fennell, Erman, & Reddy, 1974) as an environment for a speech understanding program. This system is called HEARSAY II. These two systems have a good deal in common and solve the communication problem in much the same way – namely, both systems consist of sets of totally independent asynchronous processes which communicate by means of a global, highly structured data storage device. In Kaplan's system the communication center is called a *chart,* in the HEARSAY system it is called a *blackboard.* I use the more neutral term *message center* in my development below. This development is most closely related to the HEARSAY system and could well be considered as an application of the HEARSAY model to reading. However, I also draw on aspects of GSP and the model as I develop it has the Rumelhart and Siple (1974) model of word recognition as a special case.

Following HEARSAY, the model can be characterized as consisting of a set of independent *knowledge sources.* (These knowledge sources correspond to the sources of input to the pattern synthesizer in Fig. 5.) Each knowledge source contains specialized knowledge about some aspect of the reading process. The message center keeps a running list of hypotheses about the nature of the input string. Each knowledge source constantly scans the message center for the appearance of hypotheses relevant to its own sphere of knowledge. Whenever such a hypothesis enters the message center the knowledge source in question evaluates the hypothesis in light of its own specialized knowledge. As a result of its analysis, the hypothesis may be confirmed, disconfirmed, and removed from the message center, or a new hypothesis can be added to the message center. This process continues until some decision can be reached. At that point the most probable hypothesis is determined to be the correct one. To facilitate the process, the message center is highly structured so that the knowledge sources know exactly where to find relevant hypotheses and so that dependencies among hypotheses are easily determined.

A. The Message Center

The message center can be represented as a three-dimensional space; one dimension representing the position along the line of text, one dimension representing the level of the hypothesis (word level, letter level, phrase level, etc.), and one dimension representing alternative hypotheses at the same level. Associated with each hypothesis is a running estimate of the probability that it is the correct hypothesis. Moreover, hypotheses at each level may have pointers to hypotheses at higher or lower levels on which they are dependent. Thus, for example, the hypothesis that the first word in a string is the word THE is supported by the hypothesis that the first letter of the string is "T" and supports the hypothesis that the string begins with a noun phrase. Figure 6 illustrates a two-dimensional slice of the message center at some point during the reading of the phrase, THE

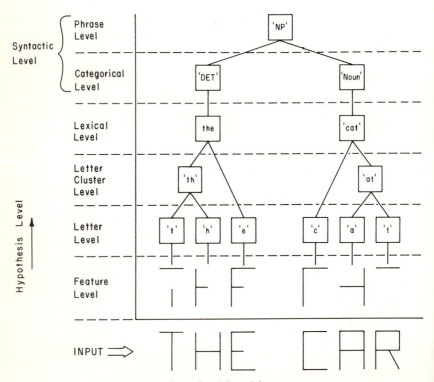

FIG. 6   A two-dimensional slice of the message center.

CAR. The figure illustrates hypotheses at five different levels (feature level, letter level, letter-cluster level, lexical level, and syntactic level). The diagram is only a two-dimensional slice inasmuch as no alternative hypotheses are illustrated. In practice, of course, many alternative hypotheses would be considered and evaluated in the course of reading this phrase. It should be pointed out that the tree-like structure should not be taken to mean that the tree was constructed either from a purely bottom-up process (starting with the features, then hypothesizing the letters, then the letter clusters, etc.), nor from a purely top-down analysis (starting with a view that we have a noun phrase and that noun phrases are made up of determiners followed by nouns, etc.). Rather, the hypotheses can be generated at any level. If it is likely that a line begins with a noun phrase, then we postulate a noun phrase and look for evidence. If we see features that suggest a "t" as the first letter we postulate a "t" in the first position and continue processing. If we later have to reject either or both of these hypotheses little is lost. The system makes the best guesses and checks out their implications. If these guesses are wrong it will take a bit longer, but the system will eventually find some hypotheses at some level that it can accept.

1. An Example

To illustrate the operation of the system, consider the following experimental procedure. A subject is presented with a picture (e.g., Fig. 7) and allowed to

FIG. 7   A scene. (Figure provided by Jean Mandler.)

view it for a few seconds. Then he is given a tachistoscopic presentation of a noun phrase which he knows will refer to one of the objects in the picture. His job is to decide which object was referred to. This experimental procedure is designed to simulate the process of reading a phrase for meaning. (An experimental procedure of this sort is currently under development in our laboratory.) I will illustrate the current model by showing the changes we might expect in the message center as the phrase THE CAR is read after viewing Fig. 7.

Figure 8 shows the message center at an early point in the processing of this phrase. The subject knows from the instructions of the experiment that the phrase will refer to some object in the picture. Thus, the semantic-level "object"

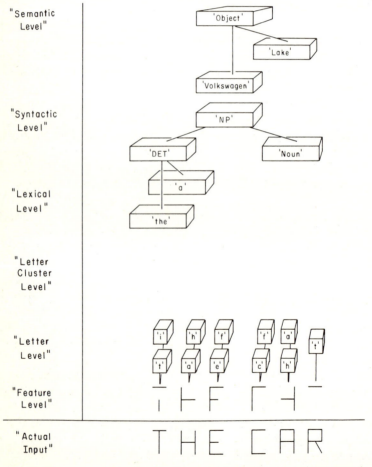

FIG. 8   The message center shortly after processing has begun on "THE CAR."

hypothesis can be entered and assigned a high likelihood value from the start. Moreover, through looking at the picture and perceiving certain aspects of it as salient, the subject will develop expectations as to the probable referent of the phrase. In this example, I have assumed that the subject noticed and set up special expectations as to the probable referent of the phrase. In this case, I have assumed that the subject set up special expectations for a phrase referring to *the lake* or to *the Volkswagen.*

Similarly, at the syntactic level, the subject can be quite certain that the input will form a noun phrase. Thus, the hypothesis "NP" is entered into the message center and assigned a high value. Noun phrases have a rather characteristic structure. About 25% of the time they begin with a determiner (DET). Thus, in the example, I have assumed that the hypothesis that the first word was a determiner was entered. Similarly, we can expect the second word of a noun phrase to be a noun about 20% of the time. Thus, I have entered the hypothesis that the second word is a noun. Now, in the case where the first word is a determiner, we could expect it to be the word "the" about 60% of the time and the word "a" about 20%. Thus, I have assumed that these two hypotheses have also been entered.

As all of these hypotheses are being entered in top-down fashion, hypotheses at the letter level are also being entered bottom-up on the basis of featural information. In the example, I have assumed that for each of the first five letter positions the two most promising letter possibilities were entered as hypotheses. For the sixth letter position, which contains very little featural information, I have assumed that only its most likely letter hypothesis has been entered.

Figure 9 illustrates the state of the message center at a later point in the processing. In the meantime, the lexical hypothesis "a" has led to a letter hypothesis which was then tested against the featural information and rejected. The hypothesization of an initial "t" has led to the hypothesization of an initial "th" at the letter cluster level — a hypothesis which is given added validity by the possible "h" in the second position. The lexical-level hypothesis of the word "the" has also led to the hypothesization of the letter cluster "th" followed by the letter "e." The prior existence of these hypotheses generated from the bottom up has led to a mutual strengthening of all of the hypotheses in question and a resultant weakening of the alternative letter hypotheses at the first three letter positions.

While this processing was taking place, lexical hypotheses were generated from the semantic level as possible nouns. In this instance I have assumed that the semantic hypothesis "lake" has led to the lexical hypothesis that the word "lake" was in the string and that the semantic hypothesis "Volkswagen" has led to the lexical hypothesis "Volkswagen" and to the lexical hypothesis "car." Meanwhile, the letter hypotheses have led to alternative letter cluster hypotheses "ch" and "at."

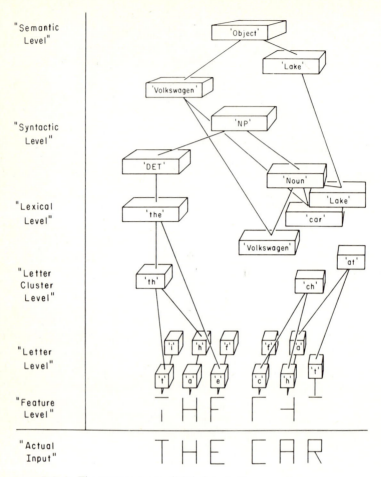

FIG. 9   The message center slightly later in the processing sequence.

Figure 10 illustrates the state of the message center at a still later point in the processing of the input. By this point the hypothesis that the first word is "the" has reached a sufficient value that further processing has ceased. No new hypotheses have been generated about the first word. On the other hand, lexical hypotheses on the second word have proliferated. The existence of the letter hypothesis "c" followed by the letter cluster hypothesis "at" has led to a hypothesization of the lexical item "cat." Similarly, the letter hypothesis "f" followed by "at" has led to hypothesizing the lexical item "fat." The lexical hypothesis "cat" is consistent with the "noun" hypothesis, thus strengthening the view that the second word is a noun. At the same time, the lexical

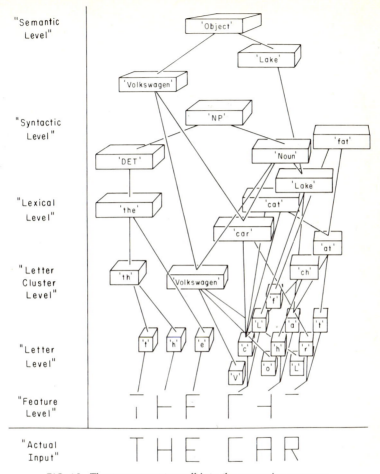

FIG. 10 The message center well into the processing sequence.

hypotheses "lake," "Volkswagen" and "car" have either strengthened existing letter hypotheses or have caused new ones to be generated. Notice, in particular, that the prior existence of the letter hypotheses "c" and "a" strengthened the semantically derived lexical hypothesis "car" which in turn strengthened the letter hypothesis "r" – even though the letter hypothesis "r" has not yet been evaluated in light of the featural information in the final position.

Finally, Fig. 11 illustrates a state of processing after the letter hypotheses have been tested against the featural information. At this point, only three lexical hypotheses for the second word remain – "fat," "cat," and "car." The lexical hypothesis "fat" has led to the syntactic hypothesis that the second word is an

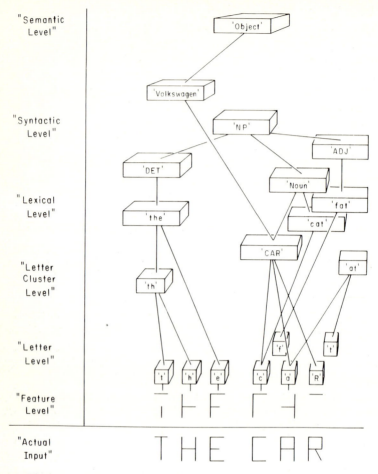

FIG. 11 The message center near the end of processing. At this point the semantics of the input has been pretty well determined.

adjective (ADJ) and the lexical hypothesis "cat" has led to the semantic level hypothesis that there should be a cat in the picture. Meanwhile, the semantic hypothesis "Volkswagen" has been strengthened by the finding that the final featural information is consistent with the hypothesis that the last letter is an "r." At this point the semantic hypothesis "Volkswagen" is probably high enough to lead to a response. If not, a test of the semantic hypothesis "cat" will lead to the rejection of that hypothesis and the consequent strengthening of the "Volkswagen" hypothesis and thus the lexical hypothesis "car" and the letter level hypotheses "c," "a," and "r."

It should be clear from this example how, in principle at least, one could build a model of reading that would actually employ constraints from all levels concurrently in the process of constructing an interpretation of an input string. Of course, this example is a long way from the specification of such a model. All I have illustrated here is the nature of the message center and how it is structured to facilitate communication among processes acting at various levels. Before a concrete model of reading can be specified, the nature of the various knowledge sources must be specified as well. I now turn to a brief discussion of the operation of the various knowledge sources.

B. The Knowledge Sources

I do not yet have a detailed model of the operation of all the knowledge sources. However, I do have ideas about a number of them and will now discuss them:

1. *Featural knowledge:* At this level, I am assuming that features are extracted according to the assumptions of the Rumelhart and Siple (1974) model. More-over, I am assuming that these critical features are the basic level of processing. In a tachistoscopic experiment, all decisions must be made with respect to the set of features extracted during and shortly after the exposure. In free-reading situations the reader can go back and get more featural information if no hypothesis gets a sufficiently high rating or if some hypothesis does get a high rating at one point and is later rejected. Such occasions probably account for regressions in eye movements.

2. *Letter-level knowledge:* This knowledge source scans the feature inputs and whenever it finds a close match to a known letter, it posits a letter hypothesis. In addition, whenever a letter hypothesis appears from a higher level, this knowledge source evaluates that hypothesis against the feature information. In addition to information about letters in various fonts, the letter-level knowledge source presumably takes into account the probabilities of letters in the language. Thus, relatively more featural evidence would be necessary to postulate a "z" or "q" than an "e" or a "t."

3. *Letter-cluster knowledge:* This knowledge source scans the incoming letter-level hypotheses looking for letter sequences that are likely and form units in the language, or single letters which are frequently followed or preceeded by another letter (e.g., as "q" is frequently followed by "u"). In either case a letter cluster is postulated. In the latter case a letter level hypothesis is also introduced. (That is, if a "q" is found a "qu" is postulated at the letter-cluster level and a "u" is postulated at the letter level.) The value associated with any of these hypotheses depends on the values of the letter-level information on which it is based and on the frequency of such clusters in the language. In addition, the letter cluster knowledge source looks for the introduction of letter cluster hypotheses from

the lexical level. Whenever it finds these it evaluates them by proposing the appropriate letter level hypotheses. For this knowledge source, as with all others, the most probable hypotheses that are unsupported from the following or that support no higher-level hypotheses are evaluated first.

4. *Lexical-level knowledge:* The lexical-level knowledge source operates in exactly the same way as the other knowledge sources. It scans the letter cluster and letter hypotheses for letter sequences which form lexical items, or which are close to lexical items. When it finds such information it posits the appropriate lexical-level hypotheses and any additional letter-cluster or letter-level hypotheses. When evaluating the goodness of any hypothesis it takes into account the goodness of the evidence on which it is based and the a priori frequency of that item in the language. In addition, whenever a lexical item is postulated from either the semantic or syntactic levels this knowledge source evaluates that hypothesis by postulating those letter-cluster and letter hypotheses that are not yet present. Those letter and letter-cluster hypotheses that are present are strengthened due to the convergence of lines of evidence. Other alternatives without such convergent information are relatively weakened.

5. *Syntactic knowledge:* Like all of the other knowledge sources this knowledge source is designed to operate in both a bottom-up and top-down mode. Thus, whenever a lexical hypothesis is suggested, one or more syntactic category hypothesis is entered into the message center. In general, not all syntactic category hypotheses consistent with the lexical form would be expected. Instead, those categories which are most probable, given that lexical item, would be entered first. Similarly, sequences of lexical category hypotheses would be scanned looking for phrase possibilities, etc. At the same time, the syntactic knowledge source would have the capacity to operate in a top-down fashion. Thus, for example, whenever a noun-phrase hypothesis was entered, the syntactic knowledge source would establish, say a determiner, syntactic-category hypothesis which in turn might initiate lexical-level hypotheses of determiner words like "a" and "the." Following Kaplan's (1973) GSP I assume that this top-down portion of the syntactic knowledge source would be well represented by an Augmented Transition Network (ATN) parser. (See Stevens & Rumelhart, 1975, for an application of an ATN to reading data.) Like all other levels, the syntactic hypotheses are given values dependent on the goodness of the evidence (or prior probabilities) of the hypotheses on which they are based. Moreover, a convergence of top-down and bottom-up hypotheses strengthens both.

6. *Semantic-level knowledge:* This is perhaps the most difficult level to characterize. Nevertheless, I assume that its operation is essentially the same as the others. Whenever strong lexical hypotheses occur, this knowledge source must have the ability to look for semantic-level correlates to evaluate the plausibility of the hypothesis (at both the lexical and syntactic levels). Moreover, it must be able to develop hypotheses about the content of the input and generate lexical-level hypotheses as possible representations of this. The experimental procedure

discussed in the previous section was designed as an attempt to reduce the complexity of the semantic component by supposing a relatively simple referential semantics.

Still, of course, after having outlined the functional characteristics of the various knowledge sources I am still far from the quantitative model I have in mind. However, it would appear that a HEARSAY type model such as this offers promise as a framework for the development of serious models of reading which nevertheless assumes a highly interactive parallel processing system.

C. A Mathematical Model of Hypothesis Evaluation

In this section I will specify in somewhat more detail the nature of the hypothesis evaluation process I envision. Figure 12 illustrates a simplified version of the message center from the primary example. This figure differs somewhat in format from the previous figures of this type in order to make clearer the sequential dependencies among hypotheses at the same level. Thus, the fact that an NP consists of a DET and NOUN and that the word "cat" consists of C + A + T is illustrated by the arrows connecting those constituents at the same level. Moreover, the dependency arrows have been drawn to only the left-hand

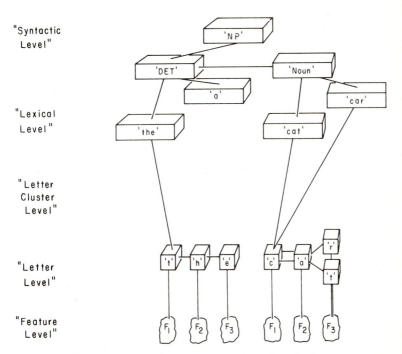

FIG. 12   An illustration of the relations among the hypotheses in the message center.

member of such hypothesis sequences. In a sense, as we shall see below, the left-hand member is representing the entire sequence of hypotheses.

There are four different types of dependency relationships among hypotheses in this model. These types are illustrated in the figure. First, an hypothesis may have one or more *daughter* hypotheses. A daughter hypothesis is one at a lower level which is connected directly to a higher-level hypothesis. In the figure the hypothesis, "DET" has two daughter hypotheses: "the" and "a." The hypothesis "the" has a single daughter, "t." An hypothesis may have any number of daughters. Each daughter is an alternative way in which the higher hypothesis can be realized. Thus, "the" and "a" are alternative ways in which "DET" can be realized. For any hypothesis, h_i, I shall use the symbol D_i to designate its set of daughters.

The reciprocal relationship to daughter is *parent*. Any hypothesis may have one or more parent hypotheses. A parent hypothesis is one to which an hypothesis can lend direct support. Thus, in the figure "NOUN" is a parent of both "car" and "cat." Similarly, the letter hypothesis "c" has two different parents "car" and "cat." Only hypotheses which are at the left most position of a sequence of hypotheses may have parents. Thus, the hypothesis "NOUN" has no parent. For each hypothesis, h_i, I shall designate the set of parents P_i.

In addition to parents and daughters, hypotheses may have *sisters*. Sisters are hypotheses in a sequence which either follow or precede a particular hypothesis at the same level. Sisters are not alternatives, but are consistent possibilities of the same level. There are two sorts of sister hypotheses; *right sisters* and *left sisters*. Right sisters are hypotheses that follow a given hypothesis in a sequence of hypotheses. Thus, "NOUN" would be a right sister of "DET" and "r" and "t" are right sisters of the letter-level hypothesis "a." I designate the set of right sisters of h_i as R_i. Left sisters are those hypotheses which precede a given hypothesis in a string of hypotheses. Although it is possible for an hypothesis to have more than one left sister, no cases of this are illustrated in the figure. I designate the set of left sisters of hypothesis h_i as L_i.

We are now in a position to develop a measure for evaluating hypotheses. The measure that I will propose is essentially the Bayesian probability that the hypothesis is true given the evidence at hand. The evidence favoring a particular hypothesis can be broken down into two parts: contextual evidence, dependent only on sister and parent hypotheses, and direct evidence dependent solely on the evidence derived from daughter hypotheses and ultimately featural evidence. Equation (1) illustrates the assumed multiplicative relationship among these two kinds of evidence:

$$s_i = v_i \cdot \beta_i.^4 \tag{1}$$

---

[4] This is the same relationship between these two sorts of evidence assumed by Luce (1959) and which is incorporated into the Rumelhart and Siple (1974) model for word recognition.

where s_i is the overall strength of the hypothesis h_i, v_i is a measure of the direct evidence for h_i, and β_i is a measure of the contextual evidence for h_i. Now, we can define the values of v_i and β_i in terms of the parents, and sisters of h_i. Equation (2) gives the value of the contextual strength of h_i:

$$\beta_i = \begin{cases} \Pr(h_i) & P_i = L_i = \phi \\ \sum_{s_k} \dfrac{\cdot\Pr(h_i|h_k)}{v_i} & \text{otherwise,} \end{cases} \tag{2}$$

where the sum is over all $h_k \epsilon P_i$ or L_i. Thus, when h_i has no parents or left sisters, its contextual strength is given by its a priori probability. Otherwise, its contextual strength is given by the sum, over all of its left sisters and parents of the strength of the left sister or parent, h_k, times the conditional probability of the hypothesis given h_k. The sum is then divided by its own direct strength so that its direct strength will not contribute to its contextual strength (since as we shall see, its own direct strength contributes to the strength of its parents and left sisters and is represented multiplicatively in s_k).

Direct evidence for an hypothesis comes only from its daughters. Equation (3) gives the direct evidence for an hypothesis as a function of a value associated with its daughters:

$$v_i = \begin{cases} \sum C_{ik} \cdot \Pr(h_k|h_i) & D_i \neq \phi \\ 1 & \text{otherwise} \end{cases} \tag{3}$$

where the sum is over all $h_k \epsilon D_i$ and where C_{ik} is the *cumulative evidence* for hypothesis h_i associated with the sequence of hypotheses whose left most member is the daughter h_k. Thus, in the diagram, the direct evidence for "car" is determined jointly by the direct evidence for "c," for "a" and for "r." The value of $C_{i,k}$ is given by the following equation:

$$C_{i,k} = \begin{cases} v_k & R_k = \phi \\ \sum_j v_k \cdot C_{i,j} \cdot \Pr(h_j|h_i, h_k) & \text{otherwise} \end{cases} \tag{4}$$

where the sum is over all $h_j \epsilon R_k$. Thus, the cumulative evidence for hypothesis h_i associated with hypothesis h_k is determined by the product of the direct evidence for h_k and the cumulative evidence for its right sister. If its probable right sisters are very strong then the cumulative evidence is very strong and thus offers good support to its parent. Otherwise, it offers support against its parent.

Finally, we must give special attention to the first level hypotheses associated with featural level inputs. For any letter hypothesis h_i featural level inputs have cumulative values of $C_{i,F}$ given by:

$$C_{i,F} = [\Pr(F)]^{-1} \tag{5}$$

where F is the set of features observed in that location. This, in effect, is a normalizer designed to keep the strengths in the 0 to 1 range.

The equations (1)–(5) define a system of evaluation which makes near optimal use of the information available at any given point in time. Whenever a new hypothesis is postulated and a new connection is drawn, new values must be computed for the entire set of hypotheses. Resources can be allotted to the knowledge sources based upon their momentary evaluations. Effort can be focused on generating hypotheses from the top down whenever we have hypotheses with strong contextual strengths and few daughter hypotheses. Effort can be focused on the generation of hypotheses from the bottom up whenever there is strong direct evidence and few parents. Moreover, the strength values can be signals to stop processing and accept an hypothesis. When some criterion strength-value is obtained an hypothesis can be accepted and no further processing need be required. Then resources can be siphoned to other more critical areas.

Of course specifying equations such as these does not fully specify our model. We must specify all of the knowledge sources and how they postulate hypotheses. They do, I feel, illustrate the model under consideration can be quantified and can generate specific predictions — in spite of the enormous complexity of a highly interactive system.

ACKNOWLEDGMENTS

Research support was provided by grant NS 07454 from the National Institute of Health.

REFERENCES

Bransford, J. D., & Johnson, M. K. Considerations of some problems of comprehension. In W. G. Chase (Ed.), *Visual information processing.* New York: Academic Press, 1973.

Brewer, W. F. Is reading a letter-by-letter process? In J. F. Kavanagh & I. G. Mattingly (Eds.), *Language by eye and ear.* Cambridge, Mass.: MIT Press, 1972.

Gough, P. B. One second of reading. In J. F. Kavanagh & I. G. Mattingly (Eds.), *Language by eye and ear.* Cambridge, Mass.: MIT Press, 1972.

Graboi, D. Physical shape, practice and meaning in visual search. Unpublished doctoral dissertation, University of California, San Diego, 1974.

Huey, E. B. The psychology and pedagogy of reading. Cambridge, Mass.: MIT Press, 1968. (Originally published 1908.)

Kaplan, R. M. A general syntactic processor. In R. Rustin (Ed.), *Natural language processing.* New York: Algorithmics Press, 1973.

Kolers, P. A. Three stages in reading. In H. Levin & J. T. Williams (Eds.), *Basic studies in reading.* New York: Basic Books, 1970.

LaBerge, D., & Samuels, S. J. Toward a theory of automatic information processing in reading. *Cognitive Psychology,* 1974, **6**, 293–323.

Lesser, V. R., Fennell, R. D., Erman, L. D., & Reddy, D. R. *Organization of the HEARSAY II speech understanding system.* (Working papers in Speech Recognition III.) Pittsburgh, Pa. Carnegie-Mellon University, 1974. Pp. 11–21.

Luce, R. D. *Individual choice behavior.* New York: Wiley, 1959.

McClelland, J. L., & Johnston, J. C. The role of familiar units in word perception. Manuscript in preparation.

Meyer, D. E., & Schvaneveldt, R. W. Facilitation in recognizing pairs of words: Evidence of a dependence between retrieval operations. *Journal of Experimental Psychology,* 1971, **90,** 227–234.

Meyer, D. E., Schvaneveldt, R. W., & Ruddy, M. G. Activation of lexical memory. Paper presented at the meeting of the Psychonomic Society, St. Louis, November, 1972.

Meyer, D. E., Schvaneveldt, R. W., & Ruddy, M. G. Functions of phonemic and graphemic codes in visual word recognition. *Memory & Cognition,* 1974, **2,** 309–321.

Miller, G. A., Bruner, J. S., & Postman, L. Familiarity of letter sequences and tachistoscopic identification. *Journal of Genetic Psychology,* 1954, **50,** 129–139.

Miller, G. A., & Isard, S. Some perceptual consequences of linguistic rules. *Journal of Verbal Learning and Verbal Behavior,* 1963, **2,** 217–228.

Nash-Weber, B. The role of semantics in automatic speech understanding. In D. G. Bobrow & A. Collins (Eds.), *Representation and understanding.* New York: Academic Press, 1975.

Pillsbury, W. B. A study in apperception. *American Journal of Psychology,* 1897, **8,** 315–393.

Reicher, G. M. Perceptual recognition as a function of meaningfulness of stimulus material. *Journal of Experimental Psychology,* 1969, **81,** 274–280.

Ruddy, M. G., Meyer, D. E., & Schvaneveldt, R. W. Context effects on phonemic encoding in visual word recognition. Paper read at the meeting of the Midwestern Psychological Association, Chicago, May 1973.

Rumelhart, D. E., & Siple, P. Process of recognizing tachistoscopically presented words. *Psychological Review,* 1974, **81,** 99–118.

Schank, R. C. Identification of conceptualizations underlying natural language. In R. C. Schank & K. M. Colby (Eds.), *Computer models of thought and language.* San Francisco: Freeman, 1973.

Schvaneveldt, R. W., & Meyer, D. E. Retrieval and comparison processes in semantic memory. In S. Kornblum (Ed.), *Attention and performance IV.* New York: Academic Press, 1973.

Stevens, A. L., & Rumelhart, D. E. Errors in reading: Analysis using an augmented network model of grammar. In D. A. Norman, D. E. Rumelhart, & the LNR Research Group, *Explorations in cognition.* San Francisco: Freeman, 1975.

Tulving, E., & Gold, C. Stimulus information and contextual information as determinants of tachistoscopic recognition of words. *Journal of Experimental Psychology,* 1963, **66,** 319–327.

Tulving, E., Mandler, G., & Baumal, R. Interaction of two sources of information in tachistoscopic word recognition. *Canadian Journal of Psychology,* 1964, **18,** 62–71.

Weber, R. M. First graders use of grammatical context in reading. In H. Levin & J. T. Williams (Eds.), *Basic studies in reading.* New York: Basic Books, 1970.

Part V

MEMORY ORGANIZATION AND RETRIEVAL

28
Does Memory Scanning Involve Implicit Speech?[1]

William G. Chase

Department of Psychology
Carnegie—Mellon University
Pittsburgh, Pennsylvania, United States

ABSTRACT

Five experiments examined the effects of acoustic similarity and syllabic word length on the rehearsal rate and three memory scanning tasks: scanning for presence, scanning for location, and metered memory search. Acoustic similarity and syllabic word length did not influence the speed of any memory scanning process, but they did slow the rehearsal rate by 15 to 25%. Acoustic similarity and syllabic word length had larger effects on larger memory sets near the memory span. It is concluded that memory scanning does not involve implicit speech. The results are discussed in terms of mechanisms underlying the management of active memory.

I. INTRODUCTION

During the past ten years, with the aid of chronometric techniques, there has been a tremendous amount of research aimed at isolating and measuring the basic processes underlying speeded mental tasks. This methodology has been successfully applied to a wide variety of tasks, including memory search (Sternberg, 1966), visual search (Neisser, 1963), mental rotation (Shepard & Metzler, 1971), mental arithmetic (Groen & Parkman, 1972), and simple verification tasks (Clark & Chase, 1972), to name a few. In each case, a basic mental process is isolated and its speed is measured. Theories have characterized the flow of

---

[1] Parts of this chapter were also presented at the meeting of the Midwestern Psychological Association, Chicago, May 1974.

information in terms of computer analogies, with flow charts and mathematical models, and they generally obtain good fits to the latencies within each task.

While this research has yielded fairly satisfying theoretical accounts of the latencies within each task, considered separately, the theoretical framework that ties these basic mental processes together across tasks is rather loose. That is, we assume that there is a relatively small set of basic mental processes underlying a wide variety of speeded mental tasks, such that any two tasks within this domain share some of these same processes. However, the control structure, the organizational processes that assemble these basic processes from task to task (Atkinson & Shiffrin, 1968; Newell, 1973), has received very little study. At present, it is not possible to make predictions across tasks; theories of high-speed mental processes, however nice, are decidedly task-specific.

The ultimate goal of this research program is to generate a theoretical account of the basic mental operations and control processes underlying the management of active memory, although the research reported here asks a very much smaller question: can we find, nontrivially, a common mental process underlying more than one memory task? More specifically, does implicit speech underlie scanning processes in active memory?

The research strategy here involves a slightly different emphasis. Instead of analyzing any one task in depth, several closely related tasks are analyzed to see if a common mental process can be identified. We make use of two techniques. One technique is to look for intersubject correlations across tasks. That is, if we are measuring the same underlying process within two tasks, then a person who is slow (or fast) in one task should also be slow (or fast) in the other task. The second technique is to see if the basic processes are affected in the same way by the same independent variables from task to task. That is, if acoustic similarity slows down a basic process within one task, then it should also slow the same basic process within another task. This research emphasizes this latter technique. Five experiments are reported here which investigate the effects of acoustic similarity and word length on various memory search tasks.

II. EXPERIMENT I

The methodology of this experiment involves measuring the time to perform three tasks: Scanning for presence, scanning for location, and rehearsal of items in active memory. The empirical question is whether all three tasks are slowed by acoustically confusable materials. The theoretical question is whether implicit speech plays a role in memory scanning. The assumption is that acoustically confusable materials will slow the implicit speech rate, and if all three tasks rely on implicit speech, then they should all be affected similarly by acoustic similarity.

Scanning for presence is the paradigm first investigated by Sternberg (1966) in which the subject is given a memory set and then a probe item, and the task is to indicate as quickly as possible whether or not the probe is a member of the memory set. The independent variable in this task is the size of the memory set, the dependent variable is the reaction time (RT) to the probe, and the typical result is a linear function relating RT and memory set size. It is generally believed that these results are due to a serial, exhaustive scanning mechanism which operates on active memory to find the probe, and the slope of the line is an estimate of the time it takes to make a single memory comparison (Sternberg, 1966).

The second task, scanning for location, is an interesting variation of Sternberg's paradigm in which the probe is always a member of the memory set and the subject's task is to name the item which follows the probe in the memory set. Again, the independent variable is the size of the memory set, the dependent variable is RT to the probe, and the typical result is a linear function relating RT and memory set size. Sternberg (1967, 1969), who first investigated this task, suggested that the results in this task are due to a serial *self-terminating* scanning mechanism which operates on active memory at a much slower rate than the mechanism underlying scanning for presence (38 msec versus 250 msec per item for digits). Again, the slope of the line relating memory set size and RT can be used to estimate the speed of the memory comparison; if the scanning process is strictly self-terminating, the slope (approximately 125 msec per item) is doubled to obtain an estimate of the memory comparison time.

Sternberg (1967) has suggested that scanning for presence and scanning for location both involve the same basic comparison process, and it is the control structure that causes this latter scan to be slower and self-terminating. Sternberg's explanation is as follows. Scanning for presence is so fast that for small sets below the memory span, it is more efficient to search the whole set before checking to see if a match has occurred. Thus, total search time is, say, 38 msec per item plus 200 msec for the match—mismatch decision. It would be much slower if a match—mismatch decision were made for each item in the set (38 plus 200 msec per item). The fact that people who are slow at scanning for presence also show a tendency to self-terminate provides some evidence for this interpretation (Sternberg, 1975).

For these purposes, we assume that if scanning for location and scanning for presence share the same comparison process, be it implicit speech or some other mechanism, then they should both be affected in the same way by acoustic similarity. It must also be assumed, somewhat tenuously, that the additional components in scanning for location won't be affected by acoustic similarity. It is also conceivable that scanning for presence and scanning for location involve entirely different mechanisms, the latter being implicit speech and the former being a much faster process. The fact that Sternberg's estimate of scanning for location (about 250 msec) is close to the implicit speech rate (Landauer, 1962), provides some evidence for this interpretation. This experiment should provide more direct evidence on this issue, one way or another, depending on how acoustic similarity has its effects.

The third task involves simply rehearsing the memory set, and the same basic methodology is applied here: the independent variable is the size of the memory set, the dependent variable is the time it takes to rehearse the memory set, and the expected outcome is a linear function relating memory set size and rehearsal time. The slope will be used to estimate the rehearsal rate.

How acoustic similarity affects these tasks is interesting because acoustic similarity has been shown to be a powerful source of interference in short-term retention of verbal materials (Conrad, 1964). The implication is that short-term retention of verbal materials relies heavily on some phonemic—articulatory code. If this is true, then implicit speech would certainly be a logical mechanism for searching active memory.

The literature on memory scanning and acoustic similarity is inconsistent. The bulk of the evidence suggests that acoustic similarity does not readily affect scanning for presence (Chase & Calfee, 1969; Chase & Posner, 1965; Monsell, 1973), although one study did find that nontarget probes were searched slower through acoustically confusable materials (Chase & Calfee, 1969, Experiment I), and Hiles (1973) found large reliable effects when subjects were instructed to overtly pronounce the memory set items. Unfortunately, Hiles used only one set size, so it is unclear whether acoustic similarity affected the memory search rate (the slope), or some other process (the intercept).

The two studies that specifically investigated the effects of acoustic similarity on scanning for location both found large effects. Chi and Chase (1972) found that acoustic similarity decreased the memory scanning rate by more than one-third, but subsequent unpublished experiments have not replicated that result. Monsell (1973) found that acoustic similarity caused about a 70 msec increment in overall RT, but since he used only one set size, it is unclear whether acoustic confusability actually affected the memory search rate.

This experiment manipulates acoustic similarity across tasks within the same experiment and with the same subjects.

A. Method

1. Scanning for Presence

After memorizing a set of 1 to 4 letters, subjects looked into a tachistoscope and pressed a button. A probe appeared 1 sec later and subjects pressed a "yes" or "no" button as quickly as possible, depending on whether the probe was in the memory set or not. Subjects performed 192 trials composed of equal numbers of "yes" and "no" responses, of the four memory set sizes, of the two types of materials (acoustically similar and neutral letters), and for the "yes" responses, each serial position was probed an equal number of times. The assignment of hands to "yes" and "no" buttons was counterbalanced across subjects.

2. Scanning for Location

The procedure was identical to scanning for presence, except that subjects memorized sets of 3 to 6 letters, the probe was always in the memory set, RTs were measured by a voice operated relay, and the task was to name the letter that followed the probe in the memory set. If the probe was the last item in the set, subjects named the first item in the list. Memory sets of fewer than three items cannot be used in this task because with two items, for example, subjects can simply name the other item without accessing any order information, thus bypassing the search process.

3. Rehearsal

Before each trial in both scanning conditions, subjects rehearsed the list 10 times as quickly as possible (subjects kept track of the number of rehearsals on their fingers). The memory sets were displayed visually (simultaneously) and subjects were allowed as much time as they wanted to inspect the memory set before they began the timed rehearsal. Rehearsal time was measured twice, once silently and once out loud, and the order was randomized over trials.

Memory sets were drawn from a population of eight acoustically confusable (BCDEPTVZ) or neutral (ADHIMQYZ) letters, after Conrad's (1964) perceptual confusion matrix. Naming time and frequency of occurrence in the English language were closely equated across letter populations. The neutral set of letters is a highly distinctive subset; in fact it rivals the digits in terms of memory span and memory scanning rate (Chase, 1965).

Six subjects performed scanning for presence and scanning for location on successive days, with the order counterbalanced over days.

B. Results and Discussion

The basic findings of this experiment are illustrated in Fig. 1. First, acoustic similarity had no effect on scanning for presence or location of verbal materials in active memory. (similarity $\times$ linear memory set size $F(1,5) = 2.9$ and 1.1, respectively.) As expected, RTs were a linear function of memory set size, with linearity accounting for over 98 and 99%, respectively, of the variance for scanning for presence and location. The slopes of 50 and 85 msec/item, respectively, are about the same magnitude as reported previously in the literature. If scanning for location is a strictly self-terminating process, then the 85 msec slope should be doubled to obtain an estimate of the memory comparison time (170 msec).

The second important result is that acoustic similarity did produce an increase in overall RTs of about 35 msec in scanning for location, although this result was not very reliable with only six subjects ($F(1,5) = 4.21, p < .10$). The implication is that acoustic similarity influences some process other than the scan mechanism during scanning to locate. More will be said about this process subsequently.

The third important result is that acoustic similarity produced about a 20–25% decrease in the rehearsal rate, from about 200 msec per item to about 250 msec per item (similarity × linear memory set size $F(1,5) = 15.3, p < .025$), and the effect was more pronounced for larger memory set sizes (similarity × quadratic memory set size $F(1,5) = 12.2, p < .025$). That is, acoustic similarity caused only about a 15% increase in the rehearsal rate over the range of 1 to 4 items, but about a 30% increase over the range of 4 to 6 items.

The fourth important result concerns the nonlinearity of the rehearsal functions. Although only 1.5% of the variance was nonlinear, it was quite reliable and almost entirely (1.42%) due to a quadratic trend (quadratic memory set size $F(1,5) = 15.8, p < .025$). This makes it difficult to estimate the rehearsal rate.

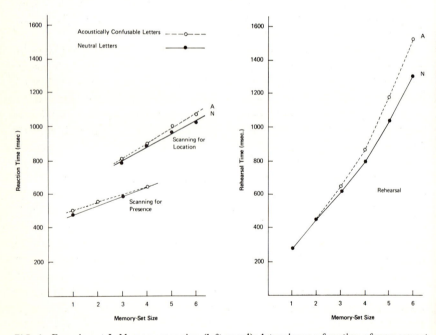

FIG. 1   Experiment I. Memory scanning (left panel): latencies as a function of memory set size for scanning for presence and location, and for both types of material. The solid lines are least-squares estimates of the best-fitting linear functions. Rehearsal (right panel): rehearsal times as a function of memory set size. The times represent the average time to rehearse a list once, computed by dividing the total rehearsal time (for 10 rehearsals) by 10.

For example, if memory sets of 1 to 4 items are used, the slope is about 185 msec per item, whereas the slope is about 290 msec per item over memory sets of 4 to 6 items. In other words, memory sets near the memory span were rehearsed over 50% slower than smaller memory sets. This is a reliable and important result which is discussed subsequently at some length.

One final result worth noting at this point is that the rehearsal rate was about 15% slower for aloud than silent rehearsal (aloud–silent $\times$ linear memory set size $F(1,5) = 11.38$, $p < .025$). This effect did not interact with anything else in the experiment. This is an interesting result because it suggests that organizing an overt articulation is an additive process (which costs about 30 msec or so of extra processing time), and it probably occurs independently of the other processes involved in rehearsal. Landauer (personal communication, 1974) reports that this effect tends to disappear with practice.

The results seem to answer the question posed by this study, namely, acoustic similarity does not slow the search in active memory for either the presence or the location of verbal items. The implication is that it is not necessary to employ implicit speech as a memory search mechanism; people can use other, faster, mechanisms to search active verbal memory. This conclusion seems particularly solid for scanning for presence because first, it is clearly too fast to be implicit speech, and second, it is unusual to find effects of acoustic similarity.

The evidence is not so solid, however, for scanning for location because the process is slow enough to be about the same magnitude as implicit speech. Furthermore, what little literature there is suggests that effects of acoustic similarity are the rule rather than the exception. The fact that here acoustic similarity influenced the overall RTs, but not the slope, suggests that phonemic–articularity codes are affecting some other process that is additive with the memory comparison. The next two experiments further investigate the possibility that implicit speech may underly scanning for location.

III. EXPERIMENT II

This experiment was designed primarily to replicate the effects of acoustic similarity on rehearsal and scanning for location. More subjects were run in order to estimate the correlation between the rehearsal rate and the memory scanning rate. Also, some of the methodological procedures were improved. In Experiment I, subjects had rehearsed the memory sets at least 20 times (10 times aloud and 10 times silently) before they performed a memory search. In this experiment, subjects performed a timed rehearsal only once, and the order of rehearsal and memory search was counterbalanced so that a more direct comparison could be made between search and rehearsal rates, as well as the relative effects of acoustic similarity.

A. Method

Twelve subjects performed two tasks – scanning for location and implicit rehearsal – on the same memory sets, and the order was counterbalanced over trials for each subject. In most respects, the procedure was similar to the session involving scanning for location in Experiment I: 192 total trials, memory sets of size 3–6, neutral and acoustically similar memory sets, and so forth. The main difference is that here, subjects rehearsed the memory set only once (implicitly) by depressing a button when they started and releasing the button when they were done.

B. Results and Discussion

The basic results for scanning for location are essentially a replication of Experiment I (Fig. 2). The results were linear (99.9%), as expected, and the slope of 136 msec per item is in accord with the literature. Again, acoustic similarity had no effect on the search rate (similarity × linear memory set size $F(1,33) = 0.53$) but acoustic similarity did cause an increase of about 50 msec in

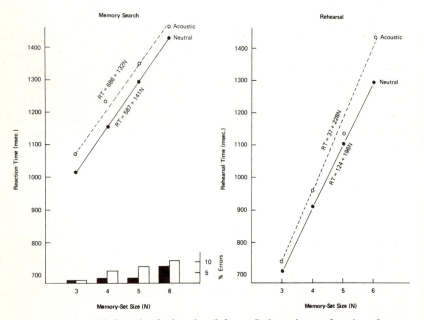

FIG. 2   Experiment II. Scanning for location (left panel): latencies as a function of memory set size for both neutral and acoustically similar materials. Error percentages are shown as a bar graph at the bottom. Rehearsal (right panel): rehearsal times as a function of memory set size for both neutral and acoustically confusable materials. The times represent the total time to rehearse the list once. The best-fitting linear equations are listed in both panels for each type of material.

overall RT ($F(1,11)$ = 13.2, $p < .01$). The implication again is that acoustic similarity does not influence the scanning mechanism itself, but it does affect some other process which operates only once, independently of memory set size.

The results involving rehearsal are also shown in Fig. 2. First, acoustic similarity caused a smaller (16%) and less reliable increase in the rehearsal rate here ($F(1,11)$ = 5.56, $p < .05$) than in Experiment I. Second, the nonlinearity is virtually gone (less than .1%; quadratic memory set size $F(1,33)$ = 1.68; similarity X quadratic memory set size $F(1,33)$ = 2.32). Only for the acoustically similar memory sets was there any hint of nonlinearity (e.g., quadratic $F(1,33)$ = 3.19, $p < .10$, for acoustically similar material) and this was due to slower rehearsals of 6-item lists.

A final analysis was performed on the data to see if the scanning rate and the rehearsal rate were correlated. The logic of the analysis is that if search and rehearsal involve a common mechanism, then a particular subject's search and rehearsal rates should be similar, hence there should be a correlation between search and rehearsal rates across subjects.[2] Four correlation coefficients were computed, two between the different types of material (neutral versus acoustic) for each task, and two between the two tasks (search versus rehearsal) for each type of material. For each task, correlations between the two types of materials were substantial: .48 for search ($p < .06$) and .77 for rehearsal ($p < .002$). The 95% confidence intervals for these two correlations are ($-.13 \leqslant p \leqslant .83$), and ($.35 \leqslant p \leqslant .93$), respectively. These correlations can be taken as an indication of the reliability of the search and rehearsal rate estimates. The interesting correlations between tasks were $-.07$ and $.03$ for neutral and acoustically similar materials, respectively, with confidence intervals of roughly $\pm .55$. Although these data should be interpreted with caution since the sample size is so small, the evidence is certainly suggestive that different mechanisms are involved in search and rehearsal.

IV. EXPERIMENT III

In the previous two experiments, part of the argument was that if search and rehearsal involve the same underlying process, namely, implicit speech, then they both should be influenced by the same variables, for example, acoustic similarity. But since acoustic similarity slowed the rehearsal rate but not the search rate, the hypothesis was rejected. Similarly, this experiment looked at search and rehearsal as a function of word length.

Baddeley, Thomson, and Buchanan (1975) have shown that word length is a major determinant of short-term retention of verbal materials. Only when words

---

[2] I am indebted to Saul Sternberg for suggesting this analysis.

were presented visually and vocalization was suppressed did the word-length effect disappear. They interpret their results as evidence for the existence of a phonemically-based temporary memory for verbal materials which seems to serve the purpose of an output buffer for speech production. They suggest that this system is separate from active memory, or central working memory, as they call it. Such a system, if it exists, would certainly underlie implicit speech, and hence, word length should certainly slow the rehearsal rate. And if memory search also involves implicit speech, word length should also affect memory search rates. In a recent experiment, Clifton and Tash (1973) showed that the rehearsal rate was slower for one-syllable than three-syllable words, but syllabic word length influenced only the intercept in scanning for presence. Presumably, three-syllabic probes were encoded slower, but both were scanned at the same rate.

In this experiment, subjects performed both rehearsal and scanning for location on the same materials used by Clifton and Tash. The expectation is that if implicit speech underlies both rehearsal and scanning to locate, then they should both be slower for three-syllable than one-syllable words.

A. Method

Memory sets of 3 to 6 items were constructed using the three types of material from Clifton and Tash (1973): ten consonants (T,H,R,S,L,D,F,M,C,Y), ten one-syllable nouns (STREET, GROWTH, LEAGUE, FRANCE, THROAT, CLOUDS, WEALTH, SCREEN, CHURCH, PHASE), and ten three-syllable nouns (PERIOD, ANIMAL, ANYONE, OXYGEN, AVENUE, MUSEUM, GENIUS, MEMORY, POLICY, VIENNA). All words were six letters in length. Eighty lists of each type of material were generated, twenty for each set size (3,4,5,6). Probes were selected from lists so that each serial position was represented approximately equally often.

Six subjects were given the full set of 240 trials, with a different random order for each subject. The experiment took three sessions of about an hour each to complete. In most other respects, the procedure was similar to that of Experiment II.

C. Results and Discussion

The important result is that syllabic word length had large effects on the rehearsal rate but no reliable effect on the search rate (Fig. 3). Statistically, three-syllable words were rehearsed significantly slower than one-syllable words (linear memory set size $\times$ 1 versus 3 syllables ($F(1,30) = 12.2$, $p < .005$), and words were rehearsed more slowly than letters (linear memory set size $\times$ letters versus words $F(1,30) = 75.7$, $p < .001$). None of these contrasts approached

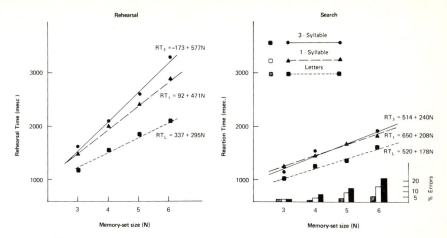

FIG. 3   Experiment III. Rehearsal (left panel): rehearsal times as a function of memory set size for letters, one-syllable words, and three-syllable words. The times represent the total time to rehearse the list once. Scanning for location (right panel): latencies as a function of memory set size for each type of material. Error percentages are shown at the bottom. The best-fitting linear equations are listed for each type of material in both panels.

significance for the search task (Fs = .6 and 1.7, respectively). These results are added proof that memory search does not involve implicit speech.

The only reliable result involving search was that overall RTs were 266 msec slower for words than letters ($F(1,10)$ = 48.6, $p < .001$). This result could be due to differences in encoding time for the probe, to naming time for the item following the probe, or some other process that occurs once during the RT interval independently of memory-set size. However, Clifton and Tash (1973) found only about a 25 msec difference in intercepts between letters and three-syllable words in the scanning for presence task, and Klapp, Anderson, and Berrian (1973) found only about a 15 msec difference in naming time for one-versus two-syllable words. These experiments would seem to rule out both encoding and naming time for the bulk of the 266 msec difference in RTs between words and letters.

There were two other interesting results in the rehearsal data. The first was the magnitude of the rehearsal rates: three-syllable words were rehearsed about 100 msec slower than one-syllable words (577 versus 471 msec, respectively), a difference of about 50 msec per syllable. Note that this is nowhere near the 3 to 1 difference one would expect if the basic unit of rehearsal were the syllable. This 50 msec difference is closer to the syllabic difference reported by Klapp *et al.* (1973) in their naming time experiment. Apparently, the basic unit of rehearsal is the word, and most of the slope is consumed by the process of activating interword associations and a smaller part of this slope — about 50 msec per syllable — is due to organization of the articulation process.

Finally, although the rehearsal times were linear (99.7%), there was a statistically significant deviation from linearity in the rehearsal of three-syllable words (quadratic three-syllable $F(1,30) = 6.35$, $p < .025$). This quadratic trend was present in at least half of the six subjects we ran.

It seems clear from the first three experiments that memory scanning for either presence or location does not involve implicit speech. The evidence consists of the following four findings: (1) acoustic similarity slows the rehearsal rate but not the scanning rate, (2) syllabic word length affects the rehearsal rate but not the scanning rate, (3) there are nonlinearities in the rehearsal functions but not in the scanning functions, and (4) there is no correlation between the rehearsal rate and the scanning rate across subjects. There are also some relevant introspective reports. Subjects typically report that in scanning to locate, they occasionally use implicit rehearsal, but most of the time they do not.

Why, then, were scanning to locate and rehearsal thought to be the same process in the first place? First, both processes are serial and proceed at about the same rate. Why should the memory system need another mechanism to locate things when it already has one that can do the job at the same speed? Second, we assumed that for verbal materials, order information is retained through rehearsal, and further that scanning for location requires sorting through this order information, hence it must involve rehearsal. The results, however, show that search and rehearsal are not always the same speed. Only for the most familiar of materials (letters and numbers) are the rates similar; for more complex materials, the rehearsal rates are substantially slower (see Experiment III). Even with letters and numbers, the search rates still may be faster than the rehearsal rates. The problem is that the memory-search slope is doubled to estimate the search rate because the search is assumed to be self-terminating. But the assumption of *strict* self-termination may not be valid (Anders, 1971; Sternberg, 1973), so that the true estimate of the search rate could be anywhere in between the slope and twice the slope.

At this point, we should raise an issue concerning errors. The theories we have been analyzing make rather extensive predictions of correct RTs, but unfortunately they do not lend themselves readily to predictions of errors. They are theories of correct performance, and they do not generally have mechanisms for producing errors. This is a defect of current theories of speeded mental tasks. However, we can say a couple of things about errors. First, errors tend to occur more frequently in the more difficult conditions which also have longer latencies. This would rule out any simple explanation of latencies in terms of speed—error tradeoffs. Second, there are three interesting results concerning errors in the scanning to locate task.

1. Sternberg (personal communication, 1974) reports that when people make errors, they are about twice as likely to name the item two away from the probe as to name the item preceding the probe. This 2:1 ratio is exactly what would be

predicted if people make the transposition error of reversing a pair of items in the list.

2. Sternberg (1967) presented the list either one, two, or three times before he presented the probe, and he found a large, systematic decline in errors with number of presentations, but latencies were invariant with number of presentations.

3. For acoustically similar lists, as one might expect, there is a strong serial-position effect with errors tending to occur in the middle of the long lists, but the latencies do not parallel these error functions.

These results are all consistent with the idea that errors are a function of associative strengths as well as complexity of the underlying mental processes, whereas latencies depend more on the latter.

V. EXPERIMENTS IV AND V

These last two experiments investigated the role of implicit speech in metered memory search, a task first investigated by Weber and his colleagues (Weber & Castleman, 1969; Weber, Cross, & Carlton, 1968). This task is a logical extension of scanning to locate, and is designed to investigate the process of finding the next item once the probe is located. In this task, the subject is presented with a probe, he scans the memory set until he finds the probe, and then he names the item 1, 2, or 3 away from the probe. This distance from the probe is called the "meter"; in Sternberg's scanning-to-locate task, the meter has always been 1. In the metered memory search task, the independent variable is the size of the meter, the dependent variable is RT to the probe, and the typical result is a linear function relating RT to meter size. Metered memory search is relatively slow and self-terminating. Searching an ordered list (e.g., abcde) proceeds at the rate of about 500 msec per item after about an hour's practice on the same list (Weber & Blagowsky, 1970, 1971; Weber & Castleman, 1969), and searching an unordered list (e.g., edacb) proceeds much more slowly (over 1 sec per item in Weber & Castleman, 1969).

Weber has suggested that implicit speech serves as the scanning mechanism in metered memory search (Weber & Blagowsky, 1970). This conclusion is based on several reasons. First, metered memory search is the same order of magnitude as implicit speech, but slower due to the concurrent place-keeping task with the meter. Second, metered memory search proceeds at the same rate, regardless of whether or not subjects overtly name each successive item following the probe. Third, metered memory search is severely disrupted with a concurrent verbal task (chanting). Finally, the process seems introspectively like implicit speech.

If metered memory search does involve implicit speech, that would explain the consistent finding that acoustic similarity causes an approximately 50 msec increase in overall RT in scanning to locate. Presumably, once the probe is found, implicit speech is employed to name the next item, and acoustic similarity, as we have seen, does cause implicit speech to slow down. These two experiments pursue this hypothesis further by seeing if metered memory search is slowed by acoustic similarity (Experiment IV) or syllabic word length (Experiment V).

A. Method

After memorizing a set of items, subjects were shown a series of 24 probes and meters. A trial began with the presentation of the meter (1, 2, or 3), which also served as the warning signal. Two seconds later, the probe appeared, and the task was to name, as quickly as possible, the item that followed the probe by 1, 2, or 3 items (the meter). If the subject reached the end of the list, he continued on to the first item in the list. After 24 trials, 8 for each meter size, a new memory set was memorized, followed by another 24 trials, and so on.

In each experiment, subjects performed a total of 144 trials, 24 trials for each of six memory sets. The six memory sets consisted of three types of material combined with two memory set sizes (4 and 8). The order of these six memory set-conditions was counterbalanced across subjects. Within each set of 24 trials, there were 8 trials for each meter size (1, 2, and 3), and, for each of these 8 trials, each serial position was probed equally often (once for 8-item lists and twice for 4-item lists).

The three types of material for Experiment IV consisted of acoustically confusable letters (BCDEPTVZ), visually confusable letters (BCDGOQRU), and neutral letters (ADHIMQYZ). These are the same stimuli used in previous experiments (Chase & Calfee, 1969; Chase & Posner, 1965; Chi & Chase, 1972), and, except for the visually confusable letters, these are the same stimuli used in Experiments I and II. The three types of material for Experiment V were letters, one-syllable words, and three-syllable words from Clifton and Tash (1973) and Experiment III. In all other respects, the procedures of Experiments IV and V were similar.

Twenty-four subjects were run, twelve in each experiment.

B. Results and Discussion

The important result was that neither acoustic similarity (Fig. 4) nor syllabic word length (Fig. 5) had a reliable effect on the metered memory search rate (acoustic versus visual and neutral N linear meter size $F(1,44) = 1.53$; and one-syllable versus three-syllable X linear meter size $F(1,44) = 1.39$). The slopes and intercepts are also listed in Table 1. As expected, the data are quite linear (over 99.5% in both experiments) with deviations from linearity not approaching significance.

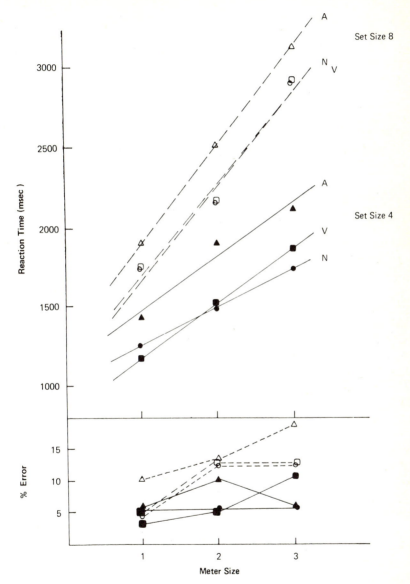

FIG. 4 Experiment IV. Metered memory-search time as a function of meter size for memory set sizes 4 and 8, and for each type of material (N = neutral, V = visually similar, A = acoustically similar). Solid lines represent the best-fitting linear functions. Error percentages are shown in the bottom panel.

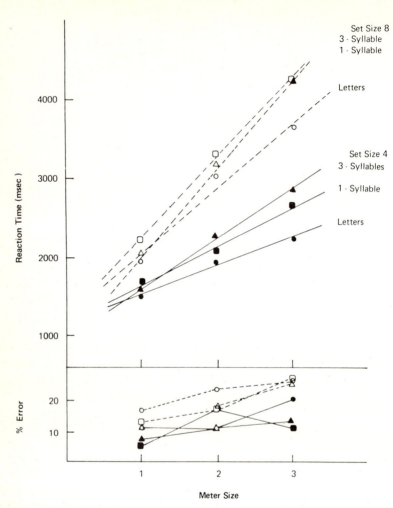

FIG. 5 Experiment V. Metered memory search time as a function of meter size for memory set sizes 4 and 8, and for each type of material. Solid lines represent the best-fitting linear functions. Error percentages are shown in the bottom panel.

There were three other important results. First, overall RTs to acoustically similar lists were 273 msec slower than visually similar or neutral lists ($F(1,22) = 12.89$, $p < .005$). As in the previous experiments, acoustic similarity seems to affect some process that occurs only once. At this point, we conclude that, contrary to expectation, even metered memory search does not rely on implicit speech.

Second, the metered memory-search rate was faster for letters than words by about 200 msec (letters versus words $\times$ linear meter size $F(1,44) = 8.60$, $p < .01$). This is roughly the same magnitude as the 266 msec difference in overall

TABLE 1
Slopes and Intercepts (in msec) of Experiments IV and
V as a Function of Set Size and Type of Material

Set size	Slope		Intercept	
	4	8	4	8
Experiment IV				
Acoustic	338	608	1112	1289
Visual	338	570	835	1125
Neutral	233	589	1020	1083
Experiment V				
Letters	346	844	1192	1169
One-syllable	495	1010	1130	1215
Three-syllable	614	1081	1004	973

RT between letters and words in the scanning-to-locate task of Experiment III. This is consistent with the view that, once the probe is located, the "find-next" process is faster for letters than words. We will tentatively suggest that interitem associations are stronger for letters than words, and this is perhaps due to greater familiarity with letters.

Finally, the metered memory search rate was almost twice as fast for 4-item lists as 8-item lists in both experiments (linear meter size $\times$ memory-set size ($F(1,22) = 32.7$ and $58.8, p < .001$, for Experiments IV and V, respectively).

VI. GENERAL DISCUSSION

It seems clear from these experiments that implicit speech is not the mechanism underlying any of the memory scanning tasks we have investigated: scanning for presence, scanning for location, and metered memory search. This is true mainly because none of the search rates was slowed either by acoustically similar items or by longer words, whereas both these variables did cause implicit speech (rehearsal) to slow down. Further, implicit speech tends to slow down with long lists near the memory span, whereas this is not true for scanning for presence or location. Finally, there does not seem to be a correlation between the implicit speech rate and the rate of scanning for location.

What can we say about the mechanisms underlying management of active memory? The most obvious thing is that there exist high-speed (and perhaps serial) mechanisms for handling various search procedures that can sort through active verbal associations or structures without recourse to implicit speech. If we assume that one purpose of implicit speech is to activate verbal information, then all we need to suppose is that this activation mechanism has operated in the recent past in order to bring the desired information into active memory. Once the desired information is active, then these search mechanisms can be brought to bear without having to reactivate the information.

We do not know whether a common mechanism is responsible for all the search tasks we have investigated, or whether a different mechanism underlies each search task. Nothing in the present experiments, however, is inconsistent with Sternberg's (1967) suggestion that scanning for presence and location both involve the same memory comparison process. This hypothesis can be tentatively extended to include metered memory search. There are additional components, of course, which cause scanning for location and metered memory search to be progressively slower and more self-terminating.

How can these search mechanisms access order information without the aid of implicit speech? We suggest that this is because order information is already built into verbal memory structures in the first place. That is, when people store unrelated verbal materials (lists of letters, numbers, etc.), they tend to group them by means of intonations, pauses, and stress patterns, and when this material is searched, this group structure information can be used to guide the search. It is also naive to believe that the rehearsal process is completely serial because, as Lashley (1951) has pointed out in his famous article on "The Problem of Serial Order in Behavior," a simple chain association model cannot account for high-speed skilled movements, spoonerisms, transposition errors in recall, and many other phenomena of serial behavior. In rehearsal, the activation of interitem associations must also involve the hierarchical grouping structures in some way (cf. Estes, 1972).

Grouping, according to Broadbent (1976), is a pervasive phenomenon, occurring in a wide variety of memories. People tend to store information in small groups of about three items, according to Broadbent, because of some fundamental capacity limitation. Baddeley et al. (1975) also postulate a similar limitation of about three items for their verbal output buffer, which they suggest is due to a decay time of approximately two seconds, and only about three items can be articulated in this amount of time. Recent evidence on the span of apprehension also suggests that only about three visual items can be grouped at any one time (Chi & Klahr, 1975). Regardless of the reason, it seems clear that there is a fundamental limit on how many verbal items can be handled together, hence grouping is a universal memory phenomenon when more than three or four unrelated items are stored. Once a string of verbal items is segmented into groups, then order information within each group can be easily identified by some sort of beginning—middle—end relations.

Although grouping has not received much attention in the memory scanning literature, there is some work that suggests that latencies are sensitive to group boundaries in scanning for presence (Bauer, 1975), scanning for location (Anders, 1971; DeRosa & Baumgarte, 1971; Walker, 1972; Wilkes & Kennedy, 1970), and metered memory search (unpublished experiments from our own laboratory). It is possible, therefore, that various memory scanning procedures do utilize information about group structure.

Another question of concern is what determines the limits of active memory. Is efficiency of memory span performance due to faster basic processes? Baddeley *et al.* (1975) suggest that the speed of the rehearsal loop determines the memory span, in large part, because verbal items (those based on a phonemic code) tend to decay away within about two seconds, and the function of rehearsal is to keep these items from decaying. Hence, memory span for verbal materials is determined by how many items can be kept active in the rehearsal loop in a two-second time span. The evidence for this hypothesis is fairly extensive. First, they found a substantial correlation between people's reading rate and their memory spans ($r = -.68$); people's memory spans are roughly equivalent to the number of words they can read in two seconds. They also cite as evidence Mackworth's (1963) finding of a high correlation between reading rate and memory span across a wide range of materials.

There is other recent evidence, however, that does not support this theory. Lyon (1975) looked at the correlation between people's rehearsal rates and their memory span, and he found a more complex relationship. The correlation between memory span and rehearsal rates for small lists of digits (3 and 4 digits) was virtually zero. However, there was a substantial correlation (about $-.50$) between memory span and rehearsal rates of larger lists (5 and 6 digits) near the memory span. When Lyon plotted his rehearsal times as a function of memory set size he found a very interesting result: the data were linear for people with high memory spans, but for people with low memory spans, he found the same kinds of nonlinearities we observed for hard-to-remember materials in Experiments I–III. The implication is that memory span is unrelated to the speed of the rehearsal process itself — the rate at which items can be articulated in active memory. The correlation is due to the fact that near the memory span, where people begin to experience difficulties in remembering, people also necessarily have trouble rehearsing.

There is also some preliminary evidence from our own laboratory that supports this interpretation. We were interested in why variables such as acoustic similarity cause nonlinearities in the rehearsal functions, so we measured interitem rehearsal times. The idea was that acoustically confusable items are normally rehearsed as fast as other items, but there are pauses in the longer lists when memory problems occur, probably at group boundaries. The data did seem to show that rehearsal time distributions are a mixture of normal rehearsals and longer pauses. These data support the idea that acoustic similarity does not directly affect the speed of the rehearsal process, but only indirectly, with longer pauses occurring when memory problems arise.

How do we account for the high correlation between reading rate and memory span found by Baddeley *et al.* (1975)? One possibility is that reading rate and memory span are both measuring some other property, such as general or verbal intelligence. For example, Jensen has reported that digit span and the WAIS intelligence test, minus the digit span subtest, correlate $r = .75$ after correction for attenuation (reported in Lyon, 1975, p. 16). It seems most likely that these correlations reflect the speed of accessing verbal material in semantic memory, depending on the accessibility, elaborateness, and quality of the semantic network, which in turn probably depends most heavily on past experience (Chi, 1975).

Where do we stand so far in our search for task-independent basic processes? The answer is not very far, but we have learned some things. First, we now know that memory scanning does not involve implicit speech. Also, it seems likely that the rate of implicit speech is not an important determiner of memory span, but it is a tenable hypothesis that memory span (and reading rate) depends upon the speed of accessing information in semantic memory. Some preliminary results from our laboratory also suggest that the various memory-scanning rates correlate only modestly with memory span, but there seem to be large correlations between memory span and overall RT (the intercepts). Perhaps these results also point to the speed of accessing knowledge in semantic memory.

ACKNOWLEDGMENTS

This research was supported in part by Public Health Service Grants MH-26073 and MH-07722 from the National Institutes of Mental Health. Part of this work was also generously supported by the Cognitive Laboratory at the University of Oregon while the author was on sabbatical leave there. I also wish to thank the National Science Foundation for providing a travel grant to Stockholm. I am indebted to many people for their help and advice in conducting this research, including Mike Bauer, Glenn Lea, Barbara Lewis, and Bill Ogden. Comments from Alan Baddeley and Saul Sternberg were greatly appreciated.

REFERENCES

Anders, T. R. Retrospective reports of retrieval from short-term memory. *Journal of Experimental Psychology,* 1971, 90, 251–257.

Atkinson, R. C., & Shiffrin, R. M. Human memory: A proposed system and its control processes. In K. W. Spence & J. T. Spence (Eds.), *The psychology of learning and motivation: Advances in research and theory.* Vol. 2. New York: Academic Press, 1968.

Baddeley, A. D., Thomson, N., & Buchanan, M. Word length and the structure of short-term memory. Journal of Verbal Learning and Verbal Behavior, 1975, 14, 575–589. November 1974.

Bauer, T. M. Organization in short-term memory. Paper presented at the meeting of the Midwestern Psychological Association, Chicago, May 1975.

Broadbent, D. E. The magic number seven after fifteen years. In A. Kennedy & A. Wilkes (Eds.), *Studies in long-term memory.* New York: Wiley, 1975.

Chase, W. G. The effect of auditory and visual confusability on visual and memory search tasks. Unpublished master's dissertation, University of Wisconsin, 1965.

Chase, W. G., & Calfee, R. C. Modality and similarity effects in short-term recognition memory. *Journal of Experimental Psychology*, 1969, **81**, 510–514.

Chase, W. G., & Posner, M. I. The effect of auditory and visual confusability on visual and memory search tasks. Paper presented at the meeting of the Midwestern Psychological Association, Chicago, May 1965.

Chi, M. T. H. Short-term memory limitations in children: Capacity or processing deficits? *Memory & Cognition*, 1976, **4**, 559–572.

Chi, M. T. H., & Chase, W. G. Effects of modality and similarity on context recall. *Journal of Experimental Psychology*, 1972, **96**, 219–222.

Chi, M. T. H., & Klahr, D. Span and rate of apprehension in children and adults. *Journal of Experimental Child Psychology*, 1975, **19**, 434–439.

Clark, H. H., & Chase, W. G. On the process of comparing sentences against pictures. *Cognitive Psychology*, 1972, **3**, 472–517.

Clifton, C., Jr., & Tash, J. Effect of syllabic word length on memory-search rate. *Journal of Experimental Psychology*, 1973, **99**, 231–235.

Conrad, R. Acoustic confusions in immediate memory. *British Journal of Psychology*, 1964, **55**, 75–84.

De Rosa, D. V., & Baumgarte, R. Probe digit recall of items from temporally organized memory sets. *Journal of Experimental Psychology*, 1971, **91**, 154–158.

Estes, W. K. An associative basis for coding and organization in memory. In A. W. Melton & E. Margin (Eds.), *Coding processes in human memory*. Washington, D.C.: Winston, 1972.

Groen, G. J., & Parkman, J. M. A chronometric analysis of simple addition. *Psychological Review*, 1972, **79**, 329–343.

Hiles, D. R. Visual encoding in short-term memory. Unpublished doctoral dissertation, McGill University, 1973.

Klapp, S. T., Anderson, W. G., & Berrian, W. Implicit speech in reading, reconsidered. *Journal of Experimental Psychology*, 1973, **100**, 368–374.

Landauer, T. Rate of implicit speech. *Perception and Motor Skills*, 1962, **15**, 646.

Lashley, K. S. The problem of serial order in behavior. In L. A. Jeffress (Ed.), *Cerebral mechanisms in behavior*. New York: Wiley, 1951.

Lyon, D. R. Sources of individual differences in digit span size. Unpublished doctoral dissertation, University of Oregon, 1975.

Mackworth, J. F. The relation between the visual image and post-perceptual immediate memory. *Journal of Verbal Learning and Verbal Behavior*, 1963, **2**, 75–85.

Monsell, S. Information processing in short-term memory tasks. Unpublished doctoral dissertation, Oxford University, 1973.

Neisser, U. Decision time without reaction time: Experiments in visual scanning. *American Journal of Psychology*, 1963, **76**, 376–385.

Newell, A. Production systems: Models of control structures. In W. G. Chase (Ed.), *Visual information processing*. New York: Academic Press, 1973.

Shepard, R., & Metzler, J. Mental rotation of three dimensional objects. *Science*, 1971, **171**, 77–110.

Sternberg, S. High speed scanning in human memory. *Science*, 1966, **153**, 652–654.

Sternberg, S. Retrieval of contextual information from memory. *Psychonomic Science*, 1967, **8**, 55–56.

Sternberg, S. Memory scanning: Mental processes revealed by reaction time experiments. *American Scientist*, 1969, **57**, 421–457.

Sternberg, S. Evidence against self-terminating memory search from properties of RT distributions. Paper presented at the meeting of the Psychonomic Society, St. Louis, November 1973.

Sternberg, S. Memory scanning: New findings and current controversies. *Quarterly Journal of Experimental Psychology,* 1975, **27**, 1–32.

Walker, E. C. T. The effect of structure on scanning strategies. *Perception & Psychophysics,* 1972, **12**, 427–429.

Weber, R. J., & Blagowsky, J. Metered memory search with implicit and explicit scanning. *Journal of Experimental Psychology,* 1970, **84**, 343–348.

Weber, R. J., & Blagowsky, J. Metered memory search and concurrent chanting. *Journal of Experimental Psychology,* 1971, **89**, 162–170.

Weber, R. J., & Castleman, J. Metered memory search. *Psychonomic Science,* 1969, **16**, 311–312.

Weber, R. J., Cross, M., & Carlton, M. Searching circular sequences. *Journal of Experimental Psychology,* 1968, **78**, 588–592.

Wilkes, A. L., & Kennedy, R. A. The relative accessibility of lists of items within different pause-defined groups. *Journal of Verbal Learning and Verbal Behavior,* 1970, **9**, 197–201.

29

Capacity Differences in Processing and Storage of Auditory and Visual Input

Lars-Göran Nilsson
Kjell Ohlsson
Jerker Rönnberg

Department of Psychology
University of Uppsala
Uppsala, Sweden

ABSTRACT

Earlier research showing superior recall of auditorily as opposed to visually presented items (the modality effect) has essentially been interpreted in favor of either
a one-store (processing theory) or a two-store theory (storage theory). Neither
theory alone seems to be capable of accounting for all of the experimental findings
in different sorts of experimental paradigms. In those cases in which list items have
been presented in one modality only (single-mode presentation) a one-store theory
has been found to be more suitable, while in those cases in which some items of a
list have been presented auditorily and others visually (mixed-mode presentation) a
two-store theory has been found to be more appropriate. In an attempt to resolve
this theoretical inconsistency a theoretical synthesis between storage and processing
theories was constructed and three experiments were conducted. The one- and
two-store theories were supported in one experiment each, while the synthesis
model gained support in all three experiment. Four other sets of data are discussed,
which previously have caused problems for the one- and two-store theories. These
data seemed to be consistent with the synthesis model. The main features of the
synthesis model were postulated to be a general memory system containing modality-specific channels or stores and a central mechanism capable of processing the
information in the modality-specific stores as well as the information in the rest of
the memory system.

I. INTRODUCTION

The modality effect in verbal memory research refers to the superior retention of auditorily as opposed to visually presented words. The effect is empirically well established and has been obtained in a wide variety of short-term memory tasks such as paired associates, free recall, probed recall, serial recall, and recognition. Needless to say, it is important to stress the generality of a phenomenon whenever there is such an opportunity. General empirical findings like the modality effect are not too common in memory research.

It is interesting to note, though, that this striking generality on the empirical level is accompanied by widespread disagreement on the theoretical level. The reason for this might be that there are several possible interpretations of the modality effects obtained in different experimental paradigms. An observation similar to this one was touched upon by Watkins, Watkins, and Crowder (1974), who argued that it was uncertain whether the origin of the modality effect is the same for different paradigms. This is indeed an interesting question to ask and it is unfortunate that Watkins and co-workers chose to walk the broad path by concluding: "The various interpretations of the modality effect may ... be considered without worrying too much about the context in which they were originally conceived" (p. 431). The two paradigms Watkins and co-workers were interested in comparing were serial and free recall.

One general purpose of this chapter is to walk the narrow path by worrying a little more about the interpretations of modality effects originating from different paradigms. The "two paradigms" examined here are usually considered in the literature to belong to the same paradigm; that of free recall. The two "versions" referred to are the single-mode and mixed-mode presentations in modality experiments. Single-mode presentation refers to the case in which all words of a list are presented in the same modality; that is, either auditorily or visually. In a mixed-mode presentation half of the words are presented in one modality, while the other half are presented in the other. The most common version of the mixed-mode presentation is probably the one where the items from the two modalities appear in a random order, sometimes with a restriction that no more than, say, two or three items from the same modality are allowed to come in succession.

A second purpose of this chapter is to present data from three experiments that will fill some of the gaps necessarily resulting from the lack of empirical and theoretical correspondence previously outlined. The final aim of the chapter is to suggest a way out of the theoretical disagreement by integrating existing theories on the modality effects and by proposing a new way of interpreting them.

Relative to the first general purpose we need some empirical and theoretical material to work with. Let us first consider the critical empirical findings obtained in conditions with single-mode and mixed-mode presentations. In single-mode presentation the modality effect is typically found only for the recency part of the serial position curve, while the auditory superiority holds for all serial positions when a mixed-mode presentation is used. This discrepancy is in itself also a reliable empirical finding whose importance may have been overlooked in the literature.

The difference between the extent of the modality effect in single-mode and mixed-mode presentations becomes interesting when one seeks to analyze it in terms of the existing theories of the modality effect. There are two theories that turn out to be especially interesting in this respect. For convenience, these two will be referred to as one- and two-store theories, respectively. The latter is probably the better known. It was originally proposed by Murdock (1967, 1968; Murdock & Walker, 1969) and states that the list items presented auditorily or visually enter separate modality-specific short-term stores. A larger capacity of the auditory as opposed to the visual store is then assumed to determine the auditory superiority.

The one-store theory, properly speaking, comprises several theories differing slightly in detail, but all with the general notion that there is only one primary memory system common to both modalities. The three versions of the one-store theory that will be presented below differ somewhat in detail, but they are all *processing* theories as opposed to the two-store notion, which is rather a *storage* theory.

Craik (1969), and Crowder and Morton (1969) have assumed that the output from primary memory is augmented by fairly unprocessed information still present in an auditory sensory register or to use their own term a precategorial acoustic store (PAS). The reason why there is no equivalent augmentation from the visual sensory store is a much faster decay of material from this store. Thus, recall of auditorily presented words for the recency part of the serial position curve is assumed to be a result of output from primary memory and PAS, while recall of visually presented words is supposed to be purely from primary memory. Hence, there is an auditory superiority for the last four or five items of the list.

In another version of the one-store theory (Sperling, 1967) the auditory superiority is assumed to be a result of the auditory or acoustic–phonological character of primary memory. Thus, it is postulated that auditorily presented items enter primary memory directly, while visually presented items have to be "translated" to an acoustic–phonological form before entering primary memory. This extra step of processing visually presented items is then assumed to suppress primary memory performance.

A third version of the one-store theory should also be mentioned. It is more general than the other two alternatives and it has some interesting implications for a direct comparison to the two-store theory. It was presented by Watkins (1972), and states that the modality effect occurs because of a larger primary memory capacity for auditory input.

As the next step, it seems appropriate to analyze how these two theories would explain the discrepancy obtained between the extent of the modality effect in single-mode and mixed-mode presentations. Considering first how such a result would be explained by the two-store notion, it is important to keep in mind the opinion that the modality effect is a short-term memory phenomenon. Thus, for the single-mode presentation, earlier items of the list are assumed to be retrieved from a long-term store that is not modality specific, while items from a later part of the list are assumed to be retrieved from the two modality-specific short-term stores. Therefore, modality differences are expected in the recency part of the serial-position curve, but not in the prerecency part of the curve.

As previously defined, in single-mode presentation the items are presented to one modality only, which according to the two-store theory would mean that only one of the two stores is utilized. Given the assumption of the two stores and the definition of single presentation, it is not clear, however, why subjects would choose to use the visual store, since this store is of a smaller capacity. It might very well be the case that subjects are using the auditory store in spite of the fact that the presentation is visual. After all, the auditory store is assumed to be of a larger capacity and as the typical subject is a competitive student he would try in all respects to maximize his recall performance. One obvious strategy would be for him to "translate" the visual input to some acoustic–phonological form that is more compatible with the characteristics of the auditory store and thus possibly more suitable for rehearsal. Such an explanation of the modality effect is definitely in line with a one-store notion (e.g., Sperling, 1967; Watkins, 1972) and therefore it seems somewhat unparsimonious to postulate two modality-specific stores. Although, it would still be possible that such modality-specific short-term stores exist, one would necessarily have to argue that no experiment suggested so far has been critical enough to test the two-store theory relative to the single presentation procedure. In an attempt to restore the credibility of the two-store notion for this type of presentation, the first two experiments of this chapter were conducted.

The one-store theory would also say that the modality effect is a short-term or primary memory phenomenon, and that the auditory superiority therefore appears in the recency part of the serial-position curve only. It is commonly agreed that primary memory capacity is limited and according to the one-store notion a larger part of this limited processing capacity is assumed to be devoted to auditory rather than to visual input (Watkins, 1972). A general idea within the one-store tradition is that this might occur because subjects have to do some extra processing of the visual information in order to make it more compatible with the phonological characteristics of primary memory.

The first experiment reported was designed with the purpose of providing a proper test of the two-store notion with respect to single-mode presentation. The idea is that the usual single-mode presentation, in which subjects know when the list is going to end, is inappropriate for testing the notion of two stores varying in capacity. It is reasonable to assume that the subjects may learn to utilize some kind of specific encoding strategy for the last items presented, if they know the length of the list. The fact that subjects learn to recall the last items presented first in free recall indicates that some specific strategy is imposed on these items. It is possible that subjects try to utilize some acoustic–phonological encoding to maximize recall of these items. Whether or not the speculation about the nature of this encoding is valid, it seems necessary to avoid such a confounding if the purpose is to study capacity differences of the hypothetical modality-specific stores. To avoid the possibility that any special attention or processing is directed towards the last items presented, a type of single-mode presentation was used, in which subjects were unaware of the length of the list prior to the presentation of the list. The assumption is, then, that recall of those items that the subjects have already encoded into memory should reflect capacity differences between the auditory and visual short-term stores much more convincingly than the conventional single presentation procedure.

Although it was concluded that the power of the two-store theory to explain the already existing single-mode presentation data was not too impressive, the theory does seem appropriate for the mixed-mode presentation. The reason for this is obvious, considering the possibility in this condition to test the capacities of the two stores at the same time. Furthermore, it is easy for the two-store notion to explain the result of an extended modality effect in this type of presentation as compared to the shorter effect in single-mode presentation. According to the two-store theory, half of the list items are assumed to enter the auditory store, while the other half of the items are assumed to enter the visual store. Since each store, will thus be loaded with only half the number of items stored in single presentation, the modality effect will extend over twice as many items. Furthermore, one would also predict a more extended recency effect if one assumes that auditory and visual items enter separate stores. This is in fact the result that has been obtained in experiments using mixed-mode presentation. For instance, the data presented by Murdock and Walker (1969), and Nilsson (1973b) show flatter serial-position curves for both modalities in mixed-mode presentation than in single-mode presentation. The fact that the auditory superiority seems to hold for the whole list in mixed-mode presentation is more or less a coincidence, since in most cases fairly short lists have been used. The critical aspect to focus on is that the auditory superiority is extended over twice as many items at most. If longer mixed-mode lists were used one would still expect more extended recency and modality effects, but one would not necessarily expect them to hold for the whole list. Unpublished data by Mike and Olga Watkins support this notion.

Data from mixed-mode experiments cause problems to the one-store theory. The modality effect is considered a primary memory phenomenon and it would therefore be predicted to occur in the recency part only, but not in the rest of the curve. The fact that the modality effect does appear for approximately twice as many items in mixed-mode as opposed to single-mode presentation thus questions the one-store theory for the former type of presentation.

As noted from the description of the theories, the concept of capacity is a basic term represented in both theories. In modality experiments reported to date this term has mainly been used as a hypothetical construct only. No systematic attempts have been made to manipulate variables that might affect the capacity of primary memory or of the modality-specific stores, according to the one- or two-store theories, respectively. Such an attempt is made here. A variable of central interest to the concept of capacity is list length. It is true that Roberts (1972) did vary list length in a modality experiment, but in that study there were no attempts to make any inferences about the concept of capacity. More or less as a byproduct of the instructions used in Experiment I it was possible to study the effect of list length in single-mode presentation. The general purpose of this experiment was to obtain an experimental condition in which the list length was unknown to the subjects before the presentation of each list. To obtain this, the subjects were instructed that the list length could vary up to 20 items. The list lengths actually given were 6, 10, and 14 items. The predictions from the two-store theory with respect to list length were that the size of the modality effect could be constant for the various list lengths. The size rather than the extent of the effect is the appropriate concept to use here, since the extent is confounded with the independent variable list length in this particular case. The *extent* of the effect is the number of serial positions in the curves for which there is an auditory superiority, while *size* of the effect refers to the difference in area between the recency parts of auditory and visual curves (see Nilsson, 1975, p. 17). If subjects do not know when the list is going to end, it seems reasonable to assume that the pure modality-specific stores could be tested with little or no influences from the type of extra encoding mentioned initially in connection with single-mode visual presentation. The prediction of a constant modality effect regardless of list length seems reasonable to make, given that the pure modality-specific stores work with little influence from such extra processing, and that the list lengths used (6, 10, and 14 items) exceed the postulated capacity of these stores.

Experiment II served as control. In order to see the effect of the instructions used in Experiment I, Experiment II was conducted applying the type of instructions that are used in the more conventional single technique. Thus, in this case any extra processing is allowed to work besides the hypothetical modality-specific stores.

II. EXPERIMENTS I AND II

Experiments I and II were conducted as two separate experiments, but are described together because of great similarities in method. Another reason for treating them together is that in order to understand the effect of the instructions used in Experiment I, it has to be directly compared to the effect of the instructions used in the conventional single-mode presentation.

A. Method

1. Experimental Design

For Experiment I, half of the subjects were presented the words auditorily, while half were given visual presentation. Thus, mode of presentation constitutes a between-subject variable. Three different list lengths (6, 10, and 14 items) were the three levels of a within-subjects variable. In Experiment II both these variables were between-subjects variables.

2. Procedure

Depending upon which condition each subject had been assigned he was instructed that he was going to hear or see 15 lists of words and that he was supposed to remember and recall the words of each list, in any order, immediately after the termination of each list presentation. In Experiment I the subjects were instructed that the length of the lists could vary up to 20 items, while the subjects of Experiment II were informed in advance about the list length. The words were presented at a .5-sec rate by means of a Ferguson tape recorder and an Eumig Super-8 film projector for auditory and visual presentation, respectively. For both experiments subjects were given a nominal time of 20 sec for oral recall of each list. The subject's responses were recorded on tape for later decoding.

3. Materials

For both experiments, the lists were composed of two-syllable, unrelated Swedish nouns randomly selected from normative data (Nilsson, 1973a). In all, 45 lists (15 lists for each list length) were constructed. Only 15 of these were used per subject; for Experiment I, 5 lists of each length were given to each subject in a random order; and for Experiment II each subject got 15 lists of the same length.

4. Subjects

A total of 112 undergraduates at the University of Uppsala participated in the two experiments for partial fulfilment of course requirements. In Experiment I, 20 subjects were given auditory and 20 were given visual presentation. In Experiment II, 12 subjects were assigned to each of the 6 between-subjects conditions. Each subject was randomly assigned to appropriate condition and tested individually.

B. Results and Discussion

Recall data for each serial input position were collapsed over lists and subjects for each modality and list length. The six serial position curves so obtained for each experiment are presented in Fig. 1. A general inspection of these data

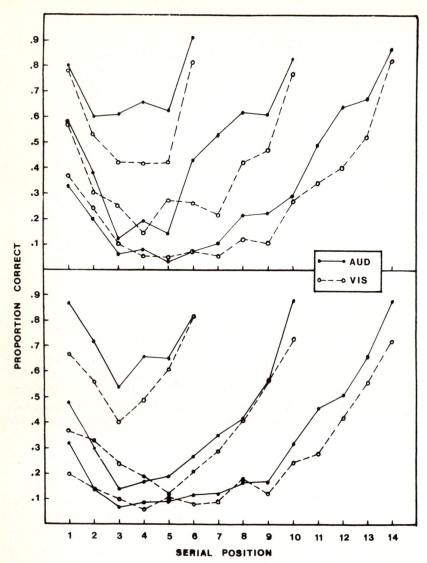

FIG. 1   Free recall performance as a function of ordinal list length and mode of presentation for Experiment I (top) and Experiment II (bottom).

confirms the presence of a modality effect for each list length in both experiments. The size and pattern of the effect, though, vary between experiments. When subjects do not know about the length of the list before presentation (Experiment I) the modality effect is generally larger than if the subjects know about the length in advance (Experiment II). The pattern of the modality effect usually obtained in single presentation is essentially the same as for the results of 10 and 14 item lists of Experiment II. The auditory superiority is usually found to be most pronounced for the last item presented. This is certainly not the case in Experiment I, where the auditory advantage is much less for the last item, compared to other items in the recency portion of the serial position curves.

These impressions are generally supported by analyses of variance carried out on data for each list length and experiment. First, there is a highly significant auditory superiority for all list lengths of Experiment I; F values of 18.37 ($p <$ .001), 9.45 ($p < .01$), and 13.57 ($p < .001$) were obtained for 6-, 1-, and 14-item lists, respectively (degrees of freedom in all cases were 1 and 38). Experiment II also yielded reliably higher recall; $F(1, 22) = 15.93$, $p < .001$ and $F(1, 22) = 7.89$, $p < .05$, for the 6- and 14-item lists respectively. A lack of significant interactions between modality and serial position for 6-item lists in both experiments suggests that the modality effect holds for all items of these lists. Statistically significant modality $\times$ serial position interactions for 14-item lists in Experiment I, $F(13, 494) = 1.96$, $p < .05$, and Experiment II, $F(13, 286) = 1.83$, $p < .05$, and for 10-item lists in Experiment I, $F(9, 342) = 3.70$, $p < .01$ suggests that the modality effect holds for the recency parts of the curves only. The lack of a significant main effect and a significant modality $\times$ serial position interaction for the 10-item lists of Experiment II is simply considered an atypical result for which there seems to be no reasonable explanation.

Taken together the results of Experiments I and II strongly support the two-store theory for single-mode presentation. The reason for this is simply that the auditory superiority was obtained in three cases in which the subjects did not know about the list length in advance, thus suggesting that it is the capacity of the stores, and not any encoding strategies, that determine the modality effect.

As mentioned in the Introduction it might be possible to draw inferences about the stores by estimating the size of the modality effect for different list lengths. It was predicted that the size of the modality effect should stay constant for the three list lengths used here, since all of them exceed what reasonably could be the limit of the capacity of the auditory and the visual stores. It can be seen from the serial position curves of Experiment I that this is indeed the case. To obtain a quantitative measure of this, the differences in proportion correct between auditory and visual items were added for those items showing a modality effect. The mean auditory superiority in Experiment I was found to be .82, .87, and .86 for the 6-, 10-, and 14-item lists respectively. The serial positions used for this purpose in Experiment I were all 6, the last 5, and the last 8 positions for 6-, 10-, and 14-item lists respectively. Since the instructions used in Experiment II did not exclude the influence of extra encoding strategies, no such homogeneity in the size of the modality effect for different list lengths should necessarily be expected. And indeed a large variation was obtained: .74, .15, and .62 for 6-, 10-, and 14-item lists, respectively.

III. EXPERIMENT III

Two important aspects of the results of Experiment I were interpreted as supporting the two-store theory: First, modality effects were obtained when specific encoding processes favoring the auditory presentation were reduced or eliminated. The modality effects obtained were assumed to reflect a larger capacity of the auditory, as opposed to the visual, store. Second, the modality effects obtained for the three different list lengths used were found to be constant, which should be the case according to the two-store notion, since the number of items used in these lists were assumed to exceed the limited capacity of the modality-specific stores.

However, the fact that modality effects were obtained in Experiment II should not pass without notice since it clearly supports the one-store theory. The most straightforward conclusion from these two experiments might simply be that both the one- and two-store theories are correct for different paradigms. When dealing with a complex subject like the human mind, such an unparsimonious conceptualization might indeed be correct in one sense. However, for the sake of theoretical advancement in mapping this subject, it seems more reasonable to abandon such a cautious approach. A more appealing account of the modality effect would depend on a synthesis of the one- and two-store theories. A general outline of such a synthesis model might be as follows.

The information that is presented to an individual is assumed to enter a general memory system containing modality-specific channels or stores. Since the problem under examination here is modality effects using verbal information, the discussion is limited to the auditory and visual modalities. The auditory and visual stores are assumed to differ in capacity in the same way as was suggested by the two-store theory; that is, a larger capacity for the auditory than the visual store. As stimuli are picked up by the perceptual system the information extracted is modality specific and for some time its memory representation will stay in a modality-specific state. Evidence has been presented that such a modality-specific persistence holds for early stages of information processing (Murdock, 1971) and for later stages. For instance, Kroll, Parks, Parkinson, Bieber, and Johnson (1970) have presented data showing that there are conditions in which the persistence of auditory and visual traces may be greater than has been previously assumed. However, for reasons previously discussed, in the context of the traditional single-mode presentation a pure storage approach does not seem satisfactory. Furthermore, an impressive amount of data have been presented that strongly argues for processing aspects of learning and remembering (see Craik & Jacoby, 1975; Craik & Lockhart, 1972; Craik, this volume). This approach to memory research should of course be taken into account when trying to conceptualize any aspect of memory.

The processing part of this synthesis model is to be seen as a function of a central processor. It is postulated that the main function of the central processor is to make the information presented more compatible with the specific demands of a current memory task. If modality of presentation is the important aspect of the task the central processor will process information in such a fashion, but if the task emphasizes other aspects the central processor will act on those. In most memory experiments verbal materials are used, which carries semantic meaning, and therefore the task for the central processor will be to "enrich" the information semantically. Independent evidence for such a viewpoint has in fact been presented (see Nilsson, 1974, Experiment II). It was demonstrated that organization by modality ceased over time, while organization by semantic category increased over time.

Now, provided that there is a common memory system, including auditory and visual stores or channels, and that the processing of all information is handled by a central processor, there is one question of main interest for the purpose of this model. Is the commonly obtained auditory superiority due to the fact that auditory items are processed more efficiently or better than visual items, or is it due to a larger capacity of the auditory than the visual store? If the former were true, any notion about modality-specific stores would be redundant. For instance, it might be enough to postulate a common memory system and a central processor that for whatever reason could handle auditory information easier or better than visual. However, there are data in the literature (e.g., those about organization by modality) suggesting this not to be the case. Instead, we would like to suggest according to the present model that the same amount of central processing is given to each item in the modality-specific stores, but, since the auditory store is in some sense larger (i.e., having a larger capacity), there will be an auditory superiority. Thus, while the same amount of central processing is given to each item in the stores, more total central processing will be given to the auditory store, since this is larger. Therefore, the auditory superiority is a function of both storage and processing.

In order to test this model a mixed-mode presentation would seem to be a necessary condition. The reason for this is that subjects must use both stores in processing each list. Furthermore, instead of presenting the same number of items in each modality this number was varied within a list of constant length. The proportion of auditorily and visually presented items in each list was always unknown to the subject prior to the presentation of the list, which was a prerequisite that a constant amount of central processing (CP_1) would be given to the auditory store and a constant amount of central processing (CP_2) would be given to the visual store where $CP_1 > CP_2$. Based on these prerequisites it was predicted that the fewer items in a store the higher the preformance would be. For instance, when one item is in a store all central processing for that store will be devoted to that item, which is a larger amount of processing as compared to the case in which, for instance, two items will have to share the central processing that is devoted to the store.

In Experiment III the number of items in the auditory store vary, while the number of items in the visual store will always be constant, that is, the number of items visually presented will actually exceed the capacity limit of the visual store. From the synthesis model it is predicted that the modality effect will increase as the number of items decreases in the auditory store, given that the limit for the visual store is reached. Thus, the ease with which this central processing can be performed is, among other things, dependent upon the size of the store and also to what extent the limited capacity of the store has been reached.

The general prediction for the one- and two-store theories is that modality effects should be obtained for all different proportions of auditory and visual items used. However, neither of these two theories give grounds for predicting that the size of the modality effect should vary as the proportions of auditory and visual items vary. As previously stated, such a variation is predicted for the synthesis model.

A. Method

1. Design and Procedure

All lists presented were 10 items long and the proportions of auditory and visual words in the lists were 3–7, 4–6, 5–5, 6–4, or 7–3, respectively. Each subject was given 4 lists of each of these 5 possible proportions for a total of 20 lists per subject. The order of the lists with these proportions was random. Half of the subjects were given one set of 20 lists and the other half were given another set of lists. These sets were identical with respect to the words but varied with respect to mode of presentation; that is, if a certain word in one set was presented auditorily it was visually presented in the other set. The words were recorded at a .5-sec rate and were presented by means of an Eumig Super-8 projector with a sound track on the film. The subjects were allowed 20 sec for oral recall after each list.

2. Materials

Each list was composed of semantically unrelated, two-syllable Swedish nouns from the same source as in Experiments I and II (Nilsson, 1973a).

3. Subjects

Sixteen undergraduates at the University of Uppsala participated in the experiment for partial fulfilment of a course requirement. The subjects were tested individually.

B. Results and Discussion

Ordinal serial-position curves for auditory and visual presentation are presented in Fig. 2. (These curves are labeled ordinal since they are not based on nominal serial positions, but rather on the order the words are presented in each modality.) More specifically, the assumption is that auditorily presented words

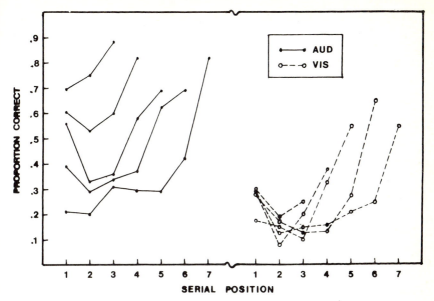

FIG. 2   Serial position curves for auditory and visual mode of presentation and ordinal list length.

enter an auditory store while visually presented words enter a visual store. For instance, in a list with 3 auditory and 7 visual items the auditory words might be at the third, sixth and ninth nominal positions and visual words for the rest of the nominal serial positions. The ordinal serial positions for such a list would be 1, 2, and 3 for auditory items and 1 through 7 for visual items. The notion of modality-specific stores is very central to the two-store theory and therefore the serial position curves should be plotted in this fashion.

As can be seen from Fig. 2, there is a very drastic difference in pattern for auditorily and visually presented items. The curves for the former vary in level quite nicely according to the variations in the length of the string of words presented to the auditory store. The recall level for three items is high and it decreases as the number of auditorily presented items increases. For visual presentation, on the other hand, the recall level stays the same independently of the number of items entering the visual store. This is interpreted as support for the synthesis model but not for the one- and two-store theories and the reason is as follows: The capacity limit for the visual store is reached already by the shortest string of words (i.e., 3), while for the auditory store the capacity is larger, and, as number of items in the store varies, recall performance varies accordingly. Given that the visual store is filled the size of the modality effect is larger the fewer the items there are that have entered the auditory store. The level of recall for visual items is essentially the same for all list lengths, as it should be, since all list lengths used exceed the limited capacity of the visual store. The level of recall for auditory items varies according to the number of items in the auditory store. Where only three items have entered this store the efficiency of the central processor is greater than in those cases where more items have entered the store.

IV. CONCLUSION

A general purpose of this chapter is to emphasize the fact that the impressive empirical generality on modality effects has been accompanied by very few advances on the theoretical level. It was suggested that the reason for this might be that there are, in fact, several possible interpretations of the modality effect obtained in different experimental paradigms. Examples of two paradigms where different theoretical interpretations seem appropriate were single- and mixed-mode presentations. From previously published data it was concluded that the theories postulating a larger processing capacity for auditorily than for visually presented items (one-store theories) could explain data from single-mode presentation far more satisfactorily than theories postulating a larger capacity for an auditory as opposed to a visual short-term store (two-store theories). For mixed-mode presentation, on the other hand, a two-store theory seemed to be more appropriate than a one-store theory. One purpose of the three experiments reported was to elucidate this very problem and it would probably be worthwhile examining other paradigms used to study the modality effect in a similar way. Examples of such experiments are those that do not use auditory and visual presentation in the traditional sense but equate auditory presentation with the subjects' vocalization of visually presented items (Watkins *et al.*, 1974). The fact that these two types of auditory presentation produce similar serial position curves, does not necessarily mean that the same memory process are involved.

A more specific purpose of the first two experiments was to restore the viability of the two-store theory relative to single presentation. This was accomplished by not informing the subjects about the length of the lists that were to be presented. Besides the manipulation of instructions given in the two experiments, list length became the variable of interest on the empirical level and capacity of the modality-specific stores became the concept of interest on the theoretical level. The list length used in these two experiments were chosen to exceed the limited capacity of the modality-specific short-term stores, and therefore the size of the modality effect should be constant. The results showed that this was indeed the case.

Due to the fact that the one- or two-store theories could not explain all the modality effects obtained in the first two experiments, a theoretical integration was proposed to cope with both sets of data. This theoretical synthesis was then tested in a third experiment using mixed-mode presentation. The results obtained seemed to be very much in line with the suggested theoretical notion of

taking both a central processor and the modality-specific stores into consideration when trying to explain the modality effects.

In order to further qualify the viability of the proposed theoretical interpretation of the modality effect, four sets of data will be discussed, which previously
have caused problems for the already existing one- and two-store theories. One
such result is the finding that subjects tend to organize auditorily presented
words together and visually presented words together in spite of the fact that
they were presented randomly in a mixed-mode list (Murdock & Walker, 1969;
Nilsson, 1973b, 1974). Such results have been used as support for the notion of
modality-specific stores and is, in this sense, also in accordance with the
theoretical synthesis suggested here. More important, however, in this context is
the finding that subjects can increase this organization by modality if they are
instructed to do so (Nilsson, 1973b, 1974). Although this result does not
disconfirm the traditional two-store theory, there is, properly speaking, no
mechanism postulated that can cope with such a result. In the synthesis model
suggested here, however, structural characteristics of the modality-specific stores
are the main determinants of the basic degree of organization by modality for
noninstructed subjects, while functional features of the central processor determine the additional degree of organization for instructed subjects (see Nilsson,
1973b, p. 252). It does not seem too farfetched that a central processor should
be sensitive to instructions of this sort.

The fact that the auditory superiority decreases with slower presentation rates
(Murdock & Walker, 1969) is another result that every now and then has been
included in the domain of either the one-store or the two-store theory. However,
neither of them has been able to assign this empirical effect to a certain
well-defined mechanism. Such an identification is possible, though, for the
synthesis theory since a slower presentation rate gives ample time for the central
processor to work on the information entering the stores.

An experimental finding that has caused serious problems for the two-store
theory was presented by Craik (1969), who found the auditory superiority to be
as great after a retention interval of 15 seconds. Such a result simply cannot be
due to a passive, rapidly decaying auditory trace. However, from the point of
view of the synthesis model it seems reasonable to expect the modality effect to
occur even after an interval of several seconds since it postulates active processing
in addition to modality-specific storage and that this processing is more
efficient and more compatible with the information in the auditory store.

From the description of the synthesis model it can be understood that the
locus of the modality effect is precategorical in terms of the modality-specific
stores and postcategorical in terms of the central processor. It is realized that
such a statement might not seem parsimonious, and therefore a few comments
are in order to clarify the matter. First, it should be noted that the original
two-store theory assumed a precategorical locus of the modality effect. Later
this assumption was questioned by Watkins (1972), who argued for a postcate-

gorical locus. Recently, Nilsson (1975) argued that the empirical test used by Watkins (1972) was not critical to rule out a precategorical notion. In order to do this, Nilsson argued that an experimental condition had to be used in which variables were manipulated that affected the modality effect if it was precategorical but not postcategorical, or vice versa. It was also stated (Nilsson, 1975) that in cases where common meaningful words were used, these words were always encoded and remembered as words and not as syllables, phonemes or as other parts of the word. There is no doubt that the processing of meaningful words is postcategorical, but that does not rule out a precategorical origin of the modality effect (Nilsson, 1975). In order to investigate this, then, an experimental test was used, which minimized the possibility of such a deeper processing of the words. The conclusion from this experiment (Nilsson, 1975) was that, indeed, the locus of the modality effect could be considered as precategorical. In the light of this synthesis theory the question of a pre- or postcategorical locus of the modality effect does not seem meaningful, since the effect of the modality-specific stores and the central processor is confounded in the usual modality experiment.

The theoretical framework proposed here may be regarded as tentative rather than definite. More empirical work is needed before the theoretical synthesis suggested can be considered as an appropriate alternative explanation of the modality effect.

ACKNOWLEDGMENTS

This study was supported by a grant from the Swedish Council for Social Science Research.

REFERENCES

Craik, F. I. M. Modality differences in short-term free recall. Paper presented to the A.A.A.S. Annual Meeting, Boston, December 1969.

Craik, F. I. M., & Jacoby, L. L. A process view of short-term retention. In R. Restle (Ed.), *Cognitive theory*. Hillsdale, N.J.: Lawrence Erlbaum Associates, 1975.

Craik, F. I. M., & Lockhart, R. S. Levels of processing: A framework for memory research. *Journal of Verbal Learning and Verbal Behavior*, 1972, **11**, 671–684.

Crowder, R. G., & Morton, J. Precategorical acoustic storage (PAS). *Perception & Psychophysics*, 1969, **5**, 365–373.

Kroll, N. E. A., Parks, T., Parkinson, S. R., Bieber, S. L., & Johnson, A. L. Short-term memory while shadowing: Recall of visually and aurally presented letters. *Journal of Experimental Psychology*, 1970, **85**, 220–224.

Murdock, B. B., Jr. Auditory and visual stores in short-term memory. *Acta Psychologica*, 1967, **27**, 316–324.

Murdock, B. B., Jr. Modality effects in short-term memory: storage or retrieval? *Journal of Experimental Psychology*, 1968, **77**, 79–86.

Murdock, B. B., Jr. Four-channel effects in short-term memory. *Psychonomic Science,* 1971, **24**, 197–198.

Murdock, B. B., Jr., & Walker, K. D. Modality effects in free recall. *Journal of Verbal Learning and Verbal Behavior,* 1969, **8**, 665–676.

Nilsson, L.-G. Category norms for verbal material (Report No. 135). Uppsala, Sweden: Department of Psychology, University of Uppsala, 1973. (a)

Nilsson, L.-G. Organization by modality in short-term memory. *Journal of Experimental Psychology,* 1973, **100**, 246–253. (b)

Nilsson, L.-G. Further evidence for organizations by modality in immediate free recall. *Journal of Experimental Psychology,* 1974, **103**, 644–648.

Nilsson, L.-G. Locus of the modality effect in free recall: A reply to Watkins. *Journal of Experimental Psychology: Human Learning and Memory,* 1975, **104**, 13–17.

Roberts, W. A. Free recall of word lists varying in length and rate of presentation: A test of total-time hypotheses. *Journal of Experimental Psychology,* 1972, **92**, 365–372.

Sperling, G. Successive approximations to a model for short-term memory. *Acta Psychologica,* 1967, **27**, 285–292.

Watkins, M. J. Locus of the modality effect in free recall. *Journal of Verbal Learning and Verbal Behavior,* 1972, **11**, 644–648.

Watkins, M. J., Watkins, O. C., & Crowder, R. G. The modality effect in free and serial recall as a function of phonological similarity. *Journal of Verbal Learning and Verbal Behavior,* 1974, **13**, 430–447.

30
Recency Reexamined

Alan D. Baddeley
Graham J. Hitch

Medical Research Council
Applied Psychology Unit
Cambridge, England

ABSTRACT

The recency effect in free recall is widely held to reflect output from a short-term storage system. Three groups of experiments are described which cast doubt on this interpretation. The first group shows marked recency effects under incidental learning conditions, a result that is inconsistent with both a rehearsal buffer and a recoding interpretation. The second group of experiments shows that recency is unaffected by both articulatory suppression and by a concurrent short-term memory load of up to six digits. This suggests that recency does not depend on a limited capacity short-term memory store. The third group of experiments show marked recency in the long-term recall of anagram solutions (with a delay of several minutes) and of rugby football games (with a delay of several weeks). It is suggested: (1) Although a short-term working memory exists, it is *not* responsible for the recency effect. (2) The recency effect probably represents a retrieval strategy based on ordinal cues. (3) Such a strategy may be applied within a memory store, or to a clearly defined subset of items within a store. (4) It may be an important factor in keeping track of events and avoiding disorientation.

I. INTRODUCTION

When subjects are presented with a list of unrelated items, and subsequently asked to recall them in any order they wish, there is a marked tendency for the last few items to be very well recalled. This phenomenon, termed the *recency effect,* has played a central role in theorizing about human memory for the past ten years. The main reason for this is shown in Fig. 1 which is taken from Postman and Phillips (1965). Subjects were presented with lists of either 10, 20,

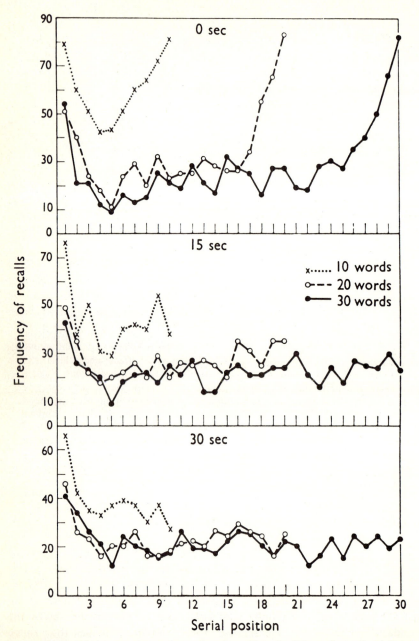

FIG. 1 Serial position curve in recall as a function of length of list and retention interval. (After Postman & Phillips, 1965.)

or 30 words, which they were required to recall either immediately, or after a delay of 15 or 30 sec filled with a rehearsal-preventing activity. Note that the recency effect is equally marked on immediate test in all three list lengths, but that after only 15 seconds of interpolated activity it has virtually disappeared, while performance on earlier items is relatively unimpaired. This result has been interpreted in a range of different ways, but by far the most common and influential has been the suggestion that the recency effect represents the contents of a labile short-term store, while performance on earlier items is based on a more durable long-term storage system (Atkinson & Shiffrin, 1968; Baddeley, 1968a; Glanzer & Cunitz, 1966). Other interpretations include the suggestion that the forgetting of the most recent items occurs because of proactive interference (PI) from earlier items (Postman & Phillips, 1965), that the recency effect represents the output of an articulatory-rehearsal buffer (Atkinson & Shiffrin, 1968), that the recency effect represents a change in the subject's strategy (Craik & Lockhart, 1972), and that it represents the application of a specific retrieval strategy (Tulving, 1968).

One way of tackling this issue might be to spell out all the various theories that have been suggested, together with the vast amount of evidence that has been produced over the last decade, and attempt to synthesize this into an adequate overall theory of recency. However, a good deal of the material has already been summarized by Shallice (1975), Watkins (1974), and Craik and Jacoby (1975). A further review would be both redundant and distinctly indigestible, and would not, alas, allow one to come up with a final convincing solution. What we propose to do instead is to present three groups of experiments that have substantially modified our own view of recency. The first of these is concerned with recency in incidental learning, in which, since the subject is not aware that he will subsequently be tested, it is unlikely that he will adopt special learning or rehearsal strategies. The second group of experiments is concerned with difficulties with the view that recency represents the output of a short-term phonemically based store, while the third group of experiments is concerned with recency effects in long-term memory.

II. RECENCY EFFECTS IN INCIDENTAL LEARNING

Back in the mists of time when memory was called verbal learning, and people still used nonsense syllables, one of us became interested in what was involved in the intention to learn. He ran a number of experiments that were concerned with the issue of whether intention to learn had any effect over and above the particular processing that it induced the subject to perform. In one of these, subjects were shown a series of low association-value nonsense syllables one at a time on cards at a rate of one syllable per 10 seconds. Four groups of 30 soldiers were tested, and required to copy down each syllable on a moving paper device which ensured that after the syllable had been written it was removed from view. Subjects were told that we were testing various code words. Two of the groups of subjects were warned that recall would subsequently be tested (the intentional-learning groups) while the other two groups were led to believe that we were only interested in their copying. One of the incidental and one of the intentional groups was simply required to write each syllable down once, while the other groups were required to copy each syllable out as often as they were able in the available 10 seconds. The question at issue was whether inducing both the incidental and intentional subjects to indulge in the same activity would lead to an equivalent amount of learning. The results are shown in Fig. 2. Equivalent written rehearsal did indeed lead to equivalent amounts of recall in the incidental and intentional groups (as was independently and rather more elegantly shown by Mechanic, 1964). Of more relevance to this issue however is the clear evidence for a marked recency effect in three of the four groups. This suggests that recency does not depend on a learning strategy adopted by the subject during input, and as such is incompatible with both Atkinson and Shiffrin's (1968) interpretation of recency as the output of a rehearsal buffer, and Craik and Lockhart's (1972) suggestion that recency represents a switch of strategy from one of semantic processing to one of phonemic processing. The apparent absence of a recency effect in the condition involving intentional free recall with no supplementary writing task is consistent with the suggestion that recency does involve a particular retrieval strategy. Recency effects typically depend on the subject's starting to recall the last few items first, and do not occur if he attempts to use a strategy of starting with earlier items. As Table 1 shows, subjects in the intentional condition with no written rehearsal were much more likely to begin by recalling the first item than were subjects in the other groups, who typically began by recalling one of the last few items presented.

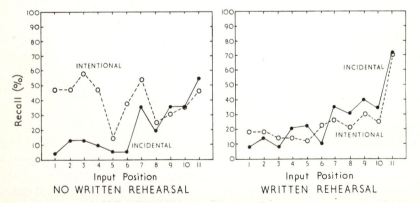

FIG. 2 Recall of nonsense syllables under incidental and intentional learning conditions, with and without "rehearsal" repeated copying during learning.

TABLE 1

Total Number of Subjects in Each Group Who Began by
Recalling the First Item Presented, the Last Item
Presented, or Some Other Item

	Item recalled first		
Condition	First presented	Last presented	Other
Intentional no written rehearsal	10	10	10
Intentional with rehearsal	0	17	13
Incidental no rehearsal	1	19	10
Incidental with rehearsal	3	15	12

Although the first experiment does indeed appear to show clear recency effects, it is a somewhat unusual experiment from a number of viewpoints. Overall level of recall was low, and in many cases subjects who did not get an item completely correct were clearly remembering part of it; furthermore it could be argued that the recall of nonsense syllables differs substantially from the meaningful material which is more typically used in free-recall experiments. A second experiment therefore used very different material, first names, and studied the effect of the rate of presentation on free recall with and without instructions to learn.

Four groups of 40–50 young soldiers were each presented with a list of 12 names. Their task was to classify each name as applicable to a man only, to a woman only, or to either. The names were read out at a rate of 2 seconds per name to two of the groups, and 10 seconds per name to the other two. At each speed, one group was instructed that they would subsequently have to recall the items, while the other was led to believe that it was simply a classification task. Immediately after the last item all groups were instructed to turn over their sheet of paper and then write down as many of the names as they could remember in any order they wished. Subjects were tested in groups, and were subsequently asked to write down whether or not they had expected to be tested. The very few subjects in the incidental conditions who said they were expecting to recall were subsequently discarded. Figure 3 shows the recall performance of the four groups. Note that all four groups show a recency effect.

They also show evidence of a primacy effect, the tendency for the initial items to be well recalled, which suggests that this too may be independent of rehearsal strategy. It is also noteworthy that the additional learning time is only useful in the

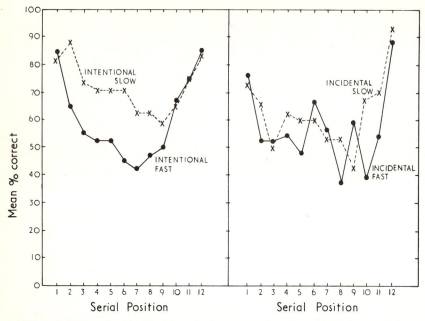

FIG. 3   Intentional and incidental recall of names as a function of rate of presentation.

condition in which subjects are actually instructed to learn. With intention to learn however, the recency portion of the two curves are completely identical. This presents something of a problem for a simple two-store view of recency, since if recent items can benefit from both the long-term and the short-term store, then their recall should be higher in the slow presentation condition, since their long-term component should be greater with slower presentation. This paradox has been discussed in more detail by Bernbach (1975), who suggests that curves of this sort represent conditions under which the subject is modifying his strategy, and relying heavily on a short-term, rather than long-term system, for retrieval of the last few items; when the subject is unable to do this, for example, because he does not know how long the list will be, then parallel curves occur, with any factor which influences the early part of the curve influencing the overall level of the recency effect to the same extent.

A third incidental-learning study took advantage of the fact that if a subject does not know he is to be tested, he will have no reason to rehearse items during a delay. If performance is based on a spontaneously fading trace, then the subject's recall score should decline after an unfilled delay, whereas if forgetting occurs because of displacement by other material, one should expect no such decline in performance. A further three groups of subjects were tested using the name classifying task, with items presented at a rate of 2 seconds per name. The subjects were young soldiers, all tested in groups, and in none of the conditions were they warned that the items would subsequently have to be recalled. In one condition ($N = 22$) they were asked for free recall immediately after presentation; in a second condition ($N = 37$) they were required to copy digits for 30 seconds and then were asked for recall; while in a third condition ($N = 31$) recall was delayed for 30 seconds but no interpolated task was presented. In order to make the delay seem plausible, the experimenter rummaged among his papers as if looking for the next experiment. The results are shown in Fig. 4. Once again there is clear evidence of recency, which is dissipated by 30 seconds of interpolated digit copying. In the absence of such activity, however, recency is quite unimpaired by the delay, suggesting that it does not depend on a spontaneously fading trace, a conclusion that is consistent with the results of Glanzer, Gia-

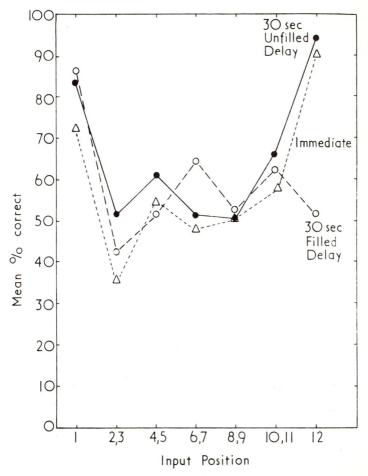

FIG. 4 Incidental recall of names tested immediately, after a 30-sec filled delay, or after a 30-sec unfilled delay.

nutsos, and Dubin (1969), who used an intentional learning paradigm. Once again, there is clear evidence of primacy, indicating that cumulative rehearsal is not the only reason for the occurrence of a primacy effect.

Taken together, these experiments suggest very strongly that although the recency effect may be enhanced by the subjects' strategy during input, it is not basically dependent on such a strategy. Both primacy and recency effects occur under conditions in which the subject has no reason to rehearse the incoming material, or to encode it in such a way as to facilitate subsequent recall.

III. THE RECENCY EFFECT AND SHORT-TERM MEMORY

The results so far described suggest that recency cannot be attributed entirely to input strategy, although such strategies may of course influence the magnitude of the effect (Shallice, 1975). They are all however compatible with the widely held view that the recency effect represents retrieval from a labile short-term memory system. Other evidence that is consistent with this view stems from the numerous studies showing that factors influencing the recall of earlier items do not affect the recency component (reviewed by Glanzer, 1972), and from evidence that amnesic patients who have grossly defective long-term memory, show an unimpaired recency effect (Baddeley & Warrington, 1970), while other patients may show an exactly opposite dissociation (Shallice & Warrington, 1970).

There is considerable evidence for an association between a labile short-term system and phonemic coding. Thus, Conrad (1964) showed that the errors in recalling sequences of consonants show a marked tendency to be phonemic in nature, hence an incorrectly recalled "C" is more likely to be recalled as "T" or "G" than it is to be recalled as "M" or "F," while the reverse is the case for intrusions to the letter "N." When subjects are required to recall sequences of unrelated words, they have considerably greater difficulty in recalling words that are similar in sound (e.g., MAN, CAN, CAP, CAT, MAP) than dissimilar words, while similarity of meaning has no such effect (Baddeley, 1966a). In long-term learning, the reverse is the case with semantic similarity causing difficulty, while phonemic similarity is unimportant (Baddeley, 1966b). If the recency effect in free recall represents the output from this phonemically based short-term system, then one might expect it to show evidence of phonemic coding. A direct test of this is difficult since the phonemic similarity effect shows up in the recall of order information, rather than item information (Wickelgren, 1965). Since order information is not required in the free-recall paradigm, a direct test is not possible. Three types of indirect evidence were however available. Craik and Levy (1970) studied the retention of clusters of related items placed at varying points within a free recall list. The relationship could be either semantic, with items coming from the same taxonomic category, or phonemic with items being similar in sound. They observed that both types of clustering enhanced recall whether the cluster occurred in the middle of the list or in the recency portion. They found no evidence, however, for the last few items to be more sensitive to the effects of phonemic similarity, such as might be expected on the assumption that the recency effect represents the output of a phonemically based store. Glanzer, Koppenaal, and Nelson (1972) came to a similar conclusion following an experiment in which the recall of the list was delayed while subjects processed a small number of interpolated words. Disruption was no greater when these words were phonemically similar to the last few items than when they were phonemically unrelated. They conclude that the recency effect does represent the output of a short-term memory system, but that this system is not based on phonemic coding. Finally, however, two studies have presented positive evidence for an association between phonemic coding and recency. Both of these have studied the nature of intrusion errors in free recall, and both find that errors that are phonemically similar to the correct item come predominantly from the last few serial positions (Craik, 1968; Shallice, 1975).

In an attempt to throw more light on this issue, Richardson and Baddeley (1975) decided to use the *articulatory suppression technique.* In this procedure the subject is presented with the material to be remembered visually, and is required at the same time to articulate some irrelevant redundant phrase such as the word "the" or the digits 1 to 6; this procedure has been shown both to impair memory span and probe memory performance, and to prevent the occurrence of the phonemic similarity effect (Levy, 1971; Murray, 1968; Peterson & Johnson, 1971). The suppression technique appears to work by preempting the articulatory–phonemic coding process; if this process is responsible for the recency effect in free recall, then suppression should have a much more dramatic effect on recency than on performance with earlier items in the list. Two experiments were performed, both involving the visual presentation of lists of unrelated words, both comparing retention under instructions to articulate irrelevant items during presentation with retention following standard presentation conditions, and both involved both immediate recall and recall after a filled delay. The results of the two studies were consistent in showing an effect of suppression on both immediate and delayed recall, but no evidence for the predicted disruption of the recency effect. Figure 5 shows the results of one of the experiments, in which words were presented at a rate of 2 per second. No evidence for a suppression of recency occurs with either visual or auditory presentation, a result which has subsequently been replicated in an unpublished study by Thomson and McNeil (personal communication, 1974).

Considering the available evidence, it therefore appears to be the case that apart from the tendency for phonemic intrusion errors to come from later items in a list, there is no evidence for the view that the recency effect in free recall represents the output of a phonemically based system. Since there is abundant

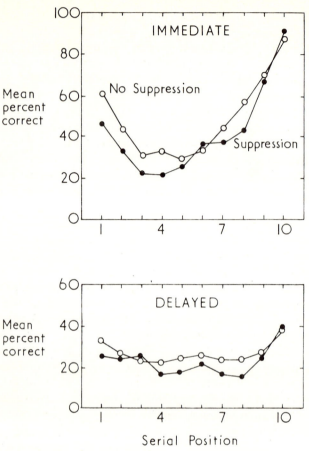

FIG. 5 Immediate and delayed recall of lists of 10 words, presented with and without concurrent articulartory suppression. (After Richardson & Baddeley, 1975.)

evidence of phonemic coding in a wide range of other short-term memory tasks including memory span (Baddeley, 1966a; Conrad & Hull, 1964), probed recall (Kintsch & Buschke, 1969), and the Brown–Peterson short-term retention task (Baddeley, 1968b), it seems likely that the recency effect is based on a different mechanism from the system underlying these tasks.

Further evidence for such a conclusion came from experiments on working memory and free recall (Baddeley & Hitch, 1974). We carried out a series of experiments aimed at testing the hypothesis that a single limited-capacity, working memory system was important for verbal reasoning, prose comprehension, and free-recall learning. Subjects were concurrently required to hold a sequence of from one to six digits, while performing the tasks in question. It was argued that if the tasks depended on the limited-capacity working memory, then occupying the system with the retention of digits should reduce the amount of available processing capacity, which in turn should impair performance. In the case of prose comprehension, we found evidence that subjects could handle up to three digits with virtually no effect on comprehension, while a load of six items did cause consistent decrements. Verbal reasoning was similarly impaired by a concurrent short-term memory load of six items. We therefore applied the same technique to immediate and delayed free recall. We had two questions in mind; first, if the limited-capacity, working memory system which was being required to hold the digits was indeed essential for long-term learning, then we might expect to find impaired retention of the earlier items in the list. Second, if the limited-capacity, working memory system is responsible for both holding the digits and for the recency effect in free recall, then recency should be drastically reduced, with the amount of reduction being a function of the number of digits concurrently being held in working memory.

We carried out a series of experiments, starting with one in which the subject was given a sequence of one, three, or six digits before the presentation of the unrelated word list, and was required to recall this either after presentation of the words, or after recall. We found evidence for impaired recall of earlier items in the list, but no evidence for impaired recency. This result is however open to the objection that the amount of attention devoted to the rehearsal of the digits may well have declined during the presentation of the list, so that the load was not consistent across serial positions. Fortunately we had included a delayed-recall condition which allowed us to check this. On examining the effect of load on delayed retention it became clear that the effect did diminish, indicating that subjects were changing their strategy throughout the list; this was confirmed by subjects' comments on the experiment. It is perhaps worth drawing attention to the fact that methods of estimating the short-term component in free recall, which rely entirely on immediate recall, all make the assumption that factors influencing performance are constant across serial positions. In our study this clearly was not the case, and we suspect it may not be the case in many others.

In a second experiment we therefore modified our task from one in which the digits were presented initially, to one in which they were presented at the same time as the words to be recalled. We achieved this by presenting the words auditorily at a rate of 1 every 2 seconds, and at the same time requiring the subject to process visually presented digits. The storage load in the digit task was manipulated by requiring the subject either to write down each digit as it appeared (Storage Load 1), or to delay his writing until three items had appeared (Storage Load 3), or until he had seen six items (Storage Load 6). This procedure equated the amount of writing across conditions, and ensured that the subject was occupied from before the beginning of the word list until its termination with the cue "Recall." Two groups of 17 students were tested, one with an immediate and the other with a delayed-recall procedure. The results are shown in Fig. 6. As in the previous experiment, there was an effect of storage

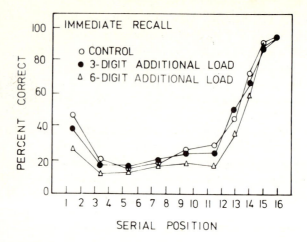

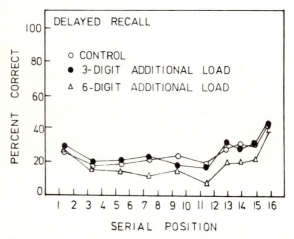

FIG. 6 The effect of a concurrent digit load on the immediate and delayed recall of auditorally presented words. (After Baddeley & Hitch, 1974.)

load on overall performance, with a storage load of 6 items causing impaired retention compared to performance with a load of 1 or 3 items, which did not differ. Performance of the group tested after a delay indicates that the storage load effect occurred throughout the list. Finally, there is no evidence that storage load disrupts the recency effect in the way that would be expected if the digits were taking up storage space in the limited capacity short-term store which is commonly assumed to be responsible for the recency effect.

Unfortunately our second experiment is also open to an objection. There is evidence that auditorily presented material may be held in an auditory buffer store, and it may be this that is responsible for the recency effect in our study.

Evidence for such an interpretation comes from a study by Anderson and Craik
(1974) which showed that auditorily presented material was resistant to disruption by the concurrent presentation of visual material, while the converse was
not the case. We therefore repeated our study with one modification; the list of
words for free recall was presented visually and the digit monitoring task
auditorily. Otherwise conditions were identical with the previous experiment.
The results are shown in Fig. 7. Considering first the delayed recall condition, it
is clear that once again a load of 6 items impairs performance throughout the
list, relative to performance when holding only 1 or 3 items. In the immediate-
recall condition, there is again no evidence that storage load interacts with serial
position. The three curves are essentially parallel. On the short-term store
interpretation of recency, the last few items should represent the output of both
the long-term store, which can be seen from earlier items to be influenced by
storage load, and the short-term store. If the latter is also impaired, as it
certainly should be, given that it is holding up to six additional items, then the
storage load effect should be particularly dramatic over the recency portion of
the curve. This is clearly not the case.

  Given the results from both the storage load and the articulatory suppression
studies, we decided to abandon our previous view that recency represents the
output of a limited-capacity short-term store. We adopted in its place a view
similar to that suggested briefly by Tulving (1968), that the recency effect
represents a retrieval strategy which relies heavily on ordinal retrieval cues
(Baddeley & Hitch, 1974). We suggested that such a strategy may be applied
within any of the range of memory stores, and indeed within long-term memory
to any given class of items, provided they are readily distinguishable as a class,

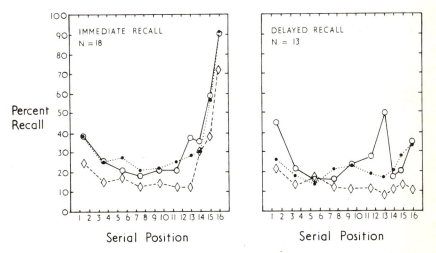

FIG. 7 The effect of a concurrent digit load on the recall of visually presented words. Open
diamonds: load = 6 items; open circles: load = 3 items; solid circles: control.

and have been presented in a clearly defined order. It follows from this view that recency effects should be observed in long-term memory, given appropriate conditions, and the last group of experiments is concerned with exploring this possibility.

IV. RECENCY EFFECTS IN LONG-TERM MEMORY

At about the time that we were completing the experiments just described, a number of reports appeared of recency effects occurring under conditions that would appear to have precluded an explanation in terms of short-term or primary memory. For example, Tzeng (1973) observed recency in a study involving the free recall of words, under conditions in which each word was both preceded and followed by 20 seconds of backward counting, a task that is generally assumed to displace any information in short-term memory. Similar phenomena were observed by Bjork and Whitten (1974) and Dalezman (1974), and had been observed in the unpublished data from a study on anagram solving (Baddeley, 1963). In this study subjects were presented with a series of five-letter anagrams. In each case the subject was allowed up to 1 minute for solution, and if he did not solve the item in that time he was told the answer and the next item presented. After 12 items the test was discontinued and the subject was debriefed and asked about any particular solution strategies he might have employed. He was then asked to recall as many of the solution words as he could in any order he wished. The results are shown in Fig. 8. There is a very marked recency effect which extends throughout the entire list.

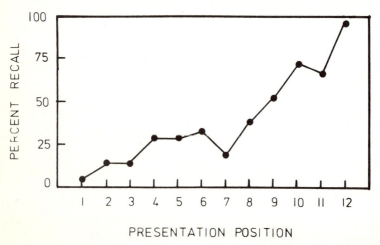

PRESENTATION POSITION

FIG. 8 The recall of anagram solutions as a function of the presentation order. (After Baddeley & Hitch, 1974.)

Although the previous result is very clear-cut, it is open to a number of possible objections; it was certainly not predicted and hence could conceivably have been a fluke result. More importantly, it is unclear what the effect of a debriefing session would be; it is possible, for instance, that subjects may have used the most recent items as illustrations of their strategies, and hence effectively rehearsed them during the debriefing. It was therefore decided to replicate the study with some slight modifications. Subjects again attempted to solve 12 anagrams, and were this time allowed a maximum of 30 seconds before being told the solution. They were then required to count backward for either 10 seconds (the "fast" condition) or for 30 seconds (the "slow" condition) before going on to the next item. After the final anagram, subjects were required to count backward for 30 seconds and were then unexpectedly asked to recall as many items as possible in any order. A total of 11 naval ratings were tested in each of the two conditions. The results are shown in Fig. 9. Although the data are somewhat noisier than in the previous study, presumably due to a smaller number of subjects tested, there is marked recency present in both the slow and the fast conditions. It was hoped that the two rates of presentation might allow us to compare the effect of number of items with that of elapsed time, but as the graphs suggest, the differences between the two conditions were not sufficiently large to allow any very confident conclusion on this point.

The position then appears to be that one can produce quite reliable recency effects under long-term memory conditions, although this is not characteristically the case in delayed free recall. Why should this be? One characteristic of all the situations in which pronounced recency has been observed in long-term

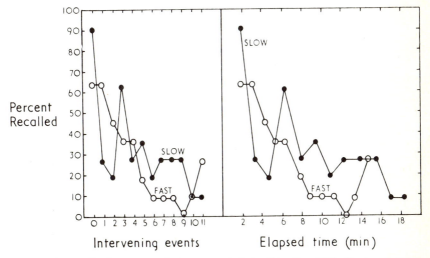

FIG. 9 The recall of anagram solutions presented at a "slow" and "fast" rate, plotted in terms of intervening events and elapsed time.

memory is that all are cases in which strong associations between items within the list do not occur, either because they are actively distrupted as by the interpolated backward counting in Tzeng's (1973) study, or by the combination of incidental learning conditions with an anagram task in which subjects would have no reason to build associations among successive items. One hypothesis might be that the strategy of using ordinal recency as a retrieval cue is one that tends only to be applied when there is no better organizational cue. In a previous study (Baddeley & Hitch, 1974) we speculated that such recency effects might appear in the recall of isolated incidents in everyday life; for example if asked to recall as many parties as possible, one suspects that subjects would show a marked tendency to recall the last few parties first, and hence a marked recency effect. Unfortunately running a controlled study along these lines proved to be beyond the scope of our research budget, and in the absence of objective evidence as to exactly who had been to what party, the hypothesis seemed difficult to test.

One situation that might allow the hypothesis to be tested is presented by the case of sportsmen who play each week for a team; a particularly convenient sport for looking at this is the Rugby Union, in which each club arranges to play a different team on each week of the season. Since most games are not organized on a league basis and are not obviously associated with a specific geographical locality, it seemed likely that complex modes of retrieval of information about games might be less common and hence an ordinal retrieval strategy more obvious. We therefore decided to look at the probability of recall of the names of opponent teams by two local rugby clubs.

The procedure was as follows; subjects were asked immediately after a game if they were prepared to take part in a short experiment, and were offered an "honorarium" of one pint of beer for participating. Virtually all members of the teams in question volunteered. Subjects were tested in groups of approximately six, and were asked to write down in any order they wished as many as possible of the names of teams they had played against that season. They were allowed 2 minutes for recall, and were then given a list of all the games played by their club, and asked to tick off those which they recognized as having played in. Two rugby clubs were tested, one ($N = 23$) was a university team, and the other ($N = 23$) was an open club.

Figure 10 shows the probability of recalling a game, given that it was recognized subsequently, as a function of the number of intervening games played for the two clubs. There is clearly a general tendency for the most recent games to be the best recalled. As a test of this each players' games were given ranks starting with the most recent game. Then the mean rank of the games recalled was compared with the mean rank of the games played for each player. In general, the recalled games had the lower ranks and were therefore the more recent ones ($p < .001$ and $p < .05$ by sign tests on each team's data). There are however considerable irregularities in the recall curves. In one of these cases, the sixth last game for the first team, the game was very well recalled because it was

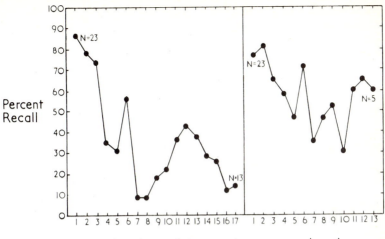

FIG. 10 Percentage recall of rugby games as a function of number of intervening games played. Data from two rugby clubs.

the club's first league win of the season. The reliability of the curves drops off after about 10 games because the numbers of players responding begins to decline rapidly, since only players who had participated in virtually every game would contribute to such points. However, the fact that not each player played in every game allows us to separate the effects of amount of elapsed time from number of interpolated games.

Two features of the season's record were estimated for each player: the mean rank of his games played (ignoring their dates), and the mean "age" of the memory of the game. Since the two measures were highly correlated for both teams (Kendall's $\tau = .65, p < .001$ and $\tau = .45, p < .01$), partial correlation coefficients were used to separate the effects of time and interpolated events on recall. The partial correlation between the proportion of games recalled and the mean ordinal rank of games played was strongly negative for both teams ($\tau = -.42$ and $-.63$), while the partial correlation between recall and the mean age of games played was virtually zero ($\tau = .04$ and $.05$). Thus recall declines as the number of intervening games increases but is largely independent of when they were played. Such a result suggests that the recency effect in long-term recall is a function of interpolated events rather than elapsed time.

V. GENERAL DISCUSSION

In this chapter we have attempted to outline some of the reasons for our dissatisfaction with existing interpretations of the recency effect. The presence of clear recency effects in incidental learning studies suggests that strategy interpretations cannot be a complete answer, although strategy at input clearly can modify the recency effect (Shallice, 1975).

The possibility that the recency effect may reflect the output from a short-term working memory seems unlikely in view of our evidence that:

1. Both working memory and memory span appear to be heavily dependent on phonemic coding, whereas recency does not appear to be sensitive to such phonemic factors as articulatory suppression or acoustic similarity.

2. Concurrent tasks such as digit span, card sorting (Baddeley, Scott, Dryan, & Smith, 1969; Murdock, 1965), and arithmetic (Shiffrin, 1970; Silverstein & Glanzer, 1971), which appear to utilize a working memory system, do not influence the recency effect.

3. Clear recency effects have been observed in a wide range of situations that are almost certainly free of short-term memory.

One is therefore left with the alternative of either attempting to modify the existing short-term store model so as to account for the available evidence, or to seek an alternative model. Our own view is that we should retain the concept of a short-term or working memory, but that we should not use this to explain recency effects. We would choose to explore the possibility of interpreting recency in terms of the utilization of ordinal retrieval cues. Such a retrieval strategy has the advantage that it is very simple and can be applied to any memory store, or any adequately delineated set of items within a store. It can thus be applied not only in the traditional free-recall situation, but also in such diverse contexts as the retention of information about specified events in long-term memory, or the retrieval of evidence from the unattended ear in echoic memory. Bryden (1971) presented digits dichotically to his subjects, instructing them to attend to one ear but subsequently requiring recall from both. He observed that items recalled from the unattended ear always showed a marked recency effect. This occurred regardless of whether subjects were asked to recall the attended or the unattended ear first. This contrasts with the retention of material on the attended ear which shows little recency, and a marked effect of order of recall, with performance being much better when the wanted message is recalled first. If one assumes that the recency strategy is being applied to the unwanted ear, since the organization within unattended material is likely to be minimal, then both the recency effect and its relative resistance to disruption by delay can be accounted for. Similarly in the typical auditory free-recall condition it seems plausible to assume that the recency strategy is applied to the auditory memory system, hence producing the phonemic intru-sions observed by Craik (1968) and by Shallice (1975) to be associated with the last few items presented, and overlapping recency curves observed by Bernbach (1975). Clearly at this stage we cannot claim to have offered an adequate model of recency. What we have attempted to do is suggest that the most commonly held existing views of the recency effect present a number of problems, and that we should perhaps be concerning ourselves with exploring possible alternatives. Such alternatives raise a number of new problems, including that of whether recency effects in long-term memory are based on the same process as in short-term memory; the evidence at the moment is not sufficient to allow one to reject this hypothesis. Second, we need to specify much more clearly under what conditions an ordinal retrieval strategy will be applied, and what limits its success. In the case of long-term recency effects we need to devise clearer tests of the relative importance of time and interpolated items. If, as our data tentatively suggest, interpolated items prove to be a more potent factor than elapsed time, the further question arises as to why this should be; is the effect entirely due to output interference as Dalezman (1974) suggests? Or is output interference itself due to the disruption of ordinal retrieval cues by recall; if so is it important whether the disruption is by recall or by subsequent input items? Finally, to what extent is such a hypothesis different from a simple retroactive-interference hypothesis?

In conclusion, we would like to suggest that although the distinction between long- and short-term memory is still a useful one, it does not present an adequate basis for interpreting the recency effect. As a number of other authors have suggested (e.g., Craik & Jacoby, 1975; Sanders, 1975; Tulving, 1968), we suspect that the recency effect is based on an ordinal retrieval strategy. Such a strategy is very widely applicable, and probably crucially important in keeping track of events and avoiding disorientation in a complex world. If so, understanding the recency effect becomes even more important than was previously suspected.

ACKNOWLEDGMENTS

A number of the experiments described were carried out at the University of Stirling, Scotland.

The authors are grateful to the Medical Research Council and the Social Science Research Council for financial support, and to Stirling County and Stirling University Rugby Clubs for their cooperation.

REFERENCES

Anderson, C. M. B., & Craik, F. I. M. The effect of a concurrent task on recall from primary memory. *Journal of Verbal Learning and Verbal Beahvior,* 1974, **13**, 107–113.

Atkinson, R. C., & Shiffrin, R. M. Human memory: A proposed system and its control processes. In K. W. Spence & J. T. Spence (Eds.), *The psychology of learning and motivation.* Vol. 2. New York: Academic Press, 1968.

Baddeley, A. D. A Zeigarnik-like effect in the recall of anagram solutions. *Quarterly Journal of Experimental Psychology,* 1963, **15**, 63–64.

Baddeley, A. D. Short-term memory for word sequences as a function of acoustic, semantic and formal similarity. *Quarterly Journal of Experimental Psychology,* 1966, **18**, 362–365. (a)

Baddeley, A. D. The influence of acoustic and semantic similarity on long-term memory for word sequences. *Quarterly Journal of Experimental Psychology,* 1966, **18,** 302–309. (b)

Baddeley, A. D. Prior recall of newly learned items and the recency effect in free recall. *Canadian Journal of Psychology,* 1968, **22,** 157–163. (a)

Baddeley, A. D. How does acoustic similarity influence short-term memory? *Quarterly Journal of Experimental Psychology,* 1968, **20,** 249–264. (b)

Baddeley, A. D., & Hitch, G. J. Working memory. In G. Bower (Ed.), *The psychology of learning and motivation.* Vol. 8. New York: Academic Press, 1974.

Baddeley, A. D., Scott, D., Dryan, R., & Smith, J. C. Short-term memory and the limited capacity hypothesis. *British Journal of Psychology,* 1969, **60,** 51–55.

Baddeley, A. D., & Warrington, E. K. Amnesia and the distinction between long- and short-term memory. *Journal of Verbal Learning and Verbal Behavior,* 1970, **9,** 176–189.

Bernbach, H. A. A problem for two-stage memory theories. *Journal of Experimental Psychology; Human Learning and Memory,* 1975, **104,** 18–22.

Bjork, R. A., & Whitten, W. B. Recency-sensitive retrieval processes in long-term free recall. *Cognitive Psychology,* 1974, **6,** 173–189.

Bryden, M. P. Attentional strategies and short-term memory in dichotic listening. *Cognitive Psychology,* 1971, **2,** 99–116.

Conrad, R. Acoustic confusions in immediate memory. *British Journal of Psychology,* 1964, **55,** 75–84.

Conrad, R., & Hull, A. J. Information, acoustic confusion and memory span. *British Journal of Psychology,* 1964, **55,** 429–432.

Craik, F. I. M. Types of error in free recall. *Psychonomic Science,* 1968, **10,** 353–354.

Craik, F. I. M. & Jacoby, L. L. A process view of short-term retention. In F. Restle (Ed.), *Cognitive theory: Volume I.* Potomac, Md.: Lawrence Erlbaum Associates, 1975.

Craik, F. I. M., & Levy, B. A. Semantic and acoustic information in primary memory. *Journal of Experimental Psychology,* 1970, **86,** 77–82.

Craik, F. I. M., & Lockhart, R. S. Levels of processing: A framework for memory research. *Journal of Verbal Learning and Verbal Behavior,* 1972, **11,** 671–684.

Dalezman, J. J. Free recall and short-term memory: A symbiotic relationship or? Unpublished doctoral dissertation, Ohio State University, 1974.

Glanzer, M. Storage mechanisms in recall. In G. H. Bower (Ed.), *The psychology of learning and motivation.* Vol. 5. New York: Academic Press, 1972.

Glanzer, M., & Cunitz, A. R. Two storage mechanisms in free recall. *Journal of Verbal Learning and Verbal Behavior,* 1966, **5,** 351–356.

Glanzer, M., Gianutsos, R., & Dubin, S. The removal of items from short-term storage. *Journal of Verbal Learning and Verbal Behavior,* 1969, **8,** 435–447.

Glanzer, M., Koppenaal, L., & Nelson, R. Effects of relations between words on short-term storage and long-term storage. *Journal of Verbal Learning and Verbal Behavior,* 1972, **11,** 403–416.

Kintsch, W., & Buschke, H. Homophones and synonyms in short-term memory. *Journal of Experimental Psychology,* 1969, **80,** 403–407.

Levy, B. A. Role of articulation in auditory and visual short-term memory. *Journal of Verbal Learning and Verbal Behavior,* 1971, **10,** 123–132.

Mechanic, A. The responses involved in the rote learning of verbal materials. *Journal of Verbal Learning and Verbal Behavior,* 1964, **3,** 30–36.

Murdock, B. B., Jr. Effects of a subsidiary task on short-term memory. *British Journal of Psychology,* 1965, **56,** 413–419.

Murray, D. J. Articulation and acoustic confusability in short-term memory. *Journal of Experimental Psychology,* 1968, **78,** 679–684.

Peterson, L. R., & Johnson, S. T. Some effects of minimizing articulation on short-term retention. *Journal of Verbal Learning and Verbal Behavior,* 1971, **10,** 346–354.

Postman, L., & Phillips, L. W. Short-term temporal changes in free recall. *Quarterly Journal of Experimental Psychology,* 1965, **17,** 132–138.

Richardson, J. T. E., & Baddeley, A. D. The effect of articulatory suppression in free recall. *Journal of Verbal Learning and Verbal Behavior,* 1975, **14,** 623–629.

Sanders, A. F. Some remarks on short-term memory. In P. M. A. Rabbitt & S. Dornic (Eds.), *Attention and performance V.* London: Academic Press, 1975.

Shallice, T. H. On the contents of primary memory. In P. M. A. Rabbitt & S. Dornic (Eds.), *Attention and performance V.* London: Academic Press, 1975.

Shallice, T. H., & Warrington, E. K. Independent functioning of verbal memory stores: A neuropsychological study. *Quarterly Journal of Experimental Psychology,* 1970, **22,** 261–273.

Shiffrin, R. M. Forgetting: Trace erosion or retrieval. *Science,* 1970, **168,** 1601–1603.

Silverstein, C., & Glanzer, M. Concurrent task in free recall: Differential effects of LTS and STS. *Psychonomic Science,* 1971, **22,** 367–368.

Tulving, E. Theoretical issues in free recall. In T. R. Dixon & D. L. Horton (Eds.), *Verbal behavior and general behavior theory.* Englewood Cliffs, N.J.: Prentice-Hall, 1968.

Tzeng, O. J. L. Positive recency effect in delayed free recall. *Journal of Verbal Learning and Verbal Behavior,* 1973, **12,** 436–439.

Watkins, M. J. The concept and measurement of primary memory. *Psychological Bulletin,* 1974, **81,** 695–711.

Wickelgren, W. A. Short-term memory for phonemically similar lists. *American Journal of Psychology,* 1965, **78,** 567–574.

31
Selective Retention in Bilingual Tasks

Stanislav Dornič

Institute of Applied Psychology
University of Stockholm
Stockholm, Sweden *

ABSTRACT

Retention of "nonattended" unilingual and bilingual lists consisting of visually presented unrelated words was studied in several experiments in which the primary task involved high or low information load. The primary task was verbal in character and was performed in one of the bilingual subjects' languages. The main finding was that in the high-load condition, retention of the nonattended lists was superior for words from that language which was used in the primary task. No such difference was found in the low-load condition. It is argued that when one of the bilingual's language systems is activated under conditions involving high mental load, the other language system becomes less operative, probably due to a more difficult interlingual switching process.

I. INTRODUCTION

The idea of an "on—off switching mechanism" (Penfield & Roberts, 1959; Kolers, 1963) operating between the bilingual's two languages has been tested in several experimental studies, and undoubtedly deserves further investigation. Briefly, it has been assumed that when the bilingual is operating in one language, the other language is "switched off," "blocked," or at least "attenuated." Hamers and Lambert (1972) referred to a general impression that "some mental or neurological switch has been thrown, making one (language) system inoperative as the other comes into play" (p. 303).

*Now at the Department of Psychology, University of Stockholm, Sweden

One way of studying the question of whether the activation of one language renders the other language system fully, or at least partly, inoperative is to use an experimental situation in which the bilingual faces a conflict due to the fact that his two languages are brought into play simultaneously (see Preston & Lambert, 1969). Such a situation arises, for example, in the bilingual version of the Stroop test.

Normally, when in the Stroop test a subject names the colors of words meaning different colors (for example, the word "blue" printed in red), only one language is used; that is, the interfering and the reading (naming) languages are identical. In an interlingual modification, however, these two languages differ: the words are written in one of the subject's languages while he names the colors in his other language. In the former case, we speak of *intralingual interference;* in the latter case, *interlingual* interference is involved.

If the idea of an "on–off switching mechanism" were correct, one would expect a bilingual to perform better in an interlingual version of the Stroop test compared to the intralingual one, since there would be no direct interference in the former case. On the other hand, if there were no separation between the two languages of a bilingual, one would expect equal interference to color naming in both conditions.

Most data reported during the last few years supported the latter assumption, that the activation of one language does *not* make the other language inoperative (Dalrymple-Alford, 1968; Dyer, 1971; Hamers & Lambert, 1972; Preston & Lambert, 1969).

Another situation, in which the processes in the bilingual's two language systems may be brought into play at the same time, is a memory experiment. A large number of studies have been performed on various topics concerning the bilingual's memory processes, and various designs with recall and recognition have been used. To quote just the most relevant studies would require much space. Most of these experiments have used lists of unrelated words from one, two, or several languages (unilingual, bilingual, or multilingual lists). Sometimes better retention was found for one of the languages (usually for the subjects' dominant language), sometimes not, but no data have been reported indicating that an "on–off switching mechanism" had been at work. It would of course be unreasonable to expect *selective* retention of words from only one language in a usual type of bilingual short-term memory experiment, in which the memory task is the only one. Even if the bilingual is instructed to try and remember selectively only words from one language, he is unable to disregard the other words, and his recall or recognition will be about the same for words from both languages.

Since our question is: "does the *activation* of one language render the other language inoperative?," we should try to find a situation in which one of the bilingual's two languages would somehow be activated while the other would not, although both languages would be brought into play in the same task.

Such a situation might be provided by employing a double task in which the subject is instructed to attend to a task requiring active use of one language; at the same time, he is presented with a "not-to-be-attended" list of unrelated words from the other language (or from both languages) to be recalled or recognized later. This technique has been used in the experiments to be briefly reported in the next section.

The experiments described in this chapter were carried out as a part of a project on the retention of nonattended tasks (Dornic, 1973, 1975a; Dornic, Svensson, & Sarnecki, 1975). The studies using bilingual tasks have been started with no well-defined hypotheses in mind. We simply wanted to know how well our bilingual subjects could remember nonattended words from their two languages while they were occupied with another task which was intended to create a continuous "language set" in one of their languages. Four of these experiments will be described here.

At this point, it may be worth citing Tulving and Colotla (1970, p. 87), who pointed out the "flexibility or immaturity" of this research field, and indicated that, for example, in an experiment on the bilingual's memory, all kinds of results might make sense. Tulving and Colotla's remark may certainly be applied to our problem. First, equal retention of words from both of the subject's languages would be in line with data from typical experiments on the bilingual's memory, and would indicate that no "on—off" mechanism is at work when one of the languages is activated. If, on the other hand, better retention from the bilingual's "nonactivated" language were found, this could be interpreted as showing that while one of his language systems is fully occupied with the main task, the storage capacity of the other language is free for coding.

Finally, if more words were retained from the language used in the primary ("to be attended to") task, one might assume that the activation of that language does render the other language less operative and reduces its storage capacity.

The present studies indicate that the latter assumption might be correct provided that the primary task, requiring activation of one language system, involves high mental load.

II. THE EXPERIMENTS

In all the experiments described in this section, a double-task technique was used. There was one task to which the subjects were instructed to pay full attention ("primary task"), and a secondary task which required no more than the subject's keeping his eyes fixed upon a spot in front of him.

Swedish—English bilinguals, with Swedish as their dominant language, ranging in age between 20 and 34 years, served as subjects. Sixteen subjects participated in Experiment I, 14 in Experiment II, and 15 in Experiments III and IV, respectively. All of them had at least 6 years of school training in English, and could use the language fluently. Only a slight dominance in Swedish could be detected using a modified version of Ervin's (1961) "language dominance test." On a 9-point self-rating scale, the subjects estimated their fluency in English to be at least 5 (average 6.7). For the purpose of these experiments, in which only high-frequency words overlearned in both languages were used, the subjects could be considered balanced bilinguals. This is in line with a view frequently expressed in the literature: bilingual subjects are considered to be balanced or "equally competent" in their languages with regard to the requirements of the particular experimental situation (see, for example, Macnamara, Krauthammer, & Bolgar, 1968; Preston & Lambert, 1969).

A.   Experiments I and II

In the first two experiments, the primary task involved high information load. It was a type of task called by Hamilton, Hockey and Rejman (in this volume) "closed system thinking" in which the required output is obtained by a series of transformations on the input. These tasks involve storage load, which makes the required mental operations considerably more difficult.

The subject was seated at about 1 m distance from a screen, fixating a point on it. The experiment began when a three-digit number was projected in the area of the fixation point. The subject immediately began performing a series of mental operations, such as counting backward by sevens, then adding together the last two digits of the resulting number, or otherwise transforming it; occasionally, he had to answer short questions which placed high demands on concentration and short-term memory. The task was performed either in Swedish or in English. Subjects were told that their major task was to perform as many correct trans-formations of the input as possible. Since it required much training to perform the task properly, subjects had to practice it thoroughly prior to the experiment.

Following a 30-sec period of backward counting, a series of 28 words — verbal labels of familiar objects — was successively projected on the screen. The subjects were told that this was a secondary task, and they were instructed to try and "not to pay any attention" to it. In Experiment I, the set was *unilingual*, that is, all the 28 words were in one language. There were four conditions, that is, four combinations of languages used in the two tasks (in the primary task, and in the word list). In two conditions, the language of both tasks was congruent (either Swedish or English). In the other two conditions, it was incongruent (Swedish in the primary task and English in the secondary task, or vice versa).

In Experiment II, the list of words in the secondary (memory) task was mixed: one-half of the words were Swedish, the other half English. The words were presented alternately: a Swedish word was always followed by an English word, and vice versa. In one condition, the primary task was performed in the subjects' dominant language, while in the other condition, the other language was used for the primary task.

In both experiments, each word in the secondary task was presented for 4 seconds. The letters in the projected words were about 7 cm high. After the last word had been presented, the subjects went on performing on the primary task for another 10 seconds.

Following the above procedure, half of the subjects were asked to free recall the words for a period of 1 min, while the other half were given a recognition test consisting of stimulus words ("old items") and distractors ("new items"). In the recognition test, subjects were asked to give a forced-choice yes/no answer. Details of the above as well as of the following experiments are given elsewhere (Dornic, in preparation). In a second session, the recall group was given a recognition test, and vice versa. Each experiment involved 10 sessions.

Table 1 shows recall and recognition scores (in percentages) for the four conditions. It is seen that both recall and recognition scores are markedly higher for the "congruent" conditions, in which the languages of the primary and secondary tasks were identical, than for the "incongruent" conditions in which the languages differed. The differences are highly significant. Thus, the results seem to indicate that some "on—off switching mechanism" was at work; although the switch obviously did not close completely, it made it more difficult for the subjects to retain words from the incongruent languages.

Table 2 concerns bilingual (mixed) lists used in Experiment II. Although all values are somewhat lower than in Experiment I, the table yields about the same picture as Table 1. Again, significantly more words were recalled and recognized from the language congruent with the language in which the primary task was performed. Thus, the retention of words from the mixed lists was clearly selective.

As can be seen in Tables 1 and 2, there was a small but consistent tendency toward a poorer retention in conditions in which the primary task was performed

TABLE 1
Recall and Recognition in Experiment I (High Information Load, Unilingual Lists)[a]

	Both tasks in DL	Both tasks in NDL	Primary task in DL, secondary task in NDL	Primary task in NDL, secondary task in DL
Percentage recalled	13.0	13.1	5.0	3.8
Percentage recognized	55.8	54.2	16.4	14.6

[a]DL = dominant language; NDL = nondominant language.

TABLE 2
Recall and Recognition in Experiment II (High
Information Load, Bilingual Lists)[a]

	Primary task in DL, secondary task mixed	Primary task in NDL, secondary task mixed
Percentage recalled		
In DL	12.7	2.1
In NDL	3.1	11.2
Percentage recognized		
In DL	51.9	12.0
In NDL	13.4	48.1

[a]DL = dominant language; NDL = nondominant language.

in the nondominant language. There is also a consistent tendency in favor of the retention of unilingual lists as compared to mixed ones. However, these differences did not reach the .05 significance level.

Since the size of the effect reported above appeared to correlate with the rate and/or quality of the subjects' performance on the primary task, the question was raised of what was the decisive factor in the findings obtained in Experiments I and II; was it the mere fact that the use (activation) of one language in the primary task somehow inhibited or "damped" the subject's other language system and reduced its storage capacity, or was it the primary task's high information load? Experiments III and IV were intended to study this question. Here the primary task involved "mechanical" verbal activity rather than high-information load.

B. Experiments III and IV

In contrast to the first two experiments, here the primary task involved low information load; it required a continuous but simple type of mental and verbal activity (such as counting forward and reciting highly overlearned verbal mate-

TABLE 3
Recall and Recognition in Experiment III (Low Information Load, Unilingual Lists)[a]

	Both tasks in DL	Both tasks in NDL	Primary task in DL, secondary task in NDL	Primary task in NDL, secondary task in DL
Percentage recalled	26.7	23.8	25.6	23.9
Percentage recognized	69.9	71.1	65.4	68.2

[a]DL = dominant language; NDL = nondominant language.

TABLE 4
Recall and Recognition in Experiment IV (Low
Information Load, Bilingual Lists)[a]

	Primary task in DL, secondary task mixed	Primary task in NDL, secondary task mixed
Percentage recalled		
In DL	24.8	25.1
In NDL	23.8	23.9
Percentage recognized		
In DL	69.1	66.3
In NDL	68.5	67.9

[a]DL = dominant language; NDL = nondominant language.

rials), which posed low demands on the subject's concentration, mental effort, and short-term memory. Other conditions were equal to those employed in the first two experiments. The secondary tasks (lists of unrelated words) in Experiments III and IV were also unilingual and mixed, respectively.

From Tables 3 and 4, a quite different picture emerges as compared to the data from the first two experiments. As expected, both recall and recognition scores are markedly higher — obviously since more "spare capacity" was left for the secondary task in Experiments III and IV. Unlike Experiments I and II, the retention in conditions in which the primary task was performed in the subjects' nondominant language was not poorer here, possibly also due to the fact that more "spare capacity" was left for processing the secondary task (see Dornic, 1975b). Also, unlike Experiments I and II, there was no consistent trend for the retention of unilingual lists to be better than that of the mixed ones.

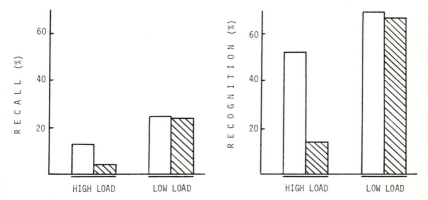

FIG. 1 Mean recall (left) and recognition (right) of words from languages congruent (blank columns) and incongruent (shaded columns) with the language used in the primary task.

The main finding is, however, that words from the language that was not used in the primary task were recalled and recognized virtually as well as words from the other language. Thus, the difficulty of the main task rather than mere language activation seems to be decisive for the phenomenon under study.

Figure 1 provides a simplified summary of the results. Scores for recall and recognition are averaged over unilingual and bilingual lists, as well as over languages.

III. CONCLUSION

The results can be summarized as follows. When the primary task involved verbal activity with high information load, better performance was found for both recall and recognition of the nonattended words from the language that was used in the primary task. This was true of both unilingual and bilingual (mixed) lists. However, when the primary task involved verbal activity with virtually no information load, the above differences were not found: the retention of nonattended words was not better for the language "activated" by the primary task than for the other language.

In short, the results indicate that when one of the bilingual's language systems is activated under conditions posing high demands on concentration, mental effort and short-term memory, and inducing strong and continuous unilingual "language set," retention of irrelevant verbal information presented in the other language is reduced considerably more than that presented in the same language.

The results seem to give some support to the idea of an "on–off switching mechanism," although it is far from clear how such a mechanism might work.

Let us assume that the differences found in retention reflect different encoding and storage (rather than different accessibility of equally stored information), and that these differences are mainly due to different conditions in input.

According to Macnamara's (1967) two switch model, a bilingual's input switch is automatic, and is controlled by the environment; it is *on* in the language of the stimuli, and automatically processes verbal information in the appropriate language. The input switch is assumed to be independent of the output switch which is subject to voluntary control. This model makes it possible to explain, for example, findings from the experiments with the interlingual form of the Stroop test.

While normally the input switch may automatically be *on* in the language of the stimuli, this need not be the case under conditions such as those used in our Experiments I and II. Here the position of the output switch (strong unilingual "language set") seems to influence the input switch,[1] which may result in better encoding and storage of words from the language activated by the primary task.

---

[1] This is not too surprising: if you are concentrated on some verbal activity in one language, and someone addresses you in a different language, it may clearly prolong your

Since in Experiment I and II some words from the nonactivated language were nevertheless encoded and stored, the input switch must occasionally also have been *on* in the other language.

According to Macnamara's model, the automatic input switch does not work instantaneously and it takes an observable amount of time to operate (Macnamara & Kushnir, 1971). It follows from the studies on comprehension of bilingually mixed texts (e.g. Kolers, 1966), that time to switch languages in input is normally very short. However, in a situation involving activation of one language system and requiring focused attention and continuous strong unilingual "language set," the amount of time necessary for switching languages in input may increase considerably. Switching from the activated to the nonactivated language may thus become a less automatic, more difficult and time-consuming process. It would not be unreasonable to assume that not enough time is available for a deeper processing and, hence, for appropriate encoding and storage of words from the nonactivated language: a shallow and superficial processing then would result in poorer retention.

ACKNOWLEDGMENTS

Most of the research work reported in this paper was supported by the Swedish Council for Social Science Research.

REFERENCES

Dalrymple-Alford, E. C. Interlingual interference in a color-naming task. *Psychonomic Science,* 1968, **10**, 215–216.

Dornic, S. Order error in attended and nonattended tasks. In S. Kornblum (Ed.), *Attention and performance IV.* New York: Academic Press, 1973.

Dornic, S. Some studies on the retention of order information. In P. Rabbitt & S. Dornic (Eds.), *Attention and performance V.* London: Academic Press, 1975. (a)

Dornic, S. Human information processing and bilingualism. *Reports from the Institute of Applied Psychology, University of Stockholm,* 1975, (Whole no. 67). (b)

Dornic, S. Language and stress. (In preparation).

Dornic, S., Svensson, J. Ch., & Sarnecki, M. Recognition of nonattended visual tasks: The difference between pictures and words. *Reports from the Institute of Applied Psychology, University of Stockholm,* 1975, (Whole No. 65).

"comprehension time." In a laboratory situation, the influence of strong "language set" on the bilingual's input switch was also demonstrated (Dornic, in preparation).

Why, in such a case, would the output switch not affect the input switch in the interlingual Stroop test which also poses high demands on concentration, mental effort, and requires strong unilingual "language set"? This may be due to the fact that the interfering language is too much a part of the same task here, or that the subject himself tries to "switch off" one of the languages involved, which is basically different from the paradigm used in the present experiments.

Dyer, F. N. Color-naming interference in monolinguals and bilinguals. *Journal of Verbal Learning and Verbal Behavior*, 1971, **10**, 297–302.

Ervin, S. M. Learning and recall in bilinguals. *American Journal of Psychology*, 1961, **74**, 446–451.

Hamers, J. F., & Lambert, W. E. Bilingual interdependencies in auditory perception. *Journal of Verbal Learning and Verbal Behavior*, 1972, **11**, 303–310.

Hamilton, P., Hockey, P., & Rejman, M. The place of the concept of activation in human information processing theory: An integrative approach. This volume.

Kolers, P. A. Interlingual word associations. *Journal of Verbal Learning and Verbal Behavior*, 1963, **2**, 291–300.

Kolers, P. A. Reading and talking bilingually. *The American Journal of Psychology*, 1966, **79**, 357–376.

Macnamara, J. The bilingual's linguistic performance – a psychological overview. *Journal of Social Issues*, 1967, **23**, 58–77.

Macnamara, J., Krauthammer, M., & Bolgar, M. Language switching in bilinguals as a function of stimulus and response uncertainty. *Journal of Experimental Psychology*, 1968, **78**, 208–215.

Macnamara, J., & Kushnir, S. L. Linguistic independence of bilinguals: the input switch. *Journal of Verbal Learning and Verbal Behavior*, 1971, **10**, 480–487.

Penfield, W., & Roberts, L. *Speech and brain mechanisms.* Princeton: Princeton University Press, 1959.

Preston, M. S., & Lambert, W. E. Interlingual interference in a bilingual version of the Stroop color–word task. *Journal of Verbal Learning and Verbal Behavior*, 1969, **8**, 295–301.

Tulving, E., & Colotla, V. A. Free recall of trilingual lists. *Cognitive Psychology*, 1970, **1**, 86–98.

32
Depth of Processing in Recall and Recognition

Fergus I. M. Craik

Erindale College
University of Toronto
Mississauga, Ontario, Canada

ABSTRACT

The levels-of-processing approach to the study of memory, advocated by Craik and Lockhart (1972), is briefly reviewed. Previous studies are described which suggest that elaboration, rather than "depth" of encoding, may provide a better description of some results. In these experiments, subjects made decisions about words at input; the decisions induced the subjects to process the words structurally, phonemically, or semantically. A retention test for the words followed the input phase. Two recent studies using the same paradigm showed that both copying down the word at input and holding the word in mind for 5 seconds before making a decision about it, led to improved retention of words encoded structurally and phonemically. These further results suggest some principles of memory function.

I. INTRODUCTION

To many people, the rate of progress toward an understanding of human memory has been disappointingly slow. This feeling of skepticism about much recent theorizing is well captured by Tulving and Madigan's (1970) pessimistic remark that in an age of great technological advancement, man "still thinks about his own memory processes in terms readily translatable into ancient Greek" (p. 437). If it is true that our understanding has developed less rapidly than it might, what are the reasons for this slow rate of advance? One possibility is that we have concentrated too much on prediction and quantitative models and have not been sufficiently concerned with description and understanding. The emphasis on prediction and curve fitting has led to premature formalization, and to an unwarranted concern with the minutiae of theory and data. Yet the short history of the psychological study of memory has taught us that the features of models that have proved enduringly useful and have carried over from one generation of models to the next, have been at the level of general principles rather than at the level of specific detail. If this is so, it might make some sense to obtain wide agreement about a set of general principles that *must* form a part of any final theory, before worrying too much about the fine detail.

Recent theoretical writings on memory have, of course, been largely concerned with limited problems rather than with large-scale theories. Thus we have theories of free recall (Tulving, 1968), imagery (Paivio, 1971), order information (Murdock, 1974), and the spacing effect in recall (Hintzman, 1974). However, the general principles to which I refer are not microtheories of delimited areas or of specific phenomena so much as notions that pervade many different aspects of memory performance. Examples of such notions are the encoding-specificity principle (Tulving & Thomson, 1973), the distinction between primary and secondary memory (James, 1890; Waugh & Norman, 1965), and the limited-capacity hypothesis (Broadbent, 1958; Miller, 1956). These broad ideas are valuable in that they focus attention on important rather than trivial aspects of behavior, provide a setting for the discovery of robust phenomena, and establish a framework for empirical research. Within the context of a search for general principles, the role of experiments is not so much to confirm predictions from theory as to provide the means for a dialogue between theoretical ideas on the one hand and the natural world on the other. In this way, experimental research serves to refine the general principles and aids the construction of a framework for the description of mental processes.

In this chapter I want to outline some of the general notions that have provided a framework for my research over the last three years. I will describe some experiments suggested by this framework and show how the original notions have necessarily been modified by the empirical results.

II. LEVELS OF PROCESSING

Craik and Lockhart (1972) proposed a framework for memory research that provided an alternative to multistore theories, although still within the information-processing tradition. Following Treisman's (1964) theory of attention, Craik and Lockhart proposed that events are analyzed to different levels or depths by hierarchically organized cognitive structures. In this view, preliminary, shallow analyses are concerned with physical aspects of the stimulus, whereas subsequent, deeper analyses are concerned more with meaning and associative relationships. The depth to which an event is processed depends on such factors as the meaningfulness of the stimulus, the attention devoted to its analysis, and the nature of the task being performed. For some tasks (such as proofreading) a superficial analysis will suffice, whereas for others (such as comprehension) a deeper analysis is necessary. Craik and Lockhart further proposed that the products of these perceptual–cognitive analyses constitute the memory trace for the event in question, and that deeper analysis yields a more durable trace. That is, the memory trace is a record of the encoding operation performed on the stimulus; no special "mnemonic" or learning operations are necessary.

The levels-of-processing viewpoint provides an account of the results of many incidental learning studies (Hyde & Jenkins, 1973; Schulman, 1974) in which semantic analysis of the material is associated with high levels of retention. The idea can also be applied to divided-attention studies in which greater attention is associated with longer retention (Treisman, 1964), and to studies of the serial-position effect in free recall, that have shown retention of end-of-list items to vary with processing demands and the subject's expectations (Craik, 1970; Jacoby, 1973). However, there is one major objection to a levels-of-processing approach, and that is its inherent circularity. Since there is no other index of depth of processing than the subsequent retention level of the material, it is too easy to define depth as "the type of processing that leads to high retention levels" and to give "deeper processing" as the answer to the question of why some events are well remembered.

In an attempt to break the circularity, Craik (1973) postulated that deeper analyses required more processing time than superficial analyses; accordingly, he devised an experimental paradigm in which response latency served as the index of depth. Subjects were informed that the experiment concerned the time required to answer various questions about words exposed singly on a tachistoscope for 200 msec. Before each word was presented, the subject was asked one of three types of question about the word. The three types concerned, first, the typescript in which the word was written ("Is the word in capital letters?"); second, the word's phonemic qualities ("Does the word rhyme with RAIN?"); and third, the word's semantic qualities ("Would the word fit the sentence: He kept the ——— in his room?"). In each case, half of the words presented led to a positive response, and half to a negative response. Examples of the questions and word stimuli are shown in Table 1. Obviously, the questions were designed to induce the subject to process the exposed words to different depths, questions about typescript leading to shallow encoding and questions about meaning leading to deep encoding. The predictions in this type of experiment were, first, that "deeper" questions would take longer to answer and, second, that deeper levels of processing would be associated with higher levels of retention in a subsequent unexpected memory test.

The results of one such experiment were reported by Craik and Tulving (1975, Experiment II). In this study, 60 words were presented, 10 under each combination of question type with response type (positive or negative). Across subjects, the same words served in all six conditions. On each trial, a question was presented auditorily to the subject, followed after 2 seconds by the word,

TABLE 1

Examples of Encoding Questions Used in these Experiments

	Yes	No
1. Is the word in capital letters?	FRIEND	ocean
2. Does the word rhyme with TRAIN?	brain	speech
3. Is the word a piece of furniture?	TABLE	string
4. Would the word fit the sentence: "He kept the ____ in his room."?	PICTURE	RAIN

presented visually for 200 msec. The subject responded "yes" or "no" by pressing the appropriate one of two telegraph keys; the latency between word onset and the subject's response was recorded from a millisecond timer. After completing the 60 trials, the subjects were given an unexpected recognition test, made up of the 60 original words plus 120 distractors; they were instructed to check all words seen in the first phase of the experiment. The results, shown in Table 2, confirmed both predictions; decision latency increased for both positive and negative responses as a function of depth of processing, and the probability of recognition also increased with depth. It may be noted that whereas positive and negative decisions were equally fast at each level of processing, positive decisions at the rhyme and semantic levels were associated with higher recognition performance. This pattern recurred in further experiments and is discussed subsequently. Craik and Tulving (1975) also found the same general relationship between initial processing and subsequent retention in both free-recall and cued-recall studies.

The data shown in Table 2 fit a depth-of-processing description reasonably well, but there may be alternative ways of accounting for the results. Since deeper levels of processing are associated both with higher retention and with longer processing times, it could be objected that the high recognition probabilities in the sentence condition are simply a function of longer "study times."

TABLE 2

Decision Latency and Proportion of Words Recognized as a Function of Depth of Processing[a]

Response type	Decision latency			Response type	Proportion recognized		
	Case	Rhyme	Sentence		Case	Rhyme	Sentence
Yes	550	635	734	Yes	.15	.48	.81
No	580	622	743	No	.19	.26	.49

[a]After Craik and Tulving (1975). Copyright 1975 by the American Psychological Association. Reprinted by permission.

This objection was countered by a further experiment in the Craik and Tulving series. Two processing tasks were devised such that the shallow, structural task was quite complex and thus took longer to accomplish than the deeper, semantic task. In both tasks a word was presented for 200 msec and was preceded by a question. Structural questions concerned the pattern of vowels and consonants in the word; for example, the word BOOK has the pattern CVVC (where C = consonant and V = vowel). On each structural trial the subject was given a card with a pattern of Cs and Vs printed on it; when the word was presented, the task was to judge whether the word fitted that particular pattern. The semantic task was the sentence-frame task described previously. Following the decision phase of the experiment, a recognition test was given. The results showed that whereas the structural task took 1.73 sec to perform on average and the semantic task took 0.81 sec, the corresponding recognition probabilities were 0.53 and 0.75.

The negative correlation between processing time and the recognition performance suggests that study time is not the major determinant of retention. It seems, rather, that the qualitative nature of the encoding operations is crucial for subsequent performance. Although this conclusion is in line with the levels-of-processing framework, the finding of a negative correlation between processing time and retention performance does mean that response latency can not be taken unequivocally as an index of depth.

Another objection to the depth-of-processing explanation could be that in the case and rhyme judgement tasks, subjects do not perceive the word properly. In one sense, of course, that is exactly what a levels-of-processing description is saying; that perception is not all or none, it is a matter of degree, and that semantic judgments necessitate deeper, fuller analysis. However, the objection could take the simpler form that when subjects judge typescript they may only read one letter and not the whole word. Similarly, for rhyme judgements, they may simply read the last few letters to perform the task. A variant of the levels-of-processing experiment, which reduces the force of this objection, was also carried out by Craik and Tulving (1975, Experiment IX). Again, words were presented serially and each word was preceded by a question, but in this case subjects were informed that their main task was to learn words for a later recognition test. That is, the experiment was run under intentional learning conditions. In addition, each word was exposed on a screen for 1 sec, with a 5-sec interval between words. Given the instructions to learn and the increased exposure time, it seemed certain that all subjects would perceive the word fully (in the sense that they would identify it). The only other modifications were that the semantic task consisted of judging whether the word fitted a taxonomic category (e.g., a form of communication? a type of fruit?) and also that, in the recognition test, subjects were instructed to check exactly 60 words.

The results, shown in Table 3, are quite similar to those obtained under shorter exposure conditions and incidental learning instructions (Table 2). It can thus be concluded, with reasonable confidence, that the original results were not due to

TABLE 3
Proportion of Words Recognized as a Function of Depth
of Processing; Intentional Learning Conditions[a]

Response type	Case	Rhyme	Category
yes	.23	.59	.81
no	.28	.33	.62

[a]After Craik and Tulving (1975). Copyright 1975 by the American Psychological Association. Reprinted by permission.

partial perception of stimulus words. Also, finding the same pattern of results under intentional learning conditions rules out the possibility that the original results are restricted to incidental learning situations.

Despite the mounting evidence that depth of processing provides a reasonable account of the results, several curious aspects of the data remain unexplained. Why are positive decisions associated with higher retention levels than negative decisions, for example? Why does this effect interact with depth, such that it is present for semantic decisions but not for case decisions? In the intentional learning study, why were subjects apparently unable to achieve higher recognition levels for case and rhyme decisions even though they had 6 sec to process each word?

Regarding the questions concerning positive and negative decisions, Craik and Tulving suggested that, for rhyme and semantic decisions at least, positive responses reflect a situation in which the word can form an integrated encoded unit with the question context. The question and the word presented are "congruous" (Schulman, 1974), and this state of affairs facilitates the formation of a richer, more elaborate memory trace. For example, if the encoding context is the sentence frame "while walking down the street he saw his ____," the word FRIEND would yield a positive response and the word SPEECH would not. From the first word, the subject can form an integrated unit comprising word and context, but cannot do so for the second word; the word and context must be stored separately. Thus for semantic and rhyme decisions, positive responses reflect situations in which words are elaborated by the context and thus, plausibly, their retention is enhanced. However, for questions concerning type-script, positive and negative decisions lead to equally poor encodings; "Is the word in capital letters?" leads to no more elaboration of TABLE than does the question "Is the word in small print?" If this analysis is valid it should be possible to devise semantic questions that lead to equal elaboration for both positive and negative decisions, and thus yield equal retention levels. Craik and Tulving (1975, Experiment VI) presented subjects with questions like "Is the object taller than a man?" followed by such words as STEEPLE (positive response) and CHILD (negative response). In this case, the words can be equally elaborated by the concept of size, and, in line with the argument just presented, the retention of "positive" and "negative" words was indeed found to be equivalent.

The question of poor recognition of case-encoded words remains unanswered, however, and some suspicion of artefact may still be present. The following experiments have recently been carried out to shed further light on the levels-of-processing paradigm.

III. EXPERIMENT I

One possible account of the recognition results shown in Tables 2 and 3 is that, in the within-subjects design, subjects may have adopted an inappropriately high recognition criterion and thus failed to recognize many case- and rhyme-encoded words. That is, if semantically encoded words are rather easy to recognize, subjects may maintain that high criterion when examining other words as well, and thus fail to recognize words they might recognize when using a more realistic criterion. This account admits to *some* differences between words encoded in different ways, but it is possible that the differences are quantitative rather than qualitative. In either case, a between-subjects study — in which the different encoding operations are performed by different groups of subjects — should reveal this source of artefact if it exists. Other departures from the standard paradigm used by Craik and Tulving were, first, the use of a forced-choice recognition procedure and, second, the requirement that subjects copy each word down as it was presented. The point of the first modification was to reduce further any bias to the decision criterion; the second modification was introduced to eliminate the possibility that subjects do not perceive the word fully under some conditions.

A. Procedure

Four groups of 10 subjects performed the experiment; each group made only one type of judgment about the words. These four tasks were judgments about case (such as "Is the word in capital letters?"), judgments about rhyme (such as "Does the word rhyme with FLOOR?"), and judgments about categorical membership (such as "Is the word a type of clergy?"). The fourth group's task was simply to learn the list of words presented. All four groups received intentional learning instructions; thus the first three groups performed an orienting task in addition to learning the words.

All subjects were presented with the same list of 60 common nouns. Each word was presented visually for 3.5 sec, followed by a further 3.5-sec interval in which the subject wrote down the word and recorded his judgment. Subjects in the first three groups read the questions relevant to each word from a printed sheet; they recorded their decision about words on the same sheet. Subjects in the fourth group performed no orienting task but simply copied each word down as it was presented. After all 60 words had been presented, subjects received an 8-alternative forced-choice recognition test. The distractor words were drawn from the same pool as the target words. Eight alternatives were used since preliminary tests had shown that ceiling effects occurred with fewer alternatives.

B. Results and Discussion

Table 4 shows that the pattern of results was similar to that obtained in previous studies, but that performance was markedly higher in the case and rhyme conditions. In regard to the three orienting task conditions, the effect of task ("level of processing") was statistically reliable, $F(2, 27) = 8.93, p < .01$, as was decision type (yes/no), $F(1, 27) = 12.63, p < .01$, and the interaction between level and decision, $F(2, 27) = 5.90, p < .01$. With regard to the fourth group, it is sufficient to note that instructions to learn yielded a retention level comparable to the semantic processing group. Thus, the "levels-of-processing" effect was still obtained under rather different conditions, although performance was improved for shallow-level tasks; also the difference between positive and negative responses was attenuated relative to the differences found in previous experiments.

Unfortunately, since several modifications were embodied in this study, it is not possible to specify which of the changes caused the improved recognition of case-encoded and rhyme-encoded words. The possible sources of improvement are: (1) the between-subjects design; (2) the forced-choice recognition test; and (3) the requirement to copy each word at presentation. It seems somewhat unlikely that the between-subjects design would modify the pattern of results radically since, in a related series of studies, Hyde and Jenkins (1973) found marked differences in retention following different orienting tasks, although the task manipulation was between subjects. Also, it does not seem likely that the forced-choice recognition test was the cause of the changed pattern, since in the intentional learning study reported by Craik and Tulving (Table 3 in this

TABLE 4
Proportion of Words Recognized; Between-Subjects
Design (Experiment I)

Response type	Case	Rhyme	Category	Learn
yes	.60	.78	.90	
				.86
no	.59	.64	.80	

chapter) subjects were instructed to check exactly 60 words on the recognition sheet. This instruction should force subjects to lower their recognition criterion once they have checked words they recognize with high confidence. On the other hand, it is quite plausible that the act of copying the words down induced subjects to process shallow-encoded words to a deeper level, and that this manipulation resulted in higher recognition levels for the case and rhyme groups, and for words associated with negative decisions. Further discussion of this possibility is deferred until a further variant of the levels-of-processing paradigm is described.

IV. EXPERIMENT II

The second experiment to be reported was an exploratory study, carried out to examine the effect of presenting the word *before* presenting its encoding question; in all previous studies the question had been presented first. Although no specific outcomes were predicted for the experiment, it was expected that the necessity to remember the word until the question was presented would lead to more processing — especially at shallow levels. A further exploratory variable in this setting was the contrast between incidental and intentional learning; given the distinction between maintenance and elaborative rehearsal (Craik & Lockhart, 1972), it seemed likely that the necessity to hold the word until the question was presented would yield even higher retention levels under intentional learning conditions. That is, under incidental conditions the subject would simply maintain the word in a relatively unprocessed form until the question was presented, whereas under intentional conditions he might use the holding interval to carry out deeper, elaborative encoding on the word.

A. Procedure

Four groups of 16 subjects were tested under the combinations of incidental or intentional instructions with word or question presented first. Subjects in incidental conditions were told that the experiment concerned perception of the words and decisions about them; subjects in the intentional conditions were informed that they would give a recognition test for all presented words at a later stage. All subjects were told that they had to answer simple questions about words and mark their responses on a sheet. In the "word-first" conditions, the sequence of events was as follows: The word appeared for 2 sec on a television screen, followed by a 5-sec blank interval; an auditory tone then instructed the subject to turn over the top card from the pile in front of him. On the card, a question about case, rhyme, or category was printed; the subject had 5 sec to read the question and circle "yes" or "no" on his answer sheet. At the end of the 5-sec period, a further tone signaled the appearance of the next word on the

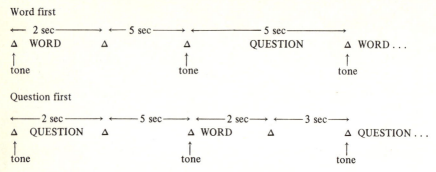

FIG. 1   Sequence of events in Experiment I.

television screen. In the "question first" conditions, the sequence was reversed: At the first tone, the subject turned the top card and read the question; he then held the question in mind for 5 sec; at the next tone the word appeared for 2 sec, followed by 3 sec in which the subject recorded his decision. The two conditions are illustrated in Fig. 1. After the completion of 60 such trials (10 positive and 10 negative decisions for each of case, rhyme, and category questions, randomly presented), all subjects were given the recognition test. In this test, 180 words were presented visually, one at a time, at a 3-sec rate; the 180 comprised the 60 original words plus 120 distractors of a similar type. Subjects checked "yes" or "no" as each word was presented.

B. Results

The findings are illustrated in Fig. 2. The figure shows that the results for incidental and intentional groups were extremely similar. For both groups the "question first" condition yielded results comparable with those of previous studies (for example, with the data shown in Tables 2 and 3). For "word-first" conditions, however, the results were more similar to the pattern of findings in Experiment I; that is, case and rhyme encodings were associated with higher levels of recognition than the equivalent conditions in the "question-first" group. Also, the difference in retention between positive and negative decisions was attenuated in the "word-first" conditions.

The reliability of the findings was assessed by analysis of variance. Of the main effects, the incidental–intentional manipulation had no reliable effect ($F < 1$), while the effects of presentation order (word first versus question first) and level of processing were both highly significant (both $ps < .001$). Thus, while the typical levels-of-processing results were obtained under both presentation orders, the word-first condition was associated with higher retention levels. Of the interactions, no interaction involving the incidental–intentional variable was significant. Two reliable interactions of interest were the interaction of level of processing and order of presentation, $F(2, 120) = 22.0$, $p < .001$, and the

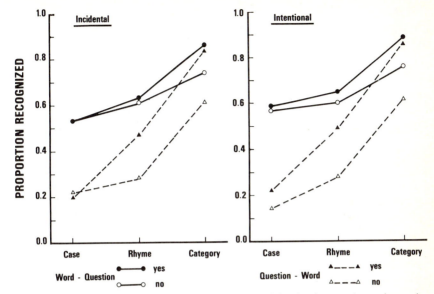

FIG. 2 Proportion of words recognized as a function of depth of processing and experimental condition (Experiment II).

interaction of response type (yes/no) and order of presentation, $F(1, 60) = 11.8$, $p < .001$. The first interaction confirms that the word-first manipulation differentially improved performance for shallower levels of processing; the second illustrates the attenuation of the difference between positive and negative decisions under word-first conditions.

C. Discussion

The major point of interest to be drawn from Experiment II is the finding that the necessity to hold the word in mind for 5 sec before the question was presented increased recognition scores — especially for shallower levels of encoding and for negative decisions. Further, it is suggested that this difference between word-first and question-first conditions is echoed in the difference between the results of Experiment I and previous studies. That is, the requirement to copy each word down as it was presented (Experiment I) and the requirement to hold the word in mind for 5 sec (Experiment II) apparently acted similarly to improve the encoding of words under conditions that normally induce rather poor encoding and thus yield low levels of retention. Although it is perfectly plausible that the extra processing necessitated by copying or remembering the word should differentially increase the retention of shallow-encoded words, it becomes even more mystifying that intentional learning instructions did not have a similar, beneficial effect on case and rhyme encodings as in the study whose results are shown in Table 2. For the moment we can only speculate that subjects are either unwilling to carry out more beneficial encoding operations on their own initiative or, more likely, are *unaware* that their memory for words given shallow encodings will be so poor; it is apparently only when the task requires some further cognitive activity that performance improves.

V.   MODIFICATIONS OF THE ORIGINAL THEORETICAL FRAMEWORK

Although some of the results reported here and by Craik and Tulving (1975) are in reasonable agreement with the levels-of-processing framework, other aspects of the data are clearly incompatible with the original formulation. Craik and Lockhart postulated that words and other events were processed to different depths, depending on the orienting task. This analysis suggests that under some conditions only the structural or phonemic qualities of the word are analyzed. However, under intentional learning conditions, it is clear that the word is always fully identified even in the structural judgment task; subjects do not perceive a pattern of strokes and curves, they perceive the word TABLE. If meaning is accessed, why is retention so poor? Another problem for the original formulation is the difference in retention between words associated with positive and negative decisions: there is no reason to believe that the two decisions necessitate different depths of analysis, yet words given positive decisions are consistently associated with higher levels of retention.

Both of these problems are resolved if it is postulated that retention is enhanced by greater degrees of trace elaboration. It is not so much the depth of processing that is important for memory, perhaps, as the richness and complexity of cognitive operations carried out on the stimulus. As a further speculation, trace elaboration may depend on the context as much as on the item to be remembered, and to the extent to which the item and the context can be integrated to form a coherent unit. Thus, a sentence frame will typically provide a richer context than a question about case or rhyme, but the degree of elaboration will also depend on the extent to which the item and the context are compatible. As argued above, subjects can form coherent encoded units when the encoding question yields a positive response. The trace will not be elaborated to the same extent when the item and the question are incompatible, as they are when the question yields a negative response. Schulman's (1974) notion of *congruity* between the encoding question and the encoded item thus seems a further necessary principle. Richer encoding contexts can lead to a greater elaboration of the item's memory trace and thus to better retention, but only when the item and the context are congruous.

B. Sentence Complexity Study

Two further studies illustrating the notions of elaboration and congruity are described briefly below. The first study, reported fully by Craik and Tulving (1975, Experiment VII), was an attempt to manipulate directly the degree of elaboration. The encoding questions were all sentence frames, but of three different degrees of complexity: simple, medium, and complex. We tried to make the complex sentence frames no more predictive of the missing word than the simple or medium frames. Examples of the three sentence types are "He dropped the – – –;" "The old man dropped the _____;" and "The old man hobbled across the room and dropped the _____." The word presented was WATCH in all cases. In outline, 60 trials were given, 20 of each sentence type, with 10 positive and 10 negative responses associated with each type. Sixty different sentence frames were used. The task was described as a decision test, to study the speed with which subjects could decide whether the word fitted the sentence frame; no mention was made of a memory test. After all 60 trials were completed, subjects were given 8 min to recall as many words as they could from the decision phase. This free-recall test was followed by a cued-recall test in which the sentence frames were re-presented as cues.

The results are shown in Fig. 3. For free recall, there is no effect of sentence complexity in the case of negative responses, but a systematic increase in recall from simple to complex for positive responses. The provision of cues had no facilitative effect upon negative responses but greatly enhanced the recall of

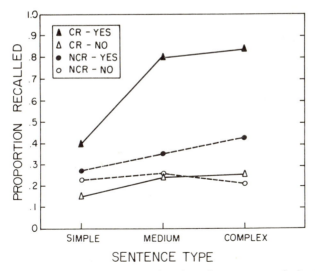

FIG. 3 Proportion of words recalled as a function of sentence complexity (CR = cued recall; NCR - noncued recall).

words associated with positive responses, especially for more complex sentence frames. The results can be interpreted as showing that when the item and the context are not congruous (negative responses), neither the elaborateness of the context, nor the provision of the context at retrieval, aided recall of the item. Both of these factors did act to enhance recall of positive items, however. In line with notions of encoding specificity (Tulving & Thomson, 1973) and redintegration (Horowitz & Prytulak, 1969), the provision of a cue associated with the item at input — in this case, the sentence context — acts to enhance recall, but only if the item and the cue can be encoded as an integrated unit. In addition, it may be concluded that the semantic richness of the context benefits the recall of congruent encodings but has no effect on "noncongruent" encodings. Extrapolating from the present findings, it would be expected that extremely simple, nonsemantic sentence frames such as "It is a _____" would yield poor retention of the presented words (Hyde & Jenkins, 1973).

B. Study on Shared and Unique Cues

The final study to be described yielded a pattern of results similar to the pattern found in the sentence-complexity experiment. Just as the similarities between Experiments I and II suggested notions accounting for these similarities, so this further example of a common pattern of findings may yield a common theoretical description. The data in question are taken from an incidental learning study by Moscovitch and Craik (1976); only the relevant portion of the experiment will be described. Subjects were asked whether the presented word rhymed with a given word or fitted a given sentence frame. As before, half of the words in each case yielded positive decisions and half gave negative decisions. After the initial phase was completed, subjects were represented with the encoding questions as cues and were asked to recall the presented words. There were two major conditions in the experiment: For one group, each of the 40 words presented for decision was associated with its own unique encoding question; for the second group of subjects, only two rhyme questions and two sentence frames were presented — that is, 10 words shared each encoding question. Thus, at retrieval, in the first group each word was associated with a unique retrieval cue, while in the second group, 10 words (5 positive and 5 negative decisions) shared each cue. The point of the experiment was to discover whether recall depended only on the level of encoding (rhyme versus sentence) or whether performance was also a function of cue uniqueness.

Table 5 shows that cued-recall levels were higher when each word was associated with its own unique cue. It also shows that unique cuing was not uniformly beneficial; the manipulation had a greater effect on sentence-encoded than on rhyme-encoded words.

Further, within sentence-encoded words, the beneficial effect of unique cues was greater for positive than for negative responses. A slightly different way of

TABLE 6
Proportion of Words Recalled as a Function of
Retrieval Cue Uniqueness[a]

	Shared cues		Unique cues	
Response type	Rhyme	Sentence	Rhyme	Sentence
yes	.33	.42	.35	.85
no	.02	.20	.10	.37

[a]After Moscovitch and Craik (1976).

looking at the results in Table 5 is to state that the provision of unique cues had a relatively small effect on negative responses, and a much larger effect on positive responses, but with the qualification that the beneficial effect of cuing on positive responses was restricted to words encoded in sentence frames. An analysis of variance on these data lends support to this interpretation. The main effects of cue condition and type of encoding question were both statistically reliable. Of greater interest, the interaction of cue condition and response type was significant as was the three-way interaction of cue condition, question type, and response type $F(1, 34) = 12.9, p < .01$.

The resemblance between these results and the results of the sentence-complexity study may be seen with a little effort. The provision of unique cues in the present experiment is like the provision of retrieval cues in the previous study; the differences between rhyme and sentence encodings are like the differences between levels of sentence complexity. I would like to suggest that the similarities are not coincidental. The provision of retrieval cues in the sentence-complexity study and of unique cues in the cue-sharing study both may be seen as the provision of more adequate retrieval information. In the sentence-complexity study, the presence of the encoding question at retrieval provides access to the encoded unit of item-plus-question; note that the retrieval cue is effective only in the case of positive responses, where item and question have been encoded as an integrated unit. The unique cues in the present study aid retrieval by specifying more precisely the trace in question; the shared-cue condition exemplifies the notion of cue overload discussed by Watkins and Watkins (1975). Again, the unique cues are more effective in the case of positive responses where the encoding question and the item have formed a congruous, integrated, encoded unit. Thus it is postulated that words associated with positive decisions in the initial phase benefit more from adequate retrieval information since that information forms an integral part of the item's memory trace — the item and cue are congruous, or to use another description, are stored as dependent rather than independent traces (Jacoby, 1974). It is further postulated that "deeper" or more complex encodings benefit more from the provision of adequate retrieval information since such encodings are richer and more elaborate — in some sense, there is more there to retrieve, once the trace has been accessed. Such elaborate traces may also be more unique and distinctive from other memory traces and their retrieval thereby enhanced, in the same way as a red dot is easily perceived in a background of green dots (see Lockhart, Craik, & Jacoby, 1975).

At a less speculative level, the Moscovitch and Craik study makes it clear that the *uniqueness* of the link between the retrieval information and the encoded item is a further important determinant of memory performance. Craik and Lockhart (1972) acknowledge the future importance of retrieval factors within a levels-of-processing framework; the present results provide a starting point for the elucidation of such factors. It should be noted, however, that although the beneficial effects of unique cues are seen at retrieval, the cue manipulation is effective only because the words were associated with one or several encoding questions at input. That is, overall performance must be viewed as an interaction of encoding and retrieval factors (Tulving, 1974). Finally in this section, it may be noted that the results of the sentence-complexity study, and the unique-cue study, qualify and extend Tulving's encoding-specificity principle. Not only must an effective retrieval cue be presented with the to-be-recalled item at input, but the cue must also: (1) be congruous with the item so that an integrated trace is formed; and (2) form a relatively unique link between that cue and the item to be retrieved.

VI.   SOME DESCRIPTIVE PRINCIPLES OF MEMORY FUNCTION

The experiments described above have served to qualify and modify the levels-of-processing notions advanced by Craik and Lockhart (1972). The notion of elaboration of encoding provides a more satisfactory account of the differences in retention between positive and negative responses, of differences due to sentence complexity, and of the intentional-learning results in the Craik and Tulving paradigm. In addition, the principles of congruity and uniqueness are necessary to handle some of the experimental observations. Does all this mean that the original notion of "depth" of processing has been superseded and should now be abandoned? It seems to me that depth of encoding still serves a useful descriptive function and is still required to account for some results. For example, words associated with negative responses show a systematic increase in retention level from structural to semantic decisions even though the word is not congruous with the context and is thus little elaborated by it. It seems that the qualitative nature of the analysis that must be carried out before the decision can be made, affects the memorability of the item. Also, retention levels were higher following a simple semantic task than after a complex structural task; again it is necessary to conclude that the qualitative nature of the task is critically important.

To summarize the argument, notes on four descriptive principles are offered. These four are chosen simply because they were suggested by these experiments; there is absolutely no suggestion that they are *the* four principles of memory function:

Depth of processing refers to qualitatively different perceptual/cognitive analyses, possibly organized in an hierarchical fashion (Rumelhart, 1977); it is postulated that deeper encodings are associated with higher levels of retention. The notion is supported by the finding that a simple semantic task yields higher retention than a complex structural task, and by the systematic increase in retention of negative responses as the decisions made at encoding require greater degrees of semantic involvement.

Elaboration of encoding refers to further, richer processing within one qualitative domain. The idea is supported by the finding of strong levels-of-processing effects under intentional-learning conditions, by the results of the sentence-complexity study, and by the finding of equal retention of positive and negative responses with such encoding questions as "Is the object larger than a table?"

Congruity between an event and its encoding context leads to the formation of an elaborate, integrated trace. The preexisting relations in semantic memory, which underlie congruity, will also facilitate reconstructive retrieval (Craik & Tulving, 1975, pp. 291–292). The generally higher retention levels associated with positive responses are attributed to the greater congruity between item and question. The notion is also supported by the differential effectiveness of cues depending (partially at least) on the congruity between the item and the retrieval information.

Uniqueness of the link between retrieval information and the encoded event is the fourth factor. Its importance is demonstrated by the experiment on shared and unique cues.

In conclusion, I should stress again that these four principles are intended as examples of important, pervasive features of memory function, but the list is tentative and incomplete. Although the principles refer to different aspects of mental functioning, they are not necessarily mutually exclusive. For example, it seems quite possible that further work will show depth and uniqueness to have much in common. The goal of the present research program is to specify such principles more precisely, and to elucidate their implications and interactions. The broad aim is not so much to predict behavior as to understand memory processes and their role in cognition.

ACKNOWLEDGMENTS

The research described in this article was supported by Grant A8261 to the author from the National Research Council of Canada. Many of the ideas discussed were developed in conversations with Larry Jacoby, Bob Lockhart, Morris Moscovitch, and Endel Tulving. The author is also grateful to these colleagues for helpful criticisms of an earlier version of the paper.

REFERENCES

Broadbent, D. E. *Perception and communication*. London: Pergamon, 1958.

Craik, F. I. M. The fate of primary memory items in free recall. *Journal of Verbal Learning and Verbal Behavior,* 1970, **9**, 143–148.

Craik, F. I. M. A 'levels of analysis' view of memory, In P. Pliner, L. Krames, & T. M. Alloway (Eds.), *Communication and affect: Language and thought.* New York: Academic Press, 1973.

Craik, F. I. M., & Lockhart, R. S. Levels of processing: A framework for memory research. *Journal of Verbal Learning and Verbal Behavior*, 1972, **11**, 671–684.

Craik, F. I. M., & Tulving, E. Depth of processing and the retention of words in episodic memory. *Journal of Experimental Psychology: General*, 1975, **104**, 268–294.

Hintzman, D. L. Theoretical implications of the spacing effect. In R. L. Solso (Ed.), *Theories in cognitive psychology: The Loyola Symposium.* Hillsdale, N.J.: Lawrence Erlbaum Associates, 1974.

Horowitz, L. M., & Prytulak, L. S. Redintegrative memory. *Psychological Review,* 1969, **76**, 519–531.

Hyde, T. S., & Jenkins, J. J. Recall for words as a function of semantic, graphic, and syntactic orienting tasks. *Journal of Verbal Learning and Verbal Behavior,* 1973, **12**, 471–480.

Jacoby, L. L. Encoding processes, rehearsal, and recall requirements. *Journal of Verbal Learning and Verbal Behavior*, 1973, **12**, 302–310.

Jacoby, L. L. The role of mental contiguity in memory: Registration and retrieval effects. *Journal of Verbal Learning and Verbal Behavior,* 1974, **13**, 483–496.

James, W. *Principles of psychology.* New York: Holt, 1890.

Lockhart, R. S., Craik, F. I. M., & Jacoby, L. L. Depth of processing and recall: Some aspects of a general memory system. In J. Brown (Ed.), *Recognition and recall.* London: Wiley, 1975.

Miller, G. A. The magical number seven, plus or minus two: Some limits on our capacity for processing information. *Psychological Review,* 1956, **63**, 81–96.

Moscovitch, M., & Craik, F. I. M. Depth of processing, retrieval cues, and uniqueness of encoding as factors in recall. *Journal of Verbal Learning and Verbal Behavior,* 1976, **15**, 447–458.

Murdock, B. B., Jr. *Human memory: Theory and data.* Hillsdale, N.J.: Lawrence Erlbaum Associates, 1974.

Paivio, A. *Imagery and verbal processes.* New York: Holt, Rinehart and Winston, 1971.

Rumelhart, D. E. Toward a complete theory of reading. In S. Dornic (Ed.), *Attention and performance VI.* Hillsdale, N.J.: Lawrence Erlbaum Associates, 1977.

Schulman, A. I. Memory for words recently classified. *Memory & Cognition,* 1974, **2**, 47–52.

Treisman, A. M. Selective attention in man. *British Medical Bulletin,* 1964, **2**, 12–15.

Tulving, E. Theoretical issues in free recall. In T. R. Dixon & D. L. Horton (Eds.), *Verbal behavior and general behavior theory*. Englewood Cliffs, N.J.: Prentice-Hall, 1968.

Tulving, E. Cue-dependent forgetting. *American Scientist*, 1974, **62**, 74–82.

Tulving, E., & Madigan, S. A. Memory and verbal learning. *Annual Review of Psychology*, 1970, **21**, 437–484.

Tulving, E., & Thomson, D. M. Encoding specificity and retrieval processes in episodic memory. *Psychological Review*, 1973, **80**, 352–373.

Watkins, O. C., & Watkins, M. J. Buildup of proactive inhibition as a cue-overload effect. *Journal of Experimental Psychology: Human Learning and Memory*, 1975, **1**, 442–452.

Waugh, N. C., & Norman, D. A. Primary memory. *Psychological Review*, 1965, **72**, 89–104.

33

Crossword Puzzles and Lexical Memory

R. S. Nickerson

Bolt Beranek and Newman Inc.
Cambridge, Massachusetts, United States

ABSTRACT

The crossword puzzle task is discussed as it relates to the question of how words are retrieved from lexical memory. Arguments are made concerning the effectiveness of semantic, orthographic, phonetic, and thematic cues. It is suggested that cues are effective in two ways: they provide information in terms of which candidate solution words can be evaluated, and they directly facilitate the search for solution words. It is further suggested that if "search" is to be used as an explanatory concept, at least two types of search processes must be assumed, one a rapid parallel process that occurs below the level of awareness and the other a slow serial process that is open to introspection.

I. INTRODUCTION

> Human minds, at least human minds that are good for much, like to play. They like to play with all sorts of things, and since words are dear to minds, notably with words. (Laird, 1953, p. 67).

Crossword puzzles are undoubtedly among the most engaging and engaged-in diversions of the western world. Acording to the *Boston Globe,* there are 30 million crossword puzzle doers in the United States alone (Miller, 1975). One can think of many reasons for the popularity of this pastime. Crossword puzzles can be done anytime, anywhere. Totally engrossing, they provide an innocuous and socially acceptable form of escapism. They are intellectually challenging, but in a pleasant and nonthreatening way — one fails in private and tears up the evidence of one's failure. They do not require intense uninterrupted concentration — as do some more creative pursuits, nor careful logical reasoning — as does the working out of some other kinds of puzzles, nor eternal vigilance against irremedial blunders — as does a game of chess. My interest in crossword puzzles, for the purposes of this chapter, is not based, however, on a desire to understand the motivation of puzzle doers, but rather on the notion that the crossword puzzle is a particularly interesting task for the investigator of lexical memory. A study of the behavior of individuals performing this task, or even an armchair analysis of how they do it, might perhaps provide some hints concerning the way memory is organized and the strategies or heuristics that people use to tease information out of it.

Several preliminary comments will help delimit the area of interest more precisely, and set the tone for what follows. First, as used in this chapter, the term *lexical memory* is given the rather broad connotation of memory not only for words and their meanings, but for linguistic rules, conventions, and associations. More generally, the concern is for the kinds of information that have been acquired during the normal course of life and have become part of the more or less permanent knowledge base that underlies one's understanding and use of speech and language.

Second, in the study of lexical memory, it is natural to focus on retrieval processes. One seldom knows the condition under which specific items of lexical information were acquired, and there seems little point in worrying about what has happened during retention intervals that are measured in years or decades. Some memory theorists make the assumption that most, if not all, of the information that finds its way into very long-term memory is stored there permanently anyway. Failure to recall is viewed as a failure of the retrieval process (Rumelhart, Lindsay, & Norman, 1972; Shiffrin & Atkinson, 1969; Tulving & Pearlstone, 1966).

Third, many of the comments in the chapter derive from the currently popular view that effective utilization of memory may reasonably be thought of, at least in some respects, as a type of problem solving. The literature contains many references to storage and retrieval "strategies" or "plans" (Banks & Atkinson, 1974; Bellezza & Walker, 1974; Bower, 1972; Norman, 1970; Santa, Ruskin, Snuttjer, & Baker, 1975; Shiffrin, 1970). Discussions of memory retrieval often make use of the notion of a search process (Mohs, Wescourt, & Atkinson, 1975; Peterson, 1967; Shiffrin, 1970); and sometimes, though not always, the search is viewed as a conscious and deliberate hunting expedition. It makes sense, therefore, to ask about the nature of the search procedure, how the search is guided, whether it is efficient, and under what conditions it is terminated. And in conceptualizing a search process one naturally thinks in terms of goals, strategies, heuristics, tricks, inferences, and rules. Searching is something one does, not something that happens. And one may do it well or badly, cleverly or incompetently, energetically or lackadaisically.

Fourth, the chapter is discursive and speculative. I have not hesitated to use introspective and anecdotal clues concerning how crossword puzzle doers go about finding target words. Experimental findings and memory theories are discussed as they relate to speculations about lexical memory that are prompted by a consideration of the crossword puzzle task; but no attempt is made to review either exhaustively or systematically the results of all the experiments that are relevant to the various issues that are raised, or all the ways in which these issues might be resolved by current theoretical treatments of memory.

II. RETRIEVAL CUES

The crossword puzzle task may be characterized as a *cued-retrieval* task. One fills in a puzzle by finding target words in one's memory that match certain cues, some of which come with the puzzle, and others of which are acquired as the solution is developed. It is easy to identify several types of effective retrieval cues. The challenge is to account for their effectiveness.

What kind of process does one evoke when asked to produce a word that has a given meaning? How does the brain use such information as the number of letters in the desired word and perhaps what some of those letters are, to facilitate the process? How is it that one can sometimes be confident, without knowing what one is looking for, that whatever it is, it does *not* have certain properties? What is it that one does when trying to think of the name of an animal that rhymes with CARE? How does one go about searching for six-letter words that begin with M, or for words that end with PT? What is the significance of the fact that one can search on the ending, or the middle, of a word as well as on the beginning?

These are the sorts of questions that a consideration of the crossword puzzle task evokes. I do not think the answers to these questions are known, although there are some hypotheses.

A. Semantic Cues

The most obvious type of cue that is provided to the puzzle doer is semantic. Typically, one is given an abbreviated definition, a synonym, or an associate of the word that is required. The fact that memory can be entered with a definition for the purpose of finding a word (as well as vice versa) is a fact that must be accounted for by any adequate model of lexical memory. It suggests that the organization of memory is unlike that of a dictionary, which is organized to facilitate the retrieval of a definition, given a word, but is ill suited to the retrieval of a word, given a definition.

Brown and McNeill (1966) make this point and note that an organizational scheme that would permit searching for a word, given a definition, is one that is used with keysort cards. Suppose a word were defined in terms of a set of semantic features. Suppose further that the definition of a word were encoded on a card in the following way: the presence of a feature is represented by a hole at a particular spot close to the edge of the card; the absence of that feature is represented by an indentation in the card at that spot (both the area of the hole and the portion of the card on edgeward side of it are removed). Thus, the definition of a word is represented by the pattern of holes and indentations on the edge of a card. Now imagine a memory comprised of a large stack of such cards. By passing a rod through the stack at the place representing a given feature, one could extract those cards that have a hole at this spot; those cards having an indentation would remain in the stack. Then, by taking the subset of cards representing words that have *this* feature, and passing the rod through them at the place representing a second feature, one would extract words that have each of two features, and so on. Eventually, one could presumably identify a single card representing a word with a unique set of features, which would be tantamount to finding a word with a given definition.

The keysort-card explanation is obviously a metaphorical one; however, the sorting principle that it embodies is readily implementable in computer software and presumably in a human brain. The idea that words are represented in memory as sets, lists, complexes, collections, or bundles of features has been proposed by several investigators (Anderson & Bower, 1972; Anisfeld & Knapp, 1968; Bower, 1967; Craik & Lockhart, 1972; Kintsch, 1970; Morton, 1970; Nelson, 1972; Nelson & Brooks, 1974; Nelson, Wheeler, Borden, & Brooks, 1974; Posner & Warren, 1972; Tulving & Watkins, 1975; Wickens, 1970). This general notion might be referred to as the feature-list hypothesis. Although theorists differ somewhat in the way they characterize feature lists, they generally agree that these lists must contain features of several different types, for example, orthographic, phonetic, and semantic. We will return to this hypothesis presently in a discussion of the utilization of multiple cues to facilitate retrieval.

Semantic cues sometimes turn out to be misleading in an interesting way. When the task is to find an associate or a synonym for a cue word that has more than one meaning, the puzzle doer may be led astray in his search if he focuses initially on a meaning other than the one that "points to" the target. To illustrate: the cue was SUPERIOR and the target word had four letters. BEST came to mind, as did BOSS, but both were ruled out by the discovery that the fourth letter in the word was E. The later discovery that the second letter was A was not enough to elicit the correct word. Only after learning that the first letter was L, and conducting a letter-by-letter search for the third and only remaining unidentified letter did it become apparent that the desired word was LAKE. Once LAKE was identified as a possibility, there was little question of its correctness because the association was obvious. Initially, however, the search was for a word that *meant* SUPERIOR. The target was assumed to be a synonym for what had been interpreted as either an adjective meaning "excellent" or "better," or a noun meaning a person who is in a position of authority over another. The possible use of the word as the name of a body of water, or even as a proper noun, had not been considered. If it had, LAKE would probably have been elicited as a possibility. This suggests that it is incorrect to talk of word associations; what are associated are not words, but meanings. LAKE – or better, one of its meanings – is highly associated with one meaning of SUPERIOR, but not at all with others.

The hypothesis that what is stored about a word in a typical list-learning memory experiment is its meaning – and, in particular, one of its meanings if it has several – has been entertained by several investigators, notably by Tulving and his colleagues (Tulving, 1974; Tulving & Thomson, 1973; Tulving & Watkins, 1975). This is one form of what Tulving refers to as the "encoding specificity principle," which states that what is stored about a word when it occurs in the context of a list-learning memory task is information about the specific encoding of the word in that particular context and situation. A stronger version of the encoding specificity principle holds that a cue will not facilitate the recall of an item unless its association or other relationship to the item is somehow represented in the encoding of that item at the time of storage (Thomson & Tulving, 1970). The principle is illustrated by the results of an unpublished study by Bobrow described by Wood (1972): When the word CARDINAL was categorized with other terms relating to the clergy (priest, minister) during acquisition, the category label CLERGY proved to be an effective retrieval cue, whereas BIRDS did not.

Support has been gathered both for and against the encoding-specificity hypothesis (Bahrick, 1969, 1970; Freund & Underwood, 1970; Lauer, 1974; Salzberg & Pellegrino, 1974; Santa & Lamwers, 1974; Tulving, 1974; Tulving & Osler, 1968; Winograd & Geis, 1974; Wood, 1967). The hypothesis has been used to account for the ability or inability to recall words that have been committed to memory during the course of an experiment. The crossword puzzle examples mentioned above, however, suggest that an even stronger version of the encoding-specificity hypothesis may be correct with respect to lexical memory; that is, that words with multiple meanings have multiple representations in the lexicon. Presumably, the associations between different meanings of the same word may vary in strength just as do the associations between different words. Thus, the association between RUN (to travel by moving the feet rapidly) and WALK may be stronger than that between RUN (to travel by moving the feet rapidly) and RUN (to manage).

B. Structural and Orthographic Cues

Next to semantic cues the cues that are probably used most by crossword puzzle doers are perhaps best described as *structural* and *orthographic*. These cues are a knowledge of the number of letters in the target word, and often of what one or more of those letters are. It is apparent that such cues provide criteria against which to judge the acceptability of potential solution words. Any candidate that results from a search on semantic cues must fit the orthographic constraints in order to remain viable. A question of theoretical interest is whether such cues also facilitate the evocation of candidate solutions.

One reason for believing they do is introspective: it *seems* in doing puzzles that structural constraints condition the search, at least that part of it that is available to introspection. If one is looking for a three-letter word, seven-letter words seldom come to mind. And other things being equal, it is much easier to find a target word if some of its letters have already been identified than if none of them has. Perhaps a more convincing reason, however, is the fact that people find it easy to generate lists of words that satisfy such varied constraints as: five letters; "T" in third position; ends in ATE; begins with SP (Nickerson & Rollins, in preparation). Again, introspectively, one has the impression in generating such lists that most of the words one thinks of at all satisfy the criterion. Try to generate a list of words with, say, R in the third position, and you will notice that relatively few words that do *not* satisfy this constraint come to mind.

Some of the uses that crossword puzzle doers make of structural cues appear to depend upon a considerable knowledge of the statistical dependencies of written English. If the first letter of a desired word is H, J, L, M, or N, for example, one assumes (though not necessarily explicitly) that the next letter is very likely to be a vowel. If a Q occurs within a word, one knows that the next letter must be U; if it occurs in the final position, one would probably assume that a mistake had been made. Presumably, knowledge of such constraints is acquired gradually as a result of language usage over many years.

Consider the following situation. The puzzle doer discovers that in the process of filling in two horizontal words he has filled in the last two squares of an eight-letter vertical word as IK. Even before looking up the cue for the vertical word, he suspects something is wrong because he does not think there are any English words that end with IK. Why does he think that? He probably never learned it explicitly. And the combination is not ruled out on the basis of unpronounceability. Certainly, he does not exhaustively test all possible combinations of the six preceding letters (there are over 300 million of them). Nevertheless, he may feel reasonably confident that the combination seldom, if ever, occurs at the end of English words.

To conclude that there are no words that satisfy some structural constraint simply because one finds oneself unable to think of any appears, on the face of it, to be risky, if not somewhat presumptuous. The inference seems to require the premise: "If there were any such words, I would be able to think of at least one of them," a premise that most people probably would not want to assert. What people probably are willing to accept as a premise is: "If there were very many such words, I would probably be able to think of some of them." One's confidence that there are very few, if any, words that end with IK is increased by another consideration, and that is the fact that one can call many words to mind that sound as they would be expected to if they did end with IK. One notes, however, that these words invariably end with something other than IK, for example, IC, ICK, or IQUE. The fact that it is easy to produce these words but impossible to produce any that end with IK leads to the strong suspicion that the convention, in English, is to use one of the forms that one can think of, and never, or very seldom, IK, to represent a word that terminates with the sound /ik/. In filling out the crossword puzzle — in deciding that _____IK is incorrect — one may not verbalize this thinking to oneself, but something like it, I believe, goes on.

This conjecture is similar to a suggestion made by Tversky and Kahneman (1973, 1974) that people resort to the "principle of availability" when attempting to estimate frequencies or probabilities. The availability principle involves the idea that estimates of frequency or probability are sometimes based on the ease with which instances are called to mind. When asked to estimate the relative likelihoods of heart-attack victims among men and women, to borrow an example from Tversky and Kahneman, one may think of heart-attack victims among one's acquaintances and take the male-to-female ratio in this sample as indicative of that of the general population. Or, more to the point of our —IK problem, if asked to judge which of certain letter combinations occurs more frequently at specified positions within words, one might attempt to think of words satisfying both criteria and make the judgment on the basis of the rapidity with which examples of each type come to mind.

C. Acoustic or Phonetic Cues

That one can readily produce words that satisfy criteria relating to the way the words sound is obvious: think of words that rhyme with ATE. The role of acoustic coding in intermediate or long-term memory is only beginning to receive attention from investigators (Bruce & Crowley, 1970; Wickens, Ory, & Graf, 1970; Wood, 1972). It is already apparent, however, that the acoustic properties of words can serve as effective retrieval cues at least when subjects are encouraged to note acoustic relationships (e.g., categories of rhyming words) at the time of acquisition.

In the crossword puzzle situation, phonemic cues usually come from partial solutions that result from the identification of row (column) targets that intersect with a column (row) target that has yet to be found. Thus, given a partial solution such as SL_____, or _____INE, one has a cue that should be useful for any process that can conduct a search on phonemic properties. Indeed, any orthographic cue has a phonemic analog, and conceivably a search might be guided by either type of property, or both.

As a particularly convincing demonstration that people tend to use phonemic features for finding target words, ask each of a few friends if there is any four-letter English word that ends with ENY.[1] It is a safe bet that a fair

---

[1] I am indebted to David Green for this example.

percentage of them will say no, and with considerable confidence in their answer. An individual may try for a few moments to think of a word without using an apparent overt search startegy, but then if he is unable to find one, he may consider each letter in the alphabet in turn, and determine whether by attaching it to the front of ENY he forms a word. As likely as not, he will proceed through the entire alphabet in this way and then announce that there is no such word. Ask him if he really means to *deny* that there is such a word, and he may suspect, simply because you asked the question, that he has been too hasty; whereupon he may run through all possibilities again and confirm his earlier conclusion that no such word exists. The reason for his failure to find the word — even though it is one with which he undoubtedly is very familiar — is that his search is based on a phonetic rendering of the cue that is misleading because it does not match the target. Of 32 adults (all high-school graduates) to whom this problem was recently given on a test with several other similar problems, only 10 produced the desired word; of those who could not produce it, 7 either felt "quite sure" or "certain" that such a word exists, 12 were either "quite sure" or "certain" that such a word does not exist, and 3 had "no opinion" on the matter.

Loftus, Wiksten, and Abelson (1974) have collected some data that raise questions about the respective roles of orthographic and phonemic factors in producing words with specified letter constraints. They found that the time required to produce a word with a specified letter in the nth position increases fairly linearly with n (at least as n goes from 1 to 4) at the rate of about 1.5 seconds per position. One might account for this result by assuming that the memory search is directed by orthographic criteria and that the time required to search memory for a word with a specified letter in the nth position increases with n. Alternatively, one might assume that the search time is relatively independent of n, but that the time required to *verify* that the desired letter is indeed in the nth position increases with n. As a specific example of the latter possibility, consider the following model. Assume one process, P1, which finds a candidate word in memory, and another, P2, which determines whether the candidate has the required letter in the specified position. Assume that P1 searches on the basis of phonemic features and, therefore, turns up words that are likely, but not certain, to meet the orthographic criterion. Assume further, that given a phonemically represented candidate word that has been found by P1, P2 generates its orthographic equivalent, counts from the left until it comes to the nth letter, and determines whether that is the required one.

There are two reasons to expect production time to increase with n, given this model. First, the time required to complete P2 for any given word would increase with n. Second, it seems likely that the frequency with which P1 would return a word that P2 would then reject would also increase with n. We would expect, however, that the majority of unacceptable words produced by P1 would have the required letter, or a homophone, in the vicinity of the nth position. Loftus *et al.* (1974) reported that most erroneous responses they obtained had the desired letter in the word, but in the wrong position.

The idea that P1 involves a search based, at least in part, on phonemic features is supported by the following observation. When a person is given the task of producing a list of words that end with TION, he is likely to report that many of the words that come to mind actually end in SSION. Or, when listing words that end with PT, one tends often to think of words that actually end with PED or PPED (Nickerson & Rollins, in preparation). One would not include such words in one's list because they do not satisfy the orthographic requirement.

That the search is not based exclusively on phonemic cues is suggested by the observation that the majority of words that come to mind do satisfy the orthographic constraint. Consider the problem of thinking of words that begin with KN. Although there are only about one-tenth as many English words that begin with this letter combination as there are that begin with the phonemically equivalent N, if the reader attempts to list all the KN- words he can think of, he will probably not feel, at least initially, that ten N- words are coming to mind for every KN- word that he lists.

D. Grammatical Cues

Sometimes the cue that is provided for the target word carries information of a grammatical nature. Part of speech, number, and tense (if it is a verb) can often be inferred. Such cues are undoubtedly effective. If the target is known to be a plural noun, one considers plural nouns in seeking a solution; if it is a past-tense verb, one thinks of past-tense verbs. On the face of it, the limitation of one's search to the appropriate grammatical category seems like an eminently reasonable and obvious thing to do. What is of interest for our purposes is that one seems, in fact, to be able to do that. How is it that one can go rummaging through memory, picking out only action words, or only adjectives, or only nouns, apparently without being bothered by anything else? If you try to generate a list of verbs, you will probably notice that for the most part only verbs come to mind (except words which can be either verbs or nouns, in which cases, you may not be conscious of the noun forms except in retrospect). That is to say, you will not be aware of having considered and explicitly rejected many nonverbs. This does not rule out the possibility that many such words are considered and rejected by a process that occurs below the level of awareness. It also seems possible, however, that this is not the case and that the accessing of words within a grammatical category does not involve the consideration and rejection of other words not in that category. The keysort-card model of Brown and McNeill (1966), or any retrieval process based on the same principle, would permit retrieval within a grammatical category without explicit consideration of words not in that category, provided that the features in terms of which the words were coded included grammatical properties.

Grammatical cues can be misleading. For example, when a cue word is given that can be, say, either a noun or a verb, the puzzle doer may, if he recognizes only the inappropriate form, be led to search a space that does not contain the target. To illustrate, a four-letter word for VIEWED proved to be difficult to find. The word that was required was SEEN. In retrospect, it was noted that VIEWED had initially been interpreted as an active, not a passive, verb. Again, the cue for a four-letter word was MIMICS. After trying in vain to come up with a plausible possibility, the puzzle doer realized that he had read the cue as a plural noun and had overlooked the fact that it can also be a third-person singular verb. Immediately upon this realization, the word APES came to mind. (APES also can be a plural noun, and might conceivably have been evoked – as a noun – by the noun MIMICS. In this case, this association was apparently not strong enough to do the trick, whereas the one between verbs was.)

E. Thematic Cues

Composers of crossword puzzles often work a theme so that several of the target words will be related in some way. The theme may not be announced, in which case the puzzle doer discovers it only as a result of identifying a number of target words and recognizing the relationship among some of them. Such a theme can function as a sort of metacue.

The following example illustrates both the discovery of a thematic cue and its use as a confirmation check on an hypothesized solution word. The target is a ten-letter word meaning practical wisdom, the second and third letters of which are O and R. The puzzle doer thinks of HORSESENSE and immediately recalls that two other compound words beginning with HORSE (HORSESHOES and HORSELAUGH) have already been used in this puzzle. The realization raises his confidence that HORSESENSE is the word because he detects a theme. But was the fact that he thought of HORSESENSE in the first place a result, at least in part, of the fact that he had recently thought of other words with the same prefix, and a strong semantic association? Was he primed, in other words, to produce such a word?

Experimental evidence of priming effects on retrieval from lexical memory has been obtained by several investigators (Collins & Quillian, 1970; Loftus, 1973; Loftus & Loftus, 1974; Meyer & Schvaneveldt, 1971). Loftus (1973), for example, has shown that when one is asked to produce a word that is the name of a member of a specified semantic category and begins with a specified letter (name of a fruit that begins with P), the act of naming a member of a category decreases the time required to produce another member of the same category on a subsequent trial, the amount of reduction falling off with the number of intervening trials involving other categories.

Collins and Quillian (1970) have found evidence of priming effects in their investigations of inferential processes in memory. Judging the truth or falsity of a sentence such as "A canary is a bird," for example, seems to shorten the time required to judge the truth or falsity of the subsequently presented statement "A canary can fly." These investigators account for part of this priming effect by assuming that the process of deciding whether a canary can fly makes inferential use of the knowledge that a canary is a bird, and that activation of the memory for that fact facilitates subsequent access to it. They note that this explanation does not entirely account for their results, however, inasmuch as determination of the truth or falsity of the assertion that a canary is a bird was also facilitated, although to a lesser degree, when the order of the sentences was reversed. Thus, it would appear that simple repetition of the subject of the sentence was enough to be facilitative.

F. Complete-the-Expression Cues

It is apparent from our ability to produce well-formed sentences that we are aware of the rules of our language, or at least of the conventions of language usage, and the results of the many experiments that have shown effects of word frequency on perception and memory demonstrate that we have at least implicit knowledge of the relative frequencies of occurrence of words and word combinations in language usage. It also appears that we have stored away in memory many phrases, figures of speech, expressions, clichés, and the like, each of which can be retrieved en toto, given a portion of it as a cue.

Crossword puzzle builders make use of this aspect of memory and frequently provide cues of the sort:

THE OLD GRAY – – – –

IF THE – – – – FITS

A – – – – – FOR YOUR – – – – – – – –

MY KINGDOM FOR A – – – – –

WHAT'S IN A – – – –

I'VE GOT SIX – – – – –

The reason the desired words are easy to identify is not because of rigid syntactic or semantic constraints. THE OLD GRAY SHOE and IF THE SOCK FITS are perfectly acceptable possibilities from either a syntactic or semantic point of view, and in some contexts would make more sense than the alternatives that are more likely to come to mind. Most (American) doers of crossword puzzles would feel unfairly treated, however, if they were to discover that THE

OLD GRAY $----$ had been used as a cue for SHOE. When one encounters a complete-the-expression type cue, one naturally assumes that what is called for is a *well-known* expression. In other words, the doer of crossword puzzles operates in accordance with certain unstated rules that, he assumes, are binding on the composer of puzzles as well as on doers. JACK'S COMPANION can *only* be JILL; HALE'S CHUM can *only* be HEARTY.

Not all complete-the-expression cues are as transparent as the above examples. If the cue is a legitimate pointer to more than one expression, the puzzle doer can be misled. Consider, for example, the cue JUST IN $----$. For some puzzle doers, the word TIME may come readily to mind. And only if unable to find confirming evidence by filling in the orthogonal rows (or columns), are they likely to lose confidence in this choice, and discover by thinking further about it, that CASE is also a possibility.

This example raises a question about how these types of cues work. When the desired word is obtained quickly, one may not be aware of any noticeable effort to obtain it. Given the failure to confirm TIME as the answer to the JUST IN $----$ cue, however, the retrieval of CASE may require some effort. Introspection suggests that one strategy that is used is to repeat to oneself "just in $----$'" pausing expectantly after "in" as though assuming that the desired word would make a grand entrance into consciousness if properly introduced. The interesting question is, what is it that one's brain is doing while one is waiting after repeating "just in $----$?" It is not searching for a synonym, nor for a word whose definition is given, nor for a word with known phonetic properties. It is after a word that will, when appended to "just in $----$," complete a familiar expression. Clearly, it does not simply sample four-letter words at random. But what does it do?

Another question that is prompted by a consideration of complete-the-expression cues concerns the way in which expressions are stored in memory. Presumably, representations of the words that comprise any given expression are stored individually. In most cases the meanings of the individual words were learned long before the expression was first encountered; moreover, each of the words is independently accessible for use in sentence construction. Possibly the memory representation for an expression is a complex associative linking of individually stored components, however, a *simple* linking of adjacent components will not do. Any given word must be associatively linked to many others, and therefore an element in many intersecting chains; so to reconstruct an expression, the choice of which link to follow at any particular point must depend not only on where one is in the chain, but how one got there. Another possibility is that expressions are represented as wholes, and independently of the words that comprise them. It is difficult to rule out the possibility that the learning of an expression involves the encoding of a new memory structure, as opposed to a new set of linkages among old ones.

III. HOW DO RETRIEVAL CUES
HAVE THEIR EFFECTS?

It is typically the case that the crossword puzzle doer has multiple cues for a target word. At a minimum, he is provided with a semantic cue and the number of letters in the word at the start. As work on the puzzle progresses, he may learn what some of the word's letters are, he may discover what the word rhymes with, he may become aware of a puzzle theme, and so on. And in general, the more cues one has, the easier is the task of finding a given word.

It is apparent that the information cues provide can be used to evaluate possible solutions that are considered. And the greater the number of cues available in a given case, the less likely will one be to accept as a solution a word that will later prove to be incorrect. As has already been noted, the really interesting question is, do the cues guide the memory search? Do they provide new entry points to memory, new paths along which to look for a solution? It is clear that they can indirectly force an exploration of new possibilities by virtue of showing a formerly viable alternative to be incorrect. But do they channel the search in a more direct way?

One obvious effect of multiple cues is that of restricting the number of words that fall within the set defined by their intersection. Consider the four cues: NAME OF A FRUIT, BEGINS WITH P, HAS FOUR LETTERS, RHYMES WITH RUM. Each of them individually delimits a set of words. A conjunction of any two of them delimits a much smaller set than does either one alone, and the conjunction of all four delimits a very small set indeed. The implication is that if one can isolate the set of words that satisfy all the cues, then searching through this set is likely to be an easy task. But, how is the set itself isolated? Does one have to search all words that begin with B and all vegetable names to generate a list of vegetables whose names begin with B? It seems unlikely. Or, does one search one of these sets exhaustively, looking for items that satisfy the other criterion (e.g., search through all vegetable names, looking for those that begin with B)? This seems unlikely, too. Again, one gets the feeling that the search is highly focused and goes rather quickly to a "region" of memory that will yield a relatively high hit rate. Names of vegetables beginning with B seem to come readily to mind, until one begins to exhaust one's repertory — which may be rather quickly — at which point one may resort to a strategy of deliberately calling to mind other vegetable names, groping for leads to B——s that may have been overlooked. I do not think much is known about how this all happens.

Or, consider the task of producing three-letter words that begin with P. There are perhaps roughly 1000 three-letter words in English (Kucera & Francis, 1967), and a few thousand words that begin with P. There are probably less than 50 three-letter words that begin with P, however, and it would seem like an inefficient strategy to search either of the larger sets exhaustively to find members of the intersection.[2] For that matter the assumption that one can confine — speaking metaphorically — one's search to a region containing three-letter words beginning with P is hardly less arbitrary than the assumption that one can limit it to a region containing words that begin with P, or to one containing those that have three letters. And unless one can make some such assumptions, one is forced to the conclusion that the search must always be through one's entire vocabulary.

Reference has already been made to the notion that words are represented in memory as sets or lists of features, and to the fact that the theorists who espouse this idea agree that the features represented in these lists are of various types. Thus, the feature list for the word TRAIN, for example, might contain such information as five letters, one syllable, spelled TRAIN, pronounced /tren/, noun, means of transportation, strongly associated with FREIGHT, PAS-SENGER, LOCOMOTIVE, etc. The same word used as a transitive verb to connote the teaching of skills would have some of these same elements on its feature list but not others. Nelson, Wheeler, Borden, and Brooks (1974) suggest that the features in terms of which words are coded are activated by different levels of stimulus processing. Sensory and semantic features are assumed to represent opposite ends of a continuum. Semantic features require more processing to be activated, but are more effective as retrieval cues, provided the sought-for item was encoded semantically during acquisition.

Morton's (1970) *logogen* model is illustrative of feature-list models as a class. A logogen is a device for accumulating information about linguistic stimuli. For each verbal unit, the logogen system contains a set of defining attributes, which we may think of as a feature list. The process of word recognition involves the gathering of information pertaining to the presence or absence of these defining features. A decision is made in favor of a particular word when the number of identified features belonging to that word's list reaches some (adjustable) threshold. Thresholds may be modified as the result of various factors. For example, prior presentation of a word is assumed to lower the threshold for that word temporarily; frequent presentation of a word is assumed to reduce its resting level.

The model is able to account for a variety of findings in word-recognition studies (Morton, 1970), and it has the advantage of being equally applicable to auditorily or visually presented words, and therefore to the study of speech perception and reading. In particular, the effects of contextual information are nicely handled, inasmuch as it is immaterial what combination of acoustic, visual, or semantic feature information accumulates to exceed a threshold. The

---

[2] A feasible strategy in this case would be to try all admissible letter combinations. Inasmuch as the first letter must be P and the second is (almost) guaranteed to be a vowel, a consideration of all psosible P-vowel-consonant and P-vowel-vowel combinations would yield almost all of the desired words. I cannot think of an analogous strategy for reducing the search space, however, for a rule such as "two-syllable animal names."

reception by the logogen system of relevant information from context (such as the fact that the sought-for word is a noun, and animate) effectively reduces the amount of additional information of other types that will be required to bring above threshold the total evidence favoring a particular word.

Morton's model seems to account as well as any other that is available for the effectiveness of crossword puzzle cues and for the way in which their effects might be mediated. According to this conceptualization, retrieval cues are effective to the extent that they prime the features of the target word. Conversely, they will be misleading to the extent that they also prime those of incorrect words. Inasmuch as associates and synonyms share semantic features, a candidate solution that is strongly associated with, or a synonym for, a target item presumably will have more of its features primed by a semantic cue than will an unrelated item, and will therefore be more likely to be called to mind by the cue than will unrelated items. Multiple cues are more effective than a single cue because they prime several features on relatively few words. NAME OF FRUIT THAT BEGINS WITH P, HAS FOUR LETTERS AND RHYMES WITH RUM, for example, would prime a very large number of words with respect to one or two features, but a very few with respect to all four.

Exactly how the priming has its effect is not clear. The possibility that seems most consistent with current theorizing is that it delimits a set of alternatives that can be isolated and searched. Imagine that all the words in a person's vocabulary were at the same "level" on a storage "surface." Then suppose that the effect of priming a feature was to move the word up one unit on the surface, and that priming n features moved it up n units. This is functionally equivalent to the keysort-card model proposed by Brown and McNeill (1966). After all the priming had been done the search could begin on the highest level to which any units had been raised. If only one or two cues had been given, there might be many items through which to search at the same (relatively low) level. If several cues had been given, there would probably be very few items to search, and they would be at a relatively high level. On this view, the effect of asking an individual to produce a list of three-syllable words that rhyme with PINE is to isolate the set by priming on the two salient features. Then all the subject needs to do is "read" the words from this isolated set. This view is certainly too simple to be valid, but it is not clear that there is yet a better explanation of how it is that people find it easy to generate such lists.

There is an interesting type of *multiple semantic cue* that is sometimes encountered in crossword puzzles. The cue consists of a pair of words whose relationship to each other is mediated by the target word. The cue SQUAD OR ACT, for example, might be given for the target word RIOT; or BOX OR BERG for ICE; or PONS OR PAD for LILY. Typically neither of the components of this type of cue is sufficiently strongly associated with the target word to elicit it by itself; it is the pairing of the words that constitutes the effective cue. The effect is suggestive of a process that simultaneously checks the associates of each of the individual cues in search of elements that are common to both sets. The notion of "spreading activation" through a semantic network that has been proposed by Quillian and Collins and their colleagues (Bell & Quillian, 1971; Collins & Quillian, 1972; Quillian, 1968) involves such a process. According to this view, a concept is represented in memory by a list of pointers to other concepts, which constitute properties of the concept represented by the list. Each of the "property" concepts is in turn represented by a list of pointers to still other concepts, and so on. Different lists contain pointers to common elements, because concepts share defining properties; so the net is richly inter-connected. (Loops and reentries, and thus circular definitions, are allowed.) Activation of a concept involves activation of those concepts represented on its pointer list, and activation of each of these concepts involves activation of those concepts to which its lists points, and so on; thus, the notion of an activation process spreading from one point of entry throughout the net. If two concepts are activated simultaneously, the activation will spread from both, and if the concepts are closely related the activation patterns will quickly involve common elements. In our example, a target word would be found by virtue of the fact that each cue would (independently) produce an activation path to this word.

A significant aspect of this account is the lack of interaction between the two cues. The way in which activation spreads from each cue is independent of the fact that the other cue has been activated, or that they share an associate. An alternative conceptualization might assume that the path from one of these cues, say ACT, to the target, RIOT, is somehow facilitated by the fact that the other cue, SQUAD, has also been given.

A precise answer to the question of how retrieval cues have their effect on memory is beyond our current level of understanding. It does seem safe to conclude, however, that such cues not only provide criteria against which candidate solutions can be evaluated, but they also facilitate the evocation of candidate words in the first place. That words are represented in memory as lists of features, that those features include qualitatively different types of proper-ties, that the encoding of these lists involves some economizing principle such as the use of pointers to avoid storing features redundantly, that similarity, synonymity and associative strength depend in some way on shared features, that activation of one word can partially activate others by virtue of the involvement of their common features, are all mutually compatible ideas. And, given our current state of ignorance of how memory for words and linguistic information works, a model that can account even for crossword puzzle solving may have to make use of all of them.

IV.   THE IDEA OF A MEMORY SEARCH

The term "search" has been used throughout this discussion to connote the process by which words are retrieved from memory. The idea that retrieval does involve a search process is a common one in the literature on memory (Peterson,

1967; Shiffrin, 1970). The term "search" is not always used in the same way, however.

Some writers, in speaking of a search process, seem to have in mind a deliberate and conscious activity that is open to introspection. Shiffrin (1970) quotes William James' summarization of a description of the search process given by the British philosopher James Mill as follows:

> In short, we make search in our memory for a forgotten idea, just as we rummage our house for a lost object. In both cases we visit what seems to us the probable *neighborhood* of that which we miss. We turn over the things under which, or within which, or along side of which, it may possibly be; and if it lies near them, it soon comes to view. (p. 375)

Sometimes, perhaps more often, the term is used to suggest a process that occurs below the level of awareness. "Search" still seems like an appropriate term, nevertheless, because one can feel quite certain the word one wants is in one's vocabulary, and that the problem is to find it, to tease it out of hiding, so to speak.

Occasionally, a deliberate, exhaustive search through a well-defined set of possibilities is an effective strategy for finding a target word for a crossword puzzle. When only one or two letters are required to complete a word, for example, a letter-by-letter scan through the alphabet is feasible. More interesting examples are those of finding a four-letter name of a continent, or the name of a number with five letters, the second of which is E. An exhaustive search – of continent names in the first instance and of number names in the second – might be an effective strategy for producing the desired word in both of these cases. Moreover, it might well make sense to do such a search to verify that there is only one candidate that satisfies the need, even if the search is not necessary to identify that candidate in the first place. What makes these latter examples interesting is the assumption that one need search *only* through continent names, or number names, to find the desired word, which seems to require the further assumption that a search is not needed to isolate the words in one of these categories as a group. Or at least, if a search is required in this case it is not the kind that is conscious and open to introspection.

An exhaustive search is possible, of course, only if the set to be searched is known in its entirety. A search that is as nearly exhaustive as possible can also be effective, however, when the set of interest is known only imperfectly. One need not be able to list the names of all woodwind instruments, for example, to make effective use of a nearly exhaustive search strategy to determine that the name of a woodwind instrument of four letters, the first of which is O, is probably OBOE.

Introspective evidence that a search occurs at a subconscious level comes from the fact that a target word often seems to come to mind at a time when one is not consciously trying to think of it. This may happen, for example, after one has tried very hard to get a word – perhaps being frustrated by the feeling that one knows the word but just cannot bring it to mind – and has finally given up and moved on. Then, when working on another part of the puzzle, the word that was so elusive when being actively pursued, turns itself in, as it were, on its own.

Perhaps various types of search processes occur more or less simultaneously at different levels. If one wants to account for crossword puzzle solving in terms of search processes, it will probably be necessary to distinguish at least two types: one a very rapid parallel process that operates below the level of awareness; and the other, a slow serial process which can be consciously guided and is open to introspection. It also seems possible, however, that thinking in terms of search processes may prove to be misleading. Much of the current thinking about how human memory may function has been heavily influenced by the design of the modern serial single-processor digital computer. Within this frame of reference it is natural to make a distinction between the storage unit, which is a passive repository of information, and the processing unit, which moves information in and out of storage and acts upon it in various ways. Until very recently, relatively little thought seems to have been given to the possibility that memory and the processor are one and the same thing. The idea that computational capability is distributed throughout the brain, that the same neural elements can be used for storing information and for processing it, is not implausible from a physiological point of view. The question of how information might be "found" in, and by, such a processor memory is worthy of more thought than it has yet received.

ACKNOWLEDGMENTS

I am grateful to Marilyn Adams for helpful comments on a draft of this paper.

REFERENCES

Anderson, D. R., & Bower, G. H. Recognition and retrieval processes in free recall. *Psychological Review,* 1972, 79, 97–123.

Anisfeld, M., & Knapp, M. Association, synonymity, and the directionality in false recognition. *Journal of Experimental Psychology,* 1968, 77, 171–179.

Bahrick, H. P. Measurement of memory by prompted recall. *Journal of Experimental Psychology,* 1969, 79, 213–219.

Bahrick, H. P. A two-phase model for prompted recall. *Psychological Review,* 1970, 77, 215–222.

Banks, W. P., & Atkinson, R. C. Accuracy and speed strategies in scanning active memory. *Memory & Cognition,* 1974, 2, 629–636.

Bell, A., & Quillian, M. R. Capturing concepts in a semantic net. In E. C. Jacks (Ed.), *Associative information techniques.* New York: American Elsevier, 1971. Pp. 3–25.

Bellezza, F. S., & Walker, R. J. Storage-coding trade-off in short-term store. *Journal of Experimental Psychology,* 1974, 102, 629–633.

Bower, G. H. A multicomponent theory of memory trace. In K. W. Spence & J. T. Spence

(Eds.), *The psychology of learning and motivation: Advances in research theory.* Vol. 1. New York: Academic Press, 1967.

Bower, G. H. A selective review of organizational factors in memory. In E. Tulving & W. Donaldson, (Eds.), *Organization of memory.* New York: Academic Press, 1972.

Brown, R., & McNeill, D. The "tip of the tongue" phenomenon. *Journal of Verbal Learning and Verbal Behavior,* 1966, **4**, 325–337.

Bruce, D., & Crowley, J. J. Acoustic similarity effects on retrieval from secondary memory. *Journal of Verbal Learning and Verbal Behavior,* 1970, **9**, 190–196.

Collins, A. M., & Quillian, M. R. Facilitating retrieval from semantic memory: The effect of repeating part of an inference. *Acta Psychologica,* 1970, **33**, 304–314.

Collins, A. M., & Quillian, M. R. How to make a language user. In E. Tulving & W. Donaldson (Eds.), *Organization of memory.* New York: Academic Press, 1972.

Craik, F. I., & Lockhart, R. S. Levels of processing: A framework for memory research. *Journal of Verbal Learning and Verbal Behavior,* 1972, **11**, 671–684.

Freund, J. S., & Underwood, B. J. Restricted associates as cues in free recall. *Journal of Verbal Learning and Verbal Behavior,* 1970, **9**, 136–141.

Kintsch, W. Models for free recall and recognition. In D. A. Norman (Ed.), *Models of human memory.* New York: Academic Press, 1970.

Kucera, H. G., & Francis, W. N. *Computational analysis of present-day American English.* Providence, R.I.: Brown University Press, 1967.

Laird, C. *The miracle of language.* Greenwich, Conn.: Fawcett, 1953.

Lauer, P. A. Encoding specificity in the cued and free recall of categorically and alphabetically organized words. *Bulletin of the Psychonomic Society,* 1974, **4**, 496–498.

Loftus, E. F. Activation of semantic memory. *American Journal of Psychology,* 1973, **86**, 331–337.

Loftus, E. F., Wiksten, S., & Abelson, R. P. Using semantic memory to find vs. create a word. *Memory & Cognition,* 1974, **2**, 479–483.

Loftus, G. R., & Loftus, E. F. The influence of one memory retrieval on a subsequent memory retrieval. *Memory & Cognition,* 1974, **2**, 467–471.

Meyer, D. E., & Schvaneveldt, R. W. Facilitation on recognizing pairs of words: Evidence of a dependence between retrieval operations. *Journal of Experimental Psychology,* 1971, **90**, 227–234.

Miller, M. Puzzling people. *Boston Globe,* July 13, 1975, B1.

Mohs, R. C., Wescourt, K. T., & Atkinson, R. C. Search processes for associative structures in long-term memory. *Journal of Experimental Psychology,* 1975, **104**, 103–121.

Morton, J. A functional model for memory. In D. A. Norman (Ed.), *Models of human memory.* New York: Academic Press, 1970.

Nelson, D. L. Words as sets of features: The role of phonological attributes. In R. F. Thompson & J. F. Voss (Eds.), *Topics in learning and performance.* New York: Academic Press, 1972.

Nelson, D. L., & Brooks, D. H. Relative effectiveness of rhymes and synonyms as retrieval cues. *Journal of Experimental Psychology,* 1974, **102**, 503–507.

Nelson, D. L., Wheeler, J. W., Jr., Borden, R. C., & Brooks, D. H. Levels of processing and cueing: Sensory versus meaning features. *Journal of Experimental Psychology,* 1974, **103**, 971–977.

Nickerson, R. S., & Rollins, A. M. On generating lists of words. In preparation.

Norman, D. A. Comments on the information structure of memory. In A. F. Sanders (Ed.), *Attention and performance III.* Amsterdam: North-Holland Publ., 1970.

Peterson, L. R. Search and judgment in memory. In B. Kleinmuntz (Ed.), *Concepts and the structure of memory.* New York: Wiley, 1967.

Posner, M. I., & Warren, R. E. Traces, concepts, and conscious constructions. In A. W.

Melton & E. Martin (Eds.), *Coding processes in human memory.* Washington, D.C.: Winston, 1972.

Quillian, M. R. Semantic memory. In M. Minsky (Ed.), *Semantic information processing.* Cambridge, Mass.: MIT Press, 1968, 227–270.

Rumelhart, D. E., Lindsay, P. H., & Norman, D. A. A process model for long-term memory. In E. Tulving & W. Donaldson (Eds.), *Organization of memory.* New York: Academic Press, 1972. Pp. 198–248.

Salzberg, P. M., & Pellegrino, J. W. The generation and recognition components of encoding specificity. *Bulletin of the Psychonomic Society,* 1974, **4,** 9–11.

Santa, J. L., & Lamwers, L. L. Encoding specificity: Fact or artifact. *Journal of Verbal Learning and Verbal Behavior,* 1974, **13,** 412–423.

Santa, J. L., Ruskin, A. B., Snuttjer, D., & Baker, L. Retrieval in cued recall. *Memory & Cognition,* 1975, **3,** 341–348.

Shiffrin, R. M. Memory search. In D. A. Norman (Ed.), *Models of human memory.* New York: Academic Press, 1970.

Shiffrin, R. M., & Atkinson, R. C. Storage and retrieval processes in long-term memory. *Psychological Review,* 1969, **76,** 179–193.

Thomson, D. M., & Tulving, E. Associative encoding and retrieval: Weak and strong cues. *Journal of Experimental Psychology,* 1970, **86,** 255–262.

Tulving, E. Recall and recognition of semantically encoded words. *Journal of Experimental Psychology,* 1974, **102,** 778–787.

Tulving, E., & Osler, S. Effectiveness of retrieval cues in memory for words. *Journal of Experimental Psychology,* 1968, **77,** 593–601.

Tulving, E., & Pearlstone, Z. Availability versus accessibility of information in memory for words. *Journal of Verbal Learning and Verbal Behavior,* 1966, **5,** 381–391.

Tulving, E., & Thomson, D. M. Encoding specificity and retrieval processes in episodic memory. *Psychological Review,* 1973, **80,** 352–373.

Tulving, E., & Watkins, M. J. Structure of memory traces. *Psychological Review,* 1975, **82,** 261–275.

Tversky, A., & Kahneman, D. Availability: A heuristic for judging frequency and probability. *Cognitive Psychology,* 1973, **5,** 207–232.

Tversky, A., & Kahneman, D. Judgment under uncertainty: Heuristics and biases. *Science,* 1974, **185,** 1124–1131.

Wickens, D. D. Encoding categories of words: An empirical approach to meaning. *Psychological Review,* 1970, **77,** 1–15.

Wickens, D. D., Ory, N. E., & Graf, S. A. Encoding by taxonomic and acoustic categories in long-term memory. *Journal of Experimental Psychology,* 1970, **84,** 462–469.

Winograd, E., & Geis, M. Semantic encoding and recognition memory. *Journal of Experimental Psychology,* 1974, **102,** 1061–1068.

Wood, G. Category names as cues for the recall of category instances. *Psychonomic Science,* 1967, **9,** 323–324.

Wood, G. Organizational processes and free recall. In E. Tulving & W. Donaldson (Eds.), *Organization of memory.* New York: Academic Press, 1972.

34

Memory Processes in Motor Control

George E. Stelmach
J. A. Scott Kelso

Motor Behavior Laboratory
University of Wisconsin
Madison, Wisconsin, United States

ABSTRACT

One of the foremost issues in motor control and memory research concerns the sources of information that contribute in the development of memory representation for movements. This somewhat diffuse literature focusing on the relative roles of peripheral and central information in movement coding is systematically reviewed. While most studies have examined the coding and retention characteristics of movement information in the proprioceptive modality, some recent experiments have explored the efferent dimension of movement reproduction. This latter work has led to the hypothesis that, when a subject is allowed to internally organize a response, there is an efference-based mechanism such as corollary discharge which operates to prepare sensory processing systems for the anticipated consequences of the motor act. Several experiments are presented which explore this hypothesis by forcing a reliance on distance cues, by manipulating the planning and efferent components of movement, and by maximizing the encoding of proprioceptive information. While it is realized that crucial experiments still need to be performed, the results are in general agreement with an efference-based mechanism. In all cases, prior response organization facilitated the reproduction of the motor act.

I. INTRODUCTION

Perhaps the major contemporary issue in motor-behavior research concerns the development of a central or internal-memory representation which is postulated as necessary for guiding and controlling movement. Whether we hypothesize this to be a perceptual trace (Adams, 1971), a schema (Pew, 1974; Schmidt, 1975), a neural model (Sokolov, 1969), a spatial reference or coordinate system (Lashley, 1951; Paillard & Brouchon, 1968), a standard (Laszlo & Bairstow, 1971), or a template (Keele, 1968; Keele & Summers, 1976) there seems to be universal agreement that some such agent is critical for governing movement. The preoccupation with the role that this "internal code" plays in motor learning, memory, and control has necessitated a consideration of the input domains by which this code is established. The fundamental concern for which sources of information are actually used in developing a memory representation for movement is the focus of this chapter.

Clearly, there are a variety of information sources which can contribute to the development of a memory representation (e.g., vision and audition). On the other hand, there are many situations in which the learner must depend on cues arising as the result of his own movements, per se. Such cues are thought to be based on proprioception, the encompassing term for the modality subserving sense of position and movement. In addition, it has been hypothesized that the central nervous system also has mechanisms available by which it can inform itself as to the intended output (Merton, 1970). Thus, movement information can be considered as "peripheral," in the sense that it arises from proprioceptive receptor organs stimulated as a result of movement; or "central," in the sense that internal information is generated prior to the occurrence of overt movement.

The relative roles of peripheral and central information in movement coding have yet to be assessed in any systematic manner. Therefore, the primary questions addressed in this study focus on the receptor and effector mechanisms involved when a subject produces a motor response and is later asked to duplicate it. What information does the subject rely on in this situation? What does he encode? And what is the nature of the storage code on which reproduction is based?

Most of the studies concerned with the coding and retention characteristics of movement information have focused on the proprioceptive modality. Much of the research emphasis has been to determine whether memory for proprioceptive information is governed by the same laws as those derived for verbal materials. Positioning tasks have been used to test predictions based on interference or trace decay theory. The underlying assumptions of this approach seem to be (1) that a movement produces some kind of "trace" which either decays as a function of time, or is lost as a result of interference from other traces, and (2) that the subject is dependent on sensory feedback upon which to base future response production. This latter approach seems to neglect the processes operating prior to, and intervening between a movement and its reproduction. Rather an approach in which the organism is considered as an active processor of information, whether it be centrally or peripherally generated, is to be desired if the dynamic aspects of memory are to be understood.

Adopting a so-called *multicue approach* to movement coding (Laabs, 1973; Marteniuk, 1973; Marteniuk & Roy, 1972), a group of studies have focused on separating proprioceptive information into distance and location cues. At issue in these investigations was the type of proprioceptive cue that is encoded by the subject. The cues potentially available to the subject might include acceleration, amplitude, direction, end location, and speed of movement. Earlier studies have utilized criterion and reproduction movements which began and ended at invariant starting points (Ascoli & Schmidt, 1969; Boswell & Bilodeau, 1964; Stelmach & Wilson, 1970); thus, the distance moved (*amplitude*) and the terminal location were both reliable cues to aid recall (Fig. 1a).

Realizing that it is practically impossible to completely isolate one movement cue from another by strictly behavioral techniques, investigators have attempted to utilize techniques which force dependence on different subsets of cues. For location, subjects are instructed to recall the endpoint of the movement with distance cues rendered unreliable by altering starting positions (Fig. 1b). For distance, subjects recall the amplitude of the movement independent of end location (Fig. 1c). With these procedures, Posner (1967), Marteniuk, Shields, and Campbell (1972), Keele and Ells (1972), and Laabs (1973) have generally found that location information can be successfully maintained if retention intervals

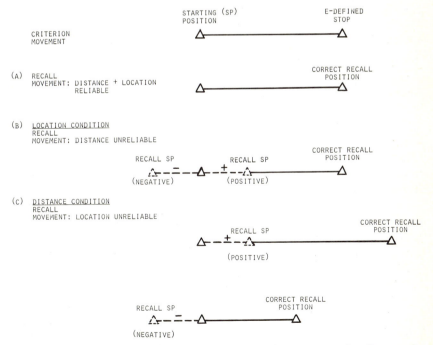

FIG. 1 Schematic representation of criterion and recall movements for distance plus location; for location; and for distance conditions.

are not filled with information-processing activity. In contrast to location cues, distance information has been found to yield larger errors and to decay spontaneously. There is some evidence that indicates that distance information is not a useful reproduction cue. Marteniuk and Roy (1972) found that randomly induced passive movements had no influence on location reproduction. Thus, the conclusion that location information is highly codable seems warranted.

As yet, there has been little consideration of the possible receptor mechanisms which could mediate location. Only Marteniuk and his students (Marteniuk *et al.*, 1972; Marteniuk & Roy, 1972; Marteniuk & Ryan, 1972) have attempted to analyze the possibilities and opted strongly for the joint-capsule receptors. Based on the early work of Browne, Lee, and Ring (1954), and Provins (1958) in which the perception of passive movement was deficient when the joint capsule was anesthetized, as well as Skoglund's (1956) classification scheme for joint receptors, there seems to be some support for this position. Nevertheless, it should be treated cautiously for a number of reasons. First, a recent study by Grigg, Finerman, and Riley (1973) on patients in which the joint capsule has been surgically removed, has indicated that *active* movements can be produced as well as those of normal subjects. This suggests that other, pericapsular sources of information can mediate location cues in active movement. Second, Marteniuk and Roy (1972) failed to consider the rule of muscular afferent and motor outflow information, both of which were available, in his analysis of the superiority due to location cues. Third, and following on from the previous two points, there as yet has been no investigation of the coding and retention characteristics of movement when joint receptors are unavailable. Thus, the exact role of joint receptors in voluntary movement control has yet to be assessed.

The contribution of "corollary discharges" to movement coding is of special interest in the light of neuroscience research which has revealed a number of possible mediating mechanisms, mostly involving cerebrocerebellar pathways (Allen & Tsukahara, 1974; Evarts, 1971; Teuber, 1972). Essentially corollary-discharge theory proposes that active, voluntary movements involve two sets of signals; one, a downward discharge to effector organs, and two, a simultaneous central discharge from motor to sensory systems preparing the latter for the anticipated consequences of the motor act. Although the notion is similar to Helmholtz's "sensation of innervation" (without necessarily implying "sensation") put forward over a century ago (see Helmholtz, 1925), the behavioral data is yet somewhat meager (see Kelso & Stelmach, 1976, for reviews) deriving primarily from three sources. Briefly, these come from (1) Teuber's extensive studies on perceptual deficits in patients with frontal lesions (e.g., Teuber, 1960, 1972; Teuber & Mishkin, 1954); (2) Held and his colleagues' work on sensorimotor adaptation (e.g., Held & Hein, 1963; Held & Freedman, 1963); and (3) the extensive work on eye-movement control which has been frequently reviewed (e.g., Festinger & Canon, 1965; Festinger & Easton, 1974; Goodwin, McCloskey, & Mathews, 1972; Gyr, 1972). Basically, these latter data suggest that the perceptual system obtains knowledge of eye position and movement via monitoring the efferent commands to the extraocular muscles rather than via proprioceptive feedback from muscle receptors. While this argument is reasonable for the eye system, it has been considered highly questionable whether the skeletal system can operate in a similar manner. Since the predictability of muscle loading in normal movements is low, an efference-based mechanism has been rejected as an accurate means of movement control, in favor of a closed-loop system stressing sensory feedback (e.g., Adams, 1971).

A recent series of studies by Jones (1972, 1974), however, suggests that proprioceptive feedback is of little importance in movement coding. Borrowing from Taub and Berman's (1968) terminology, Jones has argued that the central monitoring of efference (CME) is the primary determinant for retention of simple motor responses. According to Jones, when a subject makes a voluntary movement "as rapidly as possible," the resulting efferent discharge is centrally monitored and stored as an efference copy (von Holst, 1954), which is thought to be a motor-memory storage system operating without the requirement of peripheral feedback. The support for Jones' CME comes from the finding that subjects can duplicate voluntary movements (subject defined) more accurately than constrained or passive movements. Under the latter conditions, where the subject moves to an experimenter-defined stop, it is argued that the subjects are dependent on joint inflow since they lack the opportunity to make a preset movement. Thus, according to Jones (1974) because proprioceptive feedback has "no access to central mechanisms" (p. 38) memory loss occurs.

While Jones' hypothesis raises some important theoretical issues, it fails to accommodate much of the literature in short-term motor memory (STMM), indicating that terminal-location information can be retained under constrained conditions (Keele & Ells, 1972; Laabs, 1973; Marteniuk, 1973). In addition, and contrary to Jones, interpolated processing activity during a retention interval leads to an increase in recall error, suggesting that the location aspects of movement do require central capacity.

One of the main arguments for CME as opposed to proprioceptive-location cues rests on the finding that subjects duplicate movement extents (i.e., distance) equally well from variable and constant starting positions (Jones, 1974). Hence, as long as the efferent commands for movement extent are the same for criterion and recall movements, no deficits in motor recall occur, regardless of initial starting position. But what happens when the subject is forced to generate a different efferent output at recall from that employed in the criterion movement? This question provided the impetus for a recent series of experiments performed in my laboratory (Stelmach, Kelso, & Wallace, 1976).

The first experiment of the series examined the reproduction of either the endpoint or the distance of a rapid voluntary (preselected) movement. It was argued that the former condition, by rendering distance unreliable, would require the subject to alter the efferent output for the recall movement.

According to Jones' (1974) hypothesis, this procedure should result in less accurate recall, while distance reproduction should be superior since the motor outflow for movement extent remained a reliable cue for reproduction. The results militated against the Jones' hypothesis; the location condition evidencing relatively less variability and absolute error after a 15-sec retention interval. This finding was congruent with studies in short-term motor memory (STMM) (Keele & Ells, 1972; Laabs, 1973; Marteniuk, 1973; Marteniuk & Roy, 1972) and suggested that proprioceptive-location cues were primary for accurate recall.

A subsequent experiment examined the latter interpretation by comparing location reproduction under preselected, constrained, and passive modes; the rationale being that if location cues were primary, the response mode should not be an influential factor. However, the results revealed that providing the subject an opportunity to preselect a location prior to movement initiation, was a determining element of recall accuracy. A third experiment verified this and also showed that the processing requirements of preselected, constrained and passive location were similar. This finding agreed with much of the STMM literature but was contrary to Jones' (1972) argument that proprioceptive information fails to access central processing mechanisms.

Viewed overall, our results to date refute the notion that central monitoring of efference is a "necessary and sufficient" (Jones, 1974) condition for the coding and retention of voluntary movement. They have, however, led us to an important phenomenon, which as yet seems to have escaped the theoretical attention of researchers in the motor-memory and -control domains. We refer to this phenomenon as *preselection,* the availability of which appears to allow the subject to internally organize or "plan" his response (Miller, Gallanter, & Pribram, 1960) prior to movement initiation. The role of preselection, which clearly has an overwhelming influence on our previous data, would seem to force an empirical assessment of its theoretical importance for motor control.

II. EXPERIMENT I

The bulk of STMM studies using constrained movements have indicated that distance information, unlike location, fades over time and is unaffected by interpolated processing activity (Laabs, 1973). This finding suggested that distance information does not require central processing capacity and, along with physiological evidence derived from Skoglund's (1956) work, has led to the conclusion that distance cues are, in fact, "uncodable" (Marteniuk & Roy, 1972). On the other hand, a more recent study by Marteniuk (1973) has found that distance information may be retained over time and is subject to interpolated processing effects. The discrepancy between this finding and those earlier may be due to the response mode of the criterion presentation. That is, while previous experiments used constrained, experimenter-defined movements,

Marteniuk's (1973) subjects were allowed to define their own movement. It may be that the coding characteristics of experimenter and subject defined (preselected) movements are different, thus accounting for the discrepant distance findings. On the basis of Laabs' (1973) model, however, distance information should spontaneously decay over an unfilled retention interval and not be affected by interpolated processing activity. Such should be the case regardless of presentation mode. To assess these differential predictions, Experiment I examined the retention of distance information under three modes of presentation, preselected, constrained, and passive.

A. Method

1. Apparatus

The apparatus consisted of a linear positioning slide that is used extensively in STMM research. Two steel rods are mounted horizontally and parallel to each other with a ball-bearing sleeve running on each rod, and connected via an aluminum plate on which a handle is mounted. The handle is grasped by the blindfolded subject and displaced in a left to right manner. A pointer attached to the experimenter's side moves along a metric scale so that the subject's criterion and reproduction movements can be recorded. A removable stop peg inserted by the experimenter defined movement amplitudes and locations.

2. Procedure

In the preselected-distance condition, each trial commenced with an instruction for the subject to "grasp the handle" and covertly "select" the distance he wished to move. Selection of the criterion movement (CM) was defined by the subject with the restriction that the subject should disperse his selected movements within the demonstrated movement range. On the command "Move," the subject produced his selected movement in a rapid, yet controlled manner. After 2 seconds at the CM endpoint, the command "Release," cued the subject to remove his hand from the handle and place it by his side, while the experimenter returned the slide back to the appropriate starting position. At the end of the designated-retention interval, the subject made his recall movement (RM) and the instruction to "release" signaled the end of the trial.

The constrained-distance and passive-distance conditions were identical to the preselected-distance condition except that for the CM, the subject either actively moved to a mechanical stop or was moved by the experimenter to the mechanical stop, respectively. The movement distances presented to constrained- and passive-distance subjects were yoked to those chosen by the preselected-distance subjects. Thus, the subjects in the three conditions ($N = 48$) made the same CM distance but under different presentation modes.

In order to render location cues as unreliable as possible (Fig. 1c), 24 starting position combinations for CMs and RMs were used with the former being either

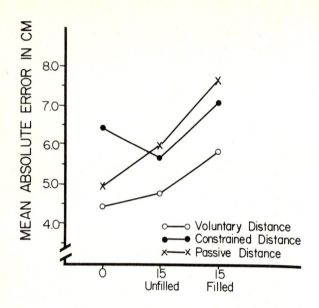

RETENTION-INTERVAL CONDITIONS

FIG. 2   Mean absolute error for the three distance conditions at each retention interval.

15, 17, 19, 21, 23, or 25 cm to the left of the zero point (subject's view) on the slide. The RM starting positions were ±5 or ±15 cm from the CM starting position. The foregoing starting position combinations were assigned in a balanced order to each of the three retention interval conditions.

The subject in all conditions attempted to recall the CM distance either immediately, after a 15-sec unfilled retention interval, or after 15 sec of interpolated verbal processing (counting backward by threes) activity. The three distance conditions received 24 trials under each of the three retention intervals. For purposes of analysis, the CM distances were categorized into short (0–19.9 cm), medium (20–39.9 cm), and long (40–59.9 cm) sectors, thus creating a 3 × 3 × 3 (groups × retention interval × sectors) factorial design.

B. Results

The results of the present experiment militated against the view the distance information is uncodable. The mean absolute error (AE) and within sector consistency (VE')[1] for distance conditions plotted as a function of retention intervals are presented in Figs. 2 and 3. Inspection of the figures reveals an

---

[1] A measure of within-sector consistency (VE') was obtained by calculating the standard deviation (SD) around the subject's mean constant error within a sector.

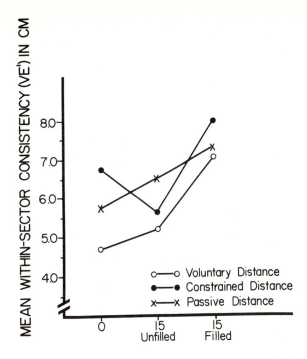

RETENTION–INTERVAL CONDITIONS

FIG. 3   Mean within-sector consistency for the three distance conditions at each retention interval.

apparent superiority of preselected distance for AE and VE′. However, while the groups main effect for AE was significant (F (2,45) = 8.43, $p < .01$), the effect for VE′ was only marginally so (F (2,45) = 2.78, $p < .10$). Tukey's post hoc test for AE supported the recall superiority of preselected distance over the passive and constrained conditions ($p < .01$) which were not different from each other. For constant error (CE), the groups main effect lacked significance (F (2,45) = 1.27, $p > .05$).

The retention intervals main effect was significant for CE, AE and VE′ with F (2,90) = 9.79, 19.60 and 15.36, $p < .01$, respectively. Post hoc analysis revealed essentially the same pattern of results, for all three dependent measures with no differences between the 0- and 15-sec retention intervals. Filling the retention interval with verbal processing activity, however, caused a positive shift in error for CE ($p < .01$) and an overall increase in AE and VE′ ($p < .01$).

The failure to find a groups X retention interval interaction for AE and VE′ was of particular interest since it indicated that the groups were not differentiated by the retention-interval manipulation. Thus, although preselected distance reproduction was superior, filling the retention interval had similar effects on all conditions. It does not appear, therefore, that preselected distance requires any more central capacity than constrained or passive distance, in spite of the fact that it seems to have a stronger representation in memory.

One further point should be emphasized from this experiment. That is, that constrained and passive distance reproduction were both retained over a 15-sec period and were similarly affected by interpolated processing activity. These findings are in direct contrast to those of Laabs (1973) and suggest that even constrained and passive distance can be retained over time and *do* require central capacity. A recent study by Diewert (1974) has shown the same result. These findings suggest that Laabs' model of two distinct storage modes in STMM, one for location and one for distance, may have to be reappraised in favor of an interpretation focusing on the central representation of both distance and location cues. As Marteniuk (1973) has suggested, it may be that both cues are centrally represented, but in varying degrees of exactness.

The preselection results of this experiment and previous studies has shown it to have an overwhelming influence on memory representation. The question is, why? Clearly the notion of CME put forward by Jones (1972, 1974) is unable to account for the findings, but this may not necessarily rule out the possibility of an efference-based mechanism such as the previously discussed corollary discharge. Here the emphasis is on facilitating the coding of sensory inputs based on a predictive signal from motor to sensory processing centers.

III.   EXPERIMENT II

The coding of movement has typically been confined to studies in which the emphasis has been on sensory information as opposed to central organizational processes. In active, voluntary movement, these may take the form of the "motor plan" (Gentile, 1974) being forwarded via such a mechanism as corollary discharge, to sensory processing centers where it can be compared with incoming inputs. Thus, under preselected conditions, sensory processing centers would be prepared to receive peripheral inputs, while with constrained movement this would not be possible since no prior information is available regarding the terminal locus of the movement. The operation of preselection would therefore be to facilitate the encoding of information which in turn could account for the greater central representation of preselected movements.

On the other hand, some have argued that because subjects in the voluntary, preselected condition are allowed to choose their own movements, they have more "task-related" information than subjects in constrained or passive conditions. Such information may allow subjects to formulate "images" (Posner, 1967) or "plans of action" (Miller, Gallanter & Pribram, 1960), which would facilitate retention (Marteniuk, 1976). These higher-order strategies would not fall within a strict definition of efference.

The principle behavioral method adopted to determine the unique role of movement information derived from central and peripheral sources has been to experimentally manipulate active and passive movement. The basic argument is simple: namely, the efferent "outflow" information is available when a subject moves actively, but is unavailable when the subject is moved by the experimenter or some mechanical device. Thus, a superiority of active reproduction supposedly reveals the contribution of an efference-based mechanism.

The impetus for this experiment is therefore to isolate the contributions of the efferent component and the planning component of movement. The latter has received minimal theoretical attention in spite of its potential importance (see Miller *et al.*, 1960, Chapter 6). Neurophysiological data indicate that the structures involved in planning a movement, and those involved in generating motor impulses (*execution*) are not the same (Allen & Tsukahara, 1974, pp. 991–993); functionally, however, these components have yet to be separated in terms of their contribution to movement coding.

This study attempts to differentiate the two positions by employing movement conditions which differ with regard to hypothesized outflow information (active versus passive) but are similar with regard to preselection, that is, both conditions can generate a potential-movement strategy. The predictions on the basis of this experimental manipulation are quite clear-cut. Since both the active-preselected and passive-preselected conditions would be allowed to preselect the movement, and if the superiority of preselection is due to the availability of a higher-order cognitive plan, there should be no differences between the reproduction responses in the two conditions. On the other hand, if preselection plays, for example, a corollary discharge role (which is unique to active, self-produced movement) the active-preselected should be superior to the passive-preselected condition, since the latter lacks the motor-to-sensory outflow which prepares sensory systems to process inputs.

A. Method

1. Apparatus

The apparatus consisted of a linear-positioning slide which is described in Experiment I.

2. Procedure

The experimental design included two groups (active and passive), each of which performed under preselected and constrained movement conditions. The subject's task ($N = 32$) was to reproduce the movement either immediately or after a 15-sec period. The active-preselected (ACT-PRE) and active-constrained (ACT-CON) conditions were identical to those described in the previous experiments, with subjects either moving to a position defined by themselves (ACT-PRE) or moving to a stop defined by the experimenter (ACT-CON). The major manipulation was with the passive group. In the passive-preselected condition (PASS-PRE), the subject was instructed to "select" the desired movement, but rather than actively moving to that position as in the ACT-PRE condition, the experimenter moved the subject along the slide until instructed to "stop." He then returned the subject to the starting position for the reproduction movement. In the passive-constrained (PASS-CON) condition, subjects were moved passively to a stop and then recalled accordingly.

Two further procedural points are worthy of emphasis. First electromyographical recordings were utilized for the purposes of training subjects in the passive group to relax while being moved and also to compare active and passive movements. Second, for the PASS-PRE condition, it was imperative that the experimenter stop the subject at the position desired. For this reason, during the intertrial interval subjects in the PASS-PRE condition were asked for a confidence rating which expressed on the scale of 1 to 10 (with 10 best), the experimenter's ability to stop the slide at the subject's selected criterion location. For example, a low-confidence rating would indicate that the subject was stopped at a position other than that which she preselected.

B. Results

The main effects of groups and response mode were significant for AE and VE' but not for CE ($F < 1$). Active movement was superior to passive, $F(1,30) = 23.63$ and $8.46, p < .01$ for AE and VE', respectively, and preselection prevailed over constrained conditions, $F(1,30) = 11.04$ (AE) and 10.50 (VE'), $p < .01$. The retention interval main effect was significant for all dependent variables, $F(1,30) = 30.08, 65.26$ ($p < .01$), and 5.11 ($p < .05$) for AE, VE', and CE, respectively. Mean AE and VE were significantly smaller for immediate recall, while CE indicated increasing negativity from 0 sec ($M = 0.11$ cm) to 15 sec ($M = -.35$ cm).

The principle interaction of interest was that of groups by response mode which was significant for AE, VE', and CE, $F(1,30) = 7.13$ ($p < .05$), 11.11, and 19.64 ($p < .01$), respectively. For AE and VE' the nature of the interaction was nearly identical and is shown in Fig. 4. Post hoc analysis using Tukey's test revealed the same findings for both dependent variables. Active preselection had significantly smaller errors than any other combination ($p < .01$). There were no significant differences between passive-preselection, passive-constrained, and active-constrained conditions. For CE, the pattern of results was somewhat different. Post hoc analysis revealed that PASS-PRE ($M = -.78$ cm) was negative and significant relative to PASS-CON ($M = .58$ cm). The opposite effect for ACT-PRE ($M = 0.31$ cm) and ACT-CON ($M = -.58$ cm) was evident but not significant.

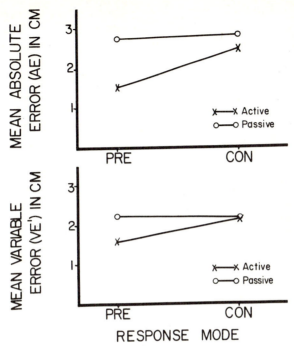

FIG. 4   Mean absolute error and variable error for the active and passive conditions plotted as a function of the three retention intervals.

Further notable findings were that the confidence ratings in the PASS-PRE condition were extremely high (M = 9.57 out of a possible 10, SD = .40) indicating that subjects were confident that the experimenter had stopped them at their selected position. Also, analysis of EMG recordings, by taking the mean amplitude (number of millivolts above and below baseline), revealed that passive conditions evidenced minimal muscular activity relative to active ($p < .0001$).

The implication from these results is that the "higher order planning process" (Marteniuk, 1976) is insufficient in *itself* to facilitate retention. The addition of an efference-based mechanism operating in voluntary movement appears also to be necessary. It is also interesting that the efferent component appears to be of little use when the subject has no idea of where the terminal location of the movement is (i.e., he lacks a motor plan) as in the ACT-CON condition. These data support our view that preselection may involve an internal "output" code such as corollary discharge (Sperry, 1950; Teuber, 1972) in which central information flows from motor to sensory systems presetting them for the anticipated consequences of the motor act. Thus, under preselection conditions sensory-processing centers would be prepared to receive peripheral inputs. The operation of preselection would therefore be to facilitate the encoding of information.

IV.   EXPERIMENT III

If prior response organization facilitates movement coding, it might be predicted that preselected movements would be less dependent on peripheral inputs than the constrained mode. It is our position that since in the constrained conditions the subjects do not know where they are going until arriving at the target, they have no efficient output code; therefore, they should be input (*sensory*) oriented and benefit from exposure to the endpoint. On the other hand, the preselected condition should be more output oriented since the subjects have an appropriate output code (efferent command) and benefit less from endpoint exposure.

This experiment sought to compare constrained and preselected conditions after varying durations at the endpoint of the criterion movement. Increasing the time at the endpoint should maximize the encoding of proprioceptive information, hence facilitating the development of the memory trace. Thus, a response mode by endpoint duration interaction would be predicted in which constrained recall improved as a function of endpoint duration, while preselected recall remained relatively unaffected.

A.   Method

1.   Apparatus

The apparatus was identical to that used in Experiments I and II.

2.   Procedure

Three groups (N = 48), varying in duration spent at the end location of the CM performed preselected and constrained movements under three retention-interval conditions. In the immediate release group (IR), the subject moved to the CM location, and, on the instruction "release" removed his hand from the slide handle and placed it by his side. Subjects in the 2-sec (TR) and 5-sec (FR) release groups remained at the CM location for the respective period of time prior to the release instruction. In order to render distance cues unreliable (Fig. 1b), 12 starting-position combinations for CMs and RMs were used, with the former being either 15, 19, or 23 cm to the left of the zero point (subject's view) on the slide. The RM starting positions were ±5 or ±15 cm from the CM starting position. The foregoing starting-position combinations were assigned in a balanced order to each of the three retention-interval conditions. The subject attempted to recall the CM location either immediately, after a 15-sec unfilled retention interval, or after 15 sec of interpolated verbal processing (counting backward by threes) activity.

B.   Results

The groups main effect for AE and VE′ was significant, F (2,45) = 8.65 and F (2,45) = 8.39, p < .01, respectively. Tukey's post hoc test indicated that the IR conditions were significantly worse than the TR (p < .05) and the FR conditions

($p < .01$) for both AE and VE$'$ measures. For CE, the groups main effect was nonsignificant, $F < 1$.

The response modes main effect was significant for AE and VE$'$, $F (1,45) =$ 15.07, $p < .01$, and $F (1,45) = 6.71$, $p < .05$, respectively. A clear superiority of preselected over constrained conditions was evident.

The retention intervals main effect was significant, for AE, VE$'$, and CE, $F (2,90)$ = 23.92, 35.16 ($p < .01$), and 3.16 ($p < .05$), respectively. For AE and VE$'$, Tukey's test revealed that all three retention intervals were significantly different from each other at or beyond the .05 significance level. For CE, a significant increase in positive errors resulted when verbal-processing activity was introduced during the 15-sec retention interval ($p < .05$).

Of considerable interest was the groups by response modes interaction since it might reflect differences in the PRE and CON conditions relative to the end-point duration manipulation. The groups by modes interaction was significant only for AE, $F (2,45) = 3.43$, $p < .05$ and can be seen in Fig. 5. A simple main-effects analysis of the two response modes as a function of the IR, TR, and FR conditions was performed. This analysis revealed that the PRE-IR recall error was only marginally greater than PRE-TR ($p < .10$). For the constrained mode however, CON-IR was significantly worse than both CON-TR and CON-FR ($p < .05$) which were not different from each other. Examining this interaction further revealed a superiority of preselected location over constrained location at

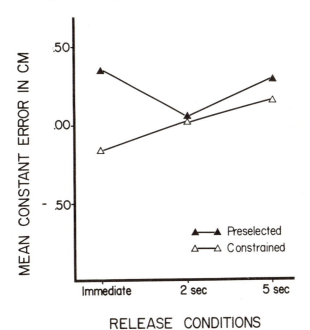

FIG. 5 Mean absolute error for the preselected and constrained conditions at the three release conditions.

the immediate and 2-sec release conditions. However, at the 5-sec release condition, reproduction of preselected and constrained location was not significantly different for AE.

The failure to obtain a significant group by modes interaction for VI' suggested that the PRE and CON modes were similarly affected by the endpoint duration manipulation. However, inspection of AE provides a slightly different perspective. Preselected movements appear more output dependent since they are relatively unaffected by the endpoint-duration manipulation. Constrained movements, on the other hand, appear more input oriented, judged by the progressive decrease in recall error as a function of resting at the endpoint. Furthermore, inspection of the AE means at the 5-sec duration, indicates that the lack of prior response organization may be compensated for by resting at the endpoint of a constrained movement. Presumably, resting at the endpoint operates to augment the memory representation to a degree comparable to that of preselected movements. Whether location information in a constrained movement requires more time to encode than preselected location, or whether constrained location is facilitated by some covert rehearsal process cannot be established from these data.

V. CONCLUSION

While this research has focused on the role of preselection and its planning and efferent components in movement coding, a principle question remains as to the contribution of proprioceptive inputs when a subject makes a voluntary movement to a chosen location. The bulk of the literature investigating constrained, input-dependent movements, has indicated that location information is primary (Marteniuk & Roy, 1972; Marteniuk et al., 1972; Keele & Ells, 1972; Laabs, 1973), thus implicating a major role for joint receptors (Marteniuk & Ryan, 1972; Marteniuk & Roy, 1972). However, in a situation where the subject knows where he wants to move to, no afferent information may be necessary to inform him that he has attained the desired position (Festinger & Cannon, 1965). As MacNeilage and MacNeilage (1973) point out in speech control, the greater the ability of the central nervous system to "predictively determine" a motor response, the less the need for peripheral sensory feedback. This essentially is a reiteration of the Lashley (1917, 1951) position that effector mechanisms can be primed or preset to discharge at a given intensity or duration in total independence of sensory control. While such central programs have been demonstrated to exist in lower phylogenetic strata (see DeLong, 1971, for review), evidence for their existence in man is sparse indeed.

One apparent way to pursue the question of whether preselected movements require proprioceptive input for effective execution, would be to directly eliminate such information and examine performance in its absence. Unfortunately, the two primary methods adopted for this purpose, are bereft with problems. The nerve-compression-block technique, for example, extensively used by Laszlo and her colleagues (e.g., Laszlo, 1966; Laszlo & Bairstow, 1971) has been clearly shown to confound sensory and motor impairment (Kelso, Stelmach, & Wanamaker, 1974; Kelso, Wallace, Stelmach, & Weitz, 1975). Similarly, it appears that the critical dosage of anesthetic required to selectively block the afferent system, without concurrently blocking efferent nerves, is extremely difficult to establish (Paintal, 1973).

If published evidence be a guide, the "wrist cuff technique" adopted by Merton (1964) and others (Goodwin, McCloskey, & Matthews, 1972) overcomes this dilemma. The beauty of this method is that the joint receptors in the hand can be rendered insentient via the inflation of a child's sphygmomanometer cuff at the wrist, while leaving the muscles responsible for finger flexion and extension unaffected since they lie above the cuff. Furthermore, it also allows for an examination of the contribution of muscle receptors to movement coding, since they too are operant, although their role remains highly controversial (Goodwin *et al.*, 1972; Granit, 1972; Merton, 1964). Theoretically, if joint afferents are eliminated, there remain only two sources of information to mediate performance; muscle receptors (primary and secondary spindle afferents and golgi tendon organs) and the hypothetical corollary discharges (Goodwin *et al.*, 1972). Experiments are necessary which seek to unravel, via neurobehavioral techniques, the individual contribution of each of these information sources to the internal representation of movement.

It would also seem intuitive to consider the question of whether organization of *input* information facilitates motor memory and control processes. The overriding influence of "trace" theories in the motor domain (see Adams, 1971, for review) has certainly not hastened a consideration of the role of organization processes. Adams (1971) closed-loop theory, for example, argues that a movement lays down a "trace" whose strength develops as a function of the sensory feedback impinging upon it. There has been a fair amount of empirical support for this theory, both in learning (Adams & Goetz, 1973; Adams, Goetz, & Marshall, 1972; Newell, 1974; Newell & Chew, 1974; Schmidt & White, 1972) and memory research (Adams, Marshall, & Goetz, 1972; Marshall, 1972; Stelmach, 1973; Stelmach & Kelso, 1975). Recently, however, there have been criticisms raised against the theory which have centered upon the potential problem of an individual "trace" being stored for each movement (if this were so the storage capacity would be immense); and the fact that the human organism is capable of making novel, creative movements depending on the environmental situation, which theoretically would be impossible unless prior development of the "trace" had occurred (Schmidt, 1975). To overcome these criticisms, Schmidt (1975) and Pew (1974) have postulated that rather than store an individual "trace," we *actively organize* and abstract incoming information into a schematic code.

Active organization has been shown to be a potent variable in verbal learning and memory (for reviews, see Tulving & Donaldson, 1972). Here the argument is that if the input (in this case a movement) is ordered in a manner meaningful to the subject then that input can be organized in such a way as to facilitate retention. The ordering of information might therefore be viewed as a variable which would facilitate the development of a schema to code information. The "trace" notion, however, would argue that organization of input should have no particular role, since all that matters is that the subject experience the feedback consequences associated with the movement. The concept of organization of output and input information in the motor domain has received minimal attention throughout the years. Our data suggest that response organization may be an important variable in retention accuracy.

The major challenge facing researchers of human motor control lies in elucidating the manner in which central and peripheral processes interact in coordinating movements. It is misleading to assume that sensory feedback, important though it may be, is always necessary to elicit further motor output. Equally unrealistic is the notion that neural networks within the central nervous system generate stored movement patterns in total independence of peripheral feedback. Both peripheral and central approaches, if accepted in isolation of each other, leave too many questions unanswered.

ACKNOWLEDGMENTS

The research reported here was supported in part from Grants NH 22081-02 from the National Institute of Mental Health, #160345 from the Graduate School, University of Wisconsin and NE-G-3-0009 from the National Institute of Education, awarded to the first author. The opinions expressed herein do not necessarily reflect the position of policies of any of the granting agencies. Travel funds to attend this conference were supplied by the National Institute of Mental Health.

REFERENCES

Adams, J. A. A closed-loop theory of motor learning. *Journal of Motor Behavior,* 1971, **3**, 111–150.

Adams, J. A., & Goetz, E. T. Feedback and practice as variables in error detection and correction. *Journal of Motor Behavior,* 1973, **5**, 217–224.

Adams, J. A., Goetz, E. T., & Marshall, P. H. Response feedback and motor learning. *Journal of Experimental Psychology,* 1972, **92**, 391–397.

Adams, J. A., Marshall, P. H., & Goetz, E. T. Response feedback and short-term motor retention. *Journal of Experimental Psychology,* 1972, **92**, 92–95.

Allen, G. I., & Tsukahara, N. Cerebrocerebellar communication systems. *Physiological Reviews,* 1974, **54**, 957–1006.

Ascoli, K. M., & Schmidt, R. A. Proactive interference in short-term motor retention. *Journal of Motor Behavior,* 1969, **1**, 29–36.

Boswell, J. J., & Bilodeau, E. A. Short-term retention of a simple motor task as a function of interpolated activity. *Perceptual and Motor Skills,* 1964, **18**, 227–230.

Browne, K., Lee, J., & Ring, P. A. The sensation of passive movement at the metatarsophalangeal joint of the great toe in man. *Journal of Physiology* (London), 1954, **126**, 448–458.

DeLong, M. Central patterning of movement. *Neurosciences Research Program Bulletin,* 1971, **9**, 10–30.

Diewert, G. L. Retention and coding in motor short-term memory: A comparison of storage codes for distance and location information. Paper presented at Sixth Canadian Symposium for Psychomotor Learning and Sport Psychology, Halifax, Nova Scotia, October, 1974.

Evarts, E. V. Feedback and corollary discharge: A merging of the concepts. *Neurosciences Research Program Bulletin,* 1971, **9**, 86–112.

Festinger, L., & Canon, L. K. Information about spatial location based on knowledge about efference. *Psychological Review,* 1965, **72**, 373–384.

Festinger, L., & Easton, A. M. Inferences about the efferent system based on a perceptual illusion produced by eye movements. *Psychological Review,* 1974, **81**, 44–58.

Gentile, A. M. Research in short-term motor memory: Methodological mire. In M. G. Wade & R. Martens (Eds.), *Psychology of motor behavior and sport.* Urbana, Ill.: Human Kinetics Publications, 1974.

Goodwin, G. M., McCloskey, D. I., & Matthews, P. B. C. The contribution of muscle afferents to kinaesthesia shown by vibration induced illusions of movement and by the effects of paralyzing joint afferents. *Brain,* 1972, **95**, 705–748.

Granit, R. Constant errors in the execution and appreciation of movement. *Brain,* 1972, **95**, 649–660.

Grigg, P., Finerman, G. A., & Riley, L. H. Joint position sense after total hip replacement. *Journal of Bone and Joint Surgery,* 1973, **55**, 1016–1025.

Gyr, J. W. Is a theory of direct visual perception adequate? *Psychological Bulletin,* 1972, **77**, 246–261.

Held, R., & Freedman, S. J. Plasticity in human sensorimotor control. *Science,* 1963, **142**, 455–462.

Held, R., & Hein, A. Movement-produced stimulation in the development of visually-guided behavior. *Journal of Comparative and Physiological Psychology,* 1963, **56**, 872–876.

Helmholtz, H. von. *Helmholtz's treatise on physiological optics* (3rd ed.). In J. P. Southall (Ed.), Menasha, Wis.: Optical Society of America, 3 (Whole No.), 1925.

Holst, E. von. Relations between the central nervous system and the peripheral organs. *British Journal of Animal Behavior,* 1954, **2**, 89–94.

Jones, B. Outflow and inflow in movement duplication. *Perception & Psychophysics,* 1972, **12**, 95–96.

Jones, B. Role of central monitoring of efference in short-term memory for movements. *Journal of Experimental Psychology,* 1974, **102**, 37–43.

Keele, S. W. Movement control in skilled motor behavior. *Psychological Bulletin,* 1968, **70**, 387–403.

Keele, S. W., & Ells, J. C. Memory characteristics of kinesthetic information. *Journal of Motor Behavior,* 1972, **4**, 127–134.

Keele, S. W., & Summers, J. The structure of motor programs. In G. E. Stelmach (Ed.), *Motor control: Issues and trends.* New York: Academic Press, 1976.

Kelso, J. A. S., & Stelmach, G. E. Central and peripheral mechanisms in motor control. In G. E. Stelmach (Ed.), *Motor control: Issues and trends.* New York: Academic Press, 1976.

Kelso, J. A. S., Stelmach, G. E., & Wanamaker, W. M. Behavioral and neurological parameters of the nerve compression block. *Journal of Motor Behavior,* 1974, **6**, 179–190.

Kelso, J. A. S., Wallace, S. A., Stelmach, G. E., & Weitz, G. A. Sensory and motor impairment in the nerve compression block. *Quarterly Journal of Experimental Psychology*, 1975, **27**, 141–147.

Laabs, G. E. Cue effects in motor short-term memory. *Journal of Experimental Psychology*, 1973, **100**, 168–177.

Lashley, K. S. Accuracy of movement in the absence of excitation from the moving organ. *American Journal of Physiology*, 1917, **43**, 169–194.

Lashley, K. S. The problem of serial order in behavior. In L. A. Jeffress (Ed.), *Cerebral mechanisms in behavior*. New York: Wiley, 1951.

Laszlo, J. I. The performance of a simple motor task with kinesthetic sense loss. *Quarterly Journal of Experimental Psychology*, 1966, **18**, 1–8.

Laszlo, J. I. & Bairstow, P. J. Accuracy of movement, peripheral feedback and efference copy. *Journal of Motor Behavior*, 1971, **3**, 241–252.

MacNeilage, P. F., & MacNeilage, L. A. Central processes controlling speech production in sleep and waking. In F. J. McGuigan (Ed.), *The psychophysiology of thinking*. New York: Academic Press, 1973.

Marshall, P. H. Recognition and recall in short-term motor memory. *Journal of Experimental Psychology*, 1972, **95**, 147–153.

Marteniuk, R. G. Retention characteristics of motor short-term memory cues. *Journal of Motor Behavior*, 1973, **5**, 249–259.

Marteniuk, R. G. Cognitive information processes in motor short-term memory and movement production. In G. E. Stelmach (Ed.), *Motor control: Issues and trends*. New York: Academic Press, 1976.

Marteniuk, R. G., & Roy, E. A. The codability of kinesthetic location and distance information. *Acta Psychologica*, 1972, **36**, 471–479.

Marteniuk, R. G., & Ryan, M. L. Psychophysics of kinesthesis: Angular movement. *Journal of Motor Behavior*, 1972, **4**, 135–142.

Marteniuk, R. G., Shields, K. W., & Campbell, S. C. Amplitude, position, timing and velocity as cues in reproduction of movement. *Perceptual and Motor Skills*, 1972, **35**, 51–58.

Merton, P. A. Human position sense and sense of effort. In *Homeostatis and feedback mechanisms*, 18th Symposium of the Society for Experimental Biology. Cambridge, England: Cambridge University Press, 1964.

Merton, P. A. The sense of effort. In R. Porter (Ed.), *Breathing: Hering-Breuer Centenary Symposium*. London: Churchill, 1970.

Miller, G. A., Galanter, E., & Pribram, K. H. *Plans and the structure of behavior*. New York: Holt, Rinehart & Winston, 1960.

Newell, K. M. Knowledge of results and motor learning. *Journal of Motor Behavior*, 1974, **6**, 235–264.

Newell, K. M., & Chew, R. A. Recall and recognition in motor learning. *Journal of Motor Behavior*, 1974, **6**, 245–253.

Paillard, J., & Brouchon, M. Active and passive movements in the calibration of positive sense. In S. J. Freedman (Ed.), *The Neuropsychology of spatially oriented behavior*. Homewood, Ill.: Dorsey Press, 1968.

Paintal, A. S. Conduction in mammalian nerve fibers. In *New developments in electromyography and clinical neurophysiology*. Basel: Karger, 1973.

Pew, R. W. Human perceptual–motor performance. In B. H. Kantowitz (Ed.), *Human information processing: Tutorials in performance and cognition*. Potomac, Md.: Lawrence Erlbaum Associates, 1974.

Posner, M. I. Characteristics of visual and kinesthetic memory codes. *Journal of Experimental Psychology*, 1967, **75**, 103–107.

Provins, K. A. The effect of peripheral nerve block on the appreciation and execution of finger movements. *Journal of Physiology*, 1958, **143**, 55–67.

Schmidt, R. A. A schema theory of discrete motor skill learning. *Psychological Review,* 1975, 82, 225–260.

Schmidt, R. A., & White, J. L. Evidence for an error detection mechanism in motor skills: A test of Adams' closed-loop theory. *Journal of Motor Behavior,* 1972, 4, 143–153.

Skoglund, S. Anatomical and physiological studies of knee joint innervation in the cat. *Acta Physiologica Scandinavica, Monogr. Supplement,* 1956, 124, 1–99.

Sokolov, E. N. The modeling properties of the nervous system. In M. Cole & I. Maltzman (Eds.), *A handbook of contemporary soviet psychology.* New York: Basic Books, 1969.

Sperry, R. W. Neural basis of the spontaneous aptokinetic response produced by visual neural inversion. *Journal of Comparative and Physiological Psychology,* 1950, 43, 482–459.

Stelmach, G. E. Feedback – A determiner of forgetting in short-term motor memory. *Acta Psychologica,* 1973, 37, 333–339.

Stelmach, G. E., & Kelso, J. A. S. Memory trace strength and response biasing in short-term motor memory. *Memory & Cognition,* 1975, 3, 58–62.

Stelmach, G. E., Kelso, J. A. S., & Wallace, S. A. Preselection in short-term motor memory. *Journal of Experimental Psychology: Human Learning and Memory,* 1976, 1, 745–755.

Stelmach, G. E., & Wilson, M. Kinesthetic retention, movement extent, and information processing. *Journal of Experimental Psychology,* 1970, 85, 425–430.

Taub, E., & Berman, A. J. Movement and learning in the absence of sensory feedback. In S. J. Freedman (Ed.), *The neuropsychology of spatially oriented behavior.* Homewood: Dorsey Press, 1968.

Teuber, H. L. Perception. In *Handbook in physiology.* Washington, D.C.: American Physiological Society, 1960.

Teuber, H. L. Unity and diversity of frontal lobe functions. *Acta Neurobiologica Experimentalis.* 1972, 32, 615–656.

Teuber, H. L., & Mishkin, M. Judgement of visual and postural vertical after brain injury. *Journal of Psychology,* 1954, 38, 161–175.

Tulving, E., & Donaldson, W. *Organization of Memory.* New York: Academic Press, 1972.

STICHTING

INTERNATIONAL ASSOCIATION FOR THE STUDY OF
ATTENTION AND PERFORMANCE

PREAMBLE TO THE CONSTITUTION

The objectives of the Association are to increase and disseminate scientific knowledge in the area of human attention, performance, and information processing, and to foster international communication in this area.

The Regular International Symposium is the Association's principal instrument in the pursuit of these goals. An Executive Committee administers and monitors the Association's activities and an Advisory Council provides the representation and accountability which are so essential to such an enterprise.

In order better to suit the Symposia to the purposes of the Association, meetings are envisioned that are small in size, have no parallel sessions, allow ample time and opportunity for detailed discussion, have broad international representation, and seek out as contributors and participants young, promising investigators as well as established scientists. Regular Symposia will normally be limited to several topics within the area specified in Article 2 so as to insure common as well as diverse interests among the participants and to encourage discussion.

In addition, the minimal set of rules that govern the affairs of the Association are conceived in a spirit that attempts to provide continuity without oppression, and refreshment without disruption.

STICHTING

INTERNATIONAL ASSOCIATION FOR THE STUDY OF ATTENTION AND PERFORMANCE

CONSTITUTION

ARTICLE 1. NAME

The name of the Stichting is: Stichting "International Association for the Study of Attention and Performance" (hereinafter referred to as the "Association"). The Stichting is established at The Hague, The Netherlands.[1]

ARTICLE 2. PURPOSE

The objectives of the Association are to increase and disseminate scientific knowledge concerning human attention, performance, and information processing, and to foster international communication in this area. The Association shall endeavor to attain its objectives by:

1. holding Regular International Scientific Symposia (hereinafter referred to as "Regular Symposia" or "Regular Symposium") and other scientific meetings;
2. publishing separate Symposium volumes consisting of papers that were presented at each Regular Symposium, as well as publishing other scientific reports;
3. promoting scientific research in the above area;
4. granting prizes and awards for outstanding publications, and other noteworthy contributions in this area;
5. any other legal means.

ARTICLE 3. EXECUTIVE COMMITTEE

1. The management of The Association shall be entrusted to an Executive Committee (hereinafter referred to as the "Committee") consisting of not fewer than five and not more than nine members. At least two members of the Committee shall have permanent residence in North America and at least two in

[1] As of January 27, 1976.

Europe. No person may be elected to the Committee if his[2] election increases the number of Committee members with permanent residence in the same country above three. Each member of the Committee shall be active in research in the area specified in Article 2.

The Committee shall appoint its own members (see this Article, Sections 7 and 8).

2. Each Committee member shall normally be elected for a term of two successive full cycles. A cycle is defined as a period of time which begins on the 30th day following the last day of a Regular Committee Meeting (see Article 4.2), and ends on the 29th day following the last day of the first Regular Committee Meeting occurring no less than 20 months later. If a member is elected between the beginning of one cycle and the next, then his term of office shall consist of the fraction of a cycle remaining after the date of his appointment together with the next full cycle. Members may serve for as many terms as they are elected to; however, a person may serve two consecutive terms only once. (See also Article 7.2).

3. At least once every two cycles a new Committee member shall be elected who has never previously served a full cycle on the Committee. If possible, Committee appointments shall be made so that at the start of every cycle at least half of the Committee members shall also have been members during the preceding cycle.

4. The Committee shall appoint as officers a Chairman, a Secretary, and a Treasurer from among its members; the offices of Secretary and Treasurer may be held by the same person.

5. The length of a term of office for Committee officers shall be one cycle. There are no restrictions on the number of successive terms to which an officer may be appointed so long as he qualifies as a Committee member (see this article, Sections 1 and 2).

6. A member's term on the Committee shall be terminated by his resignation, dismissal, or death. After a member has ceased for more than one cycle to be actively engaged in research in the area specified in Article 2 he is expected to resign. The dismissal of any of its members must be approved by at least two-thirds of the Committee.

7. The Committee is obliged to fill a vacancy within 60 days after the number of its members has declined below five.

If the number of Committee members drops below four then the Committee shall nominate candidates for membership and provide the Council with an opportunity to review the candidates as follows: The Mail Procedure (Article 4.1) shall be used to provide each member of the Advisory Council (Article 6) with the name and biographical information for each candidate together with a request that the Council member register any objections that he may have to any candidate. A candidate shall not be appointed if the Committee receives objec-

---

[2] "His" as used in this document refers to "his/her."

tions from more than 10% of the Council within 30 days of the date of the mailing.

8. If all the seats on the Committee become vacant before existing vacancies can be filled, or in the circumstances specified in Article 6.4, the Advisory Council shall appoint five new members to the Committee. If such appointment is not or cannot be effected within a reasonable time, the five new members of the Committee shall be appointed by the President of the Court of The Hague.

9. Personal financial profit resulting from services to the Association shall not accrue to members of the Committee, members of the Advisory Council, organizers of Symposia, or organizers of other scientific meetings (see Article 7).

10 The first Committee shall consist of the following members and officers:

Stanislav Dornic, Sweden: member
Sylvan Kornblum, United States: Secretary/Treasurer
Wim G. Koster, The Netherlands: member
Patrick M. A. Rabbitt, England: member
Andries F. Sanders, The Netherlands: Chairman
Saul Sternberg, United States: member
Alan T. Welford, Australia: member

ARTICLE 4. MEETINGS AND DECISIONS OF THE EXECUTIVE COMMITTEE

1. The Committee shall reach its decisions at Regular or at Special Meetings, or by a Mail Procedure that shall include the polling of members by registered mail after appropriate written consultation has taken place.

2. The Committee shall hold a Regular Meeting at or about the time of each Regular Symposium (see Articles 2 and 7). No more than 40 months shall elapse between two consecutive Regular Meetings. A Regular Meeting shall normally:

a. be announced no less than 6 months prior to the date of the meeting.
b. be attended by a majority of the Committee members.
c. include reports by the Committee Chairman, the Secretary, and the Treasurer.

In the event that any of the above three requirements of a Regular Meeting cannot be met, appropriate procedures, as specified in the Bylaws, shall be used for carrying on the Association's business.

3. At the written request of at least two Committee members who shall state the matter to be decided, the Secretary shall, if possible, call a Special Meeting of the Committee; if a Special Meeting cannot be held, at which decisions are made, then the Mail Procedure shall be used to resolve the question.

4. Minutes shall be kept of all the meetings of the Committee.

5. Unless otherwise specified in this Constitution, all decisions shall be made by an absolute majority of the Committee. Each member shall have one vote

which may be cast in person or by mail. No voting by proxy shall be allowed. Voting by secret ballot may be requested by any member of the Committee on any question.

ARTICLE 5. REPRESENTATION

1. The Association may be represented at law, and otherwise, by the Committee, by one or more of its members, or by one or more other persons. Such a person or persons must have been designated by the Committee for that purpose.

2. In the event of a decision by the Committee to empower one or more of its members, or one or more other persons to represent the Association in dealings with third parties, written notice of the said decision, duly signed by the Secretary and the Chairman, shall suffice. If the Secretary himself has been empowered to represent the Association, the notice shall also be signed by one of the other members of the Committee.

ARTICLE 6. ADVISORY COUNCIL

1. The Committee shall be responsible for forming and retaining an Advisory Council (hereinafter referred to as the "Council") consisting of not fewer than 30 and not more than 50 persons each of whom is actively engaged in research in the area specified in Article 2.

2. Each member of the Council shall be appointed by the Committee following agreement by a majority of at least two-thirds of the Committee. The term of office for each Council member shall be two cycles, with the possibility of one further term of two cycles. Termination of membership in the Council in the course of a term shall be possible by the resignation, death or dismissal of the member concerned. If the number of members on the Council drops below 30 the Committee shall appoint the required number of new members to the Council starting with the next cycle. No person may be a member of the Council and a member of the Committee at the same time.

3. The Council shall advise the Committee in matters of policy. If the number of Committee members drops below four (as mentioned in Article 3 above), the Council shall also propose candidates for membership on the Committee and on the Council. In making its decisions, the Committee shall, so far as possible, take into account the advice that it receives from members of the Council. Copies of all such advice and recommendations shall be received by and distributed to all other members of the Council and Committee by the Committee Secretary.

4. The Council may dismiss the Committee in its entirety by sending to the Secretary, by registered mail, a declaration signed by at least two-thirds of the

members of the Council stating that the signatories no longer have confidence in the Committee. The provisions of Article 3.8 shall then come into operation.

5. The Council may not dismiss individual members of the Committee.

6. The Council may dismiss one of its own members by sending to the Secretary, by registered mail, a declaration signed by at least two-thirds of the members of the Council stating that the signatories no longer have confidence in that member.

ARTICLE 7. REGULAR SCIENTIFIC SYMPOSIA

1. The Committee shall be responsible for organizing one Regular Symposium, in the area specified in Article 2, at least once every two years, if possible. No more than 40 months shall elapse between any two consecutive Regular Symposia.

In order better to suit the Symposia to the purposes of the Association, meetings are envisioned that are small in size, have no parallel sessions, allow ample time and opportunity for detailed discussion, have broad international representation, and seek out as contributors and participants young, promising investigators as well as established scientists. Regular Symposia will normally be limited to several topics within the area specified in Article 2 so as to insure common as well as diverse interests among the participants, and to encourage discussion.

2. The Committee shall appoint an Organizer for each Symposium sufficiently in advance of the actual meeting. The Organizer of a Regular Symposium shall be responsible for both the Symposium and for the Symposium volume (Article 8.2), and shall also be invited to become a member of the Committee if he is not already a member and is eligible to serve. His term shall begin with the first cycle after the symposium. If he is ineligible because of just having completed two successive terms as a member of the Committee, he shall be invited to serve as an ex officio member. A full term shall intervene between the termination of such an ex officio term and a subsequent reelection to the Committee.

3. No more than two Regular Symposia shall be convened in the same country in succession.

4. Participation in a Symposium is confined to persons who have been invited by the Organizer.

5. Papers presented at a Symposium are expected to describe work not previously published and to represent a substantial contribution to the area described in Article 2. Members of the Committee and Council shall be solicited for their nomination of participants in Regular Symposia. The Organizer shall submit the final list of proposed participants and alternates together with the source of the proposals to the Committee in time to receive their comments and concurrence prior to issuing the invitations. At the same time the Organizer shall also submit for concurrence an outline of all other essential aspects of the

Symposium including the tentative program and the dates and the place of the meeting.

ARTICLE 8. PUBLICATIONS

1. The arrangements for publishing any documents, books, journals, etc., under the Association auspices must receive prior approval by the Committee.

2. For each Regular Symposium a volume shall be published as quickly as possible after the Symposium consistent with maintaining standards of excellence. The main purpose of this volume shall be to publish papers that were presented at the symposium.

ARTICLE 9. FUNDS

1. The funds of the Association shall consist of:

a. amounts received by the Association by succession, legacy or gift;
b. contributions, subsidies, grants, contracts, etc;
c. income from Symposium publications, etc;
d. moneys received by way of loans or credits;
e. all other income.

2. At each Regular Meeting of the Committee the Treasurer shall submit a written report on his management of the Association's finances during the preceding cycle which shall have been approved and signed by two other members of the Committee who are not also officers, and who have been designated by the Committee.

ARTICLE 10. BYLAWS

The Committee shall draw up rules for the Association. The adoption and the amendment of such Bylaws shall require at least a two-thirds majority of the Committee.

ARTICLE 11. AMENDMENTS TO THE CONSTITUTION

The Committee may amend any part of the Constitution with the exception of Article 2 and Article 6, Sections 1 and 4. Amending the Constitution requires a notarial instrument and the approval of at least two-thirds of the Committee. The Committee must ascertain the Council's views on the proposed amendment prior to voting.

ARTICLE 12. DISSOLUTION

1. The Committee is entitled to dissolve the Association. The decision to do so is subject to the same voting requirements as specified in Article 11.

2. In the event of dissolution of the Association, the liquidation shall be carried out by the Committee unless other liquidators are appointed when the decision to dissolve the Association is made. The provisions of the Constitution shall, as far as possible, be applied during the liquidation process.

Any credit balance remaining shall be applied, as far as possible, in accordance with the objectives of the Association, at the discretion of the Committee.

BYLAWS

ARTICLE 1. STATUS OF THE BYLAWS

These Bylaws supplement but do not replace or supersede the Association's Constitution.

ARTICLE 2. EXECUTIVE COMMITTEE AND OFFICERS

1. Persons who are appointed as officers of the Committee shall normally have served at least one full cycle as members of the Committee before starting their term of office. Nominations for Committee officers shall be made by Committee members, and the vote shall be by secret ballot.

2. The Chairman of the Committee shall preside at the Regular Meetings and at other meetings of the Committee.

3. The Secretary shall keep and maintain the records of the Association. He shall also maintain a current list of the names and addresses of the members of the Committee and of the Council, and distribute those lists to all members at least once per year. The Secretary shall do what is necessary to insure that all Committee members are informed of other Committee members' views and Association affairs. This shall be done with the utmost dispatch when the mail procedure is used to handle Association business (cf. Constitution, Article 4) so that members may exchange views before voting.

The Secretary shall collect and tabulate mail ballots and inform Committee and/or Council members of the outcome of any mail vote without delay. The Secretary shall keep the Council informed of all decisions taken by the Committee as well as of other important developments, plans and proposals involving the Association and its work.

4. One member of the Committee shall be appointed Secretary Designate.

ARTICLE 3. THE ADVISORY COUNCIL

1. At least 30% of the members of the Council shall have permanent residence in North America, and at least 30% in Europe.

2. In addition to the responsibilities of the Council that are specified in the Constitution, Council members can expect to be asked to review manuscripts for the Association.

ARTICLE 4. DISMISSAL OF A MEMBER

Any member of the Committee or Council who faces dismissal in accordance with the provisions of either Article 6.6 or Article 3.6 of the Constitution must be given the opportunity to answer the charges that instigated the dismissal procedures both in writing and in person. If the dismissal procedures were initiated by the Committee, then that member must be allowed to appear before the Committee if he wishes. If the procedures were initiated by the Council then the Council may designate a suitable subcommittee to act as its representative in these proceedings. The vote to dismiss either by Committee or by Council must be preceded by the procedures in this section.

ARTICLE 5. REGULAR INTERNATIONAL SCIENTIFIC SYMPOSIUM

1. Participants, Contributors and Papers

a) A person who presents a paper at a Regular Symposium or whose name appears as an author or co-author on a paper in the associated volume (whether or not he was present at the Symposium) is considered as a Contributor to that Symposium.

b) A person cannot be a Contributor to more than two out of any three consecutive Regular Symposia.

c) Invited participants may attend no more than three out of any four consecutive Regular Symposia. This restriction does not apply to Committee members.

d) Invited participants are expected to attend the entire Symposium.

e) If possible the number of papers presented by persons from the same country shall not exceed half the total number of papers. Under no circumstances shall the number of papers by persons from the same country exceed two-thirds of the papers presented.

f) All the papers shall be presented in English unless other arrangements have been specifically authorized by the Committee.

g) All persons who present a paper are expected to submit the paper for consideration for inclusion in the Symposium volume by the deadline specified by the Organizer.

h) All the papers submitted for inclusion in the Symposium volume shall be subjected to review by experts in relevant fields.

i) At each Regular Symposium a minimum of four papers shall be presented by persons who have never before been Contributors (Article 5.1a) to a Regular Symposium.

j) No more than four papers may be included in the Symposium volume that were not presented at the meeting. A list of such papers, if any, shall be communicated to the Committee for their comments prior to the acceptance of such papers for publication.

k) Membership in the Committee shall not confer or appear to confer a privileged position on any of its members in the scientific program of any Symposium.

2. Symposium size (cf. Constitution, Article 7.1)

a) The total number of papers presented at any single Symposium shall not exceed forty.

b) The total number of papers presented on any one day shall not exceed eight.

c) The total number of persons present at the same time at any Symposium shall not exceed sixty-five.

3. Symposium Organizer

a) The Symposium Organizer may not be a Committee officer.

b) The Organizer must obtain the Treasurer's authorization before committing The Association to any expenditure.

c) The Organizer shall be a person who will normally have attended at least one previous Symposium.

ARTICLE 6. REGULAR COMMITTEE MEETING

If in the course of making preparations for a Regular Meeting it becomes clear that one or more of the normal requirements of a Regular Meeting cannot be met—if, in particular, it becomes clear that a majority cannot be present—then the Secretary shall alert the Committee members, inform them of the options that are available, and request their vote on the procedure that they wish to follow. The Committee must decide on one of the three options below:

1. The date of the Regular Meeting may be changed from that originally proposed so long as the new date complies with the Constitutional time requirements (Constitution, Article 4.2).

2. The meeting may be held at the time originally proposed, even though a majority is unable to attend. In that event the meeting must be explicitly designated as a Regular Meeting by a majority of the Committee. The members present at that meeting shall conduct the business of the Association in accordance with the provisions of the Constitution and Bylaws. Specific votes obtained in writing from absent members of the Committee prior to the meeting may be included in the tally of votes on specific relevant questions. Where decision cannot be reached at the meeting because of the lack of a majority, the Mail Procedure shall carry these issues to the decision stage following the meeting.

3. The Regular Meeting may be held at a nominal date without any members present where the Association business is carried out entirely by the Mail Procedure.

ARTICLE 7. RECORDS AND PUBLICATIONS

1. The Association's records and publications shall be in English. Exceptions shall require specific Committee approval.

2. The copyright of Association publications (e.g., Symposium volumes) shall be in the Association's name.

Author Index

Numbers in *italics* refer to pages on which the complete references are listed.

Subject Index